Learning Python

Other resources from O'Reilly

Related titles
Programming Python
Python Cookbook™
Python in a Nutshell

Python Pocket Reference
Twisted Network
    Programming Essentials

oreilly.com
oreilly.com is more than a complete catalog of O'Reilly books. You'll also find links to news, events, articles, weblogs, sample chapters, and code examples.

oreillynet.com is the essential portal for developers interested in open and emerging technologies, including new platforms, programming languages, and operating systems.

Conferences
O'Reilly brings diverse innovators together to nurture the ideas that spark revolutionary industries. We specialize in documenting the latest tools and systems, translating the innovator's knowledge into useful skills for those in the trenches. Visit *conferences.oreilly.com* for our upcoming events.

Safari Bookshelf (*safari.oreilly.com*) is the premier online reference library for programmers and IT professionals. Conduct searches across more than 1,000 books. Subscribers can zero in on answers to time-critical questions in a matter of seconds. Read the books on your Bookshelf from cover to cover or simply flip to the page you need. Try it today for free.

THIRD EDITION

Learning Python

Mark Lutz

O'REILLY®

Beijing · Cambridge · Farnham · Köln · Sebastopol · Taipei · Tokyo

Learning Python, Third Edition
by Mark Lutz

Published by O'Reilly Media, Inc., 1005 Gravenstein Highway North, Sebastopol, CA 95472.

O'Reilly books may be purchased for educational, business, or sales promotional use. Online editions are also available for most titles (*safari.oreilly.com*). For more information, contact our corporate/institutional sales department: (800) 998-9938 or *corporate@oreilly.com*.

Editor: Tatiana Apandi   **Indexer:** Julie Hawks
Production Editor: Sumita Mukherji   **Cover Designer:** Karen Montgomery
Copyeditor: Rachel Head   **Interior Designer:** David Futato
Proofreader: Sumita Mukherji   **Illustrator:** Robert Romano

Printing History:

March 1999:	First Edition.
December 2003:	Second Edition.
October 2007:	Third Edition.

 This book uses RepKover™, a durable and flexible lay-flat binding.

ISBN: 978-0-596-51398-6
[M] 42.5#   [4/09]

To Vera.
You are my life.

Table of Contents

Part II. Types and Operations

Part III. Statements and Syntax

Part IV. Functions

Part V. Modules

Part VII. Exceptions and Tools

Part VIII. Appendixes

Preface

This book provides an introduction to the Python programming language. Python is a popular programming language used for both standalone programs and scripting applications in a wide variety of domains. It is free, portable, powerful, and remarkably easy to use.

Whether you are new to programming or a professional developer, this book's goal is to bring you quickly up to speed on the fundamentals of the core Python language. After reading this book, you will know enough about Python to apply it in whatever application domains you choose to explore.

About This Third Edition

In the four years since the second edition of this book was published in late 2003, there have been substantial changes in Python itself, and in the topics I present in Python training sessions. Although I have attempted to retain as much of the prior version of this text as possible, this new edition reflects many recent changes in the Python language and in Python training, as well as a handful of structural changes.

This Edition's Python Language Changes

On the language front, this edition has been thoroughly updated to reflect Python 2.5 and all changes to the language since the publication of the second edition. (The second edition was based largely on Python 2.2, with some 2.3 features grafted on at the end of the project.) In addition, discussions of anticipated changes in the upcoming Python 3.0 release have been incorporated where appropriate. Here are some of the major language topics of which you'll find new or expanded coverage in this edition:

- The new B if A else C conditional expression (Chapter 12).
- with/as context managers (Chapter 27).
- try/except/finally unification (Chapter 27).
- Relative import syntax (Chapter 21).

- Generator expressions (Chapter 17).
- New generator function features (Chapter 17).
- Function decorators (Chapter 26).
- The set object type (Chapter 5).
- New built-in functions: `sorted`, `sum`, `any`, `all`, `enumerate` (Chapters 4 and 13).
- The decimal fixed-precision object type (Chapter 5).
- New and expanded material on files, list comprehensions, iterators, and more (Chapters 13 and 17).
- New development tools coverage: Eclipse, `distutils`, `unittest` and `doctest`, IDLE enhancements, Shedskin, and so on (Chapters 3 and 29).

Smaller language changes (for instance, the widespread use of `True` and `False`, the new `sys.exc_info` for fetching exception details, and the demise of string-based exceptions, string methods, and the `apply` and `reduce` built-ins) are discussed throughout the book. In addition, some of the features that were new in the prior edition enjoy substantially expanded coverage here, including three-limit slices, and the arbitrary arguments call syntax that subsumes `apply`.

This Edition's Python Training Changes

Besides such language changes, this edition has been augmented with new topics and examples presented in the Python training sessions I have held in recent years. For example, you'll find:

- A new chapter introducing built-in types (Chapter 4).
- A new chapter introducing statement syntax (Chapter 10).
- A new full chapter on dynamic typing, with enhanced coverage (Chapter 6).
- An expanded OOP introduction (Chapter 22).
- New examples for files, scopes, statement nesting, classes, exceptions, and more.

Many additions and changes were made with Python beginners in mind, and some topics have been moved to appear at the places where they have proved simplest to digest in training classes. List comprehensions and iterators, for example, now make their initial appearance in conjunction with the `for` loop statement, instead of later with functional tools.

You'll also find that the coverage of many original core language topics has been substantially expanded in this edition, with new discussions and examples added. Because this text has become something of a de facto standard resource for learning the core Python language, the presentation has been made more complete and augmented with new use cases throughout.

In addition, this entire edition integrates a new set of Python tips and tricks, gleaned from teaching classes during the last 10 years, and using Python for real work over the last 15. The exercises have also been updated and expanded to reflect current Python best practices, new language features, and common beginners' mistakes witnessed firsthand in classes. Overall, the core language coverage provided by this edition is larger than in previous editions, both because Python is larger, and because I've added contextual information that has proved to be important in practice.

This Edition's Structural Changes

As in the prior edition, to accommodate the fact that this book is now more complete, its material has been split into bite-sized chunks. That is, I've organized the core language material into many multichapter parts to make the material easier to tackle. Types and statements, for instance, are now two top-level parts, with one chapter for each major type and statement topic. This new structure is designed to allow the book to say more without intimidating readers. In the process, exercises and "gotchas" (common mistakes) were moved from chapter ends to part ends—they now appear at the end of the last chapter in each part.

In this third edition, I've also augmented the end-of-part exercises with end-of-chapter summaries and end-of-chapter quizzes to help you review chapters as you complete them. Each chapter concludes with a set of questions to help you review and test your understanding of the chapter's material. Unlike the end-of-part exercises, whose solutions are presented in Appendix B, the solutions to the end-of-chapter quizzes appear immediately after the questions; I encourage you to look at the solutions even if you're sure you've answered the questions correctly because the answers are a sort of review in themselves.

Despite all the new topics, this book is still oriented toward Python newcomers, and is designed to be a first Python text for programmers.[*] It retains much of the first two editions' material, structure, and focus. Where appropriate, I've expanded introductions for newcomers, and isolated the more advanced new topics from the main thread of discussion to avoid obscuring the fundamentals. Moreover, because it is largely based on time-tested training experience and materials, this edition, like the first two, can still serve as a self-paced introductory Python class.

---

[*] And by "programmers," I mean anyone who has written a single line of code in any programming or scripting language in the past. If this doesn't include you, you will probably find this book useful anyhow, but be aware that it will spend more time teaching Python than programming fundamentals.

This Edition's Scope Changes

This third edition is intended as a tutorial on the core Python language, and nothing else. It's about learning the language in an in-depth fashion, before applying it in application-level programming. The presentation here is bottom-up and gradual, but it provides a complete look at the entire language, in isolation from its application roles.

For some, "learning Python" involves spending an hour or two going through a tutorial on the Web. This works for already advanced programmers up to a point; Python is, after all, relatively simple by comparison to other languages. The problem with this fast-track approach is that its practitioners eventually stumble onto unusual cases and get stuck—variables change out from under them, mutable default arguments mutate inexplicably, and so on. The goal here is instead to provide a solid grounding in Python fundamentals, so that even the unusual cases will make sense when they crop up.

This scope is deliberate. By restricting our gaze to language fundamentals, we can investigate them here in more satisfying depth. Other texts, such as O'Reilly's *Programming Python*, *Python Cookbook*, *Python in a Nutshell*, and *Python Pocket Reference*, pick up where this book leaves off and provide a more complete look at application-level topics and reference materials. The purpose of the book you are reading now is solely to teach Python itself so that you can apply it to whatever domain you happen to work in.

Because of that focus change, some of the prior edition's reference and more advanced sections (that is, roughly 15 percent of the prior edition) have been cut to expand the core language sections. In exchange, readers of this edition will find a more thorough look at the core language, and a more useful first Python book. A handful of more advanced examples were also added as self-study programs as the final exercise in this edition (see Chapter 29).

About This Book

This section underscores some important points about this book in general, regardless of its edition number. No book addresses every possible audience, so it's important to understand a book's goals up front.

This Book's Prerequisites

There are no absolute prerequisites to speak of, really. Both true beginners and crusty programming veterans have used this book successfully. If you are motivated to learn Python, this text will probably work for you. In general, though, I have found that any exposure to programming or scripting before this book can be helpful, even if not required for every reader.

This book is designed to be an introductory-level Python text for programmers. It may not be an ideal text for someone who has never touched a computer before (for instance, we're not going to spend any time exploring what a computer is), but I haven't made many assumptions about your programming background or education.

On the other hand, I won't insult readers by assuming they are "dummies" either, whatever that means—it's easy to do useful things in Python, and this book will show you how. The text occasionally contrasts Python with languages such as C, C++, Java™, and Pascal, but you can safely ignore these comparisons if you haven't used such languages in the past.

This Book's Scope and Other Books

Although this book covers all the essentials of the Python language, I've kept its scope narrow in the interests of speed and size. To keep things simple, this book focuses on core concepts, uses small and self-contained examples to illustrate points, and sometimes omits the small details that are readily available in reference manuals. Because of that, this book is probably best described as an introduction and a stepping-stone to more advanced and complete texts.

For example, we won't talk much about Python/C integration—a complex topic that is nevertheless central to many Python-based systems. We also won't talk much about Python's history or development processes. And popular Python applications such as GUIs, system tools, and network scripting get only a short glance, if they are mentioned at all. Naturally, this scope misses some of the big picture.

By and large, Python is about raising the quality bar a few notches in the scripting world. Some of its ideas require more context than can be provided here, and I'd be remiss if I didn't recommend further study after you finish this book. I hope that most readers of this book will eventually go on to gain a more complete understanding of application-level programming from other texts.

Because of its beginner's focus, *Learning Python* is designed to be naturally complemented by O'Reilly's other Python books. For instance, *Programming Python*, another book I authored, provides larger and more complete examples, along with tutorials on application programming techniques, and was explicitly designed to be a follow-up text to the one you are reading now. Roughly, the current editions of *Learning Python* and *Programming Python* reflect the two halves of their author's training materials—the core language, and application programming. In addition, O'Reilly's *Python Pocket Reference* serves as a quick reference supplement for looking up some of the finer details skipped here.

Other follow-up books can also provide references, additional examples, or details about using Python in specific domains such as the Web and GUIs. For instance, O'Reilly's *Python in a Nutshell* and Sams's *Python Essential Reference* provide references, and O'Reilly's *Python Cookbook* offers a library of self-contained examples for people already familiar with application programming techniques. Because books are such a subjective experience, I encourage you to browse on your own to find advanced texts that suit your needs. Regardless of which books you choose, though, keep in mind that the rest of the Python story requires studying examples that are more realistic than there is space for here.

Having said that, I think you'll find this book to be a good first text on Python, despite its limited scope (and perhaps because of it). You'll learn everything you need to get started writing useful standalone Python programs and scripts. By the time you've finished this book, you will have learned not only the language itself, but also how to apply it well to your day-to-day tasks. And, you'll be equipped to tackle more advanced topics and examples as they come your way.

This Book's Style and Structure

This book is based on training materials developed for a three-day hands-on Python course. You'll find end-of-chapter quizzes at the end of each chapter, and end-of-part exercises at the end of the last chapter of each part. Solutions to chapter quizzes appear in the chapters themselves, and solutions to part exercises show up in Appendix B. The quizzes are designed to review material, while the exercises are designed to get you coding right away and are usually one of the highlights of the course.

I strongly recommend working through the quizzes and exercises along the way, not only to gain Python programming experience, but also because some of the exercises raise issues not covered elsewhere in the book. The solutions in the chapters and in Appendix B should help you if you get stuck (and you are encouraged to peek at the answers as much and as often as you like).

The overall structure of this book is also derived from class materials. Because this text is designed to introduce language basics quickly, I've organized the presentation by major language features, not examples. We'll take a bottom-up approach here: from built-in object types, to statements, to program units, and so on. Each chapter is fairly self-contained, but later chapters draw upon ideas introduced in earlier ones (e.g., by the time we get to classes, I'll assume you know how to write functions), so a linear reading makes the most sense for most readers.

In general terms, this book presents the Python language in a bottom-up fashion. It is organized with one part per major language feature—types, functions, and so forth—and most of the examples are small and self-contained (some might also call the examples in this text artificial, but they illustrate the points it aims to make). More specifically, here is what you will find:

Part I, *Getting Started*

We begin with a general overview of Python that answers commonly asked initial questions—why people use the language, what it's useful for, and so on. The first chapter introduces the major ideas underlying the technology to give you some background context. Then the technical material of the book begins, as we explore the ways that both we and Python run programs. The goal of this part of the book is to give you just enough information to be able to follow along with later examples and exercises.

Part II, *Types and Operations*

Next, we begin our tour of the Python language, studying Python's major built-in object types in depth: numbers, lists, dictionaries, and so on. You can get a lot done in Python with these tools alone. This is the most substantial part of the book because we lay groundwork here for later chapters. We'll also look at dynamic typing and its references—keys to using Python well—in this part.

Part III, *Statements and Syntax*

The next part moves on to introduce Python's *statements*—the code you type to create and process objects in Python. It also presents Python's general syntax model. Although this part focuses on syntax, it also introduces some related tools, such as the PyDoc system, and explores coding alternatives.

Part IV, *Functions*

This part begins our look at Python's higher-level program structure tools. Functions turn out to be a simple way to package code for reuse and avoid code redundancy. In this part, we will explore Python's scoping rules, argument-passing techniques, and more.

Part V, *Modules*

Python modules let you organize statements and functions into larger components, and this part illustrates how to create, use, and reload modules. We'll also look at some more advanced topics here, such as module packages, module reloading, and the __name__ variable.

Part VI, *Classes and OOP*

Here, we explore Python's object-oriented programming (OOP) tool, the *class*—an optional but powerful way to structure code for customization and reuse. As you'll see, classes mostly reuse ideas we will have covered by this point in the book, and OOP in Python is mostly about looking up names in linked objects. As you'll also see, OOP is optional in Python, but can shave development time substantially, especially for long-term strategic project development.

Part VII, *Exceptions and Tools*

We wrap up the text with a look at Python's exception handling model and statements, plus a brief overview of development tools that will become more useful when you start writing larger programs (debugging and testing tools, for instance). This part comes last, exceptions should now all be classes.

Part VIII, *Appendixes*

> The book ends with a pair of appendixes that give platform-specific tips for using Python on various computers (Appendix A) and provide solutions to the end-of-part exercises (Appendix B). Solutions to end-of-chapter quizzes appear in the chapters themselves.

Note that the index and table of contents can be used to hunt for details, but there are no reference appendixes in this book (this book is a tutorial, not a reference). As mentioned earlier, you can consult the *Python Pocket Reference* (O'Reilly), as well as other books, and the free Python reference manuals maintained at *http://www. python.org*, for syntax and built-in tool details.

Book Updates

Improvements happen (and so do mis^H^H^H typos). Updates, supplements, and corrections for this book will be maintained (or referenced) on the Web at one of the following sites:

> *http://www.oreilly.com/catalog/9780596513986/* (O'Reilly's web page for the book)
> *http://www.rmi.net/~lutz* (the author's site)
> *http://www.rmi.net/~lutz/about-lp.html* (the author's web page for the book)

The last of these three URLs points to a web page for this book where I will post updates, but be sure to search the Web if this link becomes invalid. If I could be more clairvoyant, I would, but the Web changes faster than printed books.

About the Programs in This Book

This book, and all the program examples in it, is based on Python version 2.5. In addition, although I won't try to predict the future, discussion of some ideas in the anticipated 3.0 release are mixed in along the way.

Because this text focuses on the core language, however, you can be fairly sure that most of what it has to say won't change very much in future releases of Python. Most of this book applies to earlier Python versions, too, except when it does not; naturally, if you try using extensions added after the release you've got, all bets are off.

As a rule of thumb, the latest Python is the best Python. Because this book focuses on the core language, most of it also applies to Jython, the Java-based Python language implementation, as well other Python implementations described in Chapter 2.

Source code for the book's examples, as well as exercise solutions, can be fetched from the book's web site at *http://www.oreilly.com/catalog/9780596513986/*. So how do you run the examples? We'll study startup details in Chapter 3, so please stay tuned for details on this front.

Preparing for Python 3.0

The first alpha release of Python 3.0 came out just before this book went to the printer, and after it had been written. Officially speaking, this edition of this book is based on the Python 2.x line (specifically, version 2.5), but it has been augmented with numerous notes about anticipated changes in the upcoming Python 3.0 release.

Version 3.0 won't be officially released until roughly one year after this book has been published, and it isn't expected to be in wide use for at least two years. Nevertheless, if you've picked up this book after 3.0 is in common use, this section provides a brief description of some of the changes in the language you will likely encounter to help you make the transition.

Although there are a few notable exceptions, most of the Python language in version 3.0 will be the same as described in this book, and the impact on typical and practical applications code will be minor. That is, the fundamentals of Python presented in this book will not change from release to release, and readers will benefit by studying those fundamentals here first before dealing with release-specific details.

To help you retarget code in the future, though, the following list highlights the major differences in Python 3.0. Pointers to the chapters in this edition that either discuss or are impacted by these changes are noted as well, and the list is ordered by relevant chapter number. Some of these changes can be coded today in Python 2.5, and some cannot. Because much of the following list won't make sense to most readers at this point, I suggest you first study this book at large to learn the fundamentals of Python, and return to this list later to see the changes in 3.0. In Python 3.0:

- The current execfile() built-in function is removed; use exec() instead (see Chapter 3).
- The reload() built-in functions may be removed; an alternative is not yet known (see Chapters 3 and 19).
- The `X` backquotes string conversion expression is removed: use repr(X) (see Chapter 5).
- The X <> Y redundant inequality expression is removed: use X != Y (see Chapter 5).
- Sets can be created with new literal syntax {1, 3, 2} equivalent to the current set([1, 3, 2]) (see Chapter 5).
- Set comprehensions may be coded: {f(x) for x in S if P(x)}, which is the same as the current generator expression: set(f(x) for x in S if P(x)) (see Chapter 5).
- True division is turned on: X / Y always returns a floating-point number that retains the remainder, even for integers; use X // Y to invoke today's truncating division (see Chapter 5).
- There is only one integer type, int, which supports the arbitrary precision of the current long type (see Chapter 5).

- Octal and binary literals: the current octal 0666 becomes an error: use 0o666 instead, and the oct() function's result has been changed accordingly; 0b1010 now equals 10, and bin(10) returns "0b1010" (see Chapter 5).

- The string type str supports wide-character Unicode text, and a new bytes type represents short-character strings (e.g, when loaded from files in binary mode); bytes is a mutable sequence of small integers with a slightly different interface than str (see Chapter 7).

- There is a new, optional technique for string formatting: "See {0}, {1} and {foo}".format("A", "B", foo="C") makes "See A, B and C" (see Chapter 7).

- The dictionary D.has_key(X) method will be removed; use X in D membership instead (see Chapters 4 and 8).

- Comparisons (and by proxy, sorts) of mixed non-numeric types raise exceptions instead of using the current arbitrary but fixed cross-type ordering (see Chapters 8 and 9).

- Dictionary methods .keys(), .items() and .values() will return iterable-like "view" objects, instead of lists; use list() to force a list to be built if needed (see Chapter 8).

- Because of the prior point, this coding pattern no longer works: k = D.keys(); k.sort(); use k = sorted(D) instead (see Chapters 4 and 8).

- The file() built-in function may be removed; use open() instead (see Chapter 9).

- The raw_input() built-in function will be renamed input(); use eval(input()) to get the behavior of today's input() function (see Chapter 10).

- The exec code-string execution statement becomes a built-in function again (Chapter 10).

- as, with, and nonlocal become new reserved words; exec no longer is reserved because of the prior point (see Chapter 11).

- Printing is a function to support more features, not a statement: use print(x, y), not print x, y, and use the new function's keyword arguments to customize printing behavior: file=sys.stdout, sep=" ", and end="\n" (see Chapter 11).

- Extended iterable unpacking: statement that supports generalized sequence assignment such as a, b, *rest = some_sequence now work, as does *rest, a = stuff; thus, the number of items on the left and right of an assignment statement no longer must match (see Chapter 11).

- Automatic tuple parameter unpacking via sequence assignment is removed for functions; you can no longer write def foo(a, (b, c)):, and must use def foo(a, bc): b, c = bc to perform sequence assignment explicitly instead (see Chapter 11).

- The current xrange() built-in function is renamed to range(); that is, there is only range() (see Chapter 13).

- In the iterator protocol, the X.next() method is renamed to X.__next__(), and a new built-in function, next(X), calls the X.__next__() method on an object (see Chapters 13 and 17).

- The built-in functions zip(), map(), and filter() return iterators; use list() to force construction of a list of results (see Chapters 13 and 17).

- Functions may optionally include annotations describing arguments and results: def foo(x: "spam", y: list(range(3))) -> 42*2:, which are simply attached to the function object's foo.func_annotations dictionary attribute at runtime: {'x': "spam", 'y': [0, 1, 2], "return": 84} (see Chapter 15).

- The new nonlocal x, y statement allows write access to variables in enclosing function scopes (see Chapter 16).

- The apply(func, args, kws) function will be removed; use the func(*args, **kws) call syntax instead (see Chapters 16 and 17).

- The reduce() built-in function is removed; code a loop like that shown in this book instead; lambda, map(), and filter() are retained in 3.0 (see Chapter 17).

- All imports become absolute by default, and skip a package's own directory: use the new syntax from . import name to invoke today's relative imports instead (see Chapter 21).

- All classes will be new style classes, and will support today's new style extensions (see Chapter 26).

- The class Spam(object) derivation required today for new style classes will not be required for classes; in 3.0, both today's standalone "classic" and derived "new-style" classes are automatically considered what is called new-style today (see Chapter 26).

- In a try statement, the form except name, value becomes except name as value (see Chapter 27).

- In a raise statement, raise E, V must be coded as raise E(V) to make an instance explicitly (see Chapter 27).

- The with/as exceptions context manager feature described in this book is turned on (see Chapter 27).

- All user-defined and built-in exceptions are identified by classes, not strings (see Chapter 28).

- User-defined exceptions must derive from the built-in BaseException, the root of the exception hierarchy (Exception is its subclass, and suffices as your root class); the built-in StandardException class is removed (see Chapter 28).

- The package structure of the standard library may be reorganized substantially (see Python 3.0 release notes).

Although this list may seem somewhat daunting on first glance, remember that most of the core Python language described in this book will be the same in 3.0; in fact, much of the above is fairly fine details that will not impact programmers much, if at all.

Also note that at this writing, the above list is still somewhat speculative, and ultimately may be neither complete nor accurate, so be sure to see Python 3.0 release notes for the official story. If you've written code for the Python 2.x line, also see the "2to3" automated 2.x to 3.0 code conversion script, which will be provided with Python 3.0.

About This Series

O'Reilly Learning books are written and designed for anyone who wants to build new skills and who prefers a structured approach to studying. Each title in this series makes use of learning principles that we (with your help) have found to be best at equipping you with the knowledge you need for joining that new project, for coping with that unexpected assignment from your manager, or for learning a new language in a hurry.

To get the most out of any book in the Learning series, we recommend you work your way through each chapter in sequence. You'll find that you can get a quick grasp of a chapter's content by reading the instructional captions we've written for its figures. You can also use the Summary to preview each chapter's key takeaways and to review what you have learned. Finally, to help you test your mastery of the material in each chapter, we conclude with a Brain Builder section, which includes a short quiz. Each Part section also includes hands-on exercises.

Learning books work with you as you learn—much as you would expect from a trusted colleague or instructor—and we strive to make your learning experience enjoyable. Tell us how we've done by sending us praise, brickbats, or suggestions for improvements to *learning@oreilly.com*.

Using Code Examples

This book is here to help you get your job done. In general, you may use the code in this book in your programs and documentation. You do not need to contact us for permission unless you're reproducing a significant portion of the code. For example, writing a program that uses several chunks of code from this book does not require permission. Selling or distributing a CD-ROM of examples from O'Reilly books *does* require permission. Answering a question by citing this book and quoting example code does not require permission. Incorporating a significant amount of example code from this book into your product's documentation *does* require permission.

We appreciate, but do not require, attribution. An attribution usually includes the title, author, publisher, and ISBN. For example: "*Learning Python*, Third Edition, by Mark Lutz. Copyright 2008 O'Reilly Media Inc., 978-0-596-51398-6."

If you feel your use of code examples falls outside fair use or the permission given above, feel free to contact us at *permissions@oreilly.com*.

Font Conventions

This book uses the following typographical conventions:

Italic
> Used for email addresses, URLs, filenames, pathnames, and emphasizing new terms when they are first introduced

`Constant width`
> Used for the contents of files and the output from commands, and to designate modules, methods, statements, and commands

`Constant width bold`
> Used in code sections to show commands or text that would be typed by the user, and, occasionally, to highlight portions of code

`Constant width italic`
> Used for replaceables and some comments in code sections

`<Constant width>`
> Indicates a syntactic unit that should be replaced with real code

 Indicates a tip, suggestion, or general note relating to the nearby text.

 Indicates a warning or caution relating to the nearby text.

In this book's examples, the % character at the start of a system command line stands for the system's prompt, whatever that may be on your machine (e.g., `C:\Python25>` in a DOS window). Don't type the % character yourself. Similarly, in interpreter interaction listings, do not type the >>> and ... characters shown at the start of lines—these are prompts that Python displays. Type just the text after these prompts. To help you remember this, user inputs are shown in bold font in this book. Also, you normally don't need to type text that starts with a # in listings; as you'll learn, these are comments, not executable code.

Safari® Books Online

 When you see a Safari® Books Online icon on the cover of your favorite technology book, that means the book is available online through the O'Reilly Network Safari Bookshelf.

Safari offers a solution that's better than e-books. It's a virtual library that lets you easily search thousands of top tech books, cut and paste code samples, download chapters, and find quick answers when you need the most accurate, current information. Try it for free at *http://safari.oreilly.com*.

How to Contact Us

Please address comments and questions concerning this book to the publisher:

O'Reilly Media, Inc.
1005 Gravenstein Highway North
Sebastopol, CA 95472
800-998-9938 (in the United States or Canada)
707-829-0515 (international or local)
707-829-0104 (fax)

We will also maintain a web page for this book, where we list errata, examples, and any additional information. You can access this page at:

http://www.oreilly.com/catalog/9780596513986

To comment or ask technical questions about this book, send email to:

bookquestions@oreilly.com

For more information about our books, conferences, Resource Centers, and the O'Reilly Network, see our web site at:

http://www.oreilly.com

For book updates, be sure to also see the other links mentioned earlier in this Preface.

Acknowledgments

As I write this third edition of this book in 2007, I can't help but be in a sort of "mission accomplished" state of mind. I have now been using and promoting Python for 15 years, and have been teaching it for 10 years. Despite the passage of time and events, I am still constantly amazed at how successful Python has been over the years. It has grown in ways that most of us could not possibly have imagined in 1992. So, at the risk of sounding like a hopelessly self-absorbed author, you'll have to pardon a few words of reminiscing, congratulations, and thanks here.

It's been a long and winding road. Looking back today, when I first discovered Python in 1992, I had no idea what an impact it would have on the next 15 years of my life. Two years after writing the first edition of *Programming Python* in 1995, I began traveling around the country and the world teaching Python to beginners and experts. Since finishing the first edition of *Learning Python* in 1999, I've been a full-time, independent Python trainer and writer, thanks largely to Python's exponentially growing popularity.

As I write these words in mid-2007, I have written nine Python books; I have also been teaching Python for more than a decade, having taught some 200 Python training sessions in the U.S., Europe, Canada, and Mexico, and having met over 3,000 students along the way. Besides racking up frequent flyer miles, these classes helped me refine this text as well as my other Python books. Over the years, teaching honed the books, and vice versa. In fact, the book you're reading is derived almost entirely from my classes.

Because of this, I'd like to thank all the students who have participated in my courses during the last 10 years. Along with changes in Python itself, your feedback played a huge role in shaping this text. (There's nothing quite as instructive as watching 3,000 students repeat the same beginner's mistakes!) This edition owes its changes primarily to classes held after 2003, though every class held since 1997 has in some way helped refine this book. I'd especially like to single out clients who hosted classes in Dublin, Mexico City, Barcelona, London, Edmonton, and Puerto Rico; better perks would be hard to imagine.

I'd also like to express my gratitude to everyone who played a part in producing this book. To the editors who worked on this project: Tatiana Apandi on this edition, and many others on prior editions. To Liza Daly for taking part in the technical review of this book. And to O'Reilly for giving me a chance to work on those nine book projects—it's been net fun (and only feels a little like the movie *Groundhog Day*).

I want to thank my original coauthor David Ascher as well for his work on earlier editions of this book. David contributed the "Outer Layers" part in prior editions, which we unfortunately had to trim to make room for new core language materials in this edition. I've added a handful of more advanced programs as a self-study final exercise in this edition, but this doesn't compensate for all the material that's been cut. See the prior notes in this Preface about follow-up application-level texts if you're feeling nostalgic about this material.

For creating such an enjoyable and useful language, I owe additional thanks to Guido van Rossum and the rest of the Python community. Like most open source systems, Python is the product of many heroic efforts. After 15 years of programming Python, I still find it to be seriously fun. It's been my privilege to watch Python grow from a new kid on the scripting languages block to a widely used tool, deployed in some fashion by almost every organization writing software. That has been an exciting endeavor to be a part of, and I'd like to thank and congratulate the entire Python community for a job well done.

I also want to thank my original editor at O'Reilly, the late Frank Willison. This book was largely Frank's idea, and it reflects the contagious vision he had. In looking back, Frank had a profound impact on both my own career and that of Python itself. It is not an exaggeration to say that Frank was responsible for much of the fun and success of Python when it was new. We miss him still.

Finally, a few personal notes of thanks. To OQO for the best toys so far. To the late Carl Sagan for inspiring an 18-year-old kid from Wisconsin. To Jon Stewart and Michael Moore for being patriots. And to all the large corporations I've come across over the years, for reminding me how lucky I have been to be self-employed.

To my children, Mike, Sammy, and Roxy, for whatever futures they will choose to make. You were children when I began with Python, and you seem to have somehow grown up along the way; I'm proud of you. Life may compel us down paths all our own, but there will always be a path home.

And most of all, to Vera, my best friend, my girlfriend, and my wife. The best day of my life was the day I finally found you. I don't know what the next 50 years hold, but I do know that I want to spend all of them holding you.

—Mark Lutz
Berthoud, Colorado
July 2007

Getting Started

## CHAPTER 1

A Python Q&A Session

If you've bought this book, you may already know what Python is, and why it's an important tool to learn. If you don't, you probably won't be sold on Python until you've learned the language by reading the rest of this book and have done a project or two. But before we jump into details, the first few pages of this book will briefly introduce some of the main reasons behind Python's popularity. To begin sculpting a definition of Python, this chapter takes the form of a question-and-answer session, which poses some of the most common questions asked by beginners.

Why Do People Use Python?

Because there are many programming languages available today, this is the usual first question of newcomers. Given that there are roughly 1 million Python users out there at the moment, there really is no way to answer this question with complete accuracy. The choice of development tools is sometimes based on unique constraints or personal preference.

But after teaching Python to roughly 200 groups and 3,000 students during the last 10 years, some common themes have emerged. The primary factors cited by Python users seem to be these:

Software quality
> For many, Python's focus on readability, coherence, and software quality in general sets it apart from other tools in the scripting world. Python code is designed to be readable, and hence, reusable and maintainable—much more so than traditional scripting languages. The uniformity of Python code makes it easy to understand, even if you did not write it. In addition, Python has deep support for more advanced software reuse mechanisms, such as object-oriented programming (OOP).

Developer productivity

Python boosts developer productivity many times beyond compiled or statically typed languages such as C, C++, and Java. Python code is typically one-third to one-fifth the size of equivalent C++ or Java code. That means there is less to type, less to debug, and less to maintain after the fact. Python programs also run immediately, without the lengthy compile and link steps of some other tools, further boosting programmer speed.

Program portability

Most Python programs run unchanged on all major computer platforms. Porting Python code between Linux and Windows, for example, is usually just a matter of copying a script's code between machines. Moreover, Python offers multiple options for coding portable graphical user interfaces, database access programs, web-based systems, and more. Even operating system interfaces, including program launches and directory processing, are as portable in Python as they can possibly be.

Support libraries

Python comes with a large collection of prebuilt and portable functionality, known as the *standard library*. This library supports an array of application-level programming tasks, from text pattern matching to network scripting. In addition, Python can be extended with both homegrown libraries and a vast collection of third-party application support software. Python's third-party domain offers tools for web site construction, numeric programming, serial port access, game development, and much more. The NumPy extension, for instance, has been described as a free and more powerful equivalent to the Matlab numeric programming system.

Component integration

Python scripts can easily communicate with other parts of an application, using a variety of integration mechanisms. Such integrations allow Python to be used as a product customization and extension tool. Today, Python code can invoke C and C++ libraries, can be called from C and C++ programs, can integrate with Java components, can communicate over frameworks such as COM and .NET, and can interact over networks with interfaces like SOAP, XML-RPC, and CORBA. It is not a standalone tool.

Enjoyment

Because of Python's ease of use and built-in toolset, it can make the act of programming more pleasure than chore. Although this may be an intangible benefit, its effect on productivity is an important asset.

Of these factors, the first two (quality and productivity) are probably the most compelling benefits to most Python users.

Software Quality

By design, Python implements a deliberately simple and readable syntax, and a highly coherent programming model. As a slogan at a recent Python conference attests, the net result is that Python seems to "fit your brain"—that is, features of the language interact in consistent and limited ways, and follow naturally from a small set of core concepts. This makes the language easier to learn, understand, and remember. In practice, Python programmers do not need to constantly refer to manuals when reading or writing code; it's a consistently designed system that many find yields surprisingly regular-looking code.

By philosophy, Python adopts a somewhat minimalist approach. This means that although there are usually multiple ways to accomplish a coding task, there is usually just one obvious way, a few less obvious alternatives, and a small set of coherent interactions everywhere in the language. Moreover, Python doesn't make arbitrary decisions for you; when interactions are ambiguous, explicit intervention is preferred over "magic." In the Python way of thinking, explicit is better than implicit, and simple is better than complex.*

Beyond such design themes, Python includes tools such as modules and OOP that naturally promote code reusability. And because Python is focused on quality, so too, naturally, are Python programmers.

Developer Productivity

During the great Internet boom of the mid-to-late 1990s, it was difficult to find enough programmers to implement software projects; developers were asked to implement systems as fast as the Internet evolved. Now, in the post-boom era of layoffs and economic recession, the picture has shifted. Today, programming staffs are often asked to accomplish the same tasks with even fewer people.

In both of these scenarios, Python has shined as a tool that allows programmers to get more done with less effort. It is deliberately optimized for *speed of development*— its simple syntax, dynamic typing, lack of compile steps, and built-in toolset allow programmers to develop programs in a fraction of the time needed when using some other tools. The net effect is that Python typically boosts developer productivity many times beyond the levels supported by traditional languages. That's good news in both boom and bust times, and everywhere the software industry goes in between.

---

* For a more complete look at the Python philosophy, type the command import this at any Python interactive prompt (you'll see how in Chapter 2). This invokes an "Easter egg" hidden in Python—a collection of design principles underlying Python. The acronym EIBTI is now fashionable jargon for the "explicit is better than implicit" rule.

Is Python a "Scripting Language"?

Python is a general-purpose programming language that is often applied in scripting roles. It is commonly defined as an *object-oriented scripting language*—a definition that blends support for OOP with an overall orientation toward scripting roles. In fact, people often use the word "script" instead of "program" to describe a Python code file. In this book, the terms "script" and "program" are used interchangeably, with a slight preference for "script" to describe a simpler top-level file, and "program" to refer to a more sophisticated multifile application.

Because the term "scripting language" has so many different meanings to different observers, some would prefer that it not be applied to Python at all. In fact, people tend to make three very different associations, some of which are more useful than others, when they hear Python labeled as such:

Shell tools

Sometimes when people hear Python described as a scripting language, they think it means that Python is a tool for coding operating-system-oriented scripts. Such programs are often launched from console command lines, and perform tasks such as processing text files and launching other programs.

Python programs can and do serve such roles, but this is just one of dozens of common Python application domains. It is not just a better shell-script language.

Control language

To others, scripting refers to a "glue" layer used to control and direct (i.e., script) other application components. Python programs are indeed often deployed in the context of larger applications. For instance, to test hardware devices, Python programs may call out to components that give low-level access to a device. Similarly, programs may run bits of Python code at strategic points to support end-user product customization without having to ship and recompile the entire system's source code.

Python's simplicity makes it a naturally flexible control tool. Technically, though, this is also just a common Python role; many Python programmers code standalone scripts without ever using or knowing about any integrated components. It is not just a control language.

Ease of use

Probably the best way to think of the term "scripting language" is that it refers to a simple language used for quickly coding tasks. This is especially true when the term is applied to Python, which allows much faster program development than compiled languages like C++. Its rapid development cycle fosters an exploratory, incremental mode of programming that has to be experienced to be appreciated.

Don't be fooled, though—Python is not just for simple tasks. Rather, it makes tasks simple by its ease of use and flexibility. Python has a simple feature set, but it allows programs to scale up in sophistication as needed. Because of that, it is commonly used for quick tactical tasks and longer-term strategic development.

So, is Python a scripting language or not? It depends on whom you ask. In general, the term "scripting" is probably best used to describe the rapid and flexible mode of development that Python supports, rather than a particular application domain.

OK, but What's the Downside?

After using Python for 15 years and teaching it for 10, the only downside to Python I've found is that, as currently implemented, its execution speed may not always be as fast as compiled languages such as C and C++.

We'll talk about implementation concepts in detail later in this book. In short, the standard implementations of Python today compile (i.e., translate) source code statements to an intermediate format known as *byte code*, and then interpret the byte code. Byte code provides portability, as it is a platform-independent format. However, because Python is not compiled all the way down to binary machine code (e.g., instructions for an Intel chip), some programs will run more slowly in Python than in a fully compiled language like C.

Whether you will ever *care* about the execution speed difference depends on what kinds of programs you write. Python has been optimized numerous times, and Python code runs fast enough by itself in most application domains. Furthermore, whenever you do something "real" in a Python script, like process a file or construct a GUI, your program is actually running at C speed, since such tasks are immediately dispatched to compiled C code inside the Python interpreter. More fundamentally, Python's speed-of-development gain is often far more important than any speed-of-execution loss, especially given modern computer speeds.

Even at today's CPU speeds, though, there still are some domains that do require optimal execution speeds. Numeric programming and animation, for example, often need at least their core number-crunching components to run at C speed (or better). If you work in such a domain, you can still use Python—simply split off the parts of the application that require optimal speed into *compiled extensions*, and link those into your system for use in Python scripts.

We won't talk about extensions much in this text, but this is really just an instance of the Python-as-control-language role that we discussed earlier. A prime example of this dual language strategy is the *NumPy* numeric programming extension for Python; by combining compiled and optimized numeric extension libraries with the Python language, NumPy turns Python into a numeric programming tool that is efficient and easy to use. You may never need to code such extensions in your own Python work, but they provide a powerful optimization mechanism if you ever do.

Who Uses Python Today?

At this writing, in 2007, the best estimate anyone can seem to make of the size of the Python user base is that there are roughly 1 million Python users around the world today (plus or minus a few). This estimate is based on various statistics, like download rates and developer surveys. Because Python is open source, a more exact count is difficult—there are no license registrations to tally. Moreover, Python is automatically included with Linux distributions, Macintosh computers, and some products and hardware, further clouding the user-base picture.

In general, though, Python enjoys a large user base, and a very active developer community. Because Python has been around for more than 15 years and has been widely used, it is also very stable and robust. Besides being employed by individual users, Python is also being applied in real revenue-generating products by real companies. For instance:

- Google makes extensive use of Python in its web search system, and employs Python's creator.
- The YouTube video sharing service is largely written in Python.
- The popular BitTorrent peer-to-peer file sharing system is a Python program.
- Intel, Cisco, Hewlett-Packard, Seagate, Qualcomm, and IBM use Python for hardware testing.
- Industrial Light & Magic, Pixar, and others use Python in the production of movie animation.
- JPMorgan Chase, UBS, Getco, and Citadel apply Python for financial market forecasting.
- NASA, Los Alamos, Fermilab, JPL, and others use Python for scientific programming tasks.
- iRobot uses Python to develop commercial robotic vacuum cleaners.
- ESRI uses Python as an end-user customization tool for its popular GIS mapping products.
- The NSA uses Python for cryptography and intelligence analysis.
- The IronPort email server product uses more than 1 million lines of Python code to do its job.
- The One Laptop Per Child (OLPC) project builds its user interface and activity model in Python.

And so on. Probably the only common thread amongst the companies using Python today is that Python is used all over the map, in terms of application domains. Its general-purpose nature makes it applicable to almost all fields, not just one. In fact, it's safe to say that Python is being used by virtually every substantial organization

writing software, whether for short-term tactical tasks such as testing and administration, or for long-term strategic product development. Python has proven to work
well in both modes.

For more details on companies using Python today, see Python's web site at *http://
www.python.org*.

What Can I Do with Python?

Besides being a well-designed programming language, Python is also useful for
accomplishing real-world tasks—the sorts of things developers do day in and day
out. It's commonly used in a variety of domains, as a tool for scripting other components and implementing standalone programs. In fact, as a general-purpose
language, Python's roles are virtually unlimited: you can use it for everything from
web site development and gaming, to robotics and spacecraft control.

However, the most common Python roles currently seem to fall into a few broad categories. The next few sections describe some of Python's most common applications
today, as well as tools used in each domain. We won't be able to explore the tools
mentioned here in any depth—if you are interested in any of these topics, see the
Python web site, or other resources for more details.

Systems Programming

Python's built-in interfaces to operating-system services make it ideal for writing portable, maintainable system-administration tools and utilities (sometimes called *shell
tools*). Python programs can search files and directory trees, launch other programs,
do parallel processing with processes and threads, and so on.

Python's standard library comes with POSIX bindings and support for all the usual
OS tools: environment variables, files, sockets, pipes, processes, multiple threads,
regular expression pattern matching, command-line arguments, standard stream
interfaces, shell-command launchers, filename expansion, and more. In addition, the
bulk of Python's system interfaces are designed to be portable; for example, a script
that copies directory trees typically runs unchanged on all major Python platforms.

GUIs

Python's simplicity and rapid turnaround also make it a good match for graphical
user interface (GUI) programming. Python comes with a standard object-oriented
interface to the Tk GUI API called *Tkinter*, which allows Python programs to implement portable GUIs with a native look and feel. Python/Tkinter GUIs run
unchanged on MS Windows, X Windows (on Unix and Linux), and the Mac OS

(both Classic and OS X). A free extension package, *PMW*, adds advanced widgets to the Tkinter toolkit. In addition, the *wxPython* GUI API, based on a C++ library, offers an alternative toolkit for constructing portable GUIs in Python.

Higher-level toolkits such as *PythonCard* and *Dabo* are built on top of base APIs such as wxPython and Tkinter. With the proper library, you can also use other GUI toolkits in Python, such as Qt, GTK, MFC, and Swing. For applications that run in web browsers, or have simple interface requirements, both Jython (the Java version of Python, described in Chapter 2) and Python server-side CGI scripts provide additional user interface options.

Internet Scripting

Python comes with standard Internet modules that allow Python programs to perform a wide variety of networking tasks, in client and server modes. Scripts can communicate over sockets; extract form information sent to server-side CGI scripts; transfer files by FTP; process XML files; send, receive, compose, and parse email; fetch web pages by URLs; parse the HTML and XML of fetched web pages; communicate over XML-RPC, SOAP, and Telnet; and more. Python's libraries make these tasks remarkably simple.

In addition, there is a large collection of third-party tools available on the Web for doing Internet programming in Python. For instance, the *HTMLGen* system generates HTML files from Python class-based descriptions, the *mod_python* package runs Python efficiently within the Apache web server and supports server-side templating with its Python Server Pages, and the Jython system provides for seamless Python/Java integration, and supports coding of server-side applets that run on clients. In addition, full-blown web development packages for Python, such as Django, Turbo-Gears, Pylons, Zope, and WebWare, support quick construction of full-featured and production-quality web sites with Python.

Component Integration

We discussed the component integration role earlier when describing Python as a control language. Python's ability to be extended by and embedded in C and C++ systems makes it useful as a flexible glue language for scripting the behavior of other systems and components. For instance, integrating a C library into Python enables Python to test and launch the library's components, and embedding Python in a product enables onsite customizations to be coded without having to recompile the entire product, or ship its source code at all.

Tools such as the SWIG and SIP code generators can automate much of the work needed to link compiled components into Python for use in scripts. And larger frameworks, such as Python's COM support on MS Windows, the Jython Java-based implementation, the IronPython .NET-based implementation, and various CORBA toolkits for Python, provide alternative ways to script components. On Windows, for example, Python scripts can use frameworks to script MS Word and Excel.

Database Programming

For traditional database demands, there are Python interfaces to all commonly used relational database systems—Sybase, Oracle, Informix, ODBC, MySQL, PostgreSQL, SQLite, and more. The Python world has also defined a *portable database API* for accessing SQL database systems from Python scripts, which looks the same on a variety of underlying database systems. For instance, because vendor interfaces implement the portable API, a script written to work with the free MySQL system will work largely unchanged on other systems (such as Oracle); all you have to do is replace the underlying vendor interface.

Python's standard pickle module provides a simple *object persistence* system—it allows programs to easily save and restore entire Python objects to files and file-like objects. On the Web, you'll also find a third-party system named ZODB that provides a complete object-oriented database system for Python scripts, and another called SQLObject that maps relational tables onto Python's class model. And, as of Python 2.5, SQLite is a standard part of Python itself.

Rapid Prototyping

To Python programs, components written in Python and C look the same. Because of this, it's possible to prototype systems in Python initially, and then move selected components to a compiled language such as C or C++ for delivery. Unlike some prototyping tools, Python doesn't require a complete rewrite once the prototype has solidified. Parts of the system that don't require the efficiency of a language such as C++ can remain coded in Python for ease of maintenance and use.

Numeric and Scientific Programming

The NumPy numeric programming extension for Python mentioned earlier includes such advanced tools as an array object, interfaces to standard mathematical libraries, and much more. By integrating Python with numeric routines coded in a compiled language for speed, NumPy turns Python into a sophisticated yet easy-to-use numeric programming tool, which can often replace existing code written in traditional compiled languages such as FORTRAN or C++. Additional numeric tools for Python support animation, 3D visualization, parallel processing, and so on.

Gaming, Images, AI, XML, Robots, and More

Python is commonly applied in more domains than can be mentioned here. For example, you can do graphics and game programming in Python with the *pygame* system; image processing with the *PIL* package and others; robot control programming with the *PyRo* toolkit; XML parsing with the xml library package, the xmlrpclib module, and third-party extensions; AI programming with neural network simulators and expert system shells; and natural language analysis with the *NLTK* package. You can even play solitaire with the *PySol* program. You'll find support for many such fields at the Vaults of Parnassus, and the newer PyPI web sites (search Google or *http://www.python.org* for links).

In general, many of these specific domains are largely just instances of Python's component integration role in action again. Adding Python as a frontend to libraries of components written in a compiled language such as C makes Python useful for scripting in a wide variety of domains. As a general-purpose language that supports integration, Python is widely applicable.

What Are Python's Technical Strengths?

Naturally, this is a developer's question. If you don't already have a programming background, the language in the next few sections may be a bit baffling—don't worry, we'll explore all of these terms in more detail as we proceed through this book. For developers, though, here is a quick introduction to some of Python's top technical features.

It's Object Oriented

Python is an object-oriented language, from the ground up. Its class model supports advanced notions such as polymorphism, operator overloading, and multiple inheritance; yet, in the context of Python's simple syntax and typing, OOP is remarkably easy to apply. In fact, if you don't understand these terms, you'll find they are much easier to learn with Python than with just about any other OOP language available.

Besides serving as a powerful code structuring and reuse device, Python's OOP nature makes it ideal as a scripting tool for object-oriented systems languages such as C++ and Java. For example, with the appropriate glue code, Python programs can subclass (specialize) classes implemented in C++, Java, and C#.

Of equal significance, OOP is an *option* in Python; you can go far without having to become an object guru all at once. Much like C++, Python supports both procedural and object-oriented programming modes. Its object-oriented tools can be applied if and when constraints allow. This is especially useful in tactical development modes, which preclude design phases.

It's Free

Python is completely free to use and distribute. As with other open source software, such as Tcl, Perl, Linux, and Apache, you can fetch the entire Python system's source code for free on the Internet. There are no restrictions on copying it, embedding it in your systems, or shipping it with your products. In fact, you can even sell Python's source code, if you are so inclined.

But don't get the wrong idea: "free" doesn't mean "unsupported." On the contrary, the Python online community responds to user queries with a speed that most commercial software vendors would do well to notice. Moreover, because Python comes with complete source code, it empowers developers, leading to the creation of a large team of implementation experts. Although studying or changing a programming language's implementation isn't everyone's idea of fun, it's comforting to know that it's available as a final resort and ultimate documentation source. You're not dependent on the whims of a commercial vendor.

Python development is performed by a community, which largely coordinates its efforts over the Internet. It consists of Python's creator—Guido van Rossum, the officially anointed Benevolent Dictator for Life (BDFL) of Python—plus a cast of thousands. Language changes must follow a formal enhancement procedure (known as the PEP process), and be scrutinized by a formal testing system and the BDFL. Happily, this tends to make Python more conservative with changes than some other languages.

It's Portable

The standard implementation of Python is written in portable ANSI C, and it compiles and runs on virtually every major platform currently in use. For example, Python programs run today on everything from PDAs to supercomputers. As a partial list, Python is available on:

- Linux and Unix systems
- Microsoft Windows and DOS (all modern flavors)
- Mac OS (both OS X and Classic)
- BeOS, OS/2, VMS, and QNX
- Real-time systems such as VxWorks
- Cray supercomputers and IBM mainframes
- PDAs running Palm OS, PocketPC, and Linux
- Cell phones running Symbian OS and Windows Mobile
- Gaming consoles and iPods
- And more

Besides the language interpreter itself, the standard library modules that ship with Python are also implemented to be as portable across platform boundaries as possible. Further, Python programs are automatically compiled to portable byte code, which runs the same on any platform with a compatible version of Python installed (more on this in the next chapter).

What that means is that Python programs using the core language and standard libraries run the same on Linux, Windows, and most other systems with a Python interpreter. Most Python ports also contain platform-specific extensions (e.g., COM support on Windows), but the core Python language and libraries work the same everywhere. As mentioned earlier, Python also includes an interface to the Tk GUI toolkit called Tkinter, which allows Python programs to implement full-featured graphical user interfaces that run on all major GUI platforms without program changes.

It's Powerful

From a features perspective, Python is something of a hybrid. Its toolset places it between traditional scripting languages (such as Tcl, Scheme, and Perl), and systems development languages (such as C, C++, and Java). Python provides all the simplicity and ease of use of a scripting language, along with more advanced software-engineering tools typically found in compiled languages. Unlike some scripting languages, this combination makes Python useful for large-scale development projects. As a preview, here are some of the main things you'll find in Python's toolbox:

Dynamic typing
> Python keeps track of the kinds of objects your program uses when it runs; it doesn't require complicated type and size declarations in your code. In fact, as you'll see in Chapter 6, there is no such thing as a type or variable declaration anywhere in Python. Because Python code does not constrain data types, it is also usually automatically applicable to a whole range of objects.

Automatic memory management
> Python automatically allocates objects and reclaims ("garbage collects") them when they are no longer used, and most grow and shrink on demand. As you'll learn, Python keeps track of low-level memory details so you don't have to.

Programming-in-the-large support
> For building larger systems, Python includes tools such as modules, classes, and exceptions. These tools allow you to organize systems into components, use OOP to reuse and customize code, and handle events and errors gracefully.

Built-in object types
> Python provides commonly used data structures such as lists, dictionaries, and strings as intrinsic parts of the language; as you'll see, they're both flexible and easy to use. For instance, built-in objects can grow and shrink on demand, can be arbitrarily nested to represent complex information, and more.

Built-in tools

To process all those object types, Python comes with powerful and standard operations, including concatenation (joining collections), slicing (extracting sections), sorting, mapping, and more.

Library utilities

For more specific tasks, Python also comes with a large collection of precoded library tools that support everything from regular-expression matching to networking. Python's library tools are where much of the application-level action occurs.

Third-party utilities

Because Python is open source, developers are encouraged to contribute precoded tools that support tasks beyond those supported by its built-ins; on the Web, you'll find free support for COM, imaging, CORBA ORBs, XML, database access, and much more.

Despite the array of tools in Python, it retains a remarkably simple syntax and design. The result is a powerful programming tool with all the usability of a scripting language.

It's Mixable

Python programs can easily be "glued" to components written in other languages in a variety of ways. For example, Python's C API lets C programs call and be called by Python programs flexibly. That means you can add functionality to the Python system as needed, and use Python programs within other environments or systems.

Mixing Python with libraries coded in languages such as C or C++, for instance, makes it an easy-to-use frontend language and customization tool. As mentioned earlier, this also makes Python good at rapid prototyping; systems may be implemented in Python first, to leverage its speed of development, and later, moved to C for delivery, one piece at a time, according to performance demands.

It's Easy to Use

To run a Python program, you simply type it and run it. There are no intermediate compile and link steps, like there are for languages such as C or C++. Python executes programs immediately, which makes for an interactive programming experience and rapid turnaround after program changes—in many cases, you can witness the effect of a program change as fast as you can type it.

Of course, development cycle turnaround is only one aspect of Python's ease of use. It also provides a deliberately simple syntax and powerful built-in tools. In fact, some have gone so far as to call Python "executable pseudocode." Because it eliminates much of the complexity in other tools, Python programs are simpler, smaller, and more flexible than equivalent programs in languages like C, C++, and Java!

Python Is Engineering, Not Art

When Python first emerged on the software scene in the early 1990s, it spawned what is now something of a classic conflict between its proponents and those of another popular scripting language, Perl. Personally, I think the debate is tired and unwarranted today—developers are smart enough to draw their own conclusions. Still, this is one of the most common topics I'm asked about on the training road, so it seems fitting to say a few words on the topic here.

The short story is this: *you can do everything in Python that you can in Perl, but you can read your code after you do it.* That's it—their domains largely overlap, but Python is more focused on producing readable code. For many, the enhanced readability of Python translates to code reusability and maintainability, making Python a better choice for programs that will not be written once and thrown away. Perl code is easy to write, but difficult to read. Given that most software has a lifespan much longer than its initial creation, many see Python as a more effective tool.

The somewhat longer story reflects the backgrounds of the designers of the two languages, and underscores some of the main reasons people choose to use Python. Python's creator is a mathematician by training; as such, he produced a language with a high degree of uniformity—its syntax and toolset are remarkably coherent. Moreover, like math, its design is orthogonal—most of the language follows from a small set of core concepts. For instance, once one grasps Python's flavor of polymorphism, the rest is largely just details.

By contrast, the creator of the Perl language is a linguist, and its design reflects this heritage. There are many ways to accomplish the same tasks in Perl, and language constructs interact in context-sensitive and sometimes quite subtle ways—much like natural language. As the well-known Perl motto states, "There's more than one way to do it." Given this design, both the Perl language and its user community have historically encouraged freedom of expression when writing code. One person's Perl code can be radically different from another's. In fact, writing unique, tricky code is often a source of pride among Perl users.

But as anyone who has done any substantial code maintenance should be able to attest, freedom of expression is great for art, but lousy for engineering. In engineering, we need a minimal feature set and predictability. In engineering, freedom of expression can lead to maintenance nightmares. As more than one Perl user has confided to me, the result of too much freedom is often code that is much easier to rewrite from scratch than to modify.

—continued—

Consider this: when people create a painting or a sculpture, they do so for themselves for purely aesthetic purposes. The possibility of someone else having to change that painting or sculpture later does not enter into it. This is a critical difference between art and engineering. When people write software, they are not writing it for themselves. In fact, they are not even writing primarily for the computer. Rather, good programmers know that code is written for the next human being who has to read it in order to maintain or reuse it. If that person cannot understand the code, it's all but useless in a realistic development scenario.

This is where many people find that Python most clearly differentiates itself from scripting languages like Perl. Because Python's syntax model almost forces users to write readable code, Python programs lend themselves more directly to the full software development cycle. And because Python emphasizes ideas such as limited interactions, uniformity, regularity, and consistency, it more directly fosters code that can be used long after it is first written.

In the long run, Python's focus on code quality in itself boosts programmer productivity, as well as programmer satisfaction. Python programmers can be creative, too, and as we'll see, the language does offer multiple solutions for some tasks. At its core, though, Python encourages good engineering in ways that other scripting languages often do not.

At least, that's the common consensus among many people who have adopted Python. You should always judge such claims for yourself, of course, by learning what Python has to offer. To help you get started, let's move on to the next chapter.

It's Easy to Learn

This brings us to a key point of this book: compared to other programming languages, the core Python language is remarkably easy to learn. In fact, you can expect to be coding significant Python programs in a matter of days (or perhaps in just hours, if you're already an experienced programmer). That's good news for professional developers seeking to learn the language to use on the job, as well as for end users of systems that expose a Python layer for customization or control. Today, many systems rely on the fact that end users can quickly learn enough Python to tailor their Python customizations' code onsite, with little or no support. Although Python does have advanced programming tools, its core language is still simple for beginners and gurus alike.

It's Named After Monty Python

OK, this isn't quite a technical strength, but it does seem to be a surprisingly well-kept secret that I wish to expose up front. Despite all the reptile icons in the Python world, the truth is that Python creator Guido van Rossum named it after the BBC comedy series *Monty Python's Flying Circus*. He is a big fan of Monty Python, as are many software developers (indeed, there seems to almost be a symmetry between the two fields).

This legacy inevitably adds a humorous quality to Python code examples. For instance, the traditional "foo" and "bar" for generic variable names become "spam" and "eggs" in the Python world. The occasional "Brian," "ni," and "shrubbery" likewise owe their appearances to this namesake. It even impacts the Python community at large: talks at Python conferences are regularly billed as "The Spanish Inquisition."

All of this is, of course, very funny if you are familiar with the show, but less so otherwise. You don't need to be familiar with the series to make sense of examples that borrow references to Monty Python (including many you will see in this book), but at least you now know their root.

How Does Python Stack Up to Language X?

Finally, to place it in the context of what you may already know, people sometimes compare Python to languages such as Perl, Tcl, and Java. We talked about performance earlier, so here we'll focus on functionality. While other languages are also useful tools to know and use, many people find that Python:

- Is more powerful than Tcl. Python's support for "programming in the large" makes it applicable to the development of larger systems.

- Has a cleaner syntax and simpler design than Perl, which makes it more readable and maintainable, and helps reduce program bugs.

- Is simpler and easier to use than Java. Python is a scripting language, but Java inherits much of the complexity and syntax of systems languages such as C++.

- Is simpler and easier to use than C++, but often doesn't compete with C++, either; as a scripting language, Python often serves different roles.

- Is both more powerful and more cross-platform than Visual Basic. Its open source nature also means it is not controlled by a single company.

- Is more mature and has a more readable syntax than Ruby. Unlike Ruby and Java, OOP is an option in Python—Python does not impose OOP on users or projects to which it may not apply.

- Has the dynamic flavor of languages like SmallTalk and Lisp, but also has a simple, traditional syntax accessible to developers as well as end users of customizable systems.

Especially for programs that do more than scan text files, and that might have to be read in the future by others (or by you!), many people find that Python fits the bill better than any other scripting or programming language available today. Furthermore, unless your application requires peak performance, Python is often a viable alternative to systems development languages such as C, C++, and Java: Python code will be much less difficult to write, debug, and maintain.

Of course, your author has been a card-carrying Python evangelist since 1992, so take these comments as you may. They do, however, reflect the common experience of many developers who have taken time to explore what Python has to offer.

Chapter Summary

And that concludes the hype portion of this book. In this chapter, we've explored some of the reasons that people pick Python for their programming tasks. We've also seen how it is applied, and a representative sample of who is using it today. My goal is to teach Python, though, not to sell it. The best way to judge a language is to see it in action, so the rest of this book focuses entirely on the language details we've glossed over here.

To get started, the next two chapters begin our technical introduction to the language. There, we explore ways to run Python programs, peek at Python's byte code execution model, and introduce the basics of module files for saving code. The goal will be to give you just enough information to run the examples and exercises in the rest of the book. You won't really start programming until Chapter 4, but make sure you have a handle on the startup details before moving on.

Chapter Quiz

In this edition of the book, we will be closing each chapter with a quick pop quiz about the material presented to help you review the key concepts. The answers for these quizzes appear immediately after the questions, and you are encouraged to read the answers once you've taken a crack at the questions yourself. In addition to these end-of-chapter quizzes, you'll find lab exercises at the end of each part of the book, designed to help you start coding Python on your own. For now, here's your first test. Good luck!

1. What are the six main reasons that people choose to use Python?
2. Name four notable companies or organizations using Python today.
3. Why might you *not* want to use Python in an application?
4. What can you do with Python?
5. What's the significance of the Python `import this` statement?
6. Why does "spam" show up in so many Python examples in books and on the Web?
7. What is your favorite color?

Quiz Answers

How did you do? Here are the answers I came up with, though there may be multiple solutions to some quiz questions. Again, even if you're sure you got a question right, I encourage you to look at these answers for additional context. See the chapter's text for more details if any of these responses don't make sense to you.

1. Software quality, developer productivity, program portability, support libraries, component integration, and enjoyment. Of these, the quality and productivity themes seem to be the main reasons that people choose to use Python.
2. Google, Industrial Light & Magic, Jet Propulsion Labs, ESRI, and many more. Almost every organization doing software development is using Python in some fashion, whether for long-term strategic product development, or for short-term tactical tasks such as testing and system administration.
3. Python's downside is performance: it won't run as quickly as fully compiled languages like C and C++. On the other hand, it's quick enough for most applications, and typical Python code runs at close to C speed anyhow because it invokes linked-in C code in the interpreter. If speed is critical, compiled extensions are available for number-crunching parts of an application.

4. You can use Python for nearly anything you can do with a computer—from web site development and gaming, to robotics and spacecraft control.

5. `import this` triggers an Easter egg inside Python that displays some of the design philosophies underlying the language. You'll learn how to run this statement in the next chapter.

6. "Spam" is a reference from a famous Monty Python skit in which people trying to order food in a cafeteria are drowned out by a chorus of Vikings singing about spam. Oh, and it's also a common variable name in Python scripts....

7. Blue. No, yellow!

CHAPTER 2

How Python Runs Programs

This chapter and the next give a quick look at program execution—how you launch code, and how Python runs it. In this chapter, we'll study the Python interpreter. Chapter 3 will then show you how to get your own programs up and running.

Startup details are inherently platform-specific, and some of the material in this chapter may not apply to the platform you work on, so you should feel free to skip parts not relevant to your intended use. Likewise, more advanced readers who have used similar tools in the past and prefer to get to the meat of the language quickly may want to file some of this chapter away as "for future reference." For the rest of you, let's learn how to run some code.

Introducing the Python Interpreter

So far, I've mostly been talking about Python as a programming language. But, as currently implemented, it's also a software package called an *interpreter*. An interpreter is a kind of program that executes other programs. When you write a Python program, the Python interpreter reads your program and carries out the instructions it contains. In effect, the interpreter is a layer of software logic between your code and the computer hardware on your machine.

When the Python package is installed on your machine, it generates a number of components—minimally, an interpreter and a support library. Depending on how you use it, the Python interpreter may take the form of an executable program, or a set of libraries linked into another program. Depending on which flavor of Python you run, the interpreter itself may be implemented as a C program, a set of Java classes, or something else. Whatever form it takes, the Python code you write must always be run by this interpreter. And, to enable that, you must install a Python interpreter on your computer.

Python installation details vary by platform, and are covered in more depth in Appendix A. In short:

- Windows users fetch and run a self-installing executable file that puts Python on their machines. Simply double-click and say Yes or Next at all prompts.

- On Windows Vista, you may need to take extra steps to use the Python 2.5 MSI installer file; see Appendix A for more details.

- Linux and Mac OS X users probably already have a usable Python preinstalled on their computers—it's a standard component on these platforms today.

- Some Linux users (and most Unix users) typically either install Python from RPM files, or compile it from its full source code distribution package.

- Other platforms have installation techniques relevant to those platforms. For instance, Python is also available on cell phones, game consoles, and iPods, but the installation details vary too widely to cover here.

Python itself may be fetched from the downloads page at Python's web site. It may also be found through various other distribution channels. Keep in mind that you should always check to see whether Python is already present before installing it. If you're working on Windows, you'll usually find Python in the Start menu, as captured in Figure 2-1 (these menu options are discussed in the next chapter). On Unix and Linux, Python probably lives in your /usr directory tree.

Figure 2-1. When installed on Windows, this is how Python shows up in your Start button menu. This can vary a bit from release to release, but IDLE starts a development GUI, and Python starts a simple interactive session. Also, here are the standard manuals, and the Pydoc documentation engine (Module Docs).

Because installation details are so platform-specific, we'll finesse the rest of this story here. For more details on the installation process, consult Appendix A. For the purposes of this chapter and the next, I'll assume that you've got Python ready to go.

Program Execution

What it means to write and run a Python script depends on whether you look at these tasks as a programmer, or as a Python interpreter. Both views offer important perspectives on Python programming.

The Programmer's View

In its simplest form, a Python program is just a text file containing Python statements. For example, the following file, named *script1.py*, is one of the simplest Python scripts we could dream up, but it passes for an official Python program:

```
print 'hello world'
print 2 ** 100
```

This file contains two Python `print` statements, which simply print a string (the text in quotes) and a numeric expression result (2 to the power 100) to the output stream. Don't worry about the syntax of this code yet—for this chapter, we're interested only in getting it to run. I'll explain the `print` statement, and why you can raise 2 to the power 100 in Python without overflowing, in later parts of this book.

You can create such a file of statements with any text editor you like. By convention, Python program files are given names that end in *.py*; technically, this naming scheme is required only for files that are "imported," as shown later in this book, but most Python files have *.py* names for consistency.

After you've typed these statements into a text file, you must tell Python to *execute* the file—which simply means to run all the statements in the file from top to bottom, one after another. As you'll see in the next chapter, you can launch Python program files by command lines, by clicking their icons, and with other standard techniques. If all goes well, when you execute the file, you'll see the results of the two `print` statements show up somewhere on your computer—by default, usually in the same window you were in when you ran the program:

```
hello world
1267650600228229401496703205376
```

For example, here's what happened when I ran this script from a DOS command line on a Windows laptop (typically called a Command Prompt window, found in the Accessories program menu), to make sure it didn't have any silly typos:

```
D:\temp> python script1.py
hello world
1267650600228229401496703205376
```

We've just run a Python script that prints a string and a number. We probably won't win any programming awards with this code, but it's enough to capture the basics of program execution.

Python's View

The brief description in the prior section is fairly standard for scripting languages, and it's usually all that most Python programmers need to know. You type code into text files, and you run those files through the interpreter. Under the hood, though, a bit more happens when you tell Python to "go." Although knowledge of Python internals is not strictly required for Python programming, a basic understanding of the runtime structure of Python can help you grasp the bigger picture of program execution.

When you instruct Python to run your script, there are a few steps that Python carries out before your code actually starts crunching away. Specifically, it's first compiled to something called "byte code" and then routed to something called a "virtual machine."

Byte code compilation

Internally, and almost completely hidden from you, when you execute a program, Python first compiles your *source code* (the statements in your file) into a format known as *byte code*. Compilation is simply a translation step, and byte code is a lower-level, platform-independent representation of your source code. Roughly, Python translates each of your source statements into a group of byte code instructions by decomposing them into individual steps. This byte code translation is performed to speed execution—byte code can be run much more quickly than the original source code statements in your text file.

You'll notice that the prior paragraph said that this is *almost* completely hidden from you. If the Python process has write access on your machine, it will store the byte code of your program in files that end with a *.pyc* extension (".pyc" means compiled ".py" source). You will see these files show up on your computer after you've run a few programs alongside the corresponding source code files (that is, in the same directories).

Python saves byte code like this as a startup speed optimization. The next time you run your program, Python will load the *.pyc* and skip the compilation step, as long as you haven't changed your source code since the byte code was last saved. Python automatically checks the timestamps of source and byte code files to know when it must recompile—if you resave your source code, byte code is automatically re-created the next time your program is run.

If Python cannot write the byte code files to your machine, your program still works—the byte code is generated in memory and simply discarded on program exit.[*] However, because *.pyc* files speed startup time, you'll want to make sure they are written for larger programs. Byte code files are also one way to ship Python programs—Python is happy to run a program if all it can find are *.pyc* files, even if the original *.py* source files are absent. (See "Frozen Binaries" later in this chapter for another shipping option.)

The Python Virtual Machine (PVM)

Once your program has been compiled to byte code (or the byte code has been loaded from existing *.pyc* files), it is shipped off for execution to something generally known as the Python Virtual Machine (PVM, for the more acronym-inclined among you). The PVM sounds more impressive than it is; really, it's not a separate program, and it need not be installed by itself. In fact, the PVM is just a big loop that iterates through your byte code instructions, one by one, to carry out their operations. The PVM is the runtime engine of Python; it's always present as part of the Python system, and it's the component that truly runs your scripts. Technically, it's just the last step of what is called the "Python interpreter."

Figure 2-2 illustrates the runtime structure described here. Keep in mind that all of this complexity is deliberately hidden from Python programmers. Byte code compilation is automatic, and the PVM is just part of the Python system that you have installed on your machine. Again, programmers simply code and run files of statements.

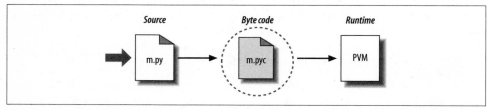

Figure 2-2. Python's traditional runtime execution model: source code you type is translated to byte code, which is then run by the Python Virtual Machine. Your code is automatically compiled, but then it is interpreted.

Performance implications

Readers with a background in fully compiled languages such as C and C++ might notice a few differences in the Python model. For one thing, there is usually no build or "make" step in Python work: code runs immediately after it is written. For another, Python byte code is not binary machine code (e.g., instructions for an Intel chip). Byte code is a Python-specific representation.

---

[*] And, strictly speaking, byte code is saved only for files that are imported, not for the top-level file of a program. We'll explore imports in Chapter 3, and again in Part V. Byte code is also never saved for code typed at the interactive prompt, which is described in Chapter 3.

This is why some Python code may not run as fast as C or C++ code, as described in Chapter 1—the PVM loop, not the CPU chip, still must interpret the byte code, and byte code instructions require more work than CPU instructions. On the other hand, unlike in classic interpreters, there is still an internal compile step—Python does not need to reanalyze and reparse each source statement repeatedly. The net effect is that pure Python code runs at speeds somewhere between those of a traditional compiled language and a traditional interpreted language. See Chapter 1 for more on Python performance implications.

Development implications

Another ramification of Python's execution model is that there is really no distinction between the development and execution environments. That is, the systems that compile and execute your source code are really one and the same. This similarity may have a bit more significance to readers with a background in traditional compiled languages, but in Python, the compiler is always present at runtime, and is part of the system that runs programs.

This makes for a much more rapid development cycle. There is no need to precompile and link before execution may begin; simply type and run the code. This also adds a much more dynamic flavor to the language—it is possible, and often very convenient, for Python programs to construct and execute other Python programs at runtime. The eval and exec built-ins, for instance, accept and run strings containing Python program code. This structure is also why Python lends itself to product customization—because Python code can be changed on the fly, users can modify the Python parts of a system onsite without needing to have or compile the entire system's code.

At a more fundamental level, keep in mind that all we really have in Python is *runtime*—there is no initial compile-time phase at all, and everything happens as the program is running. This even includes operations such as the creation of functions and classes and the linkage of modules. Such events occur before execution in more static languages, but happen as programs execute in Python. As we'll see, the net effect makes for a much more dynamic programming experience than that to which some readers may be accustomed.

Execution Model Variations

Before moving on, I should point out that the internal execution flow described in the prior section reflects the standard implementation of Python today, and is not really a requirement of the Python language itself. Because of that, the execution model is prone to changing with time. In fact, there are already a few systems that modify the picture in Figure 2-2 somewhat. Let's take a few moments to explore the most prominent of these variations.

Python Implementation Alternatives

Really, as this book is being written, there are three primary implementations of the Python language—*CPython*, *Jython*, and *IronPython*—along with a handful of secondary implementations such as *Stackless Python*. In brief, CPython is the standard implementation; all the others have very specific purposes and roles. All implement the same Python language, but execute programs in different ways.

CPython

The original, and standard, implementation of Python is usually called CPython, when you want to contrast it with the other two. Its name comes from the fact that it is coded in portable ANSI C language code. This is the Python that you fetch from *http://www.python.org*, get with the ActivePython distribution, and have automatically on most Linux and Mac OS X machines. If you've found a preinstalled version of Python on your machine, it's probably CPython, unless your company is using Python in very specialized ways.

Unless you want to script Java or .NET applications with Python, you probably want to use the standard CPython system. Because it is the reference implementation of the language, it tends to run the fastest, be the most complete, and be more robust than the alternative systems. Figure 2-2 reflects CPython's runtime architecture.

Jython

The Jython system (originally known as JPython) is an alternative implementation of the Python language, targeted for integration with the Java programming language. Jython consists of Java classes that compile Python source code to Java byte code and then route the resulting byte code to the Java Virtual Machine (JVM). Programmers still code Python statements in .*py* text files as usual; the Jython system essentially just replaces the rightmost two bubbles in Figure 2-2 with Java-based equivalents.

Jython's goal is to allow Python code to script Java applications, much as CPython allows Python to script C and C++ components. Its integration with Java is remarkably seamless. Because Python code is translated to Java byte code, it looks and feels like a true Java program at runtime. Jython scripts can serve as web applets and servlets, build Java-based GUIs, and so on. Moreover, Jython includes integration support that allows Python code to import and use Java classes as though they were coded in Python. Because Jython is slower and less robust than CPython, though, it is usually seen as a tool of interest primarily to Java developers looking for a scripting language to be a frontend to Java code.

IronPython

A third (and, at this writing, still somewhat new) implementation of Python, IronPython is designed to allow Python programs to integrate with applications coded to work with Microsoft's .NET Framework for Windows, as well as the Mono open source equivalent for Linux. .NET and its C# programming language runtime system are designed to be a language-neutral object communication layer, in the spirit of Microsoft's earlier COM model. IronPython allows Python programs to act as both client and server components, accessible from other .NET languages.

By implementation, IronPython is very much like Jython (and, in fact, is being developed by the same creator)—it replaces the last two bubbles in Figure 2-2 with equivalents for execution in the .NET environment. Also, like Jython, IronPython has a special focus—it is primarily of interest to developers integrating Python with .NET components. Because it is being developed by Microsoft, though, IronPython might also be able to leverage some important optimization tools for better performance. IronPython's scope is still evolving as I write this; for more details, consult the Python online resources, or search the Web.*

Execution Optimization Tools

CPython, Jython, and IronPython all implement the Python language in similar ways: by compiling source code to byte code, and executing the byte code on an appropriate virtual machine. Still other systems, including the Psyco just-in-time compiler, and the Shedskin C++ translator, instead attempt to optimize the basic execution model. These systems are not required knowledge at this point in your Python career, but a quick look at their place in the execution model might help demystify the model in general.

The Psyco just-in-time compiler

The Psyco system is not another Python implementation, but rather, a component that extends the byte code execution model to make programs run faster. In terms of Figure 2-2, Psyco is an enhancement to the PVM that collects and uses type information while the program runs to translate portions of the program's byte code all the way down to real binary machine code for faster execution. Psyco accomplishes this translation without requiring changes to the code or a separate compilation step during development.

---

* Jython and IronPython are completely independent implementations of Python that compile Python source for different runtime architectures. It is also possible to access Java and .NET software from standard CPython programs: the JPype and Python for .NET systems, for example, allow CPython code to call out to Java and .NET components.

Roughly, while your program runs, Psyco collects information about the kinds of objects being passed around; that information can be used to generate highly efficient machine code tailored for those object types. Once generated, the machine code then replaces the corresponding part of the original byte code to speed your program's overall execution. The net effect is that, with Psyco, your program becomes much quicker over time, and as it is running. In ideal cases, some Python code may become as fast as compiled C code under Psyco.

Because this translation from byte code happens at program runtime, Psyco is generally known as a *just-in-time* (JIT) compiler. Psyco is actually a bit different from the JIT compilers some readers may have seen for the Java language, though. Really, Psyco is a *specializing JIT compiler*—it generates machine code tailored to the data types that your program actually uses. For example, if a part of your program uses different data types at different times, Psyco may generate a different version of machine code to support each different type combination.

Psyco has been shown to speed Python code dramatically. According to its web page, Psyco provides "2x to 100x speed-ups, typically 4x, with an unmodified Python interpreter and unmodified source code, just a dynamically loadable C extension module." Of equal significance, the largest speedups are realized for algorithmic code written in pure Python—exactly the sort of code you might normally migrate to C to optimize. With Psyco, such migrations become even less important.

Psyco is not yet a standard part of Python; you will have to fetch and install it separately. It is also still something of a research project, so you'll have to track its evolution online. In fact, at this writing, although Psyco can still be fetched and installed by itself, it appears that much of the system may eventually be absorbed into the newer "PyPy" project—an attempt to reimplement Python's PVM in Python code, to better support optimizations like Psyco.

Perhaps the largest downside of Psyco is that it currently only generates machine code for Intel x86 architecture chips, though this includes Windows, Linux, and recent Macs. For more details on the Psyco extension, and other JIT efforts that may arise, consult *http://www.python.org*; you can also check out Psyco's home page, which currently resides at *http://psyco.sourceforge.net*.

The Shedskin C++ translator

Shedskin is an emerging system that takes a different approach to Python program execution—it attempts to translate Python source code to C++ code, which your computer's C++ compiler then compiles to machine code. As such, it represents a platform-neutral approach to running Python code. Shedskin is still somewhat experimental as I write these words, and it limits Python programs to an implicit statically typed constraint that is technically not normal Python, so we won't go into further detail here. Initial results, though, show that it has the potential to outperform both standard Python and the Psyco extension in terms of execution speed, and it is a promising project. Search the Web for details on the project's current status.

Frozen Binaries

Sometimes when people ask for a "real" Python compiler, what they're really seeking is simply a way to generate standalone binary executables from their Python programs. This is more a packaging and shipping idea than an execution-flow concept, but it's somewhat related. With the help of third-party tools that you can fetch off the Web, it is possible to turn your Python programs into true executables—known as *frozen binaries* in the Python world.

Frozen binaries bundle together the byte code of your program files, along with the PVM (interpreter), and any Python support files your program needs, into a single package. There are some variations on this theme, but the end result can be a single binary executable program (e.g., an *.exe* file on Windows) that can easily be shipped to customers. In Figure 2-2, it is as though the byte code and PVM are merged into a single component—a frozen binary file.

Today, three primary systems are capable of generating frozen binaries: *py2exe* (for Windows), *PyInstaller* (which is similar to py2exe, but works on Linux and Unix, too, and is also capable of generating self-installing binaries), and *freeze* (the original). You may have to fetch these tools separately from Python itself, but they are available free of charge. They are also constantly evolving, so see *http://www.python.org* and the Vaults of Parnassus web site (*http://www.vex.net/parnassus/*) for more on these tools. To give you an idea of the scope of these systems, py2exe can freeze standalone programs that use the Tkinter, Pmw, wxPython, and PyGTK GUI libraries; programs that use the *pygame* game programming toolkit; win32com client programs; and more.

Frozen binaries are not the same as the output of a true compiler—they run byte code through a virtual machine. Hence, apart from a possible startup improvement, frozen binaries run at the same speed as the original source files. Frozen binaries are not small (they contain a PVM), but by current standards, they are not unusually large either. Because Python is embedded in the frozen binary, it does not have to be installed on the receiving end to run your program. Moreover, because your code is embedded in the frozen binary, it is effectively hidden from recipients.

This single file-packaging scheme is especially appealing to developers of commercial software. For instance, a Python-coded user interface program based on the Tkinter toolkit can be frozen into an executable file and shipped as a self-contained program on a CD or on the Web. End users do not need to install (or even have to know about) Python to run the shipped program.

Future Possibilities?

Finally, note that the runtime execution model sketched here is really an artifact of the current implementation of Python, and not the language itself. For instance, it's not impossible that a full, traditional compiler for translating Python source code to machine code may appear during the shelf life of this book (although one has not in over a decade). New byte code formats and implementation variants may also be adopted in the future. For instance:

- The emerging *Parrot* project aims to provide a common byte code format, virtual machine, and optimization techniques for a variety of programming languages (see *http://www.python.org*).

- The *Stackless Python* system is a standard CPython implementation variant that does not save state on the C language call stack. This makes Python more easily ported to small stack architectures, and opens up novel programming possibilities, such as coroutines.

- The new *PyPy* project is an attempt to reimplement the PVM in Python itself to enable new implementation techniques.

Although such future implementation schemes may alter the runtime structure of Python somewhat, it seems likely that the byte code compiler will still be the standard for some time to come. The portability and runtime flexibility of byte code are important features of many Python systems. Moreover, adding type constraint declarations to support static compilation would break the flexibility, conciseness, simplicity, and overall spirit of Python coding. Due to Python's highly dynamic nature, any future implementation will likely retain many artifacts of the current PVM.

Chapter Summary

This chapter introduced the execution model of Python (how Python runs your programs) and explored some common variations on that model (just-in-time compilers and the like). Although you don't really need to come to grips with Python internals to write Python scripts, a passing acquaintance with this chapter's topics will help you truly understand how your programs run once you start coding them. In the next chapter, you'll start actually running some code of your own. First, though, here's the usual chapter quiz.

Chapter Quiz

1. What is the Python interpreter?
2. What is source code?
3. What is byte code?
4. What is the PVM?
5. Name two variations on Python's standard execution model.
6. How are CPython, Jython, and IronPython different?

Quiz Answers

1. The Python interpreter is a program that runs the Python programs you write.
2. Source code is the statements you write for your program—it consists of text in text files that normally end with a *.py* extension.
3. Byte code is the lower-level form of your program after Python compiles it. Python automatically stores byte code in files with a *.pyc* extension.
4. The PVM is the Python Virtual Machine—the runtime engine of Python that interprets your compiled code.
5. Psyco, Shedskin, and frozen binaries are all variations on the execution model.
6. CPython is the standard implementation of the language. Jython and IronPython implement Python programs for use in Java and .NET environments, respectively; they are alternative compilers for Python.

CHAPTER 3

How You Run Programs

OK, it's time to start running some code. Now that you have a handle on program execution, you're finally ready to start some real Python programming. At this point, I'll assume that you have Python installed on your computer; if not, see the prior chapter and Appendix A for installation and configuration hints.

There are a variety of ways to tell Python to execute the code you type. This chapter discusses all the program-launching techniques in common use today. Along the way, you'll learn how to type code *interactively*, and how to save it in *files* to be run with system command lines, icon clicks, module imports, IDE GUIs such as IDLE and Eclipse, and more.

If you just want to find out how to run a Python program quickly, you may be tempted to read the parts that pertain only to your platform and move on to Chapter 4. But don't skip the material on module imports, as that's essential to understanding Python's program architecture. I also encourage you at least to skim the sections on IDLE and other IDEs, so you'll know what tools are available for when you start developing more sophisticated Python programs.

Interactive Coding

Perhaps the simplest way to run Python programs is to type them at Python's interactive command line. There are a variety of ways to start this command line—in an IDE, from a system console, and so on. Assuming the interpreter is installed as an executable program on your system, the most platform-neutral way to start an interactive interpreter session is usually just to type **python** at your operating system's prompt, without any arguments. For example:

```
% python
Python 2.5 (r25:51908, Sep 19 2006, 09:52:17) [MSC v.1310 32 bit (Intel)] on win
32
Type "help", "copyright", "credits" or "license" for more information.
>>>
```

Typing the word "python" at your system shell prompt begins an interactive Python session (the "%" character stands for your system's prompt, not input that you type yourself). The notion of a system shell prompt is generic, but exactly how you access the prompt varies by platform:

- On Windows, you can type **python** in a DOS console window (a.k.a. the Command Prompt, usually found in the Accessories section of the Programs menu of your Start button) or in the Start → Run... dialog box.

- On Unix, Linux, and Mac OS X, you might type this command in a shell or terminal window (e.g., in an *xterm* or console running a shell such as *ksh* or *csh*).

- Other systems may use similar or platform-specific devices. On PalmPilots, for example, click the Python home icon to launch an interactive session.

If you have not set your shell's PATH environment variable to include Python's install directory, you may need to replace the word "python" with the full path to the Python executable on your machine. On Windows, try typing **C:\Python25\python** (for version 2.5); on Unix and Linux, **/usr/local/bin/python** (or **/usr/bin/python**) will often suffice. Alternatively, you can run a change-directory command to go to Python's install directory before typing "python" (try a **cd c:\python25** command on Windows, for instance).

The Python interactive session begins by printing two lines of informational text (which I'll omit from this book's examples to save space), then prompts for input with >>> when it's waiting for you to type a new Python statement or expression. When working interactively, the results of your code are displayed after the >>> lines. Here are the results of two Python print statements:

```
% python
>>> print 'Hello world!'
Hello world!
>>> print 2 ** 8
256
```

Again, you don't need to worry about the details of the print statements shown here yet (we'll start digging into syntax in the next chapter). In short, they print a Python string and an integer, as shown by the output lines that appear after each >>> input line.

When working interactively like this, you can type as many Python commands as you like; each is run immediately after it's entered. Moreover, because the interactive session automatically prints the results of expressions you type, you don't usually need to say "print" explicitly at this prompt:

```
>>> lumberjack = 'okay'
>>> lumberjack
'okay'
>>> 2 ** 8
256
>>>                        # Use Ctrl-D or Ctrl-Z to exit
%
```

Here, the last two lines typed are expressions (lumberjack and 2 ** 8), and their results are displayed automatically. To exit an interactive session like this one and return to your system shell prompt, type Ctrl-D on Unix-like machines; on MS-DOS and Windows systems, type Ctrl-Z to exit. In the IDLE GUI discussed later, either type Ctrl-D or simply close the window.

Now, we didn't do much in this session's code—just typed some Python print and assignment statements, and a few expressions, which we'll study in detail later. The main thing to notice is that the interpreter executes the code entered on each line immediately, when the Enter key is pressed.

For instance, when we typed the first print statement at the >>> prompt, the output (a Python string) was echoed back right away. There was no need to create a source-code file, and no need to run the code through a compiler and linker first, as you'd normally do when using a language such as C or C++. As you'll see in later chapters, you can also run multiline statements at the interactive prompt; such a statement runs immediately after you've entered all of its lines.

Besides typing **python** in a shell window, you can also begin similar interactive sessions by starting IDLE's main window or, on Windows, by selecting the "Python (command-line)" menu option from the Start button menu for Python, as shown in Figure 2-1. Both spawn a >>> prompt with equivalent functionality—code is run as it is typed.

Testing Code at the Interactive Prompt

Because code is executed immediately, the interactive prompt turns out to be a great place to *experiment* with the language. It will be used often in this book to demonstrate smaller examples. In fact, this is the first rule of thumb to remember: if you're ever in doubt about how a piece of Python code works, fire up the interactive command line and try it out to see what happens. Chances are good that you won't break anything. (You need to know more about system interfaces before you will become dangerous.)

Although you won't do the bulk of your coding in interactive sessions (because the code you type there is not saved), the interactive interpreter is also a great place to *test* code you've put in files. You can import your module files interactively and run tests on the tools they define by typing calls at the interactive prompt. More generally, the interactive prompt is a place to test program components, regardless of their source—you can type calls to linked-in C functions, exercise Java classes under Jython, and more. Partly because of this interactive nature, Python supports an experimental and exploratory programming style you'll find convenient when getting started.

Using the Interactive Prompt

Although the interactive prompt is simple to use, there are a few tips that beginners will need to keep in mind:

- **Type Python commands only.** First of all, remember that you can only type Python code at the Python prompt, not system commands. There are ways to run system commands from within Python code (e.g., with os.system), but they are not as direct as simply typing the commands themselves.

- **print statements are required only in files.** Because the interactive interpreter automatically prints the results of expressions, you do not need to type complete print statements interactively. This is a nice feature, but it tends to confuse users when they move on to writing code in files: within a code file, you must use print statements to see your output, because expression results are not automatically echoed. Remember, you must say print in files, but not interactively.

- **Don't indent at the interactive prompt (yet).** When typing Python programs, either interactively or into a text file, be sure to start all your unnested statements in column 1 (that is, all the way to the left). If you don't, Python may print a "SyntaxError" message. Until Chapter 10, all statements you write will be unnested, so this includes everything for now. This seems to be a recurring confusion in introductory Python classes. A leading space generates an error message.

- **Watch out for prompt changes and compound statements.** We won't meet compound (multiline) statements until Chapter 10, but, as a preview, you should know that when typing lines 2 and beyond of a compound statement interactively, the prompt may change. In the simple shell window interface, the interactive prompt changes to ... instead of >>> for lines 2 and beyond; in the IDLE interface, lines after the first are automatically indented. In either case, inserting a blank line (done by hitting the Enter key at the start of a line) is needed to tell interactive Python that you're done typing the multiline statement; by contrast, blank lines are ignored in files.

  You'll see why this matters in Chapter 10. For now, if you happen to come across a ... prompt or a blank line when entering your code, it probably means that you've somehow confused interactive Python into thinking you're typing a multiline statement. Try hitting the Enter key or a Ctrl-C combination to get back to the main prompt. The >>> and ... prompts can also be changed (they are available in the built-in module sys), but I'll assume they have not been, in the book's example listings.

System Command Lines and Files

Although the interactive prompt is great for experimenting and testing, it has one big disadvantage: programs you type there go away as soon as the Python interpreter executes them. The code you type interactively is never stored in a file, so you can't run it again without retyping it from scratch. Cut-and-paste and command recall can help some here, but not much, especially when you start writing larger programs. To cut and paste code from an interactive session, you have to edit out Python prompts, program outputs, and so on.

To save programs permanently, you need to write your code in files, which are usually known as *modules*. Modules are simply text files containing Python statements. Once coded, you can ask the Python interpreter to execute the statements in such a file any number of times, and in a variety of ways—by system command lines, by file icon clicks, by options in the IDLE user interface, and more. Regardless of how it is run, Python executes all the code in a module file from top to bottom each time you run the file.

Terminology in this domain can vary somewhat. For instance, module files are often referred to as *programs* in Python—that is, a program is considered to be a series of precoded statements stored in a file for repeated execution. Module files that are run directly are also sometimes called *scripts*—an informal term meaning a top-level program file. Some reserve the term "module" for a file imported from another file. (More on the meaning of "top-level" and imports in a few moments.)

Whatever you call them, the next few sections explore ways to run code typed into module files. In this section, you'll learn how to run files in the most basic way: by listing their names in a python command line entered at a system prompt. As a first example, start your favorite text editor (e.g., *vi*, Notepad, or the IDLE editor), and type two Python statements into a text file named *spam.py*:

```
print 2 ** 8                        # Raise to a power
print 'the bright side ' + 'of life'   # + means concatenation
```

This file contains two Python print statements, and some Python *comments* to the right. (Text after a # is simply ignored as a human-readable comment, and is not considered part of the statement's syntax.) Again, ignore the syntax of the code in this file for now. The point to notice is that you've typed the code into a file, rather than at the interactive prompt. In the process, you've coded a fully functional Python script.

Once you've saved this text file, you can ask Python to run it by listing its full filename as the first argument to a python command, typed at the system shell prompt:

```
% python spam.py
256
the bright side of life
```

Here again, you will type such a system shell command in whatever your system provides for command-line entry—a Windows Command Prompt window, an xterm window, or similar. Remember to replace "python" with a full directory path if your PATH setting is not configured. The output of this little script shows up after the command is typed—it's the result of the two print statements in the text file.

Notice that the module file is called *spam.py*. As for all top-level files, it could also be called simply *spam*, but files of code you want to import into a client have to end with a *.py* suffix. We'll study imports later in this chapter.

Because you may want to import a file in the future, it's a good idea to use *.py* suffixes for most Python files that you code. Also, some text editors detect Python files by their *.py* suffix; if the suffix is not present, you may not get features like syntax colorization and automatic indentation.

Because this scheme uses shell command lines to start Python programs, all the usual shell syntax applies. For instance, you can route the output of a Python script to a file to save it for later use or inspection by using special shell syntax:

```
% python spam.py > saveit.txt
```

In this case, the two output lines shown in the prior run are stored in the file *saveit.txt* instead of being printed. This is generally known as *stream redirection*; it works for input and output text, and it works on Windows and Unix-like systems. It also has little to do with Python (Python simply supports it), so we will skip further details on redirection here.

If you are working on a Windows platform, this example works the same, but the system prompt is normally different:

```
C:\Python25> python spam.py
256
the bright side of life
```

As usual, be sure to type the full path to Python if you haven't set your PATH environment variable, and haven't run a change-directory command:

```
D:\temp> C:\python25\python spam.py
256
the bright side of life
```

On newer versions of Windows, you can also type just the name of your script, regardless of the directory in which you're working. Because newer Windows systems use the Windows Registry to find a program with which to run a file, you don't need to list it on the command line explicitly. The prior command, for example, could be simplified to this on a recent version of Windows:

```
D:\temp> spam.py
```

Finally, remember to give the full path to your script file if it lives in a different directory from the one in which you are working. For example, the following system command line, run from *D:\other*, assumes Python is in your system path but runs a file located elsewhere:

```
D:\other> python c:\code\myscript.py
```

Using Command Lines and Files

Running program files from system command lines is also a fairly straightforward launch option, especially if you are familiar with command lines in general from prior work. For newcomers, though, here are a few pointers about common beginner traps:

- **Beware of automatic extensions on Windows.** If you use the Notepad program to code program files on Windows, be careful to pick the type All Files when it comes time to save your file, and give the file a *.py* suffix explicitly. Otherwise, Notepad will save your file with a *.txt* extension (e.g., as *spam.py.txt*), making it difficult to run in some launching schemes.

  Worse, Windows hides file extensions by default, so unless you have changed your view options, you may not even notice that you've coded a text file and not a Python file. The file's icon may give this away—if it doesn't have a snake on it, you may have trouble. Uncolored code in IDLE and files that open to edit instead of run when clicked are other symptoms of this problem.

  Microsoft Word similarly adds a *.doc* extension by default; much worse, it adds formatting characters that are not legal Python syntax. As a rule of thumb, always pick All Files when saving under Windows, or use more programmer-friendly text editors such as IDLE. IDLE does not even add a *.py* suffix automatically—a feature programmers tend to like, and users do not.

- **Use file extensions at system prompts, but not for imports.** Don't forget to type the full name of your file in system command lines—that is, use **python spam.py** rather than **python spam**. Python import statements, which we'll meet later in this chapter, omit both the *.py* file suffix, and the directory path (e.g., import spam). This may seem simple, but it's a common mistake.

  At the system prompt, you are in a system shell, not Python, so Python's module file search rules do not apply. Because of that, you must include the *.py* extension, and you can optionally include a full directory path leading to the file you wish to run. For instance, to run a file that resides in a different directory from the one in which you are working, you would typically list its full path (i.e., **C:\python25>python d:\tests\spam.py**). Within Python code, however, you just say **import spam**, and rely on the Python module search path to locate your file, as described later.

- **Use print statements in files.** Yes, we've already been over this, but it is such a common mistake that it's worth repeating here. Unlike in interactive coding, you generally must use print statements to see output from program files.

Unix Executable Scripts (#!)

If you are going to use Python on a Unix, Linux, or Unix-like system, you can also turn files of Python code into executable programs, much as you would for programs coded in a shell language such as *csh* or *ksh*. Such files are usually called *executable scripts*. In simple terms, Unix-style executable scripts are just normal text files containing Python statements, but with two special properties:

- **Their first line is special.** Scripts usually start with a line that begins with the characters #! (often called "hash bang"), followed by the path to the Python interpreter on your machine.

- **They usually have executable privileges.** Script files are usually marked as executable to tell the operating system that they may be run as top-level programs. On Unix systems, a command such as chmod +x file.py usually does the trick.

Let's look at an example for Unix-like systems. Use your text editor again to create a file of Python code called *brian*:

```
#!/usr/local/bin/python
print 'The Bright Side of Life...'        # Another comment here
```

The special line at the top of the file tells the system where the Python interpreter lives. Technically, the first line is a Python comment. As mentioned earlier, all comments in Python programs start with a # and span to the end of the line; they are a place to insert extra information for human readers of your code. But when a comment such as the first line in this file appears, it's special because the operating system uses it to find an interpreter for running the program code in the rest of the file.

Also, note that this file is called simply *brian*, without the *.py* suffix used for the module file earlier. Adding a *.py* to the name wouldn't hurt (and might help you remember that this is a Python program file), but because you don't plan on letting other modules import the code in this file, the name of the file is irrelevant. If you give the file executable privileges with a chmod +x brian shell command, you can run it from the operating system shell as though it were a binary program:

```
% brian
The Bright Side of Life...
```

A note for Windows users: the method described here is a Unix trick, and it may not work on your platform. Not to worry; just use the basic command-line technique explored earlier. List the file's name on an explicit python command line:*

```
C:\book\tests> python brian
The Bright Side of Life...
```

---

* As we discussed when exploring command lines, modern Windows versions also let you type just the name of a *.py* file at the system command line—they use the Registry to determine that the file should be opened with Python (e.g., typing **brian.py** is equivalent to typing **python brian.py**). This command-line mode is similar in spirit to the Unix #!. Note that some *programs* may actually interpret and use a first #! line on Windows much like on Unix, but the DOS system shell on Windows ignores it completely.

In this case, you don't need the special #! comment at the top (although Python just ignores it if it's present), and the file doesn't need to be given executable privileges. In fact, if you want to run files portably between Unix and Microsoft Windows, your life will probably be simpler if you always use the basic command-line approach, not Unix-style scripts, to launch programs.

The Unix env Lookup Trick

On some Unix systems, you can avoid hardcoding the path to the Python interpreter by writing the special first-line comment like this:

```
#!/usr/bin/env python
...script goes here...
```

When coded this way, the *env* program locates the Python interpreter according to your system search path settings (i.e., in most Unix shells, by looking in all the directories listed in the PATH environment variable). This scheme can be more portable, as you don't need to hardcode a Python install path in the first line of all your scripts.

Provided you have access to *env* everywhere, your scripts will run no matter where Python lives on your system—you need only change the PATH environment variable settings across platforms, not in the first line in all your scripts. Of course, this assumes that *env* lives in the same place everywhere (on some machines, it may also be in */sbin*, */bin*, or elsewhere); if not, all portability bets are off.

Clicking File Icons

On Windows, the Registry makes opening files with icon clicks easy. Python automatically registers itself to be the program that opens Python program files when they are clicked. Because of that, it is possible to launch the Python programs you write by simply clicking (or double-clicking) on their file icons with your mouse.

On non-Windows systems, you will probably be able to perform a similar trick, but the icons, file explorer, navigation schemes, and more may differ slightly. On some Unix systems, for instance, you may need to register the *.py* extension with your file explorer GUI, make your script executable using the #! trick discussed in the prior section, or associate the file MIME type with an application or command by editing files, installing programs, or using other tools. See your file explorer's documentation for more details if clicks do not work correctly right off the bat.

Clicking Icons on Windows

To illustrate, suppose you create the following program file with your text editor and save it as *script4.py*:

```
# A comment
import sys
print sys.platform
print 2 ** 100
```

There's not much new here—just an import and two prints again (sys.platform is just a string that identifies the kind of computer you're working on; it lives in a module called sys, which you must import to load). You can run this file from a system command line:

```
D:\LP3E\Examples> c:\python25\python script4.py
win32
1267650600228229401496703205376
```

However, icon clicks allow you to run the file without any typing at all. If you find this file's icon—for instance, by selecting My Computer and working your way down on the *D* drive—you will get the file explorer picture captured in Figure 3-1 (Windows XP is being used here). In Python 2.5, source files show up with white backgrounds on Windows, and byte code files show up with black backgrounds. You will normally want to click (or otherwise run) the source code file, in order to pick up your most recent changes. To launch the file here, simply click on the icon for *script4.py*.

Figure 3-1. On Windows, Python program files show up as icons in file explorer windows, and can automatically be run with a double-click of the mouse (though you might not see printed output or error messages this way).

The raw_input Trick

Unfortunately, on Windows, the result of clicking on a file icon may not be incredibly satisfying. In fact, as it is, this example script generates a perplexing "flash" when clicked—not the sort of feedback that budding Python programmers usually hope for! This is not a bug, but it has to do with the way the Windows port handles printed output.

By default, Python generates a pop-up black DOS console window to serve as a clicked file's input and output. If a script prints and exits, then, well, it just prints and exits—the console window appears, and text is printed there, but the console window closes and disappears on program exit. Unless you are very fast, or your machine is very slow, you won't get to see your output at all. Although this is normal behavior, it's probably not what you had in mind.

Luckily, it's easy to work around this. If you need your script's output to stick around when you launch it with an icon click, simply put a call to the built-in raw_input function at the very bottom of the script. For example:

```
# A comment
import sys
print sys.platform
print 2 ** 100
raw_input( )              # ADDED
```

In general, raw_input reads the next line of standard input, waiting if there is none yet available. The net effect in this context will be to pause the script, thereby keeping the output window shown in Figure 3-2 open until you press the Enter key.

Figure 3-2. When you click a program's icon on Windows, you will be able to see its printed output if you add a raw_input() call to the very end of the script. But you only need to do so in this context!

Now that I've shown you this trick, keep in mind that it is usually only required for Windows, and then only if your script prints text and exits, and only if you will launch the script by clicking its file icon. You should add this call to the bottom of your top-level files if and only if all of these three conditions apply. There is no reason to add this call in any other contexts.[*]

Before we move ahead, note that the `raw_input` call applied here is the input counterpart of using the `print` statement for outputs. It is the simplest way to read user input, and it is more general than this example implies. For instance, `raw_input`:

- Optionally accepts a string that will be printed as a prompt (e.g., `raw_input('Press Enter to exit')`)
- Returns to your script the line of text read as a string (e.g., `nextinput = raw_input()`)
- Supports input stream redirections at the system shell level (e.g., `python spam.py < input.txt`), just as the `print` statement does for output

We'll use `raw_input` in more advanced ways later in this text; for instance, Chapter 10 will apply it in an interactive loop.

Other Icon-Click Limitations

Even with the `raw_input` trick, clicking file icons is not without its perils. You also may not get to see Python error messages. If your script generates an error, the error message text is written to the pop-up console window—which then immediately disappears. Worse, adding a `raw_input` call to your file will not help this time because your script will likely abort long before it reaches this call. In other words, you won't be able to tell what went wrong.

Because of these limitations, it is probably best to view icon clicks as a way to launch programs after they have been debugged. Especially when starting out, use other techniques—such as system command lines and IDLE (discussed later in this chapter)—so that you can see generated error messages and view your normal output without resorting to coding tricks. When we discuss exceptions later in this book, you'll also learn that it is possible to intercept and recover from errors so that they do not terminate your programs. Watch for the discussion of the try statement later in this book for an alternative way to keep the console window from closing on errors.

Module Imports and Reloads

So far, I've been talking about "importing modules" without really explaining what this term means. We'll study modules and larger program architecture in depth in Part V, but because imports are also a way to launch programs, this section will introduce enough module basics to get you started.

---

[*] It is also possible to completely suppress the pop-up DOS console window for clicked files on Windows. Files whose names end in a *.pyw* extension will display only windows constructed by your script, not the default DOS console window. *.pyw* files are simply *.py* source files that have this special operational behavior on Windows. They are mostly used for Python-coded user interfaces that build windows of their own, often in conjunction with various techniques for saving printed output and errors to files.

In simple terms, every file of Python source code whose name ends in a *.py* extension is a module. Other files can access the items a module defines by *importing* that module; import operations essentially load another file, and grant access to that file's contents. The contents of a module are made available to the outside world through its attributes (a term I'll define in the next section).

This module-based services model turns out to be the core idea behind program architecture in Python. Larger programs usually take the form of multiple module files, which import tools from other module files. One of the modules is designated as the main or *top-level* file, and is the one launched to start the entire program.

We'll delve into such architectural issues in more detail later in this book. This chapter is mostly interested in the fact that import operations *run* the code in a file that is being loaded as a final step. Because of this, importing a file is yet another way to launch it.

For instance, if you start an interactive session (in IDLE, from a command line, or otherwise), you can run the *script4.py* file you created earlier with a simple import:

```
D:\LP3E\Examples> c:\python25\python
>>> import script4
win32
1267650600228229401496703205376
```

This works, but only once per session (really, process), by default. After the first import, later imports do nothing, even if you change and save the module's source file again in another window:

```
>>> import script4
>>> import script4
```

This is by design; imports are too expensive an operation to repeat more than once per program run. As you'll learn in Chapter 18, imports must find files, compile to byte code, and run the code.

If you really want to force Python to run the file again in the same session (without stopping and restarting the session), you need to instead call the built-in reload function:

```
>>> reload(script4)
win32
65536
<module 'script4' from 'script4.py'>
>>>
```

The reload function loads and runs the current version of your file's code if you've changed it in another window. This allows you to edit and pick up new code on the fly within the current Python interactive session. In this session, for example, the second print statement in *script4.py* was changed in another window to print 2 ** 16 between the time of the first import and the reload call.

The reload function expects the name of an already loaded module object, so you have to have successfully imported a module once before you reload it. Notice that reload also expects parentheses around the module object name, whereas import does not. reload is a function that is *called*, and import is a statement. That's why you must pass the module name to reload as an argument in parentheses, and that's why you get back an extra output line when reloading. The last output line is just print's representation of the reload call's return value, a Python module object.

Functions will be discussed further in Chapter 15.

The Grander Module Story: Attributes

Imports and reloads provide a natural program launch option because import operations execute files as a last step. In the broader scheme of things, though, modules serve the role of *libraries* of tools, as you'll learn in Part V. More generally, a module is mostly just a package of variable names, known as a *namespace*. The names within that package are called *attributes*—that is, an attribute is a variable name that is attached to a specific object.

In typical use, importers gain access to all the names assigned at the top level of a module's file. These names are usually assigned to tools exported by the module—functions, classes, variables, and so on—that are intended to be used in other files and other programs. Externally, a module file's names can be fetched with two Python statements, import and from, as well as the reload call.

To illustrate, use a text editor to create a one-line Python module file called *myfile.py* with the following contents:

```
title = "The Meaning of Life"
```

This may be one of the world's simplest Python modules (it contains a single assignment statement), but it's enough to illustrate the basics. When this file is imported, its code is run to generate the module's attribute. The assignment statement creates a module attribute named title.

You can access this module's title attribute in other components in two different ways. First, you can load the module as a whole with an import statement, and then *qualify* the module name with the attribute name to access it:

```
% python                    # Start Python
>>> import myfile           # Run file; load module as a whole
>>> print myfile.title      # Use its attribute names: '.' to qualify
The Meaning of Life
```

In general, the dot expression syntax object.attribute lets you fetch any attribute attached to any object, and this is a common operation in Python code. Here, we've used it to access the string variable title inside the module *myfile*—in other words, myfile.title.

Alternatively, you can fetch (really, copy) names out of a module with `from` statements:

```
% python
>>> from myfile import title    # Start Python
>>> print title                 # Run file; copy its names
The Meaning of Life             # Use name directly: no need to qualify
```

As you'll see in more detail later, `from` is just like an `import`, with an extra assignment to names in the importing component. Technically, `from` copies a module's *attributes*, such that they become simple *variables* in the recipient—thus, you can simply refer to the imported string this time as `title` (a variable) instead of `myfile.title` (an attribute reference).*

Whether you use `import` or `from` to invoke an import operation, the statements in the module file *myfile.py* are executed, and the importing component (here, the interactive prompt) gains access to names assigned at the top level of the file. There's only one such name in this simple example—the variable `title`, assigned to a string—but the concept will be more useful when you start defining objects such as functions and classes in your modules. Such objects become reusable software components that can be accessed by name from one or more client modules.

In practice, module files usually define more than one name to be used in and outside the files. Here's an example that defines three:

```
a = 'dead'       # Define three attributes
b = 'parrot'     # Exported to other files
c = 'sketch'
print a, b, c    # Also used in this file
```

This file, *threenames.py*, assigns three variables, and so generates three attributes for the outside world. It also uses its own three variables in a `print` statement, as we see when we run this as a top-level file:

```
% python threenames.py
dead parrot sketch
```

All of this file's code runs as usual the first time it is imported elsewhere (by either an `import` or `from`). Clients of this file that use `import` get a module with attributes, while clients that use `from` get copies of the file's names:

```
% python
>>> import threenames          # Grab the whole module
dead parrot sketch
>>>
>>> threenames.b, threenames.c
('parrot', 'sketch')
>>>
```

---

* Notice that `import` and `from` both list the name of the module file as simply *myfile* without its *.py* suffix. As you'll learn in Part V, when Python looks for the actual file, it knows to include the suffix in its search procedure. Again, you must remember to include the suffix in system shell command lines, but not in `import` statements.

```
>>> from threenames import a, b, c          # Copy multiple names
>>> b, c
('parrot', 'sketch')
```

The results here are printed in parentheses because they are really *tuples* (a kind of object covered in the next part of this book).

Once you start coding modules with multiple names like this, the built-in `dir` function starts to come in handy. You can use it to fetch a list of the names available inside a module:

```
>>> dir(threenames)
['__builtins__', '__doc__', '__file__', '__name__', 'a', 'b', 'c']
```

When the `dir` function is called with the name of an imported module passed in parentheses like this, it returns all the attributes inside that module. Some of the names it returns are names you get "for free": names with leading and trailing double underscores are built-in names that are always predefined by Python, and that have special meaning to the interpreter. The variables our code defined by assignment—a, b, and c—show up last in the `dir` result.

Modules and namespaces

Module imports are a way to run files of code, but, as we'll discuss later in the book, modules are also the largest program structure in Python programs. In general, Python programs are composed of multiple module files, linked together by `import` statements. Each module file is a self-contained package of variables—that is, a namespace. One module file cannot see the names defined in another file unless it explicitly imports that other file, so modules serve to minimize name collisions in your code—because each file is a self-contained namespace, the names in one file cannot clash with those in another, even if they are spelled the same way.

In fact, as you'll see, modules are one of a handful of ways that Python goes to great lengths to package your variables into compartments to avoid name clashes. We'll discuss modules and other namespace constructs (including classes and function scopes) further later in the book. For now, modules will come in handy as a way to run your code many times without having to retype it.

import and reload Usage Notes

For some reason, once people find out about running files using `import` and `reload`, many tend to focus on this alone and forget about other launch options that always run the current version of the code (e.g., icon clicks, IDLE menu options, and system command lines). This can quickly lead to confusion—you need to remember when you've imported to know if you can reload, you need to remember to use parentheses when you call reload (only), and you need to remember to use `reload` in the first place to get the current version of your code to run.

Because of these complications (and others we'll meet later), it's a good idea to avoid the temptation to launch by imports and reloads for now. The IDLE Run → Run Module menu option, for example, provides a simpler and less error-prone way to run your files. On the other hand, imports and reloads have proven to be a popular testing technique in Python classes. You may prefer using this approach, but if you find yourself running into a wall, stop.

There is more to the module story than we've exposed here. For instance, the execfile('module.py') built-in function is another way to launch files from the interactive prompt without having to import and later reload. It has a similar effect, but doesn't technically import the module—by default, each time you call execfile, it runs the file anew, as though you had pasted it in at the place where execfile is called. Because of that, execfile, like the from statement mentioned earlier, has the potential to silently overwrite variables you may currently be using. The basic import statement, on the other hand, runs the file only once per process, and makes the file a separate namespace so that it will not change variables in your scope.

In addition, you may run into trouble if you use modules in unusual ways at this point in the book. For instance, if you want to import a module file that is stored in a directory other than the one you're working in, you'll have to skip ahead to Chapter 18 and learn about the *module search path*. For now, if you must import, try to keep all your files in the directory you are working in to avoid complications.

 In case you can't wait until Chapter 18, the short story is that Python searches for imported modules in every directory listed in sys.path—a Python list of directory name strings in the *sys* module, which is initialized from a PYTHONPATH environment variable, plus a set of standard directories. If you want to import from a directory other than the one you are working in, that directory must generally be listed in your PYTHONPATH setting. For more details, see Chapter 18.

The IDLE User Interface

So far, we've seen how to run Python code with the interactive prompt, system command lines, icon clicks, and module imports. If you're looking for something a bit more visual, IDLE provides a graphical user interface (GUI) for doing Python development, and it's a standard and free part of the Python system. It is usually referred to as an *integrated development environment* (IDE), because it binds together various development tasks into a single view.*

In short, IDLE is a GUI that lets you edit, run, browse, and debug Python programs, all from a single interface. Moreover, because IDLE is a Python program that uses the Tkinter GUI toolkit, it runs portably on most Python platforms, including Microsoft

---

* IDLE is officially a corruption of IDE, but it's really named in honor of Monty Python member Eric Idle.

Windows, X Windows (for Linux, Unix, and Unix-like platforms), and the Mac OS (both Classic and OS X). For many, IDLE represents an easy-to-use alternative to typing command lines, and a less problem-prone alternative to clicking on icons.

IDLE Basics

Let's jump right into an example. IDLE is easy to start under Windows—it has an entry in the Start button menu for Python (see Figure 2-1), and it can also be selected by right-clicking on a Python program icon. On some Unix-like systems, you may need to launch IDLE's top-level script from a command line, or, alternatively, by clicking on the icon for the *idle.pyw* or *idle.py* file located in the *idlelib* subdirectory of Python's *Lib* directory. (On Windows, IDLE is a Python script that currently lives in *C:\Python25\Lib\idlelib*.*)

Figure 3-3 shows the scene after starting IDLE on Windows. The Python shell window that opens initially is the main window, which runs an interactive session (notice the >>> prompt). This works like all interactive sessions—code you type here is run immediately after you type it—and serves as a testing tool.

IDLE uses familiar menus with keyboard shortcuts for most of its operations. To make (or edit) a source code file under IDLE, open a text edit window: in the main window, select the File pull-down menu, and pick New Window to open a text edit window (or Open...to edit an existing file). A new window will appear. This is an IDLE text edit window, where the code for the file you are creating or changing is entered and displayed.

Although it may not show up fully in this book, IDLE uses syntax-directed *colorization* for the code typed in both the main window and all text edit windows—keywords are one color, literals are another, and so on. This helps give you a better picture of the components in your code.

To run a file of code that you are editing in IDLE, select the file's text edit window, pick that window's Run pull-down menu, and choose the Run Module option listed there (or use the equivalent keyboard shortcut, given in the menu). Python will let you know that you need to save your file first if you've changed it since it was opened or last saved.

When run this way, the output of your script and any error messages it may generate show up back in the main interactive window (the Python shell window). In Figure 3-3, for example, the last three lines in the window reflect an execution of a

---

* IDLE is a Python program that uses the standard library's Tkinter GUI toolkit to build the IDLE GUI. This makes IDLE portable, but it also means that you'll need to have Tkinter support in your Python to use IDLE. The Windows version of Python has this by default, but some Linux and Unix users may need to install the appropriate Tkinter support (a yum tkinter command may suffice on some Linux distributions, but see the installation hints in Appendix A for details). Mac OS X may have everything you need preinstalled, too; look for an idle command or script on your machine.

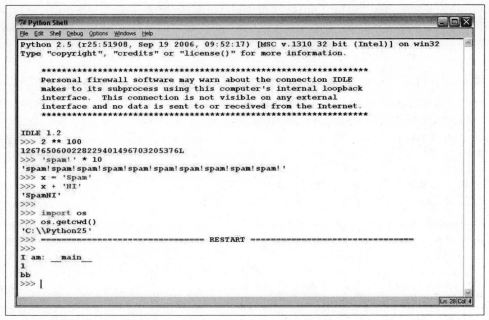

```
7 Python Shell                                                    _ □ X
File  Edit  Shell  Debug  Options  Windows  Help
Python 2.5 (r25:51908, Sep 19 2006, 09:52:17) [MSC v.1310 32 bit (Intel)] on win32
Type "copyright", "credits" or "license()" for more information.

        **********************************************************
        Personal firewall software may warn about the connection IDLE
        makes to its subprocess using this computer's internal loopback
        interface.  This connection is not visible on any external
        interface and no data is sent to or received from the Internet.
        **********************************************************

IDLE 1.2
>>> 2 ** 100
1267650600228229401496703205376L
>>> 'spam!' * 10
'spam!spam!spam!spam!spam!spam!spam!spam!spam!spam!'
>>> x = 'Spam'
>>> x + 'NI'
'SpamNI'
>>>
>>> import os
>>> os.getcwd()
'C:\\Python25'
>>> ============================== RESTART ==============================
>>>
I am: __main__
1
bb
>>> |
                                                              Ln: 28 Col: 4
```

Figure 3-3. The main Python shell window of the IDLE development GUI, shown here running on Windows. Use the File menu to begin (New Window), or change (Open…) a source file; use the file edit window's Run menu to run the code in that window (Run Module).

script opened in a separate edit window; the "RESTART" message tells us that the user-code process was restarted to run the edited script, and serves to separate script output.

 Hint of the day: if you want to repeat prior commands in IDLE's main interactive window, you can use the Alt-P key combination to scroll backward through the command history, and Alt-N to scroll forward (on some Macs, try Ctrl-P and Ctrl-N instead). Your prior commands will be recalled and displayed, and may be edited and rerun. You can also recall commands by positioning the cursor on them, or use cut-and-paste operations, but these tend to be more work. Outside IDLE, you may be able to recall commands in an interactive session with the arrow keys on Windows.

Using IDLE

IDLE is free, easy to use, portable, and automatically available on most platforms. I generally recommend it to Python newcomers because it sugarcoats some of the details, and does not assume prior experience with system command lines. But it is also somewhat limited compared to more advanced commercial IDEs. Here is a list of issues that IDLE beginners should bear in mind:

- **You must add ".py" explicitly when saving your files.** I mentioned this when talking about files in general, but it's a common IDLE stumbling block, especially for Windows users. IDLE does not automatically add a *.py* extension to filenames when files are saved. Be careful to type the *.py* extension yourself when saving a file for the first time. If you don't, you will be able to run your file from IDLE (and system command lines), but you will not be able to import your file either interactively or from other modules.

- **Run scripts by selecting Run → Run Module in text edit windows, not by interactive imports and reloads.** Earlier in this chapter, we saw that it's possible to run a file by importing it interactively. However, this scheme can grow complex because you are required to manually reload files after changes. By contrast, using the Run → Run Module menu option in IDLE always runs the most current version of your file. It also prompts you to save it first, if needed (another common mistake outside IDLE).

- **You may still have to reload nested modules.** Technically speaking, IDLE's Run → Run Module menu option always runs the current version of the top-level file only; imported files may still need to be interactively reloaded when changed. In general, though, Run → Run Module eliminates common confusions surrounding imports. If you choose to use the import and reload technique instead, remember to use Alt-P/Alt-N key combinations to recall prior commands.

- **You can customize IDLE.** To change the text fonts and colors in IDLE, select the Configure option in the Options menu of any IDLE window. You can also customize key combination actions, indentation settings, and more; see IDLE's Help pull-down menu for more hints.

- **There is currently no clear-screen option in IDLE.** This seems to be a frequent request (perhaps because it's an option available in similar IDEs), and it might be added eventually. Today, though, there is no way to clear the interactive window's text. If you want the window's text to go away, you can either press and hold the Enter key, or type a Python loop to print a series of blank lines.

- **Tkinter GUI and threaded programs may not work well with IDLE.** Because IDLE is a Python/Tkinter program, it can hang if you use it to run certain types of advanced Python/Tkinter programs. This has become less of an issue in more recent versions of IDLE that run user code in one process, and the IDLE GUI itself in another, but some programs may still hang the GUI. Your code may not exhibit such problems, but, as a rule of thumb, it's always safe if you use IDLE to edit GUI programs, but launch them using other options, such as icon clicks or system command lines. When in doubt, if your code fails in IDLE, try it outside the GUI.

- **If connection errors arise, try starting IDLE in single-process mode.** Because IDLE requires communication between its separate user and GUI processes, it can sometimes have trouble starting up on certain platforms (notably, it fails to start occasionally on some Windows machines). If you run into such connection errors, it's always possible to start IDLE with a system command line that forces it to run in single-process mode, and therefore avoids communication issues: its -n command-line flag forces this mode. On Windows, for example, start a Command Prompt window, and run the system command line idle.py -n from within the directory *C:\Python25\Lib\idlelib* (cd there first if needed).

- **Beware of some IDLE usability features.** IDLE does much to make life easier for beginners, but some of its tricks won't apply outside the IDLE GUI. For instance, IDLE runs your script in IDLE's environment, so variables in your code show up automatically in the IDLE interactive session—you don't always need to run import commands to access names at the top level of files you've already run. This can be handy, but it can also be confusing, because outside the IDLE environment, names must always be imported from files to be used.

Advanced IDLE Tools

Besides the basic edit and run functions, IDLE provides more advanced features, including a point-and-click program debugger, and an object browser. The IDLE debugger is enabled via the Debug menu, and the object browser via the File menu. The browser allows you to navigate through the module search path to files and objects in files; clicking on a file or object opens the corresponding source in a text edit window.

IDLE debugging is initiated by selecting the Debug → Debugger menu option in the main window, and then starting your script by selecting the Run → Run Module option in the text edit window; once the debugger is enabled, you can set breakpoints in your code that stop its execution by right-clicking on lines in the text edit windows, show variable values, and so on. You can also watch program execution when debugging—the current line of code is noted as you step through your code.

For simpler debugging operations, you can also right-click with your mouse on the text of an error message to quickly jump to the line of code where the error occurred—a trick that makes it simple and fast to repair and run again. In addition, IDLE's text editor offers a large collection of programmer-friendly tools, including automatic indentation, advanced text and file search operations, and more. Because IDLE uses intuitive GUI interactions, you should experiment with the system live to get a feel for its other tools.

Other IDEs

Because IDLE is free, portable, and a standard part of Python, it's a nice first development tool to become familiar with if you want to use an IDE at all. Again, I recommend that you use IDLE for this book's exercises if you're just starting out, unless you are already familiar with a command-line-based development mode. There are, however, a handful of alternative IDEs for Python developers, some of which are substantially more powerful and robust than IDLE. Here are some of the most commonly used IDEs:

Eclipse and PyDev

Eclipse is an advanced open source IDE GUI. Originally developed as a Java IDE, Eclipse also supports Python development when you install the PyDev (or similar) plug-in. Eclipse is a popular and powerful option for Python development, and it goes well beyond IDLE's feature set. Its downsides seem to be that it is a large system to install, and its PyDev plug-in requires a shareware extensions package for some features (including an integrated interactive console) that is not strictly open source. Still, when you are ready to graduate from IDLE, the Eclipse/PyDev combination is worth your attention.

Komodo

A full-featured development environment GUI for Python (and other languages), Komodo includes standard syntax-coloring, text-editing, debugging, and other features. In addition, Komodo offers many advanced features that IDLE does not, including project files, source-control integration, regular-expression debugging, and a drag-and-drop GUI builder that generates Python/Tkinter code to implement the GUIs you design interactively. At this writing, Komodo is not free; it is available at *http://www.activestate.com*.

PythonWin

PythonWin is a free Windows-only IDE for Python that ships as part of ActiveState's ActivePython distribution (and may also be fetched separately from *http://www.python.org* resources). It is roughly like IDLE, with a handful of useful Windows-specific extensions added; for example, PythonWin has support for COM objects. Today, IDLE is probably more advanced than PythonWin (for instance, IDLE's dual-process architecture more often prevents it from becoming hung). However, PythonWin still offers tools for Windows developers that IDLE does not. See *http://www.activestate.com* for more information.

Others

There are roughly half a dozen other well-known IDEs that I'm aware of (e.g., WingIDE, PythonCard), and more will probably appear over time. In fact, almost every programmer-friendly text editor has some sort of support for Python development these days, whether it be preinstalled or fetched separately. Emacs and Vim, for instance, also have substantial Python support. Rather than trying to document all such options here, see the resources available at *http://www.python.org*, or run a Google web search for "Python editors"—this should lead you to a Wiki page that maintains information about many IDE and text-editor options for Python programming.

Embedding Calls

At this point, we've seen how to run code typed interactively, and how to launch code saved in files with system command lines, Unix executable scripts, icon clicks, module imports, and IDEs like IDLE. That covers most of the cases you'll see in this book.

But, in some specialized domains, Python code may also be run by an enclosing system. In such cases, we say that the Python programs are *embedded* in (i.e., run by) another program. The Python code itself may be entered into a text file, stored in a database, fetched from an HTML page, parsed from an XML document, and so on. But from an operational perspective, another system—not you—may tell Python to run the code you've created. Such an embedded execution mode is commonly used to support end user customization—a game program, for instance, might allow for play modifications by running user-accessible embedded Python code at strategic points in time.

As an example, it's possible to create and run strings of Python code from a C program by calling functions in the Python runtime API (a set of services exported by the libraries created when Python is compiled on your machine):

```
#include <Python.h>
...
Py_Initialize();
PyRun_SimpleString("x = brave + sir + robin");
```

In this C code snippet, a program coded in the C language embeds the Python interpreter by linking in its libraries, and passes it a Python assignment statement string to run. C programs may also gain access to Python objects and process or execute them using other Python API tools.

This book isn't about Python/C integration, but you should be aware that, depending on how your organization plans to use Python, you may or may not be the one who actually starts the Python programs you create.* Regardless, you can still likely use the interactive and file-based launching techniques described here to test code in isolation from those enclosing systems that may eventually use it.

Frozen Binary Executables

Frozen binary executables, described in the preceding chapter, are packages that combine your program's byte code and the Python interpreter into a single executable program. With these, Python programs can be launched in the same ways that

---

* See *Programming Python* (O'Reilly) for more details on embedding Python in C/C++. The embedding API can call Python functions directly, load modules, and more. Also, note that the Jython system allows Java programs to invoke Python code using a Java-based API (a Python interpreter class).

you would launch any other executable program (icon clicks, command lines, etc.). While this option works well for delivery of products, it is not really intended for use during program development. You normally freeze just before shipping (after development is finished). See the prior chapter for more on this option.

Text Editor Launch Options

As mentioned previously, although not full-blown IDE GUIs, most programmer-friendly text editors have support for editing, and possibly running, Python programs. Such support may be built in or fetchable on the Web. For instance, if you are familiar with the Emacs text editor, you can do all your Python editing and launching from inside the text editor itself. See the text editor resources page at *http://www.python.org/editors* for more details, or search the Web for the phrase "Python editors."

Other Launch Options

Depending on your platform, there may be additional ways that you can start Python programs. For instance, on some Macintosh systems, you may be able to drag Python program file icons onto the Python interpreter icon to make them execute. And on Windows, you can always start Python scripts with the Run… option in the Start menu. Finally, the Python standard library has utilities that allow Python programs to be started by other Python programs (e.g., execfile, os.popen, os.system); however, these tools are beyond the scope of the present chapter.

Future Possibilities?

Although this chapter reflects current practice, much of it has been both platform- and time-specific. Indeed, many of the execution and launch details presented arose during the shelf life of this book's editions. As with program execution options, it's not impossible that new program launch options may arise over time.

New operating systems, and new versions of existing systems, may also provide execution techniques beyond those outlined here. In general, because Python keeps pace with such changes, you should be able to launch Python programs in whatever way makes sense for the machines you use, both now and in the future—be that by drawing on tablet PCs or PDAs, grabbing icons in a virtual reality, or shouting a script's name over your coworkers' conversations.

Implementation changes may also impact launch schemes somewhat (e.g., a full compiler could produce normal executables that are launched much like frozen binaries today). If I knew what the future truly held, though, I would probably be talking to a stockbroker instead of writing these words!

Which Option Should I Use?

With all these options, one question naturally arises: which one is best for me? In general, you should use the IDLE interface for development if you are just getting started with Python. It provides a user-friendly GUI environment, and can hide some of the underlying configuration details. It also comes with a platform-neutral text editor for coding your scripts, and it's a standard and free part of the Python system.

If, on the other hand, you are an experienced programmer, you might be more comfortable with simply the text editor of your choice in one window, and another window for launching the programs you edit via system command lines and icon clicks (indeed, this is how your author develops Python programs, but he has a Unix-biased past). Because development environments are a very subjective choice, I can't offer much more in the way of universal guidelines; in general, whatever environment you like to use will usually be the best for you to use.

Chapter Summary

In this chapter, we've looked at common ways to launch Python programs: by running code typed interactively, and by running code stored in files with system command lines, file-icon clicks, module imports, and IDE GUIs such as IDLE. We've covered a lot of pragmatic startup territory here. This chapter's goal was to equip you with enough information that you can start working along with the code we'll start writing in the next part of the book. There, we will start exploring the Python language itself, beginning with its core data types.

First, though, take the usual chapter quiz to exercise what you've learned here. Because this is the last chapter in this part of the book, it's followed with a set of more complete exercises that test your mastery of this entire part's topics. For help with the latter set of problems, or just for a refresher, turn to Appendix B.

Chapter Quiz

1. How can you start an interactive interpreter session?
2. Where do you type a system command line to launch a script file?
3. Name two pitfalls related to clicking file icons on Windows.
4. Why might you need to reload a module?
5. How do you run a script from within IDLE?
6. Name two pitfalls related to using IDLE.
7. What is a namespace, and how does it relate to module files?

Quiz Answers

1. You can start an interactive session on Windows by clicking your Start button, picking the All Programs option, clicking the Python entry, and selecting the "Python (command line)" menu option. You can also achieve the same effect on Windows and other platforms by typing **python** as a system command line in your system's console window (a Command Prompt window on Windows). Another alternative is to launch IDLE, as its main Python shell window is an interactive session. If you have not set your system's PATH variable to find Python, you may need to cd to where Python is installed, or type its full directory path instead of just **python** (e.g., **C:\Python25\python** on Windows).

2. You type system command lines in whatever your platform provides as a system console: a Command Prompt window on Windows; an xterm or terminal window on Unix, Linux, and Mac OS X; and so on.

3. Scripts that print and then exit cause the output file to disappear immediately, before you can view the output (which is why the raw_input trick comes in handy); error messages generated by your script also appear in an output window that closes before you can examine its contents (which is why system command lines and IDEs such as IDLE are better for most development).

4. Python only imports (loads) a module once per process, by default, so if you've changed its source code and want to run the new version without stopping and restarting Python, you'll have to reload it. You must import a module at least once before you can reload it. Running code from a system command line, or via an icon click, or an IDE such as IDLE generally makes this a nonissue, as those launch schemes usually run the current version of the source code file each time.

5. Within the text edit window of the file you wish to run, select the window's Run → Run Module menu option. This runs the window's source code as a top-level script file, and displays its output back in the interactive Python shell window.

6. IDLE can still be hung by some types of programs—especially GUI programs that perform multithreading (an advanced technique beyond this book's scope). Also, IDLE has some usability features that can burn you once you leave the IDLE GUI: a script's variables are automatically imported to the interactive scope in IDLE, for instance, but not by Python in general.

7. A namespace is just a package of variables (i.e., names). It takes the form of an object with attributes in Python. Each module file is automatically a namespace—that is, a package of variables reflecting the assignments made at the top level of the file. Namespaces help avoid name collisions in Python programs: because each module file is a self-contained namespace, files must explicitly import other files in order to use their names.

Part I Exercises

It's time to start doing a little coding on your own. This first exercise session is fairly simple, but a few of these questions hint at topics to come in later chapters. Be sure to check "Part I, Getting Started" in the solutions appendix (Appendix B) for the answers; the exercises and their solutions sometimes contain supplemental information not discussed in the main text of the part, so you should take a peek at the solutions even if you manage to answer all the questions on your own.

1. *Interaction.* Using a system command line, IDLE, or another method, start the Python interactive command line (>>> prompt), and type the expression "Hello World!" (including the quotes). The string should be echoed back to you. The purpose of this exercise is to get your environment configured to run Python. In some scenarios, you may need to first run a cd shell command, type the full path to the Python executable, or add its path to your PATH environment variable. If desired, you can set PATH in your *.cshrc* or *.kshrc* file to make Python permanently available on Unix systems; on Windows, use a *setup.bat*, *autoexec.bat*, or the environment variable GUI. See Appendix A for help with environment variable settings.

2. *Programs.* With the text editor of your choice, write a simple module file containing the single statement print 'Hello module world!' and store it as *module1.py*. Now, run this file by using any launch option you like: running it in IDLE, clicking on its file icon, passing it to the Python interpreter program on the system shell's command line (e.g., python module1.py), and so on. In fact, experiment by running your file with as many of the launch techniques discussed in this chapter as you can. Which technique seems easiest? (There is no right answer to this one.)

3. *Modules.* Next, start the Python interactive command line (>>> prompt) and import the module you wrote in exercise 2. Try moving the file to a different directory and importing it again from its original directory (i.e., run Python in the original directory when you import). What happens? (Hint: is there still a *module1.pyc* byte code file in the original directory?)

4. *Scripts.* If your platform supports it, add the #! line to the top of your *module1.py* module file, give the file executable privileges, and run it directly as an executable. What does the first line need to contain? #! usually only has meaning on Unix, Linux, and Unix-like platforms such as Mac OS X; if you're working on Windows, instead try running your file by listing just its name in a DOS console window without the word "python" before it (this works on recent versions of Windows), or via the Start → Run...dialog box.

5. *Errors.* Experiment with typing mathematical expressions and assignments at the Python interactive command line. First type the expression 1 / 0. What happens? Next, type a variable name to which you haven't yet assigned a value. What happens this time?

You may not know it yet, but you're doing exception processing (a topic we'll explore in depth in Part VII). As you'll learn there, you are technically triggering what's known as the *default exception handler*—logic that prints a standard error message. If you do not catch an error, the default handler does and prints the standard error message in response.

For full-blown source code debugging chores, IDLE includes a GUI debugging interface (introduced in the "Advanced IDLE Tools" section of this chapter), and a Python standard library module named pdb provides a command-line debugging interface (you can find more on pdb in the standard library manual). When you're first starting out, Python's default error messages will probably be as much error handling as you need—they give the cause of the error, as well as showing the lines in your code that were active when the error occurred.

6. *Breaks.* At the Python command line, type:

```
L = [1, 2]
L.append(L)
L
```

What happens? If you're using a Python newer than Release 1.5, you'll probably see a strange output that we'll describe in the next part of the book. If you're using a Python version older than 1.5.1, a Ctrl-C key combination will probably help on most platforms. Why do you think this occurs? What does Python report when you type the Ctrl-C key combination?

 If you do have a Python older than Release 1.5.1, make sure your machine can stop a program with a break-key combination of some sort before running this test, or you may be waiting a long time.

7. *Documentation.* Spend at least 17 minutes browsing the Python library and language manuals before moving on to get a feel for the available tools in the standard library and the structure of the documentation set. It takes at least this long to become familiar with the locations of major topics in the manual set; once you've done this, it's easy to find what you need. You can find this manual via the Python Start button entry on Windows, in the Python Docs option on the Help pull-down menu in IDLE, or online at *http://www.python.org/doc*. I'll also have a few more words to say about the manuals and other documentation sources available (including PyDoc and the help function) in Chapter 14. If you still have time, go explore the Python web site, as well as the Vaults of Parnassus and the PyPy third-party extension's web site. Especially check out the Python.org documentation and search pages; they can be crucial resources.

Types and Operations

## CHAPTER 4

Introducing Python Object Types

This chapter begins our tour of the Python language. In an informal sense, in Python, we do things with stuff. "Things" take the form of operations like addition and concatenation, and "stuff" refers to the objects on which we perform those operations. In this part of the book, our focus is on that stuff, and the things our programs can do with it.

Somewhat more formally, in Python, data takes the form of *objects*—either built-in objects that Python provides, or objects we create using Python or external language tools such as C extension libraries. Although we'll firm up this definition later, objects are essentially just pieces of memory, with values and sets of associated operations.

Because objects are the most fundamental notion in Python programming, we'll start this chapter with a survey of Python's built-in object types.

By way of introduction, however, let's first establish a clear picture of how this chapter fits into the overall Python picture. From a more concrete perspective, Python programs can be decomposed into modules, statements, expressions, and objects, as follows:

1. Programs are composed of modules.
2. Modules contain statements.
3. Statements contain expressions.
4. *Expressions create and process objects.*

The discussion of modules in Chapter 3 introduced the highest level of this hierarchy. This part's chapters begin at the bottom, exploring both built-in objects and the expressions you can code to use them.

Why Use Built-in Types?

If you've used lower-level languages such as C or C++, you know that much of your work centers on implementing *objects*—also known as *data structures*—to represent the components in your application's domain. You need to lay out memory structures, manage memory allocation, implement search and access routines, and so on. These chores are about as tedious (and error prone) as they sound, and they usually distract from your program's real goals.

In typical Python programs, most of this grunt work goes away. Because Python provides powerful object types as an intrinsic part of the language, there's usually no need to code object implementations before you start solving problems. In fact, unless you have a need for special processing that built-in types don't provide, you're almost always better off using a built-in object instead of implementing your own. Here are some reasons why:

- **Built-in objects make programs easy to write.** For simple tasks, built-in types are often all you need to represent the structure of problem domains. Because you get powerful tools such as collections (lists) and search tables (dictionaries) for free, you can use them immediately. You can get a lot of work done with Python's built-in object types alone.

- **Built-in objects are components of extensions.** For more complex tasks, you still may need to provide your own objects, using Python classes or C language interfaces. But as you'll see in later parts of this book, objects implemented manually are often built on top of built-in types such as lists and dictionaries. For instance, a stack data structure may be implemented as a class that manages or customizes a built-in list.

- **Built-in objects are often more efficient than custom data structures.** Python's built-in types employ already optimized data structure algorithms that are implemented in C for speed. Although you can write similar object types on your own, you'll usually be hard-pressed to get the level of performance built-in object types provide.

- **Built-in objects are a standard part of the language.** In some ways, Python borrows both from languages that rely on built-in tools (e.g., LISP) and languages that rely on the programmer to provide tool implementations or frameworks of their own (e.g., C++). Although you can implement unique object types in Python, you don't need to do so just to get started. Moreover, because Python's built-ins are standard, they're always the same; proprietary frameworks, on the other hand, tend to differ from site to site.

In other words, not only do built-in object types make programming easier, but they're also more powerful and efficient than most of what can be created from scratch. Regardless of whether you implement new object types, built-in objects form the core of every Python program.

Python's Core Data Types

Table 4-1 previews Python's built-in object types and some of the syntax used to code their *literals*—that is, the expressions that generate these objects.* Some of these types will probably seem familiar if you've used other languages; for instance, numbers and strings represent numeric and textual values, respectively, and files provide an interface for processing files stored on your computer.

Table 4-1. Built-in objects preview

Object type	Example literals/creation
Numbers	`1234, 3.1415, 999L, 3+4j, Decimal`
Strings	`'spam', "guido's"`
Lists	`[1, [2, 'three'], 4]`
Dictionaries	`{'food': 'spam', 'taste': 'yum'}`
Tuples	`(1,'spam', 4, 'U')`
Files	`myfile = open('eggs', 'r')`
Other types	Sets, types, None, Booleans

Table 4-1 isn't really complete, because everything we process in Python programs is a kind of object. For instance, when we perform text pattern matching in Python, we create pattern objects, and when we perform network scripting, we use socket objects. These other kinds of objects are generally created by importing and using modules, and they have behavior all their own.

We call the object types in Table 4-1 *core* data types because they are effectively built into the Python language—that is, there is specific syntax for generating most of them. For instance, when you run the following code:

```
>>> 'spam'
```

you are, technically speaking, running a literal expression, which generates and returns a new string object. There is specific Python language syntax to make this object. Similarly, an expression wrapped in square brackets makes a list, one in curly braces makes a dictionary, and so on. Even though, as we'll see, there are no type declarations in Python, the syntax of the expressions you run determines the types of objects you create and use. In fact, object-generation expressions like those in Table 4-1 are generally where types originate in the Python language.

Just as importantly, once you create an object, you bind its operation set for all time—you can perform only string operations on a string and list operations on a

---

* In this book, the term *literal* simply means an expression whose syntax generates an object—sometimes also called a *constant*. Note that the term "constant" does not imply objects or variables that can never be changed (i.e., this term is unrelated to C++'s const or Python's "immutable"—a topic explored later in this chapter).

list. As you'll learn, Python is *dynamically typed* (it keeps track of types for you automatically instead of requiring declaration code), but it is also *strongly typed* (you can only perform on an object operations that are valid for its type).

Functionally, the object types in Table 4-1 are more general and powerful than what you may be accustomed to. For instance, you'll find that lists and dictionaries alone are powerful data representation tools that obviate most of the work you do to support collections and searching in lower-level languages. In short, lists provide ordered collections of other objects, while dictionaries store objects by key; both lists and dictionaries may be nested, can grow and shrink on demand, and may contain objects of any type.

We'll study each of the object types in Table 4-1 in detail in upcoming chapters. Before digging into the details, though, let's begin by taking a quick look at Python's core objects in action. The rest of this chapter provides a preview of the operations we'll explore in more depth in the chapters that follow. Don't expect to find the full story here—the goal of this chapter is just to whet your appetite and introduce some key ideas. Still, the best way to get started is to get started, so let's jump right into some real code.

Numbers

If you've done any programming or scripting in the past, some of the object types in Table 4-1 will probably seem familiar. Even if you haven't, numbers are fairly straightforward. Python's core object set includes the usual suspects: integers (numbers without a fractional part), floating-point numbers (roughly, numbers with a decimal point in them), and more exotic types (unlimited-precision "long" integers, complex numbers with imaginary parts, fixed-precision decimals, and sets).

Although it offers some fancier options, Python's basic number types are, well, basic. Numbers in Python support the normal mathematical operations. For instance, the plus sign (+) performs addition, a star (*) is used for multiplication, and two stars (**) are used for exponentiation:

```
>>> 123 + 222                    # Integer addition
345
>>> 1.5 * 4                      # Floating-point multiplication
6.0
>>> 2 ** 100                     # 2 to the power 100
1267650600228229401496703205376L
```

Notice the *L* at the end of the last operation's result here: Python automatically converts up to a long integer type when extra precision is needed. You can, for instance, compute 2 to the 1,000,000 power in Python (but you probably shouldn't try to print the result—with more than 300,000 digits, you may be waiting awhile!). Watch what happens when some floating-point numbers are printed:

```
>>> 3.1415 * 2                          # repr: as code
6.2830000000000004
>>> print 3.1415 * 2                    # str: user-friendly
6.283
```

The first result isn't a bug; it's a display issue. It turns out that there are two ways to print every object: with full precision (as in the first result shown here), and in a user-friendly form (as in the second). Formally, the first form is known as an object's as-code repr, and the second is its user-friendly str. The difference can matter when we step up to using classes; for now, if something looks odd, try showing it with a print statement.

Besides expressions, there are a handful of useful numeric modules that ship with Python:

```
>>> import math
>>> math.pi
3.1415926535897931
>>> math.sqrt(85)
9.2195444572928871
```

The math module contains more advanced numeric tools as functions, while the random module performs random number generation and random selections (here, from a Python list, introduced later in this chapter):

```
>>> import random
>>> random.random( )
0.59268735266273953
>>> random.choice([1, 2, 3, 4])
1
```

Python also includes more exotic number objects—such as complex numbers, fixed-precision decimal numbers, and sets—and the third-party open source extension domain has even more (e.g., matrixes and vectors). We'll defer discussion of the details of these types until later in the book.

So far, we've been using Python much like a simple calculator; to do better justice to its built-in types, let's move on to explore strings.

Strings

Strings are used to record textual information as well as arbitrary collections of bytes. They are our first example of what we call a *sequence* in Python—that is, a positionally ordered collection of other objects. Sequences maintain a left-to-right order among the items they contain: their items are stored and fetched by their relative position. Strictly speaking, strings are sequences of one-character strings; other types of sequences include lists and tuples (covered later).

Sequence Operations

As sequences, strings support operations that assume a positional ordering among items. For example, if we have a four-character string, we can verify its length with the built-in len function and fetch its components with *indexing* expressions:

```
>>> S = 'Spam'
>>> len(S)                # Length
4
>>> S[0]                  # The first item in S, indexing by zero-based position
'S'
>>> S[1]                  # The second item from the left
'p'
```

In Python, indexes are coded as offsets from the front, and so start from 0: the first item is at index 0, the second is at index 1, and so on. In Python, we can also index backward, from the end:

```
>>> S[-1]                 # The last item from the end in S
'm'
>>> S[-2]                 # The second to last item from the end
'a'
```

Formally, a negative index is simply added to the string's size, so the following two operations are equivalent (though the first is easier to code and less easy to get wrong):

```
>>> S[-1]                 # The last item in S
'm'
>>> S[len(S)-1]           # Negative indexing, the hard way
'm'
```

Notice that we can use an arbitrary expression in the square brackets, not just a hardcoded number literal—anywhere that Python expects a value, we can use a literal, a variable, or any expression. Python's syntax is completely general this way.

In addition to simple positional indexing, sequences also support a more general form of indexing known as *slicing*, which is a way to extract an entire section (slice) in a single step. For example:

```
>>> S                     # A 4-character string
'Spam'
>>> S[1:3]                # Slice of S from offsets 1 through 2 (not 3)
'pa'
```

Probably the easiest way to think of slices is that they are a way to extract an entire *column* from a string in a single step. Their general form, X[I:J], means "give me everything in X from offset I up to but not including offset J." The result is returned in a new object. The last operation above, for instance, gives us all the characters in string S from offsets 1 through 2 (that is, 3–1) as a new string. The effect is to slice or "parse out" the two characters in the middle.

In a slice, the left bound defaults to zero, and the right bound defaults to the length of the sequence being sliced. This leads to some common usage variations:

```
>>> S[1:]              # Everything past the first (1:len(S))
'pam'
>>> S                  # S itself hasn't changed
'Spam'
>>> S[0:3]             # Everything but the last
'Spa'
>>> S[:3]              # Same as S[0:3]
'Spa'
>>> S[:-1]             # Everything but the last again, but simpler (0:-1)
'Spa'
>>> S[:]               # All of S as a top-level copy (0:len(S))
'Spam'
```

Note how negative offsets can be used to give bounds for slices, too, and how the last operation effectively copies the entire string. As you'll learn later, there is no reason to copy a string, but this form can be useful for sequences like lists.

Finally, as sequences, strings also support *concatenation* with the plus sign (joining two strings into a new string), and *repetition* (making a new string by repeating another):

```
>>> S
'Spam'
>>> S + 'xyz'          # Concatenation
'Spamxyz'
>>> S                  # S is unchanged
'Spam'
>>> S * 8              # Repetition
'SpamSpamSpamSpamSpamSpamSpamSpam'
```

Notice that the plus sign (+) means different things for different objects: addition for numbers, and concatenation for strings. This is a general property of Python that we'll call *polymorphism* later in the book—in sum, the meaning of an operation depends on the objects being operated on. As you'll see when we study dynamic typing, this polymorphism property accounts for much of the conciseness and flexibility of Python code. Because types aren't constrained, a Python-coded operation can normally work on many different types of objects automatically, as long as they support a compatible interface (like the + operation here). This turns out to be a huge idea in Python; you'll learn more about it later on our tour.

Immutability

Notice that in the prior examples, we were not changing the original string with any of the operations we ran on it. Every string operation is defined to produce a new string as its result, because strings are *immutable* in Python—they cannot be changed in-place after they are created. For example, you can't change a string by assigning to one of its positions, but you can always build a new one and assign it to the same name. Because Python cleans up old objects as you go (as you'll see later), this isn't as inefficient as it may sound:

```
>>> S
'Spam'
>>> S[0] = 'z'                    # Immutable objects cannot be changed
...error text omitted...
TypeError: 'str' object does not support item assignment

>>> S = 'z' + S[1:]              # But we can run expressions to make new objects
>>> S
'zpam'
```

Every object in Python is classified as immutable (unchangeable) or not. In terms of the core types, numbers, strings, and tuples are immutable; lists and dictionaries are not (they can be changed in-place freely). Among other things, immutability can be used to guarantee that an object remains constant throughout your program.

Type-Specific Methods

Every string operation we've studied so far is really a sequence operation—that is, these operations will work on other sequences in Python as well, including lists and tuples. In addition to generic sequence operations, though, strings also have operations all their own, available as *methods* (functions attached to the object, which are triggered with a call expression).

For example, the string find method is the basic substring search operation (it returns the offset of the passed-in substring, or -1 if it is not present), and the string replace method performs global searches and replacements:

```
>>> S.find('pa')                 # Find the offset of a substring
1
>>> S
'Spam'
>>> S.replace('pa', 'XYZ')       # Replace occurrences of a substring with another
'SXYZm'
>>> S
'Spam'
```

Again, despite the names of these string methods, we are not changing the original strings here, but creating new strings as the results—because strings are immutable, we have to do it this way. String methods are the first line of text-processing tools in Python; other methods split a string into substrings on a delimiter (handy as a simple form of parsing), perform case conversions, test the content of the string (digits, letters, and so on), and strip whitespace characters off the ends of the string:

```
>>> line = 'aaa,bbb,ccccc,dd'
>>> line.split(',')              # Split on a delimiter into a list of substrings
['aaa', 'bbb', 'ccccc', 'dd']
```

```
>>> S = 'spam'
>>> S.upper()              # Upper- and lowercase conversions
'SPAM'

>>> S.isalpha()            # Content tests: isalpha, isdigit, etc.
True

>>> line = 'aaa,bbb,ccccc,dd\n'
>>> line = line.rstrip()   # Remove whitespace characters on the right side
>>> line
'aaa,bbb,ccccc,dd'              ↗ note this is a new line
```

One note here: although sequence operations are generic, methods are not—string method operations work only on strings, and nothing else. As a rule of thumb, Python's toolset is layered: generic operations that span multiple types show up as built-in functions or expressions (e.g., len(X), X[0]), but type-specific operations are method calls (e.g., aString.upper()). Finding the tools you need among all these categories will become more natural as you use Python more, but the next section gives a few tips you can use right now.

Getting Help

The methods introduced in the prior section are a representative, but small, sample of what is available for string objects. In general, this book is not exhaustive in its look at object methods. For more details, you can always call the built-in dir function, which returns a list of all the attributes available in a given object. Because methods are function attributes, they will show up in this list:

```
>>> dir(S)
['__add__', '__class__', '__contains__', '__delattr__', '__doc__', '__eq__',
'__ge__', '__getattribute__', '__getitem__', '__getnewargs__', '__getslice__',
'__gt__', '__hash__', '__init__', '__le__', '__len__', '__lt__', '__mod__',
'__mul__', '__ne__', '__new__', '__reduce__', '__reduce_ex__', '__repr__',
'__rmod__', '__rmul__', '__setattr__', '__str__', 'capitalize', 'center',
'count', 'decode', 'encode', 'endswith', 'expandtabs', 'find', 'index',
'isalnum', 'isalpha', 'isdigit', 'islower', 'isspace', 'istitle', 'isupper',
'join', 'ljust', 'lower', 'lstrip', 'partition', 'replace', 'rfind', 'rindex',
'rjust', 'rpartition', 'rsplit', 'rstrip', 'split', 'splitlines', 'startswith',
'strip', 'swapcase', 'title', 'translate', 'upper', 'zfill']
```

You probably won't care about the names with underscores in this list until later in the book, when we study operator overloading in classes—they represent the implementation of the string object, and are available to support customization. In general, leading and trailing double underscores is the naming pattern Python uses for implementation details. The names without the underscores in this list are the callable methods on string objects.

The dir function simply gives the methods' names. To ask what they do, you can pass them to the help function:

```
>>> help(S.index)
Help on built-in function index:

index(...)
    S.index(sub [,start [,end]]) -> int

        Like S.find() but raise ValueError when the substring is not found.
```

help is one of a handful of interfaces to a system of code that ships with Python known as *PyDoc*—a tool for extracting documentation from objects. Later in the book, you'll see that PyDoc can also render its reports in HTML format.

You can also ask for help on an entire string (e.g., help(S)), but you may get more help than you want to see—i.e., information about every string method. It's generally better to ask about a specific method, as we did above.

For more details, you can also consult Python's standard library reference manual, or commercially published reference books, but dir and help are the first line of documentation in Python.

Other Ways to Code Strings

So far, we've looked at the string object's sequence operations and type-specific methods. Python also provides a variety of ways for us to code strings, which we'll explore further later (with special characters represented as backslash escape sequences, for instance):

```
>>> S = 'A\nB\tC'       # \n is end-of-line, \t is tab
>>> len(S)              # Each stands for just one character
5

>>> ord('\n')           # \n is a byte with the binary value 10 in ASCII
10

>>> S = 'A\0B\0C'       # \0, the binary zero byte, does not terminate the string
>>> len(S)
5
```

Python allows strings to be enclosed in single or double quote characters (they mean the same thing). It also has a multiline string literal form enclosed in triple quotes (single or double)—when this form is used, all the lines are concatenated together, and end-of-line characters are added where line breaks appear. This is a minor syntactic convenience, but it's useful for embedding things like HTML and XML code in a Python script:

```
>>> msg = """
aaaaaaaaaaaaa
bbb'''bbbbbbbbbb""bbbbbbb'bbbb
cccccccccccccc"""
```

```
>>> msg
'\naaaaaaaaaaaaaa\nbbb\'\'\'bbbbbbbbbb""bbbbbbb\'bbbb\nccccccccccccccc'
```

Python also supports a "raw" string literal that turns off the backslash escape mechanism (they start with the letter *r*), as well as a Unicode string form that supports internationalization (they begin with the letter *u* and contain multibyte characters). Technically, Unicode string is a different data type than normal string, but it supports all the same string operations. We'll meet all these special string forms in later chapters.

Pattern Matching

One point worth noting before we move on is that none of the string-object's methods support pattern-based text processing. Text pattern matching is an advanced tool outside this book's scope, but readers with backgrounds in other scripting languages may be interested to know that to do pattern matching in Python, we import a module called re. This module has analogous calls for searching, splitting, and replacement, but because we can use patterns to specify substrings, we can be much more general:

```
>>> import re
>>> match = re.match('Hello[ \t]*(.*)world', 'Hello    Python world')
>>> match.group(1)
'Python '
```

This example searches for a substring that begins with the word "Hello," followed by zero or more tabs or spaces, followed by arbitrary characters to be saved as a matched group, terminated by the word "world." If such as substring is found, portions of the substring matched by parts of the pattern enclosed in parentheses are available as groups. The following pattern, for example, picks out three groups separated by slashes:

```
>>> match = re.match('/(.*)/(.*)/(.*)', '/usr/home/lumberjack')
>>> match.groups()
('usr', 'home', 'lumberjack')
```

Pattern matching is a fairly advanced text-processing tool by itself, but there is also support in Python for even more advanced language processing, including natural language processing. I've already said enough about strings for this tutorial, though, so let's move on to the next type.

Lists

The Python list object is the most general sequence provided by the language. Lists are positionally ordered collections of arbitrarily typed objects, and they have no fixed size. They are also mutable—unlike strings, lists can be modified in-place by assignment to offsets as well as a variety of list method calls.

Sequence Operations

Because they are sequences, lists support all the sequence operations we discussed for strings; the only difference is that results are usually lists instead of strings. For instance, given a three-item list:

```
>>> L = [123, 'spam', 1.23]        # A list of three different-type objects
>>> len(L)                         # Number of items in the list
3
```

we can index, slice, and so on, just as for strings:

```
>>> L[0]                           # Indexing by position
123

>>> L[:-1]                         # Slicing a list returns a new list
[123, 'spam']

>>> L + [4, 5, 6]                  # Concatenation makes a new list too
[123, 'spam', 1.23, 4, 5, 6]

>>> L                              # We're not changing the original list
[123, 'spam', 1.23]
```

Type-Specific Operations

Python's lists are related to arrays in other languages, but they tend to be more powerful. For one thing, they have no fixed type constraint—the list we just looked at, for example, contains three objects of completely different types (an integer, a string, and a floating-point number). Further, lists have no fixed size. That is, they can grow and shrink on demand, in response to list-specific operations:

```
>>> L.append('NI')                 # Growing: add object at end of list  (mutated)
>>> L
[123, 'spam', 1.23, 'NI']

>>> L.pop(2)                       # Shrinking: delete an item in the middle  mutated list
1.23

>>> L                              # "del L[2]" deletes from a list too
[123, 'spam', 'NI']
```

Here, the list append method expands the list's size and inserts an item at the end; the pop method (or an equivalent del statement) then removes an item at a given offset, causing the list to shrink. Other list methods insert items at an arbitrary position (insert), remove a given item by value (remove), and so on. Because lists are mutable, most list methods also change the list object in-place, instead of creating a new one:

```
>>> M = ['bb', 'aa', 'cc']
>>> M.sort()
>>> M
['aa', 'bb', 'cc']
```

```
>>> M.reverse( )
>>> M
['cc', 'bb', 'aa']
```

 Sort (order z to A).

The list sort method here, for example, orders the list in ascending fashion by default, and reverse reverses it—in both cases, the methods modify the list directly.

Bounds Checking

Although lists have no fixed size, Python still doesn't allow us to reference items that are not present. Indexing off the end of a list is always a mistake, but so is assigning off the end:

```
>>> L
[123, 'spam', 'NI']

>>> L[99]
...error text omitted...
IndexError: list index out of range

>>> L[99] = 1
...error text omitted...
IndexError: list assignment index out of range
```

This is on purpose, as it's usually an error to try to assign off the end of a list (and a particularly nasty one in the C language, which doesn't do as much error checking as Python). Rather than silently growing the list in response, Python reports an error. To grow a list, we call list methods such as append instead.

excellent !!

Nesting

One nice feature of Python's core data types is that they support arbitrary nesting—we can nest them in any combination, and as deeply as we like (for example, we can have a list that contains a dictionary, which contains another list, and so on). One immediate application of this feature is to represent matrixes, or "multidimensional arrays" in Python. A list with nested lists will do the job for basic applications:

```
>>> M = [[1, 2, 3],          # A 3 x 3 matrix, as nested lists
         [4, 5, 6],
         [7, 8, 9]]
>>> M
[[1, 2, 3], [4, 5, 6], [7, 8, 9]]
```

Here, we've coded a list that contains three other lists. The effect is to represent a 3 × 3 matrix of numbers. Such a structure can be accessed in a variety of ways:

```
>>> M[1]                     # Get row 2
[4, 5, 6]

>>> M[1][2]                  # Get row 2, then get item 3 within the row
6
```

The first operation here fetches the entire second row, and the second grabs the third item within that row—stringing together index operations takes us deeper and deeper into our nested-object structure.[*]

List Comprehensions

In addition to sequence operations and list methods, Python includes a more advanced operation known as a *list comprehension expression*, which turns out to be a powerful way to process structures like our matrix. Suppose, for instance, that we need to extract the second column of our sample matrix. It's easy to grab rows by simple indexing because the matrix is stored by rows, but it's almost as easy to get a column with a list comprehension:

```
>>> col2 = [row[1] for row in M]          # Collect the items in column 2
>>> col2
[2, 5, 8]

>>> M                                      # The matrix is unchanged
[[1, 2, 3], [4, 5, 6], [7, 8, 9]]
```

List comprehensions derive from set notation; they are a way to build a new list by running an expression on each item in a sequence, one at a time, from left to right. List comprehensions are coded in square brackets (to tip you off to the fact that they make a list), and are composed of an expression and a looping construct that share a variable name (row, here). The preceding list comprehension means basically what it says: "Give me row[1] for each row in matrix M, in a new list." The result is a new list containing column 2 of the matrix.

List comprehensions can be more complex in practice:

```
>>> [row[1] + 1 for row in M]             # Add 1 to each item in column 2
[3, 6, 9]

>>> [row[1] for row in M if row[1] % 2 == 0]   # Filter out odd items , what if all odd ?
[2, 8]
```

The first operation here, for instance, adds 1 to each item as it is collected, and the second uses an if clause to filter odd numbers out of the result using the % modulus expression (remainder of division). List comprehensions make new lists of results, but can be used to iterate over any iterable object—here, for instance, we'll use list comprehensions to step over a hardcoded list of coordinates, and a string:

---

[*] This matrix structure works for small-scale tasks, but for more serious number crunching, you will probably want to use one of the numeric extensions to Python, such as the open source NumPy system. Such tools can store and process large matrixes much more efficiently than our nested list structure. NumPy has been said to turn Python into the equivalent of a free and more powerful version of the MatLab system, and organizations such as NASA, Los Alamos, and JPMorgan Chase use this tool for scientific and financial tasks. Search the Web for more details.

```
>>> diag = [M[i][i] for i in [0, 1, 2]]        # Collect a diagonal from matrix
>>> diag
[1, 5, 9]

>>> doubles = [c * 2 for c in 'spam']          # Repeat characters in a string
>>> doubles
['ss', 'pp', 'aa', 'mm']
```

List comprehensions are a bit too involved for me to say more about them here. The main point of this brief introduction is to illustrate that Python includes both simple and advanced tools in its arsenal. List comprehensions are an optional feature, but they tend to be handy in practice, and often provide a substantial processing speed advantage. They also work on any type that is a sequence in Python, as well as some types that are not. You'll hear more about them later in this book.

Dictionaries

Python dictionaries are something completely different (Monty Python reference intended)—they are not sequences at all, but are instead known as *mappings*. Mappings are also collections of other objects, but they store objects by key instead of by relative position. In fact, mappings don't maintain any reliable left-to-right order; they simply map keys to associated values. Dictionaries, the only mapping type in Python's core objects set, are also mutable: they may be changed in-place, and can grow and shrink on demand, like lists.

Mapping Operations

When written as literals, dictionaries are coded in curly braces, and consist of a series of "key: value" pairs. Dictionaries are useful anytime we need to associate a set of values with keys—to describe the properties of something, for instance. As an example, consider the following three-item dictionary (with keys "food," "quantity," and "color"):

```
>>> D = {'food': 'Spam', 'quantity': 4, 'color': 'pink'}
```

We can index this dictionary by key to fetch and change the keys' associated values. The dictionary index operation uses the same syntax as that used for sequences, but the item in the square brackets is a key, not a relative position:

```
>>> D['food']                                  # Fetch value of key 'food'
'Spam'

>>> D['quantity'] += 1                         # Add 1 to 'quantity' value
>>> D
{'food': 'Spam', 'color': 'pink', 'quantity': 5}
```

Although the curly-braces literal form does see use, it is perhaps more common to see dictionaries built up in different ways. The following, for example, starts with an empty dictionary, and fills it out one key at a time. Unlike out-of-bounds assignments in lists, which are forbidden, an assignment to new dictionary key creates that key:

```
>>> D = {}
>>> D['name'] = 'Bob'              # Create keys by assignment
>>> D['job']  = 'dev'
>>> D['age']  = 40

>>> D
{'age': 40, 'job': 'dev', 'name': 'Bob'}

>>> print D['name']
Bob
```

Here, we're effectively using dictionary keys as field names in a record that describes someone. In other applications, dictionaries can also be used to replace searching operations—indexing a dictionary by key is often the fastest way to code a search in Python.

Nesting Revisited

In the prior example, we used a dictionary to describe a hypothetical person, with three keys. Suppose, though, that the information is more complex. Perhaps we need to record a first name and a last name, along with multiple job titles. This leads to another application of Python's object nesting in action. The following dictionary, coded all at once as a literal, captures more structured information:

```
>>> rec = {'name': {'first': 'Bob', 'last': 'Smith'},
           'job':  ['dev', 'mgr'],
           'age':  40.5}
```

Here, we again have a three-key dictionary at the top (keys "name," "job," and "age"), but the values have become more complex: a nested dictionary for the name to support multiple parts, and a nested list for the job to support multiple roles and future expansion. We can access the components of this structure much as we did for our matrix earlier, but this time some of our indexes are dictionary keys, not list offsets:

```
>>> rec['name']                    # 'Name' is a nested dictionary
{'last': 'Smith', 'first': 'Bob'}

>>> rec['name']['last']            # Index the nested dictionary
'Smith'

>>> rec['job']                     # 'Job' is a nested list
['dev', 'mgr']
```

```
>>> rec['job'][-1]                    # Index the nested list
'mgr'

>>> rec['job'].append('janitor')      # Expand Bob's job description in-place
>>> rec
{'age': 40.5, 'job': ['dev', 'mgr', 'janitor'], 'name': {'last': 'Smith', 'first':
'Bob'}}
```

Notice how the last operation here expands the nested job list—because the job list is a separate piece of memory from the dictionary that contains it, it can grow and shrink freely (object memory layout will be discussed further later in this book).

The real reason for showing you this example is to demonstrate the flexibility of Python's core data types. As you can see, nesting allows us to build up complex information structures directly and easily. Building a similar structure in a low-level language like C would be tedious and require much more code: we would have to lay out and declare structures and arrays, fill out values, link everything together, and so on. In Python, this is all automatic—running the expression creates the entire nested object structure for us. In fact, this is one of the main benefits of scripting languages like Python.

Just as importantly, in a lower-level language, we would have to be careful to clean up all of the object's space when we no longer need it. In Python, when we lose the last reference to object—by assigning its variable to something else, for example—all of the memory space occupied by that object's structure is automatically cleaned up for us:

```
>>> rec = 0                           # Now the object's space is reclaimed
```

Technically speaking, Python has a feature known as *garbage collection* that cleans up unused memory as your program runs and frees you from having to manage such details in your code. In Python, the space is reclaimed immediately, as soon as the last reference to an object is removed. We'll study how this works later in this book; for now, it's enough to know that you can use objects freely, without worrying about creating their space or cleaning up as you go.[*]

Sorting Keys: for Loops

As mappings, as we've already seen, dictionaries only support accessing items by key. However, they also support type-specific operations with method calls that are useful in a variety of common use cases.

---

[*] One footnote here: keep in mind that the rec record we just created really could be a database record, when we employ Python's *object persistence* system—an easy way to store native Python objects in files or access-by-key databases. We won't go into more details here; see Python's pickle and shelve modules for more details.

As mentioned earlier, because dictionaries are not sequences, they don't maintain any dependable left-to-right order. This means that if we make a dictionary, and print it back, its keys may come back in a different order than how we typed them:

```
>>> D = {'a': 1, 'b': 2, 'c': 3}
>>> D
{'a': 1, 'c': 3, 'b': 2}
```

What do we do, though, if we do need to impose an ordering on a dictionary's items? One common solution is to grab a list of keys with the dictionary keys method, sort that with the list sort method, and then step through the result with a Python for loop:

```
>>> Ks = D.keys()              # Unordered keys list
>>> Ks
['a', 'c', 'b']

>>> Ks.sort()                  # Sorted keys list
>>> Ks
['a', 'b', 'c']

>>> for key in Ks:             # Iterate though sorted keys
        print key, '=>', D[key]

a => 1
b => 2
c => 3
```

This is a three-step process, though, as we'll see in later chapters, in recent versions of Python it can be done in one step with the newer sorted built-in function (sorted returns the result and sorts a variety of object types):

```
>>> D
{'a': 1, 'c': 3, 'b': 2}

>>> for key in sorted(D):
        print key, '=>', D[key]

a => 1
b => 2
c => 3
```

This case serves as an excuse to introduce the Python for loop. The for loop is a simple and efficient way to step through all the items in a sequence and run a block of code for each item in turn. A user-defined loop variable (key, here) is used to reference the current item each time through. The net effect in our example is to print the unordered dictionary's keys and values, in sorted-key order.

The for loop, and its more general cousin the while loop, are the main ways we code repetitive tasks as statements in our scripts. Really, though, the for loop, like its relative the list comprehension (which we met earlier) is a sequence operation. It works on any object that is a sequence and, also like the list comprehension, even on some things that are not. Here, for example, it is stepping across the characters in a string, printing the uppercase version of each as it goes:

```
>>> for c in 'spam':
        print c.upper()

S
P
A
M
```

We'll discuss looping statements further later in the book.

Iteration and Optimization

If the for loop looks like the list comprehension expression introduced earlier, it should: both are really general iteration tools. In fact, both will work on any object that follows the *iteration protocol*—an idea introduced recently in Python that essentially means a physically stored sequence in memory, or an object that generates one item at a time in the context of an iteration operation. This is why the sorted call used in the prior section works on the dictionary directly—we don't have to call the keys method to get a sequence because dictionaries are iterable objects.

I'll have more to say about the iteration protocol later in this book. For now, keep in mind that any list comprehension expression, such as this one, which computes the squares of a list of numbers:

```
>>> squares = [x ** 2 for x in [1, 2, 3, 4, 5]]
>>> squares
[1, 4, 9, 16, 25]
```

can always be coded as an equivalent for loop that builds the result list manually by appending as it goes:

```
>>> squares = []
>>> for x in [1, 2, 3, 4, 5]:        # This is what a list comp does
        squares.append(x ** 2)

>>> squares
[1, 4, 9, 16, 25]
```

The list comprehension, though, will generally run faster (perhaps even twice as fast)—a property that could matter in your programs for large data sets. Having said that, though, I should point out that performance measures are tricky business in Python because it optimizes so much, and can vary from release to release.

A major rule of thumb in Python is to code for simplicity and readability first, and worry about performance later, after your program is working, and after you've proved that there is a genuine performance concern. More often than not, your code will be quick enough as it is. If you do need to tweak code for performance, though, Python includes tools to help you out, including the time and timeit modules and the profile module. You'll find more on these later in this book, and in the Python manuals.

Missing Keys: if Tests

One other note about dictionaries before we move on. Although we can assign to a new key to expand a dictionary, fetching a nonexistent key is still a mistake:

```
>>> D
{'a': 1, 'c': 3, 'b': 2}

>>> D['e'] = 99                    # Assigning new keys grows dictionaries
>>> D
{'a': 1, 'c': 3, 'b': 2, 'e': 99}

>>> D['f']                         # Referencing one is an error
...error text omitted...
KeyError: 'f'
```

This is what we want—it's usually a programming error to fetch something that isn't really there. But, in some generic programs, we can't always know what keys will be present when we write our code. How do we handle such cases and avoid the errors? One trick here is to test ahead of time. The dictionary has_key method allows us to query the existence of a key and branch on the result with a Python if statement:

```
>>> D.has_key('f')
False

>>> if not D.has_key('f'):
        print 'missing'

missing
```

I'll have much more to say about the if statement and statement syntax in general later in this book, but the form we're using here is straightforward: it consists of the word if, followed by an expression that is interpreted as a true or false result, followed by a block of code to run if the test is true. In its full form, the if statement can also have an else clause for a default case, and one or more elif (else if) clauses for other tests. It's the main selection tool in Python, and it's the way we code logic in our scripts.

There are other ways to create dictionaries and avoid accessing a nonexistent dictionary key (including the get method; the in membership expression; and the try statement, a tool we'll first meet in Chapter 10 that catches and recovers from exceptions altogether), but we'll save the details on those until a later chapter. Now, let's move on to tuples.

Tuples ( )

The tuple object (pronounced "toople" or "tuhple," depending on who you ask) is roughly like a list that cannot be changed—tuples are sequences, like lists, but they are immutable, like strings. Syntactically, they are coded in parentheses instead of square brackets, and they support arbitrary types, nesting, and the usual sequence operations:

```
>>> T = (1, 2, 3, 4)              # A 4-item tuple
>>> len(T)                        # Length
4

>> T + (5, 6)                     # Concatenation → new tuple
(1, 2, 3, 4, 5, 6)

>>> T[0]                          # Indexing, slicing, and more
1
```

The only real distinction for tuples is that they cannot be changed once created. That is, they are immutable sequences:

```
>>> T[0] = 2                      # Tuples are immutable, so cant assign once exist
...error text omitted...
TypeError: 'tuple' object does not support item assignment
```

Why Tuples?

So, why have a type that is like a list, but supports fewer operations? Frankly, tuples are not generally used as often as lists in practice, but their immutability is the whole point. If you pass a collection of objects around your program as a list, it can be changed anywhere; if you use a tuple, it cannot. That is, tuples provide a sort of integrity constraint that is convenient in programs larger than those we can write here. We'll talk more about tuples later in the book. For now, though, let's jump ahead to our last major core type, the file.

Files

File objects are Python code's main interface to external files on your computer. They are a core type, but they're something of an oddball—there is no specific literal syntax for creating them. Rather, to create a file object, you call the built-in open function, passing in an external filename as a string, and a processing mode string. For example, to create an output file, you would pass in its name and the 'w' processing mode string to write data:

```
>>> f = open('data.txt', 'w')     # Make a new file in output mode
>>> f.write('Hello\n')            # Write strings of bytes to it
>>> f.write('world\n')
>>> f.close()                     # Close to flush output buffers to disk
```

This creates a file in the current directory, and writes text to it (the filename can be a full directory path if you need to access a file elsewhere on your computer). To read back what you just wrote, reopen the file in `'r'` processing mode, for reading input (this is the default if you omit the mode in the call). Then read the file's content into a string of bytes, and display it. A file's contents are always a string of bytes to your script, regardless of the type of data the file contains:

```
>>> f = open('data.txt')          # 'r' is the default processing mode
>>> bytes = f.read()              # Read entire file into a string
>>> bytes                         # shows actual bytes stored
'Hello\nworld\n'

>>> print bytes                   # Print interprets control characters
Hello
world

>>> bytes.split()                 # File content is always a string
['Hello', 'world']
```

Other file object methods support additional features we don't have time to cover here. For instance, file objects provide more ways of reading and writing (read accepts an optional byte size, readline reads one line at a time, and so on), as well as other tools (seek moves to a new file position). We'll meet the full set of file methods later in this book, but if you want a quick preview now, run a dir call on the word file (the name of the file data type), and a help on any of the names that come back:

```
>>> dir(file)
['__class__', '__delattr__', '__doc__', '__enter__', '__exit__',
'__getattribute__', '__hash__', '__init__', '__iter__', '__new__',
'__reduce__', '__reduce_ex__', '__repr__', '__setattr__', '__str__',
'close', 'closed', 'encoding', 'fileno', 'flush', 'isatty', 'mode',
'name', 'newlines', 'next', 'read', 'readinto', 'readline', 'readlines',
'seek', 'softspace', 'tell', 'truncate', 'write', 'writelines', 'xreadlines']

>>> help(file.seek)
...try it and see...
```

Other File-Like Tools

The open function is the workhorse for most file processing you will do in Python. For more advanced tasks, though, Python comes with additional file-like tools: pipes, fifos, sockets, keyed-access files, object persistence, descriptor-based files, relational and object-oriented database interfaces, and more. Descriptor files, for instance, support file locking and other low-level tools, and sockets provide an interface for networking and interprocess communication. We won't cover many of these topics in this book, but you'll find them useful once you start programming Python in earnest.

Other Core Types

Beyond the core types we've seen so far, there are others that may or may not qualify for membership, depending on how broad the category is defined to be. Sets, for example, are a recent addition to the language. Sets are containers of other objects created by calling the built-in set function, and they support the usual mathematical set operations:

```
>>> X = set('spam')
>>> Y = set(['h', 'a', 'm'])              # Make 2 sets out of sequences
>>> X, Y
(set(['a', 'p', 's', 'm']), set(['a', 'h', 'm']))   # not, implicit RE-ordering

>>> X & Y                                  # Intersection
set(['a', 'm'])

>>> X | Y                                  # Union
set(['a', 'p', 's', 'h', 'm'])

>>> X - Y                                  # Difference
set(['p', 's'])
```

In addition, Python recently added decimal numbers (fixed-precision floating-point numbers) and Booleans (with predefined True and False objects that are essentially just the integers 1 and 0 with custom display logic), and it has long supported a special placeholder object called None:

```
>>> import decimal                          # Decimals
>>> d = decimal.Decimal('3.141')
>>> d + 1
Decimal("4.141")

>>> 1 > 2, 1 < 2                            # Booleans
(False, True)
>>> bool('spam')
True

>>> X = None                               # None placeholder
>>> print X
None
>>> L = [None] * 100                        # Initialize a list of 100 Nones
>>> L
[None, None, None, None, None, None, None, None, None, None, None, None, None,
...a list of 100 Nones...]

>>> type(L)                                # Types
<type 'list'>
>>> type(type(L))                          # Even types are objects
<type 'type'>
```

How to Break Your Code's Flexibility

I'll have more to say about all these types later in the book, but the last merits a few more words here. The type object allows code to check the types of the objects it uses. In fact, there are at least three ways to do so in a Python script:

```
>>> if type(L) == type([]):              # Type testing, if you must...
        print 'yes'

yes
>>> if type(L) == list:                  # Using the type name
        print 'yes'

yes
>>> if isinstance(L, list):              # Object-oriented tests
        print 'yes'

yes
```

Now that I've shown you all these ways to do type testing, however, I must mention that, as you'll see later in the book, doing so is almost always the wrong thing to do in a Python program (and often a sign of an ex-C programmer first starting to use Python). By checking for specific types in your code, you effectively break its flexibility—you limit it to working on just one type. Without such tests, your code may be able to work on a whole range of types.

This is related to the idea of polymorphism mentioned earlier, and it stems from Python's lack of type declarations. As you'll learn, in Python, we code to object *interfaces* (operations supported), not to types. Not caring about specific types means that code is automatically applicable to many of them—any object with a compatible interface will work, regardless of its specific type. Although type checking is supported—and even required, in some rare cases—you'll see that it's not usually the "Pythonic" way of thinking. In fact, you'll find that polymorphism is probably the key idea behind using Python well.

User-Defined Classes

We'll study object-oriented programming in Python—an optional but powerful feature of the language that cuts development time by supporting programming by customization—in depth later in this book. In abstract terms, though, classes define new types of objects that extend the core set, so they merit a passing glance here. Say, for example, that you wish to have a type of object that models employees. Although there is no such specific core type in Python, the following user-defined class might fit the bill:

```
>>> class Worker:
        def __init__(self, name, pay):       # Initialize when created
            self.name = name                 # Self is the new object
            self.pay  = pay
```

```
        def lastName(self):
            return self.name.split( )[-1]          # Split string on blanks
        def giveRaise(self, percent):
            self.pay *= (1.0 + percent)            # Update pay in-place
```

This class defines a new kind of object that will have name and pay attributes (sometimes called *state information*), as well as two bits of behavior coded as functions (normally called *methods*). Calling the class like a function generates instances of our new type, and the class' methods automatically receive the instance being processed by a given method call (in the self argument):

```
>>> bob = Worker('Bob Smith', 50000)      # Make two instances
>>> sue = Worker('Sue Jones', 60000)      # Each has name and pay
>>> bob.lastName( )                       # Call method: bob is self
'Smith'
>>> sue.lastName( )                       # Sue is the self subject
'Jones'
>>> sue.giveRaise(.10)                     # Updates sue's pay
>>> sue.pay
66000.0
```

The implied "self" object is why we call this an object-oriented model: there is always an implied subject in functions within a class. In a sense, though, the class-based type simply builds on and uses core types—a user-defined Worker object here, for example, is just a collection of a string and number (name and pay, respectively), plus functions for processing those two built-in objects.

The larger story of classes is that their inheritance mechanism supports software hierarchies that lend themselves to customization by extension. We extend software by writing new classes, not by changing what already works. You should also know that classes are an optional feature of Python, and simpler built-in types such as lists and dictionaries are often better tools than user-coded classes. This is all well beyond the bounds of our introductory object-type tutorial, though, so for that tale, you'll have to read on to a later chapter.

And Everything Else

As mentioned earlier, everything you can process in a Python script is a type of object, so our object type tour is necessarily incomplete. However, even though everything in Python is an "object," only those types of objects we've met so far are considered part of Python's core type set. Other object types in Python are usually implemented by module functions, not language syntax. They also tend to have application-specific roles—text patterns, database interfaces, network connections, and so on.

Moreover, keep in mind that the objects we've met here are objects, but not necessarily *object-oriented*—a concept that usually requires inheritance and the Python class statement, which we'll meet again later in this book. Still, Python's core objects are the workhorses of almost every Python script you're likely to meet, and they usually are the basis of larger noncore types.

Chapter Summary

And that's a wrap for our concise data type tour. This chapter has offered a brief introduction to Python's core object types, and the sorts of operations we can apply to them. We've studied generic operations that work on many object types (sequence operations such as indexing and slicing, for example), as well as type-specific operations available as method calls (for instance, string splits and list appends). We've also defined some key terms along the way, such as immutability, sequences, and polymorphism.

Along the way, we've seen that Python's core object types are more flexible and powerful than what is available in lower-level languages such as C. For instance, lists and dictionaries obviate most of the work you do to support collections and searching in lower-level languages. Lists are ordered collections of other objects, and dictionaries are collections of other objects that are indexed by key instead of by position. Both dictionaries and lists may be nested, can grow and shrink on demand, and may contain objects of any type. Moreover, their space is automatically cleaned up as you go.

I've skipped most of the details here in order to provide a quick tour, so you shouldn't expect all of this chapter to have made sense yet. In the next few chapters, we'll start to dig deeper, filling in details of Python's core object types that were omitted here so you can gain a more complete understanding. We'll start off in the next chapter with an in-depth look at Python numbers. First, though, another quiz to review.

Chapter Quiz

We'll explore the concepts introduced in this chapter in more detail in upcoming chapters, so we'll just cover the big ideas here:

1. Name four of Python's core data types.
2. Why are they called "core" data types?
3. What does "immutable" mean, and which three of Python's core types are considered immutable?
4. What does "sequence" mean, and which three types fall into that category?
5. What does "mapping" mean, and which core type is a mapping?
6. What is "polymorphism," and why should you care?

Quiz Answers

1. Numbers, strings, lists, dictionaries, tuples, and files are generally considered to be the core object (data) types. Sets, types, None, and Booleans are sometimes classified this way as well. There are multiple number types (integer, long, floating point, and decimal) and two string types (normal and Unicode).

2. They are known as "core" types because they are part of the Python language itself, and are always available; to create other objects, you generally must call functions in imported modules. Most of the core types have specific syntax for generating the objects: 'spam,' for example, is an expression that makes a string and determines the set of operations that can be applied to it. Because of this, core types are hardwired into Python's syntax. In contrast, you must call the built-in open function to create a file object.

3. An "immutable" object is an object that cannot be changed after it is created. Numbers, strings, and tuples in Python fall into this category. While you cannot change an immutable object in-place, you can always make a new one by running an expression.

4. A "sequence" is a positionally ordered collection of objects. Strings, lists, and tuples are all sequences in Python. They share common sequence operations, such as indexing, concatenation, and slicing, but also have type-specific method calls.

5. The term "mapping" denotes an object that maps keys to associated values. Python's dictionary is the only mapping type in the core type set. Mappings do not maintain any left-to-right positional ordering; they support access to data stored by key, plus type-specific method calls.

6. "Polymorphism" means that the meaning of an operation (like a +) depends on the objects being operated on. This turns out to be a key idea (perhaps *the* key idea) behind using Python well—not constraining code to specific types makes that code automatically applicable to many types.

## CHAPTER 5

Numbers

This chapter begins our in-depth tour of the Python language. In Python, data takes the form of objects—either built-in objects that Python provides, or objects we create using Python tools and other languages, such as C. In fact, objects are the basis of every Python program you will ever write. Because they are the most fundamental notion in Python programming, objects are also our first focus in this book.

In the preceding chapter, we took a quick pass over Python's core object types. Although essential terms were introduced in that chapter, we avoided too many specifics in the interest of space. Here, we'll begin a more careful second look at data type concepts to fill in some of the details we glossed over earlier. We'll also explore some types related to numbers, such as sets and Booleans. Let's get started by exploring our first data type category: the Python number.

Python Numeric Types

Python's number types are fairly typical and will probably seem familiar if you've used almost any other programming language in the past. They can be used to keep track of your bank balance, the distance to Mars, the number of visitors to your web site, and just about any other numeric quantity.

In Python, numbers are not really a single object type, but a category of similar types. Python supports the usual numeric types (integers and floating points), as well as literals for creating numbers and expressions for processing them. In addition, Python provides more advanced numeric programming support, including a complex number type, an unlimited-precision integer type, a fixed-precision decimal type, sets and Booleans, and a variety of numeric tool libraries. The next few sections give an overview of the numeric support in Python.

Numeric Literals

Among its basic types, Python provides the usual numeric types: it supports integer and floating-point numbers (with a fractional part), and all their associated syntax and operations. Like the C language, Python also allows you to write integers using hexadecimal and octal literals. But, unlike C, Python additionally offers a complex number type, as well as a long integer type with unlimited precision (it can grow to have as many digits as your memory space allows). Table 5-1 shows what Python's numeric types look like when written out in a program (that is, as literals).

Table 5-1. Numeric literals

Literal	Interpretation
1234, -24, 0	Normal integers (C longs)
99999999999999999999L	Long integers (unlimited size)
1.23, 3.14e-10, 4E210, 4.0e+210	Floating-point numbers (C doubles)
0177, 0x9ff, 0XFF	Octal and hex literals for integers
3+4j, 3.0+4.0j, 3J	Complex number literals

In general, Python's numeric types are straightforward, but a few coding concepts are worth highlighting here:

Integer and floating-point literals

> Integers are written as strings of decimal digits. Floating-point numbers have an embedded decimal point, and/or an optional signed exponent introduced by an e or E. If you write a number with a decimal point or exponent, Python makes it a floating-point object, and uses floating-point (not integer) math when the object is used in an expression. The rules for writing floating-point numbers are the same in Python as in the C language.

Numeric precision and long integers

> Plain Python integers (row 1 of Table 5-1) are implemented as C "longs" internally (i.e., at least 32 bits), and Python floating-point numbers are implemented as C "doubles"; Python numbers therefore get as much precision as the C compiler used to build the Python interpreter gives to longs and doubles.[*]

Long integer literals

> If, however, an integer literal ends with an l or L, it becomes a Python long integer (not to be confused with a C long) and can grow as large as needed. In Python 2.2 and later, because integers are automatically converted to long integers when their values overflow 32 bits, you don't need to type the letter L yourself—Python automatically converts up to long integer when extra precision is needed.

---

[*] That is, the standard CPython implementation. In the Jython Java-based implementation, Python types are really Java classes.

Hexadecimal and octal literals

The rules for writing hexadecimal (base 16) and octal (base 8) integers are the same in Python as in C. Octal literals start with a leading zero (0) followed by a string of digits 0–7. Hexadecimals start with a leading 0x or 0X, followed by hexadecimal digits 0–9 and A–F. In hexadecimal literals, hex digits may be coded in lower- or uppercase. Both octal and hexadecimal literals produce integer objects; they are just alternative syntaxes for specifying values.

Complex numbers

Python complex literals are written as realpart+imaginarypart, where the imaginarypart is terminated with a j or J. The realpart is technically optional, so the imaginarypart may appear on its own. Internally, complex numbers are implemented as pairs of floating-point numbers, but all numeric operations perform complex math when applied to complex numbers.

Built-in Numeric Tools and Extensions

Besides the built-in number literals shown in Table 5-1, Python provides a set of tools for processing number objects:

Expression operators
> +, *, >>, **, etc.

Built-in mathematical functions
> pow, abs, etc.

Utility modules
> random, math, etc.

We'll meet all of these as we go along.

Finally, if you need to do serious number crunching, an optional extension for Python called *NumPy* (Numeric Python) provides advanced numeric programming tools, such as a matrix data type, vector processing, and sophisticated computation libraries. Hardcore scientific programming groups at places like Lawrence Livermore and NASA use Python with NumPy to implement the sorts of tasks they previously coded in C++, FORTRAN, or Matlab.

Because it's so advanced, we won't talk further about NumPy in this book. You can find additional support for advanced numeric programming in Python at the Vaults of Parnassus site, or by searching the Web. Also note that NumPy is currently an optional extension; it doesn't come with Python, and must be installed separately.

 In Python 3.0, the current integer and long integer types will be unified, such that there will be only one integer type, int. It will support arbitrary precision, like the current long integer type. Most programmers will see little or no change as a result of this. See the Python 3.0 release notes for more details.

Python Expression Operators

Perhaps the most fundamental tool that processes numbers is the *expression*: a combination of numbers (or other objects) and operators that computes a value when executed by Python. In Python, expressions are written using the usual mathematical notation and operator symbols. For instance, to add two numbers X and Y, say X + Y, which tells Python to apply the + operator to the values named by X and Y. The result of the expression is the sum of X and Y, another number object.

Table 5-2 lists all the operator expressions available in Python. Many are self-explanatory; for instance, the usual mathematical operators (+, -, *, /, and so on) are supported. A few will be familiar if you've used C in the past: % computes a division remainder, << performs a bitwise left-shift, & computes a bitwise AND result, etc. Others are more Python-specific, and not all are numeric in nature. For example, the is operator tests object identity (i.e., address, a strict form of equality), lambda creates unnamed functions, and so on. More on most of these later.

Table 5-2. Python expression operators and precedence

Operators	Description
`yield x`	Generator function send protocol (new in Release 2.5)
`lambda args: expression`	Anonymous function generation
`x if y else z`	Ternary selection expression (new in Release 2.5)
`x or y`	Logical OR (y is evaluated only if x is false)
`x and y`	Logical AND (y is evaluated only if x is true)
`not x`	Logical negation
`x < y,x <= y,x > y,x >= y,x == y,x <> y,x != y,x is y,x is not y,x in y,x not in y`	Comparison operators, value equality operators,[a] object identity tests, sequence membership
`x	y`	Bitwise OR
`x ^ y`	Bitwise eXclusive OR
`x & y`	Bitwise AND
`x << y,x >> y`	Shift x left or right by y bits
`-x + y,x – y`	Addition/concatenation, subtraction
`x * y,x % y,x / y,x // y`	Multiplication/repetition, remainder/format, division[b]
`-x,+x,~x,x ** y`	Unary negation, identity, bitwise complement, binary power
`x[i],x[i:j],x.attr,x(...)`	Indexing, slicing, qualification, function calls
`(...),[...],{...},`...``	Tuple, list,[c] dictionary, conversion to string[d]

[a] In Python 2.5, value inequality can be written as either X != Y or X <> Y. In Python 3.0, the latter of these options will be removed because it is redundant; use X != Y for value inequality tests.

[b] Floor division (X // Y), new in Release 2.2, always truncates fractional remainders. This is further described in "Division: Classic, Floor, and True."

[c] Beginning with Python 2.0, the list syntax ([...]) can represent either a list literal or a list comprehension expression. The latter of these performs an implied loop and collects expression results in a new list.

[d] Conversion of objects to their print strings can also be accomplished with the more readable str and repr built-in functions, which are described in the section "Numeric Display Formats" later in this chapter. Due to its obscurity, the backticks expression `X` is scheduled to be removed in Python 3.0; use repr(X) instead.

Mixed Operators Follow Operator Precedence

As in most languages, in Python, more complex expressions are coded by stringing together the operator expressions in Table 5-2. For instance, the sum of two multiplications might be written as a mix of variables and operators:

```
A * B + C * D
```

So, how does Python know which operation to perform first? The answer to this question lies in *operator precedence*. When you write an expression with more than one operator, Python groups its parts according to what are called *precedence rules*, and this grouping determines the order in which the expression's parts are computed. In Table 5-2, operators lower in the table have higher precedence, and so bind more tightly in mixed expressions.

For example, if you write X + Y * Z, Python evaluates the multiplication first (Y * Z), then adds that result to X because * has higher precedence (is lower in the table) than +. Similarly, in this section's original example, both multiplications (A * B and C * D) will happen before their results are added.

Parentheses Group Subexpressions

You can forget about precedence completely if you're careful to group parts of expressions with parentheses. When you enclose subexpressions in parentheses, you override Python's precedence rules; Python always evaluates expressions in parentheses first before using their results in the enclosing expressions.

For instance, instead of coding X + Y * Z, you could write one of the following to force Python to evaluate the expression in the desired order:

```
(X + Y) * Z
X + (Y * Z)
```

In the first case, + is applied to X and Y first, because this subexpression is wrapped in parentheses. In the second case, the * is performed first (just as if there were no parentheses at all). Generally speaking, adding parentheses in big expressions is a great idea; it not only forces the evaluation order you want, but also aids readability.

Mixed Types Are Converted Up

Besides mixing operators in expressions, you can also mix numeric types. For instance, you can add an integer to a floating-point number:

```
40 + 3.14
```

But this leads to another question: what type is the result—integer or floating-point? The answer is simple, especially if you've used almost any other language before: in mixed-type expressions, Python first converts operands *up* to the type of the most complicated operand, and then performs the math on same-type operands. If you've used C, you'll find this behavior similar to type conversions in that language.

Python ranks the complexity of numeric types like so: integers are simpler than long integers, which are simpler than floating-point numbers, which are simpler than complex numbers. So, when an integer is mixed with a floating point, as in the preceding example, the integer is converted up to a floating-point value first, and floating-point math yields the floating-point result. Similarly, any mixed-type expression, where one operand is a complex number, results in the other operand being converted up to a complex number, and the expression yields a complex result. As you'll see later in this section, as of Release 2.2, Python also automatically converts normal integers to long integers whenever their values are too large to fit in a normal integer.

You can force the issue by calling built-in functions to convert types manually:

```
>>> int(3.1415)
3
>>> float(3)
3.0
>>> long(4)
4L
```

However, you won't usually need to do this: because Python automatically converts up to the more complex type within an expression, the results are normally what you want.

Also, keep in mind that all these mixed-type conversions only apply when mixing *numeric* types (e.g., an integer and a floating-point number) around an operator or comparison. In general, Python does not convert across other type boundaries. Adding a string to an integer, for example, results in an error, unless you manually convert one or the other; watch for an example when we meet strings in Chapter 7.

Preview: Operator Overloading

Although we're focusing on built-in numbers right now, keep in mind that all Python operators may be overloaded (i.e., implemented) by Python classes and C extension types to work on objects you create. For instance, you'll see later that objects coded with classes may be added with + expressions, indexed with [i] expressions, and so on.

Furthermore, Python itself automatically overloads some operators, such that they perform different actions depending on the type of built-in objects being processed. For example, the + operator performs addition when applied to numbers, but performs concatenation when applied to sequence objects such as strings and lists. In fact, + can mean anything at all when applied to objects you define with classes.

As we saw in the prior chapter, this property is usually called *polymorphism*—a term indicating that the meaning of an operation depends on the type of objects being operated on. We'll revisit this concept when we explore functions in Chapter 15 because it becomes a much more obvious feature in that context.

Numbers in Action

Probably the best way to understand numeric objects and expressions is to see them in action. So, let's start up the interactive command line, and try some basic but illustrative operations (see Chapter 3 for pointers if you need help starting an interactive session).

Variables and Basic Expressions

First of all, let's exercise some basic math. In the following interaction, we first assign two *variables* (a and b) to integers so we can use them later in a larger expression. Variables are simply names—created by you or Python—that are used to keep track of information in your program. We'll say more about this in the next chapter, but in Python:

- Variables are created when they are first assigned values.
- Variables are replaced with their values when used in expressions.
- Variables must be assigned before they can be used in expressions.
- Variables refer to objects and are never declared ahead of time.

In other words, these assignments cause the variables a and b to spring into existence automatically:

```
% python
>>> a = 3                    # Name created
>>> b = 4
```

I've also used a *comment* here. Recall that in Python code, text after a # mark and continuing to the end of the line is considered to be a comment and is ignored. Comments are a way to write human-readable documentation for your code. Because code you type interactively is temporary, you won't normally write comments in this context, but I've added them to some of this book's examples to help explain the code.[*] In the next part of the book, we'll meet a related feature—documentation strings—that attaches the text of your comments to objects.

Now, let's use our new integer objects in expressions. At this point, the values of a and b are still 3 and 4, respectively. Variables like these are replaced with their values whenever they're used inside an expression, and the expression results are echoed back immediately when working interactively:

```
>>> a + 1, a - 1             # Addition (3 + 1), subtraction (3 - 1)
(4, 2)
>>> b * 3, b / 2             # Multiplication (4 * 3), division (4 / 2)
(12, 2)
>>> a % 2, b ** 2            # Modulus (remainder), power
(1, 16)
```

---

[*] If you're working along, you don't need to type any of the comment text from the # through the end of the line; comments are simply ignored by Python, and not required parts of the statements we're running.

```
>>> 2 + 4.0, 2.0 ** b          # Mixed-type conversions
(6.0, 16.0)
```

Technically, the results being echoed back here are *tuples* of two values because the lines typed at the prompt contain two expressions separated by commas; that's why the results are displayed in parentheses (more on tuples later). Note that the expressions work because the variables a and b within them have been assigned values. If you use a different variable that has never been assigned, Python reports an error rather than filling in some default value:

```
>>> c * 2
Traceback (most recent call last):
  File "<stdin>", line 1, in ?
NameError: name 'c' is not defined
```

You don't need to predeclare variables in Python, but they must have been assigned at least once before you can use them at all. In practice, this means you have to initialize counters to zero before you can add to them, initialize lists to an empty list before you can append to them, and so on.

Here are two slightly larger expressions to illustrate operator grouping and more about conversions:

```
>>> b / 2 + a              # Same as ((4 / 2) + 3)
5
>>> print b / (2.0 + a)    # Same as (4 / (2.0 + 3))
0.8
```

In the first expression, there are no parentheses, so Python automatically groups the components according to its precedence rules—because / is lower in Table 5-2 than +, it binds more tightly, and so is evaluated first. The result is as if the expression had parentheses as shown in the comment to the right of the code. Also, notice that all the numbers are integers in the first expression; because of that, Python performs integer division and addition.

In the second expression, parentheses are added around the + part to force Python to evaluate it first (i.e., before the /). We also made one of the operands floating-point by adding a decimal point: 2.0. Because of the mixed types, Python converts the integer referenced by a to a floating-point value (3.0) before performing the +. It also converts b to a floating-point value (4.0), and performs floating-point division; (4.0 / 5.0) yields a floating-point result of 0.8. If all the numbers in this expression were integers, it would instead invoke integer division (4 / 5), and the result would be the truncated integer 0 (in Python 2.5, at least—see the discussion of true division ahead).

Numeric Display Formats

Notice that we used a print statement in the last of the preceding examples. Without the print, you'll see something that may look a bit odd at first glance:

```
>>> b / (2.0 + a)              # Auto echo output: more digits
0.80000000000000004

>>> print b / (2.0 + a)        # Print rounds off digits
0.8
```

The full story behind this odd result has to do with the limitations of floating-point hardware, and its inability to exactly represent some values. Because computer architecture is well beyond this book's scope, though, we'll finesse this by saying that all of the digits in the first output are really there, in your computer's floating-point hardware—it's just that you're not normally accustomed to seeing them. I've used this example to demonstrate the difference in output formatting—the interactive prompt's automatic result echo shows more digits than the print statement. If you don't want to see all the digits, include the print.

Note, however, that not all values have so many digits to display:

```
>>> 1 / 2.0
0.5
```

and that there are more ways to display the bits of a number inside your computer than prints and automatic echoes:

```
>>> num = 1 / 3.0
>>> num                        # Echoes
0.33333333333333331
>>> print num                  # Print rounds
0.333333333333

>>> "%e" % num                 # String formatting
'3.333333e-001'
>>> "%2.2f" % num              # String formatting
'0.33'
```

The last two of these employ *string formatting*, an expression that allows for format flexibility, which we will explore in the upcoming chapter on strings (Chapter 7).

---

str and repr Display Formats

Technically, the difference between default interactive echoes and prints corresponds to the difference between the built-in repr and str functions:

```
>>> repr(num)                  # Used by echoes: as-code form
'0.33333333333333331'
>>> str(num)                   # Used by print: user-friendly form
'0.333333333333'
```

Both of these convert arbitrary objects to their string representations: repr (and the default interactive echo) produces results that look as though they were code; str (and the print statement) converts to a typically more user-friendly format. This notion will resurface when we study strings, and you'll find more on these built-ins in general later in the book.

Division: Classic, Floor, and True

Now that you've seen how division works, you should know that it is scheduled for a slight change in a future Python release (currently, 3.0, scheduled to appear some time after this edition is released). In Python 2.5, things work as just described, but there are actually two different division operators (one of which will change):

X / Y

> *Classic* division. In Python 2.5 and earlier, this operator truncates results for integers, and keeps remainders for floating-point numbers, as described here. This operator will be changed to *true* division—always keeping remainders regardless of types—in a future Python release (3.0).

X // Y

> *Floor* division. Added in Python 2.2, this operator always truncates fractional remainders down to their floor, regardless of types.

Floor division was added to address the fact that the results of the current classic division model are dependent on operand types, and so can be difficult to anticipate in a dynamically typed language like Python.

Due to possible backward-compatibility issues, division in Python is in a state of flux today. To recap, in version 2.5, / division works as described by default, and // floor division can be used to truncate result remainders to their floor regardless of their types:

```
>>> (5 / 2), (5 / 2.0), (5 / -2.0), (5 / -2)
(2, 2.5, -2.5, -3)

>>> (5 // 2), (5 // 2.0), (5 // -2.0), (5 // -2)
(2, 2.0, -3.0, -3)

>>> (9 / 3), (9.0 / 3), (9 // 3), (9 // 3.0)
(3, 3.0, 3, 3.0)
```

In a future Python release, / division is slated to be changed to return a *true* division result that always retains remainders, even for integers—for example, 1 / 2 will be 0.5, not 0, while 1 // 2 will still be 0.

Until this change is incorporated completely, you can see the way that the / operator will likely work in the future by using a special import of the form: from __future__ import division. This turns the / operator into a true division operator (keeping remainders), but leaves // as is. Here's how / will eventually behave:

```
>>> from __future__ import division

>>> (5 / 2), (5 / 2.0), (5 / -2.0), (5 / -2)
(2.5, 2.5, -2.5, -2.5)

>>> (5 // 2), (5 // 2.0), (5 // -2.0), (5 // -2)
(2, 2.0, -3.0, -3)
```

```
>>> (9 / 3), (9.0 / 3), (9 // 3), (9 // 3.0)
(3.0, 3.0, 3, 3.0)
```

Watch for a simple prime number while loop example in Chapter 13, and a corresponding exercise at the end of Part IV that illustrates the sort of code that may be impacted by this / change. In general, any code that depends on / truncating an integer result may be affected (use the new // instead). As I write this, this change is scheduled to occur in Python 3.0, but be sure to try these expressions in your version to see which behavior applies. Also stay tuned for more on the special from command used here; it's discussed further in Chapter 21.

Bitwise Operations

Besides the normal numeric operations (addition, subtraction, and so on), Python supports most of the numeric expressions available in the C language. For instance, here it's at work performing bitwise shift and Boolean operations:

```
>>> x = 1          # 0001
>>> x << 2         # Shift left 2 bits: 0100
4
>>> x | 2          # bitwise OR: 0011
3
>>> x & 1          # bitwise AND: 0001
1
```

In the first expression, a binary 1 (in base 2, 0001) is shifted left two slots to create a binary 4 (0100). The last two operations perform a binary OR (0001|0010 = 0011), and a binary AND (0001&0001 = 0001). Such bit-masking operations allow us to encode multiple flags and other values within a single integer.

We won't go into much more detail on "bit-twiddling" here. It's supported if you need it, and it comes in handy if your Python code must deal with things like network packets, or packed binary data produced by a C program. Be aware, though, that bitwise operations are often not as important in a high-level language such as Python as they are in a low-level language such as C. As a rule of thumb, if you find yourself wanting to flip bits in Python, you should think about which language you're really coding. In general, there are often better ways to encode information in Python than bit strings.

Long Integers

Now for something more exotic: here's a look at long integers in action. When an integer literal ends with a letter L (or lowercase l), Python creates a long integer. In Python, a long integer can be arbitrarily big. That is, it can have as many digits as you have room for in memory:

```
>>> 99999999999999999999999999999999999999L + 1
100000000000000000000000000000000000000L
```

The L at the end of the digit string tells Python to create a long integer object with unlimited precision. In fact, as of Python 2.2, even the letter L is optional—Python automatically converts a normal integer up to a long integer whenever its value is too large to fit in a normal integer (technically, when it overflows normal integer precision, which is usually 32 bits). That is, you don't need to code the L yourself, as Python will provide the extra precision if your program needs it:

```
>>> 999999999999999999999999999999999999999 + 1
1000000000000000000000000000000000000000L
```

Long integers are a convenient built-in tool. For instance, you can use them to count the national debt in pennies in Python directly (if you are so inclined, and have enough memory on your computer). They are also why we were able to raise 2 to such large powers in the examples in Chapter 3:

```
>>> 2L ** 200
1606938044258990275541962092341162602522202993782792835301376L
>>>
>>> 2 ** 200
1606938044258990275541962092341162602522202993782792835301376L
```

Because Python must do extra work to support their extended precision, long integer math is usually substantially slower than normal integer math (which usually maps directly to the hardware). However, if you need the precision, the fact that it's built-in for you to use will likely outweigh its performance penalty.

Complex Numbers

Complex numbers are a distinct core object type in Python. If you know what they are, you know why they are useful; if not, consider this section optional reading. Complex numbers are represented as two floating-point numbers—the real and imaginary parts—and are coded by adding a j or J suffix to the imaginary part. We can also write complex numbers with a nonzero real part by adding the two parts with a +. For example, the complex number with a real part of 2 and an imaginary part of -3 is written 2 + -3j. Here are some examples of complex math at work:

```
>>> 1j * 1J
(-1+0j)
>>> 2 + 1j * 3
(2+3j)
>>> (2 + 1j) * 3
(6+3j)
```

Complex numbers also allow us to extract their parts as attributes, support all the usual mathematical expressions, and may be processed with tools in the standard cmath module (the complex version of the standard math module). Complex numbers typically find roles in engineering-oriented programs. Because they are advanced tools, check Python's language reference manual for additional details.

Hexadecimal and Octal Notation

As mentioned earlier in this chapter, Python integers can be coded in hexadecimal (base 16) and octal (base 8) notation, in addition to the normal base 10 decimal coding:

- Octal literals have a leading 0, followed by a string of octal digits 0–7, each of which represents three bits.
- Hexadecimal literals have a leading 0x or 0X, followed by a string of hex digits 0–9 and upper- or lowercase A–F, each of which stands for four bits.

Keep in mind that this is simply an alternative syntax for specifying the value of an integer object. For example, the following octal and hexadecimal literals produce normal integers with the specified values:

```
>>> 01, 010, 0100          # Octal literals
(1, 8, 64)
>>> 0x01, 0x10, 0xFF       # Hex literals
(1, 16, 255)
```

Here, the octal value 0100 is decimal 64, and hex 0xFF is decimal 255. Python prints in decimal (base 10) by default but provides built-in functions that allow you to convert integers to their octal and hexadecimal digit strings:

```
>>> oct(64), hex(64), hex(255)
('0100', '0x40', '0xff')
```

The oct function converts decimal to octal, and hex converts to hexadecimal. To go the other way, the built-in int function converts a string of digits to an integer, and an optional second argument lets you specify the numeric base:

```
>>> int('0100'), int('0100', 8), int('0x40', 16)
(100, 64, 64)
```

The eval function, which you'll meet later in this book, treats strings as though they were Python code. Therefore, it has a similar effect (but usually runs more slowly—it actually compiles and runs the string as a piece of a program, and it assumes you can trust the source of the string being run; a clever user might be able to submit a string that deletes files on your machine!):

```
>>> eval('100'), eval('0100'), eval('0x40')
(100, 64, 64)
```

Finally, you can also convert integers to octal and hexadecimal strings with a string formatting expression:

```
>>> "%o %x %X" % (64, 64, 255)
'100 40 FF'
```

Again, string formatting is covered in Chapter 7.

One warning before moving on: be careful not to begin a string of digits with a leading zero in Python, unless you really mean to code an octal value. Python will treat it as base 8, which may not work as you'd expect—010 is always decimal 8, not decimal 10 (despite what you may or may not think!).

Other Built-in Numeric Tools

In addition to its core object types, Python also provides both built-in functions and built-in modules for numeric processing. The int and round built-in functions, for instance, truncate and round floating-point numbers, respectively. Here are examples of the built-in math module (which contains most of the tools in the C language's math library) and a few built-in functions at work:

```
>>> import math
>>> math.pi, math.e                          # Common constants
(3.1415926535897931, 2.7182818284590451)

>>> math.sin(2 * math.pi / 180)              # Sine, tangent, cosine
0.034899496702500969

>>> math.sqrt(144), math.sqrt(2)             # Square root
(12.0, 1.4142135623730951)

>>> abs(-42), 2**4, pow(2, 4)
(42, 16, 16)

>>> int(2.567), round(2.567), round(2.567, 2)    # Truncate, round
(2, 3.0, 2.5699999999999998)
```

As described earlier, the last output here will be (2, 3.0, 2.57) if we include print.

Notice that built-in modules such as math must be imported, but built-in functions such as abs are always available without imports. In other words, modules are external components, but built-in functions live in an implied namespace that Python automatically searches to find names used in your program. This namespace corresponds to the module called __builtin__. There is much more about name resolution in Part IV; for now, when you hear "module," think "import."

The standard library random module must be imported as well. This module provides tools for picking a random floating-point number between 0 and 1, selecting a random integer between two numbers, choosing an item at random from a sequence, and more:

```
>>> import random
>>> random.random()
0.49741978338014803
>>> random.random()
0.49354866439625611

>>> random.randint(1, 10)
5
>>> random.randint(1, 10)
4

>>> random.choice(['Life of Brian', 'Holy Grail', 'Meaning of Life'])
'Life of Brian'
>>> random.choice(['Life of Brian', 'Holy Grail', 'Meaning of Life'])
'Holy Grail'
```

The random module can be useful for shuffling cards in games, picking images at random in a slideshow GUI, performing statistical simulations, and much more. For more details, see Python's library manual.

Other Numeric Types

In this chapter, we've been using Python's core numeric types—integer, long integer, floating point, and complex. These will suffice for most of the number crunching that most programmers will ever need to do. Python comes with a handful of more exotic numeric types, though, that merit a quick look here.

Decimal Numbers

Python 2.4 introduced a new core numeric type: the decimal object. Syntactically, decimals are created by calling a function within an imported module, rather than running a literal expression. Functionally, decimals are like floating-point numbers, with a fixed number of decimal points, and hence, a fixed precision. For example, with decimals, we can have a floating-point value that always retains just two decimal digits. Furthermore, we can specify how to round or truncate the extra decimal digits beyond the object's cutoff. Although it incurs a small performance penalty compared to the normal floating-point type, the decimal type is ideal for representing fixed-precision quantities like sums of money, and for achieving better numeric accuracy.

Floating-point object math is less than exact. For example, the following should yield zero, but it does not. The result is close to zero, but there are not enough bits to be precise here:

```
>>> 0.1 + 0.1 + 0.1 - 0.3
5.5511151231257827e-017
```

Printing the result to produce the user-friendly display format doesn't completely help either, because the hardware related to floating-point math is inherently limited in terms of accuracy:

```
>>> print 0.1 + 0.1 + 0.1 - 0.3
5.55111512313e-017
```

However, with decimals, the result can be dead-on:

```
>>> from decimal import Decimal
>>> Decimal('0.1') + Decimal('0.1') + Decimal('0.1') - Decimal('0.3')
Decimal("0.0")
```

As shown here, we can make decimal objects by calling the Decimal constructor function in the decimal module, and passing in strings that have the desired number of decimal digits for the resulting object. When decimals of different precision are mixed in expressions, Python converts up to the largest number of decimal digits automatically:

```
>>> Decimal('0.1') + Decimal('0.10') + Decimal('0.10') - Decimal('0.30')
Decimal("0.00")
```

Other tools in the decimal module can be used to set the precision of all decimal numbers, and more. For instance, a context object in this module allows for specifying precision (number of decimal digits), and rounding modes (down, ceiling, etc.):

```
>>> import decimal
>>> decimal.Decimal(1) / decimal.Decimal(7)
Decimal("0.1428571428571428571428571429")
```

```
>>> decimal.getcontext().prec = 4
>>> decimal.Decimal(1) / decimal.Decimal(7)
Decimal("0.1429")
```

Because use of the decimal type is still somewhat rare in practice, I'll defer to Python's standard library manuals and interactive help for more details.

Sets

Python 2.4 also introduced a new collection type, the *set*. Because they are collections of other objects, sets are arguably outside the scope of this chapter. But because they support mathematical set operations, we'll take a look at their basic utility here. To make a set object, pass in a sequence or other iterable object to the built-in set function (similar utility is available in a module prior to Python 2.4, but no import is required as of 2.4):

```
>>> x = set('abcde')
>>> y = set('bdxyz')
```

You get back a set object, which contains all the items in the object passed in (notice that sets do not have a positional ordering, and so are not sequences):

```
>>> x
set(['a', 'c', 'b', 'e', 'd'])
```

Sets made this way support the common mathematical set operations with expression operators. Note that we can't perform these operations on plain sequences—we must create sets from them in order to apply these tools:

```
>>> 'e' in x                         # Set membership
True

>>> x - y                            # Set difference
set(['a', 'c', 'e'])

>>> x | y                            # Set union
set(['a', 'c', 'b', 'e', 'd', 'y', 'x', 'z'])

>>> x & y                            # Set intersection
set(['b', 'd'])
```

Such operations are convenient when dealing with large data sets; the intersection of two sets contains objects in common to both, for example, and the union contains all items in either set. Here's a more realistic example of set operations at work, applied to lists of people in a hypothetical company:

```
>>> engineers = set(['bob', 'sue', 'ann', 'vic'])
>>> managers  = set(['tom', 'sue'])
>>>
>>> engineers & managers              # Who is both engineer and manager?
set(['sue'])
>>>
>>> engineers | managers              # All people in either category
set(['vic', 'sue', 'tom', 'bob', 'ann'])
>>>
>>> engineers - managers              # Engineers who are not managers
set(['vic', 'bob', 'ann'])
```

In addition, the set object provides method calls that implement more exotic set operations. Although set operations can be coded manually in Python (and often were in the past), Python's built-in sets use efficient algorithms and implementation techniques to provide quick and standard operation.

For more details on sets, see Python's library reference manual.

In Python 3.0, the literal notation {1, 2, 3} is proposed to have the same effect as the current call set([1, 2, 3]), and will thus be another way to create a set object. This is a future extension, so see the 3.0 release notes for details.

Booleans

Some argue that the Python Boolean type, bool, is numeric in nature because its two values, True and False, are just customized versions of the integers 1 and 0 that print themselves differently. Although that's all most programmers need to know, let's explore this type in a bit more detail.

Python 2.3 introduced a new explicit Boolean data type called bool, with the values True and False available as new preassigned built-in names. Internally, the new names True and False are instances of bool, which is in turn just a subclass (in the object-oriented sense) of the built-in integer type int. True and False behave exactly like the integers 1 and 0, except that they have customized printing logic—they print themselves as the words True and False, instead of the digits 1 and 0 (technically, bool redefines its str and repr string formats).

Because of this customization, as of Python 2.3, the output of Boolean expressions typed at the interactive prompt prints as the words True and False instead of the older 1 and 0. In addition, Booleans make truth values more explicit. For instance, an infinite loop can now be coded as while True: instead of the less intuitive while 1:. Similarly, flags can be initialized more clearly with flag = False.

Again, though, for all other practical purposes, you can treat True and False as though they are predefined variables set to integer 1 and 0. Most programmers were preassigning True and False to 1 and 0 anyway, so the new type simply makes this a standard technique. Its implementation can lead to curious results, though—because True is just the integer 1 with a custom display format, True + 3 yields 4 in Python!

We'll revisit Booleans in Chapter 9 (to define Python's notion of truth) and again in Chapter 12 (to see how Boolean operators like and and or work).

Third-Party Extensions

Beyond Python's own numeric types, you'll find various third-party open source add-ons that provide even more exotic numeric tools. Types such as rational numbers, vectors, and matrixes can be obtained on the Web; do a search for more details.

Chapter Summary

This chapter has taken a tour of Python's numeric object types and the operations we can apply to them. Along the way, we met the standard integer and floating-point types, as well as some more exotic and less commonly used types such as complex numbers and the decimal type. We also explored Python's expression syntax, type conversions, bitwise operations, and various literal forms for coding numbers in scripts.

Later in this part of the book, I'll fill in some details about the next object type, the string. In the next chapter, however, we'll take some time to explore the mechanics of variable assignment in more detail than we have here. This turns out to be perhaps the most fundamental idea in Python, so you should read through the next chapter before moving on. First, though, take the usual chapter quiz.

Chapter Quiz

1. What is the value of the expression 2 * (3 + 4) in Python?
2. What is the value of the expression 2 * 3 + 4 in Python?
3. What is the value of the expression 2 + 3 * 4 in Python?
4. What tools can you use to find a number's square root, as well as its square?
5. What is the type of the result of the expression 1 + 2.0 + 3?
6. How could you truncate and round a floating-point number?
7. How can you convert an integer to a floating-point number?
8. How would you display an integer in octal or hexadecimal notation?
9. How might you convert an octal or hexadecimal string to a plain integer?

Quiz Answers

1. The result value will be 14, the result of 2 * 7, because the parentheses force the addition to happen before the multiplication.
2. Here, the result will be 10, the result of 6 + 4. Python's operator precedence rules are applied in the absence of parentheses, and multiplication has higher precedence than (i.e., happens before) addition, per Table 5-2.
3. This expression yields 14, the result of 2 + 12, for the same precedence reasons as in the prior question.
4. Functions for obtaining the square root, as well as *pi*, tangents, and more, are available in the imported math module. To find a number's square root, import math and call math.sqrt(N). To get a number's square, use either the exponent expression X ** 2, or the built-in function pow(X, 2).
5. The result will be a floating-point number: the integers are converted up to floating point, the most complex type in the expression, and floating-point math is used to evaluate it.
6. The int(N) function truncates, and the round(N, digits?) function rounds.
7. The float(I) function converts an integer to a floating point; mixing an integer with a floating point within an expression will result in a conversion as well.
8. The oct(I) and hex(I) built-in functions return the octal and hexadecimal string forms for an integer. The % string formatting expression also provides targets for doing this.
9. The int(S, base?) function can be used to convert from octal and hexadecimal strings to normal integers (pass in 8 or 16 for the base). The eval(S) function can be used for this purpose too, but it's more expensive to run and can have security issues. Note that integers are always stored in binary in computer memory; these are just display string format conversions.

## CHAPTER 6

The Dynamic Typing Interlude

In the prior chapter, we began exploring Python's core object types in depth with a look at Python numbers. We'll resume our object type tour in the next chapter, but before we move on, it's important that you get a handle on what may be the most fundamental idea in Python programming, and is certainly the basis of much of both the conciseness and flexibility of the Python language—dynamic typing, and the polymorphism it yields.

As you'll see here and later in the book, in Python, we do not declare the specific types of the objects our scripts use. In fact, programs should not even care about specific types; in exchange, they are naturally applicable in more contexts than we can sometimes even plan ahead for. Because dynamic typing is the root of this flexibility, let's take a brief look at the model here.

The Case of the Missing Declaration Statements

If you have a background in compiled or statically typed languages like C, C++, or Java, you might find yourself a bit perplexed at this point in the book. So far, we've been using variables without declaring their existence or their types, and it somehow works. When we type a = 3 in an interactive session or program file, for instance, how does Python know that a should stand for an integer? For that matter, how does Python know what a is at all?

Once you start asking such questions, you've crossed over into the domain of Python's *dynamic typing* model. In Python, types are determined automatically at runtime, not in response to declarations in your code. This means that you never declare variables ahead of time (a concept that is perhaps simpler to grasp if you keep in mind that it all boils down to variables, objects, and the links between them).

Variables, Objects, and References

As you've seen in many of the examples used so far in this book, when you run an assignment statement such as a = 3 in Python, it works even if you've never told

Python to use the name a as a variable, or that a should stand for an integer-type object. In the Python language, this all pans out in a very natural way, as follows:

Variable creation

A variable (i.e., name), like a, is created when your code first assigns it a value. Future assignments change the value of the already created name. Technically, Python detects some names before your code runs, but you can think of it as though initial assignments make variables.

Variable types

A variable never has any type information or constraints associated with it. The notion of type lives with objects, not names. Variables are generic in nature; they always simply refer to a particular object at a particular point in time.

Variable use

When a variable appears in an expression, it is immediately replaced with the object that it currently refers to, whatever that may be. Further, all variables must be explicitly assigned before they can be used; use of unassigned variables results in errors.

This model is strikingly different from traditional languages. When you are first starting out, dynamic typing is usually easier to understand if you keep clear the distinction between names and objects. For example, when we say this:

```
>>> a = 3
```

at least conceptually, Python will perform three distinct steps to carry out the request. These steps reflect the operation of all assignments in the Python language:

1. Create an object to represent the value 3.
2. Create the variable a, if it does not yet exist.
3. Link the variable a to the new object 3.

The net result will be a structure inside Python that resembles Figure 6-1. As sketched, variables and objects are stored in different parts of memory, and are associated by links (the link is shown as a pointer in the figure). Variables always link to objects, and never to other variables, but larger objects may link to other objects (for instance, a list object has links to the objects it contains).

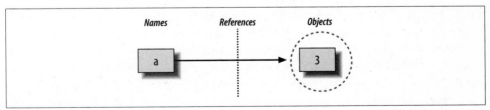

Figure 6-1. Names and objects, after running the assignment a = 3. Variable a becomes a reference to object 3. Internally, the variable is really a pointer to the object's memory space created by running literal expression 3.

These links from variables to objects are called *references* in Python—that is, a reference is a kind of association, implemented as a pointer in memory.* Whenever the variables are later used (i.e., referenced), Python automatically follows the variable-to-object links. This is all simpler than the terminology may imply. In concrete terms:

- *Variables* are entries in a system table, with spaces for links to objects.
- *Objects* are pieces of allocated memory, with enough space to represent the values for which they stand.
- *References* are automatically followed pointers from variables to objects.

At least conceptually, each time you generate a new value in your script by running an expression, Python creates a new object (i.e., a chunk of memory) to represent that value. Internally, as an optimization, Python caches and reuses certain kinds of unchangeable objects, such as small integers and strings (each 0 is not really a new piece of memory—more on this caching behavior later). But, from a logical perspective, it works as though each expression's result value is a distinct object, and each object is a distinct piece of memory.

Technically speaking, objects have more structure than just enough space to represent their values. Each object also has two standard header fields: a *type designator* used to mark the type of the object, and a *reference counter* used to determine when it's OK to reclaim the object. To understand how these two header fields factor into the model, we need to move on.

Types Live with Objects, Not Variables

To see how object types come into play, watch what happens if we assign a variable multiple times:

```
>>> a = 3            # It's an integer
>>> a = 'spam'       # Now it's a string
>>> a = 1.23         # Now it's a floating point
```

This isn't typical Python code, but it does work—a starts out as an integer, then becomes a string, and finally becomes a floating-point number. This example tends to look especially odd to ex-C programmers, as it appears as though the *type* of a changes from integer to string when we say a = 'spam'.

---

* Readers with a background in C may find Python references similar to C pointers (memory addresses). In fact, references are implemented as pointers, and they often serve the same roles, especially with objects that can be changed in-place (more on this later). However, because references are always automatically dereferenced when used, you can never actually do anything useful with a reference itself; this is a feature that eliminates a vast category of C bugs. You can think of Python references as C "void*" pointers, which are automatically followed whenever used.

However, that's not really what's happening. In Python, things work more simply: names have no types; as stated earlier, types live with objects, not names. In the preceding listing, we've simply changed a to reference different objects. Because variables have no type, we haven't actually changed the type of the variable a—we've simply made the variable reference a different type of object. In fact, again, all we can ever say about a variable in Python is that it references a particular object at a particular point in time.

Objects, on the other hand, know what type they are—each object contains a header field that tags the object with its type. The integer object 3, for example, will contain the value 3, plus a designator that tells Python that the object is an integer (strictly speaking, a pointer to an object called int, the name of the integer type). The type designator of the 'spam' string object points to the string type (called str) instead. Because objects know their types, variables don't have to.

To recap, types are associated with objects in Python, not with variables. In typical code, a given variable usually will reference just one kind of object. Because this isn't a requirement, though, you'll find that Python code tends to be much more flexible than you may be accustomed to—if you use Python well, your code might work on many types automatically.

I mentioned that objects have two header fields, a type designator and a reference counter. To understand the latter of these, we need to move on, and take a brief look at what happens at the end of an object's life.

Objects Are Garbage-Collected

In the prior section's listings, we assigned the variable a to different types of objects in each assignment. But when we reassign a variable, what happens to the value it was previously referencing? For example, after the following statements, what happens to the object 3?

```
>>> a = 3
>>> a = 'spam'
```

The answer is that in Python, whenever a name is assigned to a new object, the space held by the prior object is reclaimed (if it is not referenced by any other name or object). This automatic reclamation of objects' space is known as *garbage collection*.

To illustrate, consider the following example, which sets the name x to a different object on each assignment:

```
>>> x = 42
>>> x = 'shrubbery'      # Reclaim 42 now (unless referenced elsewhere)
>>> x = 3.1415           # Reclaim 'shrubbery' now
>>> x = [1,2,3]          # Reclaim 3.1415 now
```

First, notice that x is set to a different type of object each time. Again, though this is not really the case, the effect is as though the type of x is changing over time. In Python, types live with objects, not names. Because names are just generic references to objects, this sort of code works naturally.

Second, notice that references to objects are discarded along the way. Each time x is assigned to a new object, Python reclaims the prior object's space. For instance, when it is assigned the string 'shrubbery', the object 42 is immediately reclaimed (assuming it is not referenced anywhere else)—the object's space is automatically thrown back into the free space pool, to be reused for a future object.

Internally, Python accomplishes this feat by keeping a counter in every object that keeps track of the number of references currently pointing to that object. As soon as (and exactly when) this counter drops to zero, the object's memory space is automatically reclaimed. In the preceding listing, we're assuming that each time x is assigned to a new object, the prior object's reference counter drops to zero, causing it to be reclaimed.

The most immediately tangible benefit of garbage collection is that it means you can use objects liberally without ever needing to free up space in your script. Python will clean up unused space for you as your program runs. In practice, this eliminates a substantial amount of bookkeeping code compared to lower-level languages such as C and C++.

Shared References

So far, we've seen what happens as a single variable is assigned references to objects. Now, let's introduce another variable into our interaction, and watch what happens to its names and objects:

```
>>> a = 3
>>> b = a
```

Typing these two statements generates the scene captured in Figure 6-2. As before, the second line causes Python to create the variable b; the variable a is being used and not assigned here, so it is replaced with the object it references (3), and b is made to reference that object. The net effect is that variables a and b wind up referencing the same object (that is, pointing to the same chunk of memory). This is called a *shared reference* in Python—multiple names referencing the same object.

Next, suppose we extend the session with one more statement:

```
>>> a = 3
>>> b = a
>>> a = 'spam'
```

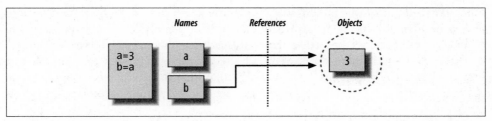

Figure 6-2. Names and objects, after next running the assignment b = a. Variable a becomes a reference to object 3. Internally, the variable is really a pointer to the object's memory space created by running literal expression 3.

As for all Python assignments, this statement simply makes a new object to represent the string value 'spam' and sets a to reference this new object. It does not, however, change the value of b; b still references the original object, the integer 3. The resulting reference structure is shown in Figure 6-3.

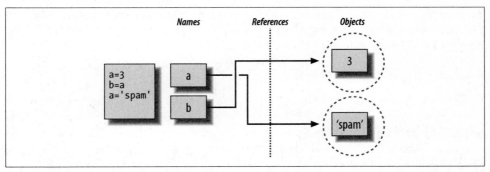

Figure 6-3. Names and objects, after finally running assignment a = 'spam'. Variable a references the new object (i.e., piece of memory) created by running literal expression 'spam', but variable b still refers to the original object 3. Because this assignment is not an in-place change to object 3, it only changes variable a, not b.

The same sort of thing would happen if we changed b to 'spam' instead—the assignment would change only b, not a. This behavior also occurs if there are no type differences at all. For example, consider these three statements:

```
>>> a = 3
>>> b = a
>>> a = a + 2
```

In this sequence, the same events transpire: Python makes the variable a reference the object 3, and makes b reference the same object as a, as in Figure 6-2; as before, the last assignment then sets a to a completely different object (in this case, the integer 5, which is the result of the + expression). It does not change b as a side effect. In fact, there is no way to ever overwrite the value of the object 3—as introduced in Chapter 4, integers are immutable, and thus can never be changed in-place.

One way to think of this is that, unlike in some languages, in Python, variables are always pointers to objects, not labels of changeable memory areas: setting a variable to a new value does not alter the original object, but rather causes the variable to reference an entirely different object. The net effect is that assignment to a variable can impact only the single variable being assigned. When mutable objects and in-place changes enter the equation, though, the picture changes somewhat; to see how, let's move on.

Shared References and In-Place Changes

As you'll see later in this part's chapters, there are objects and operations that perform in-place object changes. For instance, an assignment to an offset in a list actually changes the list object itself in-place, rather than generating a brand new list object. For objects that support such in-place changes, you need to be more aware of shared references, since a change from one name may impact others.

To further illustrate, let's take another look at the list objects introduced in Chapter 4. Recall that lists, which do support in-place assignments to positions, are simply collections of other objects, coded in square brackets:

```
>>> L1 = [2, 3, 4]
>>> L2 = L1
```

L1 here is a list containing the objects 2, 3, and 4. Items inside a list are accessed by their positions, so L1[0] refers to object 2, the first item in the list L1. Of course, lists are also objects in their own right, just like integers and strings. After running the two prior assignments, L1 and L2 reference the same object, just like a and b in the prior example (see Figure 6-2). Also, as before, if we now extend this interaction to say the following:

```
>>> L1 = 24
```

L1 is simply set to a different object; L2 still references the original list. If we change this statement's syntax slightly, however, it has radically different effect:

```
>>> L1 = [2, 3, 4]        # A mutable object
>>> L2 = L1               # Make a reference to the same object
>>> L1[0] = 24            # An in-place change

>>> L1                    # L1 is different
[24, 3, 4]
>>> L2                    # But so is L2!
[24, 3, 4]
```

Here, we haven't changed L1 itself; we've changed a component of the *object* that L1 references. This sort of change overwrites part of the list object in-place. Because the list object is shared by (referenced from) other variables, though, an in-place change like this doesn't only affect L1—that is, you must be aware that when you make such changes, they can impact other parts of your program. In this example, the effect shows up in L2 as well because it references the same object as L1. Again, we haven't actually changed L2, but its value will appear different.

This behavior is usually what you want, but you should be aware of how it works, so that it's expected. It's also just the default: if you don't want such behavior, you can request that Python *copy* objects, instead of making references. There are a variety of ways to copy a list, including the built-in list function, and the standard library copy module. Perhaps the most common way is to slice from start to finish (see Chapters 4 and 7 for more on slicing):

```
>>> L1 = [2, 3, 4]
>>> L2 = L1[:]          # Make a copy of L1
>>> L1[0] = 24

>>> L1
[24, 3, 4]
>>> L2                  # L2 is not changed
[2, 3, 4]
```

Here, the change made through L1 is not reflected in L2 because L2 references a copy of the object L1 references; that is, the two variables point to different pieces of memory.

Note that this slicing technique won't work on the other mutable core type, dictionaries, because they are not sequences—to copy a dictionary, instead use the D.copy() method. Also, note that the standard library copy module has a call for copying any object type generically, as well as a call for copying nested object structures (a dictionary with nested lists, for example):

```
import copy
X = copy.copy(Y)        # Make a top-level "shallow" copy of any object Y
X = copy.deepcopy(Y)    # Make a deep copy of any object Y: copy all nested parts
```

We'll explore lists and dictionaries in more depth, and revisit the concept of shared references and copies, in Chapter 8 and Chapter 9. For now, keep in mind that objects that can be changed in-place (that is, mutable objects) are always open to these kinds of effects. In Python, this includes lists, dictionaries, and some objects defined with class statements. If this is not the desired behavior, you can simply copy your objects as needed.

Shared References and Equality

In the interest of full disclosure, I should point out that the garbage-collection behavior described earlier in this chapter may be more conceptual than literal for certain types. Consider these statements:

```
>>> x = 42
>>> x = 'shrubbery'     # Reclaim 42 now?
```

Because Python caches and reuses small integers and small strings, as mentioned earlier, the object 42 here is probably not literally reclaimed; instead, it will likely remain in a system table to be reused the next time you generate a 42 in your code. Most kinds of objects, though, are reclaimed immediately when no longer referenced; for those that are not, the caching mechanism is irrelevant to your code.

For instance, because of Python's reference model, there are two different ways to check for equality in a Python program. Let's create a shared reference to demonstrate:

```
>>> L = [1, 2, 3]
>>> M = L              # M and L reference the same object
>>> L == M             # Same value
True
>>> L is M             # Same object
True
```

The first technique here, the == operator, tests whether the two referenced objects have the same values; this is the method almost always used for equality checks in Python. The second method, the is operator, instead tests for object identity—it returns True only if both names point to the exact same object, and so is a much stronger form of equality testing.

Really, is simply compares the pointers that implement references, and is a way to detect shared references in your code if needed. It returns False if the names point to equivalent but different objects, as is the case when we run two different literal expressions:

```
>>> L = [1, 2, 3]
>>> M = [1, 2, 3]      # M and L reference different objects
>>> L == M             # Same values
True
>>> L is M             # Different objects
False
```

Watch what happens when we perform the same operations on small numbers:

```
>>> X = 42
>>> Y = 42             # Should be two different objects
>>> X == Y
True
>>> X is Y             # Same object anyhow: caching at work!
True
```

In this interaction, X and Y should be == (same value), but not is (same object) because we ran two different literal expressions. Because small integers and strings are cached and reused, though, is tells us they reference the same single object.

In fact, if you really want a look under the hood, you can always ask Python how many references there are to an object: the getrefcount function in the standard sys module returns the object's reference count. When I ask about the integer object 1 in the IDLE GUI, for instance, it reports 837 reuses of this same object (most of which are in IDLE's system code, not mine):

```
>>> import sys
>>> sys.getrefcount(1)        # 837 pointers to this shared piece of memory
837
```

This object caching and reuse is irrelevant to your code (unless you run the is check!). Because you cannot change numbers or strings in-place, it doesn't matter how many references there are to the same object. Still, this behavior reflects one of many ways Python optimizes its model for execution speed.

Dynamic Typing Is Everywhere

You don't really need to draw name/object diagrams with circles and arrows to use Python. When you're starting out, though, it sometimes helps you understand unusual cases if you can trace their reference structures. If a mutable object changes out from under you when passed around your program, for example, chances are you are witnessing some of this chapter's subject matter firsthand.

Moreover, even if dynamic typing seems a little abstract at this point, you probably will care about it eventually. Because *everything* seems to work by assignment and references in Python, a basic understanding of this model is useful in many different contexts. As you'll see, it works the same in assignment statements, function arguments, for loop variables, module imports, and more. The good news is that there is just one assignment model in Python; once you get a handle on dynamic typing, you'll find that it works the same everywhere in the language.

At the most practical level, dynamic typing means there is less code for you to write. Just as importantly, though, dynamic typing is also the root of polymorphism—a concept we introduced in Chapter 4, and will revisit again later in this book—in Python. Because we do not constrain types in Python code, it is highly flexible. As you'll see, when used right, dynamic typing and the polymorphism it provides produce code that automatically adapts to new requirements as your systems evolve.

Chapter Summary

This chapter took a deeper look at Python's dynamic typing model—that is, the way that Python keeps track of object types for us automatically, rather than requiring us to code declaration statements in our scripts. Along the way, we learned how variables and objects are associated by references in Python; we also explored the idea of garbage collection, learned how shared references to objects can affect multiple variables, and saw how references impact the notion of equality in Python.

Because there is just one assignment model in Python, and because assignment pops up everywhere in the language, it's important that you have a handle on the model before moving on. The chapter quiz coming up should help you review some of this chapter's ideas. After that, we'll resume our object tour in the next chapter, with strings.

Chapter Quiz

1. Consider the following three statements. Do they change the value printed for A?

   ```
   A = "spam"
   B = A
   B = "shrubbery"
   ```

2. Consider these three statements. Do they change the value of A?

   ```
   A = ["spam"]
   B = A
   B[0] = "shrubbery"
   ```

3. How about these—is A changed?

   ```
   A = ["spam"]
   B = A[:]
   B[0] = "shrubbery"
   ```

Quiz Answers

1. No: A still prints as "spam". When B is assigned to the string "shrubbery", all that happens is that the variable B is reset to point to the new string object. A and B initially share (i.e., reference, or point to) the same single string object "spam", but two names are never linked together in Python. Thus, setting B to a different object has no effect on A. The same would be true if the last statement here was B = B + 'shrubbery', by the way—the concatenation makes a new object for its result, which is then assigned to B only. We can never overwrite a string (or number, or tuple) in-place, because strings are immutable.

2. Yes: A now prints as ["shrubbery"]. Technically, we haven't really changed either A or B; instead, we've changed part of the object they both reference (point to) by overwriting that object in-place through the variable B. Because A references the same object as B, the update is reflected in A as well.

3. No: A still prints as ["spam"]. The in-place assignment through B has no effect this time because the slice expression made a copy of the list object before it was assigned to B. After the second assignment statement, there are two different list objects that have the same value (in Python, we say they are ==, but not is). The third statement changes the value of the list object pointed to by B, but not that pointed to by A.

## CHAPTER 7

Strings

The next major type on our built-in object tour is the Python *string*—an ordered collection of characters used to store and represent text-based information. We looked briefly at strings in Chapter 4. Here, we will revisit them in more depth, filling in some of the details we skipped then.

From a functional perspective, strings can be used to represent just about anything that can be encoded as text: symbols and words (e.g., your name), contents of text files loaded into memory, Internet addresses, Python programs, and so on.

You may have used strings in other languages, too. Python's strings serve the same role as character arrays in languages such as C, but they are a somewhat higher-level tool than arrays. Unlike in C, in Python, strings come with a powerful set of processing tools. Also, unlike languages such as C, Python has no special type for single characters (like C's char); instead, you just use one-character strings.

Strictly speaking, Python strings are categorized as immutable sequences, meaning that the characters they contain have a left-to-right positional order, and that they cannot be changed in-place. In fact, strings are the first representative of the larger class of objects called sequences that we will study here. Pay special attention to the sequence operations introduced in this chapter, because they will work the same on other sequence types we'll explore later, such as lists and tuples.

Table 7-1 previews common string literals and operations we will discuss in this chapter. Empty strings are written as a pair of quotation marks (single or double) with nothing in between, and there are a variety of ways to code strings. For processing, strings support *expression* operations such as concatenation (combining strings), slicing (extracting sections), indexing (fetching by offset), and so on. Besides expressions, Python also provides a set of string *methods* that implement common string-specific tasks, as well as *modules* for more advanced text-processing tasks such as pattern matching. We'll explore all of these later in the chapter.

Table 7-1. Common string literals and operations

Operation	Interpretation
s1 = ''	Empty string
s2 = "spam's"	Double quotes
block = """..."""	Triple-quoted blocks
s3 = r'\temp\spam'	Raw strings
s4 = u'spam'	Unicode strings
s1 + s2 s2 * 3	Concatenate, repeat
s2[i] s2[i:j] len(s2)	Index, slice, length
"a %s parrot" % type	String formatting
s2.find('pa') s2.rstrip( ) s2.replace('pa', 'xx') s1.split(',') s1.isdigit( ) s1.lower( )	String method calls: search, remove whitespace, replacement, split on delimiter, content test, case conversion, etc.
for x in s2 'spam' in s2	Iteration, membership

Beyond the core set of string tools, Python also supports more advanced pattern-based string processing with the standard library's re (regular expression) module, introduced in Chapter 4. This chapter starts with an overview of string literal forms and basic string expressions, then looks at more advanced tools such as string methods and formatting.

String Literals

By and large, strings are fairly easy to use in Python. Perhaps the most complicated thing about them is that there are so many ways to write them in your code:

- Single quotes: 'spa"m'
- Double quotes: "spa'm"
- Triple quotes: '''... spam ...''', """... spam ..."""
- Escape sequences: "s\tp\na\0m"
- Raw strings: r"C:\new\test.spm"
- Unicode strings: u'eggs\u0020spam'

The single- and double-quoted forms are by far the most common; the others serve specialized roles. Let's take a quick look at each of these options.

Single- and Double-Quoted Strings Are the Same

Around Python strings, single and double quote characters are interchangeable. That is, string literals can be written enclosed in either two single or two double quotes—the two forms work the same and return the same type of object. For example, the following two strings are identical, once coded:

```
>>> 'shrubbery', "shrubbery"
('shrubbery', 'shrubbery')
```

The reason for including both is that it allows you to embed a quote character of the other variety inside a string without escaping it with a backslash. You may embed a single quote character in a string enclosed in double quote characters, and vice versa:

```
>>> 'knight"s', "knight's"
('knight"s', "knight's")
```

Incidentally, Python automatically concatenates adjacent string literals in any expression, although it is almost as simple to add a + operator between them to invoke concatenation explicitly:

```
>>> title = "Meaning " 'of' " Life"      # Implicit concatenation
>>> title
'Meaning of Life'
```

Notice that adding commas between these strings would make a tuple, not a string. Also, notice in all of these outputs that Python prefers to print strings in single quotes, unless they embed one. You can also embed quotes by escaping them with backslashes:

```
>>> 'knight\'s', "knight\"s"
("knight's", 'knight"s')
```

To understand why, you need to know how escapes work in general.

Escape Sequences Represent Special Bytes

The last example embedded a quote inside a string by preceding it with a backslash. This is representative of a general pattern in strings: backslashes are used to introduce special byte codings known as escape sequences.

Escape sequences let us embed byte codes in strings that cannot easily be typed on a keyboard. The character \, and one or more characters following it in the string literal, are replaced with a single character in the resulting string object, which has the binary value specified by the escape sequence. For example, here is a five-character string that embeds a newline and a tab:

```
>>> s = 'a\nb\tc'
```

The two characters \n stand for a single character—the byte containing the binary value of the newline character in your character set (usually, ASCII code 10). Similarly, the sequence \t is replaced with the tab character. The way this string looks when printed depends on how you print it. The interactive echo shows the special characters as escapes, but print interprets them instead:

```
>>> s
'a\nb\tc'
>>> print s
a
b       c
```

To be completely sure how many bytes are in this string, use the built-in len function—it returns the actual number of bytes in a string, regardless of how it is displayed:

```
>>> len(s)
5
```

This string is five bytes long: it contains an ASCII *a* byte, a newline byte, an ASCII *b* byte, and so on. Note that the original backslash characters are not really stored with the string in memory. For coding such special bytes, Python recognizes a full set of escape code sequences, listed in Table 7-2.

Table 7-2. String backslash characters

Escape	Meaning
\newline	Ignored (continuation)
\\	Backslash (keeps a \)
\'	Single quote (keeps ')
\"	Double quote (keeps ")
\a	Bell
\b	Backspace
\f	Formfeed
\n	Newline (linefeed)
\r	Carriage return
\t	Horizontal tab
\v	Vertical tab
\N{*id*}	Unicode database ID
\uhhhh	Unicode 16-bit hex
\Uhhhh...	Unicode 32-bit hex[a]
\xhh	Hex digits value
\ooo	Octal digits value
\0	Null (doesn't end string)
other	Not an escape (kept)

[a] The \Uhhhh... escape sequence takes exactly eight hexadecimal digits (h); both \u and \U can be used only in Unicode string literals.

Some escape sequences allow you to embed absolute binary values into the bytes of a string. For instance, here's a five-character string that embeds two binary zero bytes:

```
>>> s = 'a\0b\0c'
>>> s
'a\x00b\x00c'
>>> len(s)
5
```

In Python, the zero (null) byte does not terminate a string the way it typically does in C. Instead, Python keeps both the string's length and text in memory. In fact, no character terminates a string in Python. Here's a string that is all absolute binary escape codes—a binary 1 and 2 (coded in octal), followed by a binary 3 (coded in hexadecimal):

```
>>> s = '\001\002\x03'
>>> s
'\x01\x02\x03'
>>> len(s)
3
```

This becomes more important to know when you process binary data files in Python. Because their contents are represented as strings in your scripts, it's okay to process binary files that contain any sorts of binary byte values (more on files in Chapter 9).*

Finally, as the last entry in Table 7-2 implies, if Python does not recognize the character after a \ as being a valid escape code, it simply keeps the backslash in the resulting string:

```
>>> x = "C:\py\code"          # Keeps \ literally
>>> x
'C:\\py\\code'
>>> len(x)
10
```

Unless you're able to commit all of Table 7-2 to memory, though, you probably shouldn't rely on this behavior.† To code literal backslashes explicitly such that they are retained in your strings, double them up (\\ is an escape for \) or use raw strings, described in the next section.

Raw Strings Suppress Escapes

As we've seen, escape sequences are handy for embedding special byte codes within strings. Sometimes, though, the special treatment of backslashes for introducing

---

* If you're especially interested in binary data files, the chief distinction is that you open them in binary mode (using open mode flags with a b, such as 'rb', 'wb', and so on). See also the standard struct module introduced in Chapter 9, which can parse binary data loaded from a file.

† In classes, I've met people who have indeed committed most or all of this table to memory; I'd normally think that's really sick, but for the fact that I'm a member of the set, too.

escapes can lead to trouble. It's surprisingly common, for instance, to see Python newcomers in classes trying to open a file with a filename argument that looks something like this:

```
myfile = open('C:\new\text.dat', 'w')
```

thinking that they will open a file called *text.dat* in the directory *C:\new*. The problem here is that \n is taken to stand for a newline character, and \t is replaced with a tab. In effect, the call tries to open a file named *C:(newline)ew(tab)ext.dat*, with usually less than stellar results.

This is just the sort of thing that raw strings are useful for. If the letter *r* (uppercase or lowercase) appears just before the opening quote of a string, it turns off the escape mechanism. The result is that Python retains your backslashes literally, exactly as you type them. Therefore, to fix the filename problem, just remember to add the letter *r* on Windows:

```
myfile = open(r'C:\new\text.dat', 'w')
```

Alternatively, because two backslashes are really an escape sequence for one backslash, you can keep your backslashes by simply doubling them up:

```
myfile = open('C:\\new\\text.dat', 'w')
```

In fact, Python itself sometimes uses this doubling scheme when it prints strings with embedded backslashes:

```
>>> path = r'C:\new\text.dat'
>>> path                        # Show as Python code
'C:\\new\\text.dat'
>>> print path                  # User-friendly format
C:\new\text.dat
>>> len(path)                   # String length
15
```

As with numeric representation, the default format at the interactive prompt prints results as if they were code, and therefore escapes backslashes in the output. The print statement provides a more user-friendly format that shows that there is actually only one backslash in each spot. To verify this is the case, you can check the result of the built-in len function, which returns the number of bytes in the string, independent of display formats. If you count the characters in the print path output, you'll see that there really is just one character per backslash, for a total of 15.

Besides directory paths on Windows, raw strings are also commonly used for regular expressions (text pattern matching, supported with the re module introduced in Chapter 4). Also note that Python scripts can usually use *forward* slashes in directory paths on Windows and Unix because Python tries to interpret paths portably. Raw strings are useful if you code paths using native Windows backslashes, though.

Triple Quotes Code Multiline Block Strings

So far, you've seen single quotes, double quotes, escapes, and raw strings in action. Python also has a triple-quoted string literal format, sometimes called a *block string*, that is a syntactic convenience for coding multiline text data. This form begins with three quotes (of either the single or double variety), is followed by any number of lines of text, and is closed with the same triple-quote sequence that opened it. Single and double quotes embedded in the string's text may be, but do not have to be, escaped—the string does not end until Python sees three unescaped quotes of the same kind used to start the literal. For example:

```
>>> mantra = """Always look
...   on the bright
... side of life."""
>>>
>>> mantra
'Always look\n on the bright\nside of life.'
```

This string spans three lines (in some interfaces, the interactive prompt changes to ... on continuation lines; IDLE simply drops down one line). Python collects all the triple-quoted text into a single multiline string, with embedded newline characters (\n) at the places where your code has line breaks. Notice that, as in the literal, the second line in the result has a leading space, but the third does not—what you type is truly what you get.

Triple-quoted strings are useful any time you need multiline text in your program; for example, to embed multiline error messages or HTML or XML code in your source code files. You can embed such blocks directly in your scripts without resorting to external text files, or explicit concatenation and newline characters.

Triple-quoted strings are also commonly used for documentation strings, which are string literals that are taken as comments when they appear at specific points in your file (more on these later in the book). These don't have to be triple-quoted blocks, but they usually are to allow for multiline comments.

Finally, triple-quoted strings are also often used as a horribly hackish way to temporarily disable lines of code during development (OK, it's not really too horrible, and it's actually a fairly common practice). If you wish to turn off a few lines of code and run your script again, simply put three quotes above and below them, like this:

```
X = 1
"""
import os
print os.getcwd( )
"""
Y = 2
```

I said this was hackish because Python really does make a string out of the lines of code disabled this way, but this is probably not significant in terms of performance. For large sections of code, it's also easier than manually adding hash marks before each line and later removing them. This is especially true if you are using a text editor that does not have support for editing Python code specifically. In Python, practicality often beats aesthetics.

Unicode Strings Encode Larger Character Sets

The last way to write strings in your scripts is perhaps the most specialized, and it's rarely observed outside of web and XML processing. *Unicode strings* are sometimes called "wide" character strings. Because each character may be represented with more than one byte in memory, Unicode strings allow programs to encode richer character sets than standard strings.

Unicode strings are typically used to support *internationalization* of applications (sometimes referred to as "i18n," to compress the 18 characters between the first and last characters of the term). For instance, they allow programmers to directly support European or Asian character sets in Python scripts. Because such character sets have more characters than can be represented by single bytes, Unicode is normally used to process these forms of text.

In Python, you can code Unicode strings in your scripts by adding the letter *U* (lower- or uppercase) just before the opening quote:

```
>>> u'spam'
u'spam'
```

Technically, this syntax generates a Unicode string object, which is a different data type from the normal string type. However, Python allows you to freely mix Unicode and normal strings in expressions, and converts up to Unicode for mixed-type results (more on + concatenation in the next section):

```
>>> 'ni' + u'spam'          # Mixed string types
u'nispam'
```

In fact, Unicode strings are defined to support all the usual string-processing operations you'll meet in the next section, so the difference in types is often trivial to your code. Like normal strings, Unicode strings may be concatenated, indexed, sliced, matched with the re module, and so on, and cannot be changed in-place.

If you ever need to convert between the two types explicitly, you can use the built-in str and unicode functions:

```
>>> str(u'spam')            # Unicode to normal
'spam'
>>> unicode('spam')         # Normal to Unicode
u'spam'
```

Because Unicode is designed to handle multibyte characters, you can also use the special \u and \U escapes to encode binary character values that are larger than 8 bits:

```
>>> u'ab\x20cd'           # 8-bit/1-byte characters
u'ab cd'
>>> u'ab\u0020cd'         # 2-byte characters
u'ab cd'
>>> u'ab\U00000020cd'     # 4-byte characters
u'ab cd'
```

The first of these statements embeds the binary code for a space character; its binary value in hexadecimal notation is x20. The second and third statements do the same, but give the value in 2-byte and 4-byte Unicode escape notation.

Even if you don't think you will need Unicode strings, you might use them without knowing it. Because some programming interfaces (e.g., the COM API on Windows, and some XML parsers) represent text as Unicode, it may find its way into your scripts as API inputs or results, and you may sometimes need to convert back and forth between normal and Unicode types.

Because Python treats the two string types interchangeably in most contexts, though, the presence of Unicode strings is often transparent to your code—you can largely ignore the fact that text is being passed around as Unicode objects and use normal string operations.

Unicode is a useful addition to Python, and because support is built-in, it's easy to handle such data in your scripts when needed. Of course, there's a lot more to say about the Unicode story. For example:

- Unicode objects provide an encode method that converts a Unicode string into a normal 8-bit string using a specific encoding.
- The built-in function unicode and module codecs support registered Unicode "codecs" (for "COders and DECoders").
- The open function within the codecs module allows for processing Unicode text files, where each character is stored as more than one byte.
- The unicodedata module provides access to the Unicode character database.
- The sys module includes calls for fetching and setting the default Unicode encoding scheme (the default is usually ASCII).
- You may combine the raw and Unicode string formats (e.g., ur'a\b\c').

Because Unicode is a relatively advanced and not so commonly used tool, we won't discuss it further in this introductory text. See the Python standard manual for the rest of the Unicode story.

In Python 3.0, the string type will mutate somewhat: the current str string type will always be Unicode in 3.0, and there will be a new "bytes" type that will be a mutable sequence of small integers useful for representing short character strings. Some file read operations may return bytes instead of str (reading binary files, for example). This is still on the drawing board, so consult 3.0 release notes for details.

Strings in Action

Once you've created a string with the literal expressions we just met, you will almost certainly want to do things with it. This section and the next two demonstrate string basics, formatting, and methods—the first line of text-processing tools in the Python language.

Basic Operations

Let's begin by interacting with the Python interpreter to illustrate the basic string operations listed in Table 7-1. Strings can be concatenated using the + operator and repeated using the * operator:

```
% python
>>> len('abc')          # Length: number of items
3
>>> 'abc' + 'def'       # Concatenation: a new string
'abcdef'
>>> 'Ni!' * 4           # Repetition: like "Ni!" + "Ni!" + ...
'Ni!Ni!Ni!Ni!'
```

Formally, adding two string objects creates a new string object, with the contents of its operands joined. Repetition is like adding a string to itself a number of times. In both cases, Python lets you create arbitrarily sized strings; there's no need to prede-clare anything in Python, including the sizes of data structures.* The len built-in function returns the length of a string (or any other object with a length).

Repetition may seem a bit obscure at first, but it comes in handy in a surprising number of contexts. For example, to print a line of 80 dashes, you can count up to 80, or let Python count for you:

```
>>> print '------- ...more... ---'    # 80 dashes, the hard way
>>> print '-'*80                        # 80 dashes, the easy way
```

---

* Unlike C character arrays, you don't need to allocate or manage storage arrays when using Python strings; simply create string objects as needed, and let Python manage the underlying memory space. As discussed in the prior chapter, Python reclaims unused objects' memory space automatically, using a reference-count garbage-collection strategy. Each object keeps track of the number of names, data structures, etc., that reference it; when the count reaches zero, Python frees the object's space. This scheme means Python doesn't have to stop and scan all the memory to find unused space to free (an additional garbage component also collects cyclic objects).

Notice that operator overloading is at work here already: we're using the same + and * operators that perform addition and multiplication when using numbers. Python does the correct operation because it knows the types of the objects being added and multiplied. But be careful: the rules aren't quite as liberal as you might expect. For instance, Python doesn't allow you to mix numbers and strings in + expressions: 'abc'+9 raises an error instead of automatically converting 9 to a string.

As shown in the last line in Table 7-1, you can also iterate over strings in loops using for statements, and test membership with the in expression operator, which is essentially a search:

```
>>> myjob = "hacker"
>>> for c in myjob: print c,          # Step through items
...
h a c k e r
>>> "k" in myjob                      # Found
True
>>> "z" in myjob                      # Not found
False
```

The for loop assigns a variable to successive items in a sequence (here, a string), and executes one or more statements for each item. In effect, the variable c becomes a cursor stepping across the string here. We will discuss iteration tools like these in more detail later in this book.

Indexing and Slicing

Because strings are defined as ordered collections of characters, we can access their components by position. In Python, characters in a string are fetched by *indexing*— providing the numeric offset of the desired component in square brackets after the string. You get back the one-character string at the specified position.

As in the C language, Python offsets start at 0, and end at one less than the length of the string. Unlike C, however, Python also lets you fetch items from sequences such as strings using *negative* offsets. Technically, a negative offset is added to the length of a string to derive a positive offset. You can also think of negative offsets as counting backward from the end. The following interaction demonstrates:

```
>>> S = 'spam'
>>> S[0], S[-2]                       # Indexing from front or end
('s', 'a')
>>> S[1:3], S[1:], S[:-1]             # Slicing: extract a section
('pa', 'pam', 'spa')
```

The first line defines a four-character string, and assigns it the name S. The next line indexes it in two ways: S[0] fetches the item at offset 0 from the left (the one-character string 's'), and S[-2] gets the item at offset 2 from the end (or equivalently, at offset (4 + −2) from the front). Offsets and slices map to cells as shown in Figure 7-1.*

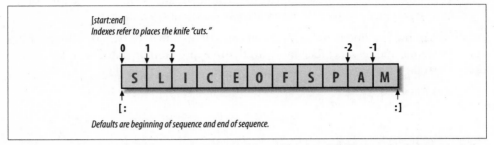

Figure 7-1. *Offsets and slices: positive offsets start from the left end (offset 0 is the first item), and negatives count back from the right end (offset −1 is the last item). Either kind of offset can be used to give positions in indexing and slicing.*

The last line in the preceding example demonstrates *slicing*. Probably the best way to think of slicing is that it is a form of *parsing* (analyzing structure), especially when applied to strings—it allows us to extract an entire section (substring) in a single step. Slices can be used to extract columns of data, chop off leading and trailing text, and more. We'll look at another slicing-as-parsing example later in this chapter.

Here's how slicing works. When you index a sequence object such as a string on a pair of offsets separated by a colon, Python returns a new object containing the contiguous section identified by the offset pair. The left offset is taken to be the lower bound (inclusive), and the right is the upper bound (noninclusive). Python fetches all items from the lower bound up to but not including the upper bound, and returns a new object containing the fetched items. If omitted, the left and right bounds default to 0, and the length of the object you are slicing, respectively.

For instance, in the example we just looked at, S[1:3] extracts the items at offsets 1 and 2. That is, it grabs the second and third items, and stops before the fourth item at offset 3. Next S[1:] gets *all items beyond the first*—the upper bound, which is not specified, defaults to the length of the string. Finally, S[:-1] fetches *all but the last item*—the lower bound defaults to 0, and −1 refers to the last item, noninclusive.

This may seem confusing at first glance, but indexing and slicing are simple and powerful tools to use, once you get the knack. Remember, if you're unsure about what a slice means, try it out interactively. In the next chapter, you'll see that it's also possible to change an entire section of a certain object in one step by assigning to a slice. Here's a summary of the details for reference:

---

* More mathematically minded readers (and students in my classes) sometimes detect a small asymmetry here: the leftmost item is at offset 0, but the rightmost is at offset −1. Alas, there is no such thing as a distinct −0 value in Python.

- Indexing (S[i]) fetches components at offsets:
  — The first item is at offset 0.
  — Negative indexes mean to count backward from the end or right.
  — S[0] fetches the first item.
  — S[-2] fetches the second item from the end (like S[len(S)-2]).
- Slicing (S[i:j]) extracts contiguous sections of a sequence:
  — The upper bound is noninclusive.
  — Slice boundaries default to 0 and the sequence length, if omitted.
  — S[1:3] fetches items at offsets 1 up to, but not including, 3.
  — S[1:] fetches items at offset 1 through the end (length).
  — S[:3] fetches items at offset 0 up to, but not including, 3.
  — S[:-1] fetches items at offset 0 up to, but not including, the last item.
  — S[:] fetches items at offsets 0 through the end—this effectively performs a top-level copy of S.

The last item listed here turns out to be a very common trick: it makes a full top-level *copy* of a sequence object—an object with the same value, but a distinct piece of memory (you'll find more on copies in Chapter 9). This isn't very useful for immutable objects like strings, but it comes in handy for objects that may be changed in-place, such as lists. In the next chapter, you'll also see that the syntax used to index by offset (square brackets) is used to index dictionaries by key as well; the operations look the same, but have different interpretations.

Extended slicing: the third limit

In Python 2.3, slice expressions grew support for an optional third index, used as a *step* (sometimes called a *stride*). The step is added to the index of each item extracted. The full-blown form of a slice is now X[I:J:K], which means "extract all the items in X, from offset I through J–1, by K." The third limit, K, defaults to 1, which is why normally all items in a slice are extracted from left to right. If you specify an explicit value, however, you can use the third limit to skip items or to reverse their order.

For instance, X[1:10:2] will fetch *every other item* in X from offsets 1–9; that is, it will collect the items at offsets 1, 3, 5, 7, and 9. As usual, the first and second limits default to 0, and the length of the sequence, respectively, so X[::2] gets every other item from the beginning to the end of the sequence:

```
>>> S = 'abcdefghijklmnop'
>>> S[1:10:2]
'bdfhj'
>>> S[::2]
'acegikmo'
```

You can also use a negative stride. For example, the slicing expression "hello"[::-1] returns the new string "olleh"—the first two bounds default to 0, and the length of the sequence, as before, and a stride of –1 indicates that the slice should go from right to left instead of the usual left to right. The effect, therefore, is to *reverse* the sequence:

```
>>> S = 'hello'
>>> S[::-1]
'olleh'
```

With a negative stride, the meanings of the first two bounds are essentially reversed. That is, the slice S[5:1:-1] fetches the items from 2 to 5, in reverse order (the result contains items from offsets 5, 4, 3, and 2):

```
>>> S = 'abcedfg'
>>> S[5:1:-1]
'fdec'
```

Skipping and reversing like this are the most common use cases for three-limit slices, but see Python's standard library manual for more details, or run a few experiments interactively—there is more to the story than we will cover here. We'll revisit three-limit slices again later in this book, in conjunction with the for loop statement.

String Conversion Tools

One of Python's design mottos is that it refuses the temptation to guess. As a prime example, you cannot add a number and a string together in Python, even if the string looks like a number (i.e., is all digits):

```
>>> "42" + 1
TypeError: cannot concatenate 'str' and 'int' objects
```

This is by design: because + can mean both addition and concatenation, the choice of conversion would be ambiguous. So, Python treats this as an error. In Python, magic is generally omitted if it will make your life more complex.

What to do, then, if your script obtains a number as a text string from a file or user interface? The trick is that you need to employ conversion tools before you can treat a string like a number, or vice versa. For instance:

```
>>> int("42"), str(42)          # Convert from/to string
(42, '42')
>>> repr(42), `42`              # Convert to as-code string
('42', '42')
```

The int function converts a string to a number, and the str function converts a number to its string representation (essentially, what it looks like when printed). The repr function and its older equivalent, the backquotes expression, also convert an object to its string representation, but these return the object as a string of code that can be rerun to recreate the object (for strings, the result has quotes around it if displayed

Throughout this book, I will include common use case sidebars (such as this one) to give you a peek at how some of the language features being introduced are typically used in real programs. Because you won't be able to make much sense of real use cases until you've seen most of the Python picture, these sidebars necessarily contain many references to topics not introduced yet; at most, you should consider them previews of ways that you may find these abstract language concepts useful for common programming tasks.

For instance, you'll see later that the argument words listed on a system command line used to launch a Python program are made available in the `argv` attribute of the built-in sys module:

```
# File echo.py
import sys
print sys.argv

% python echo.py -a -b -c
['echo.py', '-a', '-b', '-c']
```

Usually, you're only interested in inspecting the arguments that follow the program name. This leads to a very typical application of slices: a single slice expression can be used to return all but the first item of a list. Here, `sys.argv[1:]` returns the desired list, `['-a', '-b', '-c']`. You can then process this list without having to accommodate the program name at the front.

Slices are also often used to clean up lines read from input files. If you know that a line will have an end-of-line character at the end (a \n newline marker), you can get rid of it with a single expression such as `line[:-1]`, which extracts all but the last character in the line (the lower limit defaults to 0). In both cases, slices do the job of logic that must be explicit in a lower-level language.

Note that calling the `line.rstrip` method is often preferred for stripping newline characters because this call leaves the line intact if it has no newline character at the end—a common case for files created with some text-editing tools. Slicing works if you're sure the line is properly terminated.

with the `print` statement). See the "str and repr Display Formats" sidebar in Chapter 5 on the difference between `str` and `repr` for more on this topic. Of these, int and str are the generally prescribed conversion techniques.

Although you can't mix strings and number types around operators such as +, you can manually convert operands before that operation if needed:

```
>>> S = "42"
>>> I = 1
>>> S + I
TypeError: cannot concatenate 'str' and 'int' objects
```

```
>>> int(S) + I                    # Force addition
43

>>> S + str(I)                    # Force concatenation
'421'
```

Similar built-in functions handle floating-point number conversions to and from strings:

```
>>> str(3.1415), float("1.5")
('3.1415', 1.5)

>>> text = "1.234E-10"
>>> float(text)
1.2340000000000001e-010
```

Later, we'll further study the built-in eval function; it runs a string containing Python expression code, and so can convert a string to any kind of object. The functions int and float convert only to numbers, but this restriction means they are usually faster (and more secure, because they do not accept arbitrary expression code). As we saw in Chapter 5, the string formatting expression also provides a way to convert numbers to strings. We'll discuss formatting further later in this chapter.

Character code conversions

On the subject of conversions, it is also possible to convert a single character to its underlying ASCII integer code by passing it to the built-in ord function—this returns the actual binary value of the corresponding byte in memory. The chr function performs the inverse operation, taking an ASCII integer code and converting it to the corresponding character:

```
>>> ord('s')
115
>>> chr(115)
's'
```

You can use a loop to apply these functions to all characters in a string. These tools can also be used to perform a sort of string-based math. To advance to the next character, for example, convert and do the math in integer:

```
>>> S = '5'
>>> S = chr(ord(S) + 1)
>>> S
'6'
>>> S = chr(ord(S) + 1)
>>> S
'7'
```

At least for single-character strings, this provides an alternative to using the built-in int function to convert from string to integer:

```
>>> int('5')
5
>>> ord('5') - ord('0')
5
```

Such conversions can be used in conjunction with a looping statement to convert a string of binary digits to their corresponding integer values—each time through, multiply the current value by 2, and add the next digit's integer value:

```
>>> B = '1101'
>>> I = 0
>>> while B:
...     I = I * 2 + (ord(B[0]) - ord('0'))
...     B = B[1:]
...
>>> I
13
```

A left-shift operation (I << 1) would have the same effect as multiplying by 2 here. Because we haven't studied loops in detail yet, though, we'll leave implementing that as a suggested experiment.

Changing Strings

Remember the term "immutable sequence"? The immutable part means that you can't change a string in-place (e.g., by assigning to an index):

```
>>> S = 'spam'
>>> S[0] = "x"
Raises an error!
```

So how do you modify text information in Python? To change a string, you need to build and assign a new string using tools such as concatenation and slicing, and then, if desired, assign the result back to the string's original name:

```
>>> S = S + 'SPAM!'        # To change a string, make a new one
>>> S
'spamSPAM!'
>>> S = S[:4] + 'Burger' + S[-1]
>>> S
'spamBurger!'
```

The first example adds a substring at the end of S, by concatenation; really, it makes a new string and assigns it back to S, but you can think of this as "changing" the original string. The second example replaces four characters with six by slicing, indexing, and concatenating. As you'll see later in this chapter, you can achieve similar effects with string method calls like replace. Here's a sneak peek:

```
>>> S = 'splot'
>>> S = S.replace('pl', 'pamal')
>>> S
'spamalot'
```

Like every operation that yields a new string value, string methods generate new string objects. If you want to retain those objects, you can assign it to a variable name. Generating a new string object for each string change is not as inefficient as it may sound—remember, as discussed in the preceding chapter, Python automatically garbage collects (reclaims the space of) old unused string objects as you go, so newer objects reuse the space held by prior values. Python is usually more efficient than you might expect.

Finally, it's also possible to build up new text values with string formatting expressions:

```
>>> 'That is %d %s bird!' % (1, 'dead')    # Like C sprintf
That is 1 dead bird!
```

This turns out to be a powerful operation. The next section shows how it works.

String Formatting

Python defines the % binary operator to work on strings (you may recall that this is also the remainder of division, or modulus, operator for numbers). When applied to strings, this operator serves the same role as C's sprintf function; the % provides a simple way to format values as strings, according to a format definition string. In short, the % operator provides a compact way to code multiple string substitutions.

To format strings:

1. On the left of the % operator, provide a format string containing one or more embedded conversion targets, each of which starts with a % (e.g., %d).

2. On the right of the % operator, provide the object (or objects, in parentheses) that you want Python to insert into the format string on the left in place of the conversion target (or targets).

For instance, in the last example, we looked at in the prior section, the integer 1 replaces the %d in the format string on the left, and the string 'dead' replaces the %s. The result is a new string that reflects these two substitutions.

Technically speaking, string formatting expressions are usually optional—you can generally do similar work with multiple concatenations and conversions. However, formatting allows us to combine many steps into a single operation. It's powerful enough to warrant a few more examples:

```
>>> exclamation = "Ni"
>>> "The knights who say %s!" % exclamation
'The knights who say Ni!'

>>> "%d %s %d you" % (1, 'spam', 4)
'1 spam 4 you'

>>> "%s -- %s -- %s" % (42, 3.14159, [1, 2, 3])
'42 -- 3.14159 -- [1, 2, 3]'
```

The first example here plugs the string "Ni" into the target on the left, replacing the %s marker. In the second example, three values are inserted into the target string. Note that when you're inserting more than one value, you need to group the values on the right in parentheses (i.e., put them in a tuple).

The third example again inserts three values—an integer, a floating-point object, and a list object—but notice that all of the targets on the left are %s, which stands for conversion to string. As every type of object can be converted to a string (the one used when printing), every object type works with the %s conversion code. Because of this, unless you will be doing some special formatting, %s is often the only code you need to remember for the formatting expression.

Again, keep in mind that formatting always makes a new string, rather than changing the string on the left; because strings are immutable, it must work this way. As before, assign the result to a variable name if you need to retain it.

Advanced String Formatting

For more advanced type-specific formatting, you can use any of the conversion codes listed in Table 7-3 in formatting expressions. C programmers will recognize most of these because Python string formatting supports all the usual C printf format codes (but returns the result, instead of displaying it, like printf). Some of the format codes in the table provide alternative ways to format the same type; for instance, %e, %f, and %g provide alternative ways to format floating-point numbers.

Table 7-3. String-formatting codes

Code	Meaning
%s	String (or any object)
%r	s, but uses repr, not str
%c	Character
%d	Decimal (integer)
%i	Integer
%u	Unsigned (integer)
%o	Octal integer
%x	Hex integer
%X	x, but prints uppercase
%e	Floating-point exponent
%E	e, but prints uppercase
%f	Floating-point decimal
%g	Floating-point e or f
%G	Floating-point E or F
%%	Literal %

In fact, conversion targets in the format string on the expression's left side support a variety of conversion operations with a fairly sophisticated syntax all their own. The general structure of conversion targets looks like this:

```
%[(name)][flags][width][.precision]code
```

The character codes in Table 7-3 show up at the end of the target string. Between the % and the character code, you can do any of the following: provide a dictionary key; list flags that specify things like left justification (-), numeric sign (+), and zero fills (0); give a total field width and the number of digits after a decimal point; and more.

Formatting target syntax is documented in full in the Python standard manuals, but to demonstrate common usage, let's look at a few examples. This one formats integers by default, and then in a six-character field with left justification, and zero padding:

```
>>> x = 1234
>>> res = "integers: ...%d...%-6d...%06d" % (x, x, x)
>>> res
'integers: ...1234...1234  ...001234'
```

The %e, %f, and %g formats display floating-point numbers in different ways, as the following interaction demonstrates:

```
>>> x = 1.23456789
>>> x
1.2345678899999999

>>> '%e | %f | %g' % (x, x, x)
'1.234568e+000 | 1.234568 | 1.23457'
```

For floating-point numbers, you can achieve a variety of additional formatting effects by specifying left justification, zero padding, numeric signs, field width, and digits after the decimal point. For simpler tasks, you might get by with simply converting to strings with a format expression or the str built-in function shown earlier:

```
>>> '%-6.2f | %05.2f | %+06.1f' % (x, x, x)
'1.23   | 01.23 | +001.2'

>>> "%s" % x, str(x)
('1.23456789', '1.23456789')
```

Dictionary-Based String Formatting

String formatting also allows conversion targets on the left to refer to the keys in a dictionary on the right to fetch the corresponding values. I haven't told you much about dictionaries yet, so here's an example that demonstrates the basics:

```
>>> "%(n)d %(x)s" % {"n":1, "x":"spam"}
'1 spam'
```

Here, the (n) and (x) in the format string refer to keys in the dictionary literal on the right, and fetch their associated values. Programs that generate text such as HTML or XML often use this technique—you can build up a dictionary of values, and substitute them all at once with a single formatting expression that uses key-based references:

```
>>> reply = """
Greetings...
Hello %(name)s!
Your age squared is %(age)s
"""
>>> values = {'name': 'Bob', 'age': 40}
>>> print reply % values

Greetings...
Hello Bob!
Your age squared is 40
```

This trick is also used in conjunction with the vars built-in function, which returns a dictionary containing all the variables that exist in the place it is called:

```
>>> food = 'spam'
>>> age = 40
>>> vars()
{'food': 'spam', 'age': 40, ...many more... }
```

When used on the right of a format operation, this allows the format string to refer to variables by name (i.e., by dictionary key):

```
>>> "%(age)d %(food)s" % vars()
'40 spam'
```

We'll study dictionaries in more depth in Chapter 8. See also Chapter 5 for examples that convert to hexadecimal and octal number strings with the %x and %o formatting target codes.

String Methods

In addition to expression operators, strings provide a set of *methods* that implement more sophisticated text-processing tasks. Methods are simply functions that are associated with particular objects. Technically, they are attributes attached to objects that happen to reference callable functions. In Python, methods are specific to object types—string methods, for example, work only on string objects.

In finer-grained detail, functions are packages of code, and method calls combine two operations at once (an attribute fetch, and a call):

Attribute fetches
> An expression of the form *object.attribute* means "fetch the value of *attribute* in *object*."

Call expressions
> An expression of the form *function(arguments)* means "invoke the code of *function*, passing zero or more comma-separated *argument* objects to it, and return *function*'s result value."

Putting these two together allows us to call a method of an object. The method call expression *object.method(arguments)* is evaluated from left to right—that is, Python will first fetch the *method* of the *object*, and then call it, passing in the *arguments*. If the method computes a result, it will come back as the result of the entire method-call expression.

As you'll see throughout this part of the book, most objects have callable methods, and all are accessed using this same method-call syntax. To call an object method, you have to go through an existing object. Let's move on to some examples to see how.

String Method Examples: Changing Strings

Table 7-4 summarizes the call patterns for built-in string methods (be sure to check Python's standard library manual for the most up-to-date list, or run a help call on any string interactively). String methods in this table implement higher-level operations such as splitting and joining, case conversions, content tests, and substring searches.

Table 7-4. String method calls

```
S.capitalize()                              S.ljust(width)
S.center(width)                             S.lower()
S.count(sub [, start [, end]])              S.lstrip()
S.encode([encoding [,errors]])              S.replace(old, new [, maxsplit])
S.endswith(suffix [, start [, end]])        S.rfind(sub [,start [,end]])
S.expandtabs([tabsize])                     S.rindex(sub [, start [, end]])
S.find(sub [, start [, end]])               S.rjust(width)
S.index(sub [, start [, end]])              S.rstrip()
S.isalnum()                                 S.split([sep [,maxsplit]])
S.isalpha()                                 S.splitlines([keepends])
S.isdigit()                                 S.startswith(prefix [, start [, end]])
S.islower()                                 S.strip()
S.isspace()                                 S.swapcase()
S.istitle()                                 S.title()
S.isupper()                                 S.translate(table [, delchars])
S.join(seq)                                 S.upper()
```

Now, let's work through some code that demonstrates some of the most commonly used methods in action, and illustrates Python text-processing basics along the way. As we've seen, because strings are immutable, they cannot be changed in-place directly. To make a new text value from an existing string, you construct a new string with operations such as slicing and concatenation. For example, to replace two characters in the middle of a string, you can use code like this:

```
>>> S = 'spammy'
>>> S = S[:3] + 'xx' + S[5:]
>>> S
'spaxxy'
```

But, if you're really just out to replace a substring, you can use the string `replace` method instead:

```
>>> S = 'spammy'
>>> S = S.replace('mm', 'xx')
>>> S
'spaxxy'
```

The `replace` method is more general than this code implies. It takes as arguments the original substring (of any length), and the string (of any length) to replace it with, and performs a global search and replace:

```
>>> 'aa$bb$cc$dd'.replace('$', 'SPAM')
'aaSPAMbbSPAMccSPAMdd'
```

In such a role, `replace` can be used as a tool to implement template replacements (e.g., in form letters). Notice that this time we simply printed the result, instead of assigning it to a name—you need to assign results to names only if you want to retain them for later use.

If you need to replace one fixed-size string that can occur at any offset, you can do a replacement again, or search for the substring with the string `find` method and then slice:

```
>>> S = 'xxxxSPAMxxxxSPAMxxxx'
>>> where = S.find('SPAM')              # Search for position
>>> where                               # Occurs at offset 4
4
>>> S = S[:where] + 'EGGS' + S[(where+4):]
>>> S
'xxxxEGGSxxxxSPAMxxxx'
```

The `find` method returns the offset where the substring appears (by default, searching from the front), or -1 if it is not found. Another option is to use `replace` with a third argument to limit it to a single substitution:

```
>>> S = 'xxxxSPAMxxxxSPAMxxxx'
>>> S.replace('SPAM', 'EGGS')           # Replace all
'xxxxEGGSxxxxEGGSxxxx'

>>> S.replace('SPAM', 'EGGS', 1)        # Replace one
'xxxxEGGSxxxxSPAMxxxx'
```

Notice that `replace` returns a new string object each time. Because strings are immutable, methods never really change the subject strings in-place, even if they are called "replace"!

The fact that concatenation operations and the `replace` method generate new string objects each time they are run is actually a potential downside of using them to change strings. If you have to apply many changes to a very large string, you might be able to improve your script's performance by converting the string to an object that does support in-place changes:

```
>>> S = 'spammy'
>>> L = list(S)
>>> L
['s', 'p', 'a', 'm', 'm', 'y']
```

The built-in list function (or an object construction call) builds a new list out of the items in any sequence—in this case, "exploding" the characters of a string into a list. Once the string is in this form, you can make multiple changes to it without generating a new copy for each change:

```
>>> L[3] = 'x'                          # Works for lists, not strings
>>> L[4] = 'x'
>>> L
['s', 'p', 'a', 'x', 'x', 'y']
```

If, after your changes, you need to convert back to a string (e.g., to write to a file), use the string join method to "implode" the list back into a string:

```
>>> S = ''.join(L)
>>> S
'spaxxy'
```

The join method may look a bit backward at first sight. Because it is a method of strings (not of lists), it is called through the desired delimiter. join puts the list's strings together, with the delimiter between list items; in this case, it uses an empty string delimiter to convert from a list back to a string. More generally, any string delimiter and list of strings will do:

```
>>> 'SPAM'.join(['eggs', 'sausage', 'ham', 'toast'])
'eggsSPAMsausageSPAMhamSPAMtoast'
```

String Method Examples: Parsing Text

Another common role for string methods is as a simple form of text *parsing*—that is, analyzing structure and extracting substrings. To extract substrings at fixed offsets, we can employ slicing techniques:

```
>>> line = 'aaa bbb ccc'
>>> col1 = line[0:3]
>>> col3 = line[8:]
>>> col1
'aaa'
>>> col3
'ccc'
```

Here, the columns of data appear at fixed offsets, and so may be sliced out of the original string. This technique passes for parsing, as long as the components of your data have fixed positions. If instead some sort of delimiter separates the data, you can pull out its components by splitting. This will work even if the data may show up at arbitrary positions within the string:

```
>>> line = 'aaa bbb  ccc'
>>> cols = line.split( )
>>> cols
['aaa', 'bbb', 'ccc']
```

The string split method chops up a string into a list of substrings, around a delimiter string. We didn't pass a delimiter in the prior example, so it defaults to whitespace—the string is split at groups of one or more spaces, tabs, and newlines, and we get back a list of the resulting substrings. In other applications, more tangible delimiters may separate the data. This example splits (and hence parses) the string at commas, a separator common in data returned by some database tools:

```
>>> line = 'bob,hacker,40'
>>> line.split(',')
['bob', 'hacker', '40']
```

Delimiters can be longer than a single character, too:

```
>>> line = "i'mSPAMaSPAMlumberjack"
>>> line.split("SPAM")
["i'm", 'a', 'lumberjack']
```

Although there are limits to the parsing potential of slicing and splitting, both run very fast, and can handle basic text-extraction chores.

Other Common String Methods in Action

Other string methods have more focused roles—for example, to strip off whitespace at the end of a line of text, perform case conversions, test content, and test for a substring at the end:

```
>>> line = "The knights who sy Ni!\n"
>>> line.rstrip( )
'The knights who sy Ni!'
>>> line.upper( )
'THE KNIGHTS WHO SY NI!\n'
>>> line.isalpha( )
False
>>> line.endswith('Ni!\n')
True
```

Alternative techniques can also sometimes be used to achieve the same results as string methods—the in membership operator can be used to test for the presence of a substring, for instance, and length and slicing operations can be used to mimic endswith:

```
>>> line
'The knights who sy Ni!\n'

>>> line.find('Ni') != -1      # Search via method call or expression
True
```

```
>>> 'Ni' in line
True

>>> sub = 'Ni!\n'
>>> line.endswith(sub)          # End test via method call or slice
True
>>> line[-len(sub):] == sub
True
```

Because there are so many methods available for strings, we won't look at every one here. You'll see some additional string examples later in this book, but for more details, you can also turn to the Python library manual and other documentation sources, or simply experiment interactively on your own.

Note that none of the string methods accepts patterns—for pattern-based text processing, you must use the Python re standard library module, an advanced tool that was introduced in Chapter 4, but is mostly outside the scope of this text. Because of this limitation, though, string methods sometimes run more quickly than the re module's tools.

The Original string Module

The history of Python's string methods is somewhat convoluted. For roughly the first decade of Python's existence, it provided a standard library module called string that contained functions that largely mirror the current set of string object methods. In response to user requests, in Python 2.0, these functions were made available as methods of string objects. Because so many people had written so much code that relied on the original string module, however, it was retained for backward compatibility.

Today, you should use only string methods, not the original string module. In fact, the original module-call forms of today's string methods are scheduled to be deleted from Python in Release 3.0, due out soon after this edition is published. However, because you may still see the module in use in older Python code, a brief look is in order here.

The upshot of this legacy is that in Python 2.5, there technically are still two ways to invoke advanced string operations: by calling object methods, or by calling string module functions, and passing in the object as an argument. For instance, given a variable X assigned to a string object, calling an object method:

```
X.method(arguments)
```

is usually equivalent to calling the same operation through the string module (provided that you have already imported the module):

```
string.method(X, arguments)
```

Here's an example of the method scheme in action:

```
>>> S = 'a+b+c+'
>>> x = S.replace('+', 'spam')
```

```
>>> x
'aspambspamcspam'
```

To access the same operation through the `string` module, you need to import the module (at least once in your process) and pass in the object:

```
>>> import string
>>> y = string.replace(S, '+', 'spam')
>>> y
'aspambspamcspam'
```

Because the module approach was the standard for so long, and because strings are such a central component of most programs, you will probably see both call patterns in Python code you come across.

Again, though, today you should use method calls instead of the older module calls. There are good reasons for this, besides the fact that the module calls are scheduled to go away in Release 3.0. For one thing, the module call scheme requires you to import the `string` module (methods do not require imports). For another, the module makes calls a few characters longer to type (when you load the module with `import`, that is, not using `from`). And, finally, the module runs more slowly than methods (the current module maps most calls back to the methods and so incurs an extra call along the way).

The original `string` module will probably be retained in Python 3.0 because it contains additional tools, including predefined string constants, and a template object system (an advanced tool omitted here—see the Python library manual for details on template objects). Unless you really want to change your code when 3.0 rolls out, though, you should consider the basic string operation calls in it to be just ghosts from the past.

General Type Categories

Now that we've explored the first of Python's collection objects, the string, let's pause to define a few general type concepts that will apply to most of the types we look at from here on. With regard to built-in types, it turns out that operations work the same for all the types in the same category, so we'll only need to define most of these ideas once. We've only examined numbers and strings so far, but because they are representative of two of the three major type categories in Python, you already know more about other types than you might think.

Types Share Operation Sets by Categories

As you've learned, strings are immutable sequences: they cannot be changed in-place (the *immutable* part), and they are positionally ordered collections that are accessed by offset (the *sequence* part). Now, it so happens that all the sequences we'll study in this part of the book respond to the same sequence operations shown in this chapter at work on strings—concatenation, indexing, iteration, and so on. More formally, there are three type (and operation) categories in Python:

Numbers
Support addition, multiplication, etc.

Sequences
Support indexing, slicing, concatenation, etc.

Mappings
Support indexing by key, etc.

We haven't yet explored mappings on our in-depth tour (dictionaries are discussed in the next chapter), but the other types we encounter will mostly be more of the same. For example, for any sequence objects X and Y:

- X + Y makes a new sequence object with the contents of both operands.
- X * N makes a new sequence object with N copies of the sequence operand X.

In other words, these operations work the same on any kind of sequence, including strings, lists, tuples, and some user-defined object types. The only difference is that the new result object you get back is the same type as the operands X and Y—if you concatenate lists, you get back a new list, not a string. Indexing, slicing, and other sequence operations work the same on all sequences, too; the type of the objects being processed tells Python which task to perform.

Mutable Types Can Be Changed In-Place

The immutable classification is an important constraint to be aware of, yet it tends to trip up new users. If an object type is immutable, you cannot change its value in-place; Python raises an error if you try. Instead, you must run code to make a new object containing the new value. Generally, immutable types give some degree of integrity by guaranteeing that an object won't be changed by another part of a program. For a refresher on why this matters, see the discussion of shared object references in Chapter 6.

Chapter Summary

In this chapter, we took an in-depth tour of the string object type. We learned about coding string literals, and explored string operations, including sequence expressions, string formatting, and string method calls. Along the way, we studied a variety of concepts in depth, such as slicing, method calls, and triple-quoted block strings. We also defined some core ideas common to a variety of types: sequences, for example, share an entire set of operations. In the next chapter, we'll continue our types tour with a look at the most general object collections in Python—the list and dictionary. As you'll find, much of what you've learned here will apply to those types as well. First, though, here's another chapter quiz to review the material introduced here.

Chapter Quiz

1. Can the string find method be used to search a list?
2. Can a string slice expression be used on a list?
3. How would you convert a character to its ASCII integer code? How would you convert the other way, from an integer to a character?
4. How might you go about changing a string in Python?
5. Given a string S with the value "s,pa,m", name two ways to extract the two characters in the middle.
6. How many characters are there in the string "a\nb\x1f\000d"?
7. Why might you use the string module instead of string method calls?

Quiz Answers

1. No, because methods are always type-specific; that is, they only work on a single data type. Expressions are generic, though, and may work on a variety of types. In this case, for instance, the in membership expression has a similar effect, and can be used to search both strings and lists.
2. Yes. Unlike methods, expressions are generic, and apply to many types. In this case, the slice expression is really a sequence operation—it works on any type of sequence object, including strings, lists, and tuples. The only difference is that when you slice a list, you get back a new list.
3. The built-in ord(S) function converts from a one-character string to an integer character code; chr(I) converts from the integer code back to a string.
4. Strings cannot be changed; they are immutable. However, you can achieve a similar effect by creating a new string—by concatenating, slicing, running formatting expressions, or using a method call like replace—and then assigning the result back to the original variable name.
5. You can slice the string using S[2:4], or split on the comma and index the string using S.split(',')[1]. Try these interactively to see for yourself.
6. Six. The string "a\nb\x1f\000d" contains the bytes a, newline (\n), b, binary 31 (a hex escape \x1f), binary 0 (an octal escape \000), and d. Pass the string to the built-in len function to verify this, and print each of its characters' ord results to see the actual byte values. See Table 7-2 for more details.
7. You should never use the string module instead of string object method calls today—it's deprecated, and its calls are slated for removal in Python 3.0. The only reason for using the string module at all is for its other tools, such as predefined constants, and advanced template objects.

CHAPTER 8

Lists and Dictionaries

[ ]   { }

This chapter presents the list and dictionary object types, both of which are collections of other objects. These two types are the main workhorses in almost all Python scripts. As you'll see, both types are remarkably flexible: they can be changed in-place, can grow and shrink on demand, and may contain and be nested in any other kind of object. By leveraging these types, you can build up and process arbitrarily rich information structures in your scripts.

Lists

The next stop on our built-in object tour is the Python *list*. Lists are Python's most flexible ordered collection object type. Unlike strings, lists can contain any sort of object: numbers, strings, and even other lists. Also, unlike strings, lists may be changed in-place by assignment to offsets and slices, list method calls, deletion statements, and more—they are mutable objects.

Python lists do the work of most of the collection data structures you might have to implement manually in lower-level languages such as C. Here is a quick look at their main properties. Python lists are:

Ordered collections of arbitrary objects
> From a functional view, lists are just places to collect other objects so you can treat them as groups. Lists also maintain a left-to-right positional ordering among the items they contain (i.e., they are sequences).

Accessed by offset
> Just as with strings, you can fetch a component object out of a list by indexing the list on the object's offset. Because items in lists are ordered by their positions, you can also do tasks such as slicing and concatenation.

Variable-length, heterogeneous, and arbitrarily nestable

Unlike strings, lists can grow and shrink in-place (their lengths can vary), and can contain any sort of object, not just one-character strings (they're heterogeneous). Because lists can contain other complex objects, they also support arbitrary nesting; you can create lists of lists of lists, and so on.

Of the category mutable sequence

In terms of our type category qualifiers, lists can be changed in-place (they're mutable), and can respond to all the sequence operations used with strings, such as indexing, slicing, and concatenation. In fact, sequence operations work the same on lists as they do on strings; the only difference is that sequence operations such as concatenation and slicing return new lists instead of new strings when applied to lists. Because lists are mutable, however, they also support other operations that strings don't (such as deletion and index assignment operations, which change the lists in-place).

Arrays of object references

Technically, Python lists contain zero or more references to other objects. Lists might remind you of arrays of pointers (addresses). Fetching an item from a Python list is about as fast as indexing a C array; in fact, lists really are C arrays inside the standard Python interpreter, not linked structures. As we learned in Chapter 6, though, Python always follows a reference to an object whenever the reference is used, so your program deals only with objects. Whenever you assign an object to a data structure component or variable name, Python always stores a reference to that same object, not a copy of it (unless you request a copy explicitly).

Table 8-1 summarizes common and representative list object operations. As usual, for the full story, see the Python standard library manual, or run a help(list) or dir(list) call interactively for a full list of list methods—you can pass in a real list, or the word list, which is the name of the list data type.

Table 8-1. Common list literals and operations

Operation	Interpretation
L1 = []	An empty list
L2 = [0, 1, 2, 3]	Four items: indexes 0..3
L3 = ['abc', ['def', 'ghi']]	Nested sublists
L2[i] L3[i][j] L2[i:j] len(L2)	Index, index of index, slice, length
L1 + L2 L2 * 3	Concatenate, repeat

Table 8-1. Common list literals and operations (continued)

Operation	Interpretation
`for x in L2` `3 in L2`	Iteration, membership

`L2.append(4)`
`L2.extend([5,6,7])`
`L2.sort( )`
`L2.index(1)`
`L2.insert(I, X)`
`L2.reverse( )`
	Methods: grow, sort, search, insert, reverse, etc.

`del L2[k]`
`del L2[i:j]`
`L2.pop( )`
`L2.remove(2)`
`L2[i:j] = []`
	Shrinking

`L2[i] = 1` `L2[i:j] = [4,5,6]`	Index assignment, slice assignment
`range(4)` `xrange(0, 4)`	Make lists/tuples of integers
`L4 = [x**2 for x in range(5)]`	List comprehensions (Chapters 13 and 17)

When written down as a literal expression, a list is coded as a series of objects (really, expressions that return objects) in square brackets, separated by commas. For instance, the second row in Table 8-1 assigns the variable L2 to a four-item list. A nested list is coded as a nested square-bracketed series (row 3), and the empty list is just a square-bracket pair with nothing inside (row 1).*

Many of the operations in Table 8-1 should look familiar, as they are the same sequence operations we put to work on strings—indexing, concatenation, iteration, and so on. Lists also respond to list-specific method calls (which provide utilities such as sorting, reversing, adding items to the end, etc.), as well as in-place change operations (deleting items, assignment to indexes and slices, and so forth). Lists get these tools for change operations because they are a mutable object type.

Lists in Action

Perhaps the best way to understand lists is to see them at work. Let's once again turn to some simple interpreter interactions to illustrate the operations in Table 8-1.

Basic List Operations

Lists respond to the + and * operators much like strings; they mean concatenation and repetition here too, except that the result is a new list, not a string. In fact, lists

---

* In practice, you won't see many lists written out like this in list-processing programs. It's more common to see code that processes lists constructed dynamically (at runtime). In fact, although it's important to master literal syntax, most data structures in Python are built by running program code at runtime.

respond to all of the general sequence operations we used on strings in the prior chapter:

```
% python
>>> len([1, 2, 3])              # Length
3
>>> [1, 2, 3] + [4, 5, 6]       # Concatenation
[1, 2, 3, 4, 5, 6]
>>> ['Ni!'] * 4                 # Repetition
['Ni!', 'Ni!', 'Ni!', 'Ni!']
>>> 3 in [1, 2, 3]              # Membership
True
>>> for x in [1, 2, 3]: print x,   # Iteration
...
1 2 3
```

We will talk more about for iteration and the range built-ins in Chapter 13 because they are related to statement syntax. In short, for loops step through items in a sequence from left to right, executing one or more statements for each item. The last entry in Table 8-1, which is list comprehensions, are covered in Chapter 13, and expanded on in Chapter 17; as introduced in Chapter 4, they are a way to build a list by applying an expression to each item in a sequence, in a single step.

Although the + operator works the same for lists and strings, it's important to know that it expects the same sort of sequence on both sides—otherwise, you get a type error when the code runs. For instance, you cannot concatenate a list and a string unless you first convert the list to a string (using tools such as backquotes, str, or % formatting), or convert the string to a list (the list built-in function does the trick):

```
>>> str([1, 2]) + "34"          # Same as "[1, 2]" + "34"
'[1, 2]34'
>>> [1, 2] + list("34")         # Same as [1, 2] + ["3", "4"]
[1, 2, '3', '4']
```

Indexing, Slicing, and Matrixes

Because lists are sequences, indexing and slicing work the same way for lists as they do for strings. However, the result of indexing a list is whatever type of object lives at the offset you specify, while slicing a list always returns a new list:

```
>>> L = ['spam', 'Spam', 'SPAM!']
>>> L[2]                        # Offsets start at zero
'SPAM!'
>>> L[-2]                       # Negative: count from the right
'Spam'
>>> L[1:]                       # Slicing fetches sections
['Spam', 'SPAM!']
```

One note here: because you can nest lists (and other object types) within lists, you will sometimes need to string together index operations to go deeper into a data structure.

For example, one of the simplest ways to represent matrixes (multidimensional arrays) in Python is as lists with nested sublists. Here's a basic 3×3 two-dimensional list-based array:

```
>>> matrix = [[1, 2, 3], [4, 5, 6], [7, 8, 9]]
```

With one index, you get an entire row (really, a nested sublist), and with two, you get an item within the row:

```
>>> matrix[1]
[4, 5, 6]
>>> matrix[1][1]
5
>>> matrix[2][0]
7
>>> matrix = [[1, 2, 3],
...           [4, 5, 6],
...           [7, 8, 9]]
>>> matrix[1][1]
5
```

Notice in the preceding interaction that lists can naturally span multiple lines if you want them to because they are contained by a pair of brackets (more on syntax in the next part of the book). Later in this chapter, you'll also see a dictionary-based matrix representation. For high-powered numeric work, the NumPy extension mentioned in Chapter 5 provides other ways to handle matrixes.

Changing Lists In-Place

Because lists are mutable, they support operations that change a list object *in-place*. That is, the operations in this section all modify the list object directly, without forcing you to make a new copy, as you had to for strings. Because Python deals only in object references, this distinction between changing an object in-place and creating a new object matters—as discussed in Chapter 6, if you change an object in-place, you might impact more than one reference to it at the same time.

Index and slice assignments

When using a list, you can change its contents by assigning to a particular item (offset), or an entire section (slice):

```
>>> L = ['spam', 'Spam', 'SPAM!']
>>> L[1] = 'eggs'                    # Index assignment
>>> L
['spam', 'eggs', 'SPAM!']
>>> L[0:2] = ['eat', 'more']         # Slice assignment: delete+insert
>>> L                                # Replaces items 0,1
['eat', 'more', 'SPAM!']
```

Both index and slice assignments are in-place changes—they modify the subject list directly, rather than generating a new list object for the result. Index assignment in Python works much as it does in C and most other languages: Python replaces the object reference at the designated offset with a new one.

Slice assignment, the last operation in the preceding example, replaces an entire section of a list in a single step. Because it can be a bit complex, it is perhaps best thought of as a combination of two steps:

1. *Deletion*. The slice you specify to the left of the = is deleted.

2. *Insertion*. The new items contained in the object to the right of the = are inserted into the list on the left, at the place where the old slice was deleted.*

This isn't what really happens, but it tends to help clarify why the number of items inserted doesn't have to match the number of items deleted. For instance, given a list L that has the value [1,2,3], the assignment L[1:2]=[4,5] sets L to the list [1,4,5,3]. Python first deletes the 2 (a one-item slice), then inserts the 4 and 5 where the deleted 2 used to be. This also explains why L[1:2]=[] is really a deletion operation—Python deletes the slice (the item at offset 1), and then inserts nothing.

In effect, slice assignment replaces an entire section, or "column," all at once. Because the length of the sequence being assigned does not have to match the length of the slice being assigned to, slice assignment can be used to replace (by overwriting), expand (by inserting), or shrink (by deleting) the subject list. It's a powerful operation, but frankly, one that you may not see very often in practice. There are usually more straightforward ways to replace, insert, and delete (concatenation, and the insert, pop, and remove list methods, for example), which Python programmers tend to prefer in practice.

List method calls

Like strings, Python list objects also support type-specific method calls:

```
>>> L.append('please')              # Append method call
>>> L
['eat', 'more', 'SPAM!', 'please']
>>> L.sort()                        # Sort list items ('S' < 'e')
>>> L
['SPAM!', 'eat', 'more', 'please']
```

Methods were introduced in Chapter 7. In brief, they are functions (really, attributes that reference functions) that are associated with particular objects. Methods provide type-specific tools; the list methods presented here, for instance, are available only for lists.

---

* This description needs elaboration when the value and the slice being assigned overlap: L[2:5]=L[3:6], for instance, works fine because the value to be inserted is fetched before the deletion happens on the left.

Perhaps the most commonly used list method is append, which simply tacks a single item (object reference) onto the end of the list. Unlike concatenation, append expects you to pass in a single object, not a list. The effect of L.append(X) is similar to L+[X], but while the former changes L in-place, the latter makes a new list.* Another commonly seen method, sort, orders a list in-place; by default, it uses Python standard comparison tests (here, string comparisons), and sorts in ascending order. You can also pass in a comparison function of your own to sort.

 In Python 2.5 and earlier, comparisons of differently typed objects (e.g., a string and a list) work—the language defines a fixed ordering among different types, which is deterministic, if not aesthetically pleasing. That is, this ordering is based on the names of the types involved: all integers are less than all strings, for example, because "int" is less than "str". Comparisons never automatically convert types, except when comparing numeric type objects.

In Python 3.0, this may change: comparison of mixed types is scheduled to raise an exception instead of falling back on the fixed cross-type ordering. Because sorting uses comparisons internally, this means that [1, 2, 'spam'].sort( ) succeeds in Python 2.x, but will raise an exception as of Python 3.0. See the 3.0 release notes for more details.

One warning here: beware that append and sort change the associated list object in-place, but don't return the list as a result (technically, they both return a value called None). If you say something like L=L.append(X), you won't get the modified value of L (in fact, you'll lose the reference to the list altogether); when you use attributes such as append and sort, objects are changed as a side effect, so there's no reason to reassign.

Like strings, lists have other methods that perform other specialized operations. For instance, reverse reverses the list in-place, and the extend and pop methods insert multiple items at the end, and delete an item from the end of the list, respectively:

```
>>> L = [1, 2]
>>> L.extend([3,4,5])          # Append multiple items
>>> L
[1, 2, 3, 4, 5]
>>> L.pop( )                    # Delete and return last item
5
>>> L
[1, 2, 3, 4]
>>> L.reverse( )                # In-place reversal
>>> L
[4, 3, 2, 1]
```

* Unlike + concatenation, append doesn't have to generate new objects, so it's usually faster. You can also mimic append with clever slice assignments: L[len(L):]=[X] is like L.append(X), and L[:0]=[X] is like appending at the front of a list. Both delete an empty slice and insert X, changing L in-place quickly, like append.

In some types of programs, the list pop method used here is often used in conjunction with append to implement a quick last-in-first-out (LIFO) *stack* structure. The end of the list serves as the top of the stack:

```
>>> L = []
>>> L.append(1)                    # Push onto stack
>>> L.append(2)
>>> L
[1, 2]
>>> L.pop( )                       # Pop off stack
2
>>> L
[1]
```

Although not shown here, the pop method also accepts an optional offset of the item to be deleted and returned (the default is the last item). Other list methods remove an item by value (remove), insert an item at an offset (insert), search for an item's offset (index), and more; see other documentation sources, or experiment with these calls interactively on your own to learn more.

Other common list operations

Because lists are mutable, you can use the del statement to delete an item or section in-place:

```
>>> L
['SPAM!', 'eat', 'more', 'please']
>>> del L[0]                       # Delete one item
>>> L
['eat', 'more', 'please']
>>> del L[1:]                      # Delete an entire section
>>> L                              # Same as L[1:] = []
['eat']
```

Because slice assignment is a deletion plus an insertion, you can also delete a section of a list by assigning an empty list to a slice (L[i:j]=[]); Python deletes the slice named on the left, and then inserts nothing. Assigning an empty list to an index, on the other hand, just stores a reference to the empty list in the specified slot, rather than deleting it:

```
>>> L = ['Already', 'got', 'one']
>>> L[1:] = []
>>> L
['Already']
>>> L[0] = []
>>> L
[[]]
```

Although all the operations just discussed are typical, there are additional list methods and operations not illustrated here (including methods for inserting and searching). For a comprehensive and up-to-date list of type tools, you should always consult

Python's manuals, Python's dir and help functions (which we first met in Chapter 4), or the *Python Pocket Reference* (O'Reilly), and other reference texts described in the Preface.

I'd also like to remind you one more time that all the in-place change operations discussed here work only for mutable objects: they won't work on strings (or tuples, discussed in the next chapter), no matter how hard you try. Mutability is an inherent property of each object type.

Dictionaries

Apart from lists, *dictionaries* are perhaps the most flexible built-in data type in Python. If you think of lists as ordered collections of objects, you can think of dictionaries as unordered collections; the chief distinction is that in dictionaries, items are stored and fetched by *key*, instead of by positional offset.

Being a built-in type, dictionaries can replace many of the searching algorithms and data structures you might have to implement manually in lower-level languages—indexing a dictionary is a very fast search operation. Dictionaries also sometimes do the work of records and symbol tables used in other languages, can represent sparse (mostly empty) data structures, and much more. Here's a rundown of their main properties. Python dictionaries are:

Accessed by key, not offset
> Dictionaries are sometimes called *associative arrays* or *hashes*. They associate a set of values with keys, so you can fetch an item out of a dictionary using the key under which you originally stored it. You use the same indexing operation to get components in a dictionary as in a list, but the index takes the form of a key, not a relative offset.

Unordered collections of arbitrary objects
> Unlike in a list, items stored in a dictionary aren't kept in any particular order; in fact, Python randomizes their left-to-right order to provide quick lookup. Keys provide the symbolic (not physical) locations of items in a dictionary.

Variable-length, heterogeneous, and arbitrarily nestable
> Like lists, dictionaries can grow and shrink in-place (without new copies being made), they can contain objects of any type, and they support nesting to any depth (they can contain lists, other dictionaries, and so on).

Of the category mutable mapping
> Dictionaries can be changed in-place by assigning to indexes (they are mutable), but they don't support the sequence operations that work on strings and lists. Because dictionaries are unordered collections, operations that depend on a fixed positional order (e.g., concatenation, slicing) don't make sense. Instead, dictionaries are the only built-in representatives of the mapping type category (objects that map keys to values).

Tables of object references (hash tables)
   If lists are arrays of object references that support access by position, dictionaries
   are unordered tables of object references that support access by key. Internally,
   dictionaries are implemented as hash tables (data structures that support very fast
   retrieval), which start small and grow on demand. Moreover, Python employs
   optimized hashing algorithms to find keys, so retrieval is quick. Like lists, dictionaries store object references (not copies).

Table 8-2 summarizes some of the most common and representative dictionary operations (again, see the library manual or run a dir(dict) or help(dict) call for a
complete list—dict is the name of the type). When coded as a literal expression, a
dictionary is written as a series of key:value pairs, separated by commas, enclosed in
curly braces.* An empty dictionary is an empty set of braces, and dictionaries can be
nested by writing one as a value inside another dictionary, or within a list or tuple.

Table 8-2. Common dictionary literals and operations

Operation	Interpretation
D1 = {}	Empty dictionary
D2 = {'spam': 2, 'eggs': 3}	Two-item dictionary
D3 = {'food': {'ham': 1, 'egg': 2}}	Nesting
D2['eggs'] D3['food']['ham']	Indexing by key
D2.has_key('eggs') 'eggs' in D2 D2.keys() D2.values() D2.copy() D2.get(key, default) D2.update(D1) D2.pop(key)	Methods: membership test, keys list, values list, copies, defaults, merge, delete, etc.
len(D1)	Length (number of stored entries)
D2[key] = 42 del D2[key]	Adding/changing keys, deleting keys
D4 = dict.fromkeys(['a', 'b']) D5 = dict(zip(keyslist, valslist)) D6 = dict(name='Bob', age=42)	Alternative construction techniques

Dictionaries in Action

As Table 8-2 suggests, dictionaries are indexed by key, and nested dictionary entries
are referenced by a series of indexes (keys in square brackets). When Python creates

---

* As with lists, you won't often see dictionaries constructed using literals. Lists and dictionaries are grown in
  different ways, though. As you'll see in the next section, dictionaries are typically built up by assigning to
  new keys at runtime; this approach fails for lists (lists are grown with append instead).

a dictionary, it stores its items in any left-to-right order it chooses; to fetch a value back, you supply the key with which it is associated. Let's go back to the interpreter to get a feel for some of the dictionary operations in Table 8-2.

Basic Dictionary Operations

In normal operation, you create dictionaries, and store and access items by key:

```
% python
>>> d2 = {'spam': 2, 'ham': 1, 'eggs': 3}    # Make a dictionary
>>> d2['spam']                                 # Fetch a value by key
2
>>> d2                                         # Order is scrambled
{'eggs': 3, 'ham': 1, 'spam': 2}
```

Here, the dictionary is assigned to the variable d2; the value of the key 'spam' is the integer 2, and so on. We use the same square bracket syntax to index dictionaries by key as we did to index lists by offset, but here it means access by key, not by position.

Notice the end of this example: the left-to-right order of keys in a dictionary will almost always be different from what you originally typed. This is on purpose—to implement fast key lookup (a.k.a. hashing), keys need to be randomized in memory. That's why operations that assume a fixed left-to-right order (e.g., slicing, concatenation) do not apply to dictionaries; you can fetch values only by key, not by position.

The built-in len function works on dictionaries, too; it returns the number of items stored in the dictionary or, equivalently, the length of its keys list. The dictionary has_key method and the in membership operator allow you to test for key existence, and the keys method returns all the keys in the dictionary, collected in a list. The latter of these can be useful for processing dictionaries sequentially, but you shouldn't depend on the order of the keys list. Because the keys result is a normal list, however, it can always be sorted if order matters:

```
>>> len(d2)                      # Number of entries in dictionary
3
>>> d2.has_key('ham')            # Key membership test
True
>>> 'ham' in d2                  # Key membership test alternative
True
>>> d2.keys()                    # Create a new list of my keys
['eggs', 'ham', 'spam']
```

Notice the third expression in this listing. As mentioned earlier, the in membership test used for strings and lists also works on dictionaries—it checks whether a key is stored in the dictionary, like the has_key method call of the prior line. Technically, this works because dictionaries define *iterators* that step through their keys lists. Other types provide iterators that reflect their common uses; files, for example, have iterators that read line by line. We'll discuss iterators further in Chapters 17 and 24.

Later in this chapter and book, you'll learn about two alternative ways to build dictionaries, demonstrated at the end of Table 8-2: you can pass zipped lists of key/value tuples or keyword function arguments to the new dict call (really, a type constructor). We'll explore keyword arguments in Chapter 16. We'll also discuss the zip function in Chapter 13; it's a way to construct a dictionary from key and value lists in a single call. If you cannot predict the set of keys and values in your code, for instance, you can always build them up as lists and zip them together dynamically.

Changing Dictionaries In-Place

Let's continue with our interactive session. Dictionaries, like lists, are mutable, so you can change, expand, and shrink them in-place without making new dictionaries: simply assign a value to a key to change or create an entry. The del statement works here, too; it deletes the entry associated with the key specified as an index. Notice also the nesting of a list inside a dictionary in this example (the value of the key 'ham'). All collection data types in Python can nest inside each other arbitrarily:

```
>>> d2['ham'] = ['grill', 'bake', 'fry']        # Change entry
>>> d2
{'eggs': 3, 'spam': 2, 'ham': ['grill', 'bake', 'fry']}

>>> del d2['eggs']                               # Delete entry
>>> d2
{'spam': 2, 'ham': ['grill', 'bake', 'fry']}

>>> d2['brunch'] = 'Bacon'                       # Add new entry
>>> d2
{'brunch': 'Bacon', 'spam': 2, 'ham': ['grill', 'bake', 'fry']}
```

As with lists, assigning to an existing index in a dictionary changes its associated value. Unlike with lists, however, whenever you assign a *new* dictionary key (one that hasn't been assigned before), you create a new entry in the dictionary, as was done in the previous example for the key 'brunch.' This doesn't work for lists because Python considers an offset beyond the end of a list out of bounds and throws an error. To expand a list, you need to use tools such as the append method or slice assignment instead.

More Dictionary Methods

Dictionary methods provide a variety of tools. For instance, the dictionary values and items methods return lists of the dictionary's values and (key,value) pair tuples, respectively:

```
>>> d2 = {'spam': 2, 'ham': 1, 'eggs': 3}
>>> d2.values()
[3, 1, 2]
>>> d2.items()
[('eggs', 3), ('ham', 1), ('spam', 2)]
```

Such lists are useful in loops that need to step through dictionary entries one by one. Fetching a nonexistent key is normally an error, but the get method returns a default value (None, or a passed-in default) if the key doesn't exist. It's an easy way to fill in a default for a key that isn't present and avoid a missing-key error:

```
>>> d2.get('spam')                          # A key that is there
2
>>> print d2.get('toast')                     # A key that is missing
None
>>> d2.get('toast', 88)
88
```

The update method provides something similar to concatenation for dictionaries. It merges the keys and values of one dictionary into another, blindly overwriting values of the same key:

```
>>> d2
{'eggs': 3, 'ham': 1, 'spam': 2}
>>> d3 = {'toast':4, 'muffin':5}
>>> d2.update(d3)
>>> d2
{'toast': 4, 'muffin': 5, 'eggs': 3, 'ham': 1, 'spam': 2}
```

Finally, the dictionary pop method deletes a key from a dictionary, and returns the value it had. It's similar to the list pop method, but it takes a key instead of an optional position:

```
# pop a dictionary by key

>>> d2
{'toast': 4, 'muffin': 5, 'eggs': 3, 'ham': 1, 'spam': 2}
>>> d2.pop('muffin')
5
>>> d2.pop('toast')                            # Delete and return from a key
4
>>> d2
{'eggs': 3, 'ham': 1, 'spam': 2}

# pop a list by position

>>> L = ['aa', 'bb', 'cc', 'dd']
>>> L.pop()                                    # Delete and return from the end
'dd'
>>> L
['aa', 'bb', 'cc']
>>> L.pop(1)                                   # Delete from a specific position
'bb'
>>> L
['aa', 'cc']
```

Dictionaries also provide a copy method; we'll discuss this in the next chapter, as it's a way to avoid the potential side effects of shared references to the same dictionary. In fact, dictionaries come with many more methods than those listed in Table 8-2; see the Python library manual, or other documentation sources for a comprehensive list.

A Languages Table

Let's look at a more realistic dictionary example. The following example creates a table that maps programming language names (the keys) to their creators (the values). You fetch creator names by indexing on language names:

```
>>> table = {'Python':  'Guido van Rossum',
...          'Perl':    'Larry Wall',
...          'Tcl':     'John Ousterhout' }
...
>>> language = 'Python'
>>> creator  = table[language]
>>> creator
'Guido van Rossum'

>>> for lang in table.keys():
...     print lang, '\t', table[lang]
...
Tcl     John Ousterhout
Python  Guido van Rossum
Perl    Larry Wall
```

The last command uses a for loop, which we haven't covered in detail yet. If you aren't familiar with for loops, this command simply iterates through each key in the table, and prints a tab-separated list of keys and their values. We'll learn more about for loops in Chapter 13.

Because dictionaries aren't sequences, you can't iterate over them directly with a for statement in the way you can with strings and lists. But, if you need to step through the items in a dictionary, it's easy: calling the dictionary keys method returns a list of all stored keys, which you can iterate through with a for. If needed, you can index from key to value inside the for loop, as was done in this code.

In fact, Python also lets you step through a dictionary's keys list without actually calling the keys method in most for loops. For any dictionary D, saying for key in D: works the same as saying the complete for key in D.keys():. This is really just another instance of the iterators mentioned earlier, which allow the in membership operator to work on dictionaries as well (more on iterators later in this book).

Dictionary Usage Notes

Dictionaries are fairly straightforward tools once you get the hang of them, but here are a few additional pointers and reminders you should be aware of when using them:

- *Sequence operations don't work.* Dictionaries are mappings, not sequences; because there's no notion of ordering among their items, things like concatenation (an ordered joining), and slicing (extracting a contiguous section) simply don't apply. In fact, Python raises an error when your code runs if you try to do such things.

- *Assigning to new indexes adds entries.* Keys can be created when you write a dictionary literal (in which case they are embedded in the literal itself), or when you assign values to new keys of an existing dictionary object. The end result is the same.

- *Keys need not always be strings.* Our examples used strings as keys, but any other *immutable* objects (i.e., not lists) work just as well. For instance, you can use integers as keys, which makes the dictionary look much like a list (when indexing, at least). Tuples are sometimes used as dictionary keys too, allowing for compound key values. Class instance objects (discussed in Part VI) can be used as keys too, as long as they have the proper protocol methods; roughly, they need to tell Python that their values won't change, as otherwise they would be useless as fixed keys.

Using dictionaries to simulate flexible lists

The last point in the prior list is important enough to demonstrate with a few examples. When you use lists, it is illegal to assign to an offset that is off the end of the list:

```
>>> L = []
>>> L[99] = 'spam'
Traceback (most recent call last):
  File "<stdin>", line 1, in ?
IndexError: list assignment index out of range
```

Although you can use repetition to preallocate as big a list as you'll need (e.g., [0]*100), you can also do something that looks similar with dictionaries, which does not require such space allocations. By using integer keys, dictionaries can emulate lists that seem to grow on offset assignment:

```
>>> D = {}
>>> D[99] = 'spam'
>>> D[99]
'spam'
>>> D
{99: 'spam'}
```

Here, it looks as if D is a 100-item list, but it's really a dictionary with a single entry; the value of the key 99 is the string 'spam'. You can access this structure with offsets much like a list, but you don't have to allocate space for all the positions you might ever need to assign values to in the future. When used like this, dictionaries are like more flexible equivalents of lists.

Using dictionaries for sparse data structures

In a similar way, dictionary keys are also commonly leveraged to implement *sparse* data structures—for example, multidimensional arrays where only a few positions have values stored in them:

```
>>> Matrix = {}
>>> Matrix[(2, 3, 4)] = 88
>>> Matrix[(7, 8, 9)] = 99
>>>
>>> X = 2; Y = 3; Z = 4          # ; separates statements
>>> Matrix[(X, Y, Z)]
88
>>> Matrix
{(2, 3, 4): 88, (7, 8, 9): 99}
```

Here, we've used a dictionary to represent a three-dimensional array that is empty except for the two positions (2,3,4) and (7,8,9). The keys are *tuples* that record the coordinates of nonempty slots. Rather than allocating a large and mostly empty three-dimensional matrix, we can use a simple two-item dictionary. In this scheme, accessing an empty slot triggers a nonexistent key exception, as these slots are not physically stored:

```
>>> Matrix[(2,3,6)]
Traceback (most recent call last):
  File "<stdin>", line 1, in ?
KeyError: (2, 3, 6)
```

Avoiding missing-key errors

Errors for nonexistent key fetches are common in sparse matrixes, but you probably won't want them to shut down your program. There are at least three ways to fill in a default value instead of getting such an error message—you can test for keys ahead of time in if statements, use a try statement to catch and recover from the exception explicitly, or simply use the dictionary get method shown earlier to provide a default for keys that do not exist:

```
>>> if Matrix.has_key((2,3,6)):      # Check for key before fetch
...     print Matrix[(2,3,6)]
... else:
...     print 0
...
0
```

```
>>> try:
...     print Matrix[(2,3,6)]        # Try to index
... except KeyError:                 # Catch and recover
...     print 0
...
0
>>> Matrix.get((2,3,4), 0)           # Exists; fetch and return
88
>>> Matrix.get((2,3,6), 0)           # Doesn't exist; use default arg
0
```

Of these, the get method is the most concise in terms of coding requirements; we'll study the if and try statements in more detail later in this book.

Using dictionaries as "records"

As you can see, dictionaries can play many roles in Python. In general, they can replace search data structures (because indexing by key is a search operation), and can represent many types of structured information. For example, dictionaries are one of many ways to describe the properties of an item in your program's domain; that is, they can serve the same role as "records" or "structs" in other languages.

This example fills out a dictionary by assigning to new keys over time:

```
>>> rec = {}
>>> rec['name'] = 'mel'
>>> rec['age']  = 45
>>> rec['job']  = 'trainer/writer'
>>>
>>> print rec['name']
mel
```

Especially when nested, Python's built-in data types allow us to easily represent structured information. This example again uses a dictionary to capture object properties, but it codes it all at once (rather than assigning to each key separately), and nests a list and a dictionary to represent structured property values:

```
>>> mel = {'name': 'Mark',
...        'jobs': ['trainer', 'writer'],
...        'web':  'www.rmi.net/~lutz',
...        'home': {'state': 'CO', 'zip':80513}}
...
```

To fetch components of nested objects, simply string together indexing operations:

```
>>> mel['name']
'Mark'
>>> mel['jobs']
['trainer', 'writer']
>>> mel['jobs'][1]
'writer'
>>> mel['home']['zip']
80513
```

Other ways to make dictionaries

Finally, note that because dictionaries are so useful, more ways to build them have emerged over time. In Python 2.3 and later, for example, the last two calls to the dict constructor in the following have the same effect as the literal and key-assignment forms above them:

```
{'name': 'mel', 'age': 45}                # Traditional literal expression

D = {}                                    # Assign by keys dynamically
D['name'] = 'mel'
D['age']  = 45

dict(name='mel', age=45)                  # Keyword argument form

dict([('name', 'mel'), ('age', 45)])      # Key/value tuples form
```

All four of these forms create the same two-key dictionary:

- The first is handy if you can spell out the entire dictionary ahead of time.
- The second is of use if you need to create the dictionary one field at a time on the fly.
- The third keyword form is less code to type than literals, but it requires all keys to be strings.
- The last form here is useful if you need to build up keys and values as sequences at runtime.

Why You Will Care: Dictionary Interfaces

Besides being a convenient way to store information by key in your programs, some Python extensions also present interfaces that look like and work the same as dictionaries. For instance, Python's interface to DBM access-by-key files looks much like a dictionary that must be opened. Strings are stored and fetched using key indexes:

```
import anydbm
file = anydbm.open("filename")  # Link to file
file['key'] = 'data'            # Store data by key
data = file['key']              # Fetch data by key
```

Later, you'll see that you can store entire Python objects this way, too, if you replace anydbm in the preceding code with shelve (shelves are access-by-key databases of persistent Python objects). For Internet work, Python's CGI script support also presents a dictionary-like interface. A call to cgi.FieldStorage yields a dictionary-like object with one entry per input field on the client's web page:

```
import cgi
form = cgi.FieldStorage()       # Parse form data
if form.has_key('name'):
    showReply('Hello, ' + form['name'].value)
```

All of these (and dictionaries) are instances of mappings. Once you learn dictionary interfaces, you'll find that they apply to a variety of built-in tools in Python.

As suggested near the end of Table 8-2, the last form is also commonly used in conjunction with the zip function, to combine separate lists of keys and values obtained dynamically at runtime (parsed out of a data file's columns, for instance).

Provided all the key's values are the same, you can also initialize a dictionary with this special form—simply pass in a list of keys and an initial value for all of them (the default is None):

```
>>> dict.fromkeys(['a', 'b'], 0)
{'a': 0, 'b': 0}
```

Although you could get by with just literals and key assignments at this point in your Python career, you'll probably find uses for all of these dictionary-creation forms as you start applying them in realistic, flexible, and dynamic Python programs.

Chapter Summary

In this chapter, we explored the list and dictionary types—probably the two most common, flexible, and powerful collection types you will see and use in Python code. We learned that the list type supports positionally ordered collections of arbitrary objects, and that it may be freely nested, grown and shrunk on demand, and more. The dictionary type is similar, but it stores items by key instead of by position, and does not maintain any reliable left-to-right order among its items. Both lists and dictionaries are mutable, and so support a variety of in-place change operations not available for strings: for example, lists can be grown by append calls, and dictionaries by assignment to new keys.

In the next chapter, we will wrap up our in-depth core object type tour by looking at tuples and files. After that, we'll move on to statements that code the logic that processes our objects, taking us another step toward writing complete programs. Before we tackle those topics, though, here are some chapter quiz questions to review.

Chapter Quiz

1. Name two ways to build a list containing five integer zeros.

2. Name two ways to build a dictionary with two keys 'a' and 'b' each having an associated value of 0.

3. Name four operations that change a list object in-place.

4. Name four operations that change a dictionary object in-place.

Quiz Answers

1. A literal expression like [0, 0, 0, 0, 0] and a repetition expression like [0] * 5 will each create a list of five zeros. In practice, you might also build one up with a loop that starts with an empty list and appends 0 to it in each iteration: L.append(0). A list comprehension ([0 for i in range(5)]) could work here too, but this is more work than you need to do.

2. A literal expression such as {'a': 0, 'b': 0}, or a series of assignments like D = {}, D['a'] = 0, D['b'] = 0 would create the desired dictionary. You can also use the newer and simpler-to-code dict(a=0, b=0) keyword form, or the more flexible dict([('a', 0), ('b', 0)]) key/value sequences form. Or, because all the values are the same, you can use the special form dict.fromkeys(['a', 'b'], 0).

3. The append and extend methods grow a list in-place, the sort and reverse methods order and reverse lists, the insert method inserts an item at an offset, the remove and pop methods delete from a list by value and by position, the del statement deletes an item or slice, and index and slice assignment statements replace an item or entire section. Pick any four of these for the quiz.

4. Dictionaries are primarily changed by assignment to a new or existing key, which creates or changes the key's entry in the table. Also, the del statement deletes a key's entry, the dictionary update method merges one dictionary into another in-place, and D.pop(key) removes a key and returns the value it had. Dictionaries also have other, more exotic in-place change methods not listed in this chapter, such as setdefault; see reference sources for more details.

CHAPTER 9

Tuples, Files, and Everything Else

This chapter rounds out our in-depth look at the core object types in Python by exploring the *tuple* (a collection of other objects that cannot be changed), and the *file* (an interface to external files on your computer). As you'll see, the tuple is a relatively simple object that largely performs operations you've already learned about for strings and lists. The file object is a commonly used and full-featured tool for processing files; the basic overview of files here will be supplemented by further file examples that appear in later chapters of this book.

This chapter also concludes this part of the book by looking at properties common to all the core object types we've met—the notions of equality, comparisons, object copies, and so on. We'll also briefly explore other object types in the Python toolbox; as you'll see, although we've covered all the primary built-in types, the object story in Python is broader than I've implied thus far. Finally, we'll close this part of the book by taking a look at a set of common object type pitfalls, and exploring some exercises that will allow you to experiment with the ideas you've learned.

Tuples

The last collection type in our survey is the Python tuple. Tuples construct simple groups of objects. They work exactly like lists, except that tuples can't be changed in-place (they're immutable), and are usually written as a series of items in parentheses, not square brackets. Although they don't support any method calls, tuples share most of their properties with lists. Here's a quick look at their properties. Tuples are:

Ordered collections of arbitrary objects
> Like strings and lists, tuples are positionally ordered collections of objects (i.e., they maintain a left-to-right order among their contents); like lists, they can embed any kind of object.

Accessed by offset
> Like strings and lists, items in a tuple are accessed by offset (not by key); they support all the offset-based access operations, such as indexing and slicing.

Of the category immutable sequence

Like strings, tuples are immutable; they don't support any of the in-place change operations applied to lists. Like strings and lists, tuples are sequences; they support many of the same operations.

Fixed-length, heterogeneous, and arbitrarily nestable

Because tuples are immutable, you cannot change their size without making a copy. On the other hand, tuples can hold other compound objects (e.g., lists, dictionaries, other tuples), and so support arbitrary nesting.

Arrays of object references

Like lists, tuples are best thought of as object reference arrays; tuples store access points to other objects (references), and indexing a tuple is relatively quick.

Table 9-1 highlights common tuple operations. A tuple is written as a series of objects (technically, expressions that generate objects), separated by commas and enclosed in parentheses. An empty tuple is just a parentheses pair with nothing inside.

Table 9-1. Common tuple literals and operations

Operation	Interpretation
()	An empty tuple
t1 = (0,)	A one-item tuple (not an expression)
t2 = (0, 'Ni', 1.2, 3)	A four-item tuple
t2 = 0, 'Ni', 1.2, 3	Another four-item tuple (same as prior line)
t3 = ('abc', ('def', 'ghi'))	Nested tuples
t1[i] t3[i][j] t1[i:j] len(t1)	Index, index of index, slice, length
t1 + t2 t2 * 3	Concatenate, repeat
for x in t 'spam' in t2	Iteration, membership

Tuples in Action

As usual, let's start an interactive session to explore tuples at work. Notice in Table 9-1 that tuples have no methods (e.g., an append call won't work here). They do, however, support the usual sequence operations that we saw for strings and lists:

```
>>> (1, 2) + (3, 4)          # Concatenation
(1, 2, 3, 4)

>>> (1, 2) * 4               # Repetition
(1, 2, 1, 2, 1, 2, 1, 2)
```

```
>>> T = (1, 2, 3, 4)                    # Indexing, slicing
>>> T[0], T[1:3]
(1, (2, 3))
```

Tuple syntax peculiarities: commas and parentheses

The second and fourth entries in Table 9-1 merit a bit more explanation. Because parentheses can also enclose expressions (see Chapter 5), you need to do something special to tell Python when a single object in parentheses is a tuple object and not a simple expression. If you really want a single-item tuple, simply add a trailing comma after the single item, and before the closing parenthesis:

```
>>> x = (40)                            # An integer
>>> x
40
>>> y = (40,)                           # A tuple containing an integer
>>> y
(40,)
```

As a special case, Python also allows you to omit the opening and closing parentheses for a tuple in contexts where it isn't syntactically ambiguous to do so. For instance, the fourth line of the table simply lists four items separated by commas. In the context of an assignment statement, Python recognizes this as a tuple, even though it doesn't have parentheses.

Now, some people will tell you to always use parentheses in your tuples, and some will tell you to never use parentheses in tuples (and still others have lives, and won't tell you what to do with your tuples!). The only significant places where the parentheses are *required* are when a tuple is passed as a literal in a function call (where parentheses matter), and when one is listed in a print statement (where commas are significant).

For beginners, the best advice is that it's probably easier to use the parentheses than it is to figure out when they are optional. Many programmers also find that parentheses tend to aid script readability by making the tuples more explicit, but your mileage may vary.

Conversions and immutability

Apart from literal syntax differences, tuple operations (the last three rows in Table 9-1) are identical to string and list operations. The only differences worth noting are that the +, *, and slicing operations return new *tuples* when applied to tuples, and that tuples don't provide the methods you saw for strings, lists, and dictionaries. If you want to sort a tuple, for example, you'll usually have to first convert it to a list to gain access to a sorting method call and make it a mutable object:

```
>>> T = ('cc', 'aa', 'dd', 'bb')
>>> tmp = list(T)                       # Make a list from a tuple's items
>>> tmp.sort()                          # Sort the list
>>> tmp
['aa', 'bb', 'cc', 'dd']
```

```
>>> T = tuple(tmp)                  # Make a tuple from the list's items
>>> T
('aa', 'bb', 'cc', 'dd')
```

Here, the list and tuple built-in functions are used to convert to a list, and then back to a tuple; really, both calls make new objects, but the net effect is like a conversion.

List comprehensions can also be used to convert tuples. The following, for example, makes a list from a tuple, adding 20 to each item along the way:

```
>>> T = (1, 2, 3, 4, 5)
>>> L = [x + 20 for x in T]
>>> L
[21, 22, 23, 24, 25]
```

List comprehensions are really sequence operations—they always build new lists, but they may be used to iterate over any sequence objects, including tuples, strings, and other lists. As we'll see later, they even work on some things that are not physically stored sequences—any iterable objects will do, including files, which are automatically read line by line.

Also, note that the rule about tuple immutability applies only to the top level of the tuple itself, not to its contents. A list inside a tuple, for instance, can be changed as usual:

```
>>> T = (1, [2, 3], 4)

>>> T[1] = 'spam'                   # This fails: can't change tuple itself
TypeError: object doesn't support item assignment

>>> T[1][0] = 'spam'                # This works: can change mutables inside
>>> T
(1, ['spam', 3], 4)
```

For most programs, this one-level-deep immutability is sufficient for common tuple roles. Which, coincidentally, brings us to the next section.

Why Lists and Tuples?

This seems to be the first question that always comes up when teaching beginners about tuples: why do we need tuples if we have lists? Some of the reasoning may be historic; Python's creator is a mathematician by training, and has been quoted as seeing a tuple as a simple association of objects, and a list as a data structure that changes over time.

The best answer, however, seems to be that the immutability of tuples provides some *integrity*—you can be sure a tuple won't be changed through another reference elsewhere in a program, but there's no such guarantee for lists. Tuples, therefore, serve a similar role to "constant" declarations in other languages, though the notion of constant-ness is associated with objects in Python, not variables.

Tuples can also be used in places that lists cannot—for example, as dictionary keys (see the sparse matrix example in Chapter 8). Some built-in operations may also require or imply tuples, not lists. As a rule of thumb, lists are the tool of choice for ordered collections that might need to change; tuples can handle the other cases of fixed associations.

Files

You may already be familiar with the notion of files, which are named storage compartments on your computer that are managed by your operating system. The last major built-in object type that we'll examine on our in-depth tour provides a way to access those files inside Python programs.

In short, the built-in open function creates a Python file object, which serves as a link to a file residing on your machine. After calling open, you can read and write the associated external file by calling the returned file object's methods. The built-in name file is a synonym for open, and files may technically be opened by calling either open or file. open is generally preferred for opening, though, and file is mostly intended for customizations with object-oriented programming (described later in this book).

Compared to the types you've seen so far, file objects are somewhat unusual. They're not numbers, sequences, or mappings; instead, they export only methods for common file-processing tasks. Most file methods are concerned with performing input from and output to the external file associated with a file object, but other file methods allow us to seek to a new position in the file, flush output buffers, and so on.

Opening Files

Table 9-2 summarizes common file operations. To open a file, a program calls the built-in open function, with the external name first, followed by a processing mode. The mode is typically the string `'r'` to open for input (the default), `'w'` to create and open for output, or `'a'` to open for appending to the end; there are other options, but we'll omit them here. For advanced roles, adding a b to the end of the mode string allows for binary data (end-of-line translations are turned off), and adding a + means the file is opened for both input and output (i.e., we can both read and write to the same object).

Table 9-2. Common file operations

Operation	Interpretation
output = open('/tmp/spam', 'w')	Create output file ('w' means write)
input = open('data', 'r')	Create input file ('r' means read)
input = open('data')	Same as prior line ('r' is the default)

Table 9-2. Common file operations (continued)

Operation	Interpretation
`aString = input.read( )`	Read entire file into a single string
`aString = input.read(N)`	Read next N bytes (one or more) into a string
`aString = input.readline( )`	Read next line (including end-of-line marker) into a string
`aList = input.readlines( )`	Read entire file into list of line strings
`output.write(aString)`	Write a string of bytes into file
`output.writelines(aList)`	Write all line strings in a list into file
`output.close( )`	Manual close (done for you when file is collected)
`output.flush( )`	Flush output buffer to disk without closing
`anyFile.seek(N)`	Change file position to offset N for next operation

Both arguments to open must be Python strings, and an optional third argument can be used to control output buffering—passing a zero means that output is unbuffered (it is transferred to the external file immediately on a write method call). The external filename argument may include a platform-specific and absolute or relative directory path prefix; without a directory path, the file is assumed to exist in the current working directory (i.e., where the script runs).

Using Files

Once you have a file object, you can call its methods to read from or write to the associated external file. In all cases, file text takes the form of strings in Python programs; reading a file returns its text in strings, and text is passed to the write methods as strings. Reading and writing methods come in multiple flavors; Table 9-2 lists the most common.

Though the reading and writing methods in the table are common, keep in mind that probably the best way to read lines from a text file today is not to read the file at all—as we'll see in Chapter 13, files also have an *iterator* that automatically reads one line at a time in the context of a for loop, list comprehension, or other iteration context.

Notice that data read from a file always comes back to your script as a string, so you'll have to convert it to a different type of Python object if a string is not what you need. Similarly, unlike with the print statement, Python does not convert objects to strings automatically when you write data to a file—you must send an already formatted string. Therefore, the tools we have already met to convert strings to and from numbers come in handy when dealing with files (int, float, str, and string formatting expressions, for instance). Python also includes advanced standard library tools for handling generic object storage (such as the pickle module) and for dealing with packed binary data in files (such as the struct module). We'll see both of these at work later in this chapter.

Calling the file `close` method terminates your connection to the external file. As discussed in Chapter 6, in Python, an object's memory space is automatically reclaimed as soon as the object is no longer referenced anywhere in the program. When file objects are reclaimed, Python also automatically closes the files if needed. This means you don't always need to manually close your files, especially in simple scripts that don't run for long. On the other hand, manual `close` calls can't hurt, and are usually a good idea in larger systems. Also, strictly speaking, this auto-close-on-collection feature of files is not part of the language definition, and it may change over time. Consequently, manually issuing file `close` method calls is a good habit to form.

Files in Action

Let's work through a simple example that demonstrates file-processing basics. It first opens a new file for output, writes a string (terminated with a newline marker, \n), and closes the file. Later, the example opens the same file again in input mode and reads the line back. Notice that the second `readline` call returns an empty string; this is how Python file methods tell you that you've reached the end of the file (empty lines in the file come back as strings containing just a newline character, not as empty strings). Here's the complete interaction:

```
>>> myfile = open('myfile', 'w')         # Open for output (creates file)
>>> myfile.write('hello text file\n')    # Write a line of text
>>> myfile.close()                       # Flush output buffers to disk

>>> myfile = open('myfile')              # Open for input: 'r' is default
>>> myfile.readline()                    # Read the line back
'hello text file\n'
>>> myfile.readline()                    # Empty string: end of file
''
```

This example writes a single line of text as a string, including its end-of-line terminator, \n; write methods don't add the end-of-line character for us, so we must include it to properly terminate our line (otherwise the next write will simply extend the current line in the file).

Storing and parsing Python objects in files

Now, let's create a bigger file. The next example writes a variety of Python objects into a text file on multiple lines. Notice that it must convert objects to strings using conversion tools. Again, file data is always strings in our scripts, and write methods do not do any automatic to-string formatting for us:

```
>>> X, Y, Z = 43, 44, 45          # Native Python objects
>>> S = 'Spam'                    # Must be strings to store in file
>>> D = {'a': 1, 'b': 2}
>>> L = [1, 2, 3]
>>>
>>> F = open('datafile.txt', 'w')  # Create output file
>>> F.write(S + '\n')              # Terminate lines with \n
```

```
>>> F.write('%s,%s,%s\n' % (X, Y, Z))        # Convert numbers to strings
>>> F.write(str(L) + '$' + str(D) + '\n')    # Convert and separate with $
>>> F.close()
```

Once we have created our file, we can inspect its contents by opening it and reading it into a string (a single operation). Notice that the interactive echo gives the exact byte contents, while the print statement interprets embedded end-of-line characters to render a more user-friendly display:

```
>>> bytes = open('datafile.txt').read()      # Raw bytes display
>>> bytes
"Spam\n43,44,45\n[1, 2, 3]${'a': 1, 'b': 2}\n"
>>> print bytes                              # User-friendly display
Spam
43,44,45
[1, 2, 3]${'a': 1, 'b': 2}
```

We now have to use other conversion tools to translate from the strings in the text file to real Python objects. As Python never converts strings to numbers, or other types of objects automatically, this is required if we need to gain access to normal object tools like indexing, addition, and so on:

```
>>> F = open('datafile.txt')                 # Open again
>>> line = F.readline()                       # Read one line
>>> line
'Spam\n'
>>> line.rstrip()                             # Remove end-of-line
'Spam'
```

For this first line, we used the string rstrip method to get rid of the trailing end-of-line character; a line[:-1] slice would work, too, but only if we can be sure all lines have the \n character (the last line in a file sometimes does not). So far, we've read the line containing the string. Now, let's grab the next line, which contains numbers, and parse out (that is, extract) the objects on that line:

```
>>> line = F.readline()                       # Next line from file
>>> line                                      # It's a string here
'43,44,45\n'
>>> parts = line.split(',')                   # Split (parse) on commas
>>> parts
['43', '44', '45\n']
```

We used the string split method here to chop up the line on its comma delimiters; the result is a list of substrings containing the individual numbers. We still must convert from strings to integers, though, if we wish to perform math on these:

```
>>> int(parts[1])                             # Convert from string to int
44
>>> numbers = [int(P) for P in parts]         # Convert all in list at once
>>> numbers
[43, 44, 45]
```

As we have learned, int translates a string of digits into an integer object, and the list comprehension expression introduced in Chapter 4 can apply the call to each item in our list all at once (you'll find more on list comprehensions later in this book). Notice that we didn't have to run rstrip to delete the \n at the end of the last part; int and some other converters quietly ignore whitespace around digits.

Finally, to convert the stored list and dictionary in the third line of the file, we can run them through eval, a built-in function that treats a string as a piece of executable program code (technically, a string containing a Python expression):

```
>>> line = F.readline()
>>> line
"[1, 2, 3]${'a': 1, 'b': 2}\n"
>>> parts = line.split('$')              # Split (parse) on $
>>> parts
['[1, 2, 3]', "{'a': 1, 'b': 2}\n"]
>>> eval(parts[0])                        # Convert to any object type
[1, 2, 3]
>>> objects = [eval(P) for P in parts]    # Do same for all in list
>>> objects
[[1, 2, 3], {'a': 1, 'b': 2}]
```

Because the end result of all this parsing and converting is a list of normal Python objects instead of strings, we can now apply list and dictionary operations to them in our script.

Storing native Python objects with pickle

Using eval to convert from strings to objects, as demonstrated in the preceding code, is a powerful tool. In fact, sometimes it's *too* powerful. eval will happily run any Python expression—even one that might delete all the files on your computer, given the necessary permissions! If you really want to store native Python objects, but you can't trust the source of the data in the file, Python's standard library pickle module is ideal.

The pickle module is an advanced tool that allows us to store almost any Python object in a file directly, with no to- or from-string conversion requirement on our part. It's like a super-general data formatting and parsing utility. To store a dictionary in a file, for instance, we pickle it directly:

```
>>> F = open('datafile.txt', 'w')
>>> import pickle
>>> pickle.dump(D, F)                     # Pickle any object to file
>>> F.close()
```

Then, to get the dictionary back later, we simply use pickle again to recreate it:

```
>>> F = open('datafile.txt')
>>> E = pickle.load(F)                    # Load any object from file
>>> E
{'a': 1, 'b': 2}
```

We get back an equivalent dictionary object, with no manual splitting or converting required. The `pickle` module performs what is known as *object serialization*—converting objects to and from strings of bytes—but requires very little work on our part. In fact, `pickle` internally translates our dictionary to a string form, though it's not much to look at (and it can be even more convoluted if we pickle in other modes):

```
>>> open('datafile.txt').read()
"(dp0\nS'a'\np1\nI1\nsS'b'\np2\nI2\ns."
```

Because `pickle` can reconstruct the object from this format, we don't have to deal with that ourselves. For more on the `pickle` module, see the Python standard library manual, or import `pickle`, and pass it to `help` interactively. While you're exploring, also take a look at the `shelve` module. `shelve` is a tool that uses `pickle` to store Python objects in an access-by-key filesystem, which is beyond our scope here.

Storing and parsing packed binary data in files

One other file-related note before we move on: some advanced applications also need to deal with packed binary data, created perhaps by a C language program. Python's standard library includes a tool to help in this domain—the `struct` module knows how to both compose and parse packed binary data. In a sense, this is another data-conversion tool that interprets strings in files as binary data.

To create a packed binary data file, for example, open it in `'wb'` (write binary) mode, and pass `struct` a format string and some Python objects. The format string used here means pack as a 4-byte integer, a 4-character string, and a 2-byte integer, all in big-endian form (other format codes handle padding bytes, floating-point numbers, and more):

```
>>> F = open('data.bin', 'wb')                        # Open binary output file
>>> import struct
>>> bytes = struct.pack('>i4sh', 7, 'spam', 8)        # Make packed binary data
>>> bytes
'\x00\x00\x00\x07spam\x00\x08'
>>> F.write(bytes)                                    # Write byte string
>>> F.close()
```

Python creates a binary data string, which we write out to the file normally (this one consists mostly of nonprintable characters printed in hexadecimal escapes). To parse the values out to normal Python objects, we simply read the string back, and unpack it using the same format string. Python extracts the values into normal Python objects (integers and a string):

```
>>> F = open('data.bin', 'rb')
>>> data = F.read()                                   # Get packed binary data
>>> data
'\x00\x00\x00\x07spam\x00\x08'
>>> values = struct.unpack('>i4sh', data)             # Convert to Python objects
>>> values
(7, 'spam', 8)
```

Binary data files are advanced and somewhat low-level tools that we won't cover in more detail here; for more help, see the Python library manual, or import and pass struct to the help function interactively. Also note that the binary file-processing modes 'wb' and 'rb' can be used to process a simpler binary file such as an image or audio file as a whole without having to unpack its contents.

Other File Tools

There are additional, more advanced file methods shown in Table 9-2, and even more that are not in the table. For instance, seek resets your current position in a file (the next read or write happens at that position), flush forces buffered output to be written out to disk (by default, files are always buffered), and so on.

The Python standard library manual and the reference books described in the Preface provide complete lists of file methods; for a quick look, run a dir or help call interactively, passing in the word file (the name of the file object type). For more file-processing examples, watch for the sidebar "Why You Will Care: File Scanners" in Chapter 13. It sketches common file-scanning loop code patterns with statements we have not covered enough yet to use here.

Also, note that although the open function and the file objects it returns are your main interface to external files in a Python script, there are additional file-like tools in the Python toolset. Also available are descriptor files (integer file handles that support lower-level tools such as file locking), found in the os module; sockets, pipes, and FIFO files (file-like objects used to synchronize processes or communicate over networks); access-by-key files known as "shelves" (used to store unaltered Python objects directly, by key); and more. See more advanced Python texts for additional information on these file-like tools.

Type Categories Revisited

Now that we've seen all of Python's core built-in types in action, let's wrap up our object types tour by taking a look at some of the properties they share.

Table 9-3 classifies all the types we've seen according to the type categories introduced earlier. Objects share operations according to their category; for instance, strings, lists, and tuples all share sequence operations. Only mutable objects (lists and dictionaries) may be changed in-place; you cannot change numbers, strings, or tuples in-place. Files only export methods, so mutability doesn't really apply to them—they may be changed when written, but this isn't the same as Python type constraints.

Why You Will Care: Operator Overloading

Later, we'll see that objects we implement with classes can pick and choose from these categories arbitrarily. For instance, if you want to provide a new kind of specialized sequence object that is consistent with built-in sequences, code a class that overloads things like indexing and concatenation:

```
class MySequence:
    def __getitem__(self, index):
        # Called on self[index], others
    def __add__(self, other):
        # Called on self + other
```

and so on. You can also make the new object mutable or not by selectively implementing methods called for in-place change operations (e.g., __setitem__ is called on self[index]=value assignments). Although it's beyond this book's scope, it's also possible to implement new objects in an external language like C as C extension types. For these, you fill in C function pointer slots to choose between number, sequence, and mapping operation sets.

Table 9-3. Object classifications

Object type	Category	Mutable?
Numbers	Numeric	No
Strings	Sequence	No
Lists	Sequence	Yes
Dictionaries	Mapping	Yes
Tuples	Sequence	No
Files	Extension	N/A

Object Flexibility

This part of the book introduced a number of compound object types (collections with components). In general:

- Lists, dictionaries, and tuples can hold any kind of object.
- Lists, dictionaries, and tuples can be arbitrarily nested.
- Lists and dictionaries can dynamically grow and shrink.

Because they support arbitrary structures, Python's compound object types are good at representing complex information in programs. For example, values in dictionaries may be lists, which may contain tuples, which may contain dictionaries, and so on. The nesting can be as deep as needed to model the data to be processed.

Let's look at an example of nesting. The following interaction defines a tree of nested compound sequence objects, shown in Figure 9-1. To access its components, you may include as many index operations as required. Python evaluates the indexes from left to right, and fetches a reference to a more deeply nested object at each step. Figure 9-1 may be a pathologically complicated data structure, but it illustrates the syntax used to access nested objects in general:

```
>>> L = ['abc', [(1, 2), ([3], 4)], 5]
>>> L[1]
[(1, 2), ([3], 4)]
>>> L[1][1]
([3], 4)
>>> L[1][1][0]
[3]
>>> L[1][1][0][0]
3
```

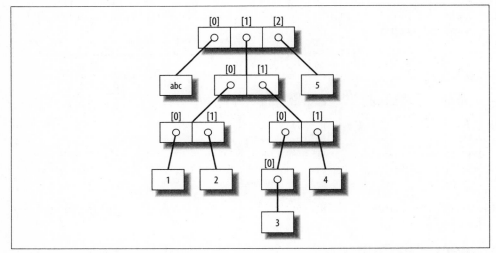

Figure 9-1. A nested object tree with the offsets of its components, created by running the literal expression ['abc', [(1, 2), ([3], 4)], 5]. Syntactically nested objects are internally represented as references (i.e., pointers) to separate pieces of memory.

References Versus Copies

Chapter 6 mentioned that assignments always store references to objects, not copies of those objects. In practice, this is usually what you want. Because assignments can generate multiple references to the same object, though, it's important to be aware that changing a mutable object in-place may affect other references to the same object elsewhere in your program. If you don't want such behavior, you'll need to tell Python to copy the object explicitly.

We studied this phenomenon in Chapter 6, but it can become more acute when larger objects come into play. For instance, the following example creates a list assigned to X, and another list assigned to L that embeds a reference back to list X. It also creates a dictionary D that contains another reference back to list X:

```
>>> X = [1, 2, 3]
>>> L = ['a', X, 'b']          # Embed references to X's object
>>> D = {'x':X, 'y':2}
```

At this point, there are three references to the first list created: from the name X, from inside the list assigned to L, and from inside the dictionary assigned to D. The situation is illustrated in Figure 9-2.

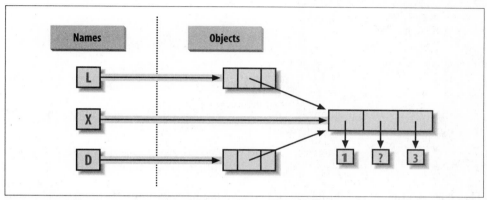

Figure 9-2. Shared object references: because the list referenced by variable X is also referenced from within the objects referenced by L and D, changing the shared list from X makes it look different from L and D, too.

Because lists are mutable, changing the shared list object from any of the three references also changes what the other two reference:

```
>>> X[1] = 'surprise'          # Changes all three references!
>>> L
['a', [1, 'surprise', 3], 'b']
>>> D
{'x': [1, 'surprise', 3], 'y': 2}
```

References are a higher-level analog of pointers in other languages. Although you can't grab hold of the reference itself, it's possible to store the same reference in more than one place (variables, lists, and so on). This is a feature—you can pass a large object around a program without generating expensive copies of it along the way. If you really do want copies, however, you can request them:

- Slice expressions with empty limits (L[:]) copy sequences.
- The dictionary copy method (D.copy()) copies a dictionary.
- Some built-in functions, such as list, make copies (list(L)).
- The copy standard library module makes full copies.

For example, say you have a list and a dictionary, and you don't want their values to be changed through other variables:

```
>>> L = [1,2,3]
>>> D = {'a':1, 'b':2}
```

To prevent this, simply assign copies to the other variables, not references to the same objects:

```
>>> A = L[:]            # Instead of A = L (or list(L))
>>> B = D.copy()        # Instead of B = D
```

This way, changes made from the other variables will change the copies, not the originals:

```
>>> A[1] = 'Ni'
>>> B['c'] = 'spam'
>>>
>>> L, D
([1, 2, 3], {'a': 1, 'b': 2})
>>> A, B
([1, 'Ni', 3], {'a': 1, 'c': 'spam', 'b': 2})
```

In terms of our original example, you can avoid the reference side effects by slicing the original list instead of simply naming it:

```
>>> X = [1, 2, 3]
>>> L = ['a', X[:], 'b']        # Embed copies of X's object
>>> D = {'x':X[:], 'y':2}
```

This changes the picture in Figure 9-2—L and D will now point to different lists than X. The net effect is that changes made through X will impact only X, not L and D; similarly, changes to L or D will not impact X.

One note on copies: empty-limit slices and the dictionary copy method still only make *top-level* copies; that is, they do not copy nested data structures, if any are present. If you need a complete, fully independent copy of a deeply nested data structure, use the standard copy module: include an import copy statement, and say X = copy.deepcopy(Y) to fully copy an arbitrarily nested object Y. This call recursively traverses objects to copy all their parts. This is the much more rare case, though (which is why you have to say more to make it go). References are usually what you will want; when they are not, slices and copy methods are usually as much copying as you'll need to do.

Comparisons, Equality, and Truth

All Python objects also respond to comparisons: tests for equality, relative magnitude, and so on. Python comparisons always inspect all parts of compound objects until a result can be determined. In fact, when nested objects are present, Python automatically traverses data structures to apply comparisons *recursively* from left to right, and as deeply as needed. The first difference found along the way determines the comparison result.

For instance, a comparison of list objects compares all their components automatically:

```
>>> L1 = [1, ('a', 3)]          # Same value, unique objects
>>> L2 = [1, ('a', 3)]
>>> L1 == L2, L1 is L2          # Equivalent? Same object?
(True, False)
```

Here, L1 and L2 are assigned lists that are equivalent but distinct objects. Because of the nature of Python references (studied in Chapter 6), there are two ways to test for equality:

- **The == operator tests value equivalence.** Python performs an equivalence test, comparing all nested objects recursively.

- **The is operator tests object identity.** Python tests whether the two are really the same object (i.e., live at the same address in memory).

In the preceding example, L1 and L2 pass the == test (they have equivalent values because all their components are equivalent), but fail the is check (they reference two different objects, and hence two different pieces of memory). Notice what happens for short strings, though:

```
>>> S1 = 'spam'
>>> S2 = 'spam'
>>> S1 == S2, S1 is S2
(True, True)
```

Here, we should again have two distinct objects that happen to have the same value: == should be true, and is should be false. But because Python internally caches and reuses short strings as an optimization, there really is just a single string 'spam' in memory, shared by S1 and S2; hence, the is identity test reports a true result. To trigger the normal behavior, we need to use longer strings:

```
>>> S1 = 'a longer string'
>>> S2 = 'a longer string'
>>> S1 == S2, S1 is S2
(True, False)
```

Of course, because strings are immutable, the object caching mechanism is irrelevant to your code—string can't be changed in-place, regardless of how many variables refer to them. If identity tests seem confusing, see Chapter 6 for a refresher on object reference concepts.

As a rule of thumb, the == operator is what you will want to use for almost all equality checks; is is reserved for highly specialized roles. We'll see cases where these operators are put to use later in the book.

Relative magnitude comparisons are also applied recursively to nested data structures:

```
>>> L1 = [1, ('a', 3)]
>>> L2 = [1, ('a', 2)]
>>> L1 < L2, L1 == L2, L1 > L2          # Less, equal, greater: tuple of results
(False, False, True)
```

Here, L1 is greater than L2 because the nested 3 is greater than 2. The result of the last line above is really a tuple of three objects—the results of the three expressions typed (an example of a tuple without its enclosing parentheses).

In general, Python compares types as follows:

- Numbers are compared by relative magnitude.
- Strings are compared lexicographically, character by character ("abc" < "ac").
- Lists and tuples are compared by comparing each component from left to right.
- Dictionaries are compared as though comparing sorted (key, value) lists.

In general, comparisons of structured objects proceed as though you had written the objects as literals and compared all their parts one at a time from left to right. In later chapters, we'll see other object types that can change the way they get compared.

The Meaning of True and False in Python

Notice that the three values in the tuple returned in the last example of the prior section represent true and false values. They print as the words True and False, but now that we're using logical tests like this one in earnest, I should be a bit more formal about what these names really mean.

In Python, as in most programming languages, an integer 0 represents false, and an integer 1 represents true. In addition, though, Python recognizes any empty data structure as false, and any nonempty data structure as true. More generally, the notions of true and false are intrinsic properties of every object in Python—each object is either true or false, as follows:

- Numbers are true if nonzero.
- Other objects are true if nonempty.

Table 9-4 gives examples of true and false objects in Python.

Table 9-4. Example object truth values

Object	Value
"spam"	True
""	False
[]	False
{}	False
1	True
0.0	False
None	False

Python also provides a special object called None (the last item in Table 9-4), which is always considered to be false. None was introduced in Chapter 4; it is the only value of a special data type in Python, and typically serves as an empty placeholder, much like a NULL pointer in C.

For example, recall that for lists you cannot assign to an offset unless that offset already exists (the list does not magically grow if you make an out-of-bounds assignment). To preallocate a 100-item list such that you can add to any of the 100 offsets, you can fill one with None objects:

```
>>> L = [None] * 100
>>>
>>> L
[None, None, None, None, None, None, None, ... ]
```

The Python Boolean type bool (introduced in Chapter 5) simply augments the notion of true and false in Python. You may have noticed that the results of tests in this chapter display as the words True and False. As we learned in Chapter 5, these are just customized versions of the integers 1 and 0. Because of the way this new type is implemented, this is really just a minor extension to the notions of true and false already described, designed to make truth values more explicit. When used explicitly in truth tests, the words True and False evaluate to true and false because they truly are just specialized versions of the integers 1 and 0. Results of tests also print as the words True and False, instead of 1 and 0.

You are not required to use only Boolean types in logical statements such as if; all objects are still inherently true or false, and all the Boolean concepts mentioned in this chapter still work as described if you use other types. We'll explore Booleans further when we study logical statements in Chapter 12.

Python's Type Hierarchies

Figure 9-3 summarizes all the built-in object types available in Python and their relationships. We've looked at the most prominent of these; most of the other kinds of objects in Figure 9-3 correspond to program units (e.g., functions and modules), or exposed interpreter internals (e.g., stack frames and compiled code).

The main point to notice here is that everything is an object type in a Python system, and may be processed by your Python programs. For instance, you can pass a class to a function, assign it to a variable, stuff it in a list or dictionary, and so on.

In fact, even types themselves are an object type in Python: a call to the built-in function type(X) returns the type object of object X. Type objects can be used for manual type comparisons in Python if statements. However, for reasons introduced in Chapter 4, manual type testing is usually not the right thing to do in Python.

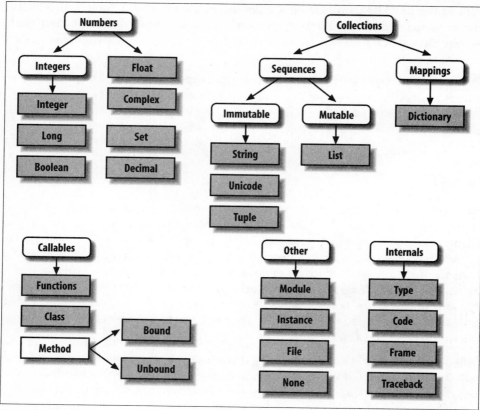

Figure 9-3. Python's major built-in object types, organized by categories. Everything is a type of object in Python, even the type of an object! The type of any object is an object of type "type."

One note on type names: as of Python 2.2, each core type has a new built-in name added to support type customization through object-oriented subclassing: `dict`, `list`, `str`, `tuple`, `int`, `long`, `float`, `complex`, `unicode`, `type`, and `file` (file is a synonym for open). Calls to these names are really object constructor calls, not simply conversion functions, though you can treat them as simple functions for basic usage.

The types standard library module also provides additional type names (now largely synonyms for the built-in type names), and it is possible to do type tests with the `isinstance` function. For example, in Python 2.2 and later, all of the following type tests are true:

```
isinstance([1],list)
type([1])==list
type([1])==type([])
type([1])==types.ListType
```

Because types can be subclassed in Python today, the isinstance technique is generally recommended. See Chapter 26 for more on subclassing built-in types in Python 2.2 and later.

Other Types in Python

Besides the core objects studied in this part of the book, a typical Python installation has dozens of other object types available as linked-in C extensions or Python classes—regular expression objects, DBM files, GUI widgets, network sockets, and so on.

The main difference between these extra tools and the built-in types we've seen so far is that the built-ins provide special language creation syntax for their objects (e.g., 4 for an integer, [1,2] for a list, and the open function for files). Other tools are generally made available in standard library modules that you must first import to use. For instance, to make a regular expression object, you import re and call re.compile( ). See Python's library reference for a comprehensive guide to all the tools available to Python programs.

Built-in Type Gotchas

That's the end of our look at core data types. We'll wrap up this part of the book with a discussion of common problems that seem to bite new users (and the occasional expert) along with their solutions. Some of this is a review of ideas we've already covered, but these issues are important enough to warn about again here.

Assignment Creates References, Not Copies

Because this is such a central concept, I'll mention it again: you need to understand what's going on with shared references in your program. For instance, in the following example, the list object assigned to the name L is referenced from L and from inside the list assigned to the name M. Changing L in-place changes what M references, too:

```
>>> L = [1, 2, 3]
>>> M = ['X', L, 'Y']          # Embed a reference to L
>>> M
['X', [1, 2, 3], 'Y']

>>> L[1] = 0                   # Changes M too
>>> M
['X', [1, 0, 3], 'Y']
```

This effect usually becomes important only in larger programs, and shared references are often exactly what you want. If they're not, you can avoid sharing objects by copying them explicitly. For lists, you can always make a top-level copy by using an empty-limits slice:

```
>>> L = [1, 2, 3]
>>> M = ['X', L[:], 'Y']          # Embed a copy of L
>>> L[1] = 0                      # Changes only L, not M
>>> L
[1, 0, 3]
>>> M
['X', [1, 2, 3], 'Y']
```

Remember, slice limits default to 0, and the length of the sequence being sliced; if both are omitted, the slice extracts every item in the sequence, and so makes a top-level copy (a new, unshared object).

Repetition Adds One Level Deep

Sequence repetition is like adding a sequence to itself a number of times. That's true, but when mutable sequences are nested, the effect might not always be what you expect. For instance, in the following example X is assigned to L repeated four times, whereas Y is assigned to a list *containing* L repeated four times:

```
>>> L = [4, 5, 6]
>>> X = L * 4                     # Like [4, 5, 6] + [4, 5, 6] + ...
>>> Y = [L] * 4                   # [L] + [L] + ... = [L, L,...]

>>> X
[4, 5, 6, 4, 5, 6, 4, 5, 6, 4, 5, 6]
>>> Y
[[4, 5, 6], [4, 5, 6], [4, 5, 6], [4, 5, 6]]
```

Because L was nested in the second repetition, Y winds up embedding references back to the original list assigned to L, and so is open to the same sorts of side effects noted in the last section:

```
>>> L[1] = 0                      # Impacts Y but not X
>>> X
[4, 5, 6, 4, 5, 6, 4, 5, 6, 4, 5, 6]
>>> Y
[[4, 0, 6], [4, 0, 6], [4, 0, 6], [4, 0, 6]]
```

The same solutions to this problem apply here as in the previous section, as this is really just another way to create the shared mutable object reference case. If you remember that repetition, concatenation, and slicing copy only the top level of their operand objects, these sorts of cases make much more sense.

Beware of Cyclic Data Structures

We actually encountered this concept in a prior exercise: if a collection object contains a reference to itself, it's called a *cyclic object*. Python prints a [...] whenever it detects a cycle in the object, rather than getting stuck in an infinite loop:

```
>>> L = ['grail']          # Append reference to same object
>>> L.append(L)            # Generates cycle in object: [...]
>>> L
['grail', [...]]
```

Besides understanding that the three dots in square brackets represent a cycle in the object, this case is worth knowing about because it can lead to gotchas—cyclic structures may cause code of your own to fall into unexpected loops if you don't anticipate them. For instance, some programs keep a list or dictionary of items already visited, and check it to determine whether they're in a cycle. See the solutions to "Part I Exercises" in Chapter 3 for more on this problem, and check out the *reloadall.py* program at the end of Chapter 21 for a solution.

Don't use a cyclic reference unless you need to. There are good reasons to create cycles, but unless you have code that knows how to handle them, you probably won't want to make your objects reference themselves very often in practice.

Immutable Types Can't Be Changed In-Place

Finally, you can't change an immutable object in-place. Instead, construct a new object with slicing, concatenation, and so on, and assign it back to the original reference, if needed:

```
T = (1, 2, 3)

T[2] = 4            # Error!

T = T[:2] + (4,)    # OK: (1, 2, 4)
```

That might seem like extra coding work, but the upside is that the previous gotchas can't happen when you're using immutable objects such as tuples and strings; because they can't be changed in-place, they are not open to the sorts of side effects that lists are.

Chapter Summary

This chapter explored the last two major core object types—the tuple and the file. We learned that tuples support all the usual sequence operations, but they have no methods, and do not allow any in-place changes because they are immutable.

We also learned that files are returned by the built-in open function and provide methods for reading and writing data. We explored how to translate Python objects to and from strings for storing in files, and we looked at the pickle and struct modules for advanced roles (object serialization and binary data). Finally, we wrapped up by reviewing some properties common to all object types (e.g., shared references) and went through a list of common mistakes ("gotchas") in the object type domain.

In the next part, we'll shift gears, turning to the topic of statement syntax in Python—we'll explore all of Python's basic procedural statements in the chapters that follow. The next chapter kicks off that part of the book with an introduction to Python's general syntax model, which is applicable to all statement types. Before moving on, though, take the chapter quiz, and then work through the end-of-part lab exercises to review type concepts. Statements largely just create and process objects, so make sure you've mastered this domain by working through all the exercises before reading on.

Chapter Quiz

1. How can you determine how large a tuple is?
2. Write an expression that changes the first item in a tuple. (4, 5, 6) should become (1, 5, 6) in the process.
3. What is the default for the processing-mode argument in a file open call?
4. What module might you use to store Python objects in a file without converting them to strings yourself?
5. How might you go about copying all parts of a nested structure at once?
6. When does Python consider an object true?
7. What is your quest?

Quiz Answers

1. The built-in `len` function returns the length (number of contained items) for any container object in Python, including tuples. It is a built-in function instead of a type method because it applies to many different types of objects.
2. Because they are immutable, you can't really change tuples in-place, but you can generate a new tuple with the desired value. Given T = (4, 5, 6), you can change the first item by making a new tuple from its parts by slicing and concatenating: T = (1,) + T[1:]. (Recall that single-item tuples require a trailing comma.) You could also convert the tuple to a list, change it in-place, and convert it back to a tuple, but this is more expensive, and is rarely required in practice—simply use a list if you know that the object will require in-place changes.
3. The default for the processing-mode argument in a file open call is 'r' for reading input. For input text files, simply pass in the external file's name.
4. The `pickle` module can be used to store Python objects in a file without explicitly converting them to strings. The `struct` module is related, but assumes the data is to be in packed binary format in the file.
5. Import the `copy` module, and call `copy.deepcopy(X)` if you need to copy all parts of a nested structure X. This is also rare to see in practice; references are usually the desired behavior, and shallow copies (e.g., `aList[:]`, `aDict.copy()`) usually suffice for most copies.
6. An object is considered true if it is either a nonzero number, or a nonempty collection object. The built-in words `True` and `False` are essentially predefined to mean integer 1 and 0, respectively.
7. Acceptable answers include "To learn Python," "To move on to the next part of the book," or "To seek the Holy Grail."

Part II Exercises

This session asks you to get your feet wet with built-in object fundamentals. As before, a few new ideas may pop up along the way, so be sure to flip to the answers in Appendix B when you're done (and even when you're not). If you have limited time, I suggest starting with exercises 10 and 11 (the most practical of the bunch), and then working from first to last as time allows. This is all fundamental material, though, so try to do as many of these as you can.

1. *The basics.* Experiment interactively with the common type operations found in the tables in Part II. To get started, bring up the Python interactive interpreter, type each of the following expressions, and try to explain what's happening in each case:

   ```
   2 ** 16
   2 / 5, 2 / 5.0

   "spam" + "eggs"
   S = "ham"
   "eggs " + S
   S * 5
   S[:0]
   "green %s and %s" % ("eggs", S)

   ('x',)[0]
   ('x', 'y')[1]

   L = [1,2,3] + [4,5,6]
   L, L[:], L[:0], L[-2], L[-2:]
   ([1,2,3] + [4,5,6])[2:4]
   [L[2], L[3]]
   L.reverse(); L
   L.sort(); L
   L.index(4)

   {'a':1, 'b':2}['b']
   D = {'x':1, 'y':2, 'z':3}
   D['w'] = 0
   D['x'] + D['w']
   D[(1,2,3)] = 4
   D.keys(), D.values(), D.has_key((1,2,3))

   [[]], ["",[],(),{},None]
   ```

2. *Indexing and slicing.* At the interactive prompt, define a list named L that contains four strings or numbers (e.g., L=[0,1,2,3]). Then, experiment with some boundary cases:

   a. What happens when you try to index out of bounds (e.g., L[4])?

   b. What about slicing out of bounds (e.g., L[-1000:100])?

c. Finally, how does Python handle it if you try to extract a sequence in reverse, with the lower bound greater than the higher bound (e.g., L[3:1])? Hint: try assigning to this slice (L[3:1]=['?']), and see where the value is put. Do you think this may be the same phenomenon you saw when slicing out of bounds?

3. *Indexing, slicing, and* del. Define another list L with four items, and assign an empty list to one of its offsets (e.g., L[2]=[]). What happens? Then, assign an empty list to a slice (L[2:3]=[]). What happens now? Recall that slice assignment deletes the slice, and inserts the new value where it used to be.

The del statement deletes offsets, keys, attributes, and names. Use it on your list to delete an item (e.g., del L[0]). What happens if you delete an entire slice (del L[1:])? What happens when you assign a nonsequence to a slice (L[1:2]=1)?

4. *Tuple assignment.* Type the following lines:

```
>>> X = 'spam'
>>> Y = 'eggs'
>>> X, Y = Y, X
```

What do you think is happening to X and Y when you type this sequence?

5. *Dictionary keys.* Consider the following code fragments:

```
>>> D = {}
>>> D[1] = 'a'
>>> D[2] = 'b'
```

You've learned that dictionaries aren't accessed by offsets, so what's going on here? Does the following shed any light on the subject? (Hint: strings, integers, and tuples share which type category?)

```
>>> D[(1, 2, 3)] = 'c'
>>> D
{1: 'a', 2: 'b', (1, 2, 3): 'c'}
```

6. *Dictionary indexing.* Create a dictionary named D with three entries, for keys 'a', 'b', and 'c'. What happens if you try to index a nonexistent key (D['d'])? What does Python do if you try to assign to a nonexistent key 'd' (e.g., D['d']='spam')? How does this compare to out-of-bounds assignments and references for lists? Does this sound like the rule for variable names?

7. *Generic operations.* Run interactive tests to answer the following questions:

a. What happens when you try to use the + operator on different/mixed types (e.g., string + list, list + tuple)?

b. Does + work when one of the operands is a dictionary?

c. Does the append method work for both lists and strings? How about using the keys method on lists? (Hint: What does append assume about its subject object?)

d. Finally, what type of object do you get back when you slice or concatenate two lists or two strings?

8. *String indexing.* Define a string S of four characters: S = "spam". Then type the following expression: S[0][0][0][0][0]. Any clue as to what's happening this time? (Hint: recall that a string is a collection of characters, but Python characters are one-character strings.) Does this indexing expression still work if you apply it to a list such as ['s', 'p', 'a', 'm']? Why?

9. *Immutable types.* Define a string S of four characters again: S = "spam". Write an assignment that changes the string to "slam", using only slicing and concatenation. Could you perform the same operation using just indexing and concatenation? How about index assignment?

10. *Nesting.* Write a data structure that represents your personal information: name (first, middle, last), age, job, address, email address, and phone number. You may build the data structure with any combination of built-in object types you like (lists, tuples, dictionaries, strings, numbers). Then, access the individual components of your data structures by indexing. Do some structures make more sense than others for this object?

11. *Files.* Write a script that creates a new output file called *myfile.txt*, and writes the string "Hello file world!" into it. Then, write another script that opens *myfile. txt* and reads and prints its contents. Run your two scripts from the system command line. Does the new file show up in the directory where you ran your scripts? What if you add a different directory path to the filename passed to open? Note: file write methods do not add newline characters to your strings; add an explicit \n at the end of the string if you want to fully terminate the line in the file.

12. *The dir function revisited.* Try typing the following expressions at the interactive prompt. Starting with version 1.5, the dir function has been generalized to list all attributes of any Python object you're likely to be interested in. If you're using an earlier version than 1.5, the __methods__ scheme has the same effect. If you're using Python 2.2, dir is probably the only of these that will work.

```
[].__methods__        # 1.4 or 1.5
dir([])               # 1.5 and later

{}.__methods__        # Dictionary
dir({})
```

Statements and Syntax

## CHAPTER 10

Introducing Python Statements

Now that you're familiar with Python's core built-in object types, this chapter begins our exploration of its fundamental statement forms. As in the previous part, we'll begin here with a general introduction to statement syntax, and follow up with more details about specific statements in the next few chapters.

In simple terms, *statements* are the things you write to tell Python what your programs should do. If programs "do things with stuff," statements are the way you specify what sort of things a program does. Python is a procedural, statement-based language; by combining statements, you specify a procedure that Python performs to satisfy a program's goals.

Python Program Structure Revisited

Another way to understand the role of statements is to revisit the concept hierarchy introduced in Chapter 4, which talked about built-in objects and the expressions used to manipulate them. This chapter climbs the hierarchy to the next level:

1. Programs are composed of modules.
2. Modules contain statements.
3. *Statements contain expressions.*
4. Expressions create and process objects.

At its core, Python syntax is composed of statements and expressions. Expressions process objects and are embedded in statements. Statements code the larger *logic* of a program's operation—they use and direct expressions to process the objects we studied in the preceding chapters. Moreover, statements are where objects spring into existence (e.g., in expressions within assignment statements), and some statements create entirely new kinds of objects (functions, classes, and so on). Statements always exist in modules, which themselves are managed with statements.

Python's Statements

Table 10-1 summarizes Python's statement set.* This part of the book deals with entries in the table from the top through break and continue. You've informally been introduced to a few of the statements in Table 10-1 already; this part of the book will fill in details that were skipped earlier, introduce the rest of Python's procedural statement set, and cover the overall syntax model. Statements lower in Table 10-1 that have to do with larger program units—functions, classes, modules, and exceptions—lead to larger programming ideas, so they will each have a section of their own. More exotic statements like exec (which compiles and executes code constructed as strings) are covered later in the book, or in Python standard documentation.

Table 10-1. Python statements

Statement	Role	Example
Assignment	Creating references	`a, b, c = 'good', 'bad', 'ugly'`
Calls	Running functions	`log.write("spam, ham\n")`
print	Printing objects	`print 'The Killer', joke`
if/elif/else	Selecting actions	`if "python" in text:` `    print text`
for/else	Sequence iteration	`for x in mylist:` `    print x`
while/else	General loops	`while X > Y:` `    print 'hello'`
pass	Empty placeholder	`while True:` `    pass`
break, continue	Loop jumps	`while True:` `    if not line: break`

try/except/finally	Catching exceptions	`try:`
		`    action( )`
		`except:`
		`    print 'action error'`

raise	Triggering exceptions	`raise endSearch, location`
import, from	Module access	`import sys` `from sys import stdin`

def, return, yield	Building functions	`def f(a, b, c=1, *d):`
		`    return a+b+c+d[0]`
		`def gen(n):`
		`    for i in n, yield i*2`

---

* Technically speaking, in Python 2.5, yield became an expression instead of a statement, and the try/except and try/finally statements were merged (the two were formerly separate statements, but we can now say both except and finally in the same try statement). Also, a new with/as statement is to be added in Python 2.6 to encode context managers—roughly speaking, it's an alternative to try/finally exception-related operations (in 2.5, with/as is an optional extension, and is not available unless you explicitly turn it on by running the statement from __future__ import with_statement). See Python manuals for more details. Further in the future, in 3.0, print and exec will become function calls instead of statements, and a new nonlocal statement will have a purpose much like that of today's global.

Table 10-1. Python statements (continued)

Statement	Role	Example
class	Building objects	`class subclass(Superclass):` `    staticData = []`

global	Namespaces	`def function():`
		`    global x, y`
		`    x = 'new'`

del	Deleting references	`del data[k]`
		`del data[i:j]`
		`del obj.attr`
		`del variable`

exec	Running code strings	`exec "import " + modName` `exec code in gdict, ldict`
assert	Debugging checks	`assert X > Y`
with/as	Context managers (2.6)	`with open('data') as myfile:` `    process(myfile)`

A Tale of Two ifs

Before we delve into the details of any of the concrete statements in Table 10-1, I want to begin our look at Python statement syntax by showing you what you are *not* going to type in Python code so you can compare and contrast it with other syntax models you might have seen in the past.

Consider the following `if` statement, coded in a C-like language:

```
if (x > y) {
    x = 1;
    y = 2;
}
```

This might be a statement in C, C++, Java, JavaScript, or Perl. Now, look at the equivalent statement in the Python language:

```
if x > y:
    x = 1
    y = 2
```

The first thing that may pop out at you is that the equivalent Python statement is less, well, cluttered—that is, there are fewer syntactic components. This is by design; as a scripting language, one of Python's goals is to make programmers' lives easier by requiring less typing.

More specifically, when you compare the two syntax models, you'll notice that Python adds one new thing to the mix, and that three items that are present in the C-like language are not present in Python code.

What Python Adds

The one new syntax component in Python is the colon character (:). All Python *compound statements* (i.e., statements that have statements nested inside them) follow the same general pattern of a header line terminated in a colon followed by a nested block of code usually indented underneath the header line, like this:

```
Header line:
    Nested statement block
```

The colon is required, and omitting it is probably the most common coding mistake among new Python programmers—it's certainly one I've witnessed thousands of times in Python training classes. In fact, if you are new to Python, you'll almost certainly forget the colon character very soon. Most Python-friendly editors make this mistake easy to spot, and including it eventually becomes an unconscious habit (so much so that you may start typing colons into your C++ code, too, generating many entertaining error messages from your C++ compiler!).

What Python Removes

Although Python requires the extra colon character, there are three things programmers in C-like languages must include that you don't generally have to in Python.

Parentheses are optional

The first of these is the set of parentheses around the tests at the top of the statement:

```
if (x < y)
```

The parentheses here are required by the syntax of many C-like languages. In Python, they are not—we simply omit the parentheses, and the statement works the same way:

```
if x < y
```

Technically speaking, because every expression can be enclosed in parentheses, including them will not hurt in this Python code, and they are not treated as an error if present. *But don't do that*: you'll be wearing out your keyboard needlessly, and broadcasting to the world that you're an ex-C programmer still learning Python (I was once, too). The Python way is to simply omit the parentheses in these kinds of statements altogether.

End of line is end of statement

The second and more significant syntax component you won't find in Python code is the semicolon. You don't need to terminate statements with semicolons in Python the way you do in C-like languages:

```
x = 1;
```

In Python, the general rule is that the end of a line automatically terminates the statement that appears on that line. In other words, you can leave off the semicolons, and it works the same way:

```
x = 1
```

There are some ways to work around this rule, as you'll see in a moment. But, in general, you write one statement per line for the vast majority of Python code, and no semicolon is required.

Here, too, if you are pining for your C programming days (if such a state is possible…), you can continue to use semicolons at the end of each statement—the language lets you get away with them if they are present. *But don't do that either* (really!); again, doing so tells the world that you're still a C programmer who hasn't quite made the switch to Python coding. The Pythonic style is to leave off the semicolons altogether.

End of indentation is end of block

The third and final syntax component that Python removes, and perhaps the most unusual one to soon-to-be-ex-C programmers (until they use it for 10 minutes, and realize it's actually a feature), is that you do not type anything explicit in your code to syntactically mark the beginning and end of a nested block of code. You don't need to include begin/end, then/endif, or braces around the nested block, as you do in C-like languages:

```
if (x > y) {
    x = 1;
    y = 2;
}
```

Instead, in Python, we consistently indent all the statements in a given single nested block the same distance to the right, and Python uses the statements' physical indentation to determine where the block starts and stops:

```
if x > y:
    x = 1
    y = 2
```

By *indentation*, I mean the blank whitespace all the way to the left of the two nested statements here. Python doesn't care how you indent (you may use either spaces or tabs), or how much you indent (you may use any number of spaces or tabs). In fact, the indentation of one nested block can be totally different from that of another. The syntax rule is only that for a given single nested block, all of its statements must be indented the same distance to the right. If this is not the case, you will get a syntax error, and your code will not run until you repair its indentation to be consistent.

Why Indentation Syntax?

The indentation rule may seem unusual at first glance to programmers accustomed to C-like languages, but it is a deliberate feature of Python, and one of the main ways that Python almost forces programmers to produce uniform, regular, and readable code. It essentially means that you must line up your code vertically, in columns, according to its logical structure. The net effect is to make your code more consistent and readable (unlike much of the code written in C-like languages).

To put that more strongly, aligning your code according to its logical structure is a major part of making it readable, and thus reusable and maintainable, by yourself and others. In fact, even if you never use Python after reading this book, you should get into the habit of aligning your code for readability in any block-structured language. Python forces the issue by making this a part of its syntax, but it's an important thing to do in any programming language, and it has a huge impact on the usefulness of your code.

Your mileage may vary, but when I was still doing development on a full-time basis, I was mostly paid to work on large old C++ programs that had been worked on by many programmers over the years. Almost invariably, each programmer had his or her own style for indenting code. For example, I'd often be asked to change a while loop coded in the C++ language that began like this:

```
while (x > 0) {
```

Before we even get into indentation, there are three or four ways that programmers can arrange these braces in a C-like language, and organizations often have political debates and write standards manuals to address the options (which seems more than a little off-topic for the problem to be solved by programming). Ignoring that, here's the scenario I often encountered in C++ code. The first person who worked on the code indented the loop four spaces:

```
while (x > 0) {
    --------;
    --------;
```

That person eventually moved on to management, only to be replaced by someone who liked to indent further to the right:

```
while (x > 0) {
    --------;
    --------;
        --------;
    --------;
```

That person later moved on to other opportunities, and someone else picked up the code who liked to indent less:

```
while (x > 0) {
    --------;
    --------;
            --------;
            --------;
--------;
--------;
}
```

And so on. Eventually, the block is terminated by a closing brace (}), which of course makes this block-structured code (he says, sarcastically). In any block-structured language, Python or otherwise, if nested blocks are not indented consistently, they become very difficult for the reader to interpret, change, or reuse. Readability matters, and indentation is a major component of readability.

Here is another example that may have burned you in the past if you've done much programming in a C-like language. Consider the following statement in C:

```
if (x)
    if (y)
        statement1;
else
    statement2;
```

Which if does the else here go with? Surprisingly, the else is paired with the nested if statement (if (y)), even though it looks visually as though it is associated with the outer if (x). This is a classic pitfall in the C language, and it can lead to the reader completely misinterpreting the code, and changing it incorrectly in ways that might not be uncovered until the Mars rover crashes into a giant rock!

This cannot happen in Python—because indentation is significant, the way the code looks is the way it will work. Consider an equivalent Python statement:

```
if x:
    if y:
        statement1
else:
    statement2
```

In this example, the if that the else lines up with vertically is the one it is associated with logically (the outer if x). In a sense, Python is a WYSIWYG language—what you see is what you get because the way code looks is the way it runs, regardless of who coded it.

If this still isn't enough to underscore the benefits of Python's syntax, here's another anecdote. Early in my career, I worked at a successful company that developed systems software in the C language, where consistent indentation is not required. Even so, when we checked our code into source control at the end of the day, this company ran an automated script that analyzed the indentation used in the code. If the script noticed that we'd indented our code inconsistently, we received an automated email about it the next morning—and so did our bosses!

My point is that even when a language doesn't require it, good programmers know that consistent use of indentation has a huge impact on code readability and quality. The fact that Python promotes this to the level of syntax is seen by most as a feature of the language.

Finally, keep in mind that nearly every programmer-friendly text editor in use today has built-in support for Python's syntax model. In the IDLE Python GUI, for example, lines of code are automatically indented when you are typing a nested block; pressing the Backspace key backs up one level of indentation, and you can customize how far to the right IDLE indents statements in a nested block.

There is no absolute standard for how to indent: four spaces or one tab per level is common, but it's up to you to decide how and how much you wish to indent. Indent further to the right for further nested blocks, and less to close the prior block. More-over, generating tabs instead of braces is no more difficult in practice for tools that must output Python code. In general, do what you should be doing in a C-like language, any-how, but get rid of the braces, and your code will satisfy Python's syntax rules.

A Few Special Cases

As mentioned previously, in Python's syntax model:

- The end of a line terminates the statement on that line (without semicolons).
- Nested statements are blocked and associated by their physical indentation (without braces).

Those rules cover almost all Python code you'll write or see in practice. However, Python also provides some special-purpose rules that allow customization of both statements and nested statement blocks.

Statement rule special cases

Although statements normally appear one per line, it is possible to squeeze more than one statement onto a single line in Python by separating them with semicolons:

```
a = 1; b = 2; print a + b          # Three statements on one line
```

This is the only place in Python where semicolons are required: as *statement separators*. This only works, though, if the statements thus combined are not themselves compound statements. In other words, you can chain together only simple statements, like assignments, prints, and function calls. Compound statements must still appear on lines of their own (otherwise, you could squeeze an entire program onto one line, which probably would not make you very popular among your coworkers!).

The other special rule for statements is essentially the inverse: you can make a single statement span across multiple lines. To make this work, you simply have to enclose part of your statement in a bracketed pair—parentheses (( )), square brackets ([ ]), or dictionary braces ({}). Any code enclosed in these constructs can cross multiple lines: your statement doesn't end until Python reaches the line containing the closing part of the pair. For instance, to continue a list literal:

```
mlist = [111,
         222,
         333]
```

Because the code is enclosed in a square brackets pair, Python simply drops down to the next line until it encounters the closing bracket. Dictionaries can also span lines this way, and parentheses handle tuples, function calls, and expressions. The indentation of the continuation lines does not matter, though common sense dictates that the lines should be aligned somehow for readability.

Parentheses are the catchall device—because any expression can be wrapped up in them, simply inserting a left parenthesis allows you to drop down to the next line and continue your statement:

```
X = (A + B +
     C + D)
```

This technique works with compound statements, too, by the way. Anywhere you need to code a large expression, simply wrap it in parentheses to continue it on the next line:

```
if (A == 1 and
    B == 2 and
    C == 3):
        print 'spam' * 3
```

An older rule also allows for continuation lines when the prior line ends in a backslash:

```
X = A + B + \
    C + D
```

But this alternative technique is dated, and somewhat frowned on today because it's difficult to notice and maintain the backslashes, and it's fairly brittle (there can be no spaces after the backslash). It's also another throwback to the C language, where it is commonly used in "#define" macros; again, when in Pythonland, do as Pythonistas do, not as C programmers do.

Block rule special case

As mentioned previously, statements in a nested block of code are normally associated by being indented the same amount to the right. As one special case here, the body of a compound statement can instead appear on the same line as the header in Python, after the colon:

```
if x > y: print x
```

This allows us to code single-line if statements, single-line loops, and so on. Here again, though, this will work only if the body of the compound statement itself does not contain any compound statements. That is, only simple statements—assignments, prints, function calls, and the like—are allowed after the colon. Larger statements must still appear on lines by themselves. Extra parts of compound statements (such as the else part of an if, which we'll meet later) must also be on separate lines of their own. The body can consist of multiple simple statements separated by semicolons, but this tends to be frowned on.

In general, even though it's not always required, if you keep all your statements on individual lines, and always indent your nested blocks, your code will be easier to read and change in the future. To see a prime and common exception to one of these rules in action, however (the use of a single-line if statement to break out of a loop), let's move on to the next section and write some real code.

A Quick Example: Interactive Loops

We'll see all these syntax rules in action when we tour Python's specific compound statements in the next few chapters, but they work the same everywhere in the Python language. To get started, let's work through a brief, realistic example that demonstrates the way that statement syntax and statement nesting come together in practice, and introduces a few statements along the way.

A Simple Interactive Loop

Suppose you're asked to write a Python program that interacts with a user in a console window. Maybe you're accepting inputs to send to a database, or reading numbers to be used in a calculation. Regardless of the purpose, you need to code a loop that reads one or more inputs from a user typing on a keyboard, and prints back a result for each. In other words, you need to write a classic read/evaluate/print loop program.

In Python, typical boilerplate code for such an interactive loop might look like this:

```
while True:
    reply = raw_input('Enter text:')
    if reply == 'stop': break
    print reply.upper()
```

This code makes use of a few new ideas:

- The code leverages the Python while loop, Python's most general looping statement. We'll study the while statement in more detail later, but in short, it consists of the word while, followed by an expression that is interpreted as a true or false result, followed by a nested block of code that is repeated while the test at the top is true (the word True here is considered always true).

- The raw_input built-in function we met earlier in the book is used here for general console input—it prints its optional argument string as a prompt, and returns the user's typed reply as a string.

- A single-line if statement that makes use of the special rule for nested blocks also appears here: the body of the if appears on the header line after the colon instead of being indented on a new line underneath it. This would work either way, but as it's coded, we've saved an extra line.

- Finally, the Python break statement is used to exit the loop immediately—it simply jumps out of the loop statement altogether, and the program continues after the loop. Without this exit statement, the while would loop forever, as its test is always true.

In effect, this combination of statements means essentially "read a line from the user and print it in uppercase until the user enters the word 'stop.'" There are other ways to code such a loop, but the form used here is very common in Python code.

Notice that all three lines nested under the while header line are indented the same amount—because they line up vertically in a column this way, they are the block of code that is associated with the while test and repeated. Either the end of the source file or a lesser-indented statement will terminate the loop body block.

When run, here is the sort of interaction we get from this code:

```
Enter text:spam
SPAM
Enter text:42
42
Enter text:stop
```

Doing Math on User Inputs

Our script works, but now suppose that instead of converting a text string to uppercase, we want to do some math with numeric input—squaring it, for example, perhaps in some misguided effort to discourage users who happen to be obsessed with youth. We might try statements like these to achieve the desired effect:

```
>>> reply = '20'
>>> reply ** 2
...error text omitted...
TypeError: unsupported operand type(s) for ** or pow(): 'str' and 'int'
```

This won't quite work in our script, though, because (as discussed in the last part of the book) Python won't convert object types in expressions unless they are all numeric, and input from a user is always returned to our script as a string. We cannot raise a string of digits to a power unless we convert it manually to an integer:

```
>>> int(reply) ** 2
400
```

Armed with this information, we can now recode our loop to perform the necessary math:

```
while True:
    reply = raw_input('Enter text:')
    if reply == 'stop': break
    print int(reply) ** 2
print 'Bye'
```

This script uses a single-line `if` statement to exit on "stop" as before, but also converts inputs to perform the required math. This version also adds an exit message at the bottom. Because the `print` statement in the last line is not indented as much as the nested block of code, it is not considered part of the loop body, and will run only once, after the loop is exited:

```
Enter text:2
4
Enter text:40
1600
Enter text:stop
Bye
```

Handling Errors by Testing Inputs

So far so good, but notice what happens when the input is invalid:

```
Enter text:xxx
...error text omitted...
ValueError: invalid literal for int() with base 10: 'xxx'
```

The built-in `int` function raises an exception here in the face of a mistake. If we want our script to be robust, we can check the string's content ahead of time with the string object's `isdigit` method:

```
>>> S = '123'
>>> T = 'xxx'
>>> S.isdigit(), T.isdigit()
(True, False)
```

This also gives us an excuse to further nest the statements in our example. The following new version of our interactive script uses a full-blown `if` statement to work around the exception on errors:

```
while True:
    reply = raw_input('Enter text:')
    if reply == 'stop':
        break
    elif not reply.isdigit():
        print 'Bad!' * 8
    else:
        print int(reply) ** 2
print 'Bye'
```

We'll study the if statement in more detail in Chapter 12, but it's a fairly light-weight tool for coding logic in scripts. In its full form, it consists of the word if followed by a test and an associated block of code, one or more optional elif ("else if") tests and code blocks, and an optional else part, with an associated block of code at the bottom to serve as a default. Python runs the block of code associated with the first test that is true, working from top to bottom, or the else part if all tests are false.

The if, elif, and else parts in the preceding example are associated as part of the same statement because they all line up vertically (i.e., share the same level of indentation). The if statement spans from the word if to the start of the print statement on the last line of the script. In turn, the entire if block is part of the while loop because all of it is indented under the loop's header line. Statement nesting is natural once you get the hang of it.

When we run our new script, its code catches errors before they occur, and prints an (arguably silly) error message to demonstrate:

```
Enter text:5
25
Enter text:xyz
Bad!Bad!Bad!Bad!Bad!Bad!Bad!Bad!
Enter text:10
100
Enter text:stop
```

Handling Errors with try Statements

The preceding solution works, but as you'll see later in the book, the most general way to handle errors in Python is to catch and recover from them completely using the Python try statement. We'll explore this statement in depth in the last part of this book, but, as a preview, using a try here can lead to code that some would claim is simpler than the prior version:

```
while True:
    reply = raw_input('Enter text:')
    if reply == 'stop': break
    try:
        num = int(reply)
    except:
        print 'Bad!' * 8
    else:
        print int(reply) ** 2
print 'Bye'
```

This version works exactly like the previous one, but we've replaced the explicit error check with code that assumes the conversion will work, and wraps it up in an exception handler for cases when it doesn't. This try statement is composed of the word try followed by the main block of code (the action we are trying to run), followed by an except part that gives the exception handler code, followed by an else part to be run if no exception is raised in the try part. Python first runs the try part, then runs either the except part (if an exception occurs), or the else part (if no exception occurs).

In terms of statement nesting, because the words try, except, and else are all indented to the same level, they are all considered part of the same single try statement. Notice that the else part is associated with the try here, not the if. As we'll see, else can appear in if statements in Python, but also in try statements and loops—its indentation tells you what statement it is a part of.

Again, we'll come back to the try statement later in the book. For now, be aware that because try can be used to intercept any error, it reduces the amount of error-checking code you have to write, and is a very general approach to dealing with unusual cases.

Nesting Code Three Levels Deep

Now, let's look at one last mutation of our script. Nesting can take us even further if we need it to—we could, for example, branch to one of a set of alternatives, based on the relative magnitude of a valid input:

```
while True:
    reply = raw_input('Enter text:')
    if reply == 'stop':
        break
    elif not reply.isdigit():
        print 'Bad!' * 8
    else:
        num = int(reply)
        if num < 20:
            print 'low'
        else:
            print num ** 2
print 'Bye'
```

This version includes an if statement nested in the else clause of another if statement, which is in turn nested in the while loop. When code is conditional, or repeated like this, we simply indent it further to the right. The net effect is like that of the prior versions, but we'll now print "low" for numbers less than 20:

```
Enter text:19
low
Enter text:20
400
Enter text:spam
Bad!Bad!Bad!Bad!Bad!Bad!Bad!Bad!
Enter text:stop
Bye
```

Chapter Summary

That concludes our quick look at Python statement syntax. This chapter introduced the general rules for coding statements and blocks of code. As you've learned, in Python, we normally code one statement per line, and indent all the statements in a nested block the same amount (indentation is part of Python's syntax). However, we also looked at a few exceptions to these rules, including continuation lines and single-line tests and loops. Finally, we put these ideas to work in an interactive script that demonstrated a handful of statements, and showed statement syntax in action.

In the next chapter, we'll start to dig deeper by going over each of Python's basic procedural statements in depth. As you'll see, though, all statements follow the same general rules introduced here.

Chapter Quiz

1. What three things are required in a C-like language, but omitted in Python?
2. How is a statement normally terminated in Python?
3. How are the statements in a nested block of code normally associated in Python?
4. How can you make a statement span over multiple lines?
5. How can you code a compound statement on a single line?
6. Is there any valid reason to type a semicolon at the end of a statement in Python?
7. What is a try statement for?
8. What is the most common coding mistake among Python beginners?

Quiz Answers

1. C-like languages require parentheses around the tests in some statements, semi-colons at the end of each statement, and braces around a nested block of code.
2. The end of a line terminates the statement that appears on that line. Alternatively, if more than one statement appears on the same line, they can be terminated with semicolons; similarly, if a statement spans many lines, you must terminate it by closing a bracketed syntactic pair.
3. The statements in a nested block are all indented the same number of tabs or spaces.
4. A statement can be made to span many lines by enclosing part of it in parentheses, square brackets, or curly braces; the statement ends when Python sees a line that contains the closing part of the pair.
5. The body of a compound statement can be moved to the header line after the colon, but only if the body consists of only noncompound statements.
6. Only when you need to squeeze more than one statement onto a single line of code. Even then, this only works if all the statements are noncompound, and it's discouraged because it can lead to code that is difficult to read.
7. The try statement is used to catch and recover from exceptions (errors) in a Python script. It's usually an alternative to manually checking for errors in your code.
8. Forgetting to type the colon character at the end of the header line in a compound statement is the most common beginner's mistake.

CHAPTER 11

Assignment, Expressions, and print

Now that we've had a quick introduction to Python statement syntax, this chapter begins our in-depth tour of specific Python statements. We'll begin with the basics—assignments, expression statements, and printing. We've already seen all these in action, but here, we'll fill in important details we've skipped so far. Although they're fairly simple, as you'll see, there are optional variations for each of these statement types that will come in handy once you begin writing real Python programs.

Assignment Statements

We've been using the Python assignment statement for a while to assign objects to names. In its basic form, you write the *target* of an assignment on the left of an equals sign, and the *object* to be assigned on the right. The target on the left may be a name or object component, and the object on the right can be an arbitrary expression that computes an object. For the most part, assignments are straightforward, but here are a few properties to keep in mind:

- **Assignments create object references.** As discussed in Chapter 6, Python assignments store references to objects in names or data structure components. They always create references to objects instead of copying the objects. Because of that, Python variables are more like pointers than data storage areas.

- **Names are created when first assigned.** Python creates variable names the first time you assign them a value (i.e., an object reference), so there's no need to predeclare names ahead of time. Some (but not all) data structure slots are created when assigned, too (e.g., dictionary entries, some object attributes). Once assigned, a name is replaced with the value it references whenever it appears in an expression.

- **Names must be assigned before being referenced.** It's an error to use a name to which you haven't yet assigned a value. Python raises an exception if you try, rather than returning some sort of ambiguous default value; if it returned a default instead, it would be more difficult for you to spot typos in your code.

- **Implicit assignments: `import`, `from`, `def`, `class`, `for`, function arguments.** In this section, we're concerned with the = statement, but assignment occurs in many contexts in Python. For instance, we'll see later that module imports, function and class definitions, for loop variables, and function arguments are all implicit assignments. Because assignment works the same everywhere it pops up, all these contexts simply bind names to object references at runtime.

Assignment Statement Forms

Although assignment is a general and pervasive concept in Python, we are primarily interested in assignment statements in this chapter. Table 11-1 illustrates the different assignment statement forms in Python.

Table 11-1. Assignment statement forms

Operation	Interpretation
spam = 'Spam'	Basic form
spam, ham = 'yum', 'YUM'	Tuple assignment (positional)
[spam, ham] = ['yum', 'YUM']	List assignment (positional)
a, b, c, d = 'spam'	Sequence assignment, generalized
spam = ham = 'lunch'	Multiple-target assignment
spams += 42	Augmented assignment (equivalent to spams = spams + 42)

The first form in Table 11-1 is by far the most common: binding a name (or data structure component) to a single object. The other table entries represent special and optional forms that programmers often find convenient:

Tuple- and list-unpacking assignments

   The second and third forms in the table are related. When you code tuples or lists on the left side of the =, Python pairs objects on the right side with targets on the left by position, and assigns them from left to right. For example, in the second line of the table, the name spam is assigned the string 'yum', and the name ham is bound to the string 'YUM'. Internally, Python makes a tuple of the items on the right first, so this is often called a tuple-unpacking assignment.

Sequence assignments

   In recent versions of Python, tuple and list assignments have been generalized into instances of what we now call sequence assignment—any sequence of names can be assigned to any sequence of values, and Python assigns the items one at a time by position. In fact, we can mix and match the types of the sequences involved. The fourth line in Table 11-1, for example, pairs a tuple of names with a string of characters: a is assigned 's', b is assigned 'p', and so on.

Multiple-target assignments

The fifth line in Table 11-1 shows the multiple-target form of assignment. In this form, Python assigns a reference to the same object (the object farthest to the right) to all the targets on the left. In the table, the names spam and ham are both assigned references to the same string object, 'lunch'. The effect is the same as if we coded ham = 'lunch' followed by spam = ham, as ham evaluates to the original string object (i.e., not a separate copy of that object).

Augmented assignments

The last line in Table 11-1 is an example of augmented assignment—a shorthand that combines an expression and an assignment in a concise way. Saying spam += 42, for example, has the same effect as spam = spam + 42, but the augmented form requires less typing, and is generally quicker to run. There's one augmented assignment statement for every binary expression operator in Python.

Sequence Assignments

We've already used basic assignments in this book. Here are a few simple examples of sequence-unpacking assignments in action:

```
% python
>>> nudge = 1
>>> wink  = 2
>>> A, B = nudge, wink        # Tuple assignment
>>> A, B                      # Like A = nudge; B = wink
(1, 2)
>>> [C, D] = [nudge, wink]    # List assignment
>>> C, D
(1, 2)
```

Notice that we really are coding two tuples in the third line in this interaction—we've just omitted their enclosing parentheses. Python pairs the values in the tuple on the right side of the assignment operator with the variables in the tuple on the left side, and assigns the values one at a time.

Tuple assignment leads to a common coding trick in Python that was introduced in a solution to the exercises from Part II. Because Python creates a temporary tuple that saves the original values of the variables on the right while the statement runs, unpacking assignments are also a way to *swap* two variables' values without creating a temporary variable of your own—the tuple on the right remembers the prior values of the variables automatically:

```
>>> nudge = 1
>>> wink  = 2
>>> nudge, wink = wink, nudge     # Tuples: swaps values
>>> nudge, wink                   # Like T = nudge; nudge = wink; wink = T
(2, 1)
```

In fact, the original tuple and list assignment forms in Python were eventually generalized to accept any type of sequence on the right as long as it is of the same length. You can assign a tuple of values to a list of variables, a string of characters to a tuple of variables, and so on. In all cases, Python assigns items in the sequence on the right to variables in the sequence on the left by position, from left to right:

```
>>> [a, b, c] = (1, 2, 3)          # Assign tuple of values to list of names
>>> a, c
(1, 3)
>>> (a, b, c) = "ABC"              # Assign string of characters to tuple
>>> a, c
('A', 'C')
```

Technically speaking, sequence assignment actually supports any iterable object on the right, not just any sequence. This is a more general concept that we will explore in Chapters 13 and 17.

Advanced sequence assignment patterns

One note here—although we can mix and match sequence types around the = symbol, we still must have the *same number* of items on the right as we have variables on the left, or we'll get an error:

```
>>> string = 'SPAM'
>>> a, b, c, d = string           # Same number on both sides
>>> a, d
('S', 'M')

>>> a, b, c = string              # Error if not
...error text omitted...
ValueError: too many values to unpack
```

To be more general, we need to slice. There are a variety of ways to employ slicing to make this last case work:

```
>>> a, b, c = string[0], string[1], string[2:]   # Index and slice
>>> a, b, c
('S', 'P', 'AM')

>>> a, b, c = list(string[:2]) + [string[2:]]    # Slice and concatenate
>>> a, b, c
('S', 'P', 'AM')

>>> a, b = string[:2]                            # Same, but simpler
>>> c = string[2:]
>>> a, b, c
('S', 'P', 'AM')

>>> (a, b), c = string[:2], string[2:]           # Nested sequences
>>> a, b, c
('S', 'P', 'AM')
```

As the last example in this interaction demonstrates, we can even assign *nested* sequences, and Python unpacks their parts according to their shape, as expected. In this case, we are assigning a tuple of two items, where the first item is a nested sequence (a string) exactly as though we had coded it this way:

```
>>> ((a, b), c) = ('SP', 'AM')        # Paired up by shape and position
>>> a, b, c
('S', 'P', 'AM')
```

Python pairs the first string on the right ('SP') with the first tuple on the left ((a, b)), and assigns one character at a time, before assigning the entire second string ('AM') to the variable c all at once. In this event, the sequence-nesting shape of the object on the left must match that of the object on the right. Nested sequence assignment like this is somewhat advanced, and rare to see, but it can be convenient for picking out the parts of data structures with known shapes. For example, this technique also works in function argument lists because function arguments are passed by assignment (as we'll see in the next part of the book).

Sequence-unpacking assignments also give rise to another common coding idiom in Python—assigning an integer series to a set of variables:

```
>>> red, green, blue = range(3)
>>> red, blue
(0, 2)
```

This initializes the three names to the integer codes 0, 1, and 2, respectively (it's Python's equivalent of the *enumerated* data types you may have seen in other languages). To make sense of this, you need to know that the range built-in function generates a list of successive integers:

```
>>> range(3)                          # Try list(range(3)) in Python 3.0
[0, 1, 2]
```

Because range is commonly used in for loops, we'll say more about it in Chapter 13. Another place you may see a tuple assignment at work is for splitting a sequence into its front and the rest in loops like this:

```
>>> L = [1, 2, 3, 4]
>>> while L:
...     front, L = L[0], L[1:]
...     print front, L
...
1 [2, 3, 4]
2 [3, 4]
3 [4]
4 []
```

The tuple assignment in the loop here could be coded as the following two lines instead, but it's often more convenient to string them together:

```
...     front = L[0]
...     L = L[1:]
```

Notice that this code is using the list as a sort of stack data structure—something we can often also achieve with the append and pop methods of list objects; here, front = L.pop(0) would have much the same effect as the tuple assignment statement, but it would be an in-place change. We'll learn more about while loops, and other (and often better) ways to step through a sequence with for loops, in Chapter 13.

Multiple-Target Assignments

A multiple-target assignment simply assigns all the given names to the object all the way to the right. The following, for example, assigns the three variables a, b, and c to the string 'spam':

```
>>> a = b = c = 'spam'
>>> a, b, c
('spam', 'spam', 'spam')
```

This form is equivalent to (but easier to code) than these three assignments:

```
>>> c = 'spam'
>>> b = c
>>> a = b
```

Multiple-target assignment and shared references

Keep in mind that there is just one object here, shared by all three variables (they all wind up pointing to the same object in memory). This behavior is fine for immutable types—initializing a set of counters to zero, for example (recall that variables must be assigned before they can be used in Python, so you must initialize counters to zero before you can start adding to them):

```
>>> a = b = 0
>>> b = b + 1
>>> a, b
(0, 1)
```

Here, changing b only changes b because numbers do not support in-place changes. As long as the object assigned is immutable, it's irrelevant if more than one name references it.

As usual, though, we have to be more cautious when initializing variables to an empty mutable object such as a list or dictionary:

```
>>> a = b = []
>>> b.append(42)
>>> a, b
([42], [42])
```

This time, because a and b reference the same object, appending to it in-place through b will impact what we see through a as well. This is really just another example of the shared reference phenomenon we first met in Chapter 6. To avoid the

---

issue, initialize mutable objects in separate statements instead, so that each creates a distinct empty object by running a distinct literal expression:

```
>>> a = []
>>> b = []
>>> b.append(42)
>>> a, b
([], [42])
```

Augmented Assignments

Beginning with Python 2.0, the set of additional assignment statement formats listed in Table 11-2 became available. Known as *augmented assignments*, and borrowed from the C language, these formats are mostly just shorthand. They imply the combination of a binary expression, and an assignment. For instance, the following two formats are now roughly equivalent:

```
X = X + Y        # Traditional form
X += Y           # Newer augmented form
```

Table 11-2. Augmented assignment statements

X += Y	X &= Y	X -= Y	X |= Y
X *= Y	X ^= Y	X /= Y	X >>= Y
X %= Y	X <<= Y	X **= Y	X //= Y

Augmented assignment works on any type that supports the implied binary expression. For example, here are two ways to add 1 to a name:

```
>>> x = 1
>>> x = x + 1        # Traditional
>>> x
2
>>> x += 1           # Augmented
>>> x
3
```

When applied to a string, the augmented form performs concatenation instead. Thus, the second line here is equivalent to typing the longer S = S + "SPAM":

```
>>> S = "spam"
>>> S += "SPAM"        # Implied concatenation
>>> S
'spamSPAM'
```

As shown in Table 11-2, there are analogous augmented assignment forms for every Python binary expression operator (i.e., each operator with values on the left and right side). For instance, X *= Y multiplies and assigns, X >>= Y shifts right and assigns, and so on. X //= Y (for floor division) was added in version 2.2.

Augmented assignments have three advantages:[*]

- There's less for you to type. Need I say more?

- The left side only has to be evaluated once. In X += Y, X may be a complicated object expression. In the augmented form, it need only be evaluated once. However, in the long form, X = X + Y, X appears twice, and must be run twice. Because of this, augmented assignments usually run faster.

- The optimal technique is automatically chosen. For objects that support in-place changes, the augmented forms automatically perform in-place change operations instead of slower copies.

The last point here requires a bit more explanation. For augmented assignments, in-place operations may be applied for mutable objects as an optimization. Recall that lists can be extended in a variety of ways. To add a single item to the end of a list, we can concatenate or call append:

```
>>> L = [1, 2]
>>> L = L + [3]          # Concatenate: slower
>>> L
[1, 2, 3]
>>> L.append(4)          # Faster, but in-place
>>> L
[1, 2, 3, 4]
```

And to add a set of items to the end, we can either concatenate again, or call the list extend method:[†]

```
>>> L = L + [5, 6]       # Concatenate: slower
>>> L
[1, 2, 3, 4, 5, 6]
>>> L.extend([7, 8])     # Faster, but in-place
>>> L
[1, 2, 3, 4, 5, 6, 7, 8]
```

In both cases, concatenation is less prone to the side effects of shared object references, but will generally run slower than the in-place equivalent. Concatenation operations must create a new object, copy in the list on the left, and then copy in the list on the right. By contrast, in-place method calls simply add items at the end of a memory block.

When we use augmented assignment to extend a list, we can forget these details—for example, Python automatically calls the quicker extend method instead of using the slower concatenation operation implied by +:

---

[*] C/C++ programmers take note: although Python now supports statements like X += Y, it still does not have C's auto-increment/decrement operators (e.g., X++, --X). These don't quite map to the Python object model because Python has no notion of in-place changes to immutable objects like numbers.

[†] As suggested in Chapter 6, we can also use slice assignment (e.g., L[len(L):] = [11,12,13]), but this works roughly the same as the simpler list extend method.

```
>>> L += [9, 10]           # Mapped to L.extend([9, 10])
>>> L
[1, 2, 3, 4, 5, 6, 7, 8, 9, 10]
```

Augmented assignment and shared references

This behavior is usually what we want, but notice that it implies the += is an in-place change for lists; thus, it is not exactly like + concatenation, which always makes a new object. As for all shared reference cases, the difference might matter if other names reference the object being changed:

```
>>> L = [1, 2]
>>> M = L                  # L and M reference the same object
>>> L = L + [3, 4]         # Concatenation makes a new object
>>> L, M                   # Changes L but not M
([1, 2, 3, 4], [1, 2])

>>> L = [1, 2]
>>> M = L
>>> L += [3, 4]            # But += really means extend
>>> L, M                   # M sees the in-place change too!
([1, 2, 3, 4], [1, 2, 3, 4])
```

This only matters for mutables like lists and dictionaries, and it is a fairly obscure case (at least, until it impacts your code!). As always, make copies of your mutable objects if you need to break the shared reference structure.

Variable Name Rules

Now that we've explored assignment statements, it's time to get more formal about the use of variable names. In Python, names come into existence when you assign values to them, but there are a few rules to follow when picking names for things in your programs:

Syntax: (underscore or letter) + (any number of letters, digits, or underscores)
Variable names must start with an underscore or letter, which can be followed by any number of letters, digits, or underscores. _spam, spam, and Spam_1 are legal names, but 1_Spam, spam$, and @#! are not.

Case matters: SPAM is not the same as spam
Python always pays attention to case in programs, both in names you create, and in reserved words. For instance, the names X and x refer to two different variables. For portability, case also matters in the names of imported module files, even on platforms where the filesystems are case insensitive.

Reserved words are off-limits

Names you define cannot be the same as words that mean special things in the Python language. For instance, if you try to use a variable name like class, Python will raise a syntax error, but klass and Class work fine. Table 11-3 lists the words that are currently reserved (and hence off-limits) in Python.

Table 11-3. Python reserved words

and	elif	if	pass
as (in 2.6 and later)	else	import	print
assert	except	in	raise
break	exec	is	return
class	finally	lambda	try
continue	for	nonlocal (in 3.0)	while
def	from	not	with (in 2.6 and later)
del	global	or	yield

 yield was an optional extension in Python 2.2, but is a standard keyword as of 2.3. It is used in conjunction with generator functions, a newer feature discussed in Chapter 17. This was one of a small handful of instances where Python broke with backward compatibility. Still, yield was phased in over time—it began generating warnings in 2.2, and was not enabled until 2.3.

Similarly, in Python 2.6, the words with and as are scheduled to become new reserved words for use in context managers (a new form of exception handling). These two words are not reserved in 2.5, unless the context manager feature is turned on manually (see Chapter 27 for details). When used in 2.5, with and as generate warnings about the upcoming change—except in the version of IDLE in Python 2.5, which appears to have enabled this feature for you (that is, using these words as variable names does generate errors in 2.5, but only in its version of the IDLE GUI).

Python's reserved words are always all lowercase, and they are truly reserved; unlike names in the built-in scope that you will meet in the next part of this book, you cannot redefine reserved words by assignment (e.g., and = 1 results in a syntax error).[*]

Furthermore, because module names in import statements become variables in your script, this constraint extends to your module filenames—you can code files called *and.py* and *my-code.py*, but you cannot import them because their names without the ".py" extension become variables in your code, and so must follow all the variable rules just outlined (reserved words are off-limits, and dashes won't work, though underscores will). We'll revisit this idea in Part V.

---

[*] In the Jython Java-based implementation of Python, though, user-defined variable names can sometimes be the same as Python reserved words.

Naming conventions

Besides these rules, there is also a set of naming *conventions*—rules that are not required, but are followed in normal practice. For instance, because names with two leading and trailing underscores (e.g., __name__) generally have special meaning to the Python interpreter, you should avoid this pattern for your own names. Here is a list of the conventions Python follows:

- Names that begin with a single underscore (_X) are not imported by a from module import * statement (described in Chapter 19).

- Names that have two leading and trailing underscores (__X__) are system-defined names that have special meaning to the interpreter.

- Names that begin with two underscores, and do not end with two more (__X) are localized ("mangled") to enclosing classes (described in Chapter 26).

- The name that is just a single underscore (_) retains the result of the last expression when working interactively.

In addition to these Python interpreter conventions, there are various other conventions that Python programmers usually follow as well. For instance, later in the book, we'll see that class names commonly start with an uppercase letter, and module names with a lowercase letter, and that the name self, though not reserved, usually has a special role in classes. In Part IV, we'll also study another, larger category of names known as the *built-ins*, which are predefined, but not reserved (and so can be reassigned: open = 42 works, though sometimes you might wish it didn't!).

Names have no type, but objects do

This is mostly review, but remember that it's crucial to keep Python's distinction between names and objects clear. As described in "The Dynamic Typing Interlude" in Chapter 6, objects have a type (e.g., integer, list), and may be mutable or not. Names (a.k.a. variables), on the other hand, are always just references to objects; they have no notion of mutability, and have no associated type information, apart from the type of the object they happen to reference at a given point in time.

It's OK to assign the same name to different kinds of objects at different times:

```
>>> x = 0           # x bound to an integer object
>>> x = "Hello"     # Now it's a string
>>> x = [1, 2, 3]   # And now it's a list
```

In later examples, you'll see that this generic nature of names can be a decided advantage in Python programming.* In Part IV, you'll learn that names also live in something called a *scope*, which defines where they can be used; the place where you assign a name determines where it is visible.

---

* If you've used C++, you may be interested to know that there is no notion of C++'s const declaration in Python; certain objects may be immutable, but names can always be assigned. Python also has ways to hide names in classes and modules, but they're not the same as C++'s declarations.

Expression Statements

In Python, you can use an expression as a statement, too (that is, on a line by itself). But because the result of the expression won't be saved, it makes sense to do so only if the expression does something useful as a side effect. Expressions are commonly used as statements in two situations:

For calls to functions and methods
> Some functions and methods do lots of work without returning a value. Such functions are sometimes called *procedures* in other languages. Because they don't return values that you might be interested in retaining, you can call these functions with expression statements.

For printing values at the interactive prompt
> Python echoes back the results of expressions typed at the interactive command line. Technically, these are expression statements, too; they serve as a shorthand for typing print statements.

Table 11-4 lists some common expression statement forms in Python. Calls to functions and methods are coded with zero or more argument objects (really, expressions that evaluate to objects) in parentheses, after the function/method name.

Table 11-4. Common Python expression statements

Operation	Interpretation
spam(eggs, ham)	Function calls
spam.ham(eggs)	Method calls
spam	Printing variables in the interactive interpreter
spam < ham and ham != eggs	Compound expressions
spam < ham < eggs	Range tests

The last line in the table is a special form: Python lets us string together magnitude comparison tests, to code chained comparisons such as range tests. For instance, the expression (A < B < C) tests whether B is between A and C; it's equivalent to the Boolean test (A < B and B < C), but is easier on the eyes (and the keyboard). Compound expressions aren't normally written as statements, but doing so is syntactically legal, and can even be useful at the interactive prompt if you're not sure of an expression's result.

Beware that although expressions can appear as statements in Python, statements can't be used as expressions. For instance, Python doesn't allow you to embed assignment statements (=) in other expressions. The rationale for this is that it avoids common coding mistakes; you can't accidentally change a variable by typing = when you really mean to use the == equality test. You'll see how to code around this when you meet the Python while loop in Chapter 13.

Expression Statements and In-Place Changes

This brings up a mistake that is common in Python work. Expression statements are often used to run list methods that change a list in-place:

```
>>> L = [1, 2]
>>> L.append(3)          # Append is an in-place change
>>> L
[1, 2, 3]
```

However, it's not unusual for Python newcomers to code such an operation as an assignment statement instead, intending to assign L to the larger list:

```
>>> L = L.append(4)      # But append returns None, not L
>>> print L              # So we lose our list!
None
```

This doesn't quite work, though—calling an in-place change operation such as append, sort, or reverse on a list always changes the list in-place, but these methods do not return the list they have changed.

In fact, they return the None object. If you assign such an operation's result back to the variable name, you effectively lose the list (and it is probably garbage collected in the process!).

So, don't do this. We'll revisit this phenomenon in the "Common Coding Gotchas" warnings section at the end of this part of the book because it can also appear in the context of some looping statements we'll meet in later chapters.

print Statements

The print statement prints things—it's simply a programmer-friendly interface to the standard output stream. Technically, it converts an object to its textual representation, and sends this to standard output.

The standard output stream is the same as the C language's stdout; it is usually mapped to the window where you started your Python program (unless redirected to a file or pipe in your system's shell).

In Chapter 9, we looked at some file methods that write text. The print statement is similar, but more focused: print writes objects to the stdout stream (with some default formatting), but file write methods write strings to arbitrary files. Because the standard output stream is available in Python as the stdout object in the built-in sys module (i.e., sys.stdout), it's possible to emulate print with file writes, but print is easier to use.

Table 11-5 lists the print statement's forms.

Table 11-5. print statement forms

Operation	Interpretation
print spam, ham	Print objects to sys.stdout; add a space between the items and a linefeed at the end
print spam, ham,	Same, but don't add linefeed at end of text
print >> myfile, spam, ham	Send text to myfile.write, not to sys.stdout.write

We've seen the basic print statement in action already. By default, it adds a space between the items separated by commas, and adds a linefeed at the end of the current output line:

```
>>> x = 'a'
>>> y = 'b'
>>> print x, y
a b
```

This formatting is just a default; you can choose to use it or not. To suppress the linefeed (so you can add more text to the current line later), end your print statement with a comma, as shown in the second line of Table 11-5. To suppress the space between items, don't print this way—instead, build up an output string yourself using the string concatenation and formatting tools covered in Chapter 7, and print the string all at once:

```
>>> print x + y
ab
>>> print '%s...%s' % (x, y)
a...b
```

The Python "Hello World" Program

To print a "hello world" message, simply print the string:

```
>>> print 'hello world'            # Print a string object
hello world
```

Because expression results are echoed on the interactive command line, you often don't even need to use a print statement there; simply type expressions you'd like to have printed, and their results are echoed back:

```
>>> 'hello world'                  # Interactive echoes
'hello world'
```

Really, the print statement is just an ergonomic feature of Python—it provides a simple interface to the sys.stdout object, with a bit of default formatting. In fact, if you like to work harder than you must, you can also code print operations this way:

```
>>> import sys                     # Printing the hard way
>>> sys.stdout.write('hello world\n')
hello world
```

This code explicitly calls the `write` method of `sys.stdout`—an attribute preset when Python starts up to an open file object connected to the output stream. The `print` statement hides most of those details, providing a simple tool for simple printing tasks.

Redirecting the Output Stream

So, why did I just show you the hard way to print? The `sys.stdout` print equivalent turns out to be the basis of a common technique in Python. In general, `print` and `sys.stdout` are related as follows. This statement:

```
print X
```

is equivalent to the longer:

```
import sys
sys.stdout.write(str(X) + '\n')
```

which manually performs a string conversion with `str`, adds a newline with +, and calls the output stream's `write` method. The long form isn't all that useful for printing by itself. However, it is useful to know that this is exactly what `print` statements do because it is possible to reassign `sys.stdout` to something different from the standard output stream. In other words, this equivalence provides a way for making your `print` statements send their text to other places. For example:

```
import sys
sys.stdout = open('log.txt', 'a')       # Redirects prints to file
...
print x, y, x                           # Shows up in log.txt
```

Here, we reset `sys.stdout` to a manually opened output file object opened in append mode. After the reset, every `print` statement anywhere in the program will write its text to the end of the file *log.txt* instead of to the original output stream. The `print` statements are happy to keep calling `sys.stdout`'s `write` method, no matter what `sys.stdout` happens to refer to. Because there is just one `sys` module in your process, assigning `sys.stdout` this way will redirect every `print` anywhere in your program.

In fact, as this chapter's upcoming sidebar on `print` and `stdout` will explain, you can even reset `sys.stdout` to a nonfile object, as long as it has the expected protocol (a `write` method); when that object is a class, printed text can be routed and processed arbitrarily.

This trick of resetting the output stream is primarily useful for programs originally coded with `print` statements. If you know that output should go to a file to begin with, you can always call file write methods instead. To redirect the output of a print-based program, though, resetting `sys.stdout` provides a convenient alternative to changing every `print` statement, or using system-shell-based redirection syntax.

The print >> file Extension

This trick of redirecting printed text by assigning sys.stdout is very commonly used in practice. But one potential problem with the last section's code is that there is no direct way to restore the original output stream should you need to switch back after printing to a file. Because sys.stdout is just a normal file object, you can always save it and restore it if needed:*

```
>>> import sys
>>> temp = sys.stdout                      # Save for restoring later
>>> sys.stdout = open('log.txt', 'a')      # Redirect prints to a file
>>> print 'spam'                           # Prints go to file, not here
>>> print 1, 2, 3
>>> sys.stdout.close()                     # Flush output to disk
>>> sys.stdout = temp                      # Restore original stream

>>> print 'back here'                      # Prints show up here again
back here
>>> print open('log.txt').read()           # Result of earlier prints
spam
1 2 3
```

This need crops up fairly regularly, and this manual saving and restoring of the original output stream is just complicated enough that a print extension was added to make it unnecessary. When a print statement begins with a >> followed by an output file (or other) object, that single print statement sends its text to the object's write method, but it does not reset sys.stdout. Because the redirection is temporary, normal print statements keep printing to the original output stream:

```
log = open('log.txt', 'a')
print >> log, x, y, z                      # Print to a file-like object
print a, b, c                              # Print to original stdout
```

The >> form of print is handy if you need to print to both files and the standard output stream in the same program. If you use this form, however, be sure to give it a file object (or an object that has the same write method as a file object), not a file's name string:

```
>>> log = open('log.txt', 'w')
>>> print >> log, 1, 2, 3
>>> print >> log, 4, 5, 6
>>> log.close()
>>> print 7, 8, 9
7 8 9
>>> print open('log.txt').read()
1 2 3
4 5 6
```

---

* You can also use the relatively new __stdout__ attribute in the sys module, which refers to the original value sys.stdout had at program startup time. You still need to restore sys.stdout to sys.__stdout__ to go back to this original stream value, though. See the sys module in the library manual for more details.

This extended form of print is also commonly used to print error messages to the standard error stream, sys.stderr. You can either use its file write methods and format the output manually, or print with redirection syntax:

```
>>> import sys
>>> sys.stderr.write(('Bad!' * 8) + '\n')
Bad!Bad!Bad!Bad!Bad!Bad!Bad!Bad!

>>> print >> sys.stderr, 'Bad!' * 8
Bad!Bad!Bad!Bad!Bad!Bad!Bad!Bad!
```

Why You Will Care: print and stdout

The equivalence between the print statement and writing to sys.stdout is important. It makes it possible to reassign sys.stdout to a user-defined object that provides the same methods as files (e.g., write). Because the print statement just sends text to the sys.stdout.write method, you can capture printed text in your programs by assigning sys.stdout to an object whose write method processes the text in arbitrary ways.

For instance, you can send printed text to a GUI window, or tee it off to multiple destinations by defining an object with a write method that does the required routing. You'll see an example of this trick when we study classes later in the book, but abstractly, it looks like this:

```
class FileFaker:
    def write(self, string):
        # Do something with the string
import sys
sys.stdout = FileFaker()
print someObjects            # Sends to class write method
```

This works because print is what we will call a *polymorphic* operation in the next part of this book—it doesn't care what sys.stdout is, only that it has a method (i.e., interface) called write. In recent versions of Python, this redirection to objects is made even simpler with the >> extended form of print because we don't need to reset sys.stdout explicitly:

```
myobj = FileFaker()          # Redirect to an object for one print
print >> myobj, someObjects  # Does not reset sys.stdout
```

Python's built-in raw_input() function reads from the sys.stdin file, so you can intercept read requests in a similar way, using classes that implement file-like read methods. See the raw_input and while loop example in Chapter 10 for more background on this.

Notice that because printed text goes to the stdout stream, it's the way to print HTML in CGI scripts. It also enables you to redirect Python script input and output at the operating system's command line, as usual:

```
python script.py < inputfile > outputfile
python script.py | filterProgram
```

In Python 3.0, the `print` statement is scheduled to become a built-in function, with equivalent utility, but slightly different syntax. The target file and end-of-line behavior are to be specified with keyword arguments. For instance, the statement `print x, y` will become the call `print(x, y)`, and `print >> f, x` will become `print(x, file=f, end=' ')`.

All of this is still in the future, so consult the 3.0 release notes for more details. Current 3.0 plans also call for including a converter script (tentatively named "2to3") that will, among a handful of other things, automatically convert `print` statements in your existing code to `print` calls. It should help, if you find yourself torn between 2.x and 3.x (like this book!).

Chapter Summary

In this chapter, we began our in-depth look at Python statements by exploring assignments, expressions, and `print`s. Although these are generally simple to use, they have some alternative forms that are optional, but often convenient in practice. Augmented assignment statements and the redirection form of `print` statements, for example, allow us to avoid some manual coding work. Along the way, we also studied the syntax of variable names, stream redirection techniques, and a variety of common mistakes to avoid, such as assigning the result of an `append` method call back to a variable.

In the next chapter, we continue our statement tour by filling in details about the `if` statement, Python's main selection tool; there, we'll also revisit Python's syntax model in more depth, and look at the behavior of Boolean expressions. Before we move on, though, the end-of-chapter quiz will test your knowledge of what you've learned here.

Chapter Quiz

1. Name three ways that you can assign three variables to the same value.
2. Why might you need to care when assigning three variables to a mutable object?
3. What's wrong with saying L = L.sort( )?
4. How might you use the print statement to send text to an external file?

Quiz Answers

1. You can use multiple-target assignments (A = B = C = 0), sequence assignment (A, B, C = 0, 0, 0), or multiple assignment statements on separate lines (A = 0, B = 0, C = 0). With the latter technique, as introduced in Chapter 10, you can also string the three separate statements together on the same line by separating them with semicolons (A = 0; B = 0; C = 0).

2. If you assign them this way:

        A = B = C = []

   all three names reference the same object, so changing it in-place from one (e.g., A.append(99)) will affect the others. This is true only for in-place changes to mutable objects like lists and dictionaries; for immutable objects, such as numbers and strings, this issue is irrelevant.

3. The list sort method is like append in that is an in-place change to the subject list—it returns None, not the list it changes. The assignment back to L sets L to None, not the sorted list. As we'll see later in this part of the book, a newer built-in function, sorted, sorts any sequence, and returns a new list with the sorting result; because it is not an in-place change, its result can be meaningfully assigned to a name.

4. You can assign sys.stdout to a manually opened file before the print, or use the extended print >> file statement form to print to a file for a single print statement. You can also redirect all of a program's printed text to a file with special syntax in the system shell, but this is outside Python's scope.

CHAPTER 12

if Tests

This chapter presents the Python if statement, which is the main statement used for selecting from alternative actions based on test results. Because this is our first in-depth look at *compound statements*—statements that embed other statements—we will also explore the general concepts behind the Python statement syntax model here in more detail than we did in the introduction in Chapter 10. And, because the if statement introduces the notion of tests, this chapter will also deal with Boolean expressions, and fill in some details on truth tests in general.

if Statements

In simple terms, the Python if statement selects actions to perform. It's the primary selection tool in Python, and represents much of the *logic* a Python program possesses. It's also our first compound statement. Like all compound Python statements, the if statement may contain other statements, including other ifs. In fact, Python lets you combine statements in a program sequentially (so that they execute one after another), and in an arbitrarily nested fashion (so that they execute only under certain conditions).

General Format

The Python if statement is typical of if statements in most procedural languages. It takes the form of an if test, followed by one or more optional elif ("else if") tests, and a final optional else block. The tests and the else part each have an associated block of nested statements, indented under a header line. When the if statement runs, Python executes the block of code associated with the first test that evaluates to true, or the else block if all tests prove false. The general form of an if statement looks like this:

```
if <test1>:              # if test
    <statements1>        # Associated block
elif <test2>:            # Optional elifs
    <statements2>
```

```
    else:                        # Optional else
        <statements3>
```

Basic Examples

To demonstrate, let's look at a few simple examples of the if statement at work. All parts are optional, except the initial if test and its associated statements; in the simplest case, the other parts are omitted:

```
>>> if 1:
...     print 'true'
...
true
```

Notice how the prompt changes to ... for continuation lines in the basic interface used here (in IDLE, you'll simply drop down to an indented line instead—hit Backspace to back up); a blank line terminates and runs the entire statement. Remember that 1 is Boolean true, so this statement's test always succeeds. To handle a false result, code the else:

```
>>> if not 1:
...     print 'true'
... else:
...     print 'false'
...
false
```

Multiway Branching

Now, here's an example of a more complex if statement, with all its optional parts present:

```
>>> x = 'killer rabbit'
>>> if x == 'roger':
...     print "how's jessica?"
... elif x == 'bugs':
...     print "what's up doc?"
... else:
...     print 'Run away! Run away!'
...
Run away! Run away!
```

This multiline statement extends from the if line through the else block. When it's run, Python executes the statements nested under the first test that is true, or the else part if all tests are false (in this example, they are). In practice, both the elif and else parts may be omitted, and there may be more than one statement nested in each section. Note that the words if, elif, and else are associated by the fact that they line up vertically, with the same indentation.

If you've used languages like C or Pascal, you might be interested to know that there is no switch or case statement in Python that selects an action based on a variable's value. Instead, *multiway branching* is coded either as a series of if/elif tests, as in the prior example, or by indexing dictionaries or searching lists. Because dictionaries and lists can be built at runtime, they're sometimes more flexible than hardcoded if logic:

```
>>> choice = 'ham'
>>> print {'spam':  1.25,          # A dictionary-based 'switch'
...         'ham':  1.99,          # Use has_key or get for default
...         'eggs': 0.99,
...         'bacon': 1.10}[choice]
1.99
```

Although it may take a few moments for this to sink in the first time you see it, this dictionary is a multiway branch—indexing on the key choice branches to one of a set of values, much like a switch in C. An almost equivalent but more verbose Python if statement might look like this:

```
>>> if choice == 'spam':
...     print 1.25
... elif choice == 'ham':
...     print 1.99
... elif choice == 'eggs':
...     print 0.99
... elif choice == 'bacon':
...     print 1.10
... else:
...     print 'Bad choice'
...
1.99
```

Notice the else clause on the if here to handle the default case when no key matches. As we saw in Chapter 8, dictionary defaults can be coded with has_key tests, get method calls, or exception catching. All of the same techniques can be used here to code a default action in a dictionary-based multiway branch. Here's the get scheme at work with defaults:

```
>>> branch = {'spam': 1.25,
...           'ham':  1.99,
...           'eggs': 0.99}
>>> print branch.get('spam', 'Bad choice')
1.25
>>> print branch.get('bacon', 'Bad choice')
Bad choice
```

Dictionaries are good for associating values with keys, but what about the more complicated actions you can code in if statements? In Part IV, you'll learn that dictionaries can also contain *functions* to represent more complex branch actions and implement general jump tables. Such functions appear as dictionary values, are often coded as lambdas, and are called by adding parentheses to trigger their actions; stay tuned for more on this topic.

Although dictionary-based multiway branching is useful in programs that deal with more dynamic data, most programmers will probably find that coding an if statement is the most straightforward way to perform multiway branching. As a rule of thumb in coding, when in doubt, err on the side of simplicity and readability.

Python Syntax Rules

I introduced Python's syntax model in Chapter 10. Now that we're stepping up to larger statements like the if, this section reviews and expands on the syntax ideas introduced earlier. In general, Python has a simple, statement-based syntax. But, there are a few properties you need to know about:

- **Statements execute one after another, until you say otherwise.** Python normally runs statements in a file or nested block in order from first to last, but statements like if (and, as you'll see, loops) cause the interpreter to jump around in your code. Because Python's path through a program is called the *control flow*, statements such as if that affect it are often called *control-flow statements*.

- **Block and statement boundaries are detected automatically.** As we've seen, there are no braces or "begin/end" delimiters around blocks of code in Python; instead, Python uses the indentation of statements under a header to group the statements in a nested block. Similarly, Python statements are not normally terminated with semicolons; rather, the end of a line usually marks the end of the statement coded on that line.

- **Compound statements = header, ":," indented statements.** All compound statements in Python follow the same pattern: a header line terminated with a colon, followed by one or more nested statements, usually indented under the header. The indented statements are called a *block* (or sometimes, a *suite*). In the if statement, the elif and else clauses are part of the if, but are also header lines with nested blocks of their own.

- **Blank lines, spaces, and comments are usually ignored.** Blank lines are ignored in files (but not at the interactive prompt). Spaces inside statements and expressions are almost always ignored (except in string literals, and when used for indentation). Comments are always ignored: they start with a # character (not inside a string literal), and extend to the end of the current line.

- **Docstrings are ignored, but saved and displayed by tools.** Python supports an additional comment form called documentation strings (*docstrings* for short), which, unlike # comments, are retained at runtime for inspection. Docstrings are simply strings that show up at the top of program files and some statements. Python ignores their contents, but they are automatically attached to objects at runtime, and may be displayed with documentation tools. Docstrings are part of Python's larger documentation strategy, and are covered in the last chapter in this part of the book.

As you've seen, there are no variable type declarations in Python; this fact alone makes for a much simpler language syntax than what you may be used to. But, for most new users, the lack of the braces and semicolons used to mark blocks and statements in many other languages seems to be the most novel syntactic feature of Python, so let's explore what this means in more detail.

Block Delimiters

Python detects block boundaries automatically, by line *indentation*—that is, the empty space to the left of your code. All statements indented the same distance to the right belong to the same block of code. In other words, the statements within a block line up vertically, as in a column. The block ends when the end of the file or a lesser-indented line is encountered, and more deeply nested blocks are simply indented further to the right than the statements in the enclosing block.

For instance, Figure 12-1 demonstrates the block structure of the following code:

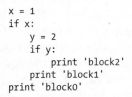
```
x = 1
if x:
    y = 2
    if y:
        print 'block2'
    print 'block1'
print 'block0'
```

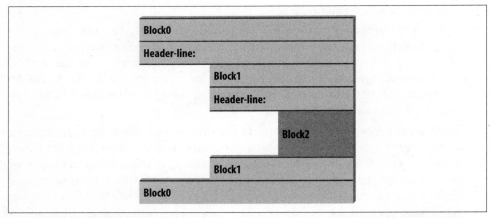

Figure 12-1. Nested blocks of code: a nested block starts with a statement indented further to the right, and ends with either a statement that is indented less, or the end of the file.

This code contains three blocks: the first (the top-level code of the file) is not indented at all, the second (within the outer if statement) is indented four spaces, and the third (the print statement under the nested if) is indented eight spaces.

In general, top-level (unnested) code must start in column 1. Nested blocks can start in any column; indentation may consist of any number of spaces and tabs, as long as it's the same for all the statements in a given single block. That is, Python doesn't care *how* you indent your code; it only cares that it's done consistently. Technically, tabs count for enough spaces to move the current column number up to a multiple of 8, but it's usually not a good idea to mix tabs and spaces within a block—use one or the other.

The only major place in Python where whitespace matters is when it's used to the left of your code, for indentation; in most other contexts, space can be coded or not. However, indentation is really part of Python syntax, not just a stylistic suggestion: all the statements within any given single block must be indented to the same level, or Python reports a syntax error. This is intentional—because you don't need to explicitly mark the start and end of a nested block of code, some of the syntactic clutter found in other languages is unnecessary in Python.

Making indentation part of the syntax model also enforces consistency, a crucial component of readability in structured programming languages like Python. Python's syntax is sometimes described as "what you see is what you get"—the indentation of each line of code unambiguously tells readers what it is associated with. This consistent appearance makes Python code easier to maintain and reuse.

Consistently indented code always satisfies Python's rules. Moreover, most text editors (including IDLE) make it easy to follow Python's indentation model by automatically indenting code as you type it.

Statement Delimiters

A statement in Python normally ends at the end of the line on which it appears. When a statement is too long to fit on a single line, though, a few special rules may be used to make it span multiple lines:

- **Statements may span multiple lines if you're continuing an open syntactic pair.** Python lets you continue typing a statement on the next line if you're coding something enclosed in a ( ), {}, or [ ] pair. For instance, expressions in parentheses, and dictionary and list literals, can span any number of lines; your statement doesn't end until the Python interpreter reaches the line on which you type the closing part of the pair (a), }, or]). Continuation lines can start at any indentation level, and should all be vertically aligned.

- **Statements may span multiple lines if they end in a backslash.** This is a somewhat outdated feature, but if a statement needs to span multiple lines, you can also add a backslash (\) at the end of the prior line to indicate you're continuing on the next line. Because you can also continue by adding parentheses around long constructs, backslashes are almost never used.

- **Triple-quoted string literals can span multiple lines.** Very long string literals can span lines arbitrarily; in fact, the triple-quoted string blocks we met in Chapter 7 are designed to do so.

- **Other rules.** There are a few other points to mention with regard to statement delimiters. Although uncommon, you can terminate statements with a semicolon—this convention is sometimes used to squeeze more than one simple (noncompound) statement onto a single line. Also, comments and blank lines can appear anywhere in a file; comments (which begin with a # character) terminate at the end of the line on which they appear.

A Few Special Cases

Here's what a continuation line looks like using the open pairs rule. You can span delimited constructs across any number of lines:

```
L = ["Good",
     "Bad",
     "Ugly"]                      # Open pairs may span lines
```

This works for anything in parentheses, too: expressions, function arguments, function headers (see Chapter 15), and so on. If you like using backslashes to continue lines, you can, but it's not common practice in Python:

```
if a == b and c == d and   \
   d == e and f == g:
    print 'olde'                  # Backslashes allow continuations...
```

Because any expression can be enclosed in parentheses, you can usually use this technique instead if you need your code to span multiple lines:

```
if (a == b and c == d and
    d == e and e == f):
    print 'new'                   # But parentheses usually do too
```

As another special case, Python allows you to write more than one noncompound statement (i.e., statements without nested statements) on the same line, separated by semicolons. Some coders use this form to save program file real estate, but it usually makes for more readable code if you stick to one statement per line for most of your work:

```
x = 1; y = 2; print x            # More than one simple statement
```

And, finally, Python lets you move a compound statement's body up to the header line, provided the body is just a simple (noncompound) statement. You'll most often see this used for simple if statements with a single test and action:

```
if 1: print 'hello'              # Simple statement on header line
```

You can combine some of these special cases to write code that is difficult to read, but I don't recommend it; as a rule of thumb, try to keep each statement on a line of its own, and indent all but the simplest of blocks. Six months down the road, you'll be happy you did.

Truth Tests

The notions of comparison, equality, and truth values were introduced in Chapter 9. Because the `if` statement is the first statement we've looked at that actually uses test results, we'll expand on some of these ideas here. In particular, Python's Boolean operators are a bit different from their counterparts in languages like C. In Python:

- Any nonzero number or nonempty object is true.
- Zero numbers, empty objects, and the special object `None` are considered false.
- Comparisons and equality tests are applied recursively to data structures.
- Comparisons and equality tests return `True` or `False` (custom versions of 1 and 0).
- Boolean and and or operators return a true or false operand object.

In short, Boolean operators are used to combine the results of other tests. There are three Boolean expression operators in Python:

X and Y
> Is true if both X and Y are true.

X or Y
> Is true if either X or Y is true.

not X
> Is true if X is false (the expression returns `True` or `False`).

Here, X and Y may be any truth value, or an expression that returns a truth value (e.g., an equality test, range comparison, and so on). Boolean operators are typed out as words in Python (instead of C's &&, ||, and !). Also, Boolean and and or operators return a true or false *object* in Python, not the values `True` or `False`. Let's look at a few examples to see how this works:

```
>>> 2 < 3, 3 < 2          # Less-than: return 1 or 0
(True, False)
```

Magnitude comparisons such as these return `True` or `False` as their truth results, which, as we learned in Chapters 5 and 9, are really just custom versions of the integers 1 and 0 (they print themselves differently, but are otherwise the same).

On the other hand, the and and or operators always return an object instead—either the object on the left side of the operator, or the object on the right. If we test their results in `if` or other statements, they will be as expected (remember, every object is inherently true or false), but we won't get back a simple `True` or `False`.

For or tests, Python evaluates the operand objects from left to right, and returns the first one that is true. Moreover, Python stops at the first true operand it finds. This is usually called *short-circuit evaluation*, as determining a result short-circuits (terminates) the rest of the expression:

```
>>> 2 or 3, 3 or 2        # Return left operand if true
(2, 3)                    # Else, return right operand (true or false)
```

```
>>> [ ] or 3
3
>>> [ ] or { }
{ }
```

In the first line of the preceding example, both operands (2 and 3) are true (i.e., are nonzero), so Python always stops and returns the one on the left. In the other two tests, the left operand is false (an empty object), so Python simply evaluates and returns the object on the right (which may happen to have either a true or false value when tested).

and operations also stop as soon as the result is known; however, in this case, Python evaluates the operands from left to right, and stops at the first *false* object:

```
>>> 2 and 3, 3 and 2      # Return left operand if false
(3, 2)                    # Else, return right operand (true or false)
>>> [ ] and { }
[ ]
>>> 3 and [ ]
[ ]
```

Here, both operands are true in the first line, so Python evaluates both sides, and returns the object on the right. In the second test, the left operand is false ([ ]), so Python stops and returns it as the test result. In the last test, the left side is true (3), so Python evaluates and returns the object on the right (which happens to be a false [ ]).

The end result of all this is the same as in C and most other languages—you get a value that is logically true or false, if tested in an if or while. However, in Python, Booleans return either the left or right object, not a simple integer flag.

This behavior of and and or may seem esoteric at first glance, but see this chapter's sidebar "Why You Will Care: Booleans" for examples of how it is sometimes used to advantage in coding by Python programmers.

The if/else Ternary Expression

One common role for Boolean operators in Python is to code an expression that runs the same as an if statement. Consider the following statement, which sets A to either Y or Z, based on the truth value of X:

```
if X:
    A = Y
else:
    A = Z
```

Sometimes, as in this example, the items involved in such a statement are so simple that it seems like overkill to spread them across four lines. At other times, we may want to nest such a construct in a larger statement instead of assigning its result to a variable. For these reasons (and, frankly, because the C language has a similar tool[*]), Python 2.5 introduced a new expression format that allows us to say the same thing in one expression:

```
A = Y if X else Z
```

This expression has the exact same effect as the preceding four-line if statement, but it's simpler to code. As in the statement equivalent, Python runs expression Y only if X turns out to be true, and runs expression Z only if X turns out to be false. That is, it short-circuits, as Boolean operators in general do. Here are some examples of it in action:

```
>>> A = 't' if 'spam' else 'f'        # Nonempty is true
>>> A
't'
>>> A = 't' if '' else 'f'
>>> A
'f'
```

Prior to Python 2.5 (and after 2.5, if you insist), the same effect can be achieved by a careful combination of the and and or operators because they return either the object on the left side or the object on the right:

```
A = ((X and Y) or Z)
```

This works, but there is a catch—you have to be able to assume that Y will be Boolean true. If that is the case, the effect is the same: the and runs first, and returns Y if X is true; if it's not, the or simply returns Z. In other words, we get "if X then Y else Z."

This and/or combination also seems to require a "moment of great clarity" to understand the first time you see it, and it's no longer required as of 2.5—use the more mnemonic Y if X else Z instead if you need this as an expression, or use a full if statement if the parts are nontrivial.

As a side note, using the following expression in Python is similar because the bool function will translate X into the equivalent of integer 1 or 0, which can then be used to pick true and false values from a list:

```
A = [Z, Y][bool(X)]
```

For example:

```
>>> ['f', 't'][bool('')]
'f'
>>> ['f', 't'][bool('spam')]
't'
```

However, this isn't exactly the same, because Python will not short-circuit—it will always run both Z and Y, regardless of the value of X. Because of such complexities, you're better off using the simpler and more easily understood if/else expression as

---

[*] In fact, Python's X if Y else Z has a slightly different order than C's Y ? X : Z. This was reportedly done in response to analysis of common use patterns in Python code, but also partially to discourage ex-C programmers from overusing it! Remember, simple is better than complex, in Python, and elsewhere.

of Python 2.5. Again, though, you should use even that sparingly, and only if its parts are all fairly simple; otherwise, you're better off coding the full if statement form to make changes easier in the future. Your coworkers will be happy you did.

Still, you may see the and/or version in code written prior to 2.5 (and in code written by C programmers who haven't quite let go of their coding pasts).

Why You Will Care: Booleans

One common way to use the somewhat unusual behavior of Python Boolean operators is to select from a set of objects with an or. A statement such as this:

```
X = A or B or C or None
```

sets X to the first nonempty (that is, true) object among A, B, and C, or to None if all of them are empty. This works because the or operator returns one of its two objects, and it turns out to be a fairly common coding paradigm in Python: to select a nonempty object from among a fixed-size set, simply string them together in an or expression.

It's also important to understand short-circuit evaluation because expressions on the right of a Boolean operator might call functions that perform substantial or important work, or have side effects that won't happen if the short-circuit rule takes effect:

```
if f1() or f2(): ...
```

Here, if f1 returns a true (or nonempty) value, Python will never run f2. To guarantee that both functions will be run, call them before the or:

```
tmp1, tmp2 = f1(), f2()
if tmp1 or tmp2: ...
```

You've already seen another application of this behavior in this chapter: because of the way Booleans work, the expression ((A and B) or C) can be used to emulate an if/else statement—almost.

Also, notice that because all objects are inherently true or false, it's common and easier in Python to test an object directly (if X:) rather than comparing it to an empty value (if X != '':). For a string, the two tests are equivalent.

Chapter Summary

In this chapter, we studied the Python if statement. Because this was our first compound and logical statement, we also reviewed Python's general syntax rules, and explored the operation of truth tests in more depth than we were able to previously. Along the way, we also looked at how to code multiway branching in Python, and learned about the if/else expression introduced in Python 2.5.

The next chapter continues our look at procedural statements by expanding on the while and for loops. There, we'll learn about alternative ways to code loops in Python, some of which may be better than others. Before that, though, here is the usual chapter quiz.

Chapter Quiz

1. How might you code a multiway branch in Python?
2. How can you code an if/else statement as an expression in Python?
3. How can you make a single statement span many lines?
4. What do the words True and False mean?

Quiz Answers

1. An if statement with multiple elif clauses is often the most straightforward way to code multiway branching, though not necessarily the most concise. Dictionary indexing can often achieve the same result, especially if the dictionary contains callable functions coded with def statements or lambda expressions.

2. In Python 2.5, the expression form Y if X else Z returns Y if X is true, or Z otherwise; it's the same as a four-line if statement. The and/or combination ((X and Y) or Z) can work the same way, but it's more obscure, and requires that the Y part be true.

3. Wrap up the statement in an open syntactic pair (( ), [ ], or { }), and it can span as many lines as you like; the statement ends when Python sees the closing, right half of the pair.

4. True and False are just custom versions of the integers 1 and 0, respectively. They always stand for Boolean true and false values in Python.

CHAPTER 13

while and for Loops

In this chapter, we'll meet Python's two main *looping* constructs—statements that repeat an action over and over. The first of these, the while statement, provides a way to code general loops; the second, the for statement, is designed for stepping through the items in a sequence object, and running a block of code for each item.

There are other kinds of looping operations in Python, but the two statements covered here are the primary syntax provided for coding repeated actions. We'll also study a few unusual statements (such as break and continue) here because they are used within loops. Additionally, this chapter will explore the related concept of Python's iteration protocol, and fill in some details on list comprehensions, a close cousin to the for loop.

while Loops

Python's while statement is the most general iteration construct in the language. In simple terms, it repeatedly executes a block of (normally indented) statements as long as a test at the top keeps evaluating to a true value. It is called a "loop" because control keeps looping back to the start of the statement until the test becomes false. When the test becomes false, control passes to the statement that follows the while block. The net effect is that the loop's body is executed repeatedly while the test at the top is true; if the test is false to begin with, the body never runs.

As I've just stated, the while statement is one of two looping statements available in Python, along with the for. Besides these statements, Python also provides a handful of tools that implicitly loop (iterate): the map, reduce, and filter functions; the in membership test; list comprehensions; and more. We'll explore some of these in Chapter 17 because they are related to functions.

General Format

In its most complex form, the while statement consists of a header line with a test expression, a body of one or more indented statements, and an optional else part that is executed if control exits the loop without a break statement being encountered. Python keeps evaluating the test at the top, and executing the statements nested in the loop body until the test returns a false value:

```
while <test>:                # Loop test
    <statements1>            # Loop body
else:                        # Optional else
    <statements2>            # Run if didn't exit loop with break
```

Examples

To illustrate, let's look at a few simple while loops in action. The first, which consists of a print statement nested in a while loop, just prints a message forever. Recall that True is just a custom version of the integer 1, and always stands for a Boolean true value; because the test is always true, Python keeps executing the body forever, or until you stop its execution. This sort of behavior is usually called an *infinite loop*:

```
>>> while True:
...     print 'Type Ctrl-C to stop me!'
```

The next example keeps slicing off the first character of a string until the string is empty and hence false. It's typical to test an object directly like this instead of using the more verbose equivalent (while x != '':). Later in this chapter, we'll see other ways to step more directly through the items in a string with a for loop. Notice the trailing comma in the print here—as we learned in Chapter 11, this makes all the outputs show up on the same line:

```
>>> x = 'spam'
>>> while x:                 # While x is not empty
...     print x,
...     x = x[1:]            # Strip first character off x
...
spam pam am m
```

The following code counts from the value of a up to, but not including, b. We'll see an easier way to do this with a Python for loop and the built-in range function later:

```
>>> a=0; b=10
>>> while a < b:             # One way to code counter loops
...     print a,
...     a += 1               # Or, a = a + 1
...
0 1 2 3 4 5 6 7 8 9
```

Finally, notice that Python doesn't have what some languages call a "do until" loop statement. However, we can simulate one with a test and break at the bottom of the loop body:

```
while True:
    ...loop body...
    if exitTest(): break
```

To fully understand how this structure works, we need to move on to the next section, and learn more about the break statement.

break, continue, pass, and the Loop else

Now that we've seen a few Python loops in action, it's time to take a look at two simple statements that have a purpose only when nested inside loops—the break and continue statements. While we're looking at oddballs, we will also study the loop else clause here because it is intertwined with break, and Python's empty placeholder statement, the pass. In Python:

break
    Jumps out of the closest enclosing loop (past the entire loop statement).

continue
    Jumps to the top of the closest enclosing loop (to the loop's header line).

pass
    Does nothing at all: it's an empty statement placeholder.

Loop else *block*
    Runs if and only if the loop is exited normally (i.e., without hitting a break).

General Loop Format

Factoring in break and continue statements, the general format of the while loop looks like this:

```
while <test1>:
    <statements1>
    if <test2>: break        # Exit loop now, skip else
    if <test3>: continue     # Go to top of loop now, to test1
else:
    <statements2>            # Run if we didn't hit a 'break'
```

break and continue statements can appear anywhere inside the while (or for) loop's body, but they are usually coded further nested in an if test to take action in response to some condition.

Examples

Let's turn to a few simple examples to see how these statements come together in practice.

pass

The pass statement is a no-operation placeholder that is used when the syntax requires a statement, but you have nothing useful to say. It is often used to code an empty body for a compound statement. For instance, if you want to code an infinite loop that does nothing each time through, do it with a pass:

```
while 1: pass                          # Type Ctrl-C to stop me!
```

Because the body is just an empty statement, Python gets stuck in this loop. pass is roughly to statements as None is to objects—an explicit nothing. Notice that here the while loop's body is on the same line as the header, after the colon; as with if statements, this only works if the body isn't a compound statement.

This example does nothing forever. It probably isn't the most useful Python program ever written (unless you want to warm up your laptop computer on a cold winter's day!); frankly, though, I couldn't think of a better pass example at this point in the book. We'll see other places where it makes sense later—for instance, to define empty classes that implement objects that behave like structs and records in other languages. A pass is also sometime coded to mean "to be filled in later," and to stub out the bodies of functions temporarily:

```
def func1():
    pass                                # Add real code here later

def func2():
    pass
```

continue

The continue statement causes an immediate jump to the top of a loop. It also sometimes lets you avoid statement nesting. The next example uses continue to skip odd numbers. This code prints all even numbers less than 10, and greater than or equal to 0. Remember, 0 means false, and % is the remainder of division operator, so this loop counts down to 0, skipping numbers that aren't multiples of 2 (it prints 8 6 4 2 0):

```
x = 10
while x:
    x = x-1                             # Or, x -= 1
    if x % 2 != 0: continue             # Odd? -- skip print
    print x,
```

Because continue jumps to the top of the loop, you don't need to nest the print statement inside an if test; the print is only reached if the continue is not run. If this sounds similar to a "goto" in other languages, it should. Python has no goto statement, but because continue lets you jump about in a program, many of the warnings about readability and maintainability you may have heard about goto apply. continue should probably be used sparingly, especially when you're first getting started with Python. For instance, the last example might be clearer if the print were nested under the if:

```
x = 10
while x:
    x = x-1
    if x % 2 == 0:                 # Even? -- print
        print x,
```

break

The break statement causes an immediate exit from a loop. Because the code that follows it in the loop is not executed if the break is reached, you can also sometimes avoid nesting by including a break. For example, here is a simple interactive loop (a variant of a larger example we studied in Chapter 10) that inputs data with raw_input, and exits when the user enters "stop" for the name request:

```
>>> while 1:
...     name = raw_input('Enter name:')
...     if name == 'stop': break
...     age  = raw_input('Enter age: ')
...     print 'Hello', name, '=>', int(age) ** 2
...
Enter name:mel
Enter age: 40
Hello mel => 1600
Enter name:bob
Enter age: 30
Hello bob => 900
Enter name:stop
```

Notice how this code converts the age input to an integer with int before raising it to the second power; as you'll recall, this is necessary because raw_input returns user input as a string. In Chapter 29, you'll see that raw_input also raises an exception at end-of-file (e.g., if the user types Ctrl-Z or Ctrl-D); if this matters, wrap raw_input in try statements.

else

When combined with the loop else clause, the break statement can often eliminate the need for the search status flags used in other languages. For instance, the following piece of code determines whether a positive integer y is prime by searching for factors greater than 1:

```
    x = y / 2                                        # For some y > 1
    while x > 1:
        if y % x == 0:                               # Remainder
            print y, 'has factor', x
            break                                    # Skip else
        x = x-1
    else:                                            # Normal exit
        print y, 'is prime'
```

Rather than setting a flag to be tested when the loop is exited, insert a break where a factor is found. This way, the loop else clause can assume that it will be executed only if no factor was found; if you don't hit the break, the number is prime.*

The loop else clause is also run if the body of the loop is never executed, as you don't run a break in that event either; in a while loop, this happens if the test in the header is false to begin with. Thus, in the preceding example, you still get the "is prime" message if x is initially less than or equal to 1 (e.g., if y is 2).

More on the loop else clause

Because the loop else clause is unique to Python, it tends to perplex some newcomers. In general terms, the loop else provides explicit syntax for a common coding scenario—it is a coding structure that lets you catch the "other" way out of a loop, without setting and checking flags or conditions.

Suppose, for instance, that you are writing a loop to search a list for a value, and you need to know whether the value was found after you exit the loop. You might code such a task this way:

```
    found = False
    while x and not found:
        if match(x[0]):                              # Value at front?
            print 'Ni'
            found = True
        else:
            x = x[1:]                                # Slice off front and repeat
    if not found:
        print 'not found'
```

Here, we initialize, set, and later test a flag to determine whether the search succeeded or not. This is valid Python code, and it does work; however, this is exactly the sort of structure that the loop else clause is there to handle. Here's an else equivalent:

```
    while x:                                         # Exit when x empty
        if match(x[0]):
```

---

* More or less. Numbers less than 2 are not considered prime by the strict mathematical definition. To be really picky, this code also fails for negative and floating-point numbers and will be broken by the future / "true division" change described in Chapter 5. If you want to experiment with this code, be sure to see the exercise at the end of Part IV, which wraps it in a function.

```
        print 'Ni'
        break                       # Exit, go around else
    x = x[1:]
else:
    print 'Not found'               # Only here if exhausted x
```

This version is more concise. The flag is gone, and we've replaced the if test at the loop end with an else (lined up vertically with the word while). Because the break inside the main part of the while exits the loop and goes around the else, this serves as a more structured way to catch the search-failure case.

Some readers might have noticed that the prior example's else clause could be replaced with a test for an empty x after the loop (e.g., if not x:). Although that's true in this example, the else provides explicit syntax for this coding pattern (it's more obviously a search-failure clause here), and such an explicit empty test may not apply in some cases. The loop else becomes even more useful when used in conjunction with the for loop—the topic of the next section—because sequence iteration is not under your control.

for Loops

The for loop is a generic sequence iterator in Python: it can step through the items in any ordered sequence object. The for statement works on strings, lists, tuples, other built-in iterables, and new objects that we'll see how to create later with classes.

General Format

The Python for loop begins with a header line that specifies an assignment target (or targets), along with the object you want to step through. The header is followed by a block of (normally indented) statements that you want to repeat:

```
for <target> in <object>:          # Assign object items to target
    <statements>                    # Repeated loop body: use target
else:
    <statements>                    # If we didn't hit a 'break'
```

When Python runs a for loop, it assigns the items in the sequence object to the target one by one, and executes the loop body for each. The loop body typically uses the assignment target to refer to the current item in the sequence as though it were a cursor stepping through the sequence.

The name used as the assignment target in a for header line is usually a (possibly new) variable in the scope where the for statement is coded. There's not much special about it; it can even be changed inside the loop's body, but it will automatically be set to the next item in the sequence when control returns to the top of the loop again. After the loop, this variable normally still refers to the last item visited, which is the last item in the sequence, unless the loop exits with a break statement.

Why You Will Care: Emulating C while Loops

The section on expression statements in Chapter 11 stated that Python doesn't allow statements such as assignments to appear in places where it expects an expression. That means this common C language coding pattern won't work in Python:

```
while ((x = next( )) != NULL) {...process x...}
```

C assignments return the value assigned, but Python assignments are just statements, not expressions. This eliminates a notorious class of C errors (you can't accidentally type = in Python when you mean ==). But, if you need similar behavior, there are at least three ways to get the same effect in Python while loops without embedding assignments in loop tests. You can move the assignment into the loop body with a break:

```
while True:
    x = next( )
    if not x: break
    ...process x...
```

or move the assignment into the loop with tests:

```
x = 1
while x:
    x = next( )
    if x:
        ...process x...
```

or move the first assignment outside the loop:

```
x = next( )
while x:
    ...process x...
    x = next( )
```

Of these three coding patterns, the first may be considered by some to be the least structured, but it also seems to be the simplest, and most commonly used. (A simple Python for loop may replace some C loops as well.)

The for statement also supports an optional else block, which works exactly as it does in a while loop—it's executed if the loop exits without running into a break statement (i.e., if all items in the sequence have been visited). The break and continue statements introduced earlier also work the same in a for loop as they do in a while. The for loop's complete format can be described this way:

```
for <target> in <object>:        # Assign object items to target
    <statements>
    if <test>: break             # Exit loop now, skip else
    if <test>: continue          # Go to top of loop now
else:
    <statements>                 # If we didn't hit a 'break'
```

Examples

Let's type a few `for` loops interactively now, so you can see how they are used in practice.

Basic usage

As mentioned earlier, a `for` loop can step across any kind of sequence object. In our first example, for instance, we'll assign the name x to each of the three items in a list in turn, from left to right, and the `print` statement will be executed for each. Inside the `print` statement (the loop body), the name x refers to the current item in the list:

```
>>> for x in ["spam", "eggs", "ham"]:
...     print x,
...
spam eggs ham
```

As noted in Chapter 11, the trailing comma in the `print` statement is responsible for making all of these strings show up on the same output line.

The next two examples compute the sum and product of all the items in a list. Later in this chapter and book, we'll meet tools that apply operations such as + and * to items in a list automatically, but it's usually just as easy to use a `for`:

```
>>> sum = 0
>>> for x in [1, 2, 3, 4]:
...     sum = sum + x
...
>>> sum
10
>>> prod = 1
>>> for item in [1, 2, 3, 4]: prod *= item
...
>>> prod
24
```

Other data types

Any sequence works in a `for`, as it's a generic tool. For example, `for` loops work on strings and tuples:

```
>>> S = "lumberjack"
>>> T = ("and", "I'm", "okay")

>>> for x in S: print x,                    # Iterate over a string
...
l u m b e r j a c k

>>> for x in T: print x,                    # Iterate over a tuple
...
and I'm okay
```

In fact, as we'll see in a moment, for loops can even work on some objects that are not sequences at all!

Tuple assignment in for

If you're iterating through a sequence of tuples, the loop target itself can actually be a *tuple* of targets. This is just another case of the tuple-unpacking assignment at work. Remember, the for loop assigns items in the sequence object to the target, and assignment works the same everywhere:

```
>>> T = [(1, 2), (3, 4), (5, 6)]
>>> for (a, b) in T:              # Tuple assignment at work
...     print a, b
...
1 2
3 4
5 6
```

Here, the first time through the loop is like writing (a,b) = (1,2), the second time is like writing (a,b) = (3,4), and so on. This isn't a special case; any assignment target works syntactically after the word for.

Nested for loops

Now, let's look at something a bit more sophisticated. The next example illustrates the loop else clause in a for, and statement nesting. Given a list of objects (items) and a list of keys (tests), this code searches for each key in the objects list, and reports on the search's outcome:

```
>>> items = ["aaa", 111, (4, 5), 2.01]    # A set of objects
>>> tests = [(4, 5), 3.14]                 # Keys to search for
>>>
>>> for key in tests:                      # For all keys
...     for item in items:                 # For all items
...         if item == key:                # Check for match
...             print key, "was found"
...             break
...     else:
...         print key, "not found!"
...
(4, 5) was found
3.14 not found!
```

Because the nested if runs a break when a match is found, the loop else clause can assume that if it is reached, the search has failed. Notice the nesting here. When this code runs, there are two loops going at the same time: the outer loop scans the keys list, and the inner loop scans the items list for each key. The nesting of the loop else clause is critical; it's indented to the same level as the header line of the inner for loop, so it's associated with the inner loop (not the if or the outer for).

Note that this example is easier to code if we employ the in operator to test membership. Because in implicitly scans a list looking for a match, it replaces the inner loop:

```
>>> for key in tests:                    # For all keys
...     if key in items:                 # Let Python check for a match
...         print key, "was found"
...     else:
...         print key, "not found!"
...
(4, 5) was found
3.14 not found!
```

In general, it's a good idea to let Python do as much of the work as possible, as in this solution, for the sake of brevity and performance.

The next example performs a typical data-structure task with a for—collecting common items in two sequences (strings). It's roughly a simple set intersection routine; after the loop runs, res refers to a list that contains all the items found in seq1 and seq2:

```
>>> seq1 = "spam"
>>> seq2 = "scam"
>>>
>>> res = []                # Start empty
>>> for x in seq1:          # Scan first sequence
...     if x in seq2:       # Common item?
...         res.append(x)   # Add to result end
...
>>> res
['s', 'a', 'm']
```

Unfortunately, this code is equipped to work only on two specific variables: seq1 and seq2. It would be nice if this loop could somehow be generalized into a tool you could use more than once. As you'll see, that simple idea leads us to functions, the topic of the next part of the book.

Iterators: A First Look

In the prior section, I mentioned that the for loop can work on any sequence type in Python, including lists, tuples, and strings, like this:

```
>>> for x in [1, 2, 3, 4]: print x ** 2,
...
1 4 9 16

>>> for x in (1, 2, 3, 4): print x ** 3,
...
1 8 27 64

>>> for x in 'spam': print x * 2,
...
ss pp aa mm
```

Why You Will Care: File Scanners

In general, loops come in handy anywhere you need to repeat an operation or process something more than once. Because files contain multiple characters and lines, they are one of the more typical use cases for loops. To load a file's contents into a string all at once, you simply call read:

```
file = open('test.txt', 'r')
print file.read( )
```

But to load a file in pieces, it's common to code either a while loop with breaks on end-of-file, or a for loop. To read by characters, either of the following codings will suffice:

```
file = open('test.txt')
while True:
    char = file.read(1)          # Read by character
    if not char: break
    print char,

for char in open('test.txt').read( ):
    print char
```

The for here also processes each character, but it loads the file into memory all at once. To read by lines or blocks with a while loop, use code like this:

```
file = open('test.txt')
while True:
    line = file.readline( )       # Read line by line
    if not line: break
    print line,

file = open('test.txt', 'rb')
while True:
    chunk = file.read(10)        # Read byte chunks
    if not chunk: break
    print chunk,
```

To read text files line by line, though, the for loop tends to be easiest to code and the quickest to run:

```
for line in open('test.txt').readlines( ):
    print line

for line in open('test.txt').xreadlines( ):
    print line

for line in open('test.txt'):
    print line
```

—continued—

readlines loads a file all at once into a line-string list, while xreadlines instead loads lines on demand to avoid filling memory for large files; the last example here relies on file *iterators* to achieve the equivalent of xreadlines (iterators are covered in the next section). The name open in all of the above can also be replaced with file as of Python 2.2. See the library manual for more on the calls used here. As a general rule of thumb, the more data you read on each step, the faster your program will run.

Actually, the for loop turns out to be even more generic than this—it works on any iterable object. In fact, this is true of all iteration tools that scan objects from left to right in Python, including for loops, list comprehensions, in membership tests, and the map built-in function.

The concept of "iterable objects" is relatively new in Python. It's essentially a generalization of the notion of sequences—an object is considered iterable if it is either a physically stored sequence, or an object that produces one result at a time in the context of an iteration tool like a for loop. In a sense, iterable objects include both physical sequences and virtual sequences computed on demand.

File Iterators

One of the easiest ways to understand what this means is to look at how it works with a built-in type such as the file. Recall that open file objects have a method called readline, which reads one line of text from a file at a time—each time we call the readline method, we advance to the next line. At the end of the file, the empty string is returned, which we can detect to break out of the loop:

```
>>> f = open('script1.py')
>>> f.readline()
'import sys\n'
>>> f.readline()
'print sys.path\n'
>>> f.readline()
'x = 2\n'
>>> f.readline()
'print 2 ** 33\n'
>>> f.readline()
''
```

Today, files also have a method named next that has a nearly identical effect—it returns the next line from a file each time it is called. The only noticeable difference is that next raises a built-in StopIteration exception at end-of-file instead of returning an empty string:

```
>>> f = open('script1.py')
>>> f.next()
'import sys\n'
```

```
>>> f.next( )
'print sys.path\n'
>>> f.next( )
'x = 2\n'
>>> f.next( )
'print 2 ** 33\n'
>>> f.next( )
Traceback (most recent call last):
  File "<pyshell#330>", line 1, in <module>
    f.next( )
StopIteration
```

This interface is exactly what we call the *iteration protocol* in Python—an object with a next method to advance to a next result, which raises StopIteration at the end of the series of results. Any such object is considered iterable in Python. Any such object may also be stepped through with a for loop or other iteration tool because all iteration tools work internally by calling next on each iteration and catching the StopIteration exception to determine when to exit.

The net effect of this magic is that, as mentioned in Chapter 9, the best way to read a text file line by line today is not to read it at all—instead, allow the for loop to automatically call next to advance to the next line on each iteration. The following, for example, reads a file line by line (printing the uppercase version of each line along the way) without ever explicitly reading from the file at all:

```
>>> for line in open('script1.py'):          # Use file iterators
...     print line.upper( ),
...
IMPORT SYS
PRINT SYS.PATH
X = 2
PRINT 2 ** 33
```

This is considered the best way to read text files by lines today, for three reasons: it's the simplest to code, the quickest to run, and the best in terms of memory usage. The older, original way to achieve the same effect with a for loop is to call the file readlines method to load the file's content into memory as a list of line strings:

```
>>> for line in open('script1.py').readlines( ):
...     print line.upper( ),
...
IMPORT SYS
PRINT SYS.PATH
X = 2
PRINT 2 ** 33
```

This readlines technique still works, but it is not best practice today, and performs poorly in terms of memory usage. In fact, because this version really does load the entire file into memory all at once, it will not even work for files too big to fit into the memory space available on your computer. On the other hand, because it reads one line at a time, the iterator-based version is immune to such memory-explosion issues.

Moreover, the iterator version has been greatly optimized by Python, so it should run faster as well.

As mentioned in the earlier sidebar "Why You Will Care: File Scanners," it's also possible to read a file line by line with a while loop:

```
>>> f = open('script1.py')
>>> while True:
...     line = f.readline()
...     if not line: break
...     print line.upper(),
...
...same output...
```

However, this will likely run slower than the iterator-based for loop version because iterators run at C language speed inside Python, whereas the while loop version runs Python byte code through the Python virtual machine. Any time we trade Python code for C code, speed tends to increase.

Other Built-in Type Iterators

Technically, there is one more piece to the iteration protocol. When the for loop begins, it obtains an iterator from the iterable object by passing it to the iter built-in function; the object returned has the required next method. This becomes obvious if we look at how for loops internally process built-in sequence types such as lists:

```
>>> L = [1, 2, 3]
>>> I = iter(L)                    # Obtain an iterator object
>>> I.next()                       # Call next to advance to next item
1
>>> I.next()
2
>>> I.next()
3
>>> I.next()
Traceback (most recent call last):
  File "<pyshell#343>", line 1, in <module>
    I.next()
StopIteration
```

Besides files and physical sequences like lists, other types have useful iterators as well. The classic way to step through the keys of a dictionary, for example, is to request its keys list explicitly:

```
>>> D = {'a':1, 'b':2, 'c':3}
>>> for key in D.keys():
...     print key, D[key]
...
a 1
c 3
b 2
```

In recent versions of Python, though, we no longer need to call the keys method—dictionaries have an iterator that automatically returns one key at a time in an iteration context, so they do not require that the keys list be physically created in memory all at once. Again, the effect is to optimize execution speed, memory use, and coding effort:

```
>>> for key in D:
...     print key, D[key]
...
a 1
c 3
b 2
```

Other Iteration Contexts

So far, I've been demonstrating iterators in the context of the for loop statement, which is one of the main subjects of this chapter. Keep in mind, though, that every tool that scans from left to right across objects uses the iteration protocol. This includes the for loops we've seen:

```
>>> for line in open('script1.py'):        # Use file iterators
...     print line.upper(),
...
IMPORT SYS
PRINT SYS.PATH
X = 2
PRINT 2 ** 33
```

However, list comprehensions, the in membership test, the map built-in function, and other built-ins, such as the sorted and sum calls, also leverage the iteration protocol:

```
>>> uppers = [line.upper() for line in open('script1.py')]
>>> uppers
['IMPORT SYS\n', 'PRINT SYS.PATH\n', 'X = 2\n', 'PRINT 2 ** 33\n']

>>> map(str.upper, open('script1.py'))
['IMPORT SYS\n', 'PRINT SYS.PATH\n', 'X = 2\n', 'PRINT 2 ** 33\n']

>>> 'y = 2\n' in open('script1.py')
False
>>> 'x = 2\n' in open('script1.py')
True

>>> sorted(open('script1.py'))
['import sys\n', 'print 2 ** 33\n', 'print sys.path\n', 'x = 2\n']
```

The map call used here, which we'll meet in the next part of this book, is a tool that applies a function call to each item in an iterable object; it's similar to list comprehensions, but more limited because it requires a function instead of an arbitrary expression. Because list comprehensions are related to for loops, we'll explore these again later in this chapter, as well as in the next part of the book.

We saw the sorted function used here at work in Chapter 4. sorted is a relatively new built-in that employs the iteration protocol—it's like the original list sort method, but it returns the new sorted list as a result, and runs on any iterable object. Other newer built-in functions support the iteration protocol as well. For example, the sum call computes the sum of all the numbers in any iterable, and the any and all built-ins return True if any or all items in an iterable are True, respectively:

```
>>> sorted([3, 2, 4, 1, 5, 0])          # More iteration contexts
[0, 1, 2, 3, 4, 5]
>>> sum([3, 2, 4, 1, 5, 0])
15
>>> any(['spam', '', 'ni'])
True
>>> all(['spam', '', 'ni'])
False
```

Interestingly, the iteration protocol is even more pervasive in Python today than the examples so far have demonstrated—everything in Python's built-in toolset that scans an object from left to right is defined to use the iteration protocol on the subject object. This even includes more esoteric tools such as the list and tuple built-in functions (which build new objects from iterables), the string join method (which puts a substring between strings contained in an iterable), and even sequence assignments. Because of that, all of these will also work on an open file, and automatically read one line at a time:

```
>>> list(open('script1.py'))
['import sys\n', 'print sys.path\n', 'x = 2\n', 'print 2 ** 33\n']

>>> tuple(open('script1.py'))
('import sys\n', 'print sys.path\n', 'x = 2\n', 'print 2 ** 33\n')

>>> '&&'.join(open('script1.py'))
'import sys\n&&print sys.path\n&&x = 2\n&&print 2 ** 33\n'

>>> a, b, c, d = open('script1.py')
>>> a, d
('import sys\n', 'print 2 ** 33\n')
```

User-Defined Iterators

I'll have more to say about iterators in Chapter 17, in conjunction with functions, and in Chapter 24, when we study classes. As you'll see later, it's possible to turn a user-defined function into an iterable object by using yield statements; list comprehensions can also support the protocol today with generator expressions, and user-defined classes can be made iterable with the __iter__ or __getitem__ operator overloading method. User-defined iterators allow arbitrary objects and operations to be used in any of the iteration contexts we've met here.

Loop Coding Techniques

The `for` loop subsumes most counter-style loops. It's generally simpler to code and quicker to run than a `while`, so it's the first tool you should reach for whenever you need to step through a sequence. But there are also situations where you will need to iterate in more specialized ways. For example, what if you need to visit every second or third item in a list, or change the list along the way? How about traversing more than one sequence in parallel, in the same `for` loop?

You can always code such unique iterations with a `while` loop and manual indexing, but Python provides two built-ins that allow you to specialize the iteration in a `for`:

- The built-in `range` function returns a list of successively higher integers, which can be used as indexes in a `for`.[*]
- The built-in `zip` function returns a list of parallel-item tuples, which can be used to traverse multiple sequences in a `for`.

Because `for` loops typically run quicker than `while`-based counter loops, it's to your advantage to use tools that allow you to use `for` when possible. Let's look at each of these built-ins in turn.

Counter Loops: while and range

The `range` function is really a general tool that can be used in a variety of contexts. Although it's used most often to generate indexes in a `for`, you can use it anywhere you need a list of integers:

```
>>> range(5), range(2, 5), range(0, 10, 2)
([0, 1, 2, 3, 4], [2, 3, 4], [0, 2, 4, 6, 8])
```

With one argument, `range` generates a list of integers from zero up to but not including the argument's value. If you pass in two arguments, the first is taken as the lower bound. An optional third argument can give a *step*; if used, Python adds the step to each successive integer in the result (steps default to 1). Ranges can also be non-positive and nonascending, if you want them to be:

```
>>> range(-5, 5)
[-5, -4, -3, -2, -1, 0, 1, 2, 3, 4]

>>> range(5, -5, -1)
[5, 4, 3, 2, 1, 0, -1, -2, -3, -4]
```

---

[*] Python today also provides a built-in called xrange that generates indexes one at a time instead of storing all of them in a list at once like range does. There's no speed advantage to xrange, but it's useful as a space optimization if you have to generate a huge number of values. At this writing, however, it seems likely that xrange may disappear in Python 3.0 altogether, and that range may become a generator object that supports the iteration protocol to produce one item at a time, instead of all at once in a list; check the 3.0 release notes for future developments on this front.

Although such range results may be useful all by themselves, they tend to come in most handy within for loops. For one thing, they provide a simple way to repeat an action a specific number of times. To print three lines, for example, use a range to generate the appropriate number of integers:

```
>>> for i in range(3):
...     print i, 'Pythons'
...
0 Pythons
1 Pythons
2 Pythons
```

range is also commonly used to iterate over a sequence indirectly. The easiest and fastest way to step through a sequence exhaustively is always with a simple for, as Python handles most of the details for you:

```
>>> X = 'spam'
>>> for item in X: print item,        # Simple iteration
...
s p a m
```

Internally, the for loop handles the details of the iteration automatically when used this way. If you really need to take over the indexing logic explicitly, you can do it with a while loop:

```
>>> i = 0
>>> while i < len(X):                  # while loop iteration
...     print X[i],; i += 1
...
s p a m
```

But, you can also do manual indexing with a for, if you use range to generate a list of indexes to iterate through:

```
>>> X
'spam'
>>> len(X)                             # Length of string
4
>>> range(len(X))                      # All legal offsets into X
[0, 1, 2, 3]
>>>
>>> for i in range(len(X)): print X[i],    # Manual for indexing
...
s p a m
```

The example here is stepping over a list of *offsets* into X, not the actual *items* of X; we need to index back into X within the loop to fetch each item.

Nonexhaustive Traversals: range

The last example in the prior section works, but it probably runs more slowly than it has to. It's also more work than we need to do. Unless you have a special indexing requirement, you're always better off using the simple for loop form in Python—use `for` instead of `while` whenever possible, and don't resort to `range` calls in `for` loops except as a last resort. This simpler solution is better:

```
>>> for item in X: print item,          # Simple iteration
...
```

However, the coding pattern used in the prior example does allow us to do more specialized sorts of traversals—for instance, to skip items as we go:

```
>>> S = 'abcdefghijk'
>>> range(0, len(S), 2)
[0, 2, 4, 6, 8, 10]

>>> for i in range(0, len(S), 2): print S[i],
...
a c e g i k
```

Here, we visit every *second* item in the string S by stepping over the generated range list. To visit every third item, change the third range argument to be 3, and so on. In effect, using `range` this way lets you skip items in loops while still retaining the simplicity of the `for`.

Still, this is probably not the ideal best-practice technique in Python today. If you really want to skip items in a sequence, the extended three-limit form of the slice expression, presented in Chapter 7, provides a simpler route to the same goal. To visit every second character in S, for example, slice with a stride of 2:

```
>>> for x in S[::2]: print x
...
```

Changing Lists: range

Another common place where you may use the `range` and `for` combination is in loops that change a list as it is being traversed. Suppose, for example, that you need to add 1 to every item in a list for some reason. Trying this with a simple `for` loop does something, but probably not what you want:

```
>>> L = [1, 2, 3, 4, 5]

>>> for x in L:
...     x += 1
...
>>> L
[1, 2, 3, 4, 5]
>>> x
6
```

This doesn't quite work—it changes the loop variable x, not the list L. The reason is somewhat subtle. Each time through the loop, x refers to the next integer already pulled out of the list. In the first iteration, for example, x is integer 1. In the next iteration, the loop body sets x to a different object, integer 2, but it does not update the list where 1 originally came from.

To really change the list as we march across it, we need to use indexes so we can assign an updated value to each position as we go. The range/len combination can produce the required indexes for us:

```
>>> L = [1, 2, 3, 4, 5]

>>> for i in range(len(L)):          # Add one to each item in L
...     L[i] += 1                    # Or L[i] = L[i] + 1
...
>>> L
[2, 3, 4, 5, 6]
```

When coded this way, the list is changed as we proceed through the loop. There is no way to do the same with a simple for x in L:-style loop here because such a loop iterates through actual items, not list positions. But what about the equivalent while loop? Such a loop requires a bit more work on our part, and likely runs more slowly:

```
>>> i = 0
>>> while i < len(L):
...     L[i] += 1
...     i += 1
...
>>> L
[3, 4, 5, 6, 7]
```

Here again, the range solution may not be ideal. A list comprehension expression of the form [x+1 for x in L] would do similar work, albeit without changing the original list in-place (we could assign the expression's new list object result back to L, but this would not update any other references to the original list). Because this is such a central looping concept, we'll revisit list comprehensions later in this chapter.

Parallel Traversals: zip and map

As we've seen, the range built-in allows us to traverse sequences with for in a nonexhaustive fashion. In the same spirit, the built-in zip function allows us to use for loops to visit multiple sequences *in parallel*. In basic operation, zip takes one or more sequences as arguments, and returns a list of tuples that pair up parallel items taken from those sequences. For example, suppose we're working with two lists:

```
>>> L1 = [1,2,3,4]
>>> L2 = [5,6,7,8]
```

To combine the items in these lists, we can use zip to create a list of tuple pairs:

```
>>> zip(L1,L2)
[(1, 5), (2, 6), (3, 7), (4, 8)]
```

Such a result may be useful in other contexts as well, but when wedded with the for loop, it supports parallel iterations:

```
>>> for (x, y) in zip(L1, L2):
...     print x, y, '--', x+y
...
1 5 -- 6
2 6 -- 8
3 7 -- 10
4 8 -- 12
```

Here, we step over the result of the zip call—that is, the pairs of items pulled from the two lists. Notice that this for loop uses tuple assignment again to unpack each tuple in the zip result. The first time through, it's as though we ran the assignment statement (x, y) = (1, 5).

The net effect is that we scan both L1 *and* L2 in our loop. We could achieve a similar effect with a while loop that handles indexing manually, but it would require more typing, and would likely be slower than the for/zip approach.

The zip function is more general than this example suggests. For instance, it accepts any type of sequence (really, any iterable object, including files), and more than two arguments:

```
>>> T1, T2, T3 = (1,2,3), (4,5,6), (7,8,9)
>>> T3
(7, 8, 9)
>>> zip(T1,T2,T3)
[(1, 4, 7), (2, 5, 8), (3, 6, 9)]
```

zip truncates result tuples at the length of the shortest sequence when the argument lengths differ:

```
>>> S1 = 'abc'
>>> S2 = 'xyz123'
>>>
>>> zip(S1, S2)
[('a', 'x'), ('b', 'y'), ('c', 'z')]
```

The related (and older) built-in map function pairs items from sequences in a similar fashion, but it pads shorter sequences with None if the argument lengths differ:

```
>>> map(None, S1, S2)
[('a', 'x'), ('b', 'y'), ('c', 'z'), (None, '1'), (None, '2'), (None,'3')]
```

This example is actually using a degenerate form of the map built-in. Normally, map takes a function, and one or more sequence arguments, and collects the results of calling the function with parallel items taken from the sequences.

When the function argument is None (as here), it simply pairs items, like zip. map and similar function-based tools are covered in Chapter 17.

Dictionary construction with zip

In Chapter 8, I suggested that the zip call used here can also be handy for generating dictionaries when the sets of keys and values must be computed at runtime. Now that we're becoming proficient with zip, I'll explain how it relates to dictionary construction. As you've learned, you can always create a dictionary by coding a dictionary literal, or by assigning to keys over time:

```
>>> D1 = {'spam':1, 'eggs':3, 'toast':5}
>>> D1
{'toast': 5, 'eggs': 3, 'spam': 1}

>>> D1 = {}
>>> D1['spam']  = 1
>>> D1['eggs']  = 3
>>> D1['toast'] = 5
```

What to do, though, if your program obtains dictionary keys and values in *lists* at runtime, after you've coded your script? For example, say you had the following keys and values lists:

```
>>> keys = ['spam', 'eggs', 'toast']
>>> vals = [1, 3, 5]
```

One solution for turning those lists into a dictionary would be to zip the lists and step through them in parallel with a for loop:

```
>>> zip(keys, vals)
[('spam', 1), ('eggs', 3), ('toast', 5)]

>>> D2 = {}
>>> for (k, v) in zip(keys, vals): D2[k] = v
...
>>> D2
{'toast': 5, 'eggs': 3, 'spam': 1}
```

It turns out, though, that in Python 2.2 and later, you can skip the for loop altogether and simply pass the zipped keys/values lists to the built-in dict constructor call:

```
>>> keys = ['spam', 'eggs', 'toast']
>>> vals = [1, 3, 5]

>>> D3 = dict(zip(keys, vals))
>>> D3
{'toast': 5, 'eggs': 3, 'spam': 1}
```

The built-in name dict is really a type name in Python (you'll learn more about type names, and subclassing them, in Chapter 26). Calling it achieves something like a list-to-dictionary conversion, but it's really an object construction request. Later in this chapter, we'll explore a related but richer concept, the *list comprehension*, which builds lists in a single expression.

Generating Both Offsets and Items: enumerate

Earlier, we discussed using range to generate the offsets of items in a string, rather than the items at those offsets. In some programs, though, we need both: the item to use, plus an offset as we go. Traditionally, this was coded with a simple for loop that also kept a counter of the current offset:

```
>>> S = 'spam'
>>> offset = 0
>>> for item in S:
...     print item, 'appears at offset', offset
...     offset += 1
...
s appears at offset 0
p appears at offset 1
a appears at offset 2
m appears at offset 3
```

This works, but in more recent Python releases, a new built-in named enumerate does the job for us:

```
>>> S = 'spam'
>>> for (offset, item) in enumerate(S):
...     print item, 'appears at offset', offset
...
s appears at offset 0
p appears at offset 1
a appears at offset 2
m appears at offset 3
```

The enumerate function returns a *generator object*—a kind of object that supports the iteration protocol we met earlier in this chapter, and will discuss in more detail in the next part of the book. It has a next method that returns an (index, value) tuple each time through the list, which we can unpack with tuple assignment in the for (much like using zip):

```
>>> E = enumerate(S)
>>> E.next()
(0, 's')
>>> E.next()
(1, 'p')
```

As usual, we don't normally see this machinery because iteration contexts—including list comprehensions, the subject of the next section—run the iteration protocol automatically:

```
>>> [c * i for (i, c) in enumerate(S)]
['', 'p', 'aa', 'mmm']
```

List Comprehensions: A First Look

In the prior section, we learned how to use range to change a list as we step across it:

```
>>> L = [1, 2, 3, 4, 5]
>>> for i in range(len(L)):
...     L[i] += 10
...
>>> L
[11, 12, 13, 14, 15]
```

This works, but as I mentioned, it may not be the optimal "best-practice" approach in Python. Today, the list comprehension expression makes many such prior use cases obsolete. Here, for example, we can replace the loop with a single expression that produces the desired result list:

```
>>> L = [x + 10 for x in L]
>>> L
[21, 22, 23, 24, 25]
```

The net result is the same, but it requires less coding on our part, and probably runs substantially faster. The list comprehension isn't exactly the same as the for loop statement version because it makes a new list object (which might matter if there are multiple references to the original list), but it's close enough for most applications, and is a common and convenient enough approach to merit a closer look here.

List Comprehension Basics

We first met the list comprehension in Chapter 4. Syntactically, list comprehensions' syntax is derived from a construct in set theory notation that applies an operation to each item in a set, but you don't have to know set theory to use them. In Python, most people find that a list comprehension simply looks like a backward for loop.

Let's look at the prior section's example in more detail. List comprehensions are written in square brackets because they are ultimately a way to construct a new list. They begin with an arbitrary expression that we make up, which uses a loop variable that we make up (x + 10). That is followed by what you should now recognize as the header of a for loop, which names the loop variable, and an iterable object (for x in L).

To run the expression, Python executes an iteration across L inside the interpreter, assigning x to each item in turn, and collects the results of running items through the expression on the left side. The result list we get back is exactly what the list comprehension says—a new list containing x + 10, for every x in L.

Technically speaking, list comprehensions are never really required because we can always build up a list of expression results manually with for loops that append results as we go:

```
>>> res = []
>>> for x in L:
...     res.append(x + 10)
...
>>> res
[21, 22, 23, 24, 25]
```

In fact, this is exactly what the list comprehension does internally.

However, list comprehensions are more concise to write, and because this code pattern of building up result lists is so common in Python work, they turn out to be very handy in many contexts. Moreover, list comprehensions can run much faster than manual for loop statements (in fact, often roughly twice as fast) because their iterations are performed at C language speed inside the interpreter, rather than with manual Python code; especially for larger data sets, there is a major performance advantage to using them.

Using List Comprehensions on Files

Let's work through another common use case for list comprehensions to explore them in more detail. Recall that the file object has a `readlines` method that loads the file into a list of line strings all at once:

```
>>> f = open('script1.py')
>>> lines = f.readlines()
>>> lines
['import sys\n', 'print sys.path\n', 'x = 2\n', 'print 2 ** 33\n']
```

This works, but the lines in the result all include the newline character (\n) at the end. For many programs, the newline character gets in the way—we have to be careful to avoid double-spacing when printing, and so on. It would be nice if we could get rid of these newlines all at once, wouldn't it?

Any time we start thinking about performing an operation on each item in a sequence, we're in the realm of list comprehensions. For example, assuming the variable `lines` is as it was in the prior interaction, the following code does the job by running each line in the list through the string `rstrip` method to remove whitespace on the right side (a `line[:-1]` slice would work, too, but only if we can be sure all lines are properly terminated):

```
>>> lines = [line.rstrip() for line in lines]
>>> lines
['import sys', 'print sys.path', 'x = 2', 'print 2 ** 33']
```

This works, but because list comprehensions are another iteration context just like simple for loops, we don't even have to open the file ahead of time. If we open it inside the expression, the list comprehension will automatically use the iteration protocol we met earlier in this chapter. That is, it will read one line from the file at a time by calling the file's next method, run the line through the rstrip expression, and add it to the result list. Again, we get what we ask for—the `rstrip` result of a line, for every line in the file:

```
>>> lines = [line.rstrip() for line in open('script1.py')]
>>> lines
['import sys', 'print sys.path', 'x = 2', 'print 2 ** 33']
```

This expression does a lot implicitly, but we're getting a lot of work for free here—Python scans the file and builds a list of operation results automatically. It's also an efficient way to code this operation: because most of this work is done inside the Python interpreter, it is likely much faster than an equivalent `for` statement. Again, especially for large files, the speed advantages of list comprehensions can be significant.

Extended List Comprehension Syntax

In fact, list comprehensions can be even more advanced in practice. As one useful extension, the `for` loop nested in the expression can have an associated `if` clause to filter out of the result items for which the test is not true.

For example, suppose we want to repeat the prior example, but we need to collect only lines that begin with the letter *p* (perhaps the first character on each line is an action code of some sort). Adding an `if` filter clause to our expression does the trick:

```
>>> lines = [line.rstrip() for line in open('script1.py') if line[0] == 'p']
>>> lines
['print sys.path', 'print 2 ** 33']
```

Here, the `if` clause checks each line read from the file, to see whether its first character is *p*; if not, the line is omitted from the result list. This is a fairly big expression, but it's easy to understand if we translate it to its simple `for` loop statement equivalent (in general, we can always translate a list comprehension to a `for` statement by appending as we go and further indenting each successive part):

```
>>> res = []
>>> for line in open('script1.py'):
...     if line[0] == 'p':
...         res.append(line.rstrip())
...
>>> res
['print sys.path', 'print 2 ** 33']
```

This `for` statement equivalent works, but it takes up four lines instead of one, and probably runs substantially slower.

List comprehensions can become even more complex if we need them to—for instance, they may also contain nested loops, coded as a series of `for` clauses. In fact, their full syntax allows for any number of `for` clauses, each of which can have an optional associated `if` clause (we'll be more formal about their syntax in Chapter 17).

For example, the following builds a list of the concatenation of x + y for every x in one string, and every y in another. It effectively collects the permutation of the characters in two strings:

```
>>> [x + y for x in 'abc' for y in 'lmn']
['al', 'am', 'an', 'bl', 'bm', 'bn', 'cl', 'cm', 'cn']
```

Again, one way to understand this expression is to convert it to statement form by indenting its parts. The following is an equivalent, but likely slower, alternative way to achieve the same effect:

```
>>> res = []
>>> for x in 'abc':
...     for y in 'lmn':
...         res.append(x + y)
...
>>> res
['al', 'am', 'an', 'bl', 'bm', 'bn', 'cl', 'cm', 'cn']
```

Beyond this complexity level, though, list comprehension expressions can become too compact for their own good. In general, they are intended for simple types of iterations; for more involved work, a simpler for statement structure will probably be easier to understand and modify in the future. As usual in programming, if something is difficult for you to understand, it's probably not a good idea.

We'll revisit iterators and list comprehensions in Chapter 17, in the context of functional programming tools; as we'll see, they turn out to be just as related to functions as they are to looping statements.

Chapter Summary

In this chapter, we explored Python's looping statements as well as some concepts related to looping in Python. We looked at the while and for loop statements in depth, and learned about their associated else clauses. We also studied the break and continue statements, which have meaning only inside loops.

Additionally, we took our first substantial look at the iteration protocol in Python—a way for nonsequence objects to take part in iteration loops—and at list comprehensions. As we saw, list comprehensions, which apply expressions to all the items in any iterable object, are similar to for loops.

This wraps up our tour of specific procedural statements. The next chapter closes out this part of the book by discussing documentation options for Python code. Documentation is also part of the general syntax model, and it's an important component of well-written programs. In the next chapter, we'll also dig into a set of exercises for this part of the book before we turn our attention to larger structures such as functions. As always, though, before moving on, first exercise what you've picked up here with a quiz.

Chapter Quiz

1. When is a loop's `else` clause executed?

2. How can you code a counter-based loop in Python?

3. How are `for` loops and iterators related?

4. How are `for` loops and list comprehensions related?

5. Name four iteration contexts in the Python language.

6. What is the best way to read line by line from a text file today?

7. What sort of weapons would you expect to see employed by the Spanish Inquisition?

Quiz Answers

1. The `else` clause in a `while` or `for` loop will be run once as the loop is exiting, if the loop exits normally (without running into a `break` statement). A `break` exits the loop immediately, skipping the `else` part on the way out (if there is one).

2. Counter loops can be coded with a `while` statement that keeps track of the index manually, or with a `for` loop that uses the `range` built-in function to generate successive integer offsets. Neither is the preferred way to work in Python, if you need to simply step across all the items in a sequence—use a simple `for` loop instead, without `range` or counters, whenever possible. It will be easier to code, and usually quicker to run.

3. The `for` loop uses the iteration protocol to step through items in the object across which it is iterating. It calls the object's `next` method on each iteration, and catches the `StopIteration` exception to determine when to stop looping.

4. Both are iteration tools. List comprehensions are a concise and efficient way to perform a common `for` loop task: collecting the results of applying an expression to all items in an iterable object. It's always possible to translate a list comprehension to a `for` loop, and part of the list comprehension expression looks like the header of a `for` loop syntactically.

5. Iteration contexts in Python include the `for` loop; list comprehensions; the `map` built-in function; the `in` membership test expression; and the built-in functions `sorted`, `sum`, `any`, and `all`. This category also includes the `list` and `tuple` built-ins, string `join` methods, and sequence assignments, all of which use the iteration protocol (the `next` method) to step across iterable objects one item at a time.

6. The best way to read lines from a text file today is to not read it explicitly at all: instead, open the file within an iteration context such as a for loop or list comprehension, and let the iteration tool automatically scan one line at a time by running the file's next method on each iteration. This approach is generally best in terms of coding simplicity, execution speed, and memory space requirements.

7. I'll accept any of the following as correct answers: fear, intimidation, nice red uniforms, a comfy couch, and soft pillows.

CHAPTER 14

The Documentation Interlude

This chapter concludes Part III with a look at techniques and tools used for documenting Python code. Although Python code is designed to be readable, a few well-placed human-readable comments can do much to help others understand the workings of your programs. Python includes syntax and tools to make documentation easier.

Although this is something of a tools-related concept, the topic is presented here partly because it involves Python's syntax model, and partly as a resource for readers struggling to understand Python's toolset. For the latter purpose, I'll expand here on documentation pointers first given in Chapter 4. As usual, this chapter ends with some warnings about common pitfalls, a chapter quiz, and a set of exercises for this part of the text.

Python Documentation Sources

By this point in the book, you're probably starting to realize that Python comes with an amazing amount of prebuilt functionality—built-in functions and exceptions, predefined object attributes and methods, standard library modules, and more. Moreover, we've really only scratched the surface of each of these categories.

One of the first questions that bewildered beginners often ask is: how do I find information on all the built-in tools? This section provides hints on the various documentation sources available in Python. It also presents documentation strings (docstrings), and the *PyDoc* system that makes use of them. These topics are somewhat peripheral to the core language itself, but they become essential knowledge as soon as your code reaches the level of the examples and exercises in this part of the book.

As summarized in Table 14-1, there are a variety of places to look for information on Python with generally increasing verbosity. Because documentation is such a crucial tool in practical programming, we'll explore each of these categories in the sections that follow.

Table 14-1. Python documentation sources

Form	Role
# comments	In-file documentation
The dir function	Lists of attributes available in objects
Docstrings: __doc__	In-file documentation attached to objects
PyDoc: The help function	Interactive help for objects
PyDoc: HTML reports	Module documentation in a browser
Standard manual set	Official language and library descriptions
Web resources	Online tutorials, examples, and so on
Published books	Commercially available reference texts

Comments

Hash-mark comments are the most basic way to document your code. Python simply ignores all the text following a # (as long as it's not inside a string literal), so you can follow this character with words and descriptions meaningful to programmers. Such comments are accessible only in your source files, though; to code comments that are more widely available, use docstrings.

In fact, current best practice generally dictates that docstings are best for larger functional documentation (e.g., "my file does this"), and # comments are best limited to smaller code documentation (e.g., "this strange expression does this"). More on docstrings in a moment.

The dir Function

The built-in dir function is an easy way to grab a list of all the attributes available inside an object (i.e., its methods and simpler data items). It can be called on any object that has attributes. For example, to find out what's available in the standard library's sys module, import it, and pass it to dir:

```
>>> import sys
>>> dir(sys)
['__displayhook__', '__doc__', '__excepthook__', '__name__',
'__stderr__', '__stdin__', '__stdout__', '_getframe', 'argv',
'builtin_module_names', 'byteorder', 'copyright', 'displayhook',
'dllhandle', 'exc_info', 'exc_type', 'excepthook',
...more names omitted...]
```

Only some of the many names are displayed here; run these statements on your machine to see the full list.

To find out what attributes are provided in built-in object types, run `dir` on a literal of the desired type. For example, to see list and string attributes, you can pass empty objects:

```
>>> dir([])
['__add__', '__class__', ...more...
'append', 'count', 'extend', 'index', 'insert', 'pop', 'remove',
'reverse', 'sort']

>>> dir('')
['__add__', '__class__', ...more...
'capitalize', 'center', 'count', 'decode', 'encode', 'endswith',
'expandtabs', 'find', 'index', 'isalnum', 'isalpha', 'isdigit',
'islower', 'isspace', 'istitle', 'isupper', 'join', 'ljust',
...more names omitted...]
```

`dir` results for any built-in type include a set of attributes that are related to the implementation of that type (technically, operator overloading methods); they all begin and end with double underscores to make them distinct, and you can safely ignore them at this point in the book.

Incidentally, you can achieve the same effect by passing a type name to `dir` instead of a literal:

```
>>> dir(str) == dir('')          # Same result as prior example
True
>>> dir(list) == dir([])
True
```

This works because functions like `str` and `list` that were once type converters are actually names of types in Python today; calling one of these invokes its constructor to generate an instance of that type. I'll have more to say about constructors and operator overloading methods when we discuss classes in Part VI.

The `dir` function serves as a sort of memory-jogger—it provides a list of attribute names, but it does not tell you anything about what those names mean. For such extra information, we need to move on to the next documentation source.

Docstrings: _ _doc_ _

Besides # comments, Python supports documentation that is automatically attached to objects, and retained at runtime for inspection. Syntactically, such comments are coded as strings at the tops of module files and function and class statements, before any other executable code (# comments are OK before them). Python automatically stuffs the string, known as a *docstring*, into the _ _doc_ _ attribute of the corresponding object.

User-defined docstrings

For example, consider the following file, *docstrings.py*. Its docstrings appear at the beginning of the file and at the start of a function and a class within it. Here, I've used triple-quoted block strings for multiline comments in the file and the function, but any sort of string will work. We haven't studied the def or class statements in detail yet, so ignore everything about them except the strings at their tops:

```
"""
Module documentation
Words Go Here
"""

spam = 40

def square(x):
    """
    function documentation
    can we have your liver then?
    """
    return x **2

class employee:
    "class documentation"
    pass

print square(4)
print square.__doc__
```

The whole point of this documentation protocol is that your comments are retained for inspection in __doc__ attributes, after the file is imported. Thus, to display the docstrings associated with the module and its objects, we simply import the file and print their __doc__ attributes, where Python has saved the text:

```
>>> import docstrings
16

    function documentation
    can we have your liver then?

>>> print docstrings.__doc__

Module documentation
Words Go Here

>>> print docstrings.square.__doc__

    function documentation
    can we have your liver then?

>>> print docstrings.employee.__doc__
    class documentation
```

Note that you will generally want to explicitly say print to docstrings; otherwise, you'll get a single string with embedded newline characters.

You can also attach docstrings to methods of classes (covered later), but because these are just def statements nested in classes, they're not a special case. To fetch the docstring of a method function inside a class within a module, follow the path, and go through the class: module.class.method.__doc__ (see the example of method docstrings in Chapter 25).

Docstring standards

There is no broad standard about what should go into the text of a docstring (although some companies have internal standards). There have been various markup language and template proposals (e.g., HTML or XML), but they don't seem to have caught on in the Python world. And, frankly, convincing programmers to document their code using handcoded HTML is probably not going to happen in our lifetimes!

Documentation tends to have a low priority amongst programmers in general. Usually, if you get any comments in a file at all, you count yourself lucky. I strongly encourage you to document your code liberally, though—it really is an important part of well-written code. The point here is that there is presently no standard on the structure of docstrings; if you want to use them, feel free to do so.

Built-in docstrings

As it turns out, built-in modules and objects in Python use similar techniques to attach documentation above and beyond the attribute lists returned by dir. For example, to see an actual human-readable description of a built-in module, import it and print its __doc__ string:

```
>>> import sys
>>> print sys.__doc__
This module provides access to some objects
used or maintained by the interpreter and to
...more text omitted...

Dynamic objects:

argv -- command line arguments; argv[0] is the script pathname if known
path -- module search path; path[0] is the script directory, else ''
modules -- dictionary of loaded modules
...more text omitted...
```

Functions, classes, and methods within built-in modules have attached descriptions in their __doc__ attributes as well:

```
>>> print sys.getrefcount.__doc__
getrefcount(object) -> integer

Return the current reference count for the object.
...more text omitted...
```

You can also read about built-in functions via their docstrings:

```
>>> print int.__doc__
int(x[, base]) -> integer

Convert a string or number to an integer, if possible.
...more text omitted...

>>> print file.__doc__
file(name[, mode[, buffering]]) -> file object

Open a file.  The mode can be 'r', 'w' or 'a' for reading
...more text omitted...
```

You can get a wealth of information about built-in tools by inspecting their docstrings this way, but you don't have to—the help function, the topic of the next section, does this automatically for you.

PyDoc: The help Function

The docstring technique has proved to be so useful that Python now ships with a tool that makes them even easier to display. The standard PyDoc tool is Python code that knows how to extract docstrings together with automatically extracted structural information, and format them into nicely arranged reports of various types.

There are a variety of ways to launch PyDoc, including command-line script options (see the Python library manual for details). Perhaps the two most prominent PyDoc interfaces are the built-in help function, and the PyDoc GUI/HTML interface. The help function invokes PyDoc to generate a simple textual report (which looks much like a "manpage" on Unix-like systems):

```
>>> import sys
>>> help(sys.getrefcount)
Help on built-in function getrefcount:

getrefcount(...)
    getrefcount(object) -> integer

    Return the current reference count for the object.
    ...more omitted...
```

Note that you do not have to import sys in order to call help, but you do have to import sys to get help on sys; it expects an object reference to be passed in. For larger objects such as modules and classes, the help display is broken down into multiple sections, a few of which are shown here. Run this interactively to see the full report:

```
>>> help(sys)
Help on built-in module sys:

NAME
    sys
```

```
FILE
    (built-in)

DESCRIPTION
    This module provides access to some objects used
    or maintained by the interpreter and to functions
    ...more omitted...

FUNCTIONS
    __displayhook__ = displayhook(...)
        displayhook(object) -> None

        Print an object to sys.stdout and also save it
    ...more omitted...
DATA
    __name__ = 'sys'
    __stderr__ = <open file '<stderr>', mode 'w' at 0x0082BEC0>
    ...more omitted...
```

Some of the information in this report is docstrings, and some of it (e.g., function call patterns) is structural information that PyDoc gleans automatically by inspecting objects' internals. You can also use help on built-in functions, methods, and types. To get help for a built-in type, use the type name (e.g., dict for dictionary, str for string, list for list). You'll get a large display that describes all the methods available for that type:

```
>>> help(dict)
Help on class dict in module __builtin__:

class dict(object)
 |  dict() -> new empty dictionary.
 ...more omitted...

>>> help(str.replace)
Help on method_descriptor:

replace(...)
    S.replace (old, new[, maxsplit]) -> string

    Return a copy of string S with all occurrences
    ...more omitted...

>>> help(ord)
Help on built-in function ord:

ord(...)
    ord(c) -> integer

    Return the integer ordinal of a one-character string.
```

Finally, the help function works just as well on your modules as built-ins. Here it is reporting on the *docstrings.py* file coded earlier; again, some of this is docstrings, and some is information automatically extracted by inspecting objects' structures:

```
>>> help(docstrings.square)
Help on function square in module docstrings:

square(x)
    function documentation
    can we have your liver then?

>>> help(docstrings.employee)
...more omitted...

>>> help(docstrings)
Help on module docstrings:

NAME
    docstrings

FILE
    c:\python22\docstrings.py

DESCRIPTION
    Module documentation
    Words Go Here

CLASSES
    employee
    ...more omitted...

FUNCTIONS
    square(x)
        function documentation
        can we have your liver then?

DATA
    __file__ = 'C:\\PYTHON22\\docstrings.pyc'
    __name__ = 'docstrings'
    spam = 40
```

PyDoc: HTML Reports

The help function is nice for grabbing documentation when working interactively. For a more grandiose display, however, PyDoc also provides a GUI interface (a simple, but portable, Python/Tkinter script), and can render its report in HTML page format, viewable in any web browser. In this mode, PyDoc can run locally or as a remote server in client/server mode; reports contain automatically created hyperlinks that allow you to click your way through the documentation of related components in your application.

To start PyDoc in this mode, you generally first launch the search engine GUI captured in Figure 14-1. You can start this either by selecting the Module Docs item in Python's Start button menu on Windows, or by launching the *pydocgui.pyw* script in Python's *Tools* directory (running pydoc.py with a -g command-line argument works, too). Enter the name of a module you're interested in, and press the Enter key; PyDoc will march down your module import search path (sys.path) looking for references to the requested module.

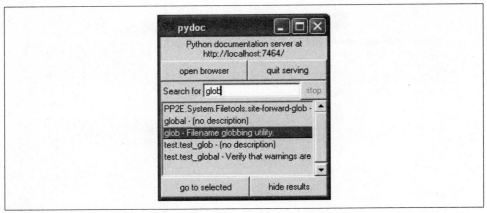

Figure 14-1. The Pydoc top-level search engine GUI: type a name of a module you want documentation for, press Enter, select the module, and then press "go to selected" (or use no module name, and press "open browser" to see all available modules).

Once you've found a promising entry, select it, and click "go to selected." PyDoc will spawn a web browser on your machine to display the report rendered in HTML format. Figure 14-2 shows the information PyDoc displays for the built-in glob module.

Notice the hyperlinks in the Modules section of this page—you can click these to jump to the PyDoc pages for related (imported) modules. For larger pages, PyDoc also generates hyperlinks to sections within the page.

Like the help function interface, the GUI interface works on user-defined modules as well. Figure 14-3 shows the page generated for our *docstrings.py* module file.

PyDoc can be customized and launched in various ways we won't cover here; see its entry in Python's standard library manual for more details. The main thing to take away from this section is that PyDoc essentially gives you implementation reports "for free"—if you are good about using docstrings in your files, PyDoc does all the work of collecting and formatting them for display. PyDoc only helps for objects like functions and modules, but it provides an easy way to access a middle level of documentation for such tools—its reports are more useful than raw attribute lists, and less exhaustive than the standard manuals.

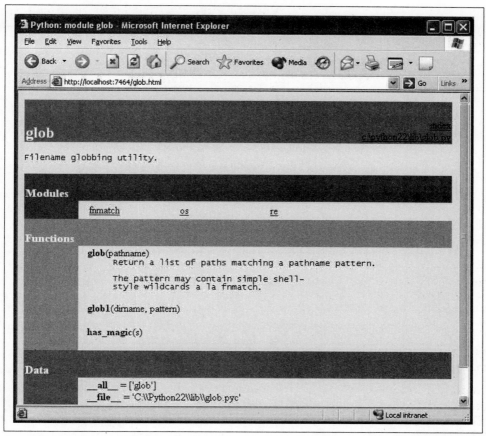

Figure 14-2. When you find a module in the Figure 14-1 GUI and press "go to selected," the module's documentation is rendered in HTML and displayed in a web browser window like this one—a built-in standard library module.

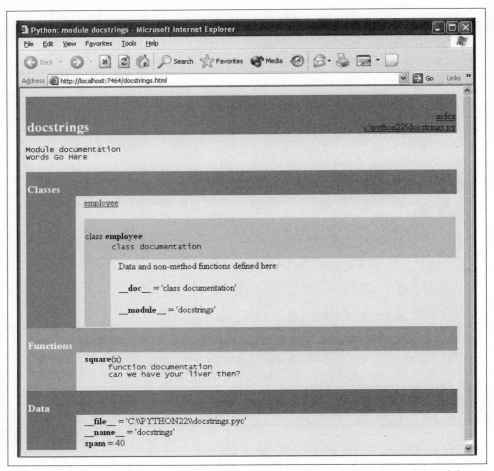

Figure 14-3. PyDoc can serve up documentation pages for both built-in and user-coded modules. Here is the page for a user-defined module, showing all its documentation strings (docstrings) extracted from the source file.

Cool PyDoc trick of the day: if you leave the module name empty in the top input field of the window in Figure 14-1 and press the Open Browser button, PyDoc will produce a web page containing a hyperlink to every module you can possibly import on your computer. This includes Python standard library modules, modules of third-party extensions you may have installed, user-defined modules on your import search path, and even statically or dynamically linked-in C-coded modules. Such information is hard to come by otherwise without writing code that inspects a set of module sources.

PyDoc can also be run to save the HTML documentation for a module in a file for later viewing or printing; see its documentation for pointers. Also, note that PyDoc might not work well if run on scripts that read from standard input—PyDoc imports the target module to inspect its contents, and there may be no connection for standard input text when it is run in GUI mode. Modules that can be imported without immediate input requirements will always work under PyDoc, though.

Standard Manual Set

For the complete and most up-to-date description of the language and its toolset, Python's standard manuals stand ready to serve. Python's manuals ship in HTML and other formats, and are installed with the Python system on Windows—they are available in your Start button's menu for Python, and they can also be opened from the Help menu within IDLE. You can also fetch the manual set separately from *http://www.python.org* in a variety of formats, or read them online at that site (follow the Documentation link). On Windows, the manuals are a compiled help file to support searches, and the online versions at Python.org include a web-based search page.

When opened, the Windows format of the manuals displays a root page like that in Figure 14-4. The two most important entries here are most likely the Library Reference (which documents built-in types, functions, exceptions, and standard library modules), and the Language Reference (which provides a formal description of language-level details). The tutorial listed on this page also provides a brief introduction for newcomers.

Web Resources

At the official Python programming language web site (*http://www.python.org*), you'll find links to various Python resources, some of which cover special topics or domains. Click the Documentation link to access an online tutorial and the Beginners Guide to Python. The site also lists non-English Python resources.

You will find numerous Python wikis, blogs, web sites, and a host of other resources on the Web today. To sample the online community, try searching for "Python programming" in Google.

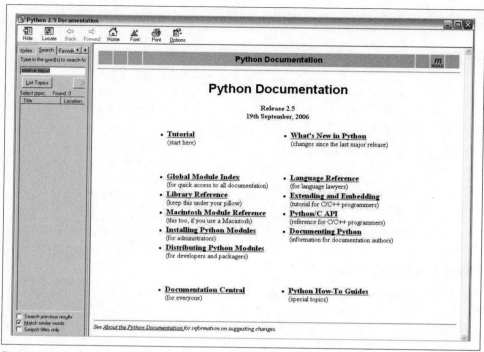

Figure 14-4. Python's standard manual set, available online at www.python.org, from IDLE's Help menu, and in the Windows Start button menu. It's a searchable help file on Windows, and there is a search engine for the online version. Of these, the Library manual is the one you'll want to use most of the time.

Published Books

As a final resource, you can choose from a large collection of reference books for Python. Bear in mind that books tend to lag behind the cutting edge of Python changes, partly because of the work involved in writing, and partly because of the natural delays built into the publishing cycle. Usually, by the time a book comes out, it's three or more months behind the current Python state. Unlike standard manuals, books are also generally not free.

Still, for many, the convenience and quality of a professionally published text is worth the cost. Moreover, Python changes so slowly that books are usually still relevant years after they are published, especially if their authors post updates on the Web. See the Preface for pointers to other Python books.

Common Coding Gotchas

Before the programming exercises for this part of the book, let's run through some of the most common mistakes beginners make when coding Python statements and programs. Many of these are warnings I've thrown out earlier in this part of the book, collected here for ease of reference. You'll learn to avoid these pitfalls once you've gained a bit of Python coding experience, but a few words now might help you avoid falling into some of these traps initially:

- **Don't forget the colons.** Always remember to type a : at the end of compound statement headers (the first line of an if, while, for, etc.). You'll probably forget at first (I did, and so have most of my 3,000 Python students over the years), but you can take some comfort from the fact that it will soon become an unconscious habit.

- **Start in column 1.** Be sure to start top-level (unnested) code in column 1. That includes unnested code typed into module files, as well as unnested code typed at the interactive prompt.

- **Blank lines matter at the interactive prompt.** Blank lines in compound statements are always ignored in module files, but when you're typing code at the interactive prompt, they end the statement. In other words, blank lines tell the interactive command line that you've finished a compound statement; if you want to continue, don't hit the Enter key at the **...** prompt (or in IDLE) until you're really done.

- **Indent consistently.** Avoid mixing tabs and spaces in the indentation of a block, unless you know what your text editor does with tabs. Otherwise, what you see in your editor may not be what Python sees when it counts tabs as a number of spaces. This is true in any block-structured language, not just Python—if the next programmer has her tabs set differently, she will not understand the structure of your code. It's safer to use all tabs or all spaces for each block.

- **Don't code C in Python.** A reminder for C/C++ programmers: you don't need to type parentheses around tests in if and while headers (e.g., if (X==1):). You can, if you like (any expression can be enclosed in parentheses), but they are fully superfluous in this context. Also, do not terminate all your statements with semicolons; it's technically legal to do this in Python as well, but it's totally useless unless you're placing more than one statement on a single line (the end of a line normally terminates a statement). And remember, don't embed assignment statements in while loop tests, and don't use {} around blocks (indent your nested code blocks consistently instead).

- **Use simple for loops instead of while or range.** Another reminder: a simple for loop (e.g., for x in seq:) is almost always simpler to code and quicker to run than a while- or range-based counter loop. Because Python handles indexing internally for a simple for, it can sometimes be twice as fast as the equivalent while. Avoid the temptation to count things in Python!

- **Beware of mutables in assignments.** I mentioned this in Chapter 11: you need to be careful about using mutables in a multiple-target assignment (a = b = [ ]), as well as in an augmented assignment (a += [1, 2]). In both cases, in-place changes may impact other variables. See Chapter 11 for details.

- **Don't expect results from functions that change objects in-place.** We encountered this one earlier, too: in-place change operations like the list.append and list.sort methods introduced in Chapter 8 do not return values (other than None), so you should call them without assigning the result. It's not uncommon for beginners to say something like mylist = mylist.append(X) to try to get the result of an append, but what this actually does is assign mylist to None, not to the modified list (in fact, you'll lose your reference to the list altogether).

  A more devious example of this pops up when trying to step through dictionary items in a sorted fashion. It's fairly common to see code like for k in D.keys( ).sort( ):. This almost works—the keys method builds a keys list, and the sort method orders it—but because the sort method returns None, the loop fails because it is ultimately a loop over None (a nonsequence). To code this correctly, either use the newer sorted built-in function, which returns the sorted list, or split the method calls out to statements: Ks = D.keys( ), then Ks.sort( ), and, finally, for k in Ks:. This, by the way, is one case where you'll still want to call the keys method explicitly for looping, instead of relying on the dictionary iterators—iterators do not sort.

- **Always use parentheses to call a function.** You must add parentheses after a function name to call it, whether it takes arguments or not (e.g., use function( ), not function). In Part IV, we'll see that functions are simply objects that have a special operation—a call that you trigger with the parentheses.

  In classes, this problem seems to occur most often with files; it's common to see beginners type file.close to close a file, rather than file.close( ). Because it's legal to reference a function without calling it, the first version with no parentheses succeeds silently, but it does not close the file!

- **Don't use extensions or paths in imports and reloads.** Omit directory paths and file suffixes in import statements (e.g., say import mod, not import mod.py). (We discussed module basics in Chapter 3, and will continue studying modules in Part V.) Because modules may have other suffixes besides *.py* (*.pyc*, for instance), hardcoding a particular suffix is not only illegal syntax, but doesn't make sense. Any platform-specific directory path syntax comes from module search path settings, not the import statement.

Chapter Summary

This chapter took us on a tour of program documentation concepts—both documentation we write ourselves for our own programs, and documentation available for built-in tools. We met doctrings, explored the online and manual resources for Python reference, and learned how PyDoc's help function and web page interface provide extra sources of documentation. Because this is the last chapter in this part of the book, we also reviewed common coding mistakes to help you avoid them.

In the next part of this book, we'll start applying what we already know to larger program constructs: functions. Before moving on, however, be sure to work through the set of lab exercises for this part of the book that appear at the end of this chapter. And even before that, let's run through this chapter's quiz.

Chapter Quiz

1. When should you use documentation strings instead of hash-mark comments?
2. Name three ways you can view documentation strings.
3. How can you obtain a list of the available attributes in an object?
4. How can you get a list of all available modules on your computer?
5. Which Python book should you purchase after this one?

Quiz Answers

1. Documentation strings (docstrings) are considered best for larger, functional documentation, describing the use of modules, functions, classes, and methods in your code. Hash-mark comments are today best limited to micro-documentation about arcane expressions or statements. This is partly because docstrings are easier to find in a source file, but also because they can be extracted and displayed by the PyDoc system.
2. You can see docstrings by printing an object's _ _doc_ _ attribute, by passing it to PyDoc's help function, and by selecting modules in PyDoc's GUI search engine in client/server mode. Additionally, PyDoc can be run to save a module's documentation in an HTML file for later viewing or printing.
3. The built-in dir(X) function returns a list of all the attributes attached to any object.
4. Run the PyDoc GUI interface, leave the module name blank, and select Open Browser; this opens a web page containing a link to every module available to your programs.
5. Mine, of course. (Seriously, the Preface lists a few recommended follow-up books, both for reference and for application tutorials.)

Part III Exercises

Now that you know how to code basic program logic, the following exercises will ask you to implement some simple tasks with statements. Most of the work is in exercise 4, which lets you explore coding alternatives. There are always many ways to arrange statements, and part of learning Python is learning which arrangements work better than others.

See "Part III, Statements and Syntax" in Appendix B for the solutions.

1. *Coding basic loops.*

    a. Write a for loop that prints the ASCII code of each character in a string named S. Use the built-in function ord(character) to convert each character to an ASCII integer. (Test it interactively to see how it works.)

    b. Next, change your loop to compute the sum of the ASCII codes of all characters in a string.

    c. Finally, modify your code again to return a new list that contains the ASCII codes of each character in the string. Does the expression map(ord, S) have a similar effect? (Hint: see Part IV.)

2. *Backslash characters.* What happens on your machine when you type the following code interactively?

```
for i in range(50):
    print 'hello %d\n\a' % i
```

Beware that if run outside of the IDLE interface, this example may beep at you, so you may not want to run it in a crowded lab. IDLE prints odd characters instead (see the backslash escape characters in Table 7-2).

3. *Sorting dictionaries.* In Chapter 8, we saw that dictionaries are unordered collections. Write a for loop that prints a dictionary's items in sorted (ascending) order. Hint: use the dictionary keys and list sort methods, or the newer sorted built-in function.

4. *Program logic alternatives.* Consider the following code, which uses a while loop and found flag to search a list of powers of 2 for the value of 2 raised to the 5th power (32). It's stored in a module file called *power.py*.

```
L = [1, 2, 4, 8, 16, 32, 64]
X = 5

found = i = 0
while not found and i < len(L):
    if 2 ** X == L[i]:
        found = 1
    else:
        i = i+1
```

```
if found:
    print 'at index', i
else:
    print X, 'not found'
```

```
C:\book\tests> python power.py
at index 5
```

As is, the example doesn't follow normal Python coding techniques. Follow the steps outlined here to improve it (for all the transformations, you may type your code interactively, or store it in a script file run from the system command line—using a file makes this exercise much easier):

a. First, rewrite this code with a while loop else clause to eliminate the found flag and final if statement.

b. Next, rewrite the example to use a for loop with an else clause, to eliminate the explicit list-indexing logic. Hint: to get the index of an item, use the list index method (L.index(X) returns the offset of the first X in list L).

c. Next, remove the loop completely by rewriting the example with a simple in operator membership expression. (See Chapter 8 for more details, or type this to test: 2 in [1,2,3].)

d. Finally, use a for loop and the list append method to generate the powers-of-2 list (L) instead of hardcoding a list literal.

Deeper thoughts:

e. Do you think it would improve performance to move the 2 ** X expression outside the loops? How would you code that?

f. As we saw in exercise 1, Python includes a map(function, list) tool that can generate the powers-of-2 list, too: map(lambda x: 2 ** x, range(7)). Try typing this code interactively; we'll meet lambda more formally in Chapter 17.

Functions

## CHAPTER 15

Function Basics

In Part III, we looked at basic procedural statements in Python. Here, we'll move on to explore a set of additional statements that we can use to create functions of our own.

In simple terms, a *function* is a device that groups a set of statements so they can be run more than once in a program. Functions also can compute a result value and let us specify parameters that serve as function inputs, which may differ each time the code is run. Coding an operation as a function makes it a generally useful tool, which we can use in a variety of contexts.

More fundamentally, functions are the alternative to programming by cutting and pasting—rather than having multiple redundant copies of an operation's code, we can factor it into a single function. In so doing, we reduce our future work radically: if the operation must be changed later, we only have one copy to update, not many.

Functions are the most basic program structure Python provides for maximizing *code reuse* and minimizing *code redundancy*. As we'll see, functions are also a design tool that lets us split complex systems into manageable parts. Table 15-1 summarizes the primary function-related tools we'll study in this part of the book.

Table 15-1. Function-related statements and expressions

Statement	Examples
Calls	`myfunc("spam", "eggs", meat=ham)`
def, return, yield	`def adder(a, b=1, *c):` `    return a+b+c[0]`
global	`def changer():` `    global x; x = 'new'`
lambda	`Funcs = [lambda x: x**2, lambda x: x*3]`

Why Use Functions?

Before we get into the details, let's establish a clear picture of what functions are all about. Functions are a nearly universal program-structuring device. You may have come across them before in other languages, where they may have been called *subroutines* or *procedures*. As a brief introduction, functions serve two primary development roles:

Maximizing code reuse and minimizing redundancy

As in most programming languages, Python functions are the simplest way to package logic you may wish to use in more than one place and more than one time. Up until now, all the code we've been writing has run immediately. Functions allow us to group and generalize code to be used arbitrarily many times later. Because they allow us to code an operation in a single place, and use it in many places, Python functions are the most basic *factoring* tool in the language: they allow us to reduce code redundancy in our programs, and thereby reduce maintenance effort.

Procedural decomposition

Functions also provide a tool for splitting systems into pieces that have well-defined roles. For instance, to make a pizza from scratch, you would start by mixing the dough, rolling it out, adding toppings, baking it, and so on. If you were programming a pizza-making robot, functions would help you divide the overall "make pizza" task into chunks—one function for each subtask in the process. It's easier to implement the smaller tasks in isolation than it is to implement the entire process at once. In general, functions are about procedure—how to do something, rather than what you're doing it to. We'll see why this distinction matters in Part VI.

In this part of the book, we'll explore the tools used to code functions in Python: function basics, scope rules, and argument passing, along with a few related concepts such as generators and functional tools. Because its importance begins to become more apparent at this level of coding, we'll also revisit the notion of polymorphism introduced earlier in the book. As you'll see, functions don't imply much new syntax, but they do lead us to some bigger programming ideas.

Coding Functions

Although it wasn't made very formal, we've already used some functions in earlier chapters. For instance, to make a file object, we called the built-in open function; similarly, we used the len built-in function to ask for the number of items in a collection object.

In this chapter, we will explore how to write *new* functions in Python. Functions we write behave the same way as the built-ins we've already seen: they are called in expressions, are passed values, and return results. But writing new functions requires the application of a few additional ideas that haven't yet been introduced. Moreover, functions behave very differently in Python than they do in compiled languages like C. Here is a brief introduction to the main concepts behind Python functions, all of which we will study in this part of the book:

- **def is executable code.** Python functions are written with a new statement, the def. Unlike functions in compiled languages such as C, def is an executable statement—your function does not exist until Python reaches and runs the def. In fact, it's legal (and even occasionally useful) to nest def statements inside if statements, while loops, and even other defs. In typical operation, def statements are coded in module files, and are naturally run to generate functions when a module file is first imported.

- **def creates an object and assigns it to a name.** When Python reaches and runs a def statement, it generates a new function object, and assigns it to the function's name. As with all assignments, the function name becomes a reference to the function object. There's nothing magic about the name of a function—as you'll see, the function object can be assigned to other names, stored in a list, and so on. Functions may also be created with the lambda expression (a more advanced concept deferred until a later chapter).

- **return sends a result object back to the caller.** When a function is called, the caller stops until the function finishes its work, and returns control to the caller. Functions that compute a value send it back to the caller with a return statement; the returned value becomes the result of the function call. Functions known as *generators* may also use the yield statement to send back a value and suspend their state such that they may be resumed later; this is another advanced topic covered later in this part of the book.

- **Arguments are passed by assignment (object reference).** In Python, arguments are passed to functions by assignment (which, as we've learned, means by object reference). As you'll see, Python's model isn't really equivalent to C's passing rules or C++'s reference parameters—the caller and function share objects by references, but there is no name aliasing. Changing an argument name does not also change a name in the caller, but changing passed-in mutable objects can change objects shared by the caller.

- **global declares module-level variables that are to be assigned.** By default, all names assigned in a function, are local to that function and exist only while the function runs. To assign a name in the enclosing module, functions need to list it in a global statement. More generally, names are always looked up in *scopes*— places where variables are stored—and assignments bind names to scopes.

- **Arguments, return values, and variables are not declared.** As with everything in Python, there are no type constraints on functions. In fact, nothing about a function needs to be declared ahead of time: you can pass in arguments of any type, return any kind of object, and so on. As one consequence, a single function can often be applied to a variety of object types—any objects that sport a compatible interface (methods and expressions) will do, regardless of their specific type.

If some of the preceding words didn't sink in, don't worry—we'll explore all of these concepts with real code in this part of the book. Let's get started by expanding on some of these ideas and looking at a few examples.

def Statements

The def statement creates a function object and assigns it to a name. Its general format is as follows:

```
def <name>(arg1, arg2,... argN):
    <statements>
```

As with all compound Python statements, def consists of a header line followed by a block of statements, usually indented (or a simple statement after the colon). The statement block becomes the function's *body*—that is, the code Python executes each time the function is called.

The def header line specifies a function *name* that is assigned the function object, along with a list of zero or more *arguments* (sometimes called parameters) in parentheses. The argument names in the header are assigned to the objects passed in parentheses at the point of call.

Function bodies often contain a return statement:

```
def <name>(arg1, arg2,... argN):
    ...
    return <value>
```

The Python return statement can show up anywhere in a function body; it ends the function call, and sends a result back to the caller. The return statement consists of an object expression that gives the function's result. The return statement is optional; if it's not present, the function exits when the control flow falls off the end of the function body. Technically, a function without a return statement returns the None object automatically, but this return value is usually ignored.

Functions may also contain yield statements, which are designed to produce a series of values over time, but we'll defer discussion of these until we survey advanced function topics in Chapter 17.

def Executes at Runtime

The Python `def` is a true executable statement: when it runs, it creates and assigns a new function object to a name. (Remember, all we have in Python is *runtime*; there is no such thing as a separate compile time.) Because it's a statement, a `def` can appear anywhere a statement can—even nested in other statements. For instance, although `defs` normally are run when the module enclosing them is imported, it's also completely legal to nest a function `def` inside an `if` statement to select between alternative definitions:

```
if test:
    def func():        # Define func this way
        ...
else:
    def func():        # Or else this way
        ...

...
func()                 # Call the version selected and built
```

One way to understand this code is to realize that the `def` is much like an = statement: it simply assigns a name at runtime. Unlike in compiled languages such as C, Python functions do not need to be fully defined before the program runs. More generally, `defs` are not evaluated until they are reached and run, and the code *inside* `defs` is not evaluated until the functions are later called.

Because function definition happens at runtime, there's nothing special about the function name. What's important is the object to which it refers:

```
othername = func       # Assign function object
othername()            # Call func again
```

Here, the function was assigned to a different name and called through the new name. Like everything else in Python, functions are just objects; they are recorded explicitly in memory at program execution time.

A First Example: Definitions and Calls

Apart from such runtime concepts (which tend to seem most unique to programmers with backgrounds in traditional compiled languages), Python functions are straightforward to use. Let's code a first real example to demonstrate the basics. As you'll see, there are two sides to the function picture: a *definition* (the `def` that creates a function), and a *call* (an expression that tells Python to run the function's body).

Definition

Here's a definition typed interactively that defines a function called `times`, which returns the product of its two arguments:

```
>>> def times(x, y):          # Create and assign function
...     return x * y          # Body executed when called
...
```

When Python reaches and runs this `def`, it creates a new function object that packages the function's code and assigns the object to the name `times`. Typically, such a statement is coded in a module file, and runs when the enclosing file is imported; for something this small, though, the interactive prompt suffices.

Calls

After the `def` has run, you can call (run) the function in your program by adding parentheses after the function's name. The parentheses may optionally contain one or more object arguments, to be passed (assigned) to the names in the function's header:

```
>>> times(2, 4)          # Arguments in parentheses
8
```

This expression passes two arguments to `times`. As mentioned previously, arguments are passed by assignment, so, in this case, the name x in the function header is assigned the value 2, y is assigned the value 4, and the function's body is run. For this function, the body is just a `return` statement that sends back the result as the value of the call expression. The returned object was printed here interactively (as in most languages, 2 * 4 is 8 in Python), but, if we needed to use it later, we could instead assign it to a variable. For example:

```
>>> x = times(3.14, 4)          # Save the result object
>>> x
12.56
```

Now, watch what happens when the function is called a third time, with very different kinds of objects passed in:

```
>>> times('Ni', 4)          # Functions are "typeless"
'NiNiNiNi'
```

This time, our function means something completely different (Monty Python reference again intended). In this third call, a string and an integer are passed to x and y, instead of two numbers. Recall that * works on both numbers and sequences; because we never declare the types of variables, arguments, or return values in Python, we can use `times` to either *multiply* numbers or *repeat* sequences.

In other words, what our `times` function means and does depends on what we pass into it. This is a core idea in Python (and perhaps the key to using the language well), which we'll explore in the next section.

Polymorphism in Python

As we just saw, the very meaning of the expression x * y in our simple `times` function depends completely upon the kinds of objects that x and y are—thus, the same function can perform multiplication in one instance, and repetition in another. Python leaves it up to the *objects* to do something reasonable for the syntax. Really, * is just a dispatch to the objects being processed.

This sort of type-dependent behavior is known as *polymorphism*, a term we first met in Chapter 4 that essentially means that the meaning of an operation depends on the objects being operated upon. Because it's a dynamically typed language, polymorphism runs rampant in Python. In fact, every operation is a polymorphic operation in Python: printing, indexing, the * operator, and much more.

This is deliberate, and it accounts for much of the language's conciseness and flexibility. A single function, for instance, can generally be applied to a whole category of object types automatically. As long as those objects support the expected interface (a.k.a. protocol), the function can process them. That is, if the objects passed into a function have the expected methods and expression operators, they are plug-and-play compatible with the function's logic.

Even in our simple `times` function, this means that *any* two objects that support a * will work, no matter what they may be, and no matter when they are coded. This function will work on two numbers (performing multiplication), or a string and a number (performing repetition), or any other combination of objects supporting the expected interface—even class-based objects we have not even coded yet.

Moreover, if the objects passed in do *not* support this expected interface, Python will detect the error when the * expression is run, and raise an exception automatically. It's therefore pointless to code error checking ourselves. In fact, doing so would limit our function's utility, as it would be restricted to work only on objects whose types we test for.

This turns out to be a crucial philosophical difference between Python and statically typed languages like C++ and Java: in Python, your code is *not supposed to care* about specific data types. If it does, it will be limited to working on just the types you anticipated when you wrote it, and it will not support other compatible object types that may be coded in the future. Although it is possible to test for types with tools like the type built-in function, doing so breaks your code's flexibility. By and large, we code to object *interfaces* in Python, not data types.

Of course, this polymorphic model of programming means we have to test our code to detect errors, rather than providing type declarations a compiler can use to detect some types of errors for us ahead of time. In exchange for an initial bit of testing, though, we radically reduce the amount of code we have to write, and radically increase our code's flexibility. As you'll learn, it's a net win in practice.

A Second Example: Intersecting Sequences

Let's look at a second function example that does something a bit more useful than multiplying arguments and further illustrates function basics.

In Chapter 13, we coded a for loop that collected items held in common in two strings. We noted there that the code wasn't as useful as it could be because it was set up to work only on specific variables and could not be rerun later. Of course, we could copy the code and paste it into each place where it needs to be run, but this solution is neither good nor general—we'd still have to edit each copy to support different sequence names, and changing the algorithm would then require changing multiple copies.

Definition

By now, you can probably guess that the solution to this dilemma is to package the for loop inside a function. Doing so offers a number of advantages:

- Putting the code in a function makes it a tool that you can run as many times as you like.
- Because callers can pass in arbitrary arguments, functions are general enough to work on any two sequences (or other iterables) you wish to intersect.
- When the logic is packaged in a function, you only have to change code in one place if you ever need to change the way the intersection works.
- Coding the function in a module file means it can be imported and reused by any program run on your machine.

In effect, wrapping the code in a function makes it a general intersection utility:

```
def intersect(seq1, seq2):
    res = []                    # Start empty
    for x in seq1:              # Scan seq1
        if x in seq2:           # Common item?
            res.append(x)       # Add to end
    return res
```

The transformation from the simple code of Chapter 13 to this function is straightforward; we've just nested the original logic under a def header, and made the objects on which it operates passed-in parameter names. Because this function computes a result, we've also added a return statement to send a result object back to the caller.

Calls

Before you can call a function, you have to make it. To do this, run its def statement, either by typing it interactively, or by coding it in a module file and importing the file. Once you've run the def, you can call the function by passing any two sequence objects in parentheses:

```
>>> s1 = "SPAM"
>>> s2 = "SCAM"

>>> intersect(s1, s2)            # Strings
['S', 'A', 'M']
```

Here, we've passed in two strings, and we get back a list containing the characters in common. The algorithm the function uses is simple: "for every item in the first argument, if that item is also in the second argument, append the item to the result." It's a little shorter to say that in Python than in English, but it works out the same.

Polymorphism Revisited

Like all functions in Python, intersect is polymorphic. That is, it works on arbitrary types, as long as they support the expected object interface:

```
>>> x = intersect([1, 2, 3], (1, 4))    # Mixed types
>>> x                                    # Saved result object
[1]
```

This time, we passed in different types of objects to our function—a list and a tuple (mixed types)—and it still picked out the common items. Because you don't have to specify the types of arguments ahead of time, the intersect function happily iterates through any kind of sequence objects you send it, as long as they support the expected interfaces.

For intersect, this means that the first argument has to support the for loop, and the second has to support the in membership test. Any two such objects will work, regardless of their specific types—that includes physically stored sequences like strings and lists; all the iterable objects we met in Chapter 13, including files and dictionaries; and even any class-based objects we code that apply operator overloading techniques (we'll discuss these later, in Part VI of this text).*

Here again, if we pass in objects that do not support these interfaces (e.g., numbers), Python will automatically detect the mismatch, and raise an exception for us—which is exactly what we want, and the best we could do on our own if we coded explicit type tests. By not coding type tests, and allowing Python to detect the mismatches for us, we both reduce the amount of code we need to write, and increase our code's flexibility.

---

* Two fine points here. One, technically a file will work as the first argument to the intersect function, but not the second, because the file will have been scanned to end-of-file after the first in membership test has been run. For instance, a call such as intersect(open('data1.txt'), ['line1\n', 'line2\n', 'line3\n']) would work, but a call like intersect(open('data1.txt'), open('data2.txt')) would not, unless the first file contained only one line—for real sequences, the call to iter made by iteration contexts to obtain an iterator always restarts from the beginning, but once a file has been opened and read, its iterator is effectively exhausted. Two, note that for classes, we would probably use the newer __iter__ or older __getitem__ operator overloading methods covered in Chapter 24 to support the expected iteration protocol. If we do this, we can define and control what iteration means for our data.

Local Variables

The variable res inside intersect is what in Python is called a *local variable*—a name that is visible only to code inside the function def, and exists only while the function runs. In fact, because all names *assigned* in any way inside a function are classified as local variables by default, nearly all the names in intersect are local variables:

- res is obviously assigned, so it is a local variable.
- Arguments are passed by assignment, so seq1 and seq2 are, too.
- The for loop assigns items to a variable, so the name x is also local.

All these local variables appear when the function is called, and disappear when the function exits—the return statement at the end of intersect sends back the result *object*, but the *name* res goes away. To fully explore the notion of locals, though, we need to move on to Chapter 16.

Chapter Summary

This chapter introduced the core ideas behind function definition—the syntax and operation of the def and return statements, the behavior of function call expressions, and the notion and benefits of polymorphism in Python functions. As we saw, a def statement is executable code that creates a function object at runtime; when the function is later called, objects are passed into it by assignment (recall that assignment means object reference in Python, which, as we learned in Chapter 6, really means pointer internally), and computed values are sent back by return. We also began exploring the concepts of local variables and scopes in this chapter, but we'll save all the details on those topics for Chapter 16. First, though, a quick quiz.

Chapter Quiz

1. What is the point of coding functions?
2. At what time does Python create a function?
3. What does a function return if it has no return statement in it?
4. When does the code nested inside the function definition statement run?
5. What's wrong with checking the types of objects passed into a function?

Quiz Answers

1. Functions are the most basic way of avoiding code *redundancy* in Python—factoring code into functions means that we have only one copy of an operation's code to update in the future. Functions are also the basic unit of code *reuse* in Python—wrapping code in functions makes it a reusable tool, callable in a variety of programs. Finally, functions allow us to divide a complex system into manageable parts, each of which may be developed individually.

2. A function is created when Python reaches and runs the def statement; this statement creates a function object, and assigns it the function's name. This normally happens when the enclosing module file is imported by another module (recall that imports run the code in a file from top to bottom, including any defs), but it can also occur when a def is typed interactively or nested in other statements, such as ifs.

3. A function returns the None object by default if the control flow falls off the end of the function body without running into a return statement. Such functions are usually called with expression statements, as assigning their None results to variables is generally pointless.

4. The function body (the code nested inside the function definition statement) is run when the function is later called with a call expression. The body runs anew each time the function is called.

5. Checking the types of objects passed into a function effectively breaks the function's flexibility, constraining the function to work on specific types only. Without such checks, the function would likely be able to process an entire range of object types—any objects that support the interface expected by the function will work. (The term *interface* means the set of methods and expression operators the function runs.)

CHAPTER 16

Scopes and Arguments

Chapter 15 introduced basic function definitions and calls. As we saw, Python's basic function model is simple to use. This chapter presents the details behind Python's *scopes*—the places where variables are defined and looked up—and behind *argument passing*—the way that objects are sent to functions as inputs.

Scope Rules

Now that you're ready to start writing your own functions, we need to get more formal about what names mean in Python. When you use a name in a program, Python creates, changes, or looks up the name in what is known as a *namespace*—a place where names live. When we talk about the search for a name's value in relation to code, the term *scope* refers to a namespace: that is, the location of a name's assignment in your code determines the scope of the name's visibility to your code.

Just about everything related to names, including scope classification, happens at assignment time in Python. As we've seen, names in Python spring into existence when they are first assigned values, and they must be assigned before they are used. Because names are not declared ahead of time, Python uses the location of the assignment of a name to associate it with (i.e., *bind* it to) a particular namespace. In other words, the place where you assign a name in your source code determines the namespace it will live in, and hence its scope of visibility.

Besides packaging code, functions add an extra namespace layer to your programs—by default, all names assigned inside a function are associated with that function's namespace, and no other. This means that:

- Names defined inside a def can only be seen by the code within that def. You cannot even refer to such names from outside the function.

- Names defined inside a def do not clash with variables outside the def, even if the same names are used elsewhere. A name X assigned outside a given def (i.e., in a different def or at the top level of a module file) is a completely different variable from a name X assigned inside that def.

In all cases, the scope of a variable (where it can be used) is always determined by where it is assigned in your source code, and has nothing to do with which functions call which. If a variable is assigned inside a def, it is *local* to that function; if assigned outside a def, it is *global* to the entire file. We call this *lexical scoping* because variable scopes are determined entirely by the locations of the variables in the source code of your program files, not by function calls.

For example, in the following module file, the X = 99 assignment creates a global variable named X (visible everywhere in this file), but the X = 88 assignment creates a local variable X (visible only within the def statement):

```
X = 99

def func( ):
    X = 88
```

Even though both variables are named X, their scopes make them different. The net effect is that function scopes help to avoid name clashes in your programs, and help to make functions more self-contained program units.

Python Scope Basics

Before we started writing functions, all the code we wrote was at the top level of a module (i.e., not nested in a def), so the names we used either lived in the module itself, or were built-ins predefined by Python (e.g., open).[*] Functions provide nested namespaces (scopes) that localize the names they use, such that names inside a function won't clash with those outside it (in a module or another function). Again, functions define a *local scope*, and modules define a *global scope*. The two scopes are related as follows:

- **The enclosing module is a global scope.** Each module is a global scope—that is, a namespace in which variables created (assigned) at the top level of the module file live. Global variables become attributes of a module object to the outside world, but can be used as simple variables within a module file.

- **The global scope spans a single file only.** Don't be fooled by the word "global" here—names at the top level of a file are only global to code within that single file. There is really no notion of a single, all-encompassing global file-based scope in Python. Instead, names are partitioned into modules, and you must always import a module explicitly if you want to be able to use the names its file defines. When you hear "global" in Python, think "module."

---

[*] Code typed at the interactive command prompt is really entered into a built-in module called __main__, so interactively created names live in a module, too, and thus follow the normal scope rules. You'll learn more about modules in Part V.

- **Each call to a function creates a new local scope.** Every time you call a function, you create a new local scope—that is, a namespace in which the names created inside that function will usually live. You can think of each def statement (and lambda expression) as defining a new local scope, but because Python allows functions to call themselves to loop (an advanced technique known as *recursion*), the local scope in fact technically corresponds to a function call—in other words, each call creates a new local namespace. Recursion is useful when processing structures whose shape can't be predicted ahead of time.

- **Assigned names are local unless declared global.** By default, all the names assigned inside a function definition are put in the local scope (the namespace associated with the function call). If you need to assign a name that lives at the top level of the module enclosing the function, you can do so by declaring it in a global statement inside the function.

- **All other names are enclosing locals, globals, or built-ins.** Names not assigned a value in the function definition are assumed to be enclosing scope locals (in an enclosing def), globals (in the enclosing module's namespace), or built-ins (in the predefined __builtin__ module Python provides).

Note that any type of assignment within a function classifies a name as local: = statements, imports, defs, argument passing, and so on. Also, notice that in-place changes to objects do not classify names as locals; only actual name assignments do. For instance, if the name L is assigned to a list at the top level of a module, a statement like L.append(X) within a function will not classify L as a local, whereas L = X will. In the former case, L will be found in the global scope as usual, and the statement will change the global list.

Name Resolution: The LEGB Rule

If the prior section sounds confusing, it really boils down to three simple rules. With a def statement:

- Name references search at most four scopes: local, then enclosing functions (if any), then global, then built-in.

- Name assignments create or change local names by default.

- Global declarations map assigned names to an enclosing module's scope.

In other words, all names assigned inside a function def statement (or a lambda, an expression we'll meet later) are locals by default; functions can use names in lexically (i.e., physically) enclosing functions and in the global scope, but they must declare globals to change them. Python's name resolution scheme is sometimes called the *LEGB rule*, after the scope names:

- When you use an unqualified name inside a function, Python searches up to four scopes—the local (*L*) scope, then the local scopes of any enclosing (*E*) defs and lambdas, then the global (*G*) scope, and then the built-in (*B*) scope—and stops at the first place the name is found. If the name is not found during this search, Python reports an error. As we learned in Chapter 6, names must be assigned before they can be used.

- When you assign a name in a function (instead of just referring to it in an expression), Python always creates or changes the name in the local scope, unless it's declared to be global in that function.

- When you assign a name outside a function (i.e., at the top level of a module file, or at the interactive prompt), the local scope is the same as the global scope—the module's namespace.

Figure 16-1 illustrates Python's four scopes. Note that the second *E* scope lookup layer—the scopes of enclosing defs or lambdas—can technically correspond to more than one lookup layer. It only comes into play when you nest functions within functions.[*]

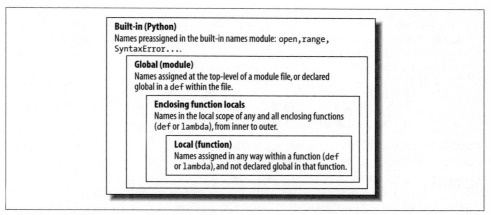

Figure 16-1. The LEGB scope lookup rule. When a variable is referenced, Python searches for it in this order: in the local scope, in any enclosing functions' local scopes, in the global scope, and, finally, in the built-in scope. The first occurrence wins. The place in your code where a variable is assigned usually determines its scope.

Also, keep in mind that these rules only apply to simple *variable* names (such as spam). In Parts V and VI, we'll see that qualified *attribute* names (such as object.spam) live in particular objects and follow a completely different set of lookup rules than the scope ideas covered here. Attribute references (names following periods) search one or more objects, not scopes, and may invoke something called "inheritance" (discussed in Part VI).

---

[*] The scope lookup rule was called the "LGB rule" in the first edition of this book. The enclosing def layer was added later in Python to obviate the task of passing in enclosing scope names explicitly—a topic usually of marginal interest to Python beginners that we'll defer until later in this chapter.

Scope Example

Let's look at a larger example that demonstrates scope ideas. Suppose we write the following code in a module file:

```
# Global scope
X = 99                  # X and func assigned in module: global

def func(Y):            # Y and Z assigned in function: locals
    # Local scope
    Z = X + Y           # X is a global
    return Z

func(1)                 # func in module: result=100
```

This module and the function it contains use a number of names to do their business. Using Python's scope rules, we can classify the names as follows:

Global names: X, func
> X is global because it's assigned at the top level of the module file; it can be referenced inside the function without being declared global. func is global for the same reason; the def statement assigns a function object to the name func at the top level of the module.

Local names: Y, Z
> Y and Z are local to the function (and exist only while the function runs) because they are both assigned values in the function definition: Z by virtue of the = statement, and Y because arguments are always passed by assignment.

The whole point behind this name segregation scheme is that local variables serve as temporary names that you need only while a function is running. For instance, in the preceding example, the argument Y and the addition result Z exist only inside the function; these names don't interfere with the enclosing module's namespace (or any other function, for that matter).

The local/global distinction also makes functions easier to understand, as most of the names a function uses appear in the function itself, not at some arbitrary place in a module. Also, because you can be sure that local names will not be changed by some remote function in your program, they tend to make programs easier to debug.

The Built-in Scope

We've been talking about the built-in scope in the abstract, but it's a bit simpler than you may think. Really, the built-in scope is just a built-in module called __builtin__, but you have to import __builtin__ to use built-in because the name builtin is not itself built-in.

No, I'm serious! The built-in scope is implemented as a standard library module named __builtin__, but that name itself is not placed in the built-in scope, so you have to import it in order to inspect it. Once you do, you can run a `dir` call to see which names are predefined:

```
>>> import __builtin__
>>> dir(__builtin__)
['ArithmeticError', 'AssertionError', 'AttributeError',
'DeprecationWarning', 'EOFError', 'Ellipsis',
    ...many more names omitted...
'str', 'super', 'tuple', 'type', 'unichr', 'unicode',
'vars', 'xrange', 'zip']
```

The names in this list constitute the built-in scope in Python; roughly the first half are built-in exceptions, and the second half are built-in functions. Because Python automatically searches this module last in its LEGB lookup rule, you get all the names in this list for free; that is, you can use them without importing any modules. Thus, there are two ways to refer to a built-in function—by taking advantage of the LEGB rule, or by manually importing the `__builtin__` module:

```
>>> zip                     # The normal way
<built-in function zip>

>>> import __builtin__      # The hard way
>>> __builtin__.zip
<built-in function zip>
```

The second of these approaches is sometimes useful in advanced work. The careful reader might also notice that because the LEGB lookup procedure takes the first occurrence of a name that it finds, names in the local scope may override variables of the same name in both the global and built-in scopes, and global names may override built-ins. A function can, for instance, create a local variable called open by assigning to it:

```
def hider():
    open = 'spam'           # Local variable, hides built-in
    ...
    open('data.txt')        # This won't open a file now in this scope!
```

However, this will hide the built-in function called open that lives in the built-in (outer) scope. It's also usually a bug, and a nasty one at that, because Python will not issue a warning message about it (there are times in advanced programming where you may really want to replace a built-in name by redefining it in your code).[*]

---

[*] Here's another thing you can do in Python that you probably shouldn't—because the names True and False are just variables in the built-in scope, it's possible to reassign them with a statement like True = False. You won't break the logical consistency of the universe in so doing! This statement merely redefines the word True for the single scope in which it appears. For more fun, though, you could say `__builtin__.True = False`, to reset True to False for the entire Python process! This may be disallowed in the future (and it sends IDLE into a strange panic state that resets the user code process). This technique is, however, useful for tool writers who must change built-ins such as open to customized functions. Also, note that third-party tools such as PyChecker will warn about common programming mistakes, including accidental assignment to built-in names (this is known as "shadowing" a built-in in PyChecker).

Functions can similarly hide global variables of the same name with locals:

```
X = 88                          # Global X

def func():
    X = 99                      # Local X: hides global

func()
print X                         # Prints 88: unchanged
```

Here, the assignment within the function creates a local X that is a completely different variable from the global X in the module outside the function. Because of this, there is no way to change a name outside a function without adding a global declaration to the def (as described in the next section).

The global Statement

The global statement is the only thing that's remotely like a declaration statement in Python. It's not a type or size declaration, though; it's a namespace declaration. It tells Python that a function plans to change one or more global names—i.e., names that live in the enclosing module's scope (namespace). We've talked about global in passing already. Here's a summary:

- Global names are names at the top level of the enclosing module file.
- Global names must be declared only if they are assigned in a function.
- Global names may be referenced in a function without being declared.

The global statement consists of the keyword global, followed by one or more names separated by commas. All the listed names will be mapped to the enclosing module's scope when assigned or referenced within the function body. For instance:

```
X = 88                          # Global X

def func():
    global X
    X = 99                      # Global X: outside def

func()
print X                         # Prints 99
```

We've added a global declaration to the example here, such that the X inside the def now refers to the X outside the def; they are the same variable this time. Here is a slightly more involved example of global at work:

```
y, z = 1, 2                     # Global variables in module

def all_global():
    global x                    # Declare globals assigned
    x = y + z                   # No need to declare y, z: LEGB rule
```

Here, x, y, and z are all globals inside the function all_global. y and z are global because they aren't assigned in the function; x is global because it was listed in a global statement to map it to the module's scope explicitly. Without the global here, x would be considered local by virtue of the assignment.

Notice that y and z are not declared global; Python's LEGB lookup rule finds them in the module automatically. Also, notice that x might not exist in the enclosing module before the function runs; if not, the assignment in the function creates x in the module.

Minimize Global Variables

By default, names assigned in functions are locals, so if you want to change names outside functions, you have to write extra code (global statements). This is by design—as is common in Python, you have to say more to do the "wrong" thing. Although there are times when globals are useful, variables assigned in a def are local by default because that is normally the best policy. Changing globals can lead to well-known software engineering problems: because the variables' values are dependent on the order of calls to arbitrarily distant functions, programs can become difficult to debug.

Consider this module file, for example:

```
X = 99

def func1():
    global X
    X = 88

def func2():
    global X
    X = 77
```

Now, imagine that it is your job to modify or reuse this module file. What will the value of X be here? Really, that question has no meaning unless qualified with a point of reference in time—the value of X is timing-dependent, as it depends on which function was called last (something we can't tell from this file alone).

The net effect is that to understand this code, you have to trace the flow of control through the entire program. And, if you need to reuse or modify the code, you have to keep the entire program in your head all at once. In this case, you can't really use one of these functions without bringing along the other. They are dependent (that is, coupled) on the global variable. This is the problem with globals—they generally make code more difficult to understand and use than code consisting of self-contained functions that rely on locals.

On the other hand, short of using object-oriented programming and classes, global variables are probably the most straightforward way to retain state information (information that a function needs to remember for use the next time it is called) in

Python—local variables disappear when the function returns, but globals do not. Other techniques, such as default mutable arguments and enclosing function scopes, can achieve this, too, but they are more complex than pushing values out to the global scope for retention.

Some programs designate a single module to collect globals; as long as this is expected, it is not as harmful. Also, programs that use multithreading to do parallel processing in Python essentially depend on global variables—they become shared memory between functions running in parallel threads, and so act as a communication device (threading is beyond this book's scope; see the follow-up texts mentioned in the Preface for more details).

For now, though, especially if you are relatively new to programming, avoid the temptation to use globals whenever you can (try to communicate with passed-in arguments and return values instead). Six months from now, both you and your coworkers will be happy you did.

Minimize Cross-File Changes

Here's another scope-related issue: although we *can* change variables in another file directly, we usually shouldn't. Consider these two module files:

```
# first.py
X = 99
```

```
# second.py
import first
first.X = 88
```

The first defines a variable X, which the second changes by assignment. Notice that we must import the first module into the second file to get to its variable—as we've learned, each module is a self-contained namespace (package of variables), and we must import one module to see inside it from another. Really, in terms of this chapter's topic, the global scope of a module file *becomes* the attribute namespace of the module object once it is imported—importers automatically have access to all of the file's global variables, so a file's global scope essentially morphs into an object's attribute namespace when it is imported.

After importing the first module, the second module assigns its variable a new value. The problem with the assignment, however, is that it is too implicit: whoever's charged with maintaining or reusing the first module probably has no clue that some arbitrarily far-removed module on the import chain can change X out from under him. In fact, the second module may be in a completely different directory, and so difficult to find. Again, this sets up too strong a coupling between the two files—because they are both dependent on the value of the variable X, it's difficult to understand or reuse one file without the other.

Here again, the best prescription is generally not to do this—the best way to communicate across file boundaries is to call functions, passing in arguments, and getting back return values. In this specific case, we would probably be better off coding an accessor function to manage the change:

```
# first.py
X = 99

def setX(new):
    global X
    X = new

# second.py
import first
first.setX(88)
```

This requires more code, but it makes a huge difference in terms of readability and maintainability—when a person reading the first module by itself sees a function, he will know that it is a point of interface, and will expect the change to the variable X. Although we cannot prevent cross-file changes from happening, common sense dictates that they should be minimized unless widely accepted across the program.

Other Ways to Access Globals

Interestingly, because global-scope variables morph into the attributes of a loaded module object, we can emulate the global statement by importing the enclosing module and assigning to its attributes, as in the following example module file. Code in this file imports the enclosing module by name, and then by indexing sys.modules, the loaded modules table (more on this table in Chapter 21):

```
# thismod.py

var = 99                              # Global variable == module attribute

def local():
    var = 0                           # Change local var

def glob1():
    global var                        # Declare global (normal)
    var += 1                          # Change global var

def glob2():
    var = 0                           # Change local var
    import thismod                    # Import myself
    thismod.var += 1                  # Change global var

def glob3():
    var = 0                           # Change local var
    import sys                        # Import system table
    glob = sys.modules['thismod']     # Get module object (or use __name__)
    glob.var += 1                     # Change global var
```

```
def test():
    print var
    local(); glob1(); glob2(); glob3()
    print var
```

When run, this adds 3 to the global variable (only the first function does not impact it):

```
>>> import thismod
>>> thismod.test()
99
102
>>> thismod.var
102
```

This works, and it illustrates the equivalence of globals to module attributes, but it's much more work than using the global statement to make your intentions explicit.

Scopes and Nested Functions

So far, I've omitted one part of Python's scope rules (on purpose, because it's relatively rarely encountered in practice). However, it's time to take a deeper look at the letter *E* in the LEGB lookup rule. The *E* layer is fairly new (it was added in Python 2.2); it takes the form of the local scopes of any and all enclosing function defs. Enclosing scopes are sometimes also called *statically nested scopes*. Really, the nesting is a lexical one—nested scopes correspond to physically nested code structures in your program's source code.

In Python 3.0, a proposed nonlocal statement is planned that will allow write access to variables in enclosing function scopes, much like the global statement does today for variables in the enclosing module scope. This statement will look like the global statement syntactically, but will use the word nonlocal instead. This is still a futurism, so see the 3.0 release notes for details.

Nested Scope Details

With the addition of nested function scopes, variable lookup rules become slightly more complex. Within a function:

- An assignment (X = value) creates or changes the name X in the current local scope, by default. If X is declared global within the function, it creates or changes the name X in the enclosing module's scope instead.

- A reference (X) looks for the name X first in the current local scope (function); then in the local scopes of any lexically enclosing functions in your source code, from inner to outer; then in the current global scope (the module file); and finally in the built-in scope (the module __builtin__). global declarations make the search begin in the global (module file) scope instead.

Notice that the global declaration still maps variables to the enclosing module. When nested functions are present, variables in enclosing functions may only be referenced, not changed. To clarify these points, let's illustrate with some real code.

Nested Scope Examples

Here is an example of a nested scope:

```
def f1():
    x = 88
    def f2():
        print x
    f2()

f1()                              # Prints 88
```

First off, this is legal Python code: the def is simply an executable statement that can appear anywhere any other statement can—including nested in another def. Here, the nested def runs while a call to the function f1 is running; it generates a function, and assigns it to the name f2, a local variable within f1's local scope. In a sense, f2 is a temporary function that only lives during the execution of (and is only visible to code in) the enclosing f1.

But, notice what happens inside f2: when it prints the variable x, it refers to the x that lives in the enclosing f1 function's local scope. Because functions can access names in all physically enclosing def statements, the x in f2 is automatically mapped to the x in f1, by the LEGB lookup rule.

This enclosing scope lookup works even if the enclosing function has already returned. For example, the following code defines a function that makes and returns another function:

```
def f1():
    x = 88
    def f2():
        print x
    return f2

action = f1()                     # Make, return function
action()                          # Call it now: prints 88
```

In this code, the call to action is really running the function we named f2 when f1 ran. f2 remembers the enclosing scope's x in f1, even though f1 is no longer active.

Factory functions

Depending on whom you ask, this sort of behavior is also sometimes called a *closure*, or *factory* function—a function object that remembers values in enclosing scopes, even though those scopes may not be around any more. Although classes (described in Part VI) are usually best at remembering state because they make it explicit with attribute assignments, such functions provide another alternative.

For instance, factory functions are sometimes used by programs that need to generate event handlers on the fly in response to conditions at runtime (e.g., user inputs that cannot be anticipated). Look at the following function, for example:

```
>>> def maker(N):
...     def action(X):
...         return X ** N
...     return action
...
```

This defines an outer function that simply generates and returns a nested function, without calling it. If we call the outer function:

```
>>> f = maker(2)                        # Pass 2 to N
>>> f
<function action at 0x014720B0>
```

what we get back is a reference to the generated nested function—the one created by running the nested def. If we now call what we got back from the outer function:

```
>>> f(3)                                # Pass 3 to X, N remembers 2
9
>>> f(4)                                # 4 ** 2
16
```

it invokes the nested function—the one called action within maker. The most unusual part of this, though, is that the nested function remembers integer 2, the value of the variable N in maker, even though maker has returned and exited by the time we call action. In effect, N from the enclosing local scope is retained as state information attached to action, and we get back its argument squared.

Now, if we call the outer function again, we get back a new nested function with different state information attached—we get the argument cubed instead of squared, but the original still squares as before:

```
>>> g = maker(3)
>>> g(3)                                # 3 ** 3
27
>>> f(3)                                # 3 ** 2
9
```

This is a fairly advanced technique that you're unlikely to see very often in practice, except among programmers with backgrounds in functional programming languages (and sometimes in lambdas, as discussed ahead). In general, classes, which we'll discuss later in the book, are better at "memory" like this because they make the state retention explicit. Short of using classes, though, globals, enclosing scope references like these, and default arguments are the main ways that Python functions can retain state information. Coincidentally, defaults are the topic of the next section.

Retaining enclosing scopes' state with defaults

In earlier versions of Python, the sort of code in the prior section failed because nested `defs` did not do anything about scopes—a reference to a variable within `f2` would search only the local (`f2`), then global (the code outside `f1`), and then built-in scopes. Because it skipped the scopes of enclosing functions, an error would result. To work around this, programmers typically used *default argument values* to pass in (remember) the objects in an enclosing scope:

```
def f1():
    x = 88
    def f2(x=x):
        print x
    f2()

f1()                              # Prints 88
```

This code works in all Python releases, and you'll still see this pattern in some existing Python code. We'll discuss defaults in more detail later in this chapter. In short, the syntax `arg = val` in a `def` header means that the argument `arg` will default to the value `val` if no real value is passed to `arg` in a call.

In the modified `f2`, the `x=x` means that the argument `x` will default to the value of `x` in the enclosing scope—because the second `x` is evaluated before Python steps into the nested `def`, it still refers to the `x` in `f1`. In effect, the default remembers what `x` was in `f1` (i.e., the object 88).

All that's fairly complex, and it depends entirely on the timing of default value evaluations. In fact, the nested scope lookup rule was added to Python to make defaults unnecessary for this role—today, Python automatically remembers any values required in the enclosing scope, for use in nested `defs`.

Of course, the best prescription is simply to avoid nesting `defs` within `defs`, as it will make your programs much simpler. The following is an equivalent of the prior example that banishes the notion of nesting. Notice that it's okay to call a function defined after the one that contains the call, like this, as long as the second `def` runs before the call of the first function—code inside a `def` is never evaluated until the function is actually called:

```
>>> def f1():
...     x = 88
...     f2(x)
...
>>> def f2(x):
...     print x
...
>>> f1()
88
```

If you avoid nesting this way, you can almost forget about the nested scopes concept in Python, unless you need to code in the factory function style discussed earlier—at least for def statements. lambdas, which almost naturally appear nested in defs, often rely on nested scopes, as the next section explains.

Nested scopes and lambdas

While they're rarely used in practice for defs themselves, you are more likely to care about nested function scopes when you start coding lambda expressions. We won't cover lambda in depth until Chapter 17, but, in short, it's an expression that generates a new function to be called later, much like a def statement. Because it's an expression, though, it can be used in places that def cannot, such as within list and dictionary literals.

Like a def, a lambda expression introduces a new local scope. Thanks to the enclosing scopes lookup layer, lambdas can see all the variables that live in the functions in which they are coded. Thus, the following code works today, but only because the nested scope rules are now applied:

```
def func():
    x = 4
    action = (lambda n: x ** n)          # x remembered from enclosing def
    return action

x = func()
print x(2)                                # Prints 16, 4 ** 2
```

Prior to the introduction of nested function scopes, programmers used defaults to pass values from an enclosing scope into lambdas, as for defs. For instance, the following works on all Python releases:

```
def func():
    x = 4
    action = (lambda n, x=x: x ** n)      # Pass x in manually
```

Because lambdas are expressions, they naturally (and even normally) nest inside enclosing defs. Hence, they are perhaps the biggest beneficiaries of the addition of enclosing function scopes in the lookup rules; in most cases, it is no longer necessary to pass values into lambdas with defaults.

Scopes versus defaults with loop variables

There is one notable exception to the rule I just gave: if a lambda or def defined within a function is nested inside a loop, and the nested function references an enclosing scope variable that is changed by the loop, all functions generated within that loop will have the same value—the value the referenced variable had in the last loop iteration.

For instance, the following attempts to build up a list of functions that each remember the current variable i from the enclosing scope:

```
>>> def makeActions():
...     acts = []
...     for i in range(5):                    # Tries to remember each i
...         acts.append(lambda x: i ** x)     # All remember same last i!
...     return acts
...
>>> acts = makeActions()
>>> acts[0]
<function <lambda> at 0x012B16B0>
```

This doesn't quite work, though—because the enclosing variable is looked up when the nested functions are later called, they all effectively remember the same value (the value the loop variable had on the last loop iteration). That is, we get back 4 to the power of 2 for each function in the list because i is the same in all of them:

```
>>> acts[0](2)                    # All are 4 ** 2, value of last i
16
>>> acts[2](2)                    # This should be 2 ** 2
16
>>> acts[4](2)                    # This should be 4 ** 2
16
```

This is the one case where we still have to explicitly retain enclosing scope values with default arguments, rather than enclosing scope references. That is, to make this sort of code work, we must pass in the current value of the enclosing scope's variable with a default. Because defaults are evaluated when the nested function is created (not when it's later called), each remembers its own value for i:

```
>>> def makeActions():
...     acts = []
...     for i in range(5):                        # Use defaults instead
...         acts.append(lambda x, i=i: i ** x)    # Remember current i
...     return acts
...
>>> acts = makeActions()
>>> acts[0](2)                    # 0 ** 2
0
>>> acts[2](2)                    # 2 ** 2
4
>>> acts[4](2)                    # 4 ** 2
16
```

This is a fairly obscure case, but it can come up in practice, especially in code that generates callback handler functions for a number of widgets in a GUI (e.g., button press handlers). We'll talk more about both defaults and lambdas in the next chapter, so you may want to return and review this section later.[*]

---

[*] In the "Function Gotchas" section for this part at the end of the next chapter, we'll also see that there is an issue with using mutable objects like lists and dictionaries for default arguments (e.g., def f(a=[]))—because defaults are implemented as single objects, mutable defaults retain state from call to call, rather then being initialized anew on each call. Depending on whom you ask, this is either considered a feature that supports state retention, or a strange wart on the language. More on this in the next chapter.

Arbitrary scope nesting

Before ending this discussion, I should note that scopes nest arbitrarily, but only enclosing functions (not classes, described in Part VI) are searched:

```
>>> def f1():
...     x = 99
...     def f2():
...         def f3():
...             print x            # Found in f1's local scope!
...         f3()
...     f2()
...
>>> f1()
99
```

Python will search the local scopes of *all* enclosing defs, from inner to outer, after the referencing function's local scope, and before the module's global scope. However, this sort of code is unlikely to pop up in practice. In Python, we say flat is better than nested—your life, and the lives of your coworkers, will generally be better if you minimize nested function definitions.

Passing Arguments

Earlier, I noted that arguments are passed by assignment. This has a few ramifications that aren't always obvious to beginners, which I'll expand on in this section. Here is a rundown of the key points in passing arguments to functions:

- **Arguments are passed by automatically assigning objects to local names.** Function arguments—references to (possibly) shared objects referenced by the caller—are just another instance of Python assignment at work. Because references are implemented as pointers, all arguments are, in effect, passed by pointer. Objects passed as arguments are never automatically copied.

- **Assigning to argument names inside a function doesn't affect the caller.** Argument names in the function header become new, local names when the function runs, in the scope of the function. There is no aliasing between function argument names and names in the caller.

- **Changing a mutable object argument in a function may impact the caller.** On the other hand, as arguments are simply assigned to passed-in objects, functions can change passed-in mutable objects, and the results may affect the caller. Mutable arguments can be input and output for functions.

For more details on references, see Chapter 6; everything we learned there also applies to function arguments, though the assignment to argument names is automatic and implicit.

Python's pass-by-assignment scheme isn't quite the same as C++'s reference parameters option, but it turns out to be very similar to the C language's argument-passing model in practice:

- **Immutable arguments are passed "by value."** Objects such as integers and strings are passed by object reference instead of by copying, but because you can't change immutable objects in-place anyhow, the effect is much like making a copy.

- **Mutable arguments are passed "by pointer."** Objects such as lists and dictionaries are also passed by object reference, which is similar to the way C passes arrays as pointers—mutable objects can be changed in-place in the function, much like C arrays.

Of course, if you've never used C, Python's argument-passing mode will seem simpler still—it just involves the assignment of objects to names, and it works the same whether the objects are mutable or not.

Arguments and Shared References

Here's an example that illustrates some of these properties at work:

```
>>> def changer(a, b):          # Function
...     a = 2                   # Changes local name's value only
...     b[0] = 'spam'           # Changes shared object in-place
...
>>> X = 1
>>> L = [1, 2]                  # Caller
>>> changer(X, L)               # Pass immutable and mutable objects
>>> X, L                        # X is unchanged, L is different
(1, ['spam', 2])
```

In this code, the changer function assigns values to argument a, and to a component in the object referenced by argument b. The two assignments within the function are only slightly different in syntax, but have radically different results:

- Because a is a local name in the function's scope, the first assignment has no effect on the caller—it simply changes the local variable a, and does not change the binding of the name X in the caller.

- b is a local name, too, but it is passed a mutable object (the list called L in the caller). As the second assignment is an in-place object change, the result of the assignment to b[0] in the function impacts the value of L after the function returns. Really, we aren't changing b, we are changing part of the object that b currently references, and this change impacts the caller.

Figure 16-2 illustrates the name/object bindings that exist immediately after the function has been called, and before its code has run.

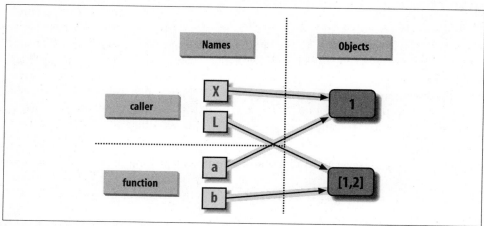

Figure 16-2. References: arguments. Because arguments are passed by assignment, argument names may share objects with variables at the call. Hence, in-place changes to mutable arguments in a function can impact the caller. Here, a and b in the function initially reference the objects referenced by variables X and L when the function is first called. Changing the list through variable b makes L appear different after the call returns.

If this example is still confusing, it may help to notice that the effect of the automatic assignments of the passed-in arguments is the same as running a series of simple assignment statements. In terms of the first argument, the assignment has no effect on the caller:

```
>>> X = 1
>>> a = X              # They share the same object
>>> a = 2              # Resets 'a' only, 'X' is still 1
>>> print X
1
```

But, the assignment through the second argument does affect a variable at the call because it is an in-place object change:

```
>>> L = [1, 2]
>>> b = L              # They share the same object
>>> b[0] = 'spam'      # In-place change: 'L' sees the change too
>>> print L
['spam', 2]
```

If you recall our discussions about shared mutable objects in Chapters 6 and 9, you'll recognize the phenomenon at work: changing a mutable object in-place can impact other references to that object. Here, the effect is to make one of the arguments work like an *output* of the function.

Avoiding Mutable Argument Changes

Arguments are passed to functions by reference (a.k.a. pointer) by default in Python because that is what we normally want—it means we can pass large objects around our programs without making multiple copies along the way, and we can easily update these objects as we go. If we don't want in-place changes within functions to impact objects we pass to them, though, we can simply make explicit copies of mutable objects, as we learned in Chapter 6. For function arguments, we can always copy the list at the point of call:

```
L = [1, 2]
changer(X, L[:])          # Pass a copy, so our 'L' does not change
```

We can also copy within the function itself, if we never want to change passed-in objects, regardless of how the function is called:

```
def changer(a, b):
    b = b[:]              # Copy input list so we don't impact caller
    a = 2
    b[0] = 'spam'         # Changes our list copy only
```

Both of these copying schemes don't stop the function from changing the object—they just prevent those changes from impacting the caller. To really prevent changes, we can always convert to immutable objects to force the issue. Tuples, for example, throw an exception when changes are attempted:

```
L = [1, 2]
changer(X, tuple(L))      # Pass a tuple, so changes are errors
```

This scheme uses the built-in tuple function, which builds a new tuple out of all the items in a sequence (really, any iterable). It's also something of an extreme—because it forces the function to be written to never change passed-in arguments, this solution might impose more limitations on the function than it should, and so should generally be avoided. You never know when changing arguments might come in handy for other calls in the future. Using this technique will also make the function lose the ability to call any list-specific methods on the argument, including methods that do not change the object in-place.

The main point to remember here is that functions might update mutable objects passed into them (e.g., lists and dictionaries). This isn't necessarily a problem, and it often serves useful purposes. But, you do have to be aware of this property—if objects change out from under you unexpectedly, check whether a called function might be responsible, and make copies when objects are passed if needed.

Simulating Output Parameters

We've already discussed the return statement and used it in a few examples. Here's a neat trick: because return can send back any sort of object, it can return multiple values by packaging them in a tuple or other collection type. In fact, although Python doesn't support what some languages label "call-by-reference" argument passing, we can usually simulate it by returning tuples and assigning the results back to the original argument names in the caller:

```
>>> def multiple(x, y):
...     x = 2                    # Changes local names only
...     y = [3, 4]
...     return x, y              # Return new values in a tuple
...
>>> X = 1
>>> L = [1, 2]
>>> X, L = multiple(X, L)        # Assign results to caller's names
>>> X, L
(2, [3, 4])
```

It looks like the code is returning two values here, but it's really just one—a two-item tuple with the optional surrounding parentheses omitted. After the call returns, we can use tuple assignment to unpack the parts of the returned tuple. (If you've forgotten why this works, flip back to "Tuples" in Chapter 4, and "Assignment Statements" in Chapter 11.) The net effect of this coding pattern is to simulate the output parameters of other languages by explicit assignments. X and L change after the call, but only because the code said so.

Special Argument-Matching Modes

As we've just seen, arguments are always passed by *assignment* in Python; names in the def header are assigned to passed-in objects. On top of this model, though, Python provides additional tools that alter the way the argument objects in a call are *matched* with argument names in the header prior to assignment. These tools are all optional, but they allow you to write functions that support more flexible calling patterns.

By default, arguments are matched by position, from left to right, and you must pass exactly as many arguments as there are argument names in the function header. You can also specify matching by name, default values, and collectors for extra arguments.

Some of this section gets complicated, and before we go into the syntactic details, I'd like to stress that these special modes are optional, and only have to do with matching objects to names; the underlying passing mechanism after the matching takes place is still assignment. In fact, some of these tools are intended more for people writing libraries than for application developers. But because you may stumble across these modes even if you don't code them yourself, here's a synopsis of the available matching modes:

Positionals: matched from left to right
   The normal case, which we've been using so far, is to match arguments by position.

Keywords: matched by argument name
   Callers can specify which argument in the function is to receive a value by using the argument's name in the call, with the name=value syntax.

Defaults: specify values for arguments that aren't passed

Functions can specify default values for arguments to receive if the call passes too few values, again using the name=value syntax.

Varargs: collect arbitrarily many positional or keyword arguments

Functions can use special arguments preceded with * characters to collect an arbitrary number of extra arguments (this feature is often referred to as *varargs*, after the varargs feature in the C language, which also supports variable-length argument lists).

Varargs: pass arbitrarily many positional or keyword arguments

Callers can also use the * syntax to unpack argument collections into discrete, separate arguments. This is the inverse of a * in a function header—in the header it means collect arbitrarily many arguments, while in the call it means pass arbitrarily many arguments.

Table 16-1 summarizes the syntax that invokes the special matching modes.

Table 16-1. Function argument-matching forms

Syntax	Location	Interpretation
func(value)	Caller	Normal argument: matched by position
func(name=value)	Caller	Keyword argument: matched by name
func(*name)	Caller	Pass all objects in name as individual positional arguments
func(**name)	Caller	Pass all key/value pairs in name as individual keyword arguments
def func(name)	Function	Normal argument: matches any by position or name
def func(name=value)	Function	Default argument value, if not passed in the call
def func(*name)	Function	Matches and collects remaining positional arguments (in a tuple)
def func(**name)	Function	Matches and collects remaining keyword arguments (in a dictionary)

In a call (the first four rows of the table), simple names are matched by position, but using the name=value form tells Python to match by name instead; these are called *keyword arguments*. Using a * or ** in a call allows us to package up arbitrarily many positional or keyword objects in sequences and dictionaries, respectively.

In a function header, a simple name is matched by position or name (depending on how the caller passes it), but the name=value form specifies a default value. The *name form collects any extra unmatched positional arguments in a tuple, and the **name form collects extra keyword arguments in a dictionary.

Of these, keyword arguments and defaults are probably the most commonly used in Python code. Keywords allow us to label arguments with their names to make calls more meaningful. We met defaults earlier, as a way to pass in values from the enclosing function's scope, but they actually are more general than that—they allow us to make any argument optional, and provide its default value in a function definition.

Special matching modes let you be fairly liberal about how many arguments must be passed to a function. If a function specifies defaults, they are used if you pass too few arguments. If a function uses the * variable argument list forms, you can pass too many arguments; the * names collect the extra arguments in a data structure.

Keyword and Default Examples

This is all simpler in code than the preceding descriptions may imply. Python matches names by position by default like most other languages. For instance, if you define a function that requires three arguments, you must call it with three arguments:

```
>>> def f(a, b, c): print a, b, c
...
```

Here, we pass them by position—a is matched to 1, b is matched to 2, and so on:

```
>>> f(1, 2, 3)
1 2 3
```

Keywords

In Python, though, you can be more specific about what goes where when you call a function. Keyword arguments allow us to match by *name*, instead of by position:

```
>>> f(c=3, b=2, a=1)
1 2 3
```

The c=3 in this call, for example, means send 3 to the argument named c. More formally, Python matches the name c in the call to the argument named c in the function definition's header, and then passes the value 3 to that argument. The net effect of this call is the same as that of the prior call, but notice that the left-to-right order of the arguments no longer matters when keywords are used because arguments are matched by name, not by position. It's even possible to combine positional and keyword arguments in a single call. In this case, all positionals are matched first from left to right in the header, before keywords are matched by name:

```
>>> f(1, c=3, b=2)
1 2 3
```

When most people see this the first time, they wonder why one would use such a tool. Keywords typically have two roles in Python. First, they make your calls a bit more self-documenting (assuming that you use better argument names than a, b, and c). For example, a call of this form:

```
func(name='Bob', age=40, job='dev')
```

is much more meaningful than a call with three naked values separated by commas—the keywords serve as labels for the data in the call. The second major use of keywords occurs in conjunction with defaults, which we'll look at next.

Defaults

We talked a little about defaults earlier, when discussing nested function scopes. In short, defaults allow us to make selected function arguments optional; if not passed a value, the argument is assigned its default before the function runs. For example, here is a function that requires one argument, and defaults two:

```
>>> def f(a, b=2, c=3): print a, b, c
...
```

When we call this function, we must provide a value for a, either by position or by keyword; however, providing values for b and c is optional. If we don't pass values to b and c, they default to 2 and 3, respectively:

```
>>> f(1)
1 2 3
>>> f(a=1)
1 2 3
```

If we pass two values, only c gets its default, and with three values, no defaults are used:

```
>>> f(1, 4)
1 4 3
>>> f(1, 4, 5)
1 4 5
```

Finally, here is how the keyword and default features interact. Because they subvert the normal left-to-right positional mapping, keywords allow us to essentially skip over arguments with defaults:

```
>>> f(1, c=6)
1 2 6
```

Here, a gets 1 by position, c gets 6 by keyword, and b, in between, defaults to 2.

Be careful not to confuse the special name=value syntax in a function header and a function call; in the call, it means a match-by-name keyword argument, and in the header, it specifies a default for an optional argument. In both cases, this is not an assignment statement; it is special syntax for these two contexts, which modifies the default argument-matching mechanics.

Arbitrary Arguments Examples

The last two matching extensions, * and **, are designed to support functions that take any number of arguments. Both can appear in either the function definition, or a function call, and they have related purposes in the two locations.

Collecting arguments

The first use, in the function definition, collects unmatched positional arguments into a tuple:

```
>>> def f(*args): print args
...
```

When this function is called, Python collects all the positional arguments into a new tuple, and assigns the variable args to that tuple. Because it is a normal tuple object, it can be indexed, stepped through with a for loop, and so on:

```
>>> f()
()
>>> f(1)
(1,)
>>> f(1,2,3,4)
(1, 2, 3, 4)
```

The ** feature is similar, but it only works for keyword arguments—it collects them into a new dictionary, which can then be processed with normal dictionary tools. In a sense, the ** form allows you to convert from keywords to dictionaries, which you can then step through with keys calls, dictionary iterators, and the like:

```
>>> def f(**args): print args
...
>>> f()
{ }
>>> f(a=1, b=2)
{'a': 1, 'b': 2}
```

Finally, function headers can combine normal arguments, the *, and the ** to implement wildly flexible call signatures:

```
>>> def f(a, *pargs, **kargs): print a, pargs, kargs
...
>>> f(1, 2, 3, x=1, y=2)
1 (2, 3) {'y': 2, 'x': 1}
```

In fact, these features can be combined in even more complex ways that may seem ambiguous at first glance—an idea we will revisit later in this chapter. First, though, let's see what happens when * and ** are coded in function calls instead of definitions.

Unpacking arguments

In recent Python releases, we can use the * syntax when we call a function, too. In this context, its meaning is the inverse of its meaning in the function definition—it unpacks a collection of arguments, rather than building a collection of arguments. For example, we can pass four arguments to a function in a tuple, and let Python unpack them into individual arguments:

```
>>> def func(a, b, c, d): print a, b, c, d
...
>>> args = (1, 2)
>>> args += (3, 4)
```

```
>>> func(*args)
1 2 3 4
```

Similarly, the ** syntax in a function call unpacks a dictionary of key/value pairs into separate keyword arguments:

```
>>> args = {'a': 1, 'b': 2, 'c': 3}
>>> args['d'] = 4
>>> func(**args)
1 2 3 4
```

Again, we can combine normal, positional, and keyword arguments in the call in very flexible ways:

```
>>> func(*(1, 2), **{'d': 4, 'c': 4})
1 2 4 4

>>> func(1, *(2, 3), **{'d': 4})
1 2 3 4

>>> func(1, c=3, *(2,), **{'d': 4})
1 2 3 4
```

This sort of code is convenient when you cannot predict the number of arguments to be passed to a function when you write your script; you can build up a collection of arguments at runtime instead, and call the function generically this way. Again, don't confuse the */** syntax in the function header and the function call—in the header, it collects any number of arguments, and in the call, it unpacks any number of arguments.

We'll revisit this form in the next chapter, when we meet the apply built-in function (a tool that this special call syntax is largely intended to subsume and replace).

Combining Keywords and Defaults

Here is a slightly larger example that demonstrates keywords and defaults in action. In the following, the caller must always pass at least two arguments (to match spam and eggs), but the other two are optional. If they are omitted, Python assigns toast and ham to the defaults specified in the header:

```
def func(spam, eggs, toast=0, ham=0):      # First 2 required
    print (spam, eggs, toast, ham)

func(1, 2)                                  # Output: (1, 2, 0, 0)
func(1, ham=1, eggs=0)                      # Output: (1, 0, 0, 1)
func(spam=1, eggs=0)                        # Output: (1, 0, 0, 0)
func(toast=1, eggs=2, spam=3)               # Output: (3, 2, 1, 0)
func(1, 2, 3, 4)                            # Output: (1, 2, 3, 4)
```

Notice again that when keyword arguments are used in the call, the order in which the arguments are listed doesn't matter; Python matches by name, not by position. The caller must supply values for spam and eggs, but they can be matched by position or by name. Also, notice that the form name=value means different things in the call and the def (a keyword in the call and a default in the header).

The min Wakeup Call

To make this more concrete, let's work through an exercise that demonstrates a practical application of argument-matching tools. Suppose you want to code a function that is able to compute the minimum value from an arbitrary set of arguments and an arbitrary set of object data types. That is, the function should accept zero or more arguments—as many as you wish to pass. Moreover, the function should work for all kinds of Python object types: numbers, strings, lists, lists of dictionaries, files, and even None.

The first requirement provides a natural example of how the * feature can be put to good use—we can collect arguments into a tuple, and step over each in turn with a simple for loop. The second part of the problem definition is easy: because every object type supports comparisons, we don't have to specialize the function per type (an application of polymorphism); we can simply compare objects blindly, and let Python perform the correct sort of comparison.

Full credit

The following file shows three ways to code this operation, at least one of which was suggested by a student at some point along the way:

- The first function fetches the first argument (args is a tuple), and traverses the rest by slicing off the first (there's no point in comparing an object to itself, especially if it might be a large structure).

- The second version lets Python pick off the first and rest of the arguments automatically, and so avoids an index and a slice.

- The third converts from a tuple to a list with the built-in list call, and employs the list sort method.

The sort method is coded in C, so it can be quicker than the others at times, but the linear scans of the first two techniques will make them faster most of the time.[*] The file *mins.py* contains the code for all three solutions:

```python
def min1(*args):
    res = args[0]
    for arg in args[1:]:
```

---

[*] Actually, this is fairly complicated. The Python sort routine is coded in C, and uses a highly optimized algorithm that attempts to take advantage of partial ordering in the items to be sorted. It's named "timsort" after Tim Peters, its creator, and in its documentation it claims to have "supernatural performance" at times (pretty good, for a sort!). Still, sorting is an inherently exponential operation (it must chop up the sequence, and put it back together many times), and the other versions simply perform one linear, left to right scan. The net effect is that sorting is quicker if the arguments are partially ordered, but likely slower otherwise. Even so, Python performance can change over time, and the fact that sorting is implemented in the C language can help greatly; for an exact analysis, you should time the alternatives with the time or timeit modules we'll meet in the next chapter.

```
        if arg < res:
            res = arg
    return res

def min2(first, *rest):
    for arg in rest:
        if arg < first:
            first = arg
    return first

def min3(*args):
    tmp = list(args)                # Or, in Python 2.4+: return sorted(args)[0]
    tmp.sort( )
    return tmp[0]

print min1(3,4,1,2)
print min2("bb", "aa")
print min3([2,2], [1,1], [3,3])
```

All three solutions produce the same result when the file is run. Try typing a few calls interactively to experiment with these on your own:

```
% python mins.py
1
aa
[1, 1]
```

Notice that none of these three variants tests for the case where no arguments are passed in. They could, but there's no point in doing so here—in all three solutions, Python will automatically raise an exception if no arguments are passed in. The first raises an exception when we try to fetch item 0; the second, when Python detects an argument list mismatch; and the third, when we try to return item 0 at the end.

This is exactly what we want to happen—because these functions support any data type, there is no valid sentinel value that we could pass back to designate an error. There are exceptions to this rule (e.g., if you have to run expensive actions before you reach the error), but, in general, it's better to assume that arguments will work in your functions' code, and let Python raise errors for you when they do not.

Bonus points

Students and readers can get bonus points here for changing these functions to compute the *maximum*, rather than minimum, values. This one's easy: the first two versions only require changing < to >, and the third simply requires that we return tmp[-1] instead of tmp[0]. For extra points, be sure to set the function name to "max" as well (though this part is strictly optional).

It's also possible to generalize a single function to compute either a minimum or a maximum value, by evaluating comparison expression strings with a tool like the eval built-in function (see the library manual), or passing in an arbitrary comparison function. The file *minmax.py* shows how to implement the latter scheme:

```
def minmax(test, *args):
    res = args[0]
    for arg in args[1:]:
        if test(arg, res):
            res = arg
    return res

def lessthan(x, y): return x < y        # See also: lambda
def grtrthan(x, y): return x > y

print minmax(lessthan, 4, 2, 1, 5, 6, 3)        # Self-test code
print minmax(grtrthan, 4, 2, 1, 5, 6, 3)

% python minmax.py
1
6
```

Functions are another kind of object that can be passed into a function like this one. To make this a max (or other) function, for example, we could simply pass in the right sort of test function. This may seem like extra work, but the main point of generalizing functions this way (instead of cutting and pasting to change just a single character) means we'll only have one version to change in the future, not two.

The punch line

Of course, all this was just a coding exercise. There's really no reason to code min or max functions because both are built-ins in Python! The built-in versions work almost exactly like ours, but they're coded in C for optimal speed.

A More Useful Example: General Set Functions

Now, let's look at a more useful example of special argument-matching modes at work. At the end of the prior chapter, we wrote a function that returned the intersection of two sequences (it picked out items that appeared in both). Here is a version that intersects an arbitrary number of sequences (one or more), by using the varargs matching form *args to collect all the passed-in arguments. Because the arguments come in as a tuple, we can process them in a simple for loop. Just for fun, we'll code a union function that also accepts an arbitrary number of arguments to collect items that appear in any of the operands:

```
def intersect(*args):
    res = []
    for x in args[0]:               # Scan first sequence
        for other in args[1:]:      # For all other args
            if x not in other: break # Item in each one?
        else:                        # No: break out of loop
            res.append(x)            # Yes: add items to end
    return res
```

```
def union(*args):
    res = []
    for seq in args:                    # For all args
        for x in seq:                   # For all nodes
            if not x in res:
                res.append(x)           # Add new items to result
    return res
```

Because these are tools worth reusing (and they're too big to retype interactively), we'll store the functions in a module file called *inter2.py* (more on modules in Part V). In both functions, the arguments passed in at the call come in as the args tuple. As in the original intersect, both work on any kind of sequence. Here, they are processing strings, mixed types, and more than two sequences:

```
% python
>>> from inter2 import intersect, union
>>> s1, s2, s3 = "SPAM", "SCAM", "SLAM"

>>> intersect(s1, s2), union(s1, s2)            # Two operands
(['S', 'A', 'M'], ['S', 'P', 'A', 'M', 'C'])

>>> intersect([1,2,3], (1,4))                   # Mixed types
[1]

>>> intersect(s1, s2, s3)                       # Three operands
['S', 'A', 'M']

>>> union(s1, s2, s3)
['S', 'P', 'A', 'M', 'C', 'L']
```

 I should note that because Python has a new set object type (described in Chapter 5), none of the set processing examples in this book are strictly required anymore; they are included only as demonstrations of coding functions. (Because it is constantly improving, Python has an uncanny way of conspiring to make my book examples obsolete over time!)

Argument Matching: The Gritty Details

If you choose to use and combine the special argument-matching modes, Python will ask you to follow these ordering rules:

- In a function call, all nonkeyword arguments (name) must appear first, followed by all keyword arguments (name=value), followed by the *name form, and, finally, the **name form, if used.

- In a function header, arguments must appear in the same order: normal arguments (name), followed by any default arguments (name=value), followed by the *name form if present, followed by **name, if used.

If you mix arguments in any other order, you will get a syntax error because the combinations can be ambiguous. Python internally carries out the following steps to match arguments before assignment:

1. Assign nonkeyword arguments by position.
2. Assign keyword arguments by matching names.
3. Assign extra nonkeyword arguments to *name tuple.
4. Assign extra keyword arguments to **name dictionary.
5. Assign default values to unassigned arguments in header.

After this, Python checks to make sure each argument is passed just one value; if not, an error is raised. This is as complicated as it looks, but tracing Python's matching algorithm will help you to understand some convoluted cases, especially when modes are mixed. We'll postpone looking at additional examples of these special matching modes until the exercises at the end of Part IV.

As you can see, advanced argument-matching modes can be complex. They are also entirely optional; you can get by with just simple positional matching, and it's probably a good idea to do so when you're starting out. However, because some Python tools make use of them, some general knowledge of these modes is important.

Why You Will Care: Keyword Arguments

Keyword arguments play an important role in Tkinter, the de facto standard GUI API for Python. We'll meet Tkinter later in this book, but as a preview, keyword arguments set configuration options when GUI components are built. For instance, a call of the form:

```
from Tkinter import *
widget = Button(text="Press me", command=someFunction)
```

creates a new button and specifies its text and callback function, using the text and command keyword arguments. Since the number of configuration options for a widget can be large, keyword arguments let you pick and choose. Without them, you might have to either list all the possible options by position or hope for a judicious positional argument defaults protocol that would handle every possible option arrangement.

Chapter Summary

In this chapter, we studied two key concepts related to functions: scopes (how variables are looked up when used), and arguments (how objects are passed into a function). As we learned, variables are considered local to the function definitions in which they are assigned, unless they are specifically declared global. As we also saw, arguments are passed into a function by assignment, which means by object reference, which really means by pointer.

For both scopes and arguments, we also studied some more advanced extensions—nested function scopes, and default and keyword arguments, for example. Finally, we looked at some general design ideas (avoiding globals and cross-file changes), and saw how mutable arguments can exhibit the same behavior as other shared references to objects—unless the object is explicitly copied when it's sent in, changing a passed-in mutable in a function can impact the caller.

The next chapter concludes our look at functions by exploring some more advanced function-related ideas: `lambda`s, generators, iterators, functional tools, such as `map`, and so on. Many of these concepts stem from the fact that functions are normal objects in Python, and so support some advanced and very flexible processing modes. Before diving into those topics, however, take this chapter's quiz to review what we've studied here.

Chapter Quiz

1. What is the output of the following code, and why?

```
>>> X = 'Spam'
>>> def func():
...     print X
...
>>> func()
```

2. What is the output of this code, and why?

```
>>> X = 'Spam'
>>> def func():
...     X = 'NI!'
...
>>> func()
>>> print X
```

3. What does this code print, and why?

```
>>> X = 'Spam'
>>> def func():
...     X = 'NI'
...     print X
...
>>> func()
>>> print X
```

4. What output does this code produce; again, why?

```
>>> X = 'Spam'
>>> def func():
...     global X
...     X = 'NI'
...
>>> func()
>>> print X
```

5. What about this code—what's the output, and why?

```
>>> X = 'Spam'
>>> def func():
...     X = 'NI'
...     def nested():
...         print X
...     nested()
...
>>> func()
>>> X
```

6. One last time: what is the output of this, and why?

```
>>> def func(a, b, c=3, d=4): print a, b, c, d
...
>>> func(1, *(5,6))
```

7. Name three or four ways to retain state information in a Python function.

8. Name three ways that functions can communicate results to a caller.

Quiz Answers

1. The output here is `'Spam'`, because the function references a global variable in the enclosing module (because it is not assigned in the function, it is considered global).

2. The output here is `'Spam'` again because assigning the variable inside the function makes it a local and effectively hides the global of the same name. The `print` statement finds the variable unchanged in the global (module) scope.

3. It prints `'NI'` on one line, and `'Spam'` on another because the reference to the variable within the function finds the assigned local, and the reference in the `print` finds the global.

4. This time it just prints `'NI'` because the global declaration forces the variable assigned inside the function to refer to the variable in the enclosing global scope.

5. The output in this case is again `'NI'` on one line, and `'Spam'` on another because the `print` statement in the nested function finds the name in the enclosing function's local scope, and the `print` at the end finds the variable in the global scope.

6. The output here is `"1 5 6 4"`: 1 matches a by position, 5 and 6 match b and c by `*name` positionals (6 overrides c's default), and d defaults to 4 because it was not passed a value.

7. Although the values of local variables go away when a function returns, state information can be retained by a Python function by using global variables, enclosing function scope references in nested functions, or default argument values. Another alternative, using OOP with classes, supports state retention better than any of the prior three techniques because it makes it explicit with attribute assignments.

8. Functions can send back results with `return` statements, by changing passed-in mutable arguments, and by setting global variables. Globals are generally frowned upon (except for very special cases, like multithreaded programs) because they can make code harder to understand and use. `return` statements are usually best, but changing mutables is fine, if expected. Functions may also communicate with system devices such as files and sockets, but these are beyond our scope here.

CHAPTER 17

Advanced Function Topics

This chapter introduces a collection of more advanced function-related topics: the lambda expression, functional programming tools such as map and list comprehensions, generator functions and expressions, and more. Part of the art of using functions lies in the interfaces between them, so we will also explore some general function design principles here. Because this is the last chapter in Part IV, we'll close with the usual sets of gotchas and exercises to help you start coding the ideas you've read about.

Anonymous Functions: lambda

You've seen what it takes to write your own basic functions in Python. The next sections deal with a few more advanced function-related ideas. Most of these are optional features, but they can simplify your coding tasks when used well.

Besides the def statement, Python also provides an expression form that generates function objects. Because of its similarity to a tool in the LISP language, it's called lambda.* Like def, this expression creates a function to be called later, but it returns the function instead of assigning it to a name. This is why lambdas are sometimes known as *anonymous* (i.e., unnamed) functions. In practice, they are often used as a way to inline a function definition, or to defer execution of a piece of code.

lambda Expressions

The lambda's general form is the keyword lambda, followed by one or more arguments (exactly like the arguments list you enclose in parentheses in a def header), followed by an expression after a colon:

```
lambda argument1, argument2,... argumentN : expression using arguments
```

---

* The name "lambda" seems to scare people more than it should. It comes from LISP, which got it from lambda calculus, which is a form of symbolic logic. In Python, though, it's really just a keyword that introduces the expression syntactically.

Function objects returned by running lambda expressions work exactly the same as those created and assigned by def, but there are a few differences that make lambdas useful in specialized roles:

- **lambda is an expression, not a statement.** Because of this, a lambda can appear in places a def is not allowed by Python's syntax—inside a list literal, or function call, for example. Also, as an expression, lambda returns a value (a new function) that can optionally be assigned a name; in contrast, the def statement always assigns the new function to the name in the header, instead of returning it as a result.

- **lambda's body is a single expression, not a block of statements.** The lambda's body is similar to what you'd put in a def body's return statement; you simply type the result as a naked expression, instead of explicitly returning it. Because it is limited to an expression, a lambda is less general than a def—you can only squeeze so much logic into a lambda body without using statements such as if. This is by design—it limits program nesting: lambda is designed for coding simple functions, and def handles larger tasks.

Apart from those distinctions, defs and lambdas do the same sort of work. For instance, we've seen how to make a function with a def statement:

```
>>> def func(x, y, z): return x + y + z
...
>>> func(2, 3, 4)
9
```

But, you can achieve the same effect with a lambda expression by explicitly assigning its result to a name through which you can later call the function:

```
>>> f = lambda x, y, z: x + y + z
>>> f(2, 3, 4)
9
```

Here, f is assigned the function object the lambda expression creates; this is how def works, too, but its assignment is automatic.

Defaults work on lambda arguments, just like in a def:

```
>>> x = (lambda a="fee", b="fie", c="foe": a + b + c)
>>> x("wee")
'weefiefoe'
```

The code in a lambda body also follows the same scope lookup rules as code inside a def. lambda expressions introduce a local scope much like a nested def, which automatically sees names in enclosing functions, the module, and the built-in scope (via the LEGB rule):

```
>>> def knights():
...     title = 'Sir'
...     action = (lambda x: title + ' ' + x)    # Title in enclosing def
...     return action                           # Return a function
...
```

```
>>> act = knights()
>>> act('robin')
'Sir robin'
```

In this example, prior to Release 2.2, the value for the name title would typically have been passed in as a default argument value instead; flip back to the scopes coverage in Chapter 16 if you've forgotten why.

Why Use lambda?

Generally speaking, lambdas come in handy as a sort of function shorthand that allows you to embed a function's definition within the code that uses it. They are entirely optional (you can always use defs instead), but they tend to be simpler coding constructs in scenarios where you just need to embed small bits of executable code.

For instance, we'll see later that callback handlers are frequently coded as inline lambda expressions embedded directly in a registration call's arguments list, instead of being defined with a def elsewhere in a file, and referenced by name (see the sidebar "Why You Will Care: Callbacks" later in this chapter for an example).

lambdas are also commonly used to code *jump tables*, which are lists or dictionaries of actions to be performed on demand. For example:

```
L = [(lambda x: x**2), (lambda x: x**3), (lambda x: x**4)]

for f in L:
    print f(2)                      # Prints 4, 8, 16

print L[0](3)                       # Prints 9
```

The lambda expression is most useful as a shorthand for def, when you need to stuff small pieces of executable code into places where statements are illegal syntactically. This code snippet, for example, builds up a list of three functions by embedding lambda expressions inside a list literal; a def won't work inside a list literal like this because it is a statement, not an expression.

You can do the same sort of thing with dictionaries and other data structures in Python to build up action tables:

```
>>> key = 'got'
>>> {'already': (lambda: 2 + 2),
...  'got':     (lambda: 2 * 4),
...  'one':     (lambda: 2 ** 6)
... }[key]()
8
```

Here, when Python makes the dictionary, each of the nested lambdas generates and leaves behind a function to be called later; indexing by key fetches one of those functions, and parentheses force the fetched function to be called. When coded this way, a dictionary becomes a more general multiway branching tool than what I could show you in Chapter 12's coverage of if statements.

To make this work without lambda, you'd need to instead code three def statements somewhere else in your file, outside the dictionary in which the functions are to be used:

```
def f1(): return 2 + 2
def f2(): return 2 * 4
def f3(): return 2 ** 6
...

key = 'one'
{'already': f1, 'got': f2, 'one': f3}[key]()
```

This works, too, but your defs may be arbitrarily far away in your file, even if they are just little bits of code. The *code proximity* that lambdas provide is especially useful for functions that will only be used in a single context—if the three functions here are not useful anywhere else, it makes sense to embed their definitions within the dictionary as lambdas. Moreover, the def form requires you to make up names for these little functions that may clash with other names in this file.

lambdas also come in handy in function argument lists as a way to inline temporary function definitions not used anywhere else in your program; we'll see some examples of such other uses later in this chapter, when we study map.

How (Not) to Obfuscate Your Python Code

The fact that the body of a lambda has to be a single expression (not a series of statements) would seem to place severe limits on how much logic you can pack into a lambda. If you know what you're doing, though, you can code most statements in Python as expression-based equivalents.

For example, if you want to print from the body of a lambda function, simply say sys.stdout.write(str(x)+'\n'), instead of print x (recall from Chapter 11 that this is what print really does). Similarly, to nest logic in a lambda, you can use the if/else ternary expression introduced in Chapter 13, or the equivalent but trickier and/or combination also described there. As you learned earlier, the following statement:

```
if a:
    b
else:
    c
```

can be emulated by either of these roughly equivalent expressions:

```
b if a else c

((a and b) or c)
```

Because expressions like these can be placed inside a lambda, they may be used to implement selection logic within a lambda function:

```
>>> lower = (lambda x, y: x if x < y else y)
>>> lower('bb', 'aa')
'aa'
>>> lower('aa', 'bb')
'aa'
```

Furthermore, if you need to perform loops within a lambda, you can also embed things like map calls and list comprehension expressions (tools we met earlier, in Chapter 13, and will revisit later in this chapter):

```
>>> import sys
>>> showall = (lambda x: map(sys.stdout.write, x))

>>> t = showall(['spam\n', 'toast\n', 'eggs\n'])
spam
toast
eggs

>>> showall = lambda x: [sys.stdout.write(line) for line in x]

>>> t = showall(('bright\n', 'side\n', 'of\n', 'life\n'))
bright
side
of
life
```

Now that I've shown you these tricks, I am required by law to ask you to please only use them as a last resort. Without due care, they can lead to unreadable (a.k.a. *obfuscated*) Python code. In general, simple is better than complex, explicit is better than implicit, and full statements are better than arcane expressions. On the other hand, you may find these techniques useful in moderation.

Nested lambdas and Scopes

lambdas are the main beneficiaries of nested function scope lookup (the E in the LEGB rule we met in Chapter 16). In the following, for example, the lambda appears inside a def—the typical case—and so can access the value that the name x had in the enclosing function's scope at the time that the enclosing function was called:

```
>>> def action(x):
...     return (lambda y: x + y)       # Make and return function, remember x
...
>>> act = action(99)
>>> act
<function <lambda> at 0x00A16A88>
>>> act(2)
101
```

What wasn't illustrated in the prior chapter's discussion of nested function scopes is that a lambda also has access to the names in any enclosing lambda. This case is somewhat obscure, but imagine if we recoded the prior def with a lambda:

```
>>> action = (lambda x: (lambda y: x + y))
>>> act = action(99)
>>> act(3)
102
>>> ((lambda x: (lambda y: x + y))(99))(4)
103
```

Here, the nested lambda structure makes a function that makes a function when called. In both cases, the nested lambda's code has access to the variable x in the enclosing lambda. This works, but it's fairly convoluted code; in the interest of readability, nested lambdas are generally best avoided.

Why You Will Care: Callbacks

Another very common application of lambda is to define inline callback functions for Python's Tkinter GUI API. For example, the following creates a button that prints a message on the console when pressed:

```
import sys
x = Button(
        text ='Press me',
        command=(lambda:sys.stdout.write('Spam\n')))
```

Here, the callback handler is registered by passing a function generated with a lambda to the command keyword argument. The advantage of lambda over def here is that the code that handles a button press is right here, embedded in the button creation call.

In effect, the lambda defers execution of the handler until the event occurs: the write call happens on button presses, not when the button is created.

Because the nested function scope rules apply to lambdas as well, they are also easier to use as callback handlers, as of Python 2.2—they automatically see names in the functions in which they are coded, and no longer require passed-in defaults in most cases. This is especially handy for accessing the special self instance argument that is a local variable in enclosing class method functions (more on classes in Part VI):

```
class MyGui:
    def makewidgets(self):
        Button(command=(lambda: self.display("spam")))
    def display(self, message):
        ...use message...
```

In prior releases, even self had to be passed in with defaults.

Applying Functions to Arguments

Some programs need to call arbitrary functions in a generic fashion, without knowing their names or arguments ahead of time (we'll see examples of where this can be useful later). Both the apply built-in function, and some special call syntax available in Python, can do the job.

 At this writing, both apply and the special call syntax described in this section can be used freely in Python 2.5, but it seems likely that apply may go away in Python 3.0. If you wish to future-proof your code, use the equivalent special call syntax, not apply.

The apply Built-in

When you need to be dynamic, you can call a generated function by passing it as an argument to apply, along with a tuple of arguments to pass to that function:

```
>>> def func(x, y, z): return x + y + z
...
>>> apply(func, (2, 3, 4))
9
>>> f = lambda x, y, z: x + y + z
>>> apply(f, (2, 3, 4))
9
```

The apply function simply calls the passed-in function in the first argument, matching the passed-in arguments tuple to the function's expected arguments. Because the arguments list is passed in as a tuple (i.e., a data structure), a program can build it at runtime.*

The real power of apply is that it doesn't need to know how many arguments a function is being called with. For example, you can use if logic to select from a set of functions and argument lists, and use apply to call any of them:

```
if <test>:
    action, args = func1, (1,)
else:
    action, args = func2, (1, 2, 3)
...
apply(action, args)
```

More generally, apply is useful any time you cannot predict the arguments list ahead of time. If your user selects an arbitrary function via a user interface, for instance, you may be unable to hardcode a function call when writing your script. To work

---

* Be careful not to confuse apply with map, the topic of the next section. apply runs a single function call, passing arguments to the function object just once. map calls a function many times instead for each item in a sequence.

around this, simply build up the arguments list with tuple operations, and call the function indirectly through apply:

```
>>> args = (2,3) + (4,)
>>> args
(2, 3, 4)
>>> apply(func, args)
9
```

Passing keyword arguments

The apply call also supports an optional third argument, where you can pass in a dictionary that represents keyword arguments to be passed to the function:

```
>>> def echo(*args, **kwargs): print args, kwargs
...
>>> echo(1, 2, a=3, b=4)
(1, 2) {'a': 3, 'b': 4}
```

This allows you to construct both positional and keyword arguments at runtime:

```
>>> pargs = (1, 2)
>>> kargs = {'a':3, 'b':4}
>>> apply(echo, pargs, kargs)
(1, 2) {'a': 3, 'b': 4}
```

apply-Like Call Syntax

Python also allows you to accomplish the same effect as an apply call with special syntax in the call. This syntax mirrors the arbitrary arguments syntax in def headers that we met in Chapter 16. For example, assuming the names in this example are still as assigned earlier:

```
>>> apply(func, args)              # Traditional: tuple
9
>>> func(*args)                    # New apply-like syntax
9
>>> echo(*pargs, **kargs)          # Keyword dictionaries too
(1, 2) {'a': 3, 'b': 4}
```

This special call syntax is newer than the apply function, and is generally preferred today. It doesn't have any obvious advantages over an explicit apply call, apart from its symmetry with def headers, and requiring a few less keystrokes. However, the new call syntax alternative also allows us to pass along real additional arguments, and so is more general:

```
>>> echo(0, *pargs, **kargs)       # Normal, *tuple, **dictionary
(0, 1, 2) {'a': 3, 'b': 4}
```

Mapping Functions over Sequences: map

One of the more common things programs do with lists and other sequences is apply an operation to each item and collect the results. For instance, updating all the counters in a list can be done easily with a for loop:

```
>>> counters = [1, 2, 3, 4]
>>>
>>> updated = []
>>> for x in counters:
...     updated.append(x + 10)          # Add 10 to each item
...
>>> updated
[11, 12, 13, 14]
```

But because this is such a common operation, Python actually provides a built-in that does most of the work for you. The map function applies a passed-in function to each item in a sequence object, and returns a list containing all the function call results. For example:

```
>>> def inc(x): return x + 10           # Function to be run
...
>>> map(inc, counters)                  # Collect results
[11, 12, 13, 14]
```

map was introduced as a parallel loop-traversal tool in Chapter 13. As you may recall, we passed in None for the function argument to pair up items. Here, we make better use of it by passing in a real function to be applied to each item in the list—map calls inc on each list item, and collects all the return values into a list.

Because map expects a function to be passed in, it also happens to be one of the places where lambdas commonly appear:

```
>>> map((lambda x: x + 3), counters)    # Function expression
[4, 5, 6, 7]
```

Here, the function adds 3 to each item in the counters list; as this function isn't needed elsewhere, it was written inline as a lambda. Because such uses of map are equivalent to for loops, with a little extra code, you can always code a general mapping utility yourself:

```
>>> def mymap(func, seq):
...     res = []
...     for x in seq: res.append(func(x))
...     return res
...
>>> map(inc, [1, 2, 3])
[11, 12, 13]
>>> mymap(inc, [1, 2, 3])
[11, 12, 13]
```

However, as map is a built-in, it's always available, always works the same way, and has some performance benefits (in short, it's faster than a manually coded for loop).

Moreover, map can be used in more advanced ways than shown here. For instance, given multiple sequence arguments, it sends items taken from sequences in parallel as distinct arguments to the function:

```
>>> pow(3, 4)
81
>>> map(pow, [1, 2, 3], [2, 3, 4])          # 1**2, 2**3, 3**4
[1, 8, 81]
```

Here, the pow function takes two arguments on each call—one from each sequence passed to map. Although we could simulate this generality, too, there is no obvious point in doing so when a speedy built-in is provided.

The map call is similar to the list comprehension expressions we studied in Chapter 13, and will meet again later in this chapter, but map applies a function call to each item instead of an arbitrary expression. Because of this limitation, it is a somewhat less general tool. However, in some cases, map is currently faster to run than a list comprehension (e.g., when mapping a built-in function), and it may require less coding. Because of that, it seems likely that map will still be available in Python 3.0. However, a recent Python 3.0 document did propose removing this call, along with the reduce and filter calls discussed in the next section, from the built-in namespace (they may show up in modules instead).

While map may stick around, it's likely that reduce and filter will be removed in 3.0, partly because they are redundant with list comprehensions (filter is subsumed by list comprehension if clauses), and partly because of their complexity (reduce is one of the most complex tools in the language and is not intuitive). I cannot predict the future on this issue, though, so be sure to watch the Python 3.0 release notes for more on these possible changes. These tools are all still included in this edition of the book because they are part of the current version of Python, and will likely be present in Python code you're likely to see for some time to come.

Functional Programming Tools: filter and reduce

The map function is the simplest representative of a class of Python built-ins used for *functional programming*—which mostly just means tools that apply functions to sequences. Its relatives filter out items based on a test function (filter), and apply functions to pairs of items and running results (reduce). For example, the following filter call picks out items in a sequence that are greater than zero:

```
>>> range(-5, 5)
[-5, -4, -3, -2, -1, 0, 1, 2, 3, 4]

>>> filter((lambda x: x > 0), range(-5, 5))
[1, 2, 3, 4]
```

Items in the sequence for which the function returns true are added to the result list. Like map, this function is roughly equivalent to a for loop, but is built-in, and fast:

```
>>> res = [  ]
>>> for x in range(-5, 5):
...     if x > 0:
...         res.append(x)
...
>>> res
[1, 2, 3, 4]
```

reduce is more complex. Here are two reduce calls computing the sum and product of items in a list:

```
>>> reduce((lambda x, y: x + y), [1, 2, 3, 4])
10
>>> reduce((lambda x, y: x * y), [1, 2, 3, 4])
24
```

At each step, reduce passes the current sum or product, along with the next item from the list, to the passed-in lambda function. By default, the first item in the sequence initializes the starting value. Here's the for loop equivalent to the first of these calls, with the addition hardcoded inside the loop:

```
>>> L = [1,2,3,4]
>>> res = L[0]
>>> for x in L[1:]:
...     res = res + x
...
>>> res
10
```

Coding your own version of reduce (for instance, if it is indeed removed in Python 3.0) is actually fairly straightforward:

```
>>> def myreduce(function, sequence):
...     tally = sequence[0]
...     for next in sequence[1:]:
...         tally = function(tally, next)
...     return tally
...
>>> myreduce((lambda x, y: x + y), [1, 2, 3, 4, 5])
15
>>> myreduce((lambda x, y: x * y), [1, 2, 3, 4, 5])
120
```

If this has sparked your interest, also see the built-in operator module, which provides functions that correspond to built-in expressions, and so comes in handy for some uses of functional tools:

```
>>> import operator
>>> reduce(operator.add, [2, 4, 6])        # Function-based +
12
>>> reduce((lambda x, y: x + y), [2, 4, 6])
12
```

Together with map, filter and reduce support powerful functional programming techniques. Some observers might also extend the functional programming toolset in Python to include lambda and apply, and list comprehensions, which are discussed in the next section.

List Comprehensions Revisited: Mappings

Because mapping operations over sequences and collecting results is such a common task in Python coding, Python 2.0 sprouted a new feature—the *list comprehension expression*—that makes it even simpler than using the tools we just studied. We met list comprehensions in Chapter 13, but because they're related to functional programming tools like the map and filter calls, we'll resurrect the topic here for one last look. Technically, this feature is not tied to functions—as we'll see, list comprehensions can be a more general tool than map and filter—but it is sometimes best understood by analogy to function-based alternatives.

List Comprehension Basics

Let's work through an example that demonstrates the basics. As we saw in Chapter 7, Python's built-in ord function returns the ASCII integer code of a single character (the chr built-in is the converse—it returns the character for an ASCII integer code):

```
>>> ord('s')
115
```

Now, suppose we wish to collect the ASCII codes of *all* characters in an entire string. Perhaps the most straightforward approach is to use a simple for loop, and append the results to a list:

```
>>> res = []
>>> for x in 'spam':
...     res.append(ord(x))
...
>>> res
[115, 112, 97, 109]
```

Now that we know about map, though, we can achieve similar results with a single function call without having to manage list construction in the code:

```
>>> res = map(ord, 'spam')          # Apply function to sequence
>>> res
[115, 112, 97, 109]
```

As of Python 2.0, however, we can get the same results from a list comprehension expression:

```
>>> res = [ord(x) for x in 'spam']       # Apply expression to sequence
>>> res
[115, 112, 97, 109]
```

List comprehensions collect the results of applying an arbitrary expression to a sequence of values and return them in a new list. Syntactically, list comprehensions are enclosed in square brackets (to remind you that they construct lists). In their simple form, within the brackets you code an expression that names a variable followed by what looks like a for loop header that names the same variable. Python then collects the expression's results for each iteration of the implied loop.

The effect of the preceding example is similar to that of the manual for loop and the map call. List comprehensions become more convenient, though, when we wish to apply an arbitrary expression to a sequence:

```
>>> [x ** 2 for x in range(10)]
[0, 1, 4, 9, 16, 25, 36, 49, 64, 81]
```

Here, we've collected the squares of the numbers 0 through 9 (we're just letting the interactive prompt print the resulting list; assign it to a variable if you need to retain it). To do similar work with a map call, we would probably invent a little function to implement the square operation. Because we won't need this function elsewhere, we'd typically (but not necessarily) code it inline, with a lambda, instead of using a def statement elsewhere:

```
>>> map((lambda x: x ** 2), range(10))
[0, 1, 4, 9, 16, 25, 36, 49, 64, 81]
```

This does the same job, and it's only a few keystrokes longer than the equivalent list comprehension. It's also only marginally more complex (at least, once you understand the lambda). For more advanced kinds of expressions, though, list comprehensions will often require considerably less typing. The next section shows why.

Adding Tests and Nested Loops

List comprehensions are even more general than shown so far. For instance, you can code an if clause after the for, to add selection logic. List comprehensions with if clauses can be thought of as analogous to the filter built-in discussed in the prior section—they skip sequence items for which the if clause is not true. Here are examples of both schemes picking up even numbers from 0 to 4; like the map list comprehension alternative we just looked at, the filter version here invents a little lambda function for the test expression. For comparison, the equivalent for loop is shown here as well:

```
>>> [x for x in range(5) if x % 2 == 0]
[0, 2, 4]

>>> filter((lambda x: x % 2 == 0), range(5))
[0, 2, 4]

>>> res = [  ]
>>> for x in range(5):
```

```
...        if x % 2 == 0:
...            res.append(x)
...
>>> res
[0, 2, 4]
```

All of these use the modulus (remainder of division) operator, %, to detect even numbers: if there is no remainder after dividing a number by two, it must be even. The filter call is not much longer than the list comprehension here either. However, we can combine an if clause, and an arbitrary expression in our list comprehension, to give it the effect of a filter *and* a map, in a single expression:

```
>>> [x ** 2 for x in range(10) if x % 2 == 0]
[0, 4, 16, 36, 64]
```

This time, we collect the squares of the even numbers from 0 through 9: the for loop skips numbers for which the attached if clause on the right is false, and the expression on the left computes the squares. The equivalent map call would require a lot more work on our part—we would have to combine filter selections with map iteration, making for a noticeably more complex expression:

```
>>> map((lambda x: x**2), filter((lambda x: x % 2 == 0), range(10)))
[0, 4, 16, 36, 64]
```

In fact, list comprehensions are more general still. You can code any number of nested for loops in a list comprehension, and each may have an optional associated if test. The general structure of list comprehensions looks like this:

```
[ expression for target1 in sequence1 [if condition]
             for target2 in sequence2 [if condition] ...
             for targetN in sequenceN [if condition] ]
```

When for clauses are nested within a list comprehension, they work like equivalent nested for loop statements. For example, the following:

```
>>> res = [x + y for x in [0, 1, 2] for y in [100, 200, 300]]
>>> res
[100, 200, 300, 101, 201, 301, 102, 202, 302]
```

has the same effect as this substantially more verbose equivalent:

```
>>> res = []
>>> for x in [0, 1, 2]:
...     for y in [100, 200, 300]:
...         res.append(x + y)
...
>>> res
[100, 200, 300, 101, 201, 301, 102, 202, 302]
```

Although list comprehensions construct lists, remember that they can iterate over any sequence or other iterable type. Here's a similar bit of code that traverses strings instead of lists of numbers, and so collects concatenation results:

```
>>> [x + y for x in 'spam' for y in 'SPAM']
['sS', 'sP', 'sA', 'sM', 'pS', 'pP', 'pA', 'pM',
 'aS', 'aP', 'aA', 'aM', 'mS', 'mP', 'mA', 'mM']
```

Finally, here is a much more complex list comprehension that illustrates the effect of attached `if` selections on nested `for` clauses:

```
>>> [(x, y) for x in range(5) if x % 2 == 0 for y in range(5) if y % 2 == 1]
[(0, 1), (0, 3), (2, 1), (2, 3), (4, 1), (4, 3)]
```

This expression permutes even numbers from 0 through 4 with odd numbers from 0 through 4. The `if` clauses filter out items in each sequence iteration. Here's the equivalent statement-based code:

```
>>> res = []
>>> for x in range(5):
...     if x % 2 == 0:
...         for y in range(5):
...             if y % 2 == 1:
...                 res.append((x, y))
...
>>> res
[(0, 1), (0, 3), (2, 1), (2, 3), (4, 1), (4, 3)]
```

Recall that if you're confused about what a complex list comprehension does, you can always nest the list comprehension's `for` and `if` clauses inside each other (indenting successively further to the right) to derive the equivalent statements. The result is longer, but perhaps clearer.

The `map` and `filter` equivalent would be wildly complex and deeply nested, so I won't even try showing it here. I'll leave its coding as an exercise for Zen masters, ex-LISP programmers, and the criminally insane.

List Comprehensions and Matrixes

Let's look at one more advanced application of list comprehensions to stretch a few synapses. One basic way to code matrixes (a.k.a. multidimensional arrays) in Python is with nested list structures. The following, for example, defines two 3×3 matrixes as lists of nested lists:

```
>>> M = [[1, 2, 3],
...      [4, 5, 6],
...      [7, 8, 9]]

>>> N = [[2, 2, 2],
...      [3, 3, 3],
...      [4, 4, 4]]
```

Given this structure, we can always index rows, and columns within rows, using normal index operations:

```
>>> M[1]
[4, 5, 6]

>>> M[1][2]
6
```

List comprehensions are powerful tools for processing such structures, though, because they automatically scan rows and columns for us. For instance, although this structure stores the matrix by rows, to collect the second column, we can simply iterate across the rows and pull out the desired column, or iterate through positions in the rows and index as we go:

```
>>> [row[1] for row in M]
[2, 5, 8]

>>> [M[row][1] for row in (0, 1, 2)]
[2, 5, 8]
```

Given positions, we can also easily perform tasks such as pulling out a diagonal. The following expression uses range to generate the list of offsets, and then indexes with the row and column the same, picking out M[0][0], then M[1][1], and so on (we assume the matrix has the same number of rows and columns):

```
>>> [M[i][i] for i in range(len(M))]
[1, 5, 9]
```

Finally, with a bit of creativity, we can also use list comprehensions to combine multiple matrixes. The following first builds a flat list that contains the result of multiplying the matrixes pairwise, and then builds a nested list structure having the same values by nesting list comprehensions:

```
>>> [M[row][col] * N[row][col] for row in range(3) for col in range(3)]
[2, 4, 6, 12, 15, 18, 28, 32, 36]

>>> [[M[row][col] * N[row][col] for col in range(3)] for row in range(3)]
[[2, 4, 6], [12, 15, 18], [28, 32, 36]]
```

This last expression works because the row iteration is an outer loop: for each row, it runs the nested column iteration to build up one row of the result matrix. It's equivalent to this statement-based code:

```
>>> res = []
>>> for row in range(3):
...     tmp = []
...     for col in range(3):
...         tmp.append(M[row][col] * N[row][col])
...     res.append(tmp)
...
>>> res
[[2, 4, 6], [12, 15, 18], [28, 32, 36]]
```

Compared to these statements, the list comprehension version requires only one line of code, will probably run substantially faster for large matrixes, and just might make your head explode! Which brings us to the next section.

Comprehending List Comprehensions

With such generality, list comprehensions can quickly become, well, incomprehensible, especially when nested. Consequently, my advice is typically to use simple for loops when getting started with Python, and map calls in most other cases (unless they get too complex). The "keep it simple" rule applies here, as always: code conciseness is a much less important goal than code readability.

However, in this case, there is currently a substantial performance advantage to the extra complexity: based on tests run under Python today, map calls are roughly twice as fast as equivalent for loops, and list comprehensions are usually slightly faster than map calls.* This speed difference is down to the fact that map and list comprehensions run at C language speed inside the interpreter, which is much faster than stepping through Python for loop code within the PVM.

Because for loops make logic more explicit, I recommend them in general on the grounds of simplicity. However, map and list comprehensions are worth knowing and using for simpler kinds of iterations, and if your application's speed is an important consideration. In addition, because map and list comprehensions are both expressions, they can show up syntactically in places that for loop statements cannot, such as in the bodies of lambda functions, within list and dictionary literals, and more. Still, you should try to keep your map calls and list comprehensions simple; for more complex tasks, use full statements instead.

Iterators Revisited: Generators

In this part of the book, we've learned about coding normal functions that receive input parameters and send back a single result immediately. It is also possible, however, to write functions that may send back a value and later be resumed, picking up where they left off. Such functions are known as *generators* because they generate a sequence of values over time.

Generator functions are like normal functions in most respects, but in Python, they are automatically made to implement the iteration protocol so that they can appear in iteration contexts. We studied iterators in Chapter 13; here, we'll revise them to see how they relate to generators.

Unlike normal functions that return a value and exit, generator functions automatically suspend and resume their execution and state around the point of value generation.

---

* These performance generalizations can depend on call patterns, as well as changes and optimizations in Python itself. Recent Python releases have sped up the simple for loop statement, for example. Usually, though, list comprehensions are still substantially faster than for loops and even faster than map (though map can still win for built-in functions). To time these alternatives yourself, see the standard library's time module's time.clock and time.time calls, the newer timeit module added in Release 2.4, or this chapter's upcoming section "Timing Iteration Alternatives."

Why You Will Care: List Comprehensions and map

Here's a more realistic example of list comprehensions and map in action (we solved this problem with list comprehensions in Chapter 13, but we'll revive it here to add map-based alternatives). Recall that the file readlines method returns lines with \n end-of-line characters at the ends:

```
>>> open('myfile').readlines()
['aaa\n', 'bbb\n', 'ccc\n']
```

If you don't want the end-of-line characters, you can slice them off all the lines in a single step with a list comprehension or a map call:

```
>>> [line.rstrip() for line in open('myfile').readlines()]
['aaa', 'bbb', 'ccc']

>>> [line.rstrip() for line in open('myfile')]
['aaa', 'bbb', 'ccc']

>>> map((lambda line: line.rstrip()), open('myfile'))
['aaa', 'bbb', 'ccc']
```

The last two of these make use of *file iterators* (which essentially means that you don't need a method call to grab all the lines in iteration contexts such as these). The map call is just slightly longer than the list comprehension, but neither has to manage result list construction explicitly.

A list comprehension can also be used as a sort of column projection operation. Python's standard SQL database API returns query results as a list of tuples much like the following—the list is the table, tuples are rows, and items in tuples are column values:

```
listoftuple = [('bob', 35, 'mgr'), ('mel', 40, 'dev')]
```

A for loop could pick up all the values from a selected column manually, but map and list comprehensions can do it in a single step, and faster:

```
>>> [age for (name, age, job) in listoftuple]
[35, 40]

>>> map((lambda (name, age, job): age), listoftuple)
[35, 40]
```

Both of these make use of tuple assignment to unpack row tuples in the list.

See other books and resources for more on Python's database API.

Because of that, they are often a useful alternative to both computing an entire series of values up front, and manually saving and restoring state in classes. Generator functions automatically retain their state when they are suspended—because this includes their entire local scope, their local variables keep state information, which is available when the functions are resumed.

The chief code difference between generator and normal functions is that a generator *yields* a value, rather than *returning* one—the `yield` statement suspends the function, and sends a value back to the caller, but retains enough state to enable the function to resume from where it left off. This allows these functions to produce a series of values over time, rather than computing them all at once, and sending them back in something like a list.

Generator functions are bound up with the notion of iterator protocols in Python. In short, functions containing a `yield` statement are compiled specially as generators; when called, they return a generator object that supports the iterator object interface. Generator functions may also have a `return` statement, which simply terminates the generation of values.

Iterator objects, in turn, define a `next` method, which either returns the next item in the iteration, or raises a special exception (`StopIteration`) to end the iteration. Iterators are fetched with the `iter` built-in function. Python `for` loops use this iteration interface protocol to step through a sequence (or sequence generator), if the protocol is supported; if not, `for` falls back on repeatedly indexing sequences instead.

Generator Function Example

Generators and iterators are advanced language features, so please see the Python library manuals for the full story. To illustrate the basics, though, the following code defines a generator function that can be used to generate the squares of a series of numbers over time:[*]

```
>>> def gensquares(N):
...     for i in range(N):
...         yield i ** 2          # Resume here later
...
```

This function yields a value, and so returns to its caller, each time through the loop; when it is resumed, its prior state is restored, and control picks up again immediately after the `yield` statement. For example, when used in the body of a `for` loop, control returns to the function after its `yield` statement each time through the loop:

```
>>> for i in gensquares(5):       # Resume the function
...     print i, ':',             # Print last yielded value
...
0 : 1 : 4 : 9 : 16 :
>>>
```

To end the generation of values, functions either use a `return` statement with no value, or simply allow control to fall off the end of the function body.

---

[*] Generators are available in Python releases after 2.2; in 2.2, they must be enabled with a special `import` statement of the form `from __future__ import generators` (see Chapter 18 for more on this statement form). Iterators were already available in 2.2, largely because the underlying protocol did not require the new, nonbackward-compatible keyword `yield`.

If you want to see what is going on inside the `for`, call the generator function directly:

```
>>> x = gensquares(4)
>>> x
<generator object at 0x0086C378>
```

You get back a generator object that supports the iterator protocol (i.e., has a `next` method that starts the function, or resumes it from where it last yielded a value, and raises a `StopIteration` exception when the end of the series of values is reached):

```
>>> x.next()
0
>>> x.next()
1
>>> x.next()
4
>>> x.next()
9
>>> x.next()

Traceback (most recent call last):
  File "<pyshell#453>", line 1, in <module>
    x.next()
StopIteration
```

`for` loops work with generators in the same way—by calling the next method repeatedly, until an exception is caught. If the object to be iterated over does not support this protocol, `for` loops instead use the indexing protocol to iterate.

Note that in this example, we could also simply build the list of yielded values all at once:

```
>>> def buildsquares(n):
...     res = []
...     for i in range(n): res.append(i**2)
...     return res
...
>>> for x in buildsquares(5): print x, ':',
...
0 : 1 : 4 : 9 : 16 :
```

For that matter, we could use any of the `for` loop, `map`, or list comprehension techniques:

```
>>> for x in [n**2 for n in range(5)]:
...     print x, ':',
...
0 : 1 : 4 : 9 : 16 :

>>> for x in map((lambda x:x**2), range(5)):
...     print x, ':',
...
0 : 1 : 4 : 9 : 16 :
```

However, generators allow functions to avoid doing all the work up front, which is especially useful when the result lists are large, or when it takes a lot of computation to produce each value. Generators distribute the time required to produce the series of values among loop iterations. Moreover, for more advanced uses, they provide a simpler alternative to manually saving the state between iterations in class objects (more on classes later in Part VI); with generators, function variables are saved and restored automatically.

Extended Generator Function Protocol: send Versus next

In Python 2.5, a send method was added to the generator function protocol. The send method advances to the next item in the series of results, just like the next method, but also provides a way for the caller to communicate with the generator, to affect its operation.

Technically, yield is now an expression form that returns the item passed to send, not a statement (though it can be called either way—as yield X, or A = (yield X)). Values are sent into a generator by calling its send(value) method. The generator's code is then resumed, and the yield expression returns the value passed to send. If the regular next( ) method is called, the yield returns None.

The send method can be used, for example, to code a generator that can be terminated by its caller. In addition, generators in 2.5 also support a throw(type) method to raise an exception inside the generator at the latest yield, and a close( ) method that raises a new GeneratorExit exception inside the generator to terminate the iteration. These are advanced features that we won't delve into in more detail here; see Python's standard manuals for more details.

Iterators and Built-in Types

As we saw in Chapter 13, built-in data types are designed to produce iterator objects in response to the iter built-in function. Dictionary iterators, for instance, produce key list items on each iteration:

```
>>> D = {'a':1, 'b':2, 'c':3}
>>> x = iter(D)
>>> x.next( )
'a'
>>> x.next( )
'c'
```

In addition, all iteration contexts (including for loops, map calls, list comprehensions, and the many other contexts we met in Chapter 13) are in turn designed to automatically call the iter function to see whether the protocol is supported. That's why you can loop through a dictionary's keys without calling its keys method, step through lines in a file without calling readlines or xreadlines, and so on:

```
>>> for key in D:
...     print key, D[key]
...
a 1
c 3
b 2
```

As we've also seen, for file iterators, Python simply loads lines from the file on demand:

```
>>> for line in open('temp.txt'):
...     print line,
...
Tis but
a flesh wound.
```

It is also possible to implement arbitrary generator objects with classes that conform to the iterator protocol, and so may be used in for loops and other iteration contexts. Such classes define a special __iter__ method that returns an iterator object (preferred over the __getitem__ indexing method). However, this is well beyond the scope of this chapter; see Part VI for more on classes in general, and Chapter 24 for an example of a class that implements the iterator protocol.

Generator Expressions: Iterators Meet List Comprehensions

In recent versions of Python, the notions of iterators and list comprehensions are combined in a new feature of the language, *generator expressions*. Syntactically, generator expressions are just like normal list comprehensions, but they are enclosed in parentheses instead of square brackets:

```
>>> [x ** 2 for x in range(4)]        # List comprehension: build a list
[0, 1, 4, 9]

>>> (x ** 2 for x in range(4))        # Generator expression: make an iterable
<generator object at 0x011DC648>
```

Operationally, however, generator expressions are very different—instead of building the result list in memory, they return a generator object, which in turn supports the iteration protocol to yield one piece of the result list at a time in any iteration context:

```
>>> G = (x ** 2 for x in range(4))
>>> G.next()
0
>>> G.next()
1
>>> G.next()
4
>>> G.next()
9
>>> G.next()
```

```
Traceback (most recent call last):
  File "<pyshell#410>", line 1, in <module>
    G.next( )
StopIteration
```

We don't typically see the next iterator machinery under the hood of a generator expression like this because for loops trigger it for us automatically:

```
>>> for num in (x ** 2 for x in range(4)):
...     print '%s, %s' % (num, num / 2.0)
...
0, 0.0
1, 0.5
4, 2.0
9, 4.5
```

In fact, every iteration context does this, including the sum, map, and sorted built-in functions, and the other iteration contexts we learned about in Chapter 13, such as the any, all, and list built-in functions.

Notice that the parentheses are not required around a generator expression if they are the sole item enclosed in other parentheses, like those of a function call. Extra parentheses are required, however, in the second call to sorted:

```
>>> sum(x ** 2 for x in range(4))
14

>>> sorted(x ** 2 for x in range(4))
[0, 1, 4, 9]

>>> sorted((x ** 2 for x in range(4)), reverse=True)
[9, 4, 1, 0]

>>> import math
>>> map(math.sqrt, (x ** 2 for x in range(4)))
[0.0, 1.0, 2.0, 3.0]
```

Generator expressions are primarily a memory space optimization—they do not require the entire result list to be constructed all at once, as the square-bracketed list comprehension does. They may also run slightly slower in practice, so they are probably best used only for very large result sets—which provides a natural segue to the next section.

Timing Iteration Alternatives

We've met a few iteration alternatives in this book. To summarize, let's take a brief look at a case study that pulls together some of the things we've learned about iteration and functions.

I've mentioned a few times that list comprehensions have a speed performance advantage over for loop statements, and that map performance can be better or worse depending on call patterns. The generator expressions of the prior section tend to be slightly slower than list comprehensions, though they minimize memory requirements.

All that's true today, but relative performance can vary over time (Python is constantly being optimized). If you want to test this for yourself, try running the following script on your own computer, and your version of Python:

```
# file timerseqs.py

import time, sys
reps = 1000
size = 10000

def tester(func, *args):
    startTime = time.time()
    for i in range(reps):
        func(*args)
    elapsed = time.time() - startTime
    return elapsed

def forStatement():
    res = []
    for x in range(size):
        res.append(abs(x))

def listComprehension():
    res = [abs(x) for x in range(size)]

def mapFunction():
    res = map(abs, range(size))

def generatorExpression():
    res = list(abs(x) for x in range(size))

print sys.version
tests = (forStatement, listComprehension, mapFunction, generatorExpression)
for testfunc in tests:
    print testfunc.__name__.ljust(20), '=>', tester(testfunc)
```

This script tests all the alternative ways to build lists of results and, as shown, executes on the order of 10 million steps for each—that is, each of the four tests builds a list of 10,000 items 1,000 times.

Notice how we have to run the generator expression though the built-in list call to force it to yield all of its values; if we did not, we would just produce a generator that never does any real work. Also, notice how the code at the bottom steps through a tuple of four function objects, and prints the __name__ of each: this is a built-in attribute that gives a function's name.

When I ran this in IDLE on Windows XP with Python 2.5, here is what I found—list comprehensions were roughly twice as fast as equivalent for loop statements, and map was slightly quicker than list comprehensions when mapping a built-in function such as abs (absolute value):

```
2.5 (r25:51908, Sep 19 2006, 09:52:17) [MSC v.1310 32 bit (Intel)]
forStatement          => 6.10899996758
listComprehension     => 3.51499986649
mapFunction           => 2.73399996758
generatorExpression   => 4.11600017548
```

But watch what happens if we change this script to perform a real operation on each iteration, such as addition:

```
...
...
def forStatement():
    res = []
    for x in range(size):
        res.append(x + 10)

def listComprehension():
    res = [x + 10 for x in range(size)]

def mapFunction():
    res = map((lambda x: x + 10), range(size))

def generatorExpression():
    res = list(x + 10 for x in range(size))
...
...
```

The function-call requirement of the map call then makes it just as slow as the for loop statements, despite the fact the looping statements version is larger in terms of code:

```
2.5 (r25:51908, Sep 19 2006, 09:52:17) [MSC v.1310 32 bit (Intel)]
forStatement          => 5.25699996948
listComprehension     => 2.68400001526
mapFunction           => 5.96900010109
generatorExpression   => 3.37400007248
```

Because the interpreter optimizes so much internally, performance analysis of Python code like this is a very tricky affair. It's virtually impossible to guess which method will perform the best—the best you can do is time your own code, on your computer, with your version of Python. In this case, all we can say for certain is that on this Python, using a user-defined function in map calls can slow it down by at least a factor of 2, and that list comprehensions run quickest for this test.

As I've mentioned before, however, performance should not be your primary concern when writing Python code—write for readability and simplicity first, then optimize later, if and only if needed. It could very well be that any of the four alternatives is quick enough for the data sets the program needs to process; if so, program clarity should be the chief goal.

For more insight, try modifying the repetition counts at the top of this script, or see the newer `timeit` module, which automates timing of code, and finesses some platform-specific issues (on some platforms, for instance, `time.time` is preferred over `time.clock`). Also, see the `profile` standard library module for a complete source code profiler tool.

Function Design Concepts

When you start using functions, you're faced with choices about how to glue components together—for instance, how to decompose a task into purposeful functions (resulting in *cohesion*), how your functions should communicate (*coupling*), and so on. You need to take into account concepts such as cohesion, coupling, and the size of the functions—some of this falls into the category of structured analysis and design. We introduced some ideas related to function and module coupling in the prior chapter, but here is a review of a few general guidelines for Python beginners:

- **Coupling: use arguments for inputs and return for outputs.** Generally, you should strive to make a function independent of things outside of it. Arguments and `return` statements are often the best ways to isolate external dependencies to a small number of well-known places in your code.

- **Coupling: use global variables only when truly necessary.** Global variables (i.e., names in the enclosing module) are usually a poor way for functions to communicate. They can create dependencies and timing issues that make programs difficult to debug and change.

- **Coupling: don't change mutable arguments unless the caller expects it.** Functions can change parts of passed-in mutable objects, but as with global variables, this implies lots of coupling between the caller and callee, which can make a function too specific and brittle.

- **Cohesion: each function should have a single, unified purpose.** When designed well, each of your functions should do one thing—something you can summarize in a simple declarative sentence. If that sentence is very broad (e.g., "this function implements my whole program"), or contains lots of conjunctions (e.g., "this function gives employee raises *and* submits a pizza order"), you might want to think about splitting it into separate and simpler functions. Otherwise, there is no way to reuse the code behind the steps mixed together in the function.

- **Size: each function should be relatively small.** This naturally follows from the preceding goal, but if your functions start spanning multiple pages on your display, it's probably time to split them. Especially given that Python code is so concise to begin with, a long or deeply nested function is often a symptom of design problems. Keep it simple, and keep it short.

- **Coupling: avoid changing variables in another module file directly.** We introduced this concept in the prior chapter, and we'll revisit it in the next part of the book when we focus on modules. For reference, though, remember that changing variables across file boundaries sets up a coupling between modules similar to how global variables couple functions—the modules become difficult to understand and reuse. Use accessor functions whenever possible, instead of direct assignment statements.

Figure 17-1 summarizes the ways functions can talk to the outside world; inputs may come from items on the left side, and results may be sent out in any of the forms on the right. Many function designers prefer to use only arguments for inputs, and `return` statements for outputs.

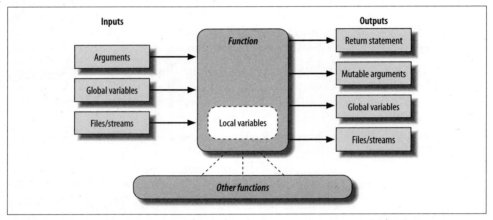

Figure 17-1. Function execution environment. Functions may obtain input and produce output in a variety of ways, though functions are usually easier to understand and maintain if you use arguments for input, and return statements and anticipated mutable argument changes for output.

Of course, there are plenty of exceptions to the preceding design rules, including some related to Python's OOP support. As you'll see in Part VI, Python classes *depend* on changing a passed-in mutable object—class functions set attributes of an automatically passed-in argument called `self` to change per-object state information (e.g., `self.name='bob'`). Moreover, if classes are not used, global variables are often the best way for functions in modules to retain state between calls. The side effects aren't dangerous if they're expected.

Functions Are Objects: Indirect Calls

Because Python functions are objects at runtime, you can write programs that process them generically. Function objects can be assigned, passed to other functions, stored in data structures, and so on, as if they were simple numbers or strings. We've seen some of these uses in earlier examples. Function objects also happen to support a special operation: they can be called by listing arguments in parentheses after a function expression. Still, functions belong to the same general category as other objects.

For instance, there's really nothing special about the name used in a def statement: it's just a variable assigned in the current scope, as if it had appeared on the left of an = sign. After a def runs, the function name is simply a reference to an object, and you can reassign that object to other names, and call it through any reference (not just the original name):

```
>>> def echo(message):          # echo assigned to a function object
...     print message
...
>>> x = echo                    # Now x references it too
>>> x('Hello world!')           # Call the object by adding ()
Hello world!
```

Because arguments are passed by assigning objects, it's just as easy to pass functions to other functions as arguments. The callee may then call the passed-in function just by adding arguments in parentheses:

```
>>> def indirect(func, arg):
...     func(arg)               # Call the object by adding ()
...
>>> indirect(echo, 'Hello jello!')   # Pass the function to a function
Hello jello!
```

You can even stuff function objects into data structures, as though they were integers or strings. Because Python compound types can contain any sort of object, there's no special case here either:

```
>>> schedule = [ (echo, 'Spam!'), (echo, 'Ham!') ]
>>> for (func, arg) in schedule:
...     func(arg)
...
Spam!
Ham!
```

This code simply steps through the schedule list, calling the echo function with one argument each time through (notice the tuple-unpacking assignment in the for loop header, introduced in Chapter 13). Python's lack of type declarations makes for an incredibly flexible programming language.

Function Gotchas

Functions have some jagged edges that you might not expect. They're all obscure, and a few have started to fall away from the language completely in recent releases, but most have been known to trip up new users.

Local Names Are Detected Statically

As you know, Python classifies names assigned in a function as locals by default; they live in the function's scope and exist only while the function is running. What I didn't tell you is that Python detects locals statically, when it compiles the def's code, rather than by noticing assignments as they happen at runtime. This leads to one of the most common oddities posted on the Python newsgroup by beginners.

Normally, a name that isn't assigned in a function is looked up in the enclosing module:

```
>>> X = 99
>>> def selector():          # X used but not assigned
...     print X              # X found in global scope
...
>>> selector()
99
```

Here, the X in the function resolves to the X in the module. But watch what happens if you add an assignment to X after the reference:

```
>>> def selector():
...     print X              # Does not yet exist!
...     X = 88               # X classified as a local name (everywhere)
...                          # Can also happen if "import X", "def X"...
>>> selector()
Traceback (most recent call last):
  File "<stdin>", line 1, in ?
  File "<stdin>", line 2, in selector
UnboundLocalError: local variable 'X' referenced before assignment
```

You get an undefined name error, but the reason is subtle. Python reads and compiles this code when it's typed interactively or imported from a module. While compiling, Python sees the assignment to X, and decides that X will be a local name everywhere in the function. But, when the function is actually run, because the assignment hasn't yet happened when the print executes, Python says you're using an undefined name. According to its name rules, it should say this; the local X is used before being assigned. In fact, any assignment in a function body makes a name local. Imports, =, nested defs, nested classes, and so on, are all susceptible to this behavior.

The problem occurs because assigned names are treated as locals everywhere in a function, not just after the statements where they are assigned. Really, the previous example is ambiguous at best: was the intention to print the global X and then create a local X, or is this a genuine programming error? Because Python treats X as a local everywhere, it is an error; if you really mean to print the global X, you need to declare it in a global statement:

```
>>> def selector():
...     global X             # Force X to be global (everywhere)
...     print X
...     X = 88
```

```
...
>>> selector()
99
```

Remember, though, that this means the assignment also changes the global X, not a local X. Within a function, you can't use both local and global versions of the same simple name. If you really meant to print the global, and then set a local of the same name, import the enclosing module, and use module attribute notation to get to the global version:

```
>>> X = 99
>>> def selector():
...     import __main__          # Import enclosing module
...     print __main__.X         # Qualify to get to global version of name
...     X = 88                   # Unqualified X classified as local
...     print X                  # Prints local version of name
...
>>> selector()
99
88
```

Qualification (the .X part) fetches a value from a namespace object. The interactive namespace is a module called __main__, so __main__.X reaches the global version of X. If that isn't clear, check out Part V.*

Defaults and Mutable Objects

Default argument values are evaluated and saved when a def statement is run, not when the resulting function is called. Internally, Python saves one object per default argument attached to the function itself.

That's usually what you want—because defaults are evaluated at def time, it lets you save values from the enclosing scope, if needed. But because a default retains an object between calls, you have to be careful about changing mutable defaults. For instance, the following function uses an empty list as a default value, and then changes it in-place each time the function is called:

```
>>> def saver(x=[]):           # Saves away a list object
...     x.append(1)            # Changes same object each time!
...     print x
...
>>> saver([2])                 # Default not used
[2, 1]
>>> saver()                    # Default used
[1]
>>> saver()                    # Grows on each call!
[1, 1]
```

---

* Python has improved on this story somewhat by issuing for this case the more specific "unbound local" error message shown in the example listing (it used to simply raise a generic name error); this gotcha is still present in general, though.

```
>>> saver( )
[1, 1, 1]
```

Some see this behavior as a feature—because mutable default arguments retain their state between function calls, they can serve some of the same roles as *static* local function variables in the C language. In a sense, they work sort of like global variables, but their names are local to the functions, and so will not clash with names elsewhere in a program.

To most observers, though, this seems like a gotcha, especially the first time they run into it. There are better ways to retain state between calls in Python (e.g., using classes, which will be discussed in Part VI).

Moreover, mutable defaults are tricky to remember (and to understand at all). They depend upon the timing of default object construction. In the prior example, there is just one list object for the default value—the one created when the def is executed. You don't get a new list every time the function is called, so the list grows with each new append; it is not reset to empty on each call.

If that's not the behavior you want, simply make a copy of the default at the start of the function body, or move the default value expression into the function body. As long as the value resides in code that's actually executed each time the function runs, you'll get a new object each time through:

```
>>> def saver(x=None):
...     if x is None:          # No argument passed?
...         x = []             # Run code to make a new list
...     x.append(1)            # Changes new list object
...     print x
...
>>> saver([2])
[2, 1]
>>> saver( )                   # Doesn't grow here
[1]
>>> saver( )
[1]
```

By the way, the if statement in this example could *almost* be replaced by the assignment x = x or [], which takes advantage of the fact that Python's or returns one of its operand objects: if no argument was passed, x would default to None, so the or would return the new empty list on the right.

However, this isn't exactly the same. If an empty list were passed in, the or expression would cause the function to extend and return a newly created list, rather than extending and returning the passed-in list like the if version. (The expression becomes [] or [], which evaluates to the new empty list on the right; see "Truth Tests" in Chapter 12, if you don't recall why). Real program requirements may call for either behavior.

Functions Without returns

In Python functions, return (and yield) statements are optional. When a function doesn't return a value explicitly, the function exits when control falls off the end of the function body. Technically, all functions return a value; if you don't provide a return statement, your function returns the None object automatically:

```
>>> def proc(x):
...     print x                    # No return is a None return
...
>>> x = proc('testing 123...')
testing 123...
>>> print x
None
```

Functions such as this without a return are Python's equivalent of what are called "procedures" in some languages. They're usually invoked as statements, and the None results are ignored, as they do their business without computing a useful result.

This is worth knowing because Python won't tell you if you try to use the result of a function that doesn't return one. For instance, assigning the result of a list append method won't raise an error, but you'll get back None, not the modified list:

```
>>> list = [1, 2, 3]
>>> list = list.append(4)         # append is a "procedure"
>>> print list                    # append changes list in-place
None
```

As mentioned in "Common Coding Gotchas" in Chapter 14, such functions do their business as a side effect, and are usually designed to be run as statements, not expressions.

Enclosing Scope Loop Variables

We described this gotcha in Chapter 16's discussion of enclosing function scopes, but, as a reminder, be careful about relying on enclosing function scope lookup for variables that are changed by enclosing loops—all such references will remember the value of the last loop iteration. Use defaults to save loop variable values instead (see Chapter 16 for more details on this topic).

Chapter Summary

This chapter took us on a tour of advanced function-related concepts—lambda expression functions; generator functions with yield statements; generator expressions; apply-like call syntax; functional tools such as map, filter, and reduce; and general function design ideas. We also revisited iterators and list comprehensions here because they are just as related to functional programming as to looping statements. As a wrap-up for iteration concepts, we also measured the performance of iteration alternatives. Finally, we reviewed common function-related mistakes to help you sidestep potential pitfalls.

This concludes the functions part of this book. In the next part, we will study modules, the topmost organizational structure in Python, and the structure in which our functions always live. After that, we will explore classes, tools that are largely packages of functions with special first arguments. As we'll see, everything we have learned here will apply when functions pop up later in the book.

Before you move on, though, make sure you've mastered function basics by working through this chapter's quiz and the exercises for this part.

Chapter Quiz

1. What is the difference between enclosing a list comprehension in square brackets and parentheses?
2. How are generators and iterators related?
3. How can you tell if a function is a generator function?
4. What does a yield statement do?
5. Given a function object, and a tuple of arguments, how might you call the function?
6. How are map calls and list comprehensions related? Compare and contrast the two.
7. How are lambda expressions and def statements related? Compare and contrast the two.

Quiz Answers

1. List comprehensions in square brackets produce the result list all at once in memory. When they are enclosed in parentheses instead, they are actually generator expressions—they have a similar meaning, but do not produce the result list all at once. Instead, generator expressions return a generator object, which yields one item in the result at a time when used in an iteration context.
2. Generators are objects that support the iteration protocol—they have a next method that repeatedly advances to the next item in a series of results, and raises an exception at the end of the series. In Python, we can code generator functions with def, generator expressions with parenthesized list comprehensions, and generator objects with classes that define a special method named __iter__ (discussed later in the book).
3. A generator function has a yield statement somewhere in its code. Generator functions are otherwise identical to normal functions.
4. When present, this statement makes Python compile the function specially as a generator; when called, it returns a generator object that supports the iteration protocol. When the yield statement is run, it sends a result back to the caller, and suspends the function's state; the function can then be resumed in response to a next method call at the caller continuing after the last yield statement. Generator functions may also have a return statement, which terminates the generator.
5. You can call the function generically with the apply-like call syntax: function(*argstuple). You can also use the built-in function apply(function, args), but this built-in will likely be removed in a future Python release, and is not as general.

6. The `map` call is similar to a list comprehension—both build a new list by collecting the results of applying an operation to each item in a sequence or other iterable, one item at a time. The main difference is that `map` applies a function call to each item, and list comprehensions apply arbitrary expressions. Because of this, list comprehensions are more general; they can apply a function call expression like `map`, but `map` requires a function to apply other kinds of expressions. List comprehensions also support extended syntax such as nested `for` loops and `if` clauses that subsume the `filter` built-in.

7. Both `lambda` and `def` create function objects to be called later. Because `lambda` is an expression, though, it can be used to nest a function definition in places where a `def` will not work syntactically. Using a `lambda` is never required—you can always code a `def` instead, and reference the function by name. `lambda`s come in handy, though, to embed small pieces of deferred code that are unlikely to be used elsewhere in a program. Syntactically, a `lambda` only allows for a single return value expression; because it does not support a block of statements, it is not ideal for larger functions.

Part IV Exercises

In these exercises, you're going to start coding more sophisticated programs. Be sure to check the solutions in "Part IV, Functions" in Appendix B, and be sure to start writing your code in module files. You won't want to retype these exercises from scratch if you make a mistake.

1. *The basics.* At the Python interactive prompt, write a function that prints its single argument to the screen and call it interactively, passing a variety of object types: string, integer, list, dictionary. Then, try calling it without passing any argument. What happens? What happens when you pass two arguments?

2. *Arguments.* Write a function called adder in a Python module file. The function should accept two arguments, and return the sum (or concatenation) of the two. Then, add code at the bottom of the file to call the adder function with a variety of object types (two strings, two lists, two floating points), and run this file as a script from the system command line. Do you have to print the call statement results to see results on your screen?

3. *varargs.* Generalize the adder function you wrote in the last exercise to compute the sum of an arbitrary number of arguments, and change the calls to pass more or less than two arguments. What type is the return value sum? (Hints: a slice such as S[:0] returns an empty sequence of the same type as S, and the type built-in function can test types; but see the min examples in Chapter 16 for a simpler approach.) What happens if you pass in arguments of different types? What about passing in dictionaries?

4. *Keywords.* Change the adder function from exercise 2 to accept and sum/concatenate three arguments: def adder(good, bad, ugly). Now, provide default values for each argument, and experiment with calling the function interactively. Try passing one, two, three, and four arguments. Then, try passing keyword arguments. Does the call adder(ugly=1, good=2) work? Why? Finally, generalize the new adder to accept and sum/concatenate an arbitrary number of keyword arguments. This is similar to what you did in exercise 3, but you'll need to iterate over a dictionary, not a tuple. (Hint: the dict.keys() method returns a list you can step through with a for or while.)

5. Write a function called copyDict(dict) that copies its dictionary argument. It should return a new dictionary containing all the items in its argument. Use the dictionary keys method to iterate (or, in Python 2.2, step over a dictionary's keys without calling keys). Copying sequences is easy (X[:] makes a top-level copy); does this work for dictionaries too?

6. Write a function called addDict(dict1, dict2) that computes the union of two dictionaries. It should return a new dictionary containing all the items in both its arguments (which are assumed to be dictionaries). If the same key appears in

both arguments, feel free to pick a value from either. Test your function by writing it in a file and running the file as a script. What happens if you pass lists instead of dictionaries? How could you generalize your function to handle this case, too? (Hint: see the type built-in function used earlier.) Does the order of the arguments passed in matter?

7. *More argument-matching examples.* First, define the following six functions (either interactively or in a module file that can be imported):

```
def f1(a, b): print a, b              # Normal args

def f2(a, *b): print a, b             # Positional varargs

def f3(a, **b): print a, b            # Keyword varargs

def f4(a, *b, **c): print a, b, c     # Mixed modes

def f5(a, b=2, c=3): print a, b, c    # Defaults

def f6(a, b=2, *c): print a, b, c     # Defaults and positional varargs
```

Now, test the following calls interactively, and try to explain each result; in some cases, you'll probably need to fall back on the matching algorithm shown in Chapter 16. Do you think mixing matching modes is a good idea in general? Can you think of cases where it would be useful?

```
>>> f1(1, 2)
>>> f1(b=2, a=1)

>>> f2(1, 2, 3)
>>> f3(1, x=2, y=3)
>>> f4(1, 2, 3, x=2, y=3)

>>> f5(1)
>>> f5(1, 4)

>>> f6(1)
>>> f6(1, 3, 4)
```

8. *Primes revisited.* Recall the following code snippet from Chapter 13, which simplistically determines whether a positive integer is prime:

```
x = y / 2                        # For some y > 1
while x > 1:
    if y % x == 0:               # Remainder
        print y, 'has factor', x
        break                    # Skip else
    x = x-1
else:                            # Normal exit
    print y, 'is prime'
```

Package this code as a reusable function in a module file, and add some calls to the function at the bottom of your file. While you're at it, replace the first line's / operator with //, so it can handle floating-point numbers, too, and is immune to the true division change planned for the / operator in Python 3.0 (described in Chapter 5). What can you do about negatives, and the values 0 and 1? How about speeding this up? Your outputs should look something like this:

```
13 is prime
13.0 is prime
15 has factor 5
15.0 has factor 5.0
```

9. *List comprehensions*. Write code to build a new list containing the square roots of all the numbers in this list: [2, 4, 9, 16, 25]. Code this as a for loop first, then as a map call, and finally as a list comprehension. Use the sqrt function in the built-in math module to do the calculation (i.e., import math and say math.sqrt(x)). Of the three, which approach do you like best?

Modules

## CHAPTER 18

Modules: The Big Picture

This chapter begins our in-depth look at the Python module, the highest-level program organization unit, which packages program code and data for reuse. In concrete terms, modules usually correspond to Python program files (or extensions coded in external languages such as C, Java, or C#). Each file is a module, and modules import other modules to use the names they define. Modules are processed with two statements, and one important built-in function:

import
> Lets a client (importer) fetch a module as a whole

from
> Allows clients to fetch particular names from a module

reload
> Provides a way to reload a module's code without stopping Python

Chapter 3 introduced module fundamentals, and we've been using them ever since. Part V begins by expanding on core module concepts, then moves on to explore more advanced module usage. This first chapter offers a general look at the role of modules in overall program structure. In the next and following chapters, we'll dig into the coding details behind the theory.

Along the way, we'll flesh out module details omitted so far: you'll learn about reloads, the _ _name_ _ and _ _all_ _ attributes, package imports, and so on. Because modules and classes are really just glorified namespaces, we'll formalize namespace concepts here as well.

Why Use Modules?

In short, modules provide an easy way to organize components into a system by serving as self-contained packages of variables known as *namespaces*. All the names defined at the top level of a module file become attributes of the imported module object. As we saw in the last part of this book, imports give access to names in a module's global scope. That is, the module file's global scope morphs into the module object's attribute namespace when it is imported. Ultimately, Python's modules allow us to link individual files into a larger program system.

More specifically, from an abstract perspective, modules have at least three roles:

Code reuse
> As discussed in Chapter 3, modules let you save code in files permanently. Unlike code you type at the Python interactive prompt, which goes away when you exit Python, code in module files is persistent—it can be reloaded and rerun as many times as needed. More to the point, modules are a place to define names, known as *attributes*, that may be referenced by multiple external clients.

System namespace partitioning
> Modules are also the highest-level program organization unit in Python. Fundamentally, they are just packages of names. Modules seal up names into self-contained packages, which helps avoid name clashes—you can never see a name in another file, unless you explicitly import that file. In fact, everything "lives" in a module—code you execute and objects you create—are always implicitly enclosed in modules. Because of that, modules are natural tools for grouping system components.

Implementing shared services or data
> From an operational perspective, modules also come in handy for implementing components that are shared across a system, and hence require only a single copy. For instance, if you need to provide a global object that's used by more than one function or file, you can code it in a module that can then be imported by many clients.

For you to truly understand the role of modules in a Python system, though, we need to digress for a moment, and explore the general structure of a Python program.

Python Program Architecture

So far in this book, I've sugarcoated some of the complexity in my descriptions of Python programs. In practice, programs usually involve more than just one file; for all but the simplest scripts, your programs will take the form of multifile systems. And even if you can get by with coding a single file yourself, you will almost certainly wind up using external files that someone else has already written.

This section introduces the general architecture of Python programs—the way you divide a program into a collection of source files (a.k.a. modules) and link the parts into a whole. Along the way, we'll also explore the central concepts of Python modules, imports, and object attributes.

How to Structure a Program

Generally, a Python program consists of multiple text files containing Python *statements*. The program is structured as one main, *top-level* file, along with zero or more supplemental files known as *modules* in Python.

In Python, the top-level file contains the main flow of control of your program—this is the file you run to launch your application. The module files are libraries of tools used to collect components used by the top-level file (and possibly elsewhere). Top-level files use tools defined in module files, and modules use tools defined in other modules.

Module files generally don't do anything when run directly; rather, they define tools intended for use in other files. In Python, a file *imports* a module to gain access to the tools it defines, which are known as its *attributes* (i.e., variable names attached to objects such as functions). Ultimately, we import modules and access their attributes to use their tools.

Imports and Attributes

Let's make this a bit more concrete. Figure 18-1 sketches the structure of a Python program composed of three files: *a.py*, *b.py*, and *c.py*. The file *a.py* is chosen to be the top-level file; it will be a simple text file of statements, which is executed from top to bottom when launched. The files *b.py* and *c.py* are modules; they are simple text files of statements as well, but they are not usually launched directly. Instead, as explained previously, modules are normally imported by other files that wish to use the tools they define.

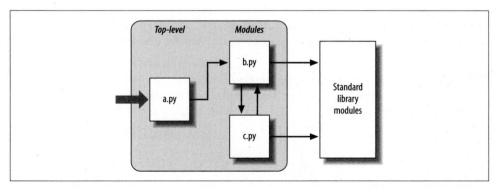

Figure 18-1. Program architecture in Python. A program is a system of modules. It has one top-level script file (launched to run the program), and multiple module files (imported libraries of tools). Scripts and modules are both text files containing Python statements, though the statements in modules usually just create objects to be used later. Python's standard library provides a collection of precoded modules.

For instance, suppose the file *b.py* in Figure 18-1 defines a function called spam, for external use. As we learned in Part IV, *b.py* will contain a Python def statement to generate the function, which can later be run by passing zero or more values in parentheses after the function's name:

```
def spam(text):
    print text, 'spam'
```

Now, suppose *a.py* wants to use spam. To this end, it might contain Python statements such as the following:

```
import b
b.spam('gumby')
```

The first of these, a Python import statement, gives the file *a.py* access to everything defined by top-level code in the file *b.py*. It roughly means "load the file *b.py* (unless it's already loaded), and give me access to all its attributes through the name b." import (and, as you'll see later, from) statements execute and load other files at runtime.

In Python, cross-file module linking is not resolved until such import statements are executed at runtime; their net effect is to assign module names—simple variables— to loaded module objects. In fact, the module name used in an import statement serves two purposes: it identifies the external file to be loaded, but it also becomes a variable assigned to the loaded module. Objects defined by a module are also created at runtime, as the import is executing: import literally runs statements in the target file one at a time to create its contents.

The second of the statements in *a.py* calls the function spam defined in the module b, using object attribute notation. The code b.spam means "fetch the value of the name spam that lives within the object b." This happens to be a callable function in our example, so we pass a string in parentheses ('gumby'). If you actually type these files, save them, and run *a.py*, the words "gumby spam" will be printed.

You'll see the object.attribute notation used throughout Python scripts—most objects have useful attributes that are fetched with the "." operator. Some are callable things like functions, and others are simple data values that give object properties (e.g., a person's name).

The notion of importing is also completely general throughout Python. Any file can import tools from any other file. For instance, the file *a.py* may import *b.py* to call its function, but *b.py* might also import *c.py* to leverage different tools defined there. Import chains can go as deep as you like: in this example, the module a can import b, which can import c, which can import b again, and so on.

Besides serving as the highest organizational structure, modules (and module packages, described in Chapter 20) are also the highest level of *code reuse* in Python. Coding components in module files makes them useful in your original program, and in any other programs you may write. For instance, if after coding the program in Figure 18-1 we discover that the function b.spam is a general-purpose tool, we can reuse it in a completely different program; all we have to do is import the file *b.py* again from the other program's files.

Standard Library Modules

Notice the rightmost portion of Figure 18-1. Some of the modules that your programs will import are provided by Python itself, and are not files you will code.

Python automatically comes with a large collection of utility modules known as the *standard library*. This collection, roughly 200 modules large at last count, contains platform-independent support for common programming tasks: operating system interfaces, object persistence, text pattern matching, network and Internet scripting, GUI construction, and much more. None of these tools are part of the Python language itself, but you can use them by importing the appropriate modules on any standard Python installation. Because they are standard library modules, you can also be reasonably sure that they will be available, and will work portably on most platforms on which you will run Python.

You will see a few of the standard library modules in action in this book's examples, but for a complete look, you should browse the standard Python library reference manual, available either with your Python installation (via IDLE or the Python Start button menu on Windows), or online at *http://www.python.org*.

Because there are so many modules, this is really the only way to get a feel for what tools are available. You can also find tutorials on Python library tools in commercial books that cover application-level programming, such as *Programming Python*, but the manuals are free, viewable in any web browser (they ship in HTML format), and updated each time Python is rereleased.

How Imports Work

The prior section talked about importing modules without really explaining what happens when you do so. Because imports are at the heart of program structure in Python, this section goes into more detail on the import operation to make this process less abstract.

Some C programmers like to compare the Python module import operation to a C #include, but they really shouldn't—in Python, imports are not just textual insertions of one file into another. They are really runtime operations that perform three distinct steps the first time a program imports a given file:

1. *Find* the module's file.
2. *Compile* it to byte code (if needed).
3. *Run* the module's code to build the objects it defines.

To better understand module imports, we'll explore these steps in turn. Bear in mind that all three of these steps are carried out only the first time a module is imported during a program's execution; later imports of the same module bypass all of these steps, and simply fetch the already loaded module object in memory.

1. Find It

First off, Python must locate the module file referenced by an `import` statement. Notice that the `import` statement in the prior section's example names the file without a *.py* suffix and without its directory path: it just says `import b`, instead of something like `import c:\dir1\b.py`. In fact, you can only list a simple name; path and suffix details are omitted on purpose, as Python uses a standard *module search path* to locate the module file corresponding to an `import` statement.[*] Because this is the main part of the import operation that programmers must know about, let's study this step in more detail.

The module search path

In many cases, you can rely on the automatic nature of the module import search path, and need not configure this path at all. If you want to be able to import files across user-defined directory boundaries, though, you will need to know how the search path works in order to customize it. Roughly, Python's module search path is composed of the concatenation of these major components, some of which are preset for you, and some of which you can tailor to tell Python where to look:

1. The home directory of the program.
2. PYTHONPATH directories (if set).
3. Standard library directories.
4. The contents of any *.pth* files (if present).

Ultimately, the concatenation of these four components becomes `sys.path`, a list of directory name strings that I'll expand upon in the next section. The first and third elements of the search path are defined automatically, but because Python searches the concatenation of these components from first to last, the second and fourth elements can be used to extend the path to include your own source code directories. Here is how Python uses each of these path components:

---

[*] It's actually syntactically illegal to include path and suffix details in a standard `import`. *Package imports*, which we'll discuss in Chapter 20, allow `import` statements to include part of the directory path leading to a file as a set of period-separated names; however, package imports still rely on the normal module search path to locate the leftmost directory in a package path (i.e., they are relative to a directory in the search path). They also cannot make use of any platform-specific directory syntax in the `import` statements; such syntax only works on the search path. Also, note that module file search path issues are not as relevant when you run *frozen executables* (discussed in Chapter 2); they typically embed byte code in the binary image.

Home directory

Python first looks for the imported file in the home directory. Depending on how you are launching code, this is either the directory containing your program's top-level file, or the directory in which you are working interactively. Because this directory is always searched first, if a program is located entirely in a single directory, all of its imports will work automatically with no path configuration required.

PYTHONPATH *directories*

Next, Python searches all directories listed in your PYTHONPATH environment variable setting, from left to right (assuming you have set this at all). In brief, PYTHONPATH is simply set to a list of user-defined and platform-specific names of directories that contain Python code files. You can add all the directories from which you wish to be able to import, and Python will use your setting to extend the module search path.

Because Python searches the home directory first, this setting is only important when importing files across directory boundaries—that is, if you need to import a file that is stored in a different directory from the file that imports it. You'll probably want to set your PYTHONPATH variable once you start writing substantial programs, but when you're first starting out, as long as you save all your module files in the directory in which you're working (i.e., the home directory), your imports will work without you needing to worry about this setting at all.

Standard library directories

Next, Python automatically searches the directories where the standard library modules are installed on your machine. Because these are always searched, they normally do not need to be added to your PYTHONPATH.

.pth file directories

Finally, a relatively new feature of Python allows users to add valid directories to the module search path by simply listing them, one per line, in a text file whose name ends with a *.pth* suffix (for "path"). These path configuration files are a somewhat advanced installation-related feature, and we will not discuss them fully here.

In short, a text file of directory names dropped in an appropriate directory can serve roughly the same role as the PYTHONPATH environment variable setting. For instance, a file named *myconfig.pth* may be placed at the top level of the Python install directory on Windows (e.g., in *C:\Python25* or *C:\Python25\Lib\site-packages*) to extend the module search path. Python will add the directories listed on each line of the file, from first to last, near the end of the module search path list. Because they are files rather than shell settings, path files can apply to all users of an installation, instead of just one user or shell.

This feature is more sophisticated than I've described here. For more details, see the Python library manual (especially its documentation for the standard library module site). I recommend that beginners use PYTHONPATH or a single *.pth* file, and then only if you must import across directories. See also Appendix A for examples of common ways to extend your module search path with PYTHONPATH or *.pth* files on various platforms.

This description of the module search path is accurate, but generic; the exact configuration of the search path is prone to changing across platforms and Python releases. Depending on your platform, additional directories may automatically be added to the module search path as well.

For instance, Python may add an entry for the *current working directory*—the directory from which you launched your program—in the search path after the PYTHONPATH directories, and before the standard library entries. When launching from a command line, the current working directory may not be the same as the home directory of your top-level file (i.e., the directory where your program file resides).* Because the current working directory can vary each time your program runs, you normally shouldn't depend on its value for import purposes.†

The sys.path list

If you want to see how the module search path is truly configured on your machine, you can always inspect the path as Python knows it by printing the built-in sys.path list (that is, the path attribute of the standard library module sys). This list of directory name strings is the actual search path within Python; on imports, Python searches each directory in this list from left to right.

Really, sys.path *is* the module search path. Python configures it at program startup, automatically merging any PYTHONPATH and *.pth* file path settings you've made into the list, and setting the first entry to identify the home directory of the top-level file (possibly as an empty string).

Python exposes this list for two good reasons. First, it provides a way to verify the search path settings you've made—if you don't see your settings somewhere in this list, you need to recheck your work. Second, if you know what you're doing, this list also provides a way for scripts to tailor their search paths manually. As you'll see later in this part of the book, by modifying the sys.path list, you can modify the search path for all future imports. Such changes only last for the duration of the script, however; PYTHONPATH and *.pth* files offer more permanent ways to modify the path.‡

---

* See Chapter 3 for more on launching programs from command lines.

† See also Chapter 21's discussion of the new *relative import syntax* in Python 2.5; this modifies the search path for from statements when "." characters are used (e.g., from . import string).

‡ Some programs really need to change sys.path, though. Scripts that run on web servers, for example, usually run as the user "nobody" to limit machine access. Because such scripts cannot usually depend on "nobody" to have set PYTHONPATH in any particular way, they often set sys.path manually to include required source directories, prior to running any import statements. A sys.path.append(dirname) will often suffice.

Module file selection

Keep in mind that filename suffixes (e.g., *.py*) are intentionally omitted from `import` statements. Python chooses the first file it can find on the search path that matches the imported name. For example, an `import` statement of the form `import b` might load:

- A source code file named *b.py*.
- A byte code file named *b.pyc*.
- A directory named *b*, for package imports (described in Chapter 20).
- A compiled extension module, usually coded in C or C++, and dynamically linked when imported (e.g., *b.so* on Linux, or *b.dll* or *b.pyd* on Cygwin and Windows).
- A compiled built-in module coded in C and statically linked into Python.
- A ZIP file component that is automatically extracted when imported.
- An in-memory image, for frozen executables.
- A Java class, in the Jython version of Python.
- A .NET component, in the IronPython version of Python.

C extensions, Jython, and package imports all extend imports beyond simple files. To importers, though, differences in the loaded file type are completely transparent, both when importing and when fetching module attributes. Saying `import b` gets whatever module b is, according to your module search path, and `b.attr` fetches an item in the module, be it a Python variable or a linked-in C function. Some standard modules we will use in this book are actually coded in C, not Python; because of this transparency, their clients don't have to care.

If you have both a *b.py* and a *b.so* in different directories, Python will always load the one found in the first (leftmost) directory of your module search path during the left-to-right search of `sys.path`. But what happens if it finds both a *b.py* and a *b.so* in the *same* directory? In this case, Python follows a standard picking order, though this order is not guaranteed to stay the same over time. In general, you should not depend on which type of file Python will choose within a given directory—make your module names distinct, or configure your module search path to make your module selection preferences more obvious.

Advanced module selection concepts

Normally, imports work as described in this section—they find and load files on your machine. However, it is possible to redefine much of what an import operation does in Python, using what are known as *import hooks*. These hooks can be used to make imports do various useful things, such as loading files from archives, performing decryption, and so on. In fact, Python itself uses these hooks to enable files to be directly imported from ZIP archives—the archived files are automatically extracted at import time when a *.zip* file is selected in the import search path. For more details, see the Python standard library manual's description of the built-in __import__ function, the customizable tool that import statements actually run.

Python also supports the notion of *.pyo* optimized byte code files, created and run with the -0 Python command-line flag; because these run only slightly faster than normal *.pyc* files (typically 5 percent faster), however, they are infrequently used. The Psyco system (see Chapter 2) provides more substantial speedups.

2. Compile It (Maybe)

After finding a source code file that matches an import statement by traversing the module search path, Python next compiles it to byte code, if necessary. (We discussed byte code in Chapter 2.)

Python checks the file timestamps and skips the source-to-byte-code compile step if it finds a *.pyc* byte code file that is not older than the corresponding *.py* source file. In addition, if Python finds only a byte code file on the search path and no source, it simply loads the byte code directly. In other words, the compile step is bypassed if possible to speed program startup. If you change the source code, Python will automatically regenerate the byte code the next time your program is run. Moreover, you can ship a program as just byte code files, and avoid sending source.

Notice that compilation happens when a file is being imported. Because of this, you will not usually see a *.pyc* byte code file for the top-level file of your program, unless it is also imported elsewhere—only imported files leave behind a *.pyc* on your machine. The byte code of top-level files is used internally and discarded; byte code of imported files is saved in files to speed future imports.

Top-level files are often designed to be executed directly and not imported at all. Later, we'll see that it is possible to design a file that serves both as the top-level code of a program, and as a module of tools to be imported. Such a file may be both executed and imported, and thus does generate a *.pyc*. To learn how this works, watch for the discussion of the special __name__ attribute and __main__ in Chapter 21.

3. Run It

The final step of an import operation executes the byte code of the module. All statements in the file are executed in turn, from top to bottom, and any assignments made to names during this step generate attributes of the resulting module object. This execution step therefore generates all the tools that the module's code defines. For instance, def statements in a file are run at import time to create functions and assign attributes within the module to those functions. The functions can then be called later in the program by the file's importers.

Because this last import step actually runs the file's code, if any top-level code in a module file does real work, you'll see its results at import time. For example, top-level print statements in a module show output when the file is imported. Function def statements simply define objects for later use.

As you can see, import operations involve quite a bit of work—they search for files, possibly run a compiler, and run Python code. Because of this, any given module is imported only once per process by default. Future imports skip all three import steps and reuse the already loaded module in memory.* If you need to import a file again after it has already been loaded (for example, to support end-user customization), you have to force the issue with a reload call—a tool we'll meet in the next chapter.

Third-Party Software: distutils

This chapter's description of module search path settings is targeted mainly at user-defined source code that you write on your own. Third-party extensions for Python typically use the distutils tools in the standard library to automatically install themselves, so no path configuration is required to use their code.

Systems that use distutils generally come with a *setup.py* script, which is run to install them; this script imports and uses distutils modules to place such systems in a directory that is automatically part of the module search path (usually in the *Lib\site-packages* subdirectory of the Python install tree, wherever that resides on the target machine).

For more details on distributing and installing with distutils, see the Python standard manual set; its use is beyond the scope of this book (for instance, it also provides ways to automatically compile C-coded extensions on the target machine). Also, see the emerging third-party open source *eggs* system, which adds dependency checking for installed Python software.

Chapter Summary

In this chapter, we covered the basics of modules, attributes, and imports, and explored the operation of import statements. We learned that imports find the designated file on the module search path, compile it to byte code, and execute all of its statements to generate its contents. We also learned how to configure the search path to be able to import from other directories than the home directory and the standard library directories, primarily with PYTHONPATH settings.

---

* Technically, Python keeps already loaded modules in the built-in sys.modules dictionary, which it checks at the start of an import operation to determine whether the referenced module is already loaded. If you want to see which modules are loaded, import sys and print sys.modules.keys( ). More on this internal table in Chapter 21.

As this chapter demonstrated, the import operation and modules are at the heart of program architecture in Python. Larger programs are divided into multiple files, which are linked together at runtime by imports. Imports in turn use the module search path to locate files, and modules define attributes for external use.

Of course, the whole point of imports and modules is to provide a structure to your program, which divides its logic into self-contained software components. Code in one module is isolated from code in another; in fact, no file can ever see the names defined in another, unless explicit import statements are run. Because of this, modules minimize name collisions between different parts of your program.

You'll see what this all means in terms of actual code in the next chapter. Before we move on, though, let's run through the chapter quiz.

Chapter Quiz

1. How does a module source code file become a module object?
2. Why might you have to set your PYTHONPATH environment variable?
3. Name the four major components of the module import search path.
4. Name four file types that Python might load in response to an import operation.
5. What is a namespace, and what does a module's namespace contain?

Quiz Answers

1. A module's source code file automatically becomes a module object when that module is imported. Technically, the module's source code is run during the import, one statement at a time, and all the names assigned in the process become attributes of the module object.

2. You only need to set PYTHONPATH to import from directories other than the one in which you are working (i.e., the current directory when working interactively, or the directory containing your top-level file).

3. The four major components of the module import search path are the top-level script's home directory (the directory containing it), all directories listed in the PYTHONPATH environment variable, standard library directories, and all directories in *.pth* path files located in standard places. Of these, programmers can customize PYTHONPATH and *.pth* files.

4. Python might load a source code (*.py*) file, a byte code (*.pyc*) file, a C extension module (e.g., a *.so* file on Linux or a *.dll* or *.pyd* file on Windows), or a directory of the same name for package imports. Imports may also load more exotic things such as ZIP file components, Java classes under the Jython version of Python, .NET components under IronPython, and statically linked C extensions that have no files present at all. With import hooks, imports can load anything.

5. A namespace is a self-contained package of variables, which are known as the attributes of the namespace object. A module's namespace contains all the names assigned by code at the top level of the module file (i.e., not nested in def or class statements). Technically, a module's global scope morphs into the module object's attributes namespace. A module's namespace may also be altered by assignments from other files that import it, though this is frowned upon (see Chapter 16 for more on this).

CHAPTER 19

Module Coding Basics

Now that we've looked at the larger ideas behind modules, let's turn to a simple example of modules in action. Python modules are easy to *create*; they're just files of Python program code created with a text editor. You don't need to write special syntax to tell Python you're making a module; almost any text file will do. Because Python handles all the details of finding and loading modules, modules are also easy to *use*; clients simply import a module, or specific names a module defines, and use the objects they reference.

Module Creation

To define a module, simply use your text editor to type some Python code into a text file, and save it with a ".py" extension; any such file is automatically considered a Python module. All the names assigned at the top level of the module become its attributes (names associated with the module object), and are exported for clients to use.

For instance, if you type the following def into a file called *module1.py* and import it, you create a module object with one attribute—the name printer, which happens to be a reference to a function object:

```
def printer(x):                    # Module attribute
    print x
```

Before we go on, I should say a few more words about module filenames. You can call modules just about anything you like, but module filenames should end in a *.py* suffix if you plan to import them. The *.py* is technically optional for top-level files that will be run but not imported, but adding it in all cases makes your files' types more obvious and allows you to import any of your files in the future.

Because module names become variable names inside a Python program (without the *.py*), they should also follow the normal variable name rules outlined in Chapter 11. For instance, you can create a module file named *if.py*, but you cannot import it because if is a reserved word—when you try to run import if, you'll get a syntax error. In fact, both the names of module files and the names of directories used in package imports (discussed in the next chapter) must conform to the rules for variable names presented in Chapter 11; they may, for instance, contain only letters, digits, and underscores. Package directories also cannot contain platform-specific syntax such as spaces in their names.

When a module is imported, Python maps the internal module name to an external filename by adding directory paths in the module search path to the front, and a *.py* or other extension at the end. For instance, a module named M ultimately maps to some external file *<directory>\M.<extension>* that contains the module's code.

As mentioned in the preceding chapter, it is also possible to create a Python module by writing code in an external language such as C or C++ (or Java, in the Jython implementation of the language). Such modules are called *extension modules*, and they are generally used to wrap up external libraries for use in Python scripts. When imported by Python code, extension modules look and feel the same as modules coded as Python source code files—they are accessed with import statements, and provide functions and objects as module attributes. Extension modules are beyond the scope of this book; see Python's standard manuals, or advanced texts such as *Programming Python* for more details.

Module Usage

Clients can use the simple module file we just wrote by running import or from statements. Both statements find, compile, and run a module file's code, if it hasn't yet been loaded. The chief difference is that import fetches the module as a whole, so you must qualify to fetch its names; in contrast, from fetches (or copies) specific names out of the module.

Let's see what this means in terms of code. All of the following examples wind up calling the printer function defined in the external module file *module1.py*, but in different ways.

The import Statement

In the first example, the name module1 serves two different purposes—it identifies an external file to be loaded, and it becomes a variable in the script, which references the module object after the file is loaded:

```
>>> import module1                      # Get module as a whole
>>> module1.printer('Hello world!')     # Qualify to get names
Hello world!
```

Because import gives a name that refers to the whole module object, we must go through the module name to fetch its attributes (e.g., module1.printer).

The from statement

By contrast, because `from` also copies names from one file over to another scope, it allows us to use the copied names directly in the script without going through the module (e.g., printer):

```
>>> from module1 import printer       # Copy out one variable
>>> printer('Hello world!')           # No need to qualify name
Hello world!
```

This has the same effect as the prior example, but because the imported name is copied into the scope where the `from` statement appears, using that name in the script requires less typing: we can use it directly instead of naming the enclosing module.

As you'll see in more detail later, the `from` statement is really just a minor extension to the `import` statement—it imports the module file as usual, but adds an extra step that copies one or more names out of the file.

The from * Statement

Finally, the next example uses a special form of `from`: when we use a `*`, we get copies of *all* the names assigned at the top level of the referenced module. Here again, we can then use the copied name `printer` in our script without going through the module name:

```
>>> from module1 import *             # Copy out all variables
>>> printer('Hello world!')
Hello world!
```

Technically, both `import` and `from` statements invoke the same import operation; the `from *` form simply adds an extra step that copies all the names in the module into the importing scope. It essentially collapses one module's namespace into another; again, the net effect is less typing for us.

And that's it—modules really are simple to use. To give you a better understanding of what really happens when you define and use modules, though, let's move on to look at some of their properties in more detail.

Imports Happen Only Once

One of the most common questions beginners seem to ask when using modules is, "Why won't my imports keep working?" They often report that the first import works fine, but later imports during an interactive session (or program run) seem to have no effect. In fact, they're not supposed to, and here's why.

Modules are loaded and run on the first `import` or `from`, and only the first. This is on purpose—because this is an expensive operation, by default, Python does it just once per file, per process. Later import operations simply fetch the already loaded module object.

As one consequence, because top-level code in a module file is usually executed only once, you can use it to initialize variables. Consider the file *simple.py*, for example:

```
print 'hello'
spam = 1                          # Initialize variable
```

In this example, the print and = statements run the first time the module is imported, and the variable spam is initialized at import time:

```
% python
>>> import simple          # First import: loads and runs file's code
hello
>>> simple.spam            # Assignment makes an attribute
1
```

Second and later imports don't rerun the module's code; they just fetch the already created module object from Python's internal modules table. Thus, the variable spam is not reinitialized:

```
>>> simple.spam = 2        # Change attribute in module
>>> import simple          # Just fetches already loaded module
>>> simple.spam            # Code wasn't rerun: attribute unchanged
2
```

Of course, sometimes you really want a module's code to be rerun on a subsequent import. We'll see how to do this with the reload built-in function later in this chapter.

import and from Are Assignments

Just like def, import and from are executable statements, not compile-time declarations. They may be nested in if tests, appear in function defs, and so on, and they are not resolved or run until Python reaches them while executing your program. In other words, imported modules and names are not available until their associated import or from statements run. Also, like def, import and from are implicit assignments:

- import assigns an entire module object to a single name.
- from assigns one or more names to objects of the same names in another module.

All the things we've already discussed about assignment apply to module access, too. For instance, names copied with a from become references to shared objects; as with function arguments, reassigning a fetched name has no effect on the module from which it was copied, but changing a fetched *mutable object* can change it in the module from which it was imported. To illustrate, consider the following file, *small.py*:

```
x = 1
y = [1, 2]

% python
>>> from small import x, y        # Copy two names out
>>> x = 42                        # Changes local x only
>>> y[0] = 42                     # Changes shared mutable in-place
```

Here, x is not a shared mutable object, but y is. The name y in the importer and the importee reference the same list object, so changing it from one place changes it in the other:

```
>>> import small                 # Get module name (from doesn't)
>>> small.x                      # Small's x is not my x
1
>>> small.y                      # But we share a changed mutable
[42, 2]
```

For a graphical picture of what from assignments do with references, flip back to Figure 16-2 (function argument passing), and mentally replace "caller" and "function" with "imported" and "importer." The effect is the same, except that here we're dealing with names in modules, not functions. Assignment works the same everywhere in Python.

Cross-File Name Changes

Recall from the prior example that the assignment to x in the interactive session changed the name x in that scope only, not the x in the file—there is no link from a name copied with from back to the file it came from. To really change a global name in another file, you must use import:

```
% python
>>> from small import x, y       # Copy two names out
>>> x = 42                       # Changes my x only

>>> import small                 # Get module name
>>> small.x = 42                 # Changes x in other module
```

This phenomenon was introduced in Chapter 16. Because changing variables in other modules like this is a common source of confusion (and often a bad design choice), we'll revisit this technique again later in this part of the book. Note that the change to y[0] in the prior session is different; it changes an object, not a name.

import and from Equivalence

Notice in the prior example that we have to execute an import statement after the from to access the small module name at all; from only copies names from one module to another, and does not assign the module name itself. At least conceptually, a from statement like this one:

```
from module import name1, name2    # Copy these two names out (only)
```

is equivalent to this statement sequence:

```
import module                      # Fetch the module object
name1 = module.name1               # Copy names out by assignment
name2 = module.name2
del module                         # Get rid of the module name
```

Like all assignments, the from statement creates new variables in the importer, which initially refer to objects of the same names in the imported file. Only the names are copied out, though, not the module itself. When we use the from * form of this statement (from module import *), the equivalence is the same, but all the top-level names in the module are copied over to the importing scope this way.

Notice that the first step of the from runs a normal import operation. Because of this, the from always imports the entire module into memory if it has not yet been imported, regardless of how many names it copies out of the file. There is no way to load just part of a module file (e.g., just one function), but because modules are byte code in Python instead of machine code, the performance implications are generally negligible.

Potential Pitfalls of the from Statement

Because the from statement makes the location of a variable more implicit and obscure (name is less meaningful to the reader than module.name), some Python users recommend using import instead of from most of the time. I'm not sure this advice is warranted, though; from is commonly and widely used, without too many dire consequences. In practice, in realistic programs, it's often convenient not to have to type a module's name every time you wish to use one of its tools. This is especially true for large modules that provide many attributes—the standard library's Tkinter GUI module, for example.

It is true that the from statement has the potential to corrupt namespaces, at least in principle—if you use it to import variables that happen to have the same names as existing variables in your scope, your variables will be silently overwritten. This problem doesn't occur with the simple import statement because you must always go through a module's name to get to its contents (module.attr will not clash with a variable named attr in your scope). As long as you understand and expect that this can happen when using from, though, this isn't a major concern in practice, especially if you list the imported names explicitly (e.g., from module import x, y, z).

On the other hand, the from statement has more serious issues when used in conjunction with the reload call, as imported names might reference prior versions of objects. Moreover, the from module import * form really can corrupt namespaces and make names difficult to understand, especially when applied to more than one file—in this case, there is no way to tell which module a name came from, short of searching the external source files. In effect, the from * form collapses one namespace into another, and so defeats the namespace partitioning feature of modules. We will explore these issues in more detail in the "Module Gotchas" section at the end of this part of the book (see Chapter 21).

Probably the best real-world advice here is to generally prefer `import` to `from` for simple modules, to explicitly list the variables you want in most `from` statements, and to limit the `from *` form to just one import per file. That way, any undefined names can be assumed to live in the module referenced with the `from *`. Some care is required when using the `from` statement, but armed with a little knowledge, most programmers find it to be a convenient way to access modules.

When import is required

The only time you really must use `import` instead of `from` is when you must use the same name defined in two different modules. For example, if two files define the same name differently:

```
# M.py

def func():
    ...do something...

# N.py

def func():
    ...do something else...
```

and you must use both versions of the name in your program, the `from` statement will fail—you can only have one assignment to the name in your scope:

```
# O.py

from M import func
from N import func            # This overwites the one we got from M
func()                        # Calls N.func only
```

An `import` will work here, though, because including the name of the enclosing module makes the two names unique:

```
# O.py

import M, N                   # Get the whole modules, not their names
M.func()                      # We can call both names now
N.func()                      # The module names make them unique
```

This case is unusual enough that you're unlikely to encounter it very often in practice.

Module Namespaces

Modules are probably best understood as simply packages of names—i.e., places to define names you want to make visible to the rest of a system. Technically, modules usually correspond to files, and Python creates a module object to contain all the names assigned in a module file. But, in simple terms, modules are just namespaces (places where names are created), and the names that live in a module are called its attributes. We'll explore how all this works in this section.

Files Generate Namespaces

So, how do files morph into namespaces? The short story is that every name that is assigned a value at the top level of a module file (i.e., not nested in a function or class body) becomes an attribute of that module.

For instance, given an assignment statement such as X = 1 at the top level of a module file *M.py*, the name X becomes an attribute of M, which we can refer to from outside the module as M.X. The name X also becomes a global variable to other code inside *M.py*, but we need to explain the notion of module loading and scopes a bit more formally to understand why:

- **Module statements run on the first import.** The first time a module is imported anywhere in a system, Python creates an empty module object, and executes the statements in the module file one after another, from the top of the file to the bottom.

- **Top-level assignments create module attributes.** During an import, statements at the top level of the file not nested in a def or class that assign names (e.g., =, def) create attributes of the module object; assigned names are stored in the module's namespace.

- **Module namespaces can be accessed via the attribute __dict__ or dir(M).** Module namespaces created by imports are dictionaries; they may be accessed through the built-in __dict__ attribute associated with module objects and may be inspected with the dir function. The dir function is roughly equivalent to the sorted keys list of an object's __dict__ attribute, but it includes inherited names for classes, may not be complete, and is prone to changing from release to release.

- **Modules are a single scope (local is global).** As we saw in Chapter 16, names at the top level of a module follow the same reference/assignment rules as names in a function, but the local and global scopes are the same (more formally, they follow the LEGB scope rule we met in Chapter 16, but without the L and E lookup layers). But, in modules, the module *scope* becomes an attribute dictionary of a module *object* after the module has been loaded. Unlike with functions (where the local namespace exists only while the function runs), a module file's scope becomes a module object's attribute namespace and lives on after the import.

Here's a demonstration of these ideas. Suppose we create the following module file in a text editor and call it *module2.py*:

```
print 'starting to load...'

import sys
name = 42

def func( ): pass

class klass: pass

print 'done loading.'
```

The first time this module is imported (or run as a program), Python executes its statements from top to bottom. Some statements create names in the module's namespace as a side effect, but others may do actual work while the import is going on. For instance, the two print statements in this file execute at import time:

```
>>> import module2
starting to load...
done loading.
```

But once the module is loaded, its scope becomes an attribute namespace in the module object we get back from import. We can then access attributes in this namespace by qualifying them with the name of the enclosing module:

```
>>> module2.sys
<module 'sys' (built-in)>

>>> module2.name
42

>>> module2.func
<function func at 0x012B1830>

>>> module2.klass
<class module2.klass at 0x011C0BA0>
```

Here, sys, name, func, and klass were all assigned while the module's statements were being run, so they are attributes after the import. We'll talk about classes in Part VI, but notice the sys attribute—import statements really *assign* module objects to names, and any type of assignment to a name at the top level of a file generates a module attribute.

Internally, module namespaces are stored as dictionary objects. These are just normal dictionary objects with the usual methods. We can access a module's namespace dictionary through the module's __dict__ attribute:

```
>>> module2.__dict__.keys()
['__file__', 'name', '__name__', 'sys', '__doc__', '__builtins__',
'klass', 'func']
```

The names we assigned in the module file become dictionary keys internally, so most of the names here reflect top-level assignments in our file. However, Python also adds some names in the module's namespace for us; for instance, __file__ gives the name of the file the module was loaded from, and __name__ gives its name as known to importers (without the *.py* extension and directory path).

Attribute Name Qualification

Now that you're becoming more familiar with modules, we should look at the notion of name *qualification* in more depth. In Python, you can access the attributes of any object that has attributes using the qualification syntax object.attribute.

Qualification is really an expression that returns the value assigned to an attribute name associated with an object. For example, the expression `module2.sys` in the previous example fetches the value assigned to `sys` in `module2`. Similarly, if we have a built-in list object `L`, `L.append` returns the append method object associated with that list.

So, what does attribute qualification do to the scope rules we studied in Chapter 16? Nothing, really: it's an independent concept. When you use qualification to access names, you give Python an explicit object from which to fetch the specified names. The LEGB rule applies only to bare, unqualified names. Here are the rules:

Simple variables
> `X` means search for the name `X` in the current scopes (following the LEGB rule).

Qualification
> `X.Y` means find `X` in the current scopes, then search for the attribute `Y` in the object `X` (not in scopes).

Qualification paths
> `X.Y.Z` means look up the name `Y` in the object `X`, then look up `Z` in the object `X.Y`.

Generality
> Qualification works on all objects with attributes: modules, classes, C extension types, etc.

In Part VI, we'll see that qualification means a bit more for classes (it's also the place where something called *inheritance* happens), but, in general, the rules outlined here apply to all names in Python.

Imports Versus Scopes

As we've learned, it is never possible to access names defined in another module file without first importing that file. That is, you never automatically get to see names in another file, regardless of the structure of imports or function calls in your program. A variable's meaning is always determined by the locations of assignments in your source code, and attributes are always requested of an object explicitly.

For example, consider the following two simple modules. The first, *moda.py*, defines a variable X global to code in its file only, along with a function that changes the global X in this file:

```
X = 88                    # My X: global to this file only

def f():
    global X              # Change this file's X
    X = 99                # Cannot see names in other modules
```

The second module, *modb.py*, defines its own global variable X, and imports and calls the function in the first module:

```
X = 11                          # My X: global to this file only

import moda                     # Gain access to names in moda
moda.f()                        # Sets moda.X, not this file's X
print X, moda.X
```

When run, `moda.f` changes the X in moda, not the X in modb. The global scope for `moda.f` is always the file enclosing it, regardless of which module it is ultimately called from:

```
% python modb.py
11 99
```

In other words, import operations never give upward visibility to code in imported files—an imported file cannot see names in the importing file. More formally:

- Functions can never see names in other functions, unless they are physically enclosing.

- Module code can never see names in other modules, unless they are explicitly imported.

Such behavior is part of the *lexical scoping* notion—in Python, the scopes surrounding a piece of code are completely determined by the code's physical position in your file. Scopes are never influenced by function calls or module imports.[*]

Namespace Nesting

In some sense, although imports do not nest namespaces upward, they do nest downward. Using attribute qualification paths, it's possible to descend into arbitrarily nested modules and access their attributes. For example, consider the next three files. *mod3.py* defines a single global name and attribute by assignment:

```
X = 3
```

mod2.py in turn defines its own X, then imports mod3 and uses qualification to access the imported module's attribute:

```
X = 2
import mod3

print X,                        # My global X
print mod3.X                    # mod3's X
```

mod1.py also defines its own X, then imports mod2, and fetches attributes in both the first and second files:

---

[*] Some languages act differently and provide for *dynamic scoping*, where scopes really may depend on runtime calls. This tends to make code trickier, though, because the meaning of a variable can differ over time.

```
X = 1
import mod2

print X,                    # My global X
print mod2.X,               # mod2's X
print mod2.mod3.X           # Nested mod3's X
```

Really, when mod1 imports mod2 here, it sets up a two-level namespace nesting. By using the path of names mod2.mod3.X, it can descend into mod3, which is nested in the imported mod2. The net effect is that mod1 can see the Xs in all three files, and hence has access to all three global scopes:

```
% python mod1.py
2 3
1 2 3
```

The reverse, however, is not true: mod3 cannot see names in mod2, and mod2 cannot see names in mod1. This example may be easier to grasp if you don't think in terms of namespaces and scopes, but instead focus on the objects involved. Within mod1, mod2 is just a name that refers to an object with attributes, some of which may refer to other objects with attributes (import is an assignment). For paths like mod2.mod3.X, Python simply evaluates from left to right, fetching attributes from objects along the way.

Note that mod1 can say import mod2, and then mod2.mod3.X, but it cannot say import mod2.mod3—this syntax invokes something called package (directory) imports, described in the next chapter. Package imports also create module namespace nesting, but their import statements are taken to reflect directory trees, not simple import chains.

Reloading Modules

As we've seen, a module's code is run only once per process by default. To force a module's code to be reloaded and rerun, you need to ask Python to do so explicitly by calling the reload built-in function. In this section, we'll explore how to use reloads to make your systems more dynamic. In a nutshell:

- Imports (via both import and from statements) load and run a module's code only the first time the module is imported in a process.

- Later imports use the already loaded module object without reloading or rerunning the file's code.

- The reload function forces an already loaded module's code to be reloaded and rerun. Assignments in the file's new code change the existing module object in-place.

Why all the fuss about reloading modules? The reload function allows parts of a program to be changed without stopping the whole program. With reload, therefore, the effects of changes in components can be observed immediately. Reloading doesn't help in every situation, but where it does, it makes for a much shorter development cycle. For instance, imagine a database program that must connect to a server on startup; because program changes or customizations can be tested immediately after reloads, you need to connect only once while debugging.

Because Python is interpreted (more or less), it already gets rid of the compile/link steps you need to go through to get a C program to run: modules are loaded dynamically when imported by a running program. Reloading offers a further performance advantage by allowing you to also change parts of running programs without stopping. Note that `reload` currently only works on modules written in Python; compiled extension modules coded in a language such as C can be dynamically loaded at runtime, too, but they can't be reloaded.

reload Basics

Unlike `import` and `from`:

- `reload` is a built-in function in Python, not a statement.
- `reload` is passed an existing module object, not a name.

Because `reload` expects an object, a module must have been previously imported successfully before you can reload it (if the import was unsuccessful, due to a syntax or other error, you may need to repeat it before you can reload the module). Furthermore, the syntax of `import` statements and `reload` calls differs: reloads require parentheses, but imports do not. Reloading looks like this:

```
import module                    # Initial import
...use module.attributes...
...                              # Now, go change the module file
...
reload(module)                   # Get updated exports
...use module.attributes...
```

The typical usage pattern is that you import a module, then change its source code in a text editor, and then reload it. When you call `reload`, Python rereads the module file's source code, and reruns its top-level statements. Perhaps the most important thing to know about `reload` is that it changes a module object *in-place*; it does not delete and re-create the module object. Because of that, every reference to a module object anywhere in your program is automatically affected by a reload. Here are the details:

- **reload runs a module file's new code in the module's current namespace.** Rerunning a module file's code overwrites its existing namespace, rather than deleting and re-creating it.
- **Top-level assignments in the file replace names with new values.** For instance, rerunning a `def` statement replaces the prior version of the function in the module's namespace by reassigning the function name.

- **Reloads impact all clients that use import to fetch modules.** Because clients that use import qualify to fetch attributes, they'll find new values in the module object after a reload.

- **Reloads impact future from clients only.** Clients that used from to fetch attributes in the past won't be affected by a reload; they'll still have references to the old objects fetched before the reload.

reload Example

Here's a more concrete example of reload in action. In the following example, we'll change and reload a module file without stopping the interactive Python session. Reloads are used in many other scenarios, too (see the sidebar "Why You Will Care: Module Reloads"), but we'll keep things simple for illustration here. First, in the text editor of your choice, write a module file named *changer.py* with the following contents:

```
message = "First version"

def printer():
    print message
```

This module creates and exports two names—one bound to a string, and another to a function. Now, start the Python interpreter, import the module, and call the function it exports. The function will print the value of the global message variable:

```
% python
>>> import changer
>>> changer.printer()
First version
```

Keeping the interpreter active, now edit the module file in another window:

```
...modify changer.py without stopping Python...
% vi changer.py
```

Change the global message variable, as well as the printer function body:

```
message = "After editing"

def printer():
    print 'reloaded:', message
```

Then, return to the Python window, and reload the module to fetch the new code. Notice in the following interaction that importing the module again has no effect; we get the original message, even though the file's been changed. We have to call reload in order to get the new version:

```
...back to the Python interpreter/program...

>>> import changer
>>> changer.printer()          # No effect: uses loaded module
First version
```

```
>>> reload(changer)              # Forces new code to load/run
<module 'changer'>
>>> changer.printer()            # Runs the new version now
reloaded: After editing
```

Notice that reload actually returns the module object for us—its result is usually ignored, but because expression results are printed at the interactive prompt, Python shows a default <module 'name'> representation.

Why You Will Care: Module Reloads

Besides allowing you to reload (and hence rerun) modules at the interactive prompt, module reloads are also useful in larger systems, especially when the cost of restarting the entire application is prohibitive. For instance, systems that must connect to servers over a network on startup are prime candidates for dynamic reloads.

They're also useful in GUI work (a widget's callback action can be changed while the GUI remains active), and when Python is used as an embedded language in a C or C++ program (the enclosing program can request a reload of the Python code it runs, without having to stop). See *Programming Python* for more on reloading GUI callbacks and embedded Python code.

More generally, reloads allow programs to provide highly dynamic interfaces. For instance, Python is often used as a *customization* language for larger systems—users can customize products by coding bits of Python code on-site, without having to recompile the entire product (or even having its source code at all). In such worlds, the Python code already adds a dynamic flavor by itself.

To be even more dynamic, though, such systems can automatically reload the Python customization code periodically at runtime. That way, users' changes are picked up while the system is running; there is no need to stop and restart each time the Python code is modified. Not all systems require such a dynamic approach, but for those that do, module reloads provide an easy-to-use dynamic customization tool.

Chapter Summary

This chapter delved into the basics of module coding tools—the import and from statements, and the reload call. We learned how the from statement simply adds an extra step that copies names out of a file after it has been imported, and how reload forces a file to be imported again without stopping and restarting Python. We also surveyed namespace concepts, saw what happens when imports are nested, explored the way files become module namespaces, and learned about some potential pitfalls of the from statement.

Although we've already seen enough to handle module files in our programs, the next chapter extends our coverage of the import model by presenting package imports—a way for our `import` statements to specify part of the directory path leading to the desired module. As we'll see, package imports give us a hierarchy that is useful in larger systems, and allow us to break conflicts between same-named modules. Before we move on, though, here's a quick quiz on the concepts presented here.

Chapter Quiz

1. How do you make a module?
2. How is the `from` statement related to the `import` statement?
3. How is the `reload` function related to imports?
4. When must you use `import` instead of `from`?
5. Name three potential pitfalls of the `from` statement.
6. What is the airspeed velocity of an unladen swallow?

Quiz Answers

1. To create a module, you just write a text file containing Python statements; every source code file is automatically a module, and there is no syntax for declaring one. Import operations load module files into module objects in memory. You can also make a module by writing code in an external language like C or Java, but such extension modules are beyond the scope of this book.

2. The `from` statement imports an entire module, like the `import` statement, but as an extra step, it also copies one or more variables from the imported module into the scope where the `from` appears. This enables you to use the imported names directly (name) instead of having to go through the module (module.name).

3. By default, a module is imported only once per process. The `reload` function forces a module to be imported again. It is mostly used to pick up new versions of a module's source code during development, and in dynamic customization scenarios.

4. You must use `import` instead of `from` only when you need to access the same name in two different modules; because you'll have to specify the names of the enclosing modules, the two names will be unique.

5. The `from` statement can obscure the meaning of a variable (which module it is defined in), can have problems with the `reload` call (names may reference prior versions of objects), and can corrupt namespaces (it might silently overwrite names you are using in your scope). The `from *` form is worse in most regards— it can seriously corrupt namespaces, and obscure the meaning of variables; it is probably best used sparingly.

6. What do you mean? An African or European swallow?

## CHAPTER 20

Module Packages

So far, when we've imported modules, we've been loading files. This represents typical module usage, and is probably the technique you'll use for most imports you'll code early on in your Python career. However, the module import story is a bit richer than I have thus far implied.

In addition to a module name, an import can name a directory path. A directory of Python code is said to be a *package*, so such imports are known as *package imports*. In effect, a package import turns a directory on your computer into another Python namespace, with attributes corresponding to the subdirectories and module files that the directory contains.

This is a somewhat advanced feature, but the hierarchy it provides turns out to be handy for organizing the files in a large system, and tends to simplify module search path settings. As we'll see, package imports are also sometimes required to resolve import ambiguities when multiple program files of the same name are installed on a single machine.

Package Import Basics

So, how do package imports work? In the place where you have been naming a simple file in your import statements, you can instead list a path of names separated by periods:

```
import dir1.dir2.mod
```

The same goes for from statements:

```
from dir1.dir2.mod import x
```

The "dotted" path in these statements is assumed to correspond to a path through the directory hierarchy on your machine, leading to the file *mod.py* (or similar; the extension may vary). That is, the preceding statements indicate that on your machine there is a directory *dir1*, which has a subdirectory *dir2*, which contains a module file *mod.py* (or similar).

Furthermore, these imports imply that *dir1* resides within some container directory *dir0*, which is accessible on the Python module search path. In other words, the two import statements imply a directory structure that looks something like this (shown with DOS backslash separators):

```
dir0\dir1\dir2\mod.py          # Or mod.pyc, mod.so, etc.
```

The container directory *dir0* needs to be added to your module search path (unless it's the home directory of the top-level file), exactly as if *dir1* were a module file. From there down, the import statements in your script give the directory paths leading to the modules explicitly.

Packages and Search Path Settings

If you use this feature, keep in mind that the directory paths in your import statements can only be variables separated by periods. You cannot use any platform-specific path syntax in your import statements, such as C:\dir1, My Documents.dir2, or ../dir1—these do not work syntactically. Instead, use platform-specific syntax in your module search path settings to name the container directories.

For instance, in the prior example, *dir0*—the directory name you add to your module search path—can be an arbitrarily long and platform-specific directory path leading up to *dir1*. Instead of using an invalid statement like this:

```
import C:\mycode\dir1\dir2\mod          # Error: illegal syntax
```

add *C:\mycode* to your PYTHONPATH variable or a *.pth* file (assuming it is not the program's home directory, in which case this step is not necessary), and say this:

```
import dir1.dir2.mod
```

In effect, entries on the module search path provide platform-specific directory path prefixes, which lead to the leftmost names in import statements. Import statements provide directory path tails in a platform-neutral fashion.*

Package _ _init_ _.py Files

If you choose to use package imports, there is one more constraint you must follow: each directory named within the path of a package import statement must contain a file named _ _init_ _.py, or your package imports will fail. That is, in the example we've been using, both *dir1* and *dir2* must contain a file called _ _init_ _.py; the container directory *dir0* does not require such a file because it's not listed in the import statement itself. More formally, for a directory structure such as this:

---

* The dot path syntax was chosen partly for platform neutrality, but also because paths in import statements become real nested object paths. This syntax also means that you get odd error messages if you forget to omit the *.py* in your import statements. For example, import mod.py is assumed to be a directory path import—it loads *mod.py*, then tries to load a *mod\py.py*, and ultimately issues a potentially confusing error message.

⟹   dir0\dir1\dir2\mod.py

and an import statement of the form:

⟹   import dir1.dir2.mod

the following rules apply:

- *dir1* and *dir2* both must contain an *__init__.py* file.
- *dir0*, the container, does not require an *__init__.py* file; this file will simply be ignored if present.
- *dir0*, not *dir0\dir1*, must be listed on the module search path (i.e., it must be the home directory, or be listed in your PYTHONPATH, etc.).

The net effect is that this example's directory structure should be as follows, with indentation designating directory nesting:

⟹
```
dir0\                       # Container on module search path
    dir1\
        __init__.py
        dir2\
            __init__.py
            mod.py
```

The *__init__.py* files can contain Python code, just like normal module files. They are partly present as a declaration to Python, however, and can be completely empty. As declarations, these files serve to prevent directories with common names from unintentionally hiding true modules that appear later on the module search path. Without this safeguard, Python might pick a directory that has nothing to do with your code, just because it appears in an earlier directory on the search path.

More generally, the *__init__.py* file serves as a hook for package initialization-time actions, generates a module namespace for a directory, and implements the behavior of from * (i.e., from ... import *) statements when used with directory imports:

Package initialization

The first time Python imports through a directory, it automatically runs all the code in the directory's *__init__.py* file. Because of that, these files are a natural place to put code to initialize the state required by files in the package. For instance, a package might use its initialization file to create required data files, open connections to databases, and so on. Typically, *__init__.py* files are not meant to be useful if executed directly; they are run automatically when a package is first accessed.

Module namespace initialization

In the package import model, the directory paths in your script become real nested object paths after an import. For instance, in the preceding example, after the import, the expression dir1.dir2 works and returns a module object whose namespace contains all the names assigned by *dir2*'s *__init__.py* file. Such files provide a namespace for module objects created for directories, which have no real associated module files.

from * *statement behavior*

As an advanced feature, you can use _ _all_ _ lists in _ _*init*_ _.py files to define what is exported when a directory is imported with the from * statement form. (We'll meet _ _all_ _ in Chapter 21.) In an _ _*init*_ _.py file, the _ _all_ _ list is taken to be the list of submodule names that should be imported when from * is used on the package (directory) name. If _ _all_ _ is not set, the from * statement does not automatically load submodules nested in the directory; instead, it loads just names defined by assignments in the directory's _ _*init*_ _.py file, including any submodules explicitly imported by code in this file. For instance, the statement from submodule import X in a directory's _ _*init*_ _.py makes the name X available in that directory's namespace.

You can also simply leave these files empty, if their roles are beyond your needs. They must exist, though, for your directory imports to work at all.

Package Import Example

Let's actually code the example we've been talking about to show how initialization files and paths come into play. The following three files are coded in a directory *dir1*, and its subdirectory *dir2*:

```
# File: dir1\__init__.py
print 'dir1 init'
x = 1

# File: dir1\dir2\__init__.py
print 'dir2 init'
y = 2

# File: dir1\dir2\mod.py
print 'in mod.py'
z = 3
```

Here, *dir1* will either be a subdirectory of the one we're working in (i.e., the home directory), or a subdirectory of a directory that is listed on the module search path (technically, on sys.path). Either way, *dir1*'s container does not need an _ _*init*_ _.py file.

import statements run each directory's initialization file the first time that directory is traversed, as Python descends the path; print statements are included here to trace their execution. Also, as with module files, an already imported directory may be passed to reload to force re-execution of that single item. As shown here, reload accepts a dotted path name to reload nested directories and files:

```
% python
>>> import dir1.dir2.mod        # First imports run init files
dir1 init
dir2 init
in mod.py
>>>
```

```
>>> import dir1.dir2.mod          # Later imports do not
>>>
>>> reload(dir1)
dir1 init
<module 'dir1' from 'dir1\__init__.pyc'>
>>>
>>> reload(dir1.dir2)
dir2 init
<module 'dir1.dir2' from 'dir1\dir2\__init__.pyc'>
```

Once imported, the path in your import statement becomes a *nested object path* in your script. Here, mod is an object nested in the object dir2, which in turn is nested in the object dir1:

```
>>> dir1
<module 'dir1' from 'dir1\__init__.pyc'>
>>> dir1.dir2
<module 'dir1.dir2' from 'dir1\dir2\__init__.pyc'>
>>> dir1.dir2.mod
<module 'dir1.dir2.mod' from 'dir1\dir2\mod.pyc'>
```

In fact, each directory name in the path becomes a variable assigned to a module object whose namespace is initialized by all the assignments in that directory's *__init__.py* file. dir1.x refers to the variable x assigned in *dir1__init__.py*, much as mod.z refers to the variable z assigned in *mod.py*:

```
>>> dir1.x
1
>>> dir1.dir2.y
2
>>> dir1.dir2.mod.z
3
```

from Versus import with Packages

import statements can be somewhat inconvenient to use with packages because you may have to retype the paths frequently in your program. In the prior section's example, for instance, you must retype and rerun the full path from dir1 each time you want to reach z. If you try to access dir2 or mod directly, you'll get an error:

```
>>> dir2.mod
NameError: name 'dir2' is not defined
>>> mod.z
NameError: name 'mod' is not defined
```

It's often more convenient, therefore, to use the from statement with packages to avoid retyping the paths at each access. Perhaps more importantly, if you ever restructure your directory tree, the from statement requires just one path update in your code, whereas the import may require many. The import as extension, discussed in the next chapter, can also help here by providing a shorter synonym for the full path:

```
% python
>>> from dir1.dir2 import mod        # Code path here only
dir1 init
dir2 init
in mod.py
>>> mod.z                            # Don't repeat path
3
>>> from dir1.dir2.mod import z
>>> z
3
>>> import dir1.dir2.mod as mod      # Use shorter name
>>> mod.z
3
```

Why Use Package Imports?

If you're new to Python, make sure that you've mastered simple modules before stepping up to packages, as they are a somewhat advanced feature. They do serve useful roles, though, especially in larger programs: they make imports more informative, serve as an organizational tool, simplify your module search path, and can resolve ambiguities.

First of all, because package imports give some directory information in program files, they both make it easier to locate your files and serve as an organizational tool. Without package paths, you must often resort to consulting the module search path to find files. Moreover, if you organize your files into subdirectories for functional areas, package imports make it more obvious what role a module plays, and so make your code more readable. For example, a normal import of a file in a directory somewhere on the module search path, like this:

```
import utilities
```

offers much less information than an import that includes the path:

```
import database.client.utilities
```

Package imports can also greatly simplify your PYTHONPATH and *.pth* file search path settings. In fact, if you use package imports for all your cross-directory imports, and you make those package imports relative to a common root directory, where all your Python code is stored, you really only need a single entry on your search path: the common root. Finally, package imports serve to resolve ambiguities by making explicit exactly which files you want to import. The next section explores this role in more detail.

A Tale of Three Systems

The only time package imports are actually required is to resolve ambiguities that may arise when multiple programs with same-named files are installed on a single machine. This is something of an install issue, but it can also become a concern in general practice. Let's turn to a hypothetical scenario to illustrate.

Suppose that a programmer develops a Python program that contains a file called *utilities.py* for common utility code, and a top-level file named *main.py* that users launch to start the program. All over this program, its files say import utilities to load and use the common code. When the program is shipped, it arrives as a single *.tar* or *.zip* file containing all the program's files, and when it is installed, it unpacks all its files into a single directory named *system1* on the target machine:

```
system1\
    utilities.py          # Common utility functions, classes
    main.py               # Launch this to start the program
    other.py              # Import utilities to load my tools
```

Now, suppose that a second programmer develops a different program with files also called *utilities.py* and *main.py*, and again uses import utilities throughout the program to load the common code file. When this second system is fetched and installed on the same computer as the first system, its files will unpack into a new directory called *system2* somewhere on the receiving machine so that they do not overwrite same-named files from the first system:

```
system2\
    utilities.py          # Common utilities
    main.py               # Launch this to run
    other.py              # Imports utilities
```

So far, there's no problem: both systems can coexist and run on the same machine. In fact, you won't even need to configure the module search path to use these programs on your computer—because Python always searches the home directory first (that is, the directory containing the top-level file), imports in either system's files will automatically see all the files in that system's directory. For instance, if you click on *system1\main.py*, all imports will search *system1* first. Similarly, if you launch *system2\main.py*, *system2* will be searched first instead. Remember, module search path settings are only needed to import across directory boundaries.

However, suppose that after you've installed these two programs on your machine, you decide that you'd like to use some of the code in each of the *utilities.py* files in a system of your own. It's common utility code, after all, and Python code by nature wants to be reused. In this case, you want to be able to say the following from code that you're writing in a third directory to load one of the two files:

```
import utilities
utilities.func('spam')
```

Now the problem starts to materialize. To make this work at all, you'll have to set the module search path to include the directories containing the *utilities.py* files. But which directory do you put first in the path—*system1* or *system2?*

The problem is the *linear* nature of the search path. It is always scanned from left to right, so no matter how long you ponder this dilemma, you will always get *utilities.py* from the directory listed first (leftmost) on the search path. As is, you'll never be able to import it from the other directory at all. You could try changing sys.path within your script before each import operation, but that's both extra work, and highly error-prone. By default, you're stuck.

This is the issue that packages actually fix. Rather than installing programs as flat lists of files in standalone directories, you can package and install them as *subdirectories* under a common root. For instance, you might organize all the code in this example as an install hierarchy that looks like this:

```
root\
    system1\
        __init__.py
        utilities.py
        main.py
        other.py
    system2\
        __init__.py
        utilities.py
        main.py
        other.py
    system3\                    # Here or elsewhere
        __init__.py             # Your new code here
        myfile.py
```

Now, add just the common root directory to your search path. If your code's imports are all relative to this common root, you can import *either* system's utility file with a package import—the enclosing directory name makes the path (and hence, the module reference) unique. In fact, you can import *both* utility files in the same module, as long as you use an import statement, and repeat the full path each time you reference the utility modules:

```
import system1.utilities
import system2.utilities
system1.utilities.function('spam')
system2.utilities.function('eggs')
```

The name of the enclosing directory here makes the module references unique.

Note that you have to use import instead of from with packages only if you need to access the same attribute in two or more paths. If the name of the called function here was different in each path, from statements could be used to avoid repeating the full package path whenever you call one of the functions, as described earlier.

Also, notice in the install hierarchy shown earlier that *__init__.py* files were added to the *system1* and *system2* directories to make this work, but not to the *root* directory. Only directories listed within import statements in your code require these files; as you'll recall, they are run automatically the first time the Python process imports through a package directory.

Technically, in this case, the *system3* directory doesn't have to be under *root*—just the packages of code from which you will import. However, because you never know when your own modules might be useful in other programs, you might as well place them under the common *root* directory to avoid similar name-collision problems in the future.

Finally, notice that both of the two original systems' imports will keep working unchanged. Because their *home* directories are searched first, the addition of the common root on the search path is irrelevant to code in *system1* and *system2*; they can keep saying just import utilities, and expect to find their own files. Moreover, if you're careful to unpack all your Python systems under a common root like this, path configuration becomes simple: you'll only need to add the common root directory, once.

Why You Will Care: Module Packages

Now that packages are a standard part of Python, it's common to see larger third-party extensions shipped as a set of package directories, rather than a flat list of modules. The *win32all* Windows extensions package for Python, for instance, was one of the first to jump on the package bandwagon. Many of its utility modules reside in packages imported with paths. For instance, to load client-side COM tools, you use a statement like this:

```
from win32com.client import constants, Dispatch
```

This line fetches names from the client module of the win32com package (an install subdirectory).

Package imports are also pervasive in code run under the Jython Java-based implementation of Python because Java libraries are organized into hierarchies as well. In recent Python releases, the email and XML tools are likewise organized into packaged subdirectories in the standard library. Whether you create package directories, you will probably import from them eventually.

Chapter Summary

This chapter introduced Python's package import model—an optional but useful way to explicitly list part of the directory path leading up to your modules. Package imports are still relative to a directory on your module import search path, but rather than relying on Python to traverse the search path manually, your script gives the rest of the path to the module explicitly.

As we've seen, packages not only make imports more meaningful in larger systems, but also simplify import search path settings (if all cross-directory imports are relative to a common root directory), and resolve ambiguities when there is more than one module of the same name (including the name of the enclosing directory in a package import helps distinguish between them).

In the next chapter, we will survey a handful of more advanced module-related topics, such as relative import syntax, and the _ _name_ _ usage mode variable. As usual, though, we'll close out this chapter with a short quiz to test what you've learned here.

Chapter Quiz

1. What is the purpose of an _ _init_ _.py file in a module package directory?
2. How can you avoid repeating the full package path every time you reference a package's content?
3. Which directories require _ _init_ _.py files?
4. When must you use import instead of from with packages?

Quiz Answers

1. The _ _init_ _.py file serves to declare and initialize a module package; Python automatically runs its code the first time you import through a directory in a process. Its assigned variables become the attributes of the module object created in memory to correspond to that directory. It is also not optional—you can't import through a directory with package syntax, unless it contains this file.

2. Use the from statement with a package to copy names out of the package directly, or use the as extension with the import statement to rename the path to a shorter synonym. In both cases, the path is listed in only one place, in the from or import statement.

3. Each directory listed in an import or from statement must contain an _ _init_ _.py file. Other directories, including the directory containing the leftmost component of a package path, do not need to include this file.

4. You must use import instead of from with packages only if you need to access the same name defined in more than one path. With import, the path makes the references unique, but from allows only one version of any given name.

## CHAPTER 21

Advanced Module Topics

This chapter concludes Part V with a collection of more advanced module-related topics—relative import syntax, data hiding, the __future__ module, the __name__ variable, sys.path changes, and so on—along with the standard set of gotchas and exercises related to what we've covered in this part of the book. Like functions, modules are more effective when their interfaces are well defined, so this chapter also briefly reviews module design concepts, some of which we have explored in prior chapters.

Despite the word "advanced" in this chapter's title, some of the topics discussed here (such as the __name__ trick) are widely used, so be sure you take a look before moving on to classes in the next part of the book.

Data Hiding in Modules

As we've seen, a Python module exports all the names assigned at the top level of its file. There is no notion of declaring which names should and shouldn't be visible outside the module. In fact, there's no way to prevent a client from changing names inside a module if it wants to.

In Python, data hiding in modules is a convention, not a syntactical constraint. If you want to break a module by trashing its names, you can, but fortunately, I've yet to meet a programmer who would. Some purists object to this liberal attitude toward data hiding, and claim that it means Python can't implement encapsulation. However, encapsulation in Python is more about packaging than about restricting.

Minimizing from * Damage: _X and __all__

As a special case, you can prefix names with a single underscore (e.g., _X) to prevent them from being copied out when a client imports a module's names with a from * statement. This really is intended only to minimize namespace pollution; because from * copies out all names, the importer may get more than it's bargained for (including names that overwrite names in the importer). Underscores aren't "private" declarations: you can still see and change such names with other import forms, such as the import statement.

Alternatively, you can achieve a hiding effect similar to the _X naming convention by assigning a list of variable name strings to the variable _ _all_ _ at the top level of the module. For example:

```
__all__ = ["Error", "encode", "decode"]      # Export these only
```

When this feature is used, the from * statement will copy out only those names listed in the _ _all_ _ list. In effect, this is the converse of the _X convention: _ _all_ _ identifies names to be copied, while _X identifies names not to be copied. Python looks for an _ _all_ _ list in the module first; if one is not defined, from * copies all names without a single leading underscore.

Like the _X convention, the _ _all_ _ list has meaning only to the from * statement form, and does not amount to a privacy declaration. Module writers can use either trick to implement modules that are well behaved when used with from *. (See also the discussion of _ _all_ _ lists in package _ _init_ _.py files in Chapter 20; there, these lists declare submodules to be loaded for a from *.)

Enabling Future Language Features

Changes to the language that may potentially break existing code are introduced gradually. Initially, they appear as optional extensions, which are disabled by default. To turn on such extensions, use a special import statement of this form:

```
from __future__ import featurename
```

This statement should generally appear at the top of a module file (possibly after a docstring) because it enables special compilation of code on a per-module basis. It's also possible to submit this statement at the interactive prompt to experiment with upcoming language changes; the feature will then be available for the rest of the interactive session.

For example, in prior editions of this book, we had to use this statement form to demonstrate generator functions, which required a keyword that was not yet enabled by default (they use a *featurename* of generators). We also used this statement to activate true division for numbers in Chapter 5, and we'll use it again in this chapter to turn on absolute imports and again later in Part VII to demonstrate context managers.

All of these changes have the potential to break existing code, and so are being phased in gradually as optional features presently enabled with this special import.

Mixed Usage Modes: _ _name_ _ and _ _main_ _

Here's a special module-related trick that lets you import a file as a module, and run it as a standalone program. Each module has a built-in attribute called _ _name_ _, which Python sets automatically as follows:

- If the file is being run as a top-level program file, _ _name_ _ is set to the string "_ _main_ _" when it starts.
- If the file is being imported, _ _name_ _ is instead set to the module's name as known by its clients.

The upshot is that a module can test its own _ _name_ _ to determine whether it's being run or imported. For example, suppose we create the following module file, named *runme.py*, to export a single function called tester:

```
def tester():
    print "It's Christmas in Heaven..."

if __name__ == '__main__':         # Only when run
    tester()                       # Not when imported
```

This module defines a function for clients to import and use as usual:

```
% python
>>> import runme
>>> runme.tester()
It's Christmas in Heaven...
```

But, the module also includes code at the bottom that is set up to call the function when this file is run as a program:

```
% python runme.py
It's Christmas in Heaven...
```

Perhaps the most common place you'll see the _ _name_ _ test applied is for *self-test* code. In short, you can package code that tests a module's exports in the module itself by wrapping it in a _ _name_ _ test at the bottom of the file. This way, you can use the file in clients by importing it, and test its logic by running it from the system shell, or via another launching scheme. In practice, self-test code at the bottom of a file under the _ _name_ _ test is probably the most common and simplest unit-testing protocol in Python. (Chapter 29 will discuss other commonly used options for testing Python code—as you'll see, the unittest and doctest standard library modules provide more advanced testing tools.)

The _ _name_ _ trick is also commonly used when writing files that can be used both as command-line utilities, and as tool libraries. For instance, suppose you write a file finder script in Python. You can get more mileage out of your code if you package it in functions, and add a _ _name_ _ test in the file to automatically call those functions when the file is run standalone. That way, the script's code becomes reusable in other programs.

Unit Tests with _ _name_ _

In fact, we've already seen a prime example in this book of an instance where the _ _name_ _ check could be useful. In the section on arguments in Chapter 16, we coded a script that computed the minimum value from the set of arguments sent in:

```
def minmax(test, *args):
    res = args[0]
    for arg in args[1:]:
        if test(arg, res):
            res = arg
    return res

def lessthan(x, y): return x < y
def grtrthan(x, y): return x > y

print minmax(lessthan, 4, 2, 1, 5, 6, 3)        # Self-test code
print minmax(grtrthan, 4, 2, 1, 5, 6, 3)
```

This script includes self-test code at the bottom, so we can test it without having to retype everything at the interactive command line each time we run it. The problem with the way it is currently coded, however, is that the output of the self-test call will appear every time this file is imported from another file to be used as a tool—not exactly a user-friendly feature! To improve it, we can wrap up the self-test call in a _ _name_ _ check, so that it will be launched only when the file is run as a top-level script, not when it is imported:

```
print 'I am:', __name__

def minmax(test, *args):
    res = args[0]
    for arg in args[1:]:
        if test(arg, res):
            res = arg
    return res

def lessthan(x, y): return x < y
def grtrthan(x, y): return x > y

if __name__ == '__main__':
    print minmax(lessthan, 4, 2, 1, 5, 6, 3)     # Self-test code
    print minmax(grtrthan, 4, 2, 1, 5, 6, 3)
```

We're also printing the value of _ _name_ _ at the top here to trace its value. Python creates and assigns this usage-mode variable as soon as it starts loading a file. When we run this file as a top-level script, its name is set to _ _main_ _, so its self-test code kicks in automatically:

```
% python min.py
I am: __main__
1
6
```

But, if we import the file, its name is not __main__, so we must explicitly call the function to make it run:

```
>>> import min
I am: min
>>> min.minmax(min.lessthan, 's', 'p', 'a', 'm')
'a'
```

Again, regardless of whether this is used for testing, the net effect is that we get to use our code in two different roles—as a library module of tools, or as an executable program.

Changing the Module Search Path

In Chapter 18, we learned that the module search path is a list of directories that can be customized via the environment variable PYTHONPATH, and possibly *.pth* path files. What I haven't shown you until now is how a Python program itself can actually change the search path by changing a built-in list called sys.path (the path attribute in the built-in sys module). sys.path is initialized on startup, but thereafter, you can delete, append, and reset its components however you like:

```
>>> import sys
>>> sys.path
['', 'D:\\PP3ECD-Partial\\Examples', 'C:\\Python25', ...more deleted...]

>>> sys.path.append('C:\\sourcedir')          # Extend module search path
>>> import string                             # All imports search the new dir
```

Once you've made such a change, it will impact future imports anywhere in the Python program, as all imports and all files share the single sys.path list. In fact, this list may be changed arbitrarily:

```
>>> sys.path = [r'd:\temp']                    # Change module search path
>>> sys.path.append('c:\\lp3e\\examples')      # For this process only
>>> sys.path
['d:\\temp', 'c:\\lp3e\\examples']

>>> import string
Traceback (most recent call last):
  File "<stdin>", line 1, in ?
ImportError: No module named string
```

Thus, you can use this technique to dynamically configure a search path inside a Python program. Be careful, though: if you delete a critical directory from the path, you may lose access to critical utilities. In the prior example, for instance, we no longer have access to the string module because we deleted the Python source library's directory from the path.

Also, remember that such sys.path settings only endure for the Python session or program (technically, process) that made them; they are not retained after Python exits. PYTHONPATH and *.pth* file path configurations live in the operating system instead of a running Python program, and so are more global: they are picked up by every program on your machine, and live on after a program completes.

The import as Extension

Both the `import` and `from` statements have been extended to allow a module to be given a different name in your script. The following `import` statement:

```
import longmodulename as name
```

is equivalent to:

```
import longmodulename
name = longmodulename
del longmodulename                      # Don't keep original name
```

After such an `import`, you can (and in fact must) use the name listed after the as to refer to the module. This works in a `from` statement, too, to assign a name imported from a file to a different name in your script:

```
from module import longname as name
```

This extension is commonly used to provide short synonyms for longer names, and to avoid name clashes when you are already using a name in your script that would otherwise be overwritten by a normal import statement. It also comes in handy for providing a short, simple name for an entire directory path when using the package import feature described in Chapter 20.

Relative Import Syntax

Python 2.5 modifies the import search path semantics of some `from` statements when they are applied to the module packages we studied in the previous chapter. Some aspects of this change will not become apparent until a later Python release (currently this is planned for version 2.7 and version 3.0), though some are already present today.

In short, `from` statements can now use dots (".") to specify that they prefer modules located within the same package (known as *package-relative imports*) to modules located elsewhere on the module import search path (called *absolute imports*). That is:

- Today, you can use dots to indicate that imports should be *relative* to the containing package—such imports will prefer modules located inside the package to same-named modules located elsewhere on the import search path, sys.path.

- Normal imports in a package's code (without dots) currently default to a relative-then-absolute search path order. However, in the future, Python will make imports absolute by default—in the absence of any special dot syntax, imports will skip the containing package itself and look elsewhere on the sys.path search path.

For example, presently, a statement of the form:

```
from .spam import name
```

means "from a module named spam located in the same package that this statement is contained in, import the variable name." A similar statement without the leading dot will still default to the current relative-then-absolute search path order, unless a statement of the following form is included in the importing file:

```
from __future__ import absolute_import    # Required until 2.7?
```

If present, this statement enables the future absolute default path change. It causes all imports without extra dots to skip the relative components of the module import search path, and look instead in the absolute directories that sys.path contains. For instance, when absolute imports are thus enabled, a statement of the following form will always find the standard library's string module, instead of a module of the same name in the package:

```
import string                             # Always finds standard lib's version
```

Without the from __future__ statement, if there's a string module in the package, it will be imported instead. To get the same behavior when the future absolute import change is enabled, run a statement of the following form (which also works in Python today) to force a relative import:

```
from . import string                      # Searches this package first
```

Note that leading dots can only be used with the from statement, not the import statement. The import modname statement form still performs relative imports today, but these will become absolute in Python 2.7.

Other dot-based relative reference patterns are possible, too. Given a package named mypkg, the following alternative import forms used by code within the package work as described:

```
from .string import name1, name2         # Imports names from mypkg.string
from . import string                      # Imports mypkg.string
from .. import string                     # Imports string from parent directory
```

To understand these latter forms better, we need to understand the rationale behind this change.

Why Relative Imports?

This feature is designed to allow scripts to resolve ambiguities that can arise when a same-named file appears in multiple places on the module search path. Consider the following package directory:

```
mypkg\
     __init__.py
     main.py
     string.py
```

This defines a package named `mypkg` containing modules named `mypkg.main` and `mypkg.string`. Now, suppose that the `main` module tries to import a module named `string`. In Python 2.4 and earlier, Python will first look in the *mypkg* directory to perform a *relative* import. It will find and import the *string.py* file located there, assigning it to the name `string` in the `mypkg.main` module's namespace.

It could be, though, that the intent of this import was to load the Python standard library's `string` module instead. Unfortunately, in these versions of Python, there's no straightforward way to ignore `mypkg.string` and look for the standard library's `string` module located further to the right on the module search path. We cannot depend on any extra package directory structure above the standard library being present on every machine.

In other words, imports in packages can be ambiguous—within a package, it's not clear whether an `import spam` statement refers to a module within or outside the package. More accurately, a local module or package can hide another hanging directly off of `sys.path`, whether intentionally or not.

In practice, Python users can avoid reusing the names of standard library modules they need for modules of their own (if you need the standard `string`, don't name a new module `string`). But this doesn't help if a package accidentally hides a standard module; moreover, Python might add a new standard library module in the future that has the same name as a module of your own. Code that relies on relative imports is also less easy to understand because the reader may be confused about which module is intended to be used. It's better if the resolution can be made explicit in code.

In Python 2.5, we can control the behavior of imports, forcing them to be absolute by using the `from __future__` import directive listed earlier. Again, bear in mind that this absolute-import behavior will become the default in a future version (planned currently for Python 2.7). When absolute imports are enabled, a statement of the following form in our example file *mypkg/main.py* will always find the standard library's version of `string`, via an absolute import search:

```
import string                          # Imports standard lib string
```

You should get used to using absolute imports now, so you're prepared when the change takes effect. That is, if you really want to import a module from your package, to make this explicit and absolute, you should begin writing statements like this in your code (`mypkg` will be found in an absolute directory on `sys.path`):

```
from mypkg import string               # Imports mypkg.string (absolute)
```

Relative imports are still possible by using the dot pattern in the `from` statement:

```
from . import string                   # Imports mypkg.string (relative)
```

This form imports the string module relative to the current package, and is the relative equivalent to the prior example's absolute form (the package's directory is automatically searched first).

We can also copy specific names from a module with relative syntax:

```
from .string import name1, name2        # Imports names from mypkg.string
```

This statement again refers to the string module relative to the current package. If this code appears in our mypkg.main module, for example, it will import name1 and name2 from mypkg.string. An additional leading dot performs the relative import starting from the parent of the current package. For example:

```
from .. import spam                     # Imports a sibling of mypkg
```

will load a sibling of mypkg—i.e., the spam module located in the parent directory, next to mypkg. More generally, code located in some module A.B.C can do any of these:

```
from . import D                         # Imports A.B.D
from .. import E                        # Imports A.E
from ..F import G                       # Imports A.F.G
```

Relative import syntax and the proposed absolute-by-default imports change are advanced concepts, and these features are still only partially present in Python 2.5. Because of that, we'll omit further details here; see Python's standard manual set for more information.

Module Design Concepts

Like functions, modules present design tradeoffs: you have to think about which functions go in which modules, module communication mechanisms, and so on. All of this will become clearer when you start writing bigger Python systems, but here are a few general ideas to keep in mind:

- **You're always in a module in Python.** There's no way to write code that doesn't live in some module. In fact, code typed at the interactive prompt really goes in a built-in module called __main__; the only unique things about the interactive prompt are that code runs and is discarded immediately, and expression results are printed automatically.

- **Minimize module coupling: global variables.** Like functions, modules work best if they're written to be closed boxes. As a rule of thumb, they should be as independent of global names in other modules as possible.

- **Maximize module cohesion: unified purpose.** You can minimize a module's couplings by maximizing its cohesion; if all the components of a module share a general purpose, you're less likely to depend on external names.

- **Modules should rarely change other modules' variables.** We illustrated this with code in Chapter 16, but it's worth repeating here: it's perfectly OK to use globals defined in another module (that's how clients import services, after all), but changing globals in another module is often a symptom of a design problem. There are exceptions, of course, but you should try to communicate results through devices such as function argument return values, not cross-module changes. Otherwise, your globals' values become dependent on the order of arbitrarily remote assignments in other files, and your modules become harder to understand and reuse.

As a summary, Figure 21-1 sketches the environment in which modules operate. Modules contain variables, functions, classes, and other modules (if imported). Functions have local variables of their own. You'll meet classes—other objects that live within modules—in Chapter 22.

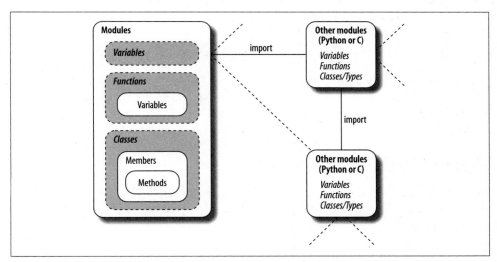

Figure 21-1. Module execution environment. Modules are imported, but modules also import and use other modules, which may be coded in Python or another language such as C. Modules in turn contain variables, functions, and classes to do their work, and their functions and classes may contain variables and other items of their own. At the top, though, programs are just a set of modules.

Modules Are Objects: Metaprograms

Because modules expose most of their interesting properties as built-in attributes, it's easy to write programs that manage other programs. We usually call such manager programs *metaprograms* because they work on top of other systems. This is also referred to as *introspection* because programs can see and process object internals. Introspection is an advanced feature, but it can be useful for building programming tools.

For instance, to get to an attribute called name in a module called M, we can use qualification, or index the module's attribute dictionary (exposed in the built-in __dict__
attribute). Python also exports the list of all loaded modules as the sys.modules dictionary (that is, the modules attribute of the sys module) and provides a built-in
called getattr that lets us fetch attributes from their string names (it's like saying
object.attr, but attr is a runtime string). Because of that, all the following expressions reach the same attribute and object:

```
M.name                          # Qualify object
M.__dict__['name']              # Index namespace dictionary manually
sys.modules['M'].name           # Index loaded-modules table manually
getattr(M, 'name')              # Call built-in fetch function
```

By exposing module internals like this, Python helps you build programs about programs.* For example, here is a module named *mydir.py* that puts these ideas to work
to implement a customized version of the built-in dir function. It defines and exports
a function called listing, which takes a module object as an argument, and prints a
formatted listing of the module's namespace:

```
# A module that lists the namespaces of other modules

verbose = 1

def listing(module):
    if verbose:
        print "-"*30
        print "name:", module.__name__, "file:", module.__file__
        print "-"*30

    count = 0
    for attr in module.__dict__.keys():        # Scan namespace
        print "%02d) %s" % (count, attr),
        if attr[0:2] == "__":
            print "<built-in name>"            # Skip __file__, etc.
        else:
            print getattr(module, attr)        # Same as .__dict__[attr]
        count = count+1

    if verbose:
        print "-"*30
        print module.__name__, "has %d names" % count
        print "-"*30

if __name__ == "__main__":
    import mydir
    listing(mydir)                             # Self-test code: list myself
```

---

* As we saw in Chapter 16, because a function can access its enclosing module by going through the sys.modules
table like this, it's possible to emulate the effect of the global statement. For instance, the effect of global X;
X=0 can be simulated (albeit with much more typing!) by saying this inside a function: import sys; glob=sys.
modules[__name__]; glob.X=0. Remember, each module gets a __name__ attribute for free; it's visible as a global name inside the functions within the module. This trick provides another way to change both local and
global variables of the same name inside a function.

We've also provided self-test logic at the bottom of this module, which narcissistically imports and lists itself. Here's the sort of output produced:

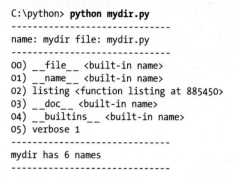

```
C:\python> python mydir.py
-----------------------------
name: mydir file: mydir.py
-----------------------------
00) __file__ <built-in name>
01) __name__ <built-in name>
02) listing <function listing at 885450>
03) __doc__ <built-in name>
04) __builtins__ <built-in name>
05) verbose 1
-----------------------------
mydir has 6 names
-----------------------------
```

We'll meet getattr and its relatives again later. The point to notice here is that mydir is a program that lets you browse other programs. Because Python exposes its internals, you can process objects generically.[*]

Module Gotchas

In this section, we'll take a look at the usual collection of boundary cases that make life interesting for Python beginners. Some are so obscure that it was hard to come up with examples, but most illustrate something important about the language.

Statement Order Matters in Top-Level Code

When a module is first imported (or reloaded), Python executes its statements one by one, from the top of the file to the bottom. This has a few subtle implications regarding forward references that are worth underscoring here:

- Code at the top level of a module file (not nested in a function) runs as soon as Python reaches it during an import; because of that, it can't reference names assigned lower in the file.

- Code inside a function body doesn't run until the function is called; because names in a function aren't resolved until the function actually runs, they can usually reference names anywhere in the file.

---

[*] Tools such as mydir.listing can be preloaded into the interactive namespace by importing them in the file referenced by the PYTHONSTARTUP environment variable. Because code in the startup file runs in the interactive namespace (module __main__), importing common tools in the startup file can save you some typing. See Appendix A for more details.

Generally, forward references are only a concern in top-level module code that executes immediately; functions can reference names arbitrarily. Here's an example that illustrates forward reference:

```
func1( )                          # Error: "func1" not yet assigned

def func1( ):
    print func2( )                # OK:  "func2" looked up later

func1( )                          # Error: "func2" not yet assigned

def func2( ):
    return "Hello"

func1( )                          # Okay: "func1" and "func2" assigned
```

When this file is imported (or run as a standalone program), Python executes its statements from top to bottom. The first call to func1 fails because the func1 def hasn't run yet. The call to func2 inside func1 works as long as func2's def has been reached by the time func1 is called (it hasn't when the second top-level func1 call is run). The last call to func1 at the bottom of the file works because func1 and func2 have both been assigned.

Mixing defs with top-level code is not only hard to read, it's dependent on statement ordering. As a rule of thumb, if you need to mix immediate code with defs, put your defs at the top of the file, and top-level code at the bottom. That way, your functions are guaranteed to be defined and assigned by the time code that uses them runs.

Importing Modules by Name String

The module name in an import or from statement is a hardcoded variable name. Sometimes, though, your program will get the name of a module to be imported as a string at runtime (e.g., if a user selects a module name from within a GUI). Unfortunately, you can't use import statements directly to load a module given its name as a string—Python expects a variable name here, not a string. For instance:

```
>>> import "string"
  File "<stdin>", line 1
    import "string"
                  ^
SyntaxError: invalid syntax
```

It also won't work to simply assign the string to a variable name:

```
x = "string"
import x
```

Here, Python will try to import a file *x.py*, not the string module.

To get around this, you need to use special tools to load a module dynamically from a string that is generated at runtime. The most general approach is to construct an import statement as a string of Python code, and pass it to the exec statement to run:

```
>>> modname = "string"
>>> exec "import " + modname          # Run a string of code
>>> string                            # Imported in this namespace
<module 'string'>
```

The exec statement (and its cousin for expressions, the eval function) compiles a string of code, and passes it to the Python interpreter to be executed. In Python, the byte code compiler is available at runtime, so you can write programs that construct and run other programs like this. By default, exec runs the code in the current scope, but you can get more specific by passing in optional namespace dictionaries.

The only real drawback to exec is that it must compile the import statement each time it runs; if it runs many times, your code may run quicker if it uses the built-in __import__ function to load from a name string instead. The effect is similar, but __import__ returns the module object, so assign it to a name here to keep it:

```
>>> modname = "string"
>>> string = __import__(modname)
>>> string
<module 'string'>
```

from Copies Names but Doesn't Link

Although it's commonly used, the from statement is the source of a variety of potential gotchas in Python. The from statement is really an assignment to names in the importer's scope—a name-copy operation, not a name aliasing. The implications of this are the same as for all assignments in Python, but subtle, especially given that the code that shares the objects lives in different files. For instance, suppose we define the following module (*nested1.py*):

```
X = 99
def printer(): print X
```

If we import its two names using from in another module (*nested2.py*), we get copies of those names, not links to them. Changing a name in the importer resets only the binding of the local version of that name, not the name in *nested1.py*:

```
from nested1 import X, printer    # Copy names out
X = 88                            # Changes my "X" only!
printer()                         # nested1's X is still 99

% python nested2.py
99
```

If we use import to get the whole module, and then assign to a qualified name, however, we change the name in *nested1.py*. Qualification directs Python to a name in the module object, rather than a name in the importer (*nested3.py*):

```
import nested1               # Get module as a whole
nested1.X = 88               # OK: change nested1's X
nested1.printer( )

% python nested3.py
88
```

from * Can Obscure the Meaning of Variables

I mentioned this in Chapter 19, but saved the details for here. Because you don't list the variables you want when using the from module import * statement form, it can accidentally overwrite names you're already using in your scope. Worse, it can make it difficult to determine where a variable comes from. This is especially true if the from * form is used on more than one imported file.

For example, if you use from * on three modules, you'll have no way of knowing what a raw function call really means, short of searching all three external module files (all of which may be in other directories):

```
>>> from module1 import *    # Bad: may overwrite my names silently
>>> from module2 import *    # Worse: no way to tell what we get!
>>> from module3 import *
>>> . . .

>>> func( )                  # Huh???
```

The solution again is not to do this: try to explicitly list the attributes you want in your from statements, and restrict the from * form to at most one imported module per file. That way, any undefined names must by deduction be in the module named in the single from *. You can avoid the issue altogether if you always use import instead of from, but that advice is too harsh; like much else in programming, from is a convenient tool if used wisely.

reload May Not Impact from Imports

Here's another from-related gotcha: as discussed previously, because from copies (assigns) names when run, there's no link back to the module where the names came from. Names imported with from simply become references to objects, which happen to have been referenced by the same names in the importee when the from ran.

Because of this behavior, reloading the importee has no effect on clients that import its names using from. That is, the client's names will still reference the original objects fetched with from, even if the names in the original module are later reset:

```
from module import X          # X may not reflect any module reloads!
. . .
reload(module)                # Changes module, but not my names
X                             # Still references old object
```

To make reloads more effective, use `import` and name qualification instead of `from`. Because qualifications always go back to the module, they will find the new bindings of module names after reloading:

```
import module                 # Get module, not names
. . .
reload(module)                # Changes module in-place
module.X                      # Get current X: reflects module reloads
```

reload, from, and Interactive Testing

Chapter 3 warned that it's usually better not to launch programs with imports and reloads because of the complexities involved. Things get even worse when `from` is brought into the mix. Python beginners often encounter the gotcha described here. After opening a module file in a text edit window, say you launch an interactive session to load and test your module with `from`:

```
from module import function
function(1, 2, 3)
```

Finding a bug, you jump back to the edit window, make a change, and try to reload the module this way:

```
reload(module)
```

But this doesn't work—the `from` statement assigned the name `function`, not `module`. To refer to the module in a `reload`, you have to first load it with an `import` statement at least once:

```
import module
reload(module)
function(1, 2, 3)
```

However, this doesn't quite work either—reload updates the module object, but as discussed in the preceding section, names like `function` that were copied out of the module in the past still refer to the old objects (in this instance, the original version of the function). To really get the new function, you must call it `module.function` after the reload, or rerun the `from`:

```
import module
reload(module)
from module import function
function(1, 2, 3)
```

Now, the new version of the function will finally run.

As you can see, there are problems inherent in using reload with from: not only do you have to remember to reload after imports, but you also have to remember to rerun your from statements after reloads. This is complex enough to trip up even an expert once in a while.

You should not expect reload and from to play together nicely. The best policy is not to combine them at all—use reload with import, or launch your programs other ways, as suggested in Chapter 3 (e.g., using the Run → Run Module menu option in IDLE, file icon clicks, or system command lines).

reload Isn't Applied Transitively

When you reload a module, Python only reloads that particular module's file; it doesn't automatically reload modules that the file being reloaded happens to import. For example, if you reload some module A, and A imports modules B and C, the reload applies only to A, not to B and C. The statements inside A that import B and C are rerun during the reload, but they just fetch the already loaded B and C module objects (assuming they've been imported before). In actual code, here's the file *A.py*:

```
import B          # Not reloaded when A is
import C          # Just an import of an already loaded module

% python
>>> . . .
>>> reload(A)
```

Don't depend on transitive module reloads—instead, use multiple reload calls to update subcomponents independently. If desired, you can design your systems to reload their subcomponents automatically by adding reload calls in parent modules like A.

Better still, you could write a general tool to do transitive reloads automatically by scanning modules' __dict__ attributes (see "Modules Are Objects: Metaprograms" earlier in this chapter) and checking each item's type (see Chapter 9) to find nested modules to reload recursively. Such a utility function could call itself recursively to navigate arbitrarily shaped import dependency chains.

For example, the module *reloadall.py* listed below has a reload_all function that automatically reloads a module, every module that the module imports, and so on, all the way to the bottom of each import chain. It uses a dictionary to keep track of already reloaded modules; recursion to walk the import chains; and the standard library's types module (introduced at the end of Chapter 9), which simply pre-defines type results for built-in types.

To use this utility, import its reload_all function, and pass it the name of an already loaded module (like you would the built-in reload function). When the file runs standalone, its self-test code will test itself—it has to import itself because its own name is not defined in the file without an import. I encourage you to study and experiment with this example on your own:

```
import types

def status(module):
    print 'reloading', module.__name__

def transitive_reload(module, visited):
    if not visited.has_key(module):               # Trap cycles, dups
        status(module)                            # Reload this module
        reload(module)                            # And visit children
        visited[module] = None
        for attrobj in module.__dict__.values():  # For all attrs
            if type(attrobj) == types.ModuleType:  # Recur if module
                transitive_reload(attrobj, visited)

def reload_all(*args):
    visited = { }
    for arg in args:
        if type(arg) == types.ModuleType:
            transitive_reload(arg, visited)

if __name__ == '__main__':
    import reloadall                              # Test code: reload myself
    reload_all(reloadall)                         # Should reload this, types
```

Recursive from Imports May Not Work

I saved the most bizarre (and, thankfully, obscure) gotcha for last. Because imports execute a file's statements from top to bottom, you need to be careful when using modules that import each other (known as *recursive imports*). Because the statements in a module may not all have been run when it imports another module, some of its names may not yet exist.

If you use import to fetch the module as a whole, this may or may not matter; the module's names won't be accessed until you later use qualification to fetch their values. But, if you use from to fetch specific names, you must bear in mind that you will only have access to names in that module that have already been assigned.

For instance, take the following modules, recur1 and recur2. recur1 assigns a name X, and then imports recur2 before assigning the name Y. At this point, recur2 can fetch recur1 as a whole with an import (it already exists in Python's internal modules table), but if it uses from, it will be able to see only the name X; the name Y, which is assigned below the import in recur1, doesn't yet exist, so you get an error:

```
# File: recur1.py
X = 1
import recur2                          # Run recur2 now if it doesn't exist
Y = 2


# File: recur2.py
from recur1 import X                   # OK: "X" already assigned
from recur1 import Y                   # Error: "Y" not yet assigned
```

```
>>> import recur1
Traceback (innermost last):
  File "<stdin>", line 1, in ?
  File "recur1.py", line 2, in ?
    import recur2
  File "recur2.py", line 2, in ?
    from recur1 import Y                    # Error: "Y" not yet assigned
ImportError: cannot import name Y
```

Python avoids rerunning recur1's statements when they are imported recursively from recur2 (or else the imports would send the script into an infinite loop), but recur1's namespace is incomplete when imported by recur2.

The solution? Don't use from in recursive imports (no, really!). Python won't get stuck in a cycle if you do, but your programs will once again be dependent on the order of the statements in the modules.

There are two ways out of this gotcha:

- You can usually eliminate import cycles like this by careful design—maximizing cohesion, and minimizing coupling are good first steps.
- If you can't break the cycles completely, postpone module name accesses by using import and qualification (instead of from), or by running your froms either inside functions (instead of at the top level of the module), or near the bottom of your file to defer their execution.

Chapter Summary

This chapter surveyed some more advanced module-related concepts. We studied data hiding techniques, enabling new language features with the __future__ module, the __name__ usage mode variable, package-relative import syntax, and more. We also explored and summarized module design issues, and looked at common mistakes related to modules to help you avoid them in your code.

The next chapter begins our look at Python's object-oriented programming tool, the class. Much of what we've covered in the last few chapters will apply there, too—classes live in modules, and are namespaces as well, but they add an extra component to attribute lookup called "inheritance search." As this is the last chapter in this part of the book, however, before we dive into that topic, be sure to work through this part's set of lab exercises. And, before that, here is this chapter's quiz to review the topics covered here.

Chapter Quiz

1. What is significant about variables at the top level of a module whose names begin with a single underscore?

2. What does it mean when a module's `__name__` variable is the string `"__main__"`?

3. What is the difference between `from mypkg import spam` and `from . import spam`?

4. If the user interactively types the name of a module to test, how can you import it?

5. How is changing `sys.path` different from setting `PYTHONPATH` to modify the module search path?

6. If the module `__future__` allows us to import from the future, can we also import from the past?

Quiz Answers

1. Variables at the top level of a module whose names begin with a single underscore are not copied out to the importing scope when the `from *` statement form is used. They can still be accessed by an `import`, or the normal `from` statement form, though.

2. If a module's `__name__` variable is the string `"__main__"`, it means that the file is being executed as a top-level script, instead of being imported from another file in the program. That is, the file is being used as a program, not a library.

3. `from mypkg import spam` is an absolute import—`mypkg` is located in an absolute directory in `sys.path`. `from . import spam`, on the other hand, is a relative import—`spam` is looked up relative to the package in which this statement is contained before `sys.path` is searched.

4. User input usually comes into a script as a string; to import the referenced module given its string name, you can build and run an `import` statement with `exec`, or pass the string name in a call to the `__import__` function.

5. Changing `sys.path` only affects one running program, and is temporary—the change goes away when the program ends. `PYTHONPATH` settings live in the operating system—they are picked up globally by all programs on a machine, and changes to these settings endure after programs exit.

6. No, we can't import from the past in Python. We can install (or stubbornly use) an older version of the language, but the latest Python is generally the best Python.

Part V Exercises

See "Part V, Modules" in Appendix B for the solutions.

1. *Import basics.* Write a program that counts the lines and characters in a file (similar in spirit to *wc* on Unix). With your text editor, code a Python module called *mymod.py* that exports three top-level names:

   - A countLines(name) function that reads an input file and counts the number of lines in it (hint: file.readlines does most of the work for you, and len does the rest).

   - A countChars(name) function that reads an input file and counts the number of characters in it (hint: file.read returns a single string).

   - A test(name) function that calls both counting functions with a given input filename. Such a filename generally might be passed in, hardcoded, input with raw_input, or pulled from a command line via the sys.argv list; for now, assume it's a passed-in function argument.

   All three mymod functions should expect a filename string to be passed in. If you type more than two or three lines per function, you're working much too hard— use the hints I just gave!

   Next, test your module interactively, using import and name qualification to fetch your exports. Does your PYTHONPATH need to include the directory where you created *mymod.py*? Try running your module on itself: e.g., test("mymod.py"). Note that test opens the file twice; if you're feeling ambitious, you may be able to improve this by passing an open file object into the two count functions (hint: file.seek(0) is a file rewind).

2. from/from *. Test your mymod module from exercise 1 interactively by using from to load the exports directly, first by name, then using the from * variant to fetch everything.

3. __main__. Add a line in your mymod module that calls the test function automatically only when the module is run as a script, not when it is imported. The line you add will probably test the value of __name__ for the string "__main__" as shown in this chapter. Try running your module from the system command line; then, import the module and test its functions interactively. Does it still work in both modes?

4. *Nested imports.* Write a second module, *myclient.py*, that imports mymod, and tests its functions; then, run myclient from the system command line. If myclient uses from to fetch from mymod, will mymod's functions be accessible from the top level of myclient? What if it imports with import instead? Try coding both variations in myclient and test interactively by importing myclient and inspecting its __dict__ attribute.

5. *Package imports*. Import your file from a package. Create a subdirectory called *mypkg* nested in a directory on your module import search path, move the *mymod.py* module file you created in exercise 1 or 3 into the new directory, and try to import it with a package import of the form import mypkg.mymod.

You'll need to add an _ _init_ _.py file in the directory your module was moved to make this go, but it should work on all major Python platforms (that's part of the reason Python uses "." as a path separator). The package directory you create can be simply a subdirectory of the one you're working in; if it is, it will be found via the home directory component of the search path, and you won't have to configure your path. Add some code to your _ _init_ _.py, and see if it runs on each import.

6. *Reloads*. Experiment with module reloads: perform the tests in Chapter 19's *changer.py* example, changing the called function's message, and/or behavior repeatedly, without stopping the Python interpreter. Depending on your system, you might be able to edit changer in another window, or suspend the Python interpreter, and edit in the same window (on Unix, a Ctrl-Z key combination usually suspends the current process, and an fg command later resumes it).

7. *Circular imports*.* In the section on recursive import gotchas, importing recur1 raised an error. But, if you restart Python, and import recur2 interactively, the error doesn't occur—test and see this for yourself. Why do you think it works to import recur2, but not recur1? (Hint: Python stores new modules in the built-in sys.modules table (a dictionary) before running their code; later imports fetch the module from this table first, whether the module is "complete" yet or not.) Now, try running recur1 as a top-level script file: **python recur1.py**. Do you get the same error that occurs when recur1 is imported interactively? Why? (Hint: when modules are run as programs, they aren't imported, so this case has the same effect as importing recur2 interactively; recur2 is the first module imported.) What happens when you run recur2 as a script?

---

* Note that circular imports are extremely rare in practice. In fact, this author has never coded or come across a circular import in a decade of Python coding. On the other hand, if you can understand why they are a potential problem, you know a lot about Python's import semantics.

Classes and OOP

## CHAPTER 22

OOP: The Big Picture

So far in this book, we've been using the term "object" generically. Really, the code written up to this point has been *object-based*—we've passed objects around our scripts, used them in expressions, called their methods, and so on. For our code to qualify as being truly object-oriented (OO), though, our objects will generally need to also participate in something called an *inheritance hierarchy*.

This chapter begins our exploration of the Python *class*—a device used to implement new kinds of objects in Python that support inheritance. Classes are Python's main object-oriented programming (OOP) tool, so we'll also look at OOP basics along the way in this part of the book. OOP offers a different and often more effective way of looking at programming, in which we factor code to minimize redundancy, and write new programs by *customizing* existing code instead of changing it in-place.

In Python, classes are created with a new statement: the `class` statement. As you'll see, the objects defined with classes can look a lot like the built-in types we studied earlier in the book. In fact, classes really just apply and extend the ideas we've already covered; roughly, they are packages of functions that largely use and process built-in object types. Classes, though, are designed to create and manage new objects, and they also support inheritance—a mechanism of code customization and reuse above and beyond anything we've seen so far.

One note up front: in Python, OOP is entirely optional, and you don't need to use classes just to get started. In fact, you can get plenty of work done with simpler constructs such as functions, or even simple top-level script code. Because using classes well requires some up-front planning, they tend to be of more interest to people who work in *strategic* mode (doing long-term product development) than to people who work in *tactical* mode (where time is in very short supply).

Still, as you'll see in this part of the book, classes turn out to be one of the most useful tools Python provides. When used well, classes can actually cut development time radically. They're also employed in popular Python tools like the Tkinter GUI API, so most Python programmers will usually find at least a working knowledge of class basics helpful.

Why Use Classes?

Remember when I told you that programs "do things with stuff"? In simple terms, classes are just a way to define new sorts of stuff, reflecting real objects in a program's domain. For instance, suppose we decide to implement that hypothetical pizza-making robot we used as an example in Chapter 15. If we implement it using classes, we can model more of its real-world structure and relationships. Two aspects of OOP prove useful here:

Inheritance
> Pizza-making robots are kinds of robots, so they possess the usual robot-y properties. In OOP terms, we say they "inherit" properties from the general category of all robots. These common properties need to be implemented only once for the general case, and can be reused by all types of robots we may build in the future.

Composition
> Pizza-making robots are really collections of components that work together as a team. For instance, for our robot to be successful, it might need arms to roll dough, motors to maneuver to the oven, and so on. In OOP parlance, our robot is an example of composition; it contains other objects that it activates to do its bidding. Each component might be coded as a class, which defines its own behavior and relationships.

General OOP ideas like inheritance and composition apply to any application that can be decomposed into a set of objects. For example, in typical GUI systems, interfaces are written as collections of widgets—buttons, labels, and so on—which are all drawn when their container is drawn (*composition*). Moreover, we may be able to write our own custom widgets—buttons with unique fonts, labels with new color schemes, and the like—which are specialized versions of more general interface devices (*inheritance*).

From a more concrete programming perspective, classes are Python program units, just like functions and modules: they are another compartment for packaging logic and data. In fact, classes also define new namespaces, much like modules. But, compared to other program units we've already seen, classes have three critical distinctions that make them more useful when it comes to building new objects:

Multiple instances
> Classes are essentially factories for generating one or more objects. Every time we call a class, we generate a new object with a distinct namespace. Each object generated from a class has access to the class' attributes *and* gets a namespace of its own for data that varies per object.

Customization via inheritance
> Classes also support the OOP notion of inheritance; we can extend a class by redefining its attributes outside the class itself. More generally, classes can build up namespace hierarchies, which define names to be used by objects created from classes in the hierarchy.

Operator overloading
> By providing special protocol methods, classes can define objects that respond to the sorts of operations we saw at work on built-in types. For instance, objects made with classes can be sliced, concatenated, indexed, and so on. Python provides hooks that classes can use to intercept and implement any built-in type operation.

OOP from 30,000 Feet

Before we see what this all means in terms of code, I'd like to say a few words about the general ideas behind OOP. If you've never done anything object-oriented in your life before now, some of the terminology in this chapter may seem a bit perplexing on the first pass. Moreover, the motivation for these terms may be elusive until you've had a chance to study the ways that programmers apply them in larger systems. OOP is as much an experience as a technology.

Attribute Inheritance Search

The good news is that OOP is much simpler to understand and use in Python than in other languages such as C++ or Java. As a dynamically typed scripting language, Python removes much of the syntactic clutter and complexity that clouds OOP in other tools. In fact, most of the OOP story in Python boils down to this expression:

```
object.attribute
```

We've been using this expression throughout the book to access module attributes, call methods of objects, and so on. When we say this to an object that is derived from a `class` statement, however, the expression kicks off a *search* in Python—it searches a tree of linked objects, looking for the first appearance of `attribute` that it can find. When classes are involved, the preceding Python expression effectively translates to the following in natural language:

> Find the first occurrence of `attribute` by looking in `object`, then in all classes above it, from bottom to top, and left to right.

In other words, attribute fetches are simply tree searches. We call this search procedure *inheritance* because objects lower in a tree inherit attributes attached to objects higher in a tree. As this search proceeds from the bottom up, in a sense, the objects linked into a tree are the union of all the attributes defined in all their tree parents, all the way up the tree.

In Python, this is all very literal: we really do build up trees of linked objects with code, and Python really does climb this tree at runtime searching for attributes every time we use the object.attribute expression. To make this more concrete, Figure 22-1 sketches an example of one of these trees.

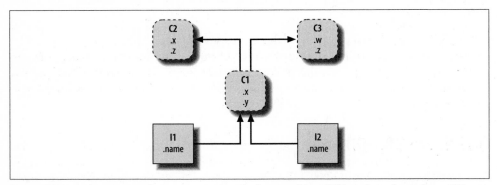

Figure 22-1. A class tree, with two instances at the bottom (I1 and I2), a class above them (C1), and two superclasses at the top (C2 and C3). All of these objects are namespaces (packages of variables), and inheritance is simply a search of the tree from bottom to top to find the lowest occurrence of an attribute name. Code implies the shape of such trees.

In this figure, there is a tree of five objects labeled with variables, all of which have attached attributes, ready to be searched. More specifically, this tree links together three *class objects* (the ovals C1, C2, and C3), and two *instance objects* (the rectangles I1 and I2) into an inheritance search tree. Notice that in the Python object model, classes and the instances you generate from them are two distinct object types:

Classes

Serve as instance factories. Their attributes provide behavior—data and functions—that is inherited by all the instances generated from them (e.g., a function to compute an employee's salary from pay and hours).

Instances

Represent the concrete items in a program's domain. Their attributes record data that varies per specific object (e.g., an employee's Social Security number).

In terms of search trees, an instance inherits attributes from its class, and a class inherits attributes from all classes above it in the tree.

In Figure 22-1, we can further categorize the ovals by their relative positions in the tree. We usually call classes higher in the tree (like C2 and C3) *superclasses*; classes lower in the tree (like C1) are known as *subclasses*.[*] These terms refer to relative tree positions and roles. Superclasses provide behavior shared by all their subclasses, but

---

[*] In other literature, you may also occasionally see the terms *base classes* and *derived classes* used to describe superclasses and subclasses, respectively.

because the search proceeds bottom-up, subclasses may override behavior defined in their superclasses by redefining superclass names lower in the tree.

As these last few words are really the crux of the matter of software customization in OOP, let's expand on this concept. Suppose we build up the tree in Figure 22-1, and then say this:

```
I2.w
```

Right away, this code invokes inheritance. Because this is an `object.attribute` expression, it triggers a search of the tree in Figure 22-1—Python will search for the attribute w by looking in I2 and above. Specifically, it will search the linked objects in this order:

```
I2, C1, C2, C3
```

and stop at the first attached w it finds (or raise an error if w isn't found at all). In this case, w won't be found until C3 is searched because it appears only in that object. In other words, I2.w resolves to C3.w by virtue of the automatic search. In OOP terminology, I2 "inherits" the attribute w from C3.

Ultimately, the two instances inherit four attributes from their classes: w, x, y, and z. Other attribute references will wind up following different paths in the tree. For example:

- I1.x and I2.x both find x in C1 and stop because C1 is lower than C2.
- I1.y and I2.y both find y in C1 because that's the only place y appears.
- I1.z and I2.z both find z in C2 because C2 is further to the left than C3.
- I2.name finds name in I2 without climbing the tree at all.

Trace these searches through the tree in Figure 22-1 to get a feel for how inheritance searches work in Python.

The first item in the preceding list is perhaps the most important to notice—because C1 redefines the attribute x lower in the tree, it effectively *replaces* the version above it in C2. As you'll see in a moment, such redefinitions are at the heart of software customization in OOP—by redefining and replacing the attribute, C1 effectively customizes what it inherits from its superclasses.

Classes and Instances

Although they are technically two separate object types in the Python model, the classes and instances we put in these trees are almost identical—each type's main purpose is to serve as another kind of *namespace*—a package of variables, and a place where we can attach attributes. If classes and instances therefore sound like modules, they should; however, the objects in class trees also have automatically searched links to other namespace objects, and classes correspond to statements, not entire files.

The primary difference between classes and instances is that classes are a kind of *factory* for generating instances. For example, in a realistic application, we might have an Employee class that defines what it means to be an employee; from that class, we generate actual Employee instances. This is another difference between classes and modules: we only ever have one instance of a given module in memory (that's why we have to reload a module to get its new code), but with classes, we can make as many instances as we need.

Operationally, classes will usually have functions attached to them (e.g., computeSalary), and the instances will have more basic data items used by the class' functions (e.g., hoursWorked). In fact, the object-oriented model is not that different from the classic data-processing model of *programs* plus *records*; in OOP, instances are like records with "data," and classes are the "programs" for processing those records. In OOP, though, we also have the notion of an inheritance hierarchy, which supports software customization better than earlier models.

Class Method Calls

In the prior section, we saw how the attribute reference I2.w in our example class tree was translated to C3.w by the inheritance search procedure in Python. Perhaps just as important to understand as the inheritance of attributes, though, is what happens when we try to call methods (i.e., functions attached to classes as attributes).

If this I2.w reference is a function call, what it really means is "call the C3.w function to process I2." That is, Python will automatically map the call I2.w( ) into the call C3.w(I2), passing in the instance as the first argument to the inherited function.

In fact, whenever we call a function attached to a class, an instance of the class is always implied. This implied subject or context is part of the reason we refer to this as an object-oriented model—there is always a subject object when an operation is run. In a more realistic example, we might invoke a method called giveRaise attached as an attribute to an Employee class; such a call has no meaning unless qualified with the employee to whom the raise should be given.

As we'll see later, Python passes in the implied instance to a special first argument in the method, called self by convention. As we'll also learn, methods can be called through either an instance (e.g., bob.giveRaise( )) or a class (e.g., Employee.giveRaise(bob)), and both forms serve purposes in our scripts. To see how methods receive their subjects, though, we need to move on to some code.

Coding Class Trees

Although we are speaking in the abstract here, there is tangible code behind all these ideas. We construct trees, and their objects with class statements and class calls, which we'll meet in more detail later. In short:

- Each `class` statement generates a new class object.
- Each time a class is called, it generates a new instance object.
- Instances are automatically linked to the classes from which they are created.
- Classes are linked to their superclasses by listing them in parentheses in a `class` header line; the left-to-right order there gives the order in the tree.

To build the tree in Figure 22-1, for example, we would run Python code of this form (I've omitted the guts of the `class` statements here):

```
class C2: ...                  # Make class objects (ovals)
class C3: ...
class C1(C2, C3): ...          # Linked to superclasses

I1 = C1( )                     # Make instance objects (rectangles)
I2 = C1( )                     # Linked to their classes
```

Here, we build the three class objects by running three `class` statements, and make the two instance objects by calling the class `C1` twice, as though it were a function. The instances remember the class they were made from, and the class `C1` remembers its listed superclasses.

Technically, this example is using something called *multiple inheritance*, which simply means that a class has more than one superclass above it in the class tree. In Python, if there is more than one superclass listed in parentheses in a `class` statement (like `C1`'s here), their left-to-right order gives the order in which those superclasses will be searched.

Because of the way inheritance searches proceed, the object to which you attach an attribute turns out to be crucial—it determines the name's scope. Attributes attached to instances pertain only to those single instances, but attributes attached to classes are shared by all their subclasses and instances. Later, we'll study the code that hangs attributes on these objects in depth. As we'll find:

- Attributes are usually attached to classes by assignments made within `class` statements, not nested inside function `def` statements.
- Attributes are usually attached to instances by assignments to a special argument passed to functions inside classes, called `self`.

For example, classes provide behavior for their instances with functions created by coding `def` statements inside `class` statements. Because such nested `def`s assign names within the class, they wind up attaching attributes to the class object that will be inherited by all instances and subclasses:

```
class C1(C2, C3):              # Make and link class C1
    def setname(self, who):    # Assign name: C1.setname
        self.name = who        # Self is either I1 or I2

I1 = C1( )                     # Make two instances
I2 = C1( )
```

```
I1.setname('bob')          # Sets I1.name to 'bob'
I2.setname('mel')          # Sets I2.name to 'mel'
print I1.name              # Prints 'bob'
```

There's nothing syntactically unique about def in this context. Operationally, when a def appears inside a class like this, it is usually known as a *method*, and it automatically receives a special first argument—called self by convention—that provides a handle back to the instance to be processed.*

Because classes are factories for multiple instances, their methods usually go through this automatically passed-in self argument whenever they need to fetch or set attributes of the particular instance being processed by a method call. In the preceding code, self is used to store a name in one of two instances.

Like simple variables, attributes of classes and instances are not declared ahead of time, but spring into existence the first time they are assigned values. When a method assigns to a self attribute, it creates or changes an attribute in an instance at the bottom of the class tree (i.e., one of the rectangles) because self automatically refers to the instance being processed.

In fact, because all the objects in class trees are just namespace objects, we can fetch or set any of their attributes by going through the appropriate names. Saying C1. setname is as valid as saying I1.setname, as long as the names C1 and I1 are in your code's scopes.

As currently coded, our C1 class doesn't attach a name attribute to an instance until the setname method is called. In fact, referencing I1.name before calling I1.setname would produce an undefined name error. If a class wants to guarantee that an attribute like name is always set in its instances, it more typically will fill out the attribute at construction time, like this:

```
class C1(C2, C3):
    def __init__(self, who):    # Set name when constructed
        self.name = who         # Self is either I1 or I2

I1 = C1('bob')                  # Sets I1.name to 'bob'
I2 = C1('mel')                  # Sets I2.name to 'mel'
print I1.name                   # Prints 'bob'
```

If it's coded and inherited, Python automatically calls a method named __init__ each time an instance is generated from a class. The new instance is passed in to the self argument of __init__ as usual, and any values listed in parentheses in the class call go to arguments two and beyond. The effect here is to initialize instances when they are made, without requiring extra method calls.

---

* If you've ever used C++ or Java, you'll recognize that Python's self is the same as the this pointer, but self is always explicit in Python to make attribute accesses more obvious.

The `__init__` method is known as the *constructor* because of when it is run. It's the most commonly used representative of a larger class of methods called *operator overloading methods*, which we'll discuss in more detail in the chapters that follow. Such methods are inherited in class trees as usual and have double underscores at the start and end of their names to make them distinct. Python runs them automatically when instances that support them appear in the corresponding operations, and they are mostly an alternative to using simple method calls. They're also optional: if omitted, the operations are not supported.

For example, to implement set intersection, a class might either provide a method named `intersect`, or overload the & expression operator to dispatch to the required logic by coding a method named `__and__`. Because the operator scheme makes instances look and feel more like built-in types, it allows some classes to provide a consistent and natural interface, and be compatible with code that expects a built-in type.

OOP Is About Code Reuse

And that, along with a few syntax details, is most of the OOP story in Python. Of course, there's a bit more to it than just inheritance. For example, operator overloading is much more general than I've described so far—classes may also provide their own implementations of operations such as indexing, fetching attributes, printing, and more. By and large, though, OOP is about looking up attributes in trees.

So why would we be interested in building and searching trees of objects? Although it takes some experience to see how, when used well, classes support code *reuse* in ways that other Python program components cannot. With classes, we code by customizing existing software, instead of either changing existing code in-place or starting from scratch for each new project.

At a fundamental level, classes are really just packages of functions and other names, much like modules. However, the automatic attribute inheritance search that we get with classes supports customization of software above and beyond what we can do with modules and functions. Moreover, classes provide a natural structure for code that localizes logic and names, and so aids in debugging.

For instance, because methods are simply functions with a special first argument, we can mimic some of their behavior by manually passing objects to be processed to simple functions. The participation of methods in class inheritance, though, allows us to naturally customize existing software by coding subclasses with new method definitions, rather than changing existing code in-place. There is really no such concept with modules and functions.

As an example, suppose you're assigned the task of implementing an employee database application. As a Python OOP programmer, you might begin by coding a general superclass that defines default behavior common to all the kinds of employees in your organization:

```
class Employee:                          # General superclass
    def computeSalary(self): ...         # Common or default behavior
    def giveRaise(self): ...
    def promote(self): ...
    def retire(self): ...
```

Once you've coded this general behavior, you can specialize it for each specific kind of employee to reflect how the various types differ from the norm. That is, you can code subclasses that customize just the bits of behavior that differ per employee type; the rest of the employee types' behavior will be inherited from the more general class. For example, if engineers have a unique salary computation rule (i.e., not hours times rate), you can replace just that one method in a subclass:

```
class Engineer(Employee):                # Specialized subclass
    def computeSalary(self): ...         # Something custom here
```

Because the computeSalary version here appears lower in the class tree, it will replace (override) the general version in Employee. You then create instances of the kinds of employee classes that the real employees belong to, to get the correct behavior:

```
bob = Employee( )                        # Default behavior
mel = Engineer( )                        # Custom salary calculator
```

Notice that you can make instances of any class in a tree, not just the ones at the bottom—the class you make an instance from determines the level at which the attribute search will begin. Ultimately, these two instance objects might wind up embedded in a larger container object (e.g., a list, or an instance of another class) that represents a department or company using the composition idea mentioned at the start of this chapter.

When you later ask for these employees' salaries, they will be computed according to the classes from which the objects were made, due to the principles of the inheritance search:*

```
company = [bob, mel]                     # A composite object
for emp in company:
    print emp.computeSalary( )           # Run this object's version
```

---

* Note that the company list in this example could be stored in a file with Python object pickling, introduced in Chapter 9 when we met files, to yield a persistent employee database. Python also comes with a module named shelve, which would allow you to store the pickled representation of the class instances in an access-by-key filesystem; the third-party open source ZODB system does the same but has better support for production-quality object-oriented databases.

This is yet another instance of the idea of polymorphism introduced in Chapter 4 and revisited in Chapter 15. Recall that polymorphism means that the meaning of an operation depends on the object being operated on. Here, the method `computeSalary` is located by inheritance search in each object before it is called. In other applications, polymorphism might also be used to hide (i.e., *encapsulate*) interface differences. For example, a program that processes data streams might be coded to expect objects with input and output methods, without caring what those methods actually do:

```
def processor(reader, converter, writer):
    while 1:
        data = reader.read()
        if not data: break
        data = converter(data)
        writer.write(data)
```

By passing in instances of subclasses that specialize the required `read` and `write` method interfaces for various data sources, we can reuse the `processor` function for any data source we need to use, both now and in the future:

```
class Reader:
    def read(self): ...          # Default behavior and tools
    def other(self): ...
class FileReader(Reader):
    def read(self): ...          # Read from a local file
class SocketReader(Reader):
    def read(self): ...          # Read from a network socket
...
processor(FileReader(...),   Converter,  FileWriter(...))
processor(SocketReader(...), Converter,  TapeWriter(...))
processor(FtpReader(...),    Converter,  XmlWriter(...))
```

Moreover, because the internal implementations of those `read` and `write` methods have been factored into single locations, they can be changed without impacting code such as this that uses them. In fact, the `processor` function might itself be a class to allow the conversion logic of `converter` to be filled in by inheritance, and to allow readers and writers to be embedded by composition (we'll see how this works later in this part of the book).

Once you get used to programming this way (by software customization), you'll find that when it's time to write a new program, much of your work may already be done—your task largely becomes one of mixing together existing superclasses that already implement the behavior required by your program. For example, someone else might have written the `Employee`, `Reader`, and `Writer` classes in this example for use in a completely different program. If so, you get all of that person's code "for free."

In fact, in many application domains, you can fetch or purchase collections of superclasses, known as *frameworks*, that implement common programming tasks as classes, ready to be mixed into your applications. These frameworks might provide database interfaces, testing protocols, GUI toolkits, and so on. With frameworks, you often simply code a subclass that fills in an expected method or two; the framework classes higher in the tree do most of the work for you. Programming in such an OOP world is just a matter of combining and specializing already debugged code by writing subclasses of your own.

Of course, it takes a while to learn how to leverage classes to achieve such OOP utopia. In practice, object-oriented work also entails substantial design work to fully realize the code reuse benefits of classes—to this end, programmers have begun cataloging common OOP structures, known as *design patterns*, to help with design issues. The actual code you write to do OOP in Python, though, is so simple that it will not in itself pose an additional obstacle to your OOP quest. To see why, you'll have to move on to Chapter 23.

Chapter Summary

We took an abstract look at classes and OOP in this chapter, taking in the big picture before we dive into syntax details. As we've seen, OOP is mostly about looking up attributes in trees of linked objects; we call this lookup an inheritance search. Objects at the bottom of the tree inherit attributes from objects higher up in the tree—a feature that enables us to program by customizing code, rather than changing it, or starting from scratch. When used well, this model of programming can cut development time radically.

The next chapter will begin to fill in the coding details behind the picture painted here. As we get deeper into Python classes, though, keep in mind that the OOP model in Python is very simple; as I've already stated, it's really just about looking up attributes in object trees. Before we move on, here's a quick quiz to review what we've covered here.

Chapter Quiz

1. What is the main point of OOP in Python?
2. Where does an inheritance search look for an attribute?
3. What is the difference between a class object and an instance object?
4. Why is the first argument in a class method function special?
5. What is the __init__ method used for?
6. How do you create a class instance?
7. How do you create a class?
8. How do you specify a class' superclasses?

Quiz Answers

1. OOP is about code reuse—you factor code to minimize redundancy and program by customizing what already exists instead of changing code in-place or starting from scratch.

2. An inheritance search looks for an attribute first in the instance object, then in the class the instance was created from, then in all higher superclasses, progressing from the bottom to the top of the object tree, and from left to right (by default). The search stops at the first place the attribute is found. Because the lowest version of a name found along the way wins, class hierarchies naturally support customization by extension.

3. Both class and instance objects are namespaces (packages of variables that appear as attributes). The main difference between them is that classes are a kind of factory for creating multiple instances. Classes also support operator overloading methods, which instances inherit, and treat any functions nested within them as special methods for processing instances.

4. The first argument in a class method function is special because it always receives the instance object that is the implied subject of the method call. It's usually called self by convention. Because method functions always have this implied subject object context by default, we say they are "object oriented"—i.e., designed to process or change objects.

5. If the __init__ method is coded or inherited in a class, Python calls it automatically each time an instance of that class is created. It's known as the constructor method; it is passed the new instance implicitly, as well as any arguments passed explicitly to the class name. It's also the most commonly used operator overloading method. If no __init__ method is present, instances simply begin life as empty namespaces.

6. You create a class instance by calling the class name as though it were a function; any arguments passed into the class name show up as arguments two and beyond in the __init__ constructor method. The new instance remembers the class it was created from for inheritance purposes.

7. You create a class by running a class statement; like function definitions, these statements normally run when the enclosing module file is imported (more on this in the next chapter).

8. You specify a class' superclasses by listing them in parentheses in the class statement, after the new class' name. The left-to-right order in which the classes are listed in the parentheses gives the left-to-right inheritance search order in the class tree.

## CHAPTER 23

Class Coding Basics

Now that we've talked about OOP in the abstract, it's time to see how this translates to actual code. This chapter and the next will fill in the syntax details behind the class model in Python.

If you've never been exposed to OOP in the past, classes can seem somewhat complicated if taken in a single dose. To make class coding easier to absorb, we'll begin our detailed exploration of OOP by taking a first look at some basic classes in action in this chapter. We'll expand on the details introduced here in later chapters of this part of the book, but in their basic form, Python classes are easy to understand.

Classes have three primary distinctions. At a base level, they are mostly just namespaces, much like the modules we studied in Part V. But, unlike modules, classes also have support for generating multiple objects, for namespace inheritance, and for operator overloading. Let's begin our class statement tour by exploring each of these three distinctions in turn.

Classes Generate Multiple Instance Objects

To understand how the multiple objects idea works, you have to first understand that there are two kinds of objects in Python's OOP model: *class* objects, and *instance* objects. Class objects provide default behavior, and serve as factories for instance objects. Instance objects are the real objects your programs process—each is a namespace in its own right, but inherits (i.e., has automatic access to) names in the class from which it was created. Class objects come from statements, and instances from calls; each time you call a class, you get a new instance of that class.

This object-generation concept is very different from any of the other program constructs we've seen so far in this book. In effect, classes are factories for generating multiple instances. By contrast, only one copy of each module is ever imported into a single program (in fact, one reason that we have to call reload is to update the single module object so that changes are reflected once they've been made).

The following is a quick summary of the bare essentials of Python OOP. As you'll see, Python classes are in some ways similar to both defs and modules, but they may be quite different from what you're used to in other languages.

Class Objects Provide Default Behavior

When we run a class statement, we get a class object. Here's a rundown of the main properties of Python classes:

- **The class statement creates a class object and assigns it a name.** Just like the function def statement, the Python class statement is an *executable* statement. When reached and run, it generates a new class object, and assigns it to the name in the class header. Also, like defs, class statements typically run when the files they are coded in are first imported.

- **Assignments inside class statements make class attributes.** Just like in module files, top-level assignments within a class statement (not nested in a def) generate attributes in a class object. Technically, the class statement scope morphs into the attribute namespace of the class object, just like a module's global scope. After running a class statement, class attributes are accessed by name qualification: object.name.

- **Class attributes provide object state and behavior.** Attributes of a class object record state information and behavior to be shared by all instances created from the class; function def statements nested inside a class generate *methods*, which process instances.

Instance Objects Are Concrete Items

When we call a class object, we get an instance object. Here's an overview of the key points behind class instances:

- **Calling a class object like a function makes a new instance object.** Each time a class is called, it creates and returns a new instance object. Instances represent concrete items in your program's domain.

- **Each instance object inherits class attributes and gets its own namespace.** Instance objects created from classes are new namespaces; they start out empty, but inherit attributes that live in the class objects from which they were generated.

- **Assignments to attributes of self in methods make per-instance attributes.** Inside class method functions, the first argument (called self by convention) references the instance object being processed; assignments to attributes of self create or change data in the instance, not the class.

A First Example

Let's turn to a real example to show how these ideas work in practice. To begin, let's define a class named FirstClass by running a Python class statement interactively:

```
>>> class FirstClass:              # Define a class object
...     def setdata(self, value):  # Define class methods
...         self.data = value      # self is the instance
...     def display(self):
...         print self.data        # self.data: per instance
...
```

We're working interactively here, but typically, such a statement would be run when the module file it is coded in is imported. Like functions created with defs, this class won't even exist until Python reaches and runs this statement.

Like all compound statements, the class starts with a header line that lists the class name, followed by a body of one or more nested and (usually) indented statements. Here, the nested statements are defs; they define functions that implement the behavior the class means to export. As we've learned, def is really an assignment; here, it assigns function objects to the names setdata and display in the class statement's scope, and so generates attributes attached to the class: FirstClass.setdata, and FirstClass.display. In fact, any name assigned at the top level of the class's nested block becomes an attribute of the class.

Functions inside a class are usually called *methods*. They're normal defs, and they support everything we've learned about functions already (they can have defaults, return values, and so on). But, in a method function, the first argument automatically receives an implied instance object when called—the subject of the call. We need to create a couple of instances to see how this works:

```
>>> x = FirstClass()              # Make two instances
>>> y = FirstClass()              # Each is a new namespace
```

By *calling* the class this way (notice the parentheses), we generate instance objects, which are just namespaces that have access to their class' attributes. Properly speaking, at this point, we have three objects—two instances, and a class. Really, we have three linked namespaces, as sketched in Figure 23-1. In OOP terms, we say that x "is a" FirstClass, as is y.

The two instances start empty, but have links back to the class from which they were generated. If we qualify an instance with the name of an attribute that lives in the class object, Python fetches the name from the class by inheritance search (unless it also lives in the instance):

```
>>> x.setdata("King Arthur")      # Call methods: self is x
>>> y.setdata(3.14159)            # Runs: FirstClass.setdata(y, 3.14159)
```

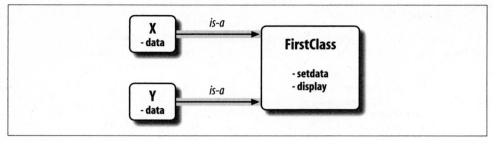

Figure 23-1. Classes and instances are linked namespace objects in a class tree that is searched by inheritance. Here, the "data" attribute is found in instances, but "setdata" and "display" are in the class above them.

Neither x nor y has a setdata attribute of its own, so to find it, Python follows the link from instance to class. And that's about all there is to inheritance in Python: it happens at attribute qualification time, and it just involves looking up names in linked objects (e.g., by following the is-a links in Figure 23-1).

In the setdata function inside FirstClass, the value passed in is assigned to self.data. Within a method, self—the name given to the leftmost argument by convention—automatically refers to the instance being processed (x or y), so the assignments store values in the instances' namespaces, not the class' (that's how the data names in Figure 23-1 are created).

Because classes generate multiple instances, methods must go through the self argument to get to the instance to be processed. When we call the class' display method to print self.data, we see that it's different in each instance; on the other hand, the name display itself is the same in x and y, as it comes (is inherited) from the class:

```
>>> x.display( )                    # self.data differs in each instance
King Arthur
>>> y.display( )
3.14159
```

Notice that we stored different object types in the data member in each instance (a string, and a floating point). As with everything else in Python, there are no declarations for instance attributes (sometimes called *members*); they spring into existence the first time they are assigned values, just like simple variables. In fact, if we were to call display on one of our instances before calling setdata, we would trigger an undefined name error—the attribute named data doesn't even exist in memory until it is assigned within the setdata method.

As another way to appreciate how dynamic this model is, consider that we can change instance attributes in the class itself, by assigning to self in methods, or outside the class, by assigning to an explicit instance object:

```
>>> x.data = "New value"           # Can get/set attributes
>>> x.display( )                   # Outside the class too
New value
```

Although less common, we could even generate a brand new attribute in the instance's namespace by assigning to its name outside the class's method functions:

```
>>> x.anothername = "spam"          # Can set new attributes here too
```

This would attach a new attribute called anothername, which may or may not be used by any of the class' methods to the instance object x. Classes usually create all of the instance's attributes by assignment to the self argument, but they don't have to; programs can fetch, change, or create attributes on any objects to which they have references.

Classes Are Customized by Inheritance

Besides serving as factories for generating multiple instance objects, classes also allow us to make changes by introducing new components (called *subclasses*), instead of changing existing components in-place. Instance objects generated from a class inherit the class' attributes. Python also allows classes to inherit from other classes, opening the door to coding *hierarchies* of classes that specialize behavior by overriding existing attributes lower in the hierarchy. Here, too, there is no parallel with modules: their attributes live in a single, flat namespace.

In Python, instances inherit from classes, and classes inherit from superclasses. Here are the key ideas behind the machinery of attribute inheritance:

- **Superclasses are listed in parentheses in a class header.** To inherit attributes from another class, just list the class in parentheses in a class statement's header. The class that inherits is called a *subclass*, and the class that is inherited from is its *superclass*.

- **Classes inherit attributes from their superclasses.** Just as instances inherit the attribute names defined in their classes, classes inherit all the attribute names defined in their superclasses; Python finds them automatically when they're accessed, if they don't exist in the subclasses.

- **Instances inherit attributes from all accessible classes.** Each instance gets names from the class it's generated from, as well as all of that class' superclasses. When looking for a name, Python checks the instance, then its class, then all superclasses.

- **Each object.attribute reference invokes a new, independent search.** Python performs an independent search of the class tree for each attribute fetch expression. This includes references to instances and classes made outside class statements (e.g., X.attr), as well as references to attributes of the self instance argument in class method functions. Each self.attr expression in a method invokes a new search for attr in self and above.

- **Logic changes are made by subclassing, not by changing superclasses.** By redefining superclass names in subclasses lower in the hierarchy (tree), subclasses replace and thus customize inherited behavior.

The net effect, and the main purpose of all this searching, is that classes support factoring and customization of code better than any other language tool we've seen so far. On the one hand, they allow us to minimize code redundancy (and so reduce maintenance costs) by factoring operations into a single, shared implementation; on the other, they allow us to program by customizing what already exists, rather than changing it in-place or starting from scratch.

A Second Example

This next example builds on the previous one. First, we'll define a new class, SecondClass, that inherits all of FirstClass' names and provides one of its own:

```
>>> class SecondClass(FirstClass):          # Inherits setdata
...     def display(self):                   # Changes display
...         print 'Current value = "%s"' % self.data
...
```

SecondClass defines the display method to print with a different format. By defining an attribute with the same name as an attribute in FirstClass, SecondClass effectively replaces the display attribute in its superclass.

Recall that inheritance searches proceed upward from instances, to subclasses, to superclasses, stopping at the first appearance of the attribute name that it finds. In this case, since the display name in SecondClass will be found before the one in FirstClass, we say that SecondClass *overrides* FirstClass's display. Sometimes we call this act of replacing attributes by redefining them lower in the tree *overloading*.

The net effect here is that SecondClass specializes FirstClass, by changing the behavior of the display method. On the other hand, SecondClass (and any instances created from it) still inherits the setdata method in FirstClass verbatim. Let's make an instance to demonstrate:

```
>>> z = SecondClass()
>>> z.setdata(42)          # Finds setdata in FirstClass
>>> z.display()            # Finds overridden method in SecondClass
Current value = "42"
```

As before, we make a SecondClass instance object by calling it. The setdata call still runs the version in FirstClass, but this time the display attribute comes from SecondClass and prints a custom message. Figure 23-2 sketches the namespaces involved.

Here's a very important thing to notice about OOP: the specialization introduced in SecondClass is completely *external* to FirstClass. That is, it doesn't affect existing or future FirstClass objects, like the x from the prior example:

```
>>> x.display()            # x is still a FirstClass instance (old message)
New value
```

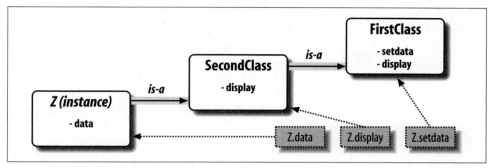

Figure 23-2. Specialization by overriding inherited names by redefining them in extensions lower in the class tree. Here, SecondClass redefines and so customizes the "display" method for its instances.

Rather than *changing* FirstClass, we *customized* it. Naturally, this is an artificial example, but as a rule, because inheritance allows us to make changes like this in external components (i.e., in subclasses), classes often support extension and reuse better than functions or modules can.

Classes Are Attributes in Modules

Before we move on, remember that there's nothing magic about a class name. It's just a variable assigned to an object when the class statement runs, and the object can be referenced with any normal expression. For instance, if our FirstClass was coded in a module file instead of being typed interactively, we could import it and use its name normally in a class header line:

```
from modulename import FirstClass        # Copy name into my scope
class SecondClass(FirstClass):           # Use class name directly
    def display(self): ...
```

Or, equivalently:

```
import modulename                        # Access the whole module
class SecondClass(modulename.FirstClass): # Qualify to reference
    def display(self): ...
```

Like everything else, class names always live within a module, and so must follow all the rules we studied in Part V. For example, more than one class can be coded in a single module file—like other statements in a module, class statements are run during imports to define names, and these names become distinct module attributes. More generally, each module may arbitrarily mix any number of variables, functions, and classes, and all names in a module behave the same way. The file *food.py* demonstrates:

```
# food.py

var = 1                                  # food.var
def func( ):                             # food.func
```

```
         ...
     class spam:                              # food.spam
         ...
     class ham:                               # food.ham
         ...
     class eggs:                              # food.eggs
         ...
```

This holds true even if the module and class happen to have the same name. For example, given the following file, *person.py*:

```
     class person:
         ...
```

we need to go through the module to fetch the class as usual:

```
     import person                            # Import module
     x = person.person( )                     # Class within module
```

Although this path may look redundant, it's required: `person.person` refers to the person class inside the person module. Saying just person gets the module, not the class, unless the `from` statement is used:

```
     from person import person                # Get class from module
     x = person( )                            # Use class name
```

Like any other variable, we can never see a class in a file without first importing and somehow fetching it from its enclosing file. If this seems confusing, don't use the same name for a module and a class within it.

Also, keep in mind that although classes and modules are both namespaces for attaching attributes, they correspond to very different source code structures: a module reflects an entire file, but a class is a statement within a file. We'll say more about such distinctions later in this part of the book.

Classes Can Intercept Python Operators

Now, let's take a look at the third major difference between classes and modules: operator overloading. In simple terms, operator overloading lets objects coded with classes intercept and respond to operations that work on built-in types: addition, slicing, printing, qualification, and so on. It's mostly just an automatic dispatch mechanism: expressions and other built-in operations route control to implementations in classes. Here, too, there is nothing similar in modules: modules can implement function calls, but not the behavior of expressions.

Although we could implement all class behavior as method functions, operator overloading lets objects be more tightly integrated with Python's object model. Moreover, because operator overloading makes our own objects act like built-ins, it tends to foster object interfaces that are more consistent and easier to learn, and it allows class-based objects to be processed by code written to expect a built-in type's interface. Here is a quick rundown of the main ideas behind overloading operators:

- **Methods named with double underscores (__X__) are special hooks.** Python operator overloading is implemented by providing specially named methods to intercept operations. The Python language defines a fixed and unchangeable mapping from each of these operations to a specially named method.

- **Such methods are called automatically when instances appear in built-in operations.** For instance, if an instance object inherits an __add__ method, that method is called whenever the object appears in a + expression. The method's return value becomes the result of the corresponding expression.

- **Classes may override most built-in type operations.** There are dozens of special operator overloading method names for intercepting and implementing nearly every operation available for built-in types. This includes expressions, but also basic operations like printing and object creation.

- **There are no defaults for operator overloading methods, and none are required.** If a class does not define or inherit an operator overloading method, it just means that the corresponding operation is not supported for the class' instances. If there is no __add__, for example, + expressions raise exceptions.

- **Operators allow classes to integrate with Python's object model.** By overloading type operations, user-defined objects implemented with classes act just like built-ins, and so provide consistency as well as compatibility with expected interfaces.

Operator overloading is an optional feature; it's used primarily by people developing tools for other Python programmers, not by application developers. And, candidly, you probably shouldn't try to use it just because it seems "cool." Unless a class needs to mimic built-in type interfaces, it should usually stick to simpler named methods. Why would an employee database application support expressions like * and +, for example? Named methods like giveRaise and promote would usually make more sense.

Because of this, we won't go into details on every operator overloading method available in Python in this book. Still, there is one operator overloading method you are likely to see in almost every realistic Python class: the __init__ method, which is known as the *constructor* method, and is used to initialize objects' state. You should pay special attention to this method, because __init__, along with the self argument, turns out to be one of the keys to understanding OOP code in Python.

A Third Example

On to another example. This time, we'll define a subclass of SecondClass that implements three specially named attributes that Python will call automatically: `__init__` is called when a new instance object is being constructed (self is the new ThirdClass object), and `__add__` and `__mul__` are called when a ThirdClass instance appears in a + or * expression, respectively. Here's our new subclass:

```
>>> class ThirdClass(SecondClass):          # Is a SecondClass
...     def __init__(self, value):          # On "ThirdClass(value)"
...         self.data = value
...     def __add__(self, other):           # On "self + other"
...         return ThirdClass(self.data + other)
...     def __mul__(self, other):
...         self.data = self.data * other   # On "self * other"
...
>>> a = ThirdClass("abc")        # New __init__ called
>>> a.display()                  # Inherited method
Current value = "abc"

>>> b = a + 'xyz'                # New __add__: makes a new instance
>>> b.display()
Current value = "abcxyz"

>>> a * 3                        # New __mul__: changes instance in-place
>>> a.display()
Current value = "abcabcabc"
```

ThirdClass "is a" SecondClass, so its instances inherit the display method from SecondClass. But, ThirdClass generation calls pass an argument now (e.g., "abc"); it's passed to the value argument in the `__init__` constructor and assigned to self.data there. Further, ThirdClass objects can show up in + and * expressions; Python passes the instance object on the left to the self argument, and the value on the right to other, as illustrated in Figure 23-3.

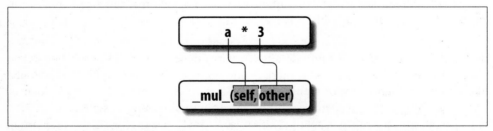

Figure 23-3. In operator overloading, expression operators and other built-on operations performed on class instances are mapped back to specially named methods in the class. These special methods are optional, and may be inherited as usual. Here, a "*" expression triggers the "_mul_" method.

Specially named methods such as __init__ and __add__ are inherited by subclasses and instances, just like any other names assigned in a class. If the methods are not coded in a class, Python looks for such names in all its superclasses, as usual. Operator overloading method names are also not built-in or reserved words; they are just attributes that Python looks for when objects appear in various contexts. Python usually calls them automatically, but they may occasionally be called by your code as well (more on this later; the __init__ method, for example, is often called manually to trigger superclass constructors).

Notice that the __add__ method makes and returns a *new* instance object of its class (by calling ThirdClass with the result value), but __mul__ *changes* the current instance object in-place (by reassigning the self attribute). This is different from the behavior of built-in types such as numbers and strings, which always make new objects for the * operator. Because operator overloading is really just an expression-to-method dispatch mechanism, you can interpret operators any way you like in your own class objects.*

Why Use Operator Overloading?

As a class designer, you can choose to use operator overloading or not. Your choice simply depends on how much you want your object to look and feel like a built-in type. As mentioned earlier, if you omit an operator overloading method, and do not inherit it from a superclass, the corresponding operation will not be supported for your instances; if it's attempted, an exception will be thrown (or a standard default will be used).

Frankly, many operator overloading methods tend to be used only when implementing objects that are mathematical in nature; a vector or matrix class may overload the addition operator, for example, but an employee class likely would not. For simpler classes, you might not use overloading at all, and would rely instead on explicit method calls to implement your objects' behavior.

On the other hand, you might decide to use operator overloading if you need to pass a user-defined object to a function that was coded to expect the operators available on a built-in type like a list or a dictionary. Implementing the same operator set in your class will ensure that your objects support the same expected object interface, and so are compatible with the function.

One overloading method seems to show up in almost every realistic class: the __init__ constructor method. Because it allows classes to fill out the attributes in their newly created instances immediately, the constructor is useful for almost every kind of class

---

* But you probably shouldn't. Common practice dictates that overloaded operators should work the same way the built-in operator implementations do. In this case, that means our __mul__ method should also return a new object as its result, rather than changing the instance (self) in place; for in-place changes, a mul method call may be better style than a * overload here (e.g., a.mul(3) instead of a * 3).

you might code. In fact, even though instance attributes are not declared in Python, you can usually find out which attributes an instance will have by inspecting its class' __init__ method code. We won't go into too much detail on this advanced feature in this book, but we'll see some additional inheritance and operator overloading techniques in action in Chapter 24.

The World's Simplest Python Class

We've begun studying class statement syntax in detail in this chapter, but I'd again like to remind you that the basic inheritance model that classes produce is very simple—all it really involves is searching for attributes in trees of linked objects. In fact, we can create a class with nothing in it at all. The following statement makes a class with no attributes attached (an empty namespace object):

```
>>> class rec: pass                    # Empty namespace object
```

We need the no-operation pass statement (discussed in Chapter 13) here because we don't have any methods to code. After we make the class by running this statement interactively, we can start attaching attributes to the class by assigning names to it completely outside of the original class statement:

```
>>> rec.name = 'Bob'                   # Just objects with attributes
>>> rec.age  = 40
```

And, after we've created these attributes by assignment, we can fetch them with the usual syntax. When used this way, a class is roughly similar to a "struct" in C, or a "record" in Pascal—an object with field names attached to it (we can do similar work with dictionary keys, but it requires extra characters):

```
>>> print rec.name                     # Like a C struct or a record
Bob
```

Notice that this works even though there are no instances of the class yet; classes are objects in their own right, even without instances. In fact, they are just self-contained namespaces, so as long as we have a reference to a class, we can set or change its attributes anytime we wish. Watch what happens when we do create two instances, though:

```
>>> x = rec( )                         # Instances inherit class names
>>> y = rec( )
```

These instances begin their lives as completely empty namespace objects. Because they remember the class they were made from, though, they will obtain the attributes we attached to the class by inheritance:

```
>>> x.name, y.name                     # Name is stored on the class only here
('Bob', 'Bob')
```

Really, these instances have no attributes of their own; they simply fetch the `name` attribute from the class object where it is stored. If we do assign an attribute to an instance, though, it creates (or changes) the attribute in that object, and no other—attribute references kick off inheritance searches, but attribute assignments affect only the objects in which the attributes are assigned. Here, x gets its own `name`, but y still inherits the `name` attached to the class above it:

```
>>> x.name = 'Sue'                    # But assignment changes x only
>>> rec.name, x.name, y.name
('Bob', 'Sue', 'Bob')
```

In fact, as we'll explore in more detail in the next chapter, the attributes of a namespace object are usually implemented as dictionaries, and class inheritance trees are (generally speaking) just dictionaries with links to other dictionaries. If you know where to look, you can see this explicitly. The `__dict__` attribute is the namespace dictionary for most class-based objects:

```
>>> rec.__dict__.keys()
['age', '__module__', '__doc__', 'name']

>>> x.__dict__.keys()
['name']

>>> y.__dict__.keys()
[]
```

Here, the class' dictionary shows the `name` and `age` attributes we assigned to it, x has its own `name`, and y is still empty. Each instance has a link to its class for inheritance, though—it's called `__class__`, if you want to inspect it:

```
>>> x.__class__
<class __main__.rec at 0x00BAFF60>
```

Classes also have a `__bases__` attribute, which is a tuple of their superclasses; these two attributes are how class trees are literally represented in memory by Python.

The main point to take away from this look under the hood is that Python's class model is extremely dynamic. Classes and instances are just namespace objects, with attributes created on the fly by assignment. Those assignments usually happen within the `class` statements you code, but they can occur anywhere you have a reference to one of the objects in the tree.

Even methods, normally created by a `def` nested in a `class`, can be created completely independent of any class object. The following, for example, defines a simple function outside of any class that takes one argument:

```
>>> def upperName(self):
...     return self.name.upper()     # Still needs a self
```

There is nothing about a class here yet—it's a simple function, and it can be called as such at this point, provided we pass in an object with a name attribute (the name self does not make this special in any way). If we assign this simple function to an attribute of our class, though, it becomes a method, callable through any instance (as well as through the class name itself, as long as we pass in an instance manually):[*]

```
>>> rec.method = upperName

>>> x.method( )                    # Run  method to process x
'SUE'

>>> y.method( )                    # Same, but  pass y to self
'BOB'

>>> rec.method(x)                  # Can call through instance or class
'SUE'
```

Normally, classes are filled out by class statements, and instance attributes are created by assignments to self attributes in method functions. The point again, though, is that they don't have to be; OOP in Python really is mostly about looking up attributes in linked namespace objects.

Chapter Summary

This chapter introduced the basics of coding classes in Python. We studied the syntax of the class statement, and saw how to use it to build up a class inheritance tree. We also studied how Python automatically fills in the first argument in method functions, how attributes are attached to objects in a class tree by simple assignment, and how specially named operator overloading methods intercept and implement built-in operations for our instances (e.g., expressions and printing).

In the next chapter, we'll continue our look at class coding, taking a second pass over the model to fill in some of the details that were omitted here to keep things simple. We'll also start to explore some larger and more realistic classes. First, though, let's work through a quiz to review the basics we've covered so far.

---

[*] In fact, this is one of the reasons the self argument must always be explicit in Python methods—because methods can be created as simple functions independent of a class, they need to make the implied instance argument explicit. Python cannot otherwise guess that a simple function might eventually become a class method. The main reason for the explicit self argument, though, is to make the meanings of names more obvious: names not referenced through self are simple variables, while names referenced through self are obviously instance attributes.

Chapter Quiz

1. How are classes related to modules?
2. How are instances and classes created?
3. Where and how are class attributes created?
4. Where and how are instance attributes created?
5. What does self mean in a Python class?
6. How is operator overloading coded in a Python class?
7. When might you want to support operator overloading in your classes?
8. Which operator overloading method is most commonly used?
9. What are the two most important concepts in Python OOP code?

Quiz Answers

1. Classes are always nested inside a module; they are attributes of a module object. Classes and modules are both namespaces, but classes correspond to statements (not entire files), and support the OOP notions of multiple instances, inheritance, and operator overloading. In a sense, a module is like a single-instance class without inheritance that corresponds to an entire file of code.

2. Classes are made by running class statements; instances are created by calling a class as though it were a function.

3. Class attributes are created by assigning attributes to a class object. They are normally generated by top-level assignments nested in a class statement—each name assigned in the class statement block becomes an attribute of the class object (technically, the class statement scope morphs into the class object's attribute namespace). Class attributes can also be created, though, by assigning attributes to the class anywhere a reference to the class object exists—i.e., even outside the class statement.

4. Instance attributes are created by assigning attributes to an instance object. They are normally created within class method functions inside the class statement by assigning attributes to the self argument (which is always the implied instance). Again, though, they may be created by assignment anywhere a reference to the instance appears, even outside the class statement. Normally, all instance attributes are initialized in the __init__ constructor method; that way, later method calls can assume the attributes already exist.

5. `self` is the name commonly given to the first (leftmost) argument in a class method function; Python automatically fills it in with the instance object that is the implied subject of the method call. This argument need not be called `self`; its position is what is significant. (Ex-C++ or Java programmers might prefer to call it `this` because in those languages that name reflects the same idea; in Python, though, this argument must always be explicit.)

6. Operator overloading is coded in a Python class with specially named methods; they all begin and end with double underscores to make them unique. These are not built-in or reserved names; Python just runs them automatically when an instance appears in the corresponding operation. Python defines the mappings from operations to special method names.

7. Operator overloading is useful to implement objects that resemble built-in types (e.g., sequences or numeric objects such as matrixes), and to mimic the built-in type interface expected by a piece of code. Mimicking built-in type interfaces enables you to pass in class instances that also have state information—i.e., attributes that remember data between operation calls. You shouldn't use operator overloading when a simple named method will suffice, though.

8. The `__init__` constructor method is the most commonly used; almost every class uses this method to set initial values for instance attributes and perform other startup tasks.

9. The special `self` argument in method functions and the `__init__` constructor method are the two cornerstones of OOP code in Python.

## CHAPTER 24

Class Coding Details

If you did not understand all of Chapter 23, don't worry; now that we've had a quick tour, we're going to dig a bit deeper and study the concepts introduced earlier in further detail. In this chapter, we'll take another look at classes and methods, inheritance, and operator overloading, formalizing and expanding on some of the class coding ideas introduced in Chapter 23. Because the class is our last namespace tool, we'll summarize the concepts of namespaces in Python here as well. This chapter will also present some larger and more realistic classes than those we have seen so far, including a final example that ties together much of what we've learned about OOP.

The class Statement

Although the Python class statement may seem similar to tools in other OOP languages on the surface, on closer inspection, it is quite different from what some programmers are used to. For example, as in C++, the class statement is Python's main OOP tool, but unlike in C++, Python's class is not a declaration. Like a def, a class statement is an object builder, and an implicit assignment—when run, it generates a class object, and stores a reference to it in the name used in the header. Also, like a def, a class statement is true executable code—your class doesn't exist until Python reaches and runs the class statement that defines it (typically while importing the module it is coded in, but not before).

General Form

class is a compound statement, with a body of indented statements typically appearing under the header. In the header, superclasses are listed in parentheses after the class name, separated by commas. Listing more than one superclass leads to multiple inheritance (which we'll discuss further in the next chapter). Here is the statement's general form:

```
class <name>(superclass,...):      # Assign to name
    data = value                   # Shared class data
```

```
    def method(self,...):              # Methods
        self.member = value            # Per-instance data
```

Within the class statement, any assignments generate class attributes, and specially named methods overload operators; for instance, a function called __init__ is called at instance object construction time, if defined.

Example

As we've seen, classes are mostly just namespaces—that is, tools for defining names (i.e., attributes) that export data and logic to clients. So, how do you get from the class statement to a namespace?

Here's how. Just like in a module file, the statements nested in a class statement body create its attributes. When Python executes a class statement (not a call to a class), it runs all the statements in its body, from top to bottom. Assignments that happen during this process create names in the class' local scope, which become attributes in the associated class object. Because of this, classes resemble both modules and functions:

- Like functions, class statements are local scopes where names created by nested assignments live.

- Like names in a module, names assigned in a class statement become attributes in a class object.

The main distinction for classes is that their namespaces are also the basis of inheritance in Python; reference attributes that are not found in a class or instance object are fetched from other classes.

Because class is a compound statement, any sort of statement can be nested inside its body—print, =, if, def, and so on. All the statements inside the class statement run when the class statement itself runs (not when the class is later called to make an instance). Assigning names inside the class statement makes class attributes, and nested defs make class methods, but other assignments make attributes, too.

For example, assignments of simple nonfunction objects to class attributes produce *data attributes*, shared by all instances:

```
>>> class SharedData:
...     spam = 42                      # Generates a class data attribute
...
>>> x = SharedData( )                  # Make two instances
>>> y = SharedData( )
>>> x.spam, y.spam                     # They inherit and share spam
(42, 42)
```

Here, because the name spam is assigned at the top level of a class statement, it is attached to the class, and so will be shared by all instances. We can change it by going through the class name, and refer to it through either instances or the class.*

```
>>> SharedData.spam = 99
>>> x.spam, y.spam, SharedData.spam
(99, 99, 99)
```

Such class attributes can be used to manage information that spans all the instances—a counter of the number of instances generated, for example (we'll expand on this idea in Chapter 26). Now, watch what happens if we assign the name spam through an instance instead of the class:

```
>>> x.spam = 88
>>> x.spam, y.spam, SharedData.spam
(88, 99, 99)
```

Assignments to instance attributes create or change the names in the instance, rather than in the shared class. More generally, inheritance searches occur only on attribute *references*, not on assignment: assigning to an object's attribute always changes that object, and no other.† For example, y.spam is looked up in the class by inheritance, but the assignment to x.spam attaches a name to x itself.

Here's a more comprehensive example of this behavior that stores the same name in two places. Suppose we run the following class:

```
class MixedNames:                         # Define class
    data = 'spam'                         # Assign class attr
    def __init__(self, value):            # Assign method name
        self.data = value                 # Assign instance attr
    def display(self):
        print self.data, MixedNames.data  # Instance attr, class attr
```

This class contains two defs, which bind class attributes to method functions. It also contains an = assignment statement; because this assignment assigns the name data inside the class, it lives in the class' local scope, and becomes an attribute of the class object. Like all class attributes, this data is inherited, and shared by all instances of the class that don't have data attributes of their own.

When we make instances of this class, the name data is attached to those instances by the assignment to self.data in the constructor method:

```
>>> x = MixedNames(1)         # Make two instance objects
>>> y = MixedNames(2)         # Each has its own data
>>> x.display(); y.display()  # self.data differs, MixedNames.data is the same
```

---

* If you've used C++ you may recognize this as similar to the notion of C++'s "static" data members—members that are stored in the class, independent of instances. In Python, it's nothing special: all class attributes are just names assigned in the class statement, whether they happen to reference functions (C++'s "methods") or something else (C++'s "members").

† Unless the class has redefined the attribute assignment operation to do something unique with the __setattr__ operator overloading method.

```
1 spam
2 spam
```

The net result is that data lives in two places: in the instance objects (created by the self.data assignment in __init__), and in the class from which they inherit names (created by the data assignment in the class). The class' display method prints both versions, by first qualifying the self instance, and then the class.

By using these techniques to store attributes in different objects, we determine their scope of visibility. When attached to classes, names are shared; in instances, names record per-instance data, not shared behavior or data. Although inheritance searches look up names for us, we can always get to an attribute anywhere in a tree by accessing the desired object directly.

In the preceding example, for instance, specifying x.data or self.data will return an instance name, which normally hides the same name in the class; however, MixedNames.data grabs the class name explicitly. We'll see various roles for such coding patterns later; the next section describes one of the most common.

Methods

Because you already know about functions, you also know about methods in classes. Methods are just function objects created by def statements nested in a class statement's body. From an abstract perspective, methods provide behavior for instance objects to inherit. From a programming perspective, methods work in exactly the same way as simple functions, with one crucial exception: a method's first argument always receives the instance object that is the implied subject of the method call.

In other words, Python automatically maps instance method calls to class method functions as follows. Method calls made through an instance, like this:

```
instance.method(args...)
```

are automatically translated to class method function calls of this form:

```
class.method(instance, args...)
```

where the class is determined by locating the method name using Python's inheritance search procedure. In fact, both call forms are valid in Python.

Besides the normal inheritance of method attribute names, the special first argument is the only real magic behind method calls. In a class method, the first argument is usually called self by convention (technically, only its position is significant, not its name). This argument provides methods with a hook back to the instance that is the subject of the call—because classes generate many instance objects, they need to use this argument to manage data that varies per instance.

C++ programmers may recognize Python's self argument as being similar to C++'s this pointer. In Python, though, self is always explicit in your code: methods must always go through `self` to fetch or change attributes of the instance being processed by the current method call. This explicit nature of `self` is by design—the presence of this name makes it obvious that you are using instance attribute names in your script, not names in the local or global scope.

Example

To clarify these concepts, let's turn to an example. Suppose we define the following class:

```
class NextClass:                    # Define class
    def printer(self, text):        # Define method
        self.message = text         # Change instance
        print self.message          # Access instance
```

The name `printer` references a function object; because it's assigned in the class statement's scope, it becomes a class object attribute, and is inherited by every instance made from the class. Normally, because methods like `printer` are designed to process instances, we call them through instances:

```
>>> x = NextClass( )                # Make instance

>>> x.printer('instance call')      # Call its method
instance call

>>> x.message                       # Instance changed
'instance call'
```

When we call it by qualifying an instance like this, `printer` is first located by inheritance, and then its `self` argument is automatically assigned the instance object (x); the text argument gets the string passed at the call (`'instance call'`). Notice that because Python automatically passes the first argument to `self` for us, we only actually have to pass in one argument. Inside `printer`, the name `self` is used to access or set per-instance data because it refers back to the instance currently being processed.

Methods may be called in one of two ways—through an instance, or through the class itself. For example, we can also call `printer` by going through the class name, provided we pass an instance to the `self` argument explicitly:

```
>>> NextClass.printer(x, 'class call')    # Direct class call
class call

>>> x.message                             # Instance changed again
'class call'
```

Calls routed through the instance and the class have the exact same effect, as long as we pass the same instance object ourselves in the class form. By default, in fact, you get an error message if you try to call a method without any instance:

```
>>> NextClass.printer('bad call')
TypeError: unbound method printer( ) must be called with NextClass instance...
```

Calling Superclass Constructors

Methods are normally called through instances. Calls to methods through the class, though, do show up in a variety of special roles. One common scenario involves the constructor method. The __init__ method, like all attributes, is looked up by inheritance. This means that at construction time, Python locates and calls just one __init__. If subclass constructors need to guarantee that superclass construction-time logic runs, too, they generally must call the superclass's __init__ method explicitly through the class:

```
class Super:
    def __init__(self, x):
        ...default code...

class Sub(Super):
    def __init__(self, x, y):
        Super.__init__(self, x)          # Run superclass __init__
        ...custom code...                # Do my init actions

I = Sub(1, 2)
```

This is one of the few contexts in which your code is likely to call an operator overloading method directly. Naturally, you should only call the superclass constructor this way if you really want it to run—without the call, the subclass replaces it completely. For a more realistic illustration of this technique in action, stay tuned for the final example in this chapter.[*]

Other Method Call Possibilities

This pattern of calling methods through a class is the general basis of extending (instead of completely replacing) inherited method behavior. In Chapter 26, we'll also meet a new option added in Python 2.2, *static* methods, that allow you to code methods that do not expect instance objects in their first arguments. Such methods can act like simple instanceless functions, with names that are local to the classes in which they are coded. This is an advanced and optional extension, though; normally, you must always pass an instance to a method, whether it is called through an instance or a class.

Inheritance

The whole point of a namespace tool like the class statement is to support name inheritance. This section expands on some of the mechanisms and roles of attribute inheritance in Python.

---

[*] On a somewhat related note, you can also code multiple __init__ methods within the same class, but only the last definition will be used; see Chapter 25 for more details.

In Python, inheritance happens when an object is qualified, and it involves searching an attribute definition tree (one or more namespaces). Every time you use an expression of the form object.attr (where object is an instance or class object), Python searches the namespace tree from bottom to top, beginning with object, looking for the first attr it can find. This includes references to self attributes in your methods. Because lower definitions in the tree override higher ones, inheritance forms the basis of specialization.

Attribute Tree Construction

Figure 24-1 summarizes the way namespace trees are constructed and populated with names. Generally:

- Instance attributes are generated by assignments to self attributes in methods.
- Class attributes are created by statements (assignments) in class statements.
- Superclass links are made by listing classes in parentheses in a class statement header.

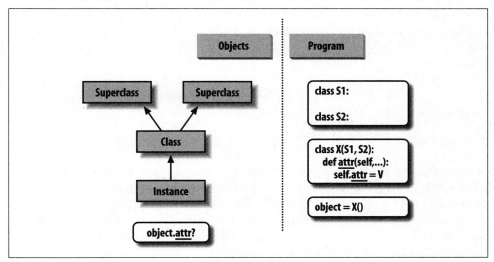

Figure 24-1. Program code creates a tree of objects in memory to be searched by attribute inheritance. Calling a class creates a new instance that remembers its class, running a class statement creates a new class, and superclasses are listed in parentheses in the class statement header. Each attribute reference triggers a new bottom-up tree search—even self attributes within a class' methods.

The net result is a tree of attribute namespaces that leads from an instance, to the class it was generated from, to all the superclasses listed in the class header. Python searches upward in this tree, from instances to superclasses, each time you use qualification to fetch an attribute name from an instance object.*

Specializing Inherited Methods

The tree-searching model of inheritance just described turns out to be a great way to specialize systems. Because inheritance finds names in subclasses before it checks superclasses, subclasses can replace default behavior by redefining their superclasses' attributes. In fact, you can build entire systems as hierarchies of classes, which are extended by adding new external subclasses rather than changing existing logic in-place.

The idea of redefining inherited names leads to a variety of specialization techniques. For instance, subclasses may *replace* inherited attributes completely, *provide* attributes that a superclass expects to find, and *extend* superclass methods by calling back to the superclass from an overridden method. We've already seen replacement in action. Here's an example that shows how extension works:

```
>>> class Super:
...     def method(self):
...         print 'in Super.method'
...
>>> class Sub(Super):
...     def method(self):                   # Override method
...         print 'starting Sub.method'     # Add actions here
...         Super.method(self)              # Run default action
...         print 'ending Sub.method'
...
```

Direct superclass method calls are the crux of the matter here. The Sub class replaces Super's method function with its own specialized version. But, within the replacement, Sub calls back to the version exported by Super to carry out the default behavior. In other words, Sub.method just extends Super.method's behavior, rather than replacing it completely:

```
>>> x = Super()          # Make a Super instance
>>> x.method()           # Runs Super.method
in Super.method

>>> x = Sub()            # Make a Sub instance
>>> x.method()           # Runs Sub.method, which calls Super.method
starting Sub.method
in Super.method
ending Sub.method
```

---

* This description isn't 100 percent complete because we can also create instance and class attributes by assigning to objects outside class statements—but that's a much less common and sometimes more error-prone approach (changes aren't isolated to class statements). In Python, all attributes are always accessible by default; we'll talk more about name privacy in Chapter 26.

This extension coding pattern is also commonly used with constructors; see the earlier section, "Methods," for an example.

Class Interface Techniques

Extension is only one way to interface with a superclass. The file shown below, *specialize.py*, defines multiple classes that illustrate a variety of common techniques:

Super
   Defines a method function and a delegate that expects an action in a subclass.

Inheritor
   Doesn't provide any new names, so it gets everything defined in Super.

Replacer
   Overrides Super's method with a version of its own.

Extender
   Customizes Super's method by overriding and calling back to run the default.

Provider
   Implements the action method expected by Super's delegate method.

Study each of these subclasses to get a feel for the various ways they customize their common superclass. Here's the file:

```
class Super:
    def method(self):
        print 'in Super.method'            # Default behavior
    def delegate(self):
        self.action()                       # Expected to be defined

class Inheritor(Super):                     # Inherit method verbatim
    pass

class Replacer(Super):                      # Replace method completely
    def method(self):
        print 'in Replacer.method'

class Extender(Super):                      # Extend method behavior
    def method(self):
        print 'starting Extender.method'
        Super.method(self)
        print 'ending Extender.method'

class Provider(Super):                      # Fill in a required method
    def action(self):
        print 'in Provider.action'

if __name__ == '__main__':
    for klass in (Inheritor, Replacer, Extender):
        print '\n' + klass.__name__ + '...'
        klass().method()
```

```
      print '\nProvider...'
      x = Provider( )
      x.delegate( )
```

A few things are worth pointing out here. First, the self-test code at the end of this example creates instances of three different classes in a for loop. Because classes are objects, you can put them in a tuple, and create instances generically (more on this idea later). Classes also have the special __name__ attribute, like modules; it's preset to a string containing the name in the class header. Here's what happens when we run the file:

```
% python specialize.py

Inheritor...
in Super.method

Replacer...
in Replacer.method

Extender...
starting Extender.method
in Super.method
ending Extender.method

Provider...
in Provider.action
```

Abstract Superclasses

Notice how the Provider class in the prior example works. When we call the delegate method through a Provider instance, *two* independent inheritance searches occur:

1. On the initial x.delegate call, Python finds the delegate method in Super by searching the Provider instance and above. The instance x is passed into the method's self argument as usual.

2. Inside the Super.delegate method, self.action invokes a new, independent inheritance search of self and above. Because self references a Provider instance, the action method is located in the Provider subclass.

This "filling in the blanks" sort of coding structure is typical of OOP frameworks. At least in terms of the delegate method, the superclass in this example is what is sometimes called an *abstract superclass*—a class that expects parts of its behavior to be provided by its subclasses. If an expected method is not defined in a subclass, Python raises an undefined name exception when the inheritance search fails. Class coders sometimes make such subclass requirements more obvious with assert statements, or by raising the built-in NotImplementedError exception:

```
class Super:
    def method(self):
        print 'in Super.method'
```

```
        def delegate(self):
            self.action()
        def action(self):
            assert 0, 'action must be defined!'
```

We'll meet assert in Chapter 27; in short, if its expression evaluates to false, it raises an exception with an error message. Here, the expression is always false (0) so as to trigger an error message if a method is not redefined, and inheritance locates the version here. Alternatively, some classes simply raise a NotImplemented exception directly in such method stubs. We'll study the raise statement in Chapter 27.

For a somewhat more realistic example of this section's concepts in action, see exercise 8 at the end of Chapter 26, and its solution in "Part VI, Classes and OOP" (in Appendix B). Such taxonomies are a traditional way to introduce OOP, but they're a bit removed from most developers' job descriptions.

Operator Overloading

We looked briefly at operator overloading in the prior chapter; here, we'll fill in more details, and look at a few commonly used overloading methods. Here's a review of the key ideas behind overloading:

- Operator overloading lets classes intercept normal Python operations.
- Classes can overload all Python expression operators.
- Classes can also overload operations such as printing, function calls, attribute qualifications, etc.
- Overloading makes class instances act more like built-in types.
- Overloading is implemented by providing specially named class methods.

Let's look at a simple example of overloading at work. If certain specially named methods are provided in a class, Python automatically calls them when instances of the class appear in expressions related to the associated operations. For instance, the Number class in the following file, *number.py*, provides a method to intercept instance construction (__init__), as well as one for catching subtraction expressions (__sub__). Special methods such as these are the hooks that let you tie into built-in operations:

```
class Number:
    def __init__(self, start):         # On Number(start)
        self.data = start
    def __sub__(self, other):          # On instance - other
        return Number(self.data - other)   # Result is a new instance

>>> from number import Number          # Fetch class from module
>>> X = Number(5)                      # Number.__init__(X, 5)
>>> Y = X - 2                          # Number.__sub__(X, 2)
>>> Y.data                            # Y is new Number instance
3
```

As discussed previously, the __init__ constructor method seen in this code is the most commonly used operator overloading method in Python; it's present in most classes. In this section, we will sample some of the other tools available in this domain, and look at example code that applies them in common use cases.

Common Operator Overloading Methods

Just about everything you can do to built-in objects such as integers and lists has a corresponding specially named method for overloading in classes. Table 24-1 lists a few of the most common; there are many more. In fact, many overloading methods come in multiple versions (e.g., __add__, __radd__, and __iadd__ for addition). See other Python books, or the Python language reference manual, for an exhaustive list of the special method names available.

Table 24-1. Common operator overloading methods

Method	Overloads	Called for
__init__	Constructor	Object creation: X = Class( )
__del__	Destructor	Object reclamation
__add__	Operator +	X + Y, X += Y
__or__	Operator | (bitwise OR)	X | Y, X |= Y
__repr__, __str__	Printing, conversions	print X, repr(X), str(X)
__call__	Function calls	X( )
__getattr__	Qualification	X.undefined
__setattr__	Attribute assignment	X.any = value
__getitem__	Indexing	X[key], for loops and other iterations if no __iter__
__setitem__	Index assignment	X[key] = value
__len__	Length	len(X), truth tests
__cmp__	Comparison	X == Y, X < Y
__lt__	Specific comparison	X < Y (or else __cmp__)
__eq__	Specific comparison	X == Y (or else __cmp__)
__radd__	Right-side operator +	Noninstance + X
__iadd__	In-place (augmented) addition	X += Y (or else __add__)
__iter__	Iteration contexts	for loops, in tests, list comprehensions, map, others

All overloading methods have names that start and end with two underscores to keep them distinct from other names you define in your classes. The mappings from special method names to expressions or operations are predefined by the Python language (and documented in the standard language manual). For example, the name __add__ always maps to + expressions by Python language definition, regardless of what an __add__ method's code actually does.

All operator overloading methods are optional—if you don't code one, that operation is simply unsupported by your class (and may raise an exception if attempted). Most overloading methods are used only in advanced programs that require objects to behave like built-ins; the __init__ constructor tends to appear in most classes, however. We've already met the __init__ initialization-time constructor method, and a few of the others in Table 24-1. Let's explore some of the additional methods in the table by example.

__getitem__ Intercepts Index References

The __getitem__ method intercepts instance-indexing operations. When an instance X appears in an indexing expression like X[i], Python calls the __getitem__ method inherited by the instance (if any), passing X to the first argument, and the index in brackets to the second argument. For instance, the following class returns the square of an index value:

```
>>> class indexer:
...     def __getitem__(self, index):
...         return index ** 2
...
>>> X = indexer()
>>> X[2]                          # X[i] calls __getitem__(X, i).
4
>>> for i in range(5):
...     print X[i],
...
0 1 4 9 16
```

__getitem__ and __iter__ Implement Iteration

Here's a trick that isn't always obvious to beginners, but turns out to be incredibly useful. The for statement works by repeatedly indexing a sequence from zero to higher indexes, until an out-of-bounds exception is detected. Because of that, __getitem__ also turns out to be one way to overload iteration in Python—if this method is defined, for loops call the class' __getitem__ each time through, with successively higher offsets. It's a case of "buy one, get one free"—any built-in or user-defined object that responds to indexing also responds to iteration:

```
>>> class stepper:
...     def __getitem__(self, i):
...         return self.data[i]
...
>>> X = stepper()                 # X is a stepper object
>>> X.data = "Spam"
>>>
>>> X[1]                          # Indexing calls __getitem__
'p'
>>> for item in X:                # for loops call __getitem__
...     print item,               # for indexes items 0..N
...
S p a m
```

In fact, it's really a case of "buy one, get a bunch free." Any class that supports for loops automatically supports all iteration contexts in Python, many of which we've seen in earlier chapters (see Chapter 13 for other iteration contexts). For example, the in membership test, list comprehensions, the map built-in, list and tuple assignments, and type constructors will also call __getitem__ automatically, if it's defined:

```
>>> 'p' in X                    # All call __getitem__ too
True

>>> [c for c in X]              # List comprehension
['S', 'p', 'a', 'm']

>>> map(None, X)                # map calls
['S', 'p', 'a', 'm']

>>> (a, b, c, d) = X            # Sequence assignments
>>> a, c, d
('S', 'a', 'm')

>>> list(X), tuple(X), ''.join(X)
(['S', 'p', 'a', 'm'], ('S', 'p', 'a', 'm'), 'Spam')

>>> X
<__main__.stepper instance at 0x00A8D5D0>
```

In practice, this technique can be used to create objects that provide a sequence interface and to add logic to built-in sequence type operations; we'll revisit this idea when extending built-in types in Chapter 26.

User-Defined Iterators

Today, all iteration contexts in Python will try the __iter__ method first, before trying __getitem__. That is, they prefer the iteration protocol we learned about in Chapter 13 to repeatedly indexing an object; if the object does not support the iteration protocol, indexing is attempted instead.

Technically, iteration contexts work by calling the iter built-in function to try to find an __iter__ method, which is expected to return an iterator object. If it's provided, Python then repeatedly calls this iterator object's next method to produce items until a StopIteration exception is raised. If no such __iter__ method is found, Python falls back on the __getitem__ scheme, and repeatedly indexes by offsets as before, until an IndexError exception is raised.

In the new scheme, classes implement user-defined iterators by simply implementing the iterator protocol introduced in Chapters 13 and 17 (refer back to those chapters for more background details on iterators). For example, the following file, *iters.py*, defines a user-defined iterator class that generates squares:

```
class Squares:
    def __init__(self, start, stop):    # Save state when created
        self.value = start - 1
        self.stop  = stop
```

```
        def __iter__(self):              # Get iterator object on iter()
            return self
        def next(self):                   # Return a square on each iteration
            if self.value == self.stop:
                raise StopIteration
            self.value += 1
            return self.value ** 2

% python
>>> from iters import Squares
>>> for i in Squares(1, 5):              # for calls iter(), which calls __iter__()
...     print i,                          # Each iteration calls next()
...
1 4 9 16 25
```

Here, the iterator object is simply the instance self because the next method is part of this class. In more complex scenarios, the iterator object may be defined as a separate class and object with its own state information to support multiple active iterations over the same data (we'll see an example of this in a moment). The end of the iteration is signaled with a Python raise statement (more on raising exceptions in the next part of this book).

An equivalent coding with __getitem__ might be less natural because the for would then iterate through all offsets zero and higher; the offsets passed in would be only indirectly related to the range of values produced (0..N would need to map to start..stop). Because __iter__ objects retain explicitly managed state between next calls, they can be more general than __getitem__.

On the other hand, __iter__-based iterators can sometimes be more complex and less convenient than __getitem__. They are really designed for iteration, not random indexing—in fact, they don't overload the indexing expression at all:

```
>>> X = Squares(1, 5)
>>> X[1]
AttributeError: Squares instance has no attribute '__getitem__'
```

The __iter__ scheme is also the implementation for all the other iteration contexts we saw in action for __getitem__ (membership tests, type constructors, sequence assignment, and so on). However, unlike __getitem__, __iter__ is designed for a single traversal, not many. For example, the Squares class is a one-shot iteration; once iterated, it's empty. You need to make a new iterator object for each new iteration:

```
>>> X = Squares(1, 5)
>>> [n for n in X]                        # Exhausts items
[1, 4, 9, 16, 25]
>>> [n for n in X]                        # Now it's empty
[]
>>> [n for n in Squares(1, 5)]            # Make a new iterator object
[1, 4, 9, 16, 25]
>>> list(Squares(1, 3))
[1, 4, 9]
```

Notice that this example would probably be simpler if coded with generator functions (a topic introduced in Chapter 17 and related to iterators):

```
>>> from __future__ import generators        # Needed in Python 2.2, but not later
>>>
>>> def gsquares(start, stop):
...     for i in range(start, stop+1):
...         yield i ** 2
...
>>> for i in gsquares(1, 5):
...     print i,
...
1 4 9 16 25
```

Unlike the class, the function automatically saves its state between iterations. Of course, for this artificial example, you could, in fact, skip both techniques and simply use a for loop, map, or list comprehension to build the list all at once. The best and fastest way to accomplish a task in Python is often also the simplest:

```
>>> [x ** 2 for x in range(1, 6)]
[1, 4, 9, 16, 25]
```

However, classes may be better at modeling more complex iterations, especially when they can benefit from state information and inheritance hierarchies. The next section explores one such use case.

Multiple iterators on one object

Earlier, I mentioned that the iterator object may be defined as a separate class with its own state information to support multiple active iterations over the same data. Consider what happens when we step across a built-in type like a string:

```
>>> S = 'ace'
>>> for x in S:
...     for y in S:
...         print x + y,
...
aa ac ae ca cc ce ea ec ee
```

Here, the outer loop grabs an iterator from the string by calling iter, and each nested loop does the same to get an independent iterator. Because each active iterator has its own state information, each loop can maintain its own position in the string, regardless of any other active loops. To achieve the same effect with user-defined iterators, __iter__ simply needs to define a new stateful object for the iterator, instead of returning self.

The following, for instance, defines an iterator class that skips every other item on iterations; because the iterator object is created anew for each iteration, it supports multiple active loops:

```
    class SkipIterator:
        def __init__(self, wrapped):
            self.wrapped = wrapped            # Iterator state information
            self.offset  = 0
        def next(self):
            if self.offset >= len(self.wrapped):    # Terminate iterations
                raise StopIteration
            else:
                item = self.wrapped[self.offset]    # else return and skip
                self.offset += 2
                return item

    class SkipObject:
        def __init__(self, wrapped):            # Save item to be used
            self.wrapped = wrapped
        def __iter__(self):
            return SkipIterator(self.wrapped)    # New iterator each time

    if __name__ == '__main__':
        alpha = 'abcdef'
        skipper = SkipObject(alpha)             # Make container object
        I = iter(skipper)                       # Make an iterator on it
        print I.next(), I.next(), I.next()      # Visit offsets 0, 2, 4

        for x in skipper:              # for calls __iter__ automatically
            for y in skipper:          # Nested fors call __iter__ again each time
                print x + y,           # Each iterator has its own state, offset
```

When run, this example works like the nested loops with built-in strings—each active loop has its own position in the string because each obtains an independent iterator object that records its own state information:

```
% python skipper.py
a c e
aa ac ae ca cc ce ea ec ee
```

By contrast, our earlier Squares example supports just one active iteration, unless we call Squares again in nested loops to obtain new objects. Here, there is just one SkipObject, with multiple iterator objects created from it.

As before, we could achieve similar results with built-in tools—for example, slicing with a third bound to skip items:

```
>>> S = 'abcdef'
>>> for x in S[::2]:
...     for y in S[::2]:            # New objects on each iteration
...         print x + y,
...
aa ac ae ca cc ce ea ec ee
```

This isn't quite the same, though, for two reasons. First, each slice expression here will physically store the result list all at once in memory; iterators, on the other hand, produce just one value at a time, which can save substantial space for large result lists. Second, slices produce new objects, so we're not really iterating over the same object in multiple places here. To be closer to the class, we would need to make a single object to step across by slicing ahead of time:

```
>>> S = 'abcdef'
>>> S = S[::2]
>>> S
'ace'
>>> for x in S:
...     for y in S:                    # Same object, new iterators
...         print x + y,
...
aa ac ae ca cc ce ea ec ee
```

This is more similar to our class-based solution, but it still stores the slice result in memory all at once (there is no generator form of slicing today), and it's only equivalent for this particular case of skipping every other item.

Because iterators can do anything a class can do, they are much more general than this example may imply. Whether our applications require such generality, user-defined iterators are a powerful tool—they allow us to make arbitrary objects look and feel like the other sequences and iterables we have met in this book. We could use this technique with a database object, for example, to make iterations to database fetches, with multiple cursors into the same query result.

_ _getattr_ _ and _ _setattr_ _ Catch Attribute References

The _ _getattr_ _ method intercepts attribute qualifications. More specifically, it's called with the attribute name as a string whenever you try to qualify an instance with an *undefined* (nonexistent) attribute name. It is not called if Python can find the attribute using its inheritance tree search procedure. Because of its behavior, _ _getattr_ _ is useful as a hook for responding to attribute requests in a generic fashion. For example:

```
>>> class empty:
...     def __getattr__(self, attrname):
...         if attrname == "age":
...             return 40
...         else:
...             raise AttributeError, attrname
...
>>> X = empty()
>>> X.age
40
>>> X.name
...error text omitted...
AttributeError: name
```

Here, the empty class and its instance X have no real attributes of their own, so the access to X.age gets routed to the _ _getattr_ _ method; self is assigned the instance (X), and attrname is assigned the undefined attribute name string ("age"). The class makes age look like a real attribute by returning a real value as the result of the X.age qualification expression (40). In effect, age becomes a *dynamically computed* attribute.

For attributes that the class doesn't know how to handle, this __getattr__ raises the built-in AttributeError exception to tell Python that these are bona fide undefined names; asking for X.name triggers the error. You'll see __getattr__ again when we see delegation and properties at work in the next two chapters, and I'll say more about exceptions in Part VII.

A related overloading method, __setattr__, intercepts *all* attribute assignments. If this method is defined, self.attr = value becomes self.__setattr__('attr', value). This is a bit trickier to use because assigning to any self attributes within __setattr__ calls __setattr__ again, causing an infinite recursion loop (and eventually, a stack overflow exception!). If you want to use this method, be sure that it assigns any instance attributes by indexing the attribute dictionary, discussed in the next section. Use self.__dict__['name'] = x, not self.name = x:

```
>>> class accesscontrol:
...     def __setattr__(self, attr, value):
...         if attr == 'age':
...             self.__dict__[attr] = value
...         else:
...             raise AttributeError, attr + ' not allowed'
...
>>> X = accesscontrol()
>>> X.age = 40                                      # Calls __setattr__
>>> X.age
40
>>> X.name = 'mel'
...text omitted...
AttributeError: name not allowed
```

These two attribute-access overloading methods allow you to control or specialize access to attributes in your objects. They tend to play highly specialized roles, some of which we'll explore later in this book.

Emulating Privacy for Instance Attributes

The following code generalizes the previous example, to allow each subclass to have its own list of private names that cannot be assigned to its instances:

```
class PrivateExc(Exception): pass              # More on exceptions later

class Privacy:
    def __setattr__(self, attrname, value):        # On self.attrname = value
        if attrname in self.privates:
            raise PrivateExc(attrname, self)
        else:
            self.__dict__[attrname] = value        # Self.attrname = value loops!
```

```
class Test1(Privacy):
    privates = ['age']

class Test2(Privacy):
    privates = ['name', 'pay']
    def __init__(self):
        self.__dict__['name'] = 'Tom'

x = Test1()
y = Test2()

x.name = 'Bob'
y.name = 'Sue'      # <== fails

y.age  = 30
x.age  = 40         # <== fails
```

In fact, this is first-cut solution for an implementation of attribute privacy in Python (i.e., disallowing changes to attribute names outside a class). Although Python doesn't support private declarations per se, techniques like this can emulate much of their purpose. This is a partial solution, though; to make it more effective, it must be augmented to allow subclasses to set private attributes too and to use __getattr__ and a wrapper (sometimes called a proxy) class to check for private attribute fetches.

I'll leave the complete solution as a suggested exercise, because even though privacy can be emulated this way, it almost never is in practice. Python programmers are able to write large OOP frameworks and applications without private declarations—an interesting finding about access controls in general that is beyond the scope of our purposes here.

Catching attribute references and assignments is generally a useful technique; it supports *delegation*, a design technique that allows controller objects to wrap up embedded objects, add new behaviors, and route other operations back to the wrapped objects (more on delegation and wrapper classes in the next chapter).

__repr__ and __str__ Return String Representations

The next example exercises the __init__ constructor, and the __add__ overload method we've already seen, but also defines a __repr__ method that returns a string representation for instances. String formatting is used to convert the managed self.data object to a string. If defined, __repr__ (or its sibling, __str__) is called automatically when class instances are printed or converted to strings. These methods allow you to define a better display format for your objects than the default instance display:

```
>>> class adder:
...     def __init__(self, value=0):
...         self.data = value          # Initialize data
...     def __add__(self, other):
...         self.data += other          # Add other in-place
...
```

```
>>> class addrepr(adder):                      # Inherit __init__, __add__
...     def __repr__(self):                     # Add string representation
...         return 'addrepr(%s)' % self.data    # Convert to string as code
...
>>> x = addrepr(2)                              # Runs __init__
>>> x + 1                                       # Runs __add__
>>> x                                           # Runs __repr__
addrepr(3)
>>> print x                                     # Runs __repr__
addrepr(3)
>>> str(x), repr(x)                             # Runs __repr__
('addrepr(3)', 'addrepr(3)')
```

So why two display methods? Roughly, `__str__` is tried first for user-friendly displays, such as the print statement, and the str built-in function. The `__repr__` method should in principle return a string that could be used as executable code to re-create the object; it's used for interactive prompt echoes, and the repr function. If no `__str__` is present, Python falls back on `__repr__` (but not vice versa):

```
>>> class addstr(adder):
...     def __str__(self):                      # __str__ but no __repr__
...         return '[Value: %s]' % self.data    # Convert to nice string
...
>>> x = addstr(3)
>>> x + 1
>>> x                                           # Default repr
<__main__.addstr instance at 0x00B35EF0>
>>> print x                                     # Runs __str__
[Value: 4]
>>> str(x), repr(x)
('[Value: 4]', '<__main__.addstr instance at 0x00B35EF0>')
```

Because of this, `__repr__` may be best if you want a single display for all contexts. By defining both methods, though, you can support different displays in different contexts—for example, an end-user display with `__str__`, and a low-level display for programmers to use during development with `__repr__`:

```
>>> class addboth(adder):
...     def __str__(self):
...         return '[Value: %s]' % self.data    # User-friendly string
...     def __repr__(self):
...         return 'addboth(%s)' % self.data    # As-code string
...
>>> x = addboth(4)
>>> x + 1
>>> x                                           # Runs __repr__
addboth(5)
>>> print x                                     # Runs __str__
[Value: 5]
>>> str(x), repr(x)
('[Value: 5]', 'addboth(5)')
```

In practice, `__str__` (or its low-level relative, `__repr__`) seems to be the second most commonly used operator overloading method in Python scripts, behind `__init__`; any time you can print an object and see a custom display, one of these two tools is probably in use.

__radd__ Handles Right-Side Addition

Technically, the `__add__` method that appeared in the prior example does not support the use of instance objects on the right side of the + operator. To implement such expressions, and hence support *commutative*-style operators, code the `__radd__` method as well. Python calls `__radd__` only when the object on the right side of the + is your class instance, but the object on the left is not an instance of your class. The `__add__` method for the object on the left is called instead in all other cases:

```
>>> class Commuter:
...     def __init__(self, val):
...         self.val = val
...     def __add__(self, other):
...         print 'add', self.val, other
...     def __radd__(self, other):
...         print 'radd', self.val, other
...
>>> x = Commuter(88)
>>> y = Commuter(99)
>>> x + 1                       # __add__: instance + noninstance
add 88 1
>>> 1 + y                       # __radd__: noninstance + instance
radd 99 1
>>> x + y                       # __add__: instance + instance
add 88 <__main__.Commuter instance at 0x0086C3D8>
```

Notice how the order is reversed in `__radd__`: self is really on the right of the +, and other is on the left. Every binary operator has a similar right-side overloading method (e.g., `__mul__` and `__rmul__`). Typically, a right-side method like `__radd__` just converts if needed, and reruns a + to trigger `__add__`, where the main logic is coded. Also, note that x and y are instances of the same class here; when instances of different classes appear mixed in an expression, Python prefers the class of the one on the left.

Right-side methods are an advanced topic, and tend to be fairly rarely used in practice; you only code them when you need operators to be commutative, and then only if you need to support operators at all. For instance, a Vector class may use these tools, but an Employee or Button class probably would not.

__call__ Intercepts Calls

The `__call__` method is called when your instance is called. No, this isn't a circular definition—if defined, Python runs a `__call__` method for function call expressions applied to your instances. This allows class instances to emulate the look and feel of things like functions:

```
>>> class Prod:
...     def __init__(self, value):
...         self.value = value
...     def __call__(self, other):
...         return self.value * other
...
>>> x = Prod(2)
>>> x(3)
6
>>> x(4)
8
```

In this example, the __call__ may seem a bit gratuitous. A simple method provides similar utility:

```
>>> class Prod:
...     def __init__(self, value):
...         self.value = value
...     def comp(self, other):
...         return self.value * other
...
>>> x = Prod(3)
>>> x.comp(3)
9
>>> x.comp(4)
12
```

However, __call__ can become more useful when interfacing with APIs that expect functions—it allows us to code objects that conform to an expected function call interface, but also retain state information. In fact, it's probably the third most commonly used operator overloading method, behind the __init__ constructor, and the __str__ and __repr__ display-format alternatives.

Function Interfaces and Callback-Based Code

As an example, the Tkinter GUI toolkit, which we'll meet later in this book, allows you to register functions as event handlers (a.k.a. callbacks); when events occur, Tkinter calls the registered objects. If you want an event handler to retain state between events, you can register either a class' *bound method*, or an *instance* that conforms to the expected interface with __call__. In this section's code, both x.comp from the second example, and x from the first, can pass as function-like objects this way.

I'll have more to say about bound methods in the next chapter, but for now, here's a hypothetical example of __call__ applied to the GUI domain. The following class defines an object that supports a function-call interface, but also has state information that remembers the color a button should change to when it is later pressed:

```
class Callback:
    def __init__(self, color):          # Function + state information
        self.color = color
    def __call__(self):                 # Support calls with no arguments
        print 'turn', self.color
```

Now, in the context of a GUI, we can register instances of this class as event handlers for buttons, even though the GUI expects to be able to invoke event handlers as simple functions with no arguments:

```
cb1 = Callback('blue')                    # 'Remember' blue
cb2 = Callback('green')

B1 = Button(command=cb1)                  # Register handlers
B2 = Button(command=cb2)                  # Register handlers
```

When the button is later pressed, the instance object is called as a simple function, exactly like in the following calls. Because it retains state as instance attributes, though, it remembers what to do:

```
cb1()                                     # On events: prints 'blue'
cb2()                                     # Prints 'green'
```

In fact, this is probably the best way to retain state information in the Python language—better than the techniques discussed earlier for functions (global variables, enclosing-function scope references, and default mutable arguments). With OOP, the state remembered is made explicit with attribute assignments.

Before we move on, there are two other ways that Python programmers sometimes tie information to a callback function like this. One option is to use default arguments in lambda functions:

```
cb3 = (lambda color='red': 'turn ' + color)   # Or: defaults
print cb3()
```

The other is to use bound methods of a class—a kind of object that remembers the self instance and the referenced function, such that it may be called as a simple function without an instance later:

```
class Callback:
    def __init__(self, color):            # Class with state information
        self.color = color
    def changeColor(self):                # A normal named method
        print 'turn', self.color

cb1 = Callback('blue')
cb2 = Callback('yellow')

B1 = Button(command=cb1.changeColor)      # Reference, but don't call
B2 = Button(command=cb2.changeColor)      # Remembers function+self
```

When this button is later pressed, it's as if the GUI does this, which invokes the changeColor method to process the object's state information:

```
object = Callback('blue')
cb = object.changeColor                   # Registered event handler
cb()                                      # On event prints 'blue'
```

This technique is simpler, but less general than overloading calls with __call__; again, watch for more about bound methods in the next chapter.

You'll also see another __call__ example in Chapter 26, where we will use it to implement something known as a *function decorator*—a callable object that adds a layer of logic on top of an embedded function. Because __call__ allows us to attach state information to a callable object, it's a natural implementation technique for a function that must remember and call another function.

__del__ Is a Destructor

The __init__ constructor is called whenever an instance is generated. Its counterpart, the destructor method __del__, is run automatically when an instance's space is being reclaimed (i.e., at "garbage collection" time):

```
>>> class Life:
...     def __init__(self, name='unknown'):
...         print 'Hello', name
...         self.name = name
...     def __del__(self):
...         print 'Goodbye', self.name
...
>>> brian = Life('Brian')
Hello Brian
>>> brian = 'loretta'
Goodbye Brian
```

Here, when brian is assigned a string, we lose the last reference to the Life instance, and so trigger its destructor method. This works, and it may be useful for implementing some cleanup activities (such as terminating server connections). However, destructors are not as commonly used in Python as in some OOP languages, for a number of reasons.

For one thing, because Python automatically reclaims all space held by an instance when the instance is reclaimed, destructors are not necessary for space management.[*] For another, because you cannot always easily predict when an instance will be reclaimed, it's often better to code termination activities in an explicitly called method (or try/finally statement, described in the next part of the book); in some cases, there may be lingering references to your objects in system tables that prevent destructors from running.

That's as many overloading examples as we have space for here. Most of the other operator overloading methods work similarly to the ones we've explored, and all are just hooks for intercepting built-in type operations; some overloading methods, for example, have unique argument lists or return values. You'll see a few others in action later in the book, but for complete coverage, I'll defer to other documentation sources.

---

[*] In the current C implementation of Python, you also don't need to close file objects held by the instance in destructors because they are automatically closed when reclaimed. However, as mentioned in Chapter 9, it's better to explicitly call file close methods because auto-close-on-reclaim is a feature of the implementation, not of the language itself (this behavior can vary under Jython).

Namespaces: The Whole Story

Now that we've examined class and instance objects, the Python namespace story is complete. For reference, I'll quickly summarize all the rules used to resolve names here. The first things you need to remember are that qualified and unqualified names are treated differently, and that some scopes serve to initialize object namespaces:

- Unqualified names (e.g., X) deal with scopes.
- Qualified attribute names (e.g., object.X) use object namespaces.
- Some scopes initialize object namespaces (for modules and classes).

Simple Names: Global Unless Assigned

Unqualified simple names follow the LEGB lexical scoping rule outlined for functions in Chapter 16:

Assignment (X = value)
 Makes names local: creates or changes the name X in the current local scope, unless declared global.

Reference (X)
 Looks for the name X in the current local scope, then any and all enclosing functions, then the current global scope, then the built-in scope.

Attribute Names: Object Namespaces

Qualified attribute names refer to attributes of specific objects, and obey the rules for modules and classes. For class and instance objects, the reference rules are augmented to include the inheritance search procedure:

Assignment (object.X = value)
 Creates or alters the attribute name X in the namespace of the object being qualified, and none other. Inheritance-tree climbing happens only on attribute reference, not on attribute assignment.

Reference (object.X)
 For class-based objects, searches for the attribute name X in object, then in all accessible classes above it, using the inheritance search procedure. For nonclass objects such as modules, fetches X from object directly.

The "Zen" of Python Namespaces: Assignments Classify Names

With distinct search procedures for qualified and unqualified names, and multiple lookup layers for both, it can sometimes be difficult to tell where a name will wind up going. In Python, the place where you *assign* a name is crucial—it fully determines the scope or object in which a name will reside. The file *manynames.py* illustrates how this principle translates to code, and summarizes the namespace ideas we have seen throughout this book:

```python
# manynames.py

X = 11                    # Global (module) name/attribute (X, or manynames.X)

def f():
    print X               # Access global X (11)

def g():
    X = 22                # Local (function) variable (X, hides module X)
    print X

class C:
    X = 33                # Class attribute (C.X)
    def m(self):
        X = 44            # Local variable in method (X)
        self.X = 55       # Instance attribute (instance.X)
```

This file assigns the same name, X, five times. Because this name is assigned in five different locations, though, all five Xs in this program are completely different variables. From top to bottom, the assignments to X here generate: a module attribute (11), a local variable in a function (22), a class attribute (33), a local variable in a method (44), and an instance attribute (55). Although all five are named X, the fact that they are all assigned at different places in the source code or to different objects makes all of these unique variables.

You should take the time to study this example carefully because it collects ideas we've been exploring throughout the last few parts of this book. When it makes sense to you, you will have achieved a sort of Python namespace nirvana. Of course, an alternative route to nirvana is to simply run the program and see what happens. Here's the remainder of this source file, which makes an instance, and prints all the Xs that it can fetch:

```python
# manynames.py, continued

if __name__ == '__main__':
    print X               # 11: module (a.k.a. manynames.X outside file)
    f()                   # 11: global
    g()                   # 22: local
    print X               # 11: module name unchanged

    obj = C()             # Make instance
    print obj.X           # 33: class name inherited by instance

    obj.m()               # Attach attribute name X to instance now
    print obj.X           # 55: instance
    print C.X             # 33: class (a.k.a. obj.X if no X in instance)

    #print C.m.X          # FAILS: only visible in method
    #print f.X            # FAILS: only visible in function
```

The outputs that are printed when the file is run are noted in the comments in the code; trace through them to see which variable named X is being accessed each time. Notice in particular that we can go through the class to fetch its attribute (C.X), but we can never fetch local variables in functions, or methods from outside their def statements. Locals are only visible to other code within the def, and, in fact, only live in memory while a call to the function or method is executing.

Some of the names defined by this file are visible outside the file to other modules, but recall that we must always import before we can access names in another file—that is the main point of modules, after all:

```
# otherfile.py

import manynames

X = 66
print X                     # 66: the global here
print manynames.X           # 11: globals become attributes after imports

manynames.f( )              # 11: manynames's X, not the one here!
manynames.g( )              # 22: local in other file's function

print manynames.C.X         # 33: attribute of class in other module
I = manynames.C( )
print I.X                   # 33: still from class here
I.m( )
print I.X                   # 55: now from instance!
```

Notice here how manynames.f( ) prints the X in manynames, not the X assigned in this file—scopes are always determined by the position of assignments in your source code (i.e., lexically), and are never influenced by what imports what, or who imports whom. Also, notice that the instance's own X is not created until we call I.m( )—attributes, like all variables, spring into existence when assigned, and not before. Normally we create instance attributes by assigning them in class __init__ constructor methods, but this isn't the only option.

You generally shouldn't use the same name for every variable in your script, of course! But as this example demonstrates, even if you do, Python's namespaces will work to keep names used in one context from accidentally clashing with those used in another.

Namespace Dictionaries

In Chapter 19, we learned that module namespaces are actually implemented as dictionaries, and exposed with the built-in __dict__ attribute. The same holds for class and instance objects: attribute qualification is really a dictionary indexing operation internally, and attribute inheritance is just a matter of searching linked dictionaries. In fact, instance and class objects are mostly just dictionaries with links inside Python. Python exposes these dictionaries, as well as the links between them, for use in advanced roles (e.g., for coding tools).

To help you understand how attributes work internally, let's work through an interactive session that traces the way namespace dictionaries grow when classes are involved. First, let's define a superclass and a subclass with methods that will store data in their instances:

```
>>> class super:
...     def hello(self):
...         self.data1 = 'spam'
...
>>> class sub(super):
...     def hola(self):
...         self.data2 = 'eggs'
...
```

When we make an instance of the subclass, the instance starts out with an empty namespace dictionary, but has links back to the class for the inheritance search to follow. In fact, the inheritance tree is explicitly available in special attributes, which you can inspect. Instances have a __class__ attribute that links to their class, and classes have a __bases__ attribute that is a tuple containing links to higher superclasses:

```
>>> X = sub()
>>> X.__dict__
{ }

>>> X.__class__
<class __main__.sub at 0x00A48448>

>>> sub.__bases__
(<class __main__.super at 0x00A3E1C8>,)

>>> super.__bases__
()
```

As classes assign to self attributes, they populate the instance objects—that is, attributes wind up in the instances' attribute namespace dictionaries, not in the classes'. An instance object's namespace records data that can vary from instance to instance, and self is a hook into that namespace:

```
>>> Y = sub()

>>> X.hello()
>>> X.__dict__
{'data1': 'spam'}

>>> X.hola()
>>> X.__dict__
{'data1': 'spam', 'data2': 'eggs'}

>>> sub.__dict__
{'__module__': '__main__', '__doc__': None, 'hola': <function hola at
0x00A47048>}
```

```
>>> super.__dict__
{'__module__': '__main__', 'hello': <function hello at 0x00A3C5A8>,
 '__doc__': None}

>>> sub.__dict__.keys(), super.__dict__.keys()
(['__module__', '__doc__', 'hola'], ['__module__', 'hello', '__doc__'])

>>> Y.__dict__
{ }
```

Notice the extra underscore names in the class dictionaries; Python sets these auto-matically. Most are not used in typical programs, but there are tools that use some of them (e.g., __doc__ holds the docstrings discussed in Chapter 14).

Also, observe that Y, a second instance made at the start of this series, still has an empty namespace dictionary at the end, even though X's dictionary has been popu-lated by assignments in methods. Again, each instance has an independent namespace dictionary, which starts out empty, and can record completely different attributes than those recorded by the namespace dictionaries of other instances of the same class.

Because attributes are actually dictionary keys inside Python, there are really two ways to fetch and assign their values—by qualification, or by key indexing:

```
>>> X.data1, X.__dict__['data1']
('spam', 'spam')

>>> X.data3 = 'toast'
>>> X.__dict__
{'data1': 'spam', 'data3': 'toast', 'data2': 'eggs'}

>>> X.__dict__['data3'] = 'ham'
>>> X.data3
'ham'
```

This equivalence applies only to attributes actually attached to the instance, though. Because attribute qualification also performs an inheritance search, it can access attributes that namespace dictionary indexing cannot. The inherited attribute X.hello, for instance, cannot be accessed by X.__dict__['hello'].

Finally, here is the built-in dir function we met in Chapters 4 and 14 at work on class and instance objects. This function works on anything with attributes: dir(object) is similar to an object.__dict__.keys() call. Notice, though, that dir sorts its list and includes some system attributes—as of Python 2.2, dir also collects inherited attributes automatically:[*]

---

[*] The contents of attribute dictionaries and dir call results may change over time. For example, because Python now allows built-in types to be subclassed like classes, the contents of dir results for built-in types have expanded to include operator overloading methods. In general, attribute names with leading and trail-ing double underscores are interpreter-specific. Type subclasses will be discussed further in Chapter 26.

```
>>> X.__dict__
{'data1': 'spam', 'data3': 'ham', 'data2': 'eggs'}
>>> X.__dict__.keys()
['data1', 'data3', 'data2']

>>>> dir(X)
['__doc__', '__module__', 'data1', 'data2', 'data3', 'hello', 'hola']
>>> dir(sub)
['__doc__', '__module__', 'hello', 'hola']
>>> dir(super)
['__doc__', '__module__', 'hello']
```

Experiment with these special attributes on your own to get a better feel for how namespaces actually do their attribute business. Even if you will never use these in the kinds of programs you write, seeing that they are just normal dictionaries will help demystify the notion of namespaces in general.

Namespace Links

The prior section introduced the special __class__ and __bases__ instance and class attributes, without really explaining why you might care about them. In short, these attributes allow you to inspect inheritance hierarchies within your own code. For example, they can be used to display a class tree, as in the following example:

```
# classtree.py

def classtree(cls, indent):
    print '.'*indent, cls.__name__        # Print class name here
    for supercls in cls.__bases__:        # Recur to all superclasses
        classtree(supercls, indent+3)     # May visit super > once

def instancetree(inst):
    print 'Tree of', inst                 # Show instance
    classtree(inst.__class__, 3)          # Climb to its class

def selftest():
    class A: pass
    class B(A): pass
    class C(A): pass
    class D(B,C): pass
    class E: pass
    class F(D,E): pass
    instancetree(B())
    instancetree(F())

if __name__ == '__main__': selftest()
```

The classtree function in this script is *recursive*—it prints a class' name using __name__, and then climbs up to the superclasses by calling itself. This allows the function to traverse arbitrarily shaped class trees; the recursion climbs to the top, and stops at root superclasses that have empty __bases__ attributes. Most of this file is self-test code; when run standalone, it builds an empty class tree, makes two instances from it, and prints their class tree structures:

```
% python classtree.py
Tree of <__main__.B instance at 0x00ACB438>
... B
...... A
Tree of <__main__.F instance at 0x00AC4DA8>
... F
...... D
......... B
............ A
......... C
............ A
...... E
```

Here, indentation marked by periods is used to denote class tree height. Of course, we could improve on this output format, and perhaps even sketch it in a GUI display.

We can import these functions anywhere we want a quick class tree display:

```
>>> class Emp: pass
...
>>> class Person(Emp): pass
...
>>> bob = Person()
>>> import classtree
>>> classtree.instancetree(bob)
Tree of <__main__.Person instance at 0x00AD34E8>
... Person
...... Emp
```

Whether you will ever code or use such tools, this example demonstrates one of the many ways that you can make use of special attributes that expose interpreter internals. You'll see another when we code a general-purpose attribute-listing class in the "Multiple Inheritance" section of Chapter 25.

A More Realistic Example

Most of the examples we've looked at so far have been artificial and self-contained to help you focus on the basics. However, we'll close out this chapter with a larger example that pulls together much of what we've studied here. I'm including this mostly as a self-study exercise—try to trace through this example's code to see how method calls are resolved.

In short, the following module, *person.py*, defines three classes:

• GenericDisplay is a mix-in class that provides a generic __str__ method; for any class that inherits from it, this method returns a string giving the name of the class from which the instance was created, as well as "name=value" pairs for every attribute in the instance. It uses the __dict__ attribute namespace dictionary to build up the list of "name=value" pairs for each attribute in the class instance and the built-in __name__ of an instance's built-in __class__ to determine the class name. Because the print statement triggers __str__, this class' result is the custom print format displayed for all instances that derive from the class. It's a generic tool.

- Person records general information about people, and provides two processing methods to use and change instance object state information; it also inherits the custom print format logic from its superclass. A person object has two attributes and two methods managed by this class.

- Employee is a customization of Person that inherits the last-name extraction and custom print format, but adds a new method for giving a raise, and redefines the birthday operation to customize it (apparently, employees age faster than other people). Notice how the superclass constructor is invoked manually; we need to run the superclass version above in order to fill out the name and age.

As you study this module's code, you'll see that each instance has its own state information. Notice how inheritance is used to mix in and customize behavior, and how operator overloading is used to initialize and print instances:

```python
# person.py

class GenericDisplay:
    def gatherAttrs(self):
        attrs = '\n'
        for key in self.__dict__:
            attrs += '\t%s=%s\n' % (key, self.__dict__[key])
        return attrs
    def __str__(self):
        return '<%s: %s>' % (self.__class__.__name__, self.gatherAttrs())

class Person(GenericDisplay):
    def __init__(self, name, age):
        self.name = name
        self.age  = age
    def lastName(self):
        return self.name.split()[-1]
    def birthDay(self):
        self.age += 1

class Employee(Person):
    def __init__(self, name, age, job=None, pay=0):
        Person.__init__(self, name, age)
        self.job  = job
        self.pay  = pay
    def birthDay(self):
        self.age += 2
    def giveRaise(self, percent):
        self.pay *= (1.0 + percent)
```

```
if __name__ == '__main__':
    bob = Person('Bob Smith', 40)
    print bob
    print bob.lastName()
    bob.birthDay()
    print bob

    sue = Employee('Sue Jones', 44, job='dev', pay=100000)
    print sue
    print sue.lastName()
    sue.birthDay()
    sue.giveRaise(.10)
    print sue
```

To test the code, we can import the module and make instances interactively. Here, for example, is the Person class in action. Creating an instance triggers __init__, calling a named method uses or changes instance state information (attributes), and printing an instance invokes the inherited __str__ to print all attributes generically:

```
>>> from person import Person
>>> ann = Person('Ann Smith', 45)
>>> ann.lastName()
'Smith'
>>> ann.birthDay()
>>> ann.age
46
>>> print ann
<Person:
    age=46
    name=Ann Smith
>
```

Finally, here is the output of the file's self-test logic (the code at the bottom, under the __name__ test), which creates a person and an employee, and changes each of them. As usual, this self-test code is run only when the file is run as a top-level script, not when it is being imported as a library module. Notice how employees inherit print formats and last-name extraction, have more state information, have an extra method for getting a raise, and run a customized version of the birthday method (they age by two!):

```
% python person.py
<Person:
    age=40
    name=Bob Smith
>
Smith
<Person:
    age=41
    name=Bob Smith
>
```

```
<Employee:
    job=dev
    pay=100000
    age=44
    name=Sue Jones
>
Jones
<Employee:
    job=dev
    pay=110000.0
    age=46
    name=Sue Jones
>
```

Trace through the code in this example to see how this output reflects method calls; it summarizes most of the ideas behind the mechanisms of OOP in Python.

Now that you know about Python classes, you can probably appreciate the fact that the classes used here are not much more than packages of functions, which embed and manage built-in objects attached to instance attributes as state information. When the `lastName` method splits and indexes, for example, it is simply applying built-in string and list processing operations to an object managed by the class.

Operator overloading and inheritance—the automatic lookup of attributes in the implied class tree—are the main tools OOP adds to the picture. Ultimately, this allows the `Employee` class at the bottom of the tree to obtain quite a bit of behavior "for free"—which is, at the end of the day, the main idea behind OOP.

Chapter Summary

This chapter took us on a second, more in-depth tour of the OOP mechanisms of the Python language. We learned more about classes and methods, inheritance, and additional operator overloading methods; we also wrapped up the namespace story in Python by extending it to cover its application to classes. Along the way, we looked at some more advanced concepts, such as abstract superclasses, class data attributes, and manual calls to superclass methods and constructors. Finally, we studied a larger example that tied together much of what we've learned about OOP so far.

Now that we've learned all about the mechanics of coding classes in Python, the next chapter turns to common design patterns—some of the ways that classes are commonly used and combined to optimize code reuse. Some of the material in the next chapter is not specific to the Python language, but is important for using classes well. Before you read on, though, be sure to work though the usual chapter quiz to review what we've covered here.

Chapter Quiz

1. What is an abstract superclass?

2. What two operator overloading methods can you use to support iteration in your classes?

3. What happens when a simple assignment statement appears at the top level of a class statement?

4. Why might a class need to manually call the __init__ method in a superclass?

5. How can you augment, instead of completely replacing, an inherited method?

6. In this chapter's final example, what methods are run when the sue Employee instance is printed?

7. What...was the capital of Assyria?

Quiz Answers

1. An abstract superclass is a class that calls a method, but does not inherit or define it—it expects the method to be filled in by a subclass. This is often used as a way to generalize classes when behavior cannot be predicted until a more specific subclass is coded. OOP frameworks also use this as a way to dispatch to client-defined, customizable operations.

2. Classes can support iteration by defining (or inheriting) __getitem__ or __iter__. In all iteration contexts, Python tries to use __iter__ (which returns an object that supports the iteration protocol with a next method) first: if no __iter__ is found by inheritance search, Python falls back on the __getitem__ indexing method (which is called repeatedly, with successively higher indexes).

3. When a simple assignment statement (X = Y) appears at the top level of a class statement, it attaches a data attribute to the class (Class.X). Like all class attributes, this will be shared by all instances; data attributes are not callable method functions, though.

4. A class must manually call the __init__ method in a superclass if it defines an __init__ constructor of its own, but must still kick off the superclass' construction code. Python itself automatically runs just one constructor—the lowest one in the tree. Superclass constructors are called through the class name, passing in the self instance manually: Superclass.__init__(self, ...).

5. To augment instead of completely replacing an inherited method, redefine it in a subclass, but call back to the superclass' version of the method manually from the new version of the method in the subclass. That is, pass the self instance to the superclass' version of the method manually: Superclass.method(self, ...).

6. Printing sue ultimately runs the GenericDisplay.__str__ method and the GenericDisplay.gatherAttrs method it calls. In more detail, to print sue, the print statement converts her to her user-friendly display string by passing her to the built-in str function. In a class, this means look for a __str__ operator over-loading method by inheritance search, and run it if it is found. sue's class, Employee, does not have a __str__ method; Person is searched next, and eventually __str__ is found in the GenericDisplay class.

7. Ashur (or Qalat Sherqat), Calah (or Nimrud), the short-lived Dur Sharrukin (or Khorsabad), and finally Nineveh.

CHAPTER 25

Designing with Classes

So far in this part of the book, we've concentrated on using Python's OOP tool, the class. But OOP is also about design issues—i.e., how to use classes to model useful objects. This chapter will touch on a few core OOP ideas, and present some additional examples that are more realistic than those shown so far. Many of the design terms mentioned here (delegation, composition, factories, and more) require more explanation than I can provide in this book; if this material sparks your curiosity, I suggest exploring a text on OOP design, or design patterns as a next step.

Python and OOP

Python's implementation of OOP can be summarized by three ideas:

Inheritance
> Inheritance is based on attribute lookup in Python (in X.name expressions).

Polymorphism
> In X.method, the meaning of method depends on the type (class) of X.

Encapsulation
> Methods and operators implement behavior; data hiding is a convention by default.

By now, you should have a good feel for what inheritance is all about in Python. We've also talked about Python's polymorphism a few times already; it flows from Python's lack of type declarations. Because attributes are always resolved at runtime, objects that implement the same interfaces are interchangeable; clients don't need to know what sorts of objects are implementing the methods they call.

Encapsulation means packaging in Python—that is, hiding implementation details behind an object's interface. It does not mean enforced privacy, as you'll see in Chapter 26. Encapsulation allows the implementation of an object's interface to be changed without impacting the users of that object.

Overloading by Call Signatures (or Not)

Some OOP languages also define polymorphism to mean overloading functions based on the type signatures of their arguments. But because there are no type declarations in Python, this concept doesn't really apply; polymorphism in Python is based on object *interfaces*, not types.

You can try to overload methods by their argument lists, like this:

```
class C:
    def meth(self, x):
        ...
    def meth(self, x, y, z):
        ...
```

This code will run, but because the def simply assigns an object to a name in the class' scope, the last definition of the method function is the only one that will be retained (it's just as if you say X = 1, and then X = 2; X will be 2).

Type-based selections can always be coded using the type testing ideas we met in Chapters 4 and 9, or the argument list tools in Chapter 16:

```
class C:
    def meth(self, *args):
        if len(args) == 1:
            ...
        elif type(arg[0]) == int:
            ...
```

You normally shouldn't do this, though—as described in Chapter 15, you should write your code to expect an object interface, not a specific data type. That way, it will be useful for a broader category of types and applications, both now and in the future:

```
class C:
    def meth(self, x):
        x.operation()          # Assume x does the right thing
```

It's also generally considered better to use distinct method names for distinct operations, rather than relying on call signatures (no matter what language you code in).

Classes As Records

Chapter 8 showed how to use dictionaries to record properties of entities in our programs. Let's explore this in more detail. Here is the example for dictionary-based records used earlier:

```
>>> rec = {}
>>> rec['name'] = 'mel'
>>> rec['age']  = 40
>>> rec['job']  = 'trainer/writer'
>>>
>>> print rec['name']
mel
```

This code emulates tools like records and structs in other languages. As we saw in Chapter 23, though, there are also multiple ways to do the same with classes. Perhaps the simplest is this:

```
>>> class rec: pass
...
>>> rec.name = 'mel'
>>> rec.age  = 40
>>> rec.job  = 'trainer/writer'
>>>
>>> print rec.age
40
```

This code has substantially less syntax than the dictionary equivalent. It uses an empty class statement to generate an empty namespace object (notice the pass statement—we need a statement syntactically even though there is no logic to code in this case). Once we make the empty class, we fill it out by assigning to class attributes over time.

This works, but a new class statement will be required for each distinct record we will need. Perhaps more typically, we can instead generate *instances* of an empty class to represent each distinct entity:

```
>>> class rec: pass
...
>>> pers1 = rec()
>>> pers1.name = 'mel'
>>> pers1.job  = 'trainer'
>>> pers1.age  = 40
>>>
>>> pers2 = rec()
>>> pers2.name = 'dave'
>>> pers2.job  = 'developer'
>>>
>>> pers1.name, pers2.name
('mel', 'dave')
```

Here, we make two records from the same class—instances start out life empty, just like classes. We then fill in the records by assigning to attributes. This time, though, there are two separate objects, and hence, two separate name attributes. In fact, instances of the same class don't even have to have the same set of attribute names; in this example, one has a unique age name. Instances really are distinct namespaces: each has a distinct attribute dictionary. Although they are normally filled out consistently by class methods, they are more flexible than you might expect.

Finally, we might instead code a more full-blown class to implement the record:

```
>>> class Person:
...     def __init__(self, name, job):
...         self.name = name
...         self.job  = job
...     def info(self):
...         return (self.name, self.job)
...
```

```
>>> mark = Person('ml', 'trainer')
>>> dave = Person('da', 'developer')
>>>
>>> mark.job, dave.info()
('trainer', ('da', 'developer'))
```

This scheme also makes multiple instances, but the class is not empty this time: we've added logic (methods) to initialize instances at construction time and collect attributes into a tuple. The constructor imposes some consistency on instances here by always setting name and job attributes.

We could further extend this code by adding logic to compute salaries, parse names, and so on (see the end of Chapter 24 for an example that does this). Ultimately, we might link the class into a larger hierarchy to inherit an existing set of methods via the automatic attribute search of classes, or perhaps even store instances of the class in a file with Python object pickling to make them persistent (more on pickling and persistence in the sidebar "Why You Will Care: Classes and Persistence," and again later in the book). In the end, although types like dictionaries are flexible, classes allow us to add behavior to objects in ways that built-in types and simple functions do not directly support.

OOP and Inheritance: "Is-a" Relationships

We've explored the mechanics of inheritance in depth already, but I'd like to show you an example of how it can be used to model real-world relationships. From a programmer's point of view, inheritance is kicked off by attribute qualifications, which trigger searches for names in instances, their classes, and then any superclasses. From a designer's point of view, inheritance is a way to specify set membership: a class defines a set of properties that may be inherited and customized by more specific sets (i.e., subclasses).

To illustrate, let's put that pizza-making robot we talked about at the start of this part of the book to work. Suppose we've decided to explore alternative career paths and open a pizza restaurant. One of the first things we'll need to do is hire employees to serve customers, prepare the food, and so on. Being engineers at heart, we've decided to build a robot to make the pizzas; but being politically and cybernetically correct, we've also decided to make our robot a full-fledged employee with a salary.

Our pizza shop team can be defined by the four classes in the example file, *employees.py*. The most general class, Employee, provides common behavior such as bumping up salaries (giveRaise) and printing (__repr__). There are two kinds of employees, and so two subclasses of Employee: Chef and Server. Both override the inherited work method to print more specific messages. Finally, our pizza robot is modeled by an even more specific class: PizzaRobot is a kind of Chef, which is a kind of Employee. In OOP terms, we call these relationships "is-a" links: a robot is a chef, which is a(n) employee. Here's the *employees.py* file:

```python
class Employee:
    def __init__(self, name, salary=0):
        self.name   = name
        self.salary = salary
    def giveRaise(self, percent):
        self.salary = self.salary + (self.salary * percent)
    def work(self):
        print self.name, "does stuff"
    def __repr__(self):
        return "<Employee: name=%s, salary=%s>" % (self.name, self.salary)

class Chef(Employee):
    def __init__(self, name):
        Employee.__init__(self, name, 50000)
    def work(self):
        print self.name, "makes food"

class Server(Employee):
    def __init__(self, name):
        Employee.__init__(self, name, 40000)
    def work(self):
        print self.name, "interfaces with customer"

class PizzaRobot(Chef):
    def __init__(self, name):
        Chef.__init__(self, name)
    def work(self):
        print self.name, "makes pizza"

if __name__ == "__main__":
    bob = PizzaRobot('bob')          # Make a robot named bob
    print bob                        # Run inherited __repr__
    bob.work()                       # Run type-specific action
    bob.giveRaise(0.20)              # Give bob a 20% raise
    print bob; print

    for klass in Employee, Chef, Server, PizzaRobot:
        obj = klass(klass.__name__)
        obj.work()
```

When we run the self-test code included in this module, we create a pizza-making robot named bob, which inherits names from three classes: PizzaRobot, Chef, and Employee. For instance, printing bob runs the Employee.__repr__ method, and giving bob a raise invokes Employee.giveRaise because that's where the inheritance search finds that method:

```
C:\python\examples> python employees.py
<Employee: name=bob, salary=50000>
bob makes pizza
<Employee: name=bob, salary=60000.0>
```

```
Employee does stuff
Chef makes food
Server interfaces with customer
PizzaRobot makes pizza
```

In a class hierarchy like this, you can usually make instances of any of the classes, not just the ones at the bottom. For instance, the for loop in this module's self-test code creates instances of all four classes; each responds differently when asked to work because the work method is different in each. Really, these classes just simulate real-world objects; work prints a message for the time being, but it could be expanded to do real work later.

OOP and Composition: "Has-a" Relationships

The notion of composition was introduced in Chapter 22. From a programmer's point of view, composition involves embedding other objects in a container object, and activating them to implement container methods. To a designer, composition is another way to represent relationships in a problem domain. But, rather than set membership, composition has to do with components—parts of a whole.

Composition also reflects the relationships between parts, which is usually called a "has-a" relationship. Some OOP design texts refer to composition as *aggregation* (or distinguish between the two terms by using aggregation to describe a weaker dependency between container and contained); in this text, a "composition" simply refers to a collection of embedded objects. The composite class generally provides an interface all its own, and implements it by directing the embedded objects.

Now that we've implemented our employees, let's put them in the pizza shop and let them get busy. Our pizza shop is a composite object: it has an oven, and it has employees like servers and chefs. When a customer enters and places an order, the components of the shop spring into action—the server takes the order, the chef makes the pizza, and so on. The following example (the file *pizzashop.py*) simulates all the objects and relationships in this scenario:

```python
from employees import PizzaRobot, Server

class Customer:
    def __init__(self, name):
        self.name = name
    def order(self, server):
        print self.name, "orders from", server
    def pay(self, server):
        print self.name, "pays for item to", server

class Oven:
    def bake(self):
        print "oven bakes"
```

```
class PizzaShop:
    def __init__(self):
        self.server = Server('Pat')          # Embed other objects
        self.chef   = PizzaRobot('Bob')      # A robot named bob
        self.oven   = Oven()

    def order(self, name):
        customer = Customer(name)            # Activate other objects
        customer.order(self.server)          # Customer orders from server
        self.chef.work()
        self.oven.bake()
        customer.pay(self.server)

if __name__ == "__main__":
    scene = PizzaShop()                      # Make the composite
    scene.order('Homer')                     # Simulate Homer's order
    print '...'
    scene.order('Shaggy')                    # Simulate Shaggy's order
```

The PizzaShop class is a container and controller; its constructor makes and embeds instances of the employee classes we wrote in the last section, as well as an Oven class defined here. When this module's self-test code calls the PizzaShop order method, the embedded objects are asked to carry out their actions in turn. Notice that we make a new Customer object for each order, and we pass on the embedded Server object to Customer methods; customers come and go, but the server is part of the pizza shop composite. Also, notice that employees are still involved in an inheritance relationship; composition and inheritance are complementary tools. When we run this module, our pizza shop handles two orders—one from Homer, and then one from Shaggy:

```
C:\python\examples> python pizzashop.py
Homer orders from <Employee: name=Pat, salary=40000>
Bob makes pizza
oven bakes
Homer pays for item to <Employee: name=Pat, salary=40000>
...
Shaggy orders from <Employee: name=Pat, salary=40000>
Bob makes pizza
oven bakes
Shaggy pays for item to <Employee: name=Pat, salary=40000>
```

Again, this is mostly just a toy simulation, but the objects and interactions are representative of composites at work. As a rule of thumb, classes can represent just about any objects and relationships you can express in a sentence; just replace *nouns* with classes, and *verbs* with methods, and you'll have a first cut at a design.

Stream Processors Revisited

For a more realistic composition example, recall the generic data stream processor function we partially coded in the introduction to OOP in Chapter 22:

```
def processor(reader, converter, writer):
    while 1:
        data = reader.read()
        if not data: break
        data = converter(data)
        writer.write(data)
```

Rather than using a simple function here, we might code this as a class that uses composition to do its work to provide more structure and support inheritance. The following file, *streams.py*, demonstrates one way to code the class:

```
class Processor:
    def __init__(self, reader, writer):
        self.reader = reader
        self.writer = writer
    def process(self):
        while 1:
            data = self.reader.readline()
            if not data: break
            data = self.converter(data)
            self.writer.write(data)
    def converter(self, data):
        assert 0, 'converter must be defined'
```

Coded this way, reader and writer objects are embedded within the class instance (*composition*), and we supply the converter logic in a subclass rather than passing in a converter function (*inheritance*). The file *converters.py* shows how:

```
from streams import Processor

class Uppercase(Processor):
    def converter(self, data):
        return data.upper()

if __name__ == '__main__':
    import sys
    Uppercase(open('spam.txt'), sys.stdout).process()
```

Here, the Uppercase class inherits the stream-processing loop logic (and anything else that may be coded in its superclasses). It needs to define only the thing that is unique about it—the data conversion logic. When this file is run, it makes and runs an instance, which reads from the file *spam.txt*, and writes the uppercase equivalent of that file to the stdout stream:

```
C:\lp3e> type spam.txt
spam
Spam
SPAM!

C:\lp3e> python converters.py
SPAM
SPAM
SPAM!
```

To process different sorts of streams, pass in different sorts of objects to the class construction call. Here, we use an output file instead of a stream:

```
C:\lp3e> python
>>> import converters
>>> prog = converters.Uppercase(open('spam.txt'), open('spamup.txt', 'w'))
>>> prog.process()

C:\lp3e> type spamup.txt
SPAM
SPAM
SPAM!
```

But, as suggested earlier, we could also pass in arbitrary objects wrapped up in classes that define the required input and output method interfaces. Here's a simple example that passes in a writer class that wraps up the text inside HTML tags:

```
C:\lp3e> python
>>> from converters import Uppercase
>>>
>>> class HTMLize:
...     def write(self, line):
...         print '<PRE>%s</PRE>' % line[:-1]
...
>>> Uppercase(open('spam.txt'), HTMLize()).process()
<PRE>SPAM</PRE>
<PRE>SPAM</PRE>
<PRE>SPAM!</PRE>
```

If you trace through this example's control flow, you'll see that we get both uppercase conversion (by inheritance), and HTML formatting (by composition), even though the core processing logic in the original Processor superclass knows nothing about either step. The processing code only cares that writers have a write method, and that a method named convert is defined; it doesn't care what those calls do. Such polymorphism and encapsulation of logic is behind much of the power of classes.

As is, the Processor superclass only provides a file-scanning loop. In more real work, we might extend it to support additional programming tools for its subclasses, and, in the process, turn it into a full-blown framework. Coding such a tool once in a superclass enables you to reuse it in all of your programs. Even in this simple example, because so much is packaged and inherited with classes, all we had to code was the HTML formatting step; the rest was free.

For another example of composition at work, see exercise 9 at the end of Chapter 26 and its solution in Appendix B; it's similar to the pizza shop example. We've focused on inheritance in this book because that is the main tool that the Python language itself provides for OOP. But, in practice, composition is used as much as inheritance as a way to structure classes, especially in larger systems. As we've seen, inheritance and composition are often complementary (and sometimes alternative) techniques.

Because composition is a design issue outside the scope of the Python language and this book, though, I'll defer to other resources for more on this topic.

Why You Will Care: Classes and Persistence

I've mentioned pickling a few times in this part of the book because it works especially well with class instances. For example, besides allowing us to simulate real-world interactions, the pizza shop classes developed here could also be used as the basis of a persistent restaurant database. Instances of classes can be stored away on disk in a single step using Python's pickle or shelve modules. The object pickling interface is remarkably easy to use:

```
import pickle
object = someClass()
file   = open(filename, 'wb')       # Create external file
pickle.dump(object, file)           # Save object in file

import pickle
file   = open(filename, 'rb')
object = pickle.load(file)          # Fetch it back later
```

Pickling converts in-memory objects to serialized byte streams, which may be stored in files, sent across a network, and so on; unpickling converts back from byte streams to identical in-memory objects. Shelves are similar, but they automatically pickle objects to an access-by-key database, which exports a dictionary-like interface:

```
import shelve
object = someClass()
dbase  = shelve.open('filename')
dbase['key'] = object               # Save under key

import shelve
dbase  = shelve.open('filename')
object = dbase['key']               # Fetch it back later
```

In our example, using classes to model employees means we can get a simple database of employees and shops with little extra work: pickling such instance objects to a file makes them persistent across Python program executions. See the standard library manual and later examples for more on pickling.

OOP and Delegation

Object-oriented programmers often also talk about something called *delegation*, which usually implies controller objects that embed other objects to which they pass off operation requests. The controllers can take care of administrative activities, such as keeping track of accesses, and so on. In Python, delegation is often implemented with the __getattr__ method hook; because it intercepts accesses to nonexistent attributes, a *wrapper* class (sometimes called a *proxy* class) can use __getattr__ to route arbitrary accesses to a wrapped object. The wrapper class retains the interface of the wrapped object, and may add additional operations of its own.

Consider the file *trace.py*, for instance:

```
class wrapper:
    def __init__(self, object):
        self.wrapped = object                   # Save object
    def __getattr__(self, attrname):
        print 'Trace:', attrname                # Trace fetch
        return getattr(self.wrapped, attrname)  # Delegate fetch
```

Recall from Chapter 24 that __getattr__ gets the attribute name as a string. This code makes use of the getattr built-in function to fetch an attribute from the wrapped object by name string—getattr(X,N) is like X.N, except that N is an expression that evaluates to a string at runtime, not a variable. In fact, getattr(X,N) is similar to X.__dict__[N], but the former also performs an inheritance search, like X.N, while the latter does not (see "Namespace Dictionaries" in Chapter 24 for more on the __dict__ attribute).

You can use the approach of this module's wrapper class to manage access to any object with attributes—lists, dictionaries, and even classes and instances. Here, the wrapper class simply prints a trace message on each attribute access, and delegates the attribute request to the embedded wrapped object:

```
>>> from trace import wrapper
>>> x = wrapper([1,2,3])              # Wrap a list
>>> x.append(4)                       # Delegate to list method
Trace: append
>>> x.wrapped                         # Print my member
[1, 2, 3, 4]

>>> x = wrapper({"a": 1, "b": 2})     # Wrap a dictionary
>>> x.keys()                          # Delegate to dictionary method
Trace: keys
['a', 'b']
```

The net effect is to augment the entire interface of the wrapped object, with additional code in the wrapper class. We can use this to log our method calls, route method calls to extra or custom logic, and so on.

We'll revive the notions of wrapped objects and delegated operations as one way to extend built-in types in Chapter 26. If you are interested in the delegation design pattern, also watch for the discussion of *function decorators* in Chapter 26—this is a strongly related concept, designed to augment a specific function or method call, rather than the entire interface of an object.

Multiple Inheritance

In a class statement, more than one superclass can be listed in parentheses in the header line. When you do this, you use something called *multiple inheritance*—the class and its instances inherit names from all listed superclasses.

When searching for an attribute, Python searches superclasses in the class header from left to right until a match is found. Technically, the search proceeds depth-first all the way to the top of the inheritance tree, and then from left to right, as any of the superclasses may have superclasses of their own.

In general, multiple inheritance is good for modeling objects that belong to more than one set. For instance, a person may be an engineer, a writer, a musician, and so on, and inherit properties from all such sets.

Perhaps the most common way multiple inheritance is used is to "mix in" general-purpose methods from superclasses. Such superclasses are usually called *mix-in classes*—they provide methods you add to application classes by inheritance. For instance, Python's default way to print a class instance object isn't incredibly useful:

```
>>> class Spam:
...     def __init__(self):            # No __repr__
...         self.data1 = "food"
...
>>> X = Spam()
>>> print X                             # Default: class, address
<__main__.Spam instance at 0x00864818>
```

As seen in the previous section on operator overloading, you can provide a __repr__ method to implement a custom string representation of your own. But, rather than coding a __repr__ in each and every class you wish to print, why not code it once in a general-purpose tool class and inherit it in all your classes?

That's what mix-ins are for. The following file, *mytools.py*, defines a mix-in class called Lister that overloads the __repr__ method for each class that includes Lister in its header line. It simply scans the instance's attribute dictionary (remember, it's exported in __dict__) to build up a string showing the names and values of all instance attributes. Because classes are objects, Lister's formatting logic can be used for instances of any subclass; it's a generic tool.[*]

Lister uses two special tricks to extract the instance's class name and address. Each instance has a built-in __class__ attribute that references the class from which it was created, and each class has a __name__ attribute that references the name in the header, so self.__class__.__name__ fetches the name of an instance's class. You get

---

[*] For an alternative way to do this, see the *person.py* module example at the end of Chapter 24. It also scans attribute namespace dictionaries, but assumes there are no double-underscore names to be skipped.

the instance's memory address by calling the built-in `id` function, which returns any object's address (by definition, a unique object identifier):

```
#############################################
# Lister can be mixed into any class to
# provide a formatted print of instances
# via inheritance of __repr__ coded here;
# self is the instance of the lowest class.
#############################################

class Lister:
    def __repr__(self):
        return ("<Instance of %s, address %s:\n%s>" %
                        (self.__class__.__name__,      # My class's name
                         id(self),                     # My address
                         self.attrnames()) )           # name=value list
    def attrnames(self):
        result = ''
        for attr in self.__dict__.keys():              # Instance namespace dict
            if attr[:2] == '__':
                result = result + "\tname %s=<built-in>\n" % attr
            else:
                result = result + "\tname %s=%s\n" % (attr, self.__dict__ [attr])
        return result
```

Instances derived from this class display their attributes automatically when printed, giving a bit more information than a simple address:

```
>>> from mytools import Lister
>>> class Spam(Lister):
...     def __init__(self):
...         self.data1 = 'food'
...
>>> x = Spam( )
>>> x
<Instance of Spam, address 8821568:
        name data1=food
>
```

The `Lister` class is useful for any classes you write—even classes that already have a superclass. This is where multiple inheritance comes in handy: by adding `Lister` to the list of superclasses in a class header (mixing it in), you get its `__repr__` for free while still inheriting from the existing superclass. The file *testmixin.py* demonstrates:

```
from mytools import Lister          # Get tool class

class Super:
    def __init__(self):             # superclass __init__
        self.data1 = "spam"

class Sub(Super, Lister):           # Mix in a __repr__
    def __init__(self):             # Lister has access to self
        Super.__init__(self)
        self.data2 = "eggs"         # More instance attrs
        self.data3 = 42
```

```
if __name__ == "__main__":
    X = Sub()
    print X                        # Mixed-in repr
```

Here, Sub inherits names from both Super and Lister; it's a composite of its own names and names in both its superclasses. When you make a Sub instance and print it, you automatically get the custom representation mixed in from Lister:

```
C:\lp3e> python testmixin.py
<Instance of Sub, address 7833392:
        name data3=42
        name data2=eggs
        name data1=spam
>
```

Lister works in any class it's mixed into because self refers to an instance of the subclass that pulls Lister in, whatever that may be. If you later decide to extend Lister's __repr__ to also print all the class attributes that an instance inherits, you're safe; because it's an inherited method, changing Lister.__repr__ automatically updates the display of each subclass that imports the class and mixes it in.*

In a sense, mix-in classes are the class equivalent of modules—packages of methods useful in a variety of clients. Here is Lister working again in single-inheritance mode on a different class's instances:

```
>>> from mytools import Lister
>>> class x(Lister):
...     pass
...
>>> t = x()
>>> t.a = 1; t.b = 2; t.c = 3
>>> t
<Instance of x, address 7797696:
        name b=2
        name a=1
        name c=3
>
```

OOP is all about code reuse, and mix-in classes are a powerful tool. Like almost everything else in programming, multiple inheritance can be a useful device when applied well; however, in practice, it is an advanced feature and can become complicated if used carelessly or excessively. We'll revisit this topic as a gotcha at the end of the next chapter. In that chapter, we'll also meet an option (new-style classes) that modifies the search order for one special multiple inheritance case.

---

* If you're curious how, flip back to "Namespace Dictionaries" in Chapter 24 for hints. We saw there that each class has a built-in attribute called __bases__, which is a tuple of the class' superclass objects. A general-purpose class hierarchy lister or browser can traverse the inheritance tree from an instance's __class__ to its class, and then from the class' __bases__ to all superclasses recursively, much like the classtree.py example shown earlier. In Python 2.2 and later, it's even simpler, as the built-in dir function now includes inherited attribute names automatically. If you don't care about displaying the tree structure, you can just scan the dir list instead of the dictionary keys list, and use getattr to fetch attributes by name string instead of dictionary-key indexing. We'll rehash this idea in one of this part's closing exercises.

Classes Are Objects: Generic Object Factories

Because classes are objects, it's easy to pass them around a program, store them in data structures, and so on. You can also pass classes to functions that generate arbitrary kinds of objects; such functions are sometimes called *factories* in OOP design circles. They are a major undertaking in a strongly typed language such as C++, but almost trivial to implement in Python. The apply function and newer alternative syntax we met in Chapter 17 can call any class with any number of constructor arguments in one step to generate any sort of instance:[*]

```
def factory(aClass, *args):              # varargs tuple
    return apply(aClass, args)           # Call aClass, or: aClass(*args)

class Spam:
    def doit(self, message):
        print message

class Person:
    def __init__(self, name, job):
        self.name = name
        self.job  = job

object1 = factory(Spam)                  # Make a Spam object
object2 = factory(Person, "Guido", "guru")   # Make a Person object
```

In this code, we define an object generator function called factory. It expects to be passed a class object (any class will do) along with one or more arguments for the class' constructor. The function uses apply to call the function and return an instance.

The rest of the example simply defines two classes, and generates instances of both by passing them to the factory function. And that's the only factory function you'll ever need to write in Python; it works for any class, and any constructor arguments.

One possible improvement worth noting is that to support keyword arguments in constructor calls, the factory can collect them with a **args argument, and pass them as a third argument to apply:

```
def factory(aClass, *args, **kwargs):    # +kwargs dict
    return apply(aClass, args, kwargs)   # Call aClass
```

By now, you should know that everything is an "object" in Python, including things like classes, which are just compiler input in languages like C++. However, as mentioned at the start of Part VI, only objects derived from classes are OOP objects in Python.

---

[*] Actually, apply can call any callable object, including functions, classes, and methods. The factory function here can also run any callable object, not just a class (despite the argument name). Also, note that in recent Python versions, the aClass(*args) call syntax is generally preferred to the apply(aClass, args) built-in call.

Why Factories?

So what good is the factory function (besides providing an excuse to illustrate class objects in this book)? Unfortunately, it's difficult to show applications of this design pattern without listing much more code than we have space for here. In general, though, such a factory might allow code to be insulated from the details of dynamically configured object construction.

For example, recall the processor example presented in the abstract in Chapter 22, and then again as a has-a composition example in this chapter. It accepted reader and writer objects for processing arbitrary data streams.

The original version of this example manually passed in instances of specialized classes like FileWriter and SocketReader to customize the data streams being processed; later, we passed in hardcoded file, stream, and formatter objects. In a more dynamic scenario, external devices such as configuration files or GUIs might be used to configure the streams.

In such a dynamic world, we might not be able to hardcode the creation of stream interface objects in our script, but might instead create them at runtime according to the contents of a configuration file.

For instance, the file might simply give the string name of a stream class to be imported from a module, plus an optional constructor call argument. Factory-style functions or code might come in handy here because they would allow us to fetch and pass in classes that are not hardcoded in our program ahead of time. Indeed, those classes might not even have existed at all when we wrote our code:

```
classname = ...parse from config file...
classarg  = ...parse from config file...

import streamtypes                          # Customizable code
aclass = getattr(streamtypes, classname)    # Fetch from module
reader = factory(aclass, classarg)          # Or aclass(classarg)
processor(reader, ...)
```

Here, the getattr built-in is again used to fetch a module attribute given a string name (it's like saying obj.attr, but attr is a string). Because this code snippet assumes a single constructor argument, it doesn't strictly need factory or apply—we could make an instance with just aclass(classarg). They may prove more useful in the presence of unknown argument lists, however, and the general factory coding pattern can improve the code's flexibility. For more details on this topic, please consult books that cover OOP design and design patterns.

Methods Are Objects: Bound or Unbound

Methods are a kind of object, much like functions. Class methods can be accessed from an instance or a class, and hence, they actually come in two flavors in Python:

Unbound class method objects: no `self`

> Accessing a function attribute of a class by qualifying a class returns an unbound method object. To call the method, you must provide an instance object explicitly as the first argument.

Bound instance method objects: `self` + *function pairs*

> Accessing a function attribute of a class by qualifying an instance returns a bound method object. Python automatically packages the instance with the function in the bound method object, so you don't need to pass an instance to call the method.

Both kinds of methods are full-fledged objects; they can be passed around, stored in lists, and so on. Both also require an instance in their first argument when run (i.e., a value for `self`). This is why we had to pass in an instance explicitly when calling superclass methods from subclass methods in the previous chapter; technically, such calls produce unbound method objects.

When calling a bound method object, Python provides an instance for you automatically—the instance used to create the bound method object. This means that bound method objects are usually interchangeable with simple function objects, and makes them especially useful for interfaces originally written for functions (see the sidebar "Why You Will Care: Bound Methods and Callbacks" for a realistic example).

To illustrate, suppose we define the following class:

```
class Spam:
    def doit(self, message):
        print message
```

Now, in normal operation, we make an instance, and call its method in a single step to print the passed-in argument:

```
object1 = Spam( )
object1.doit('hello world')
```

Really, though, a *bound* method object is generated along the way, just before the method call's parentheses. In fact, we can fetch a bound method without actually calling it. An `object.name` qualification is an object expression. In the following, it returns a bound method object that packages the instance (`object1`) with the method function (`Spam.doit`). We can assign this bound method to another name, and then call it as though it were a simple function:

```
object1 = Spam( )
x = object1.doit              # Bound method object: instance+function
x('hello world')              # Same effect as object1.doit('...')
```

On the other hand, if we qualify the class to get to doit, we get back an *unbound* method object, which is simply a reference to the function object. To call this type of method, we must pass in an instance as the leftmost argument:

```
object1 = Spam()
t = Spam.doit          # Unbound method object
t(object1, 'howdy')    # Pass in instance
```

By extension, the same rules apply within a class' method if we reference self attributes that refer to functions in the class. A self.method expression is a bound method object because self is an instance object:

```
class Eggs:
    def m1(self, n):
        print n
    def m2(self):
        x = self.m1        # Another bound method object
        x(42)              # Looks like a simple function

Eggs().m2()                # Prints 42
```

Most of the time, you call methods immediately after fetching them with qualification, so you don't always notice the method objects generated along the way. But if you start writing code that calls objects generically, you need to be careful to treat unbound methods specially—they normally require an explicit instance object to be passed in.*

Now that you understand the method object model, for other examples of bound methods at work, see this chapter's sidebar "Why You Will Care: Bound Methods and Callbacks," and the prior chapter's discussion of callback handlers in the section "__call__ Intercepts Calls."

Documentation Strings Revisited

Docstrings, which we covered in detail in Chapter 14, are string literals that show up at the top of various structures, and are automatically saved by Python in the corresponding objects' __doc__ attributes. This works for module files, function defs, and classes and methods. Now that we know more about classes and methods, the file *docstr.py* provides a quick but comprehensive example that summarizes the places where docstrings can show up in your code. All of these can be triple-quoted blocks:

```
"I am: docstr.__doc__"

class spam:
    "I am: spam.__doc__ or docstr.spam.__doc__"
```

---

* See the discussion of static and class methods in Chapter 26 for an optional exception to this rule. Like bound methods, both of these can masquerade as basic functions, too, because they do not expect instances when called.

```
        def method(self, arg):
            "I am: spam.method.__doc__ or self.method.__doc__"
            pass

    def func(args):
        "I am: docstr.func.__doc__"
        pass
```

Why You Will Care: Bound Methods and Callbacks

Because bound methods automatically pair an instance with a class method function, you can use them anywhere a simple function is expected. One of the most common places you'll see this idea put to work is in code that registers methods as event callback handlers in the Tkinter GUI interface. Here's the simple case:

```
def handler():
    ...use globals for state...
...
widget = Button(text='spam', command=handler)
```

To register a handler for button click events, we usually pass a callable object that takes no arguments to the command keyword argument. Function names (and lambdas) work here, and so do class methods, as long as they are bound methods:

```
class MyWidget:
    def handler(self):
        ...use self.attr for state...
    def makewidgets(self):
        b = Button(text='spam', command=self.handler)
```

Here, the event handler is self.handler—a bound method object that remembers both self and MyGui.handler. Because self will refer to the original instance when handler is later invoked on events, the method will have access to instance attributes that can retain state between events. With simple functions, state normally must be retained in global variables instead. See also the discussion of __call__ operator overloading in Chapter 24 for another way to make classes compatible with function-based APIs.

The main advantage of documentation strings is that they stick around at runtime. Thus, if it's been coded as a docstring, you can qualify an object with its __doc__ attribute to fetch its documentation:

```
>>> import docstr
>>> docstr.__doc__
'I am: docstr.__doc__'

>>> docstr.spam.__doc__
'I am: spam.__doc__ or docstr.spam.__doc__'

>>> docstr.spam.method.__doc__
'I am: spam.method.__doc__ or self.method.__doc__'
```

```
>>> docstr.func.__doc__
'I am: docstr.func.__doc__'
```

A discussion of the PyDoc tool, which knows how to format all these strings in reports, appears in Chapter 14.

Documentation strings are available at runtime, but they are less flexible syntactically than # comments (which can appear anywhere in a program). Both forms are useful tools, and any program documentation is good (as long as it's accurate).

Classes Versus Modules

We'll wrap up this chapter by briefly comparing the topics of this book's last two parts: modules and classes. Because they're both about namespaces, the distinction can be confusing. In short:

Modules

- Are data/logic packages.
- Are created by writing Python files or C extensions.
- Are used by being imported.

Classes

- Implement new objects.
- Are created by class statements.
- Are used by being called.
- Always live within a module.

Classes also support extra features that modules don't, such as operator overloading, multiple instance generation, and inheritance. Although both classes and modules are namespaces, you should be able to tell by now that they are very different things.

Chapter Summary

In this chapter, we sampled common ways to use and combine classes to optimize their reusability and factoring benefits—what are usually considered design issues that are often independent of any particular programming language (though Python can make them easier to implement). We studied delegation (wrapping objects in proxy classes), composition (controlling embedded objects), inheritance (acquiring behavior from other classes), and some more esoteric concepts such as multiple inheritance, bound methods, and factories.

The next chapter ends our look at classes and OOP by surveying more advanced class-related topics; some of its material may be of more interest to tool writers than application programmers, but it still merits a review by most people who will do OOP in Python. First, though, another quick chapter quiz.

Chapter Quiz

1. What is multiple inheritance?
2. What is delegation?
3. What is composition?
4. What are bound methods?

Quiz Answers

1. Multiple inheritance occurs when a class inherits from more than one super-class; it's useful for mixing together multiple packages of class-based code.

2. Delegation involves wrapping an object in a proxy class, which adds extra behavior, and passes other operations to the wrapped object. The proxy retains the interface of the wrapped object.

3. Composition is a technique whereby a controller class embeds and directs a number of objects, and provides an interface all its own; it's a way to build up larger structures with classes.

4. Bound methods combine an instance and a method function; you can call them without passing in an instance object explicitly because the original instance is still available.

## CHAPTER 26

Advanced Class Topics

This chapter concludes Part VI and our look at OOP in Python by presenting a few more advanced class-related topics: we will survey subclassing built-in types, pseudoprivate attributes, new-style classes, static methods, function decorators, and more.

As we've seen, Python's OOP model is, at its core, very simple, and some of the topics presented in this chapter are so advanced and optional that you may not encounter them very often in your Python applications-programming career. In the interest of completeness, though, we'll round out our discussion of classes with a brief look at these advanced tools for advanced OOP work.

As usual, because this is the last chapter in this part of the book, it ends with a section on class-related gotchas, and the set of lab exercises for this part. I encourage you to work through the exercises to help cement the ideas we've studied here. I also suggest working on or studying larger OOP Python projects as a supplement to this book. As with much in computing, the benefits of OOP tend to become more apparent with practice.

Extending Built-in Types

Besides implementing new kinds of objects, classes are sometimes used to extend the functionality of Python's built-in types to support more exotic data structures. For instance, to add queue insert and delete methods to lists, you can code classes that wrap (embed) a list object, and export insert and delete methods that process the list specially, like the delegation technique studied in Chapter 25. As of Python 2.2, you can also use inheritance to specialize built-in types. The next two sections show both techniques in action.

Extending Types by Embedding

Remember those set functions we wrote in Part IV? Here's what they look like brought back to life as a Python class. The following example (the file *setwrapper.py*) implements a new set object type by moving some of the set functions to methods, and adding some basic operator overloading. For the most part, this class just wraps a Python list with extra set operations. Because it's a class, it also supports multiple instances and customization by inheritance in subclasses:

```
class Set:
    def __init__(self, value = []):     # Constructor
        self.data = []                  # Manages a list
        self.concat(value)

    def intersect(self, other):         # other is any sequence
        res = []                        # self is the subject
        for x in self.data:
            if x in other:              # Pick common items
                res.append(x)
        return Set(res)                 # Return a new Set

    def union(self, other):             # other is any sequence
        res = self.data[:]              # Copy of my list
        for x in other:                 # Add items in other
            if not x in res:
                res.append(x)
        return Set(res)

    def concat(self, value):            # value: list, Set...
        for x in value:                 # Removes duplicates
            if not x in self.data:
                self.data.append(x)

    def __len__(self):          return len(self.data)            # len(self)
    def __getitem__(self, key): return self.data[key]            # self[i]
    def __and__(self, other):   return self.intersect(other)     # self & other
    def __or__(self, other):    return self.union(other)         # self | other
    def __repr__(self):         return 'Set:' + `self.data`       # Print
```

Overloading indexing enables instances of our Set class to masquerade as real lists. Because you will interact with and extend this class in an exercise at the end of this chapter, I won't say much more about this code until Appendix B.

Extending Types by Subclassing

Beginning with Python 2.2, all the built-in types can now be subclassed directly. Type-conversion functions such as list, str, dict, and tuple have become built-in type names—although transparent to your script, a type-conversion call (e.g., list('spam')) is now really an invocation of a type's object constructor.

This change allows you to customize or extend the behavior of built-in types with user-defined class statements: simply subclass the new type names to customize them. Instances of your type subclasses can be used anywhere that the original built-in type can appear. For example, suppose you have trouble getting used to the fact that Python list offsets begin at 0 instead of 1. Not to worry—you can always code your own subclass that customizes this core behavior of lists. The file *typesubclass.py* shows how:

```
# Subclass built-in list type/class.
# Map 1..N to 0..N-1; call back to built-in version.

class MyList(list):
    def __getitem__(self, offset):
        print '(indexing %s at %s)' % (self, offset)
        return list.__getitem__(self, offset - 1)

if __name__ == '__main__':
    print list('abc')
    x = MyList('abc')                    # __init__ inherited from list
    print x                              # __repr__ inherited from list

    print x[1]                           # MyList.__getitem__
    print x[3]                           # Customizes list superclass method

    x.append('spam'); print x            # Attributes from list superclass
    x.reverse();      print x
```

In this file, the MyList subclass extends the built-in list's __getitem__ indexing method only to map indexes 1 to N back to the required 0 to N–1. All it really does is decrement the index submitted, and call back to the superclass' version of indexing, but it's enough to do the trick:

```
% python typesubclass.py
['a', 'b', 'c']
['a', 'b', 'c']
(indexing ['a', 'b', 'c'] at 1)
a
(indexing ['a', 'b', 'c'] at 3)
c
['a', 'b', 'c', 'spam']
['spam', 'c', 'b', 'a']
```

This output also includes tracing text the class prints on indexing. Whether changing indexing this way is a good idea in general is another issue—users of your MyList class may very well be confused by such a core departure from Python sequence behavior. The fact that you can customize built-in types this way can be a powerful tool though, in general.

For instance, this coding pattern gives rise to an alternative way to code sets—as a subclass of the built-in list type, rather than a standalone class that manages an embedded list object. The following class, coded in the file *setsubclass.py*, customizes lists to add just methods and operators related to set processing. Because all other behavior is inherited from the built-in list superclass, this makes for a shorter and simpler alternative:

```python
class Set(list):
    def __init__(self, value = []):       # Constructor
        list.__init__([])                 # Customizes list
        self.concat(value)                # Copies mutable defaults

    def intersect(self, other):           # other is any sequence
        res = []                          # self is the subject
        for x in self:
            if x in other:                # Pick common items
                res.append(x)
        return Set(res)                   # Return a new Set

    def union(self, other):               # other is any sequence
        res = Set(self)                   # Copy me and my list
        res.concat(other)
        return res

    def concat(self, value):              # value: list, Set...
        for x in value:                   # Removes duplicates
            if not x in self:
                self.append(x)

    def __and__(self, other): return self.intersect(other)
    def __or__(self, other):  return self.union(other)
    def __repr__(self):       return 'Set:' + list.__repr__(self)

if __name__ == '__main__':
    x = Set([1,3,5,7])
    y = Set([2,1,4,5,6])
    print x, y, len(x)
    print x.intersect(y), y.union(x)
    print x & y, x | y
    x.reverse(); print x
```

Here is the output of the self-test code at the end of this file. Because subclassing core types is an advanced feature, I'll omit further details here, but I invite you to trace through these results in the code to study its behavior:

```
% python setsubclass.py
Set:[1, 3, 5, 7] Set:[2, 1, 4, 5, 6] 4
Set:[1, 5] Set:[2, 1, 4, 5, 6, 3, 7]
Set:[1, 5] Set:[1, 3, 5, 7, 2, 4, 6]
Set:[7, 5, 3, 1]
```

There are more efficient ways to implement sets with dictionaries in Python, which replace the linear scans in the set implementations shown here with dictionary index operations (hashing), and so run much quicker. (For more details, see *Programming Python*.) If you're interested in sets, also take another look at the set object type we explored in Chapter 5; this type provides set operations as built-in tools. Set implementations are fun to experiment with, but they are no longer strictly required in Python today.

For another type subclassing example, see the implementation of the new bool type in Python 2.3: as mentioned earlier in the book, bool is a subclass of int with two instances (True and False) that behave like the integers 1 and 0, but inherit custom string-representation methods that display their names.

Pseudoprivate Class Attributes

In Part IV, we learned that every name assigned at the top level of a module file is exported. By default, the same holds for classes—data hiding is a convention, and clients may fetch or change any class or instance attribute they like. In fact, attributes are all "public" and "virtual" in C++ terms; they're all accessible everywhere, and looked up dynamically at runtime.*

That's still true today. However, Python also supports the notion of name "mangling" (i.e., expansion) to localize some names in classes. Mangled names are sometimes misleadingly called "private attributes," but really this is just a way to *localize* a name to the class that created it—name mangling does not prevent access by code outside the class. This feature is mostly intended to avoid namespace collisions in instances, not to restrict access to names in general; mangled names are therefore better called "pseudoprivate" than "private."

Pseudoprivate names are an advanced and entirely optional feature, and you probably won't find them very useful until you start writing large class hierarchies in multi-programmer projects. But, because you may see this feature in other people's code, you need to be somewhat aware of it, even if you don't use it yourself.

Name Mangling Overview

Here's how name mangling works: names inside a class statement that start with two underscores, but don't end with two underscores, are automatically expanded to include the name of the enclosing class. For instance, a name like __X within a class named Spam is changed to _Spam__X automatically: the original name is prefixed with a single underscore, and the enclosing class' name. Because the modified name contains the name of the enclosing class, it's somewhat unique; it won't clash with similar names created by other classes in a hierarchy.

---

* This tends to scare C++ people unnecessarily. In Python, it's even possible to change or completely delete a class method at runtime. On the other hand, almost nobody ever does in practical programs. As a scripting language, Python is more about enabling than restricting. Also, recall from our discussion of operator overloading in Chapter 24 that __getattr__ and __setattr__ can be used to emulate privacy, but are generally not used for this in practice.

Name mangling happens only in class statements, and only for names that begin with two leading underscores. However, it happens for *every* name preceded with double underscores, including method names and instance attribute names (for example, in our Spam class, the instance attribute reference self.__X would be transformed to self._Spam__X). Because more than one class may add attributes to an instance, this mangling helps avoid clashes—but we need to move on to an example to see how.

Why Use Pseudoprivate Attributes?

The problem that the pseudoprivate attribute feature is meant to alleviate has to do with the way instance attributes are stored. In Python, all instance attributes wind up in the single instance object at the bottom of the class tree. This is very different from the C++ model, where each class gets its own space for data members it defines.

Within a class method in Python, whenever a method assigns to a self attribute (e.g., self.attr = value), it changes or creates an attribute in the instance (inheritance searches only happen on reference, not on assignment). Because this is true even if multiple classes in a hierarchy assign to the same attribute, collisions are possible.

For example, suppose that when a programmer codes a class, she assumes that she owns the attribute name X in the instance. In this class' methods, the name is set, and later fetched:

```
class C1:
    def meth1(self): self.X = 88        # Assume X is mine
    def meth2(self): print self.X
```

Suppose further that another programmer, working in isolation, makes the same assumption in a class that she codes:

```
class C2:
    def metha(self): self.X = 99        # Me too
    def methb(self): print self.X
```

Both of these classes work by themselves. The problem arises if the two classes are ever mixed together in the same class tree:

```
class C3(C1, C2): ...
I = C3( )                               # Only 1 X in I!
```

Now, the value that each class gets back when it says self.X will depend on which class assigned it last. Because all assignments to self.X refer to the same single instance, there is only one X attribute—I.X—no matter how many classes use that attribute name.

To guarantee that an attribute belongs to the class that uses it, prefix the name with double underscores everywhere it is used in the class, as in this file, *private.py*:

```
class C1:
    def meth1(self): self.__X = 88      # Now X is mine
    def meth2(self): print self.__X     # Becomes _C1__X in I
```

```
class C2:
    def metha(self): self.__X = 99          # Me too
    def methb(self): print self.__X         # Becomes _C2__X in I

class C3(C1, C2): pass
I = C3()                                     # Two X names in I

I.meth1(); I.metha()
print I.__dict__
I.meth2(); I.methb()
```

When thus prefixed, the X attributes will be expanded to include the names of their classes before being added to the instance. If you run a dir call on I, or inspect its namespace dictionary after the attributes have been assigned, you'll see the expanded names, _C1__X and _C2__X, but not X. Because the expansion makes the names unique within the instance, the class coders can safely assume that they truly own any names that they prefix with two underscores:

```
% python private.py
{'_C2__X': 99, '_C1__X': 88}
88
99
```

This trick can avoid potential name collisions in the instance, but note that it does not amount to true privacy. If you know the name of the enclosing class, you can still access either of these attributes anywhere you have a reference to the instance by using the fully expanded name (e.g., I._C1__X = 77). On the other hand, this feature makes it less likely that you will *accidentally* step on a class' names.

Again, I should note that this feature tends to be more useful for larger, multi-programmer projects, and then only for selected names. Don't be tempted to clutter your code unnecessarily; only use this feature for names that truly need to be controlled by a single class. For simpler programs, it's probably overkill.

 Also, see the emulation of private instance attributes sketched in Chapter 24, in the __getattr__ section. Although it's possible to emulate access controls in Python classes, this is rarely done in practice, even for large systems.

New-Style Classes

In Release 2.2, Python introduced a new flavor of classes, known as "new-style" classes; the classes covered so far in this part of the book are known as "classic classes" when comparing them to the new kind.

New-style classes are only slightly different from classic classes, and the ways in which they differ are completely irrelevant to the vast majority of Python users. Moreover, the classic class model, which has been with Python for some 15 years, still works exactly as I've described previously.

New-style classes are almost completely backward compatible with classic classes in syntax and behavior; they mostly just add a few advanced new features. However, because they modify one special case of inheritance, they had to be introduced as a distinct tool so as to avoid impacting any existing code that depends on the prior behavior.

New-style classes are coded with all the normal class syntax we have studied. The chief coding difference is that you subclass from a built-in type (e.g., list) to produce a new-style class. A new built-in name, object, is provided to serve as a superclass for new-style classes if no other built-in type is appropriate to use:

```
class newstyle(object):
    ...normal code...
```

More generally, any class derived from object, or any other built-in type, is automatically treated as a new-style class. (By *derived*, I mean that this includes subclasses of object, subclasses of subclasses of object, and so on—as long as a built-in is somewhere in the superclass tree, the new class will be treated as a new-style class.) Classes not derived from built-ins are considered classic.

> Per Python creator Guido van Rossum, in Python 3.0, all classes will automatically be new-style, so the requirement of being derived from a built-in superclass will no longer exist. Because even standalone classes will be considered new-style, and because new-style classes are almost completely backward compatible with classic classes, for most programmers, the change will be transparent.
>
> In the past, there was some concern that top-level classes might need to derive from object in Python 3.0, but Guido has recently stated that this won't be required. To most programmers, all classes in 3.0 will work as described in this book, but with the additional new-style features available. I can't predict the future completely, though, so be sure to check the 3.0 release notes for more on this front.

Diamond Inheritance Change

Perhaps the most visible change in new-style classes is their slightly different treatment of inheritance for the so-called *diamond* pattern of multiple inheritance trees, where more than one superclass leads to the same higher superclass further above. The diamond pattern is an advanced design concept that we have not even discussed for normal classes.

In short, with classic classes, the inheritance search procedure is strictly depth first, and then left to right—Python climbs all the way to the top, hugging the left side of the tree, before it backs up, and begins to look further to the right. In new-style classes, the search is more breadth-first in such cases—Python first looks in any superclasses to the right of the first one searched before ascending all the way to the common superclass at the top. Because of this change, lower superclasses can overload attributes of higher superclasses, regardless of the sort of multiple inheritance trees they are mixed into.

Diamond inheritance example

To illustrate, consider this simplistic incarnation of the diamond inheritance pattern for classic classes:

```
>>> class A:        attr = 1        # Classic
>>> class B(A):     pass
>>> class C(A):     attr = 2
>>> class D(B,C):   pass            # Tries A before C
>>> x = D()
>>> x.attr
1
```

The attribute here was found in superclass A, because with classic classes, the inheritance search climbs as high as it can before backing up and moving right—Python will search D, B, A, and then C (but will stop when attr is found in A, above B). With the new-style classes derived from a built-in like object, though, Python looks in C (to the right of B) before A (above B)—that is, it searches D, B, C, and then A (and in this case, stops in C):

```
>>> class A(object): attr = 1      # New style
>>> class B(A):      pass
>>> class C(A):      attr = 2
>>> class D(B,C):    pass           # Tries C before A
>>> x = D()
>>> x.attr
2
```

This change in the inheritance search procedure is based upon the assumption that if you mix in C lower in the tree, you probably intend to grab its attributes in preference to A's. It also assumes that C is always intended to override A's attributes, which is probably true when it's used standalone, but may not be when it's mixed into a diamond with classic classes—you might not even know that C may be mixed in like this when you code it.

Explicit conflict resolution

Of course, the problem with assumptions is that they assume things. If this search order deviation seems too subtle to remember, or if you want more control over the search process, you can always force the selection of an attribute from anywhere in the tree by assigning or otherwise naming the one you want at the place where the classes are mixed together:

```
>>> class A:        attr = 1        # Classic
>>> class B(A):     pass
>>> class C(A):     attr = 2
>>> class D(B,C):   attr = C.attr   # Choose C, to the right
>>> x = D()
>>> x.attr                          # Works like new style
2
```

Here, a tree of classic classes is emulating the search order of new-style classes: the assignment to the attribute in D picks the version in C, thereby subverting the normal inheritance search path (D.attr will be lowest in the tree). New-style classes can similarly emulate classic classes by choosing the attribute above at the place where the classes are mixed together:

```
>>> class A(object): attr = 1          # New style
>>> class B(A):       pass
>>> class C(A):       attr = 2
>>> class D(B,C):     attr = B.attr     # Choose A.attr, above
>>> x = D( )
>>> x.attr                             # Works like classic
1
```

If you are willing to always resolve conflicts like this, you can largely ignore the search order difference, and not rely on assumptions about what you meant when you coded your classes. Naturally, attributes picked this way can also be method functions—methods are normal, assignable objects:

```
>>> class A:
...     def meth(s): print 'A.meth'
>>> class C(A):
...     def meth(s): print 'C.meth'
>>> class B(A):
...     pass
>>> class D(B,C): pass                  # Use default search order
>>> x = D( )                            # Will vary per class type
>>> x.meth( )                           # Defaults to classic order
A.meth

>>> class D(B,C): meth = C.meth         # Pick C's method: new style
>>> x = D( )
>>> x.meth( )
C.meth

>>> class D(B,C): meth = B.meth         # Pick B's method: classic
>>> x = D( )
>>> x.meth( )
A.meth
```

Here, we select methods by explicitly assigning to names lower in the tree. We might also simply call the desired class explicitly; in practice, this pattern might be more common, especially for things like constructors:

```
class D(B,C):
    def meth(self):                     # Redefine lower
        ...
        C.meth(self)                    # Pick C's method by calling
```

Such selections by assignment or call at mix-in points can effectively insulate your code from this difference in class flavors. Explicitly resolving the conflicts this way ensures that your code won't vary per Python version in the future (apart from perhaps needing to derive classes from a built-in type for the new style).*

In sum, by default, the diamond pattern is searched differently for classic and new-style classes, and this is a nonbackward-compatible change. However, keep in mind that this change only affects diamond pattern cases; new-style class inheritance works unchanged for all other inheritance tree structures. Further, it's not impossible that this entire issue may be of more theoretical than practical importance—because it wasn't significant enough to change until 2.2, it seems unlikely to impact much Python code.

Other New-Style Class Extensions

Beyond this change in the diamond inheritance search pattern (which is itself too obscure to matter to most readers of this book), new-style classes open up a handful of even more advanced possibilities. Here's a brief look at each.

Static and class methods

As of Python 2.2, it is possible to define methods within a class that can be called without an instance: *static* methods work roughly like simple instanceless functions inside a class, and *class* methods are passed a class instead of an instance. Special built-in functions called `staticmethod` and `classmethod` must be called within the class to enable these method modes. Although this feature was added in conjunction with new-style classes, static and class methods work for classic classes, too. Because of that, we'll save this topic for the next section.

Instance slots

By assigning a list of string attribute names to a special `__slots__` class attribute, it is possible for a new-style class to limit the set of legal attributes that instances of the class will have. This special attribute is typically set by assigning to the variable `__slots__` at the top level of a `class` statement: only those names in the `__slots__` list can be assigned as instance attributes. However, like all names in Python, instance attribute names must still be assigned before they can be referenced, even if listed in `__slots__`. Here's an example to illustrate:

```
>>> class limiter(object):
...     __slots__ = ['age', 'name', 'job']
...
```

---

* Even without the classic/new divergence, this technique may sometimes come in handy in multiple inheritance scenarios in general. If you want part of a superclass on the left and part of a superclass on the right, you might need to tell Python which same-named attributes to choose by using explicit assignments in subclasses. We'll revisit this notion in a gotcha at the end of this chapter. Also note that diamond inheritance patterns can be more problematic in some cases than I've implied here (e.g., what if B and C both have required constructors that call to A's?), but this is beyond this book's scope.

```
>>> x = limiter()
>>> x.age                                    # Must assign before use
AttributeError: age

>>> x.age = 40
>>> x.age
40
>>> x.ape = 1000                             # Illegal: not in slots
AttributeError: 'limiter' object has no attribute 'ape'
```

This feature was envisioned as a way to catch "typo" errors (assignments to illegal attribute names not in __slots__ are detected), and as an optimization mechanism (slot attributes may be stored in a tuple instead of a dictionary for quicker lookup).

Slots are something of a break with Python's dynamic nature, which dictates that any name may be created by assignment. They also have additional constraints and implications that are far too complex for us to discuss here. For example, some instances with slots may not have a __dict__ attribute dictionary, which can make some of the metaprograms we've coded in this book more complex; tools that generically list attributes, for instance, may have to inspect two sources instead of one. See the Python 2.2 release documents and Python's standard manual set for more details.

Class properties

A mechanism known as *properties* provides another way for new-style classes to define automatically called methods for access or assignment to instance attributes. This feature is an alternative to many current uses of the __getattr__ and __setattr__ overloading methods we studied in Chapter 24. Properties have a similar effect to these two methods, but they incur an extra method call only for accesses to names that require dynamic computation. Properties (and slots) are based on a new notion of attribute descriptors, which is too advanced for us to cover here.

In short, properties are a type of object assigned to class attribute names. They are generated by calling a property built-in with three methods (handlers for get, set, and delete operations), as well as a docstring; if any argument is passed as None or omitted, that operation is not supported. Properties are typically assigned at the top level of a class statement [e.g., name = property(...)]. When thus assigned, accesses to the class attribute itself (e.g., obj.name) are automatically routed to one of the accessor methods passed into the property. For example, the __getattr__ method allows classes to intercept undefined attribute references:

```
>>> class classic:
...     def __getattr__(self, name):
...         if name == 'age':
...             return 40
...         else:
...             raise AttributeError
...
```

```
>>> x = classic()
>>> x.age                                    # Runs __getattr__
40
>>> x.name                                   # Runs __getattr__
AttributeError
```

Here is the same example, coded with properties instead:

```
>>> class newprops(object):
...     def getage(self):
...         return 40
...     age = property(getage, None, None, None)   # get,set,del,docs
...
>>> x = newprops()
>>> x.age                                    # Runs getage
40
>>> x.name                                   # Normal fetch
AttributeError: newprops instance has no attribute 'name'
```

For some coding tasks, properties can be less complex and quicker to run than the traditional techniques. For example, when we add attribute *assignment* support, properties become more attractive—there's less code to type, and no extra method calls are incurred for assignments to attributes we don't wish to compute dynamically:

```
>>> class newprops(object):
...     def getage(self):
...         return 40
...     def setage(self, value):
...         print 'set age:', value
...         self._age = value
...     age = property(getage, setage, None, None)
...
>>> x = newprops()
>>> x.age                                    # Runs getage
40
>>> x.age = 42                               # Runs setage
set age: 42
>>> x._age                                   # Normal fetch; no getage call
42
>>> x.job = 'trainer'                        # Normal assign; no setage call
>>> x.job                                    # Normal fetch; no getage call
'trainer'
```

The equivalent classic class might trigger extra method calls, and may need to route attribute assignments through the attribute dictionary to avoid loops:

```
>>> class classic:
...     def __getattr__(self, name):         # On undefined reference
...         if name == 'age':
...             return 40
...         else:
...             raise AttributeError
...     def __setattr__(self, name, value):  # On all assignments
...         print 'set:', name, value
```

```
...            if name == 'age':
...                self.__dict__['_age'] = value
...            else:
...                self.__dict__[name] = value
...
>>> x = classic()
>>> x.age                              # Runs __getattr__
40
>>> x.age = 41                         # Runs __setattr__
set: age 41
>>> x._age                             # Defined: no __getattr__ call
41
>>> x.job = 'trainer'                  # Runs __setattr__ again
>>> x.job                              # Defined: no __getattr__ call
```

Properties seem like a win for this simple example. However, some applications of __getattr__ and __setattr__ may still require more dynamic or generic interfaces than properties directly provide. For example, in many cases, the set of attributes to be supported cannot be determined when the class is coded, and may not even exist in any tangible form (e.g., when delegating arbitrary method references to a wrapped/embedded object generically). In such cases, a generic __getattr__ or a __setattr__ attribute handler with a passed-in attribute name may be preferable. Because such generic handlers can also handle simpler cases, properties are largely an optional extension.

New __getattribute__ overloading method

The __getattribute__ method, available for new-style classes only, allows a class to intercept *all* attribute references, not just undefined references (like __getattr__). It is also substantially trickier to use than __getattr__ and __setattr__ (it is prone to loops). I'll defer to Python's standard documentation for more details on this method.

Besides all these feature additions, new-style classes integrate with the notion of sub-classable types mentioned earlier in this chapter; subclassable types and new-style classes were introduced in conjunction with a merging of the type/class dichotomy in Python 2.2 and beyond.

Because new-style class features are all advanced topics, we won't go into further details in this introductory text. Please see the Python 2.2 release documentation and the language reference for more information.

Static and Class Methods

In Python releases prior to 2.2, class method functions can never be called without an instance. In Python 2.2 and later, this is also the default behavior, but it can be modified with a new optional feature known as *static methods*—simple functions with no self argument that appear nested in a class, and are designed to work on class attributes instead of instance attributes. Such methods usually keep track of information that spans all instances (e.g., the number created), rather than providing behavior for instances.

In the prior chapter, we talked about *unbound* methods: when we fetch a method function by qualifying a class (instead of an instance), we get an unbound method object. Even though they are defined with `def` statements, unbound method objects are not simple functions; they cannot be called without an instance.

For example, suppose we want to use class attributes to count how many instances are generated from a class (as in the following file, *spam.py*). Remember, class attributes are shared by all instances, so we can store the counter in the class object itself:

```
class Spam:
    numInstances = 0
    def __init__(self):
        Spam.numInstances = Spam.numInstances + 1
    def printNumInstances():
        print "Number of instances created: ", Spam.numInstances
```

But this won't work—the `printNumInstances` method still expects an instance to be passed in when called because the function is associated with a class (even though there are no arguments in the `def` header):

```
>>> from spam import *
>>> a = Spam()
>>> b = Spam()
>>> c = Spam()
>>> Spam.printNumInstances()
Traceback (innermost last):
  File "<stdin>", line 1, in ?
TypeError: unbound method must be called with class instance 1st argument
```

The problem here is that unbound instance methods aren't exactly the same as simple functions. This is mostly a knowledge issue, but if you want to call functions that access class members without an instance, probably the most straightforward idea is to just make them simple functions, not class methods. This way, an instance isn't expected in the call:

```
def printNumInstances():
    print "Number of instances created: ", Spam.numInstances

class Spam:
    numInstances = 0
    def __init__(self):
        Spam.numInstances = Spam.numInstances + 1

>>> import spam
>>> a = spam.Spam()
>>> b = spam.Spam()
>>> c = spam.Spam()
```

```
>>> spam.printNumInstances()
Number of instances created:  3
>>> spam.Spam.numInstances
3
```

Because the class name is accessible to the simple function as a global variable, this works fine. Also, note that the name of the function becomes global, but only to this single module; it will not clash with names in other files of the program.

We can also make this work by calling the function through an instance, as usual, although this can be inconvenient if making an instance changes the class data:

```
class Spam:
    numInstances = 0
    def __init__(self):
        Spam.numInstances = Spam.numInstances + 1
    def printNumInstances(self):
        print "Number of instances created: ", Spam.numInstances

>>> from spam import Spam
>>> a, b, c = Spam(), Spam(), Spam()
>>> a.printNumInstances()
Number of instances created:  3
>>> b.printNumInstances()
Number of instances created:  3
>>> Spam().printNumInstances()
Number of instances created:  4
```

Prior to Python 2.2's static method extension, some language theorists claimed that the availability of this technique meant that Python didn't have class methods, only instance methods. I suspect they really meant that Python classes don't work the same as classes in some other languages. What Python really has are bound and unbound method objects, with well-defined semantics; qualifying a class gets you an unbound method, which is a special kind of function. Python does have class attributes, but functions in classes expect an instance argument.

Moreover, because Python already provides modules as a namespace-partitioning tool, there's usually no need to package functions in classes unless they implement object behavior. Simple functions within modules usually do most of what instance-less class methods could. For example, in the first code sample in this section, printNumInstances is already associated with the class because it lives in the same module. The only lost functionality is that the function name has a broader scope—the entire module, rather than the class.

Using Static and Class Methods

Today, there is another option for coding simple functions associated with a class. As of Python 2.2, you can code classes with static and class methods, neither of which requires an instance argument to be passed in when they are invoked. To designate

---

such methods, classes call the built-in functions staticmethod and classmethod, as hinted in the earlier discussion of new-style classes. For example:

```
class Multi:
    def imeth(self, x):           # Normal instance method
        print self, x
    def smeth(x):                 # Static: no instance passed
        print x
    def cmeth(cls, x):            # Class: gets class, not instance
        print cls, x
    smeth = staticmethod(smeth)   # Make smeth a static method
    cmeth = classmethod(cmeth)    # Make cmeth a class method.
```

Notice how the last two assignments in this code simply *reassign* the method names smeth and cmeth. Attributes are created and changed by any assignment in a class statement, so these final assignments overwrite the assignments made earlier by the defs.

Technically, Python now supports three kinds of class-related methods: instance, static, and class. *Instance methods* are the normal (and default) case that we've seen in this book. You must always call an instance method with an instance object. When you call it through an instance, Python passes the instance to the first (leftmost) argument automatically; when you call it through a class, you pass along the instance manually:

```
>>> obj = Multi()             # Make an instance
>>> obj.imeth(1)              # Normal call, through instance
<__main__.Multi instance...> 1
>>> Multi.imeth(obj, 2)       # Normal call, through class
<__main__.Multi instance...> 2
```

By contrast, *static methods* are called without an instance argument; their names are local to the scopes of the classes in which they are defined, and may be looked up by inheritance. Mostly, they work like simple functions that happen to be coded inside a class:

```
>>> Multi.smeth(3)            # Static call, through class
3
>>> obj.smeth(4)             # Static call, through instance
4
```

Class methods are similar, but Python automatically passes the class (not an instance) in to a class method's first (leftmost) argument:

```
>>> Multi.cmeth(5)            # Class call, through class
__main__.Multi 5
>>> obj.cmeth(6)             # Class call, through instance
__main__.Multi 6
```

Static and class methods are new and advanced features of the language, with highly specialized roles that we don't have space to document fully here. Static methods are commonly used in conjunction with class attributes to manage information that spans all instances generated from the class. For example, to keep track of the number of instances generated from a class (as in the earlier example), we could use static methods to manage a counter attached as a class attribute. Because such a count has nothing to do with any particular instance, it would be inconvenient to have to access methods that process it through an instance (especially since making an instance to access the counter might change the counter). Moreover, static methods' proximity to the class provides a more natural solution than coding class-oriented functions outside the class.

Here is the static method equivalent of this section's original example:

```
class Spam:
    numInstances = 0
    def __init__(self):
        Spam.numInstances += 1
    def printNumInstances():
        print "Number of instances:", Spam.numInstances
    printNumInstances = staticmethod(printNumInstances)
```

```
>>> a = Spam()
>>> b = Spam()
>>> c = Spam()
>>> Spam.printNumInstances()
Number of instances: 3
>>> a.printNumInstances()
Number of instances: 3
```

Compared to simply moving printNumInstances outside the class, as prescribed earlier, this version requires an extra staticmethod call; however, it localizes the function name in the class scope (it won't clash with other names in the module) and moves the function code closer to where it is used (inside the class statement). You should judge for yourself whether this is a net improvement or not.

In recent Python versions, the static method designation has become even simpler; the next section explains how.

Function Decorators

Because the staticmethod call technique described in the prior section seemed obscure to some users, a feature was added to make the operation simpler. *Function decorators* provide a way to specify special operation modes for functions, by wrapping them in an extra layer of logic implemented as another function.

Function decorators turn out to be general tools: they are useful for adding many types of logic to functions besides the static method use case. For instance, they may be used to augment functions with code that logs calls made to them, checks the types of passed arguments during debugging, and so on. In some ways, function decorators are similar to the *delegation* design pattern we explored in Chapter 25, but they are designed to augment a specific function or method call, not an entire object interface.

Python provides some built-in function decorators for operations such as marking static methods, but programmers can also code arbitrary decorators of their own. Although they are not strictly tied to classes, user-defined function decorators often are coded as classes to save the original functions, along with other data, as state information.

Syntactically, a function decorator is a sort of runtime declaration about the function that follows. A function decorator is coded on a line just before the def statement that defines a function or method and consists of the @ symbol, followed by what we call a *metafunction*—a function (or other callable object) that manages another function. Static methods today, for example, may be coded with decorator syntax like this:

```
class C:
    @staticmethod
    def meth( ):
        ...
```

Internally, this syntax has the same effect as the following (passing the function through the decorator and assigning the result back to the original name):

```
class C:
    def meth( ):
        ...
    meth = staticmethod(meth)              # Rebind name
```

The net effect is that calling the method function's name actually triggers the result of its staticmethod decorator first. Because a decorator can return any sort of object, this allows the decorator to insert a layer of logic to be run on every call. The decorator function is free to return the original function itself or a new object that saves the original function passed to the decorator to be invoked indirectly after the extra logic layer runs.

In fact, decorator syntax supports adding multiple layers of wrapper logic to a decorated function or method. A decorator line of this form:

```
@A @B @C
def f( ):
    ...
```

runs the same as the following:

```
def f( ):
    ...
f = A(B(C(f)))
```

It passes the original function through three different decorators, and assigns the result back to the original name. Again, the net effect is that when the original function name is called, three layers of logic can be invoked to augment the original function.

Decorator Example

Here is an example of a user-defined decorator at work. Recall from Chapter 24 that the __call__ operator overloading method implements a function-call interface for class instances. The following code uses this to define a class that saves the decorated function in the instance and catches calls to the original name. Because this is a class, it also has state information (a counter of calls made):

```
class tracer:
    def __init__(self, func):
        self.calls = 0
        self.func  = func
    def __call__(self, *args):
        self.calls += 1
        print 'call %s to %s' % (self.calls, self.func.__name__)
        self.func(*args)

@tracer
def spam(a, b, c):                  # Wrap spam in a decorator object
    print a, b, c

spam(1, 2, 3)                       # Really calls the tracer wrapper object
spam('a', 'b', 'c')                 # Invokes __call__ in class
spam(4, 5, 6)                       # __call__ adds logic and runs original object
```

Because the spam function is run through the tracer decorator, when the original spam name is called, it actually triggers the __call__ method in the class. This method counts and logs the call, and then dispatches to the original wrapped function. Note how the *name argument syntax is used to pack and unpack arguments passed in; because of this, this decorator can be used to wrap any function with any number of arguments.

The net effect, again, is to add a layer of logic to the original spam function. Here is the script's output—the first line comes from the tracer class, and the second comes from the spam function:

```
call 1 to spam
1 2 3
call 2 to spam
a b c
call 3 to spam
4 5 6
```

Trace through this example's code for more insight.

Although they are a general mechanism, function decorators are an advanced feature of interest primarily to tool writers, not application programmers, so I'll again defer to Python's standard manual set for more details on this subject.

Class Gotchas

Most class issues can usually be boiled down to namespace issues (which makes sense, given that classes are just namespaces with a few extra tricks). Some of the topics we'll cover in this section are more like case studies of advanced class usage than problems, and one or two of these gotchas have been eased by recent Python releases.

Changing Class Attributes Can Have Side Effects

Theoretically speaking, classes (and class instances) are *mutable* objects. Like built-in lists and dictionaries, they can be changed in-place by assigning to their attributes—and, as with lists and dictionaries, this means that changing a class or instance object may impact multiple references to it.

That's usually what we want (and is how objects change their state in general), but this becomes especially critical to know when changing class attributes. Because all instances generated from a class share the class' namespace, any changes at the class level are reflected in all instances unless they have their own versions of the changed class attributes.

Because classes, modules, and instances are all just objects with attribute namespaces, you can normally change their attributes at runtime by assignments. Consider the following class. Inside the class body, the assignment to the name a generates an attribute X.a, which lives in the class object at runtime, and will be inherited by all of X's instances:

```
>>> class X:
...     a = 1          # Class attribute
...
>>> I = X()
>>> I.a                # Inherited by instance
1
>>> X.a
1
```

So far, so good—this is the normal case. But notice what happens when we change the class attribute dynamically outside the class statement: it also changes the attribute in every object that inherits from the class. Moreover, new instances created from the class during this session or program run get the dynamically set value, regardless of what the class' source code says:

```
>>> X.a = 2            # May change more than X
>>> I.a                # I changes too
2
>>> J = X()            # J inherits from X's runtime values
>>> J.a                # (but assigning to J.a changes a in J, not X or I)
2
```

Is this a useful feature or a dangerous trap? You be the judge. You can actually get work done by changing class attributes without ever making a single instance; this technique can simulate "records" or "structs" in other languages. As a refresher, consider the following unusual but legal Python program:

```
class X: pass                    # Make a few attribute namespaces
class Y: pass

X.a = 1                          # Use class attributes as variables
X.b = 2                          # No instances anywhere to be found
X.c = 3
Y.a = X.a + X.b + X.c

for X.i in range(Y.a): print X.i    # Prints 0..5
```

Here, the classes X and Y work like "fileless" modules—namespaces for storing variables we don't want to clash. This is a perfectly legal Python programming trick, but it's less appropriate when applied to classes written by others; you can't always be sure that class attributes you change aren't critical to the class' internal behavior. If you're out to simulate a C struct, you may be better off changing instances than classes, as that way, only one object is affected:

```
class Record: pass
X = Record()
X.name = 'bob'
X.job  = 'Pizza maker'
```

Multiple Inheritance: Order Matters

This may be obvious, but it's worth underscoring: if you use multiple inheritance, the order in which superclasses are listed in the class statement header can be critical. Python always searches superclasses from left to right, according to their order in the header line.

For instance, in the multiple inheritance example we saw in Chapter 25, suppose that the Super class implemented a __repr__ method, too; would we want to inherit Lister's or Super's? We would get it from whichever class is listed first in Sub's class header, as inheritance searches proceed from left to right. Presumably, we would list Lister first because its whole purpose is its custom __repr__:

```
class Lister:
    def __repr__(self): ...

class Super:
    def __repr__(self): ...

class Sub(Lister, Super):        # Get Lister's __repr__ by listing it first
```

But now suppose Super and Lister have their own versions of other same-named attributes, too. If we want one name from Super, and another from Lister, the order in which we list them in the class header won't help—we will have to override inheritance by manually assigning to the attribute name in the Sub class:

```
class Lister:
    def __repr__(self): ...
    def other(self): ...

class Super:
    def __repr__(self): ...
    def other(self): ...

class Sub(Lister, Super):       # Get Lister's __repr__ by listing it first
    other = Super.other         # But explicitly pick Super's version of other
    def __init__(self):
        ...

x = Sub( )                      # Inheritance searches Sub before Super/Lister
```

Here, the assignment to `other` within the `Sub` class creates `Sub.other`—a reference back to the `Super.other` object. Because it is lower in the tree, `Sub.other` effectively hides `Lister.other`, the attribute that the inheritance search would normally find. Similarly, if we listed `Super` first in the class header to pick up its `other`, we would need to select `Lister`'s method explicitly:

```
class Sub(Super, Lister):           # Get Super's other by order
    __repr__ = Lister.__repr__      # Explicitly pick Lister.__repr__
```

Multiple inheritance is an advanced tool. Even if you understood the last paragraph, it's still a good idea to use it sparingly and carefully. Otherwise, the meaning of a name may come to depend on the order in which classes are mixed in an arbitrarily far-removed subclass. (For another example of the technique shown here in action, see the discussion of explicit conflict resolution in "New-Style Classes" earlier in this chapter.)

As a rule of thumb, multiple inheritance works best when your mix-in classes are as self-contained as possible—because they may be used in a variety of contexts, they should not make assumptions about names related to other classes in a tree. The pseudoprivate attributes feature we studied earlier can help by localizing names that a class relies on owning, and limiting the names that your mix-in classes add to the mix. In this example, for instance, if `Lister` only means to export its custom `__repr__`, it can name its other method `__other` to avoid clashing with other classes.

Methods, Classes, and Nested Scopes

This gotcha went away in Python 2.2, with the introduction of nested function scopes, but I've retained it here for historical perspective, for readers working with older Python releases, and because it demonstrates what happens to the new nested function scope rules when one layer of the nesting is a class.

Classes introduce local scopes, just as functions do, so the same sorts of scope behavior can happen in a class statement body. Moreover, methods are further nested functions, so the same issues apply. Confusion seems to be especially common when classes are nested.

In the following example (the file *nester.py*), the generate function returns an instance of the nested Spam class. Within its code, the class name Spam is assigned in the generate function's local scope. But, in versions of Python prior to 2.2, within the class' method function, the class name Spam is not visible—method has access only to its own local scope, the module surrounding generate, and built-in names:

```
def generate():
    class Spam:
        count = 1
        def method(self):             # Name Spam not visible:
            print Spam.count          # Not local(def), global(module), built-in
    return Spam()

generate().method()


C:\python\examples> python nester.py
Traceback (innermost last):
  File "nester.py", line 8, in ?
    generate().method()
  File "nester.py", line 5, in method
    print Spam.count                  # Not local(def), global(module), built-in
NameError: Spam
```

This example works in Python 2.2 and later because the local scopes of all enclosing function defs are automatically visible to nested defs (including nested method defs, as in this example). But, it doesn't work before 2.2 (see below for some possible solutions).

Note that even in 2.2, method defs cannot see the local scope of the enclosing *class*; they can only see the local scopes of enclosing defs. That's why methods must go through the self instance or the class name to reference methods and other attributes defined in the enclosing class statement. For example, code in the method must use self.count, or Spam.count, not just count.

If you're using a release prior to 2.2, there are a variety of ways to get the preceding example to work. One of the simplest is to move the name Spam out to the enclosing module's scope with a global declaration. Because method sees global names in the enclosing module, references to Spam will work:

```
def generate():
    global Spam                       # Force Spam to module scope
    class Spam:
        count = 1
        def method(self):
            print Spam.count          # Works: in global (enclosing module)
    return Spam()

generate().method()                   # Prints 1
```

A better alternative would be to restructure the code such that the class `Spam` is defined at the top level of the module by virtue of its nesting level, rather than using global declarations. The nested `method` function and the top-level `generate` will then find `Spam` in their global scopes:

```
def generate():
    return Spam()

class Spam:                      # Define at top level of module
    count = 1
    def method(self):
        print Spam.count         # Works: in global (enclosing module)

generate().method()
```

In fact, this approach is recommended for all Python releases—code tends to be simpler in general if you avoid nesting classes and functions.

If you want to get complicated and tricky, you can also get rid of the `Spam` reference in method altogether by using the special `__class__` attribute, which returns an instance's class object:

```
def generate():
    class Spam:
        count = 1
        def method(self):
            print self.__class__.count      # Works: qualify to get class
    return Spam()

generate().method()
```

"Overwrapping-itis"

When used well, the code reuse features of OOP make it excel at cutting development time. Sometimes, though, OOP's abstraction potential can be abused to the point of making code difficult to understand. If classes are layered too deeply, code can become obscure; you may have to search through many classes to discover what an operation does.

For example, I once worked in a C++ shop with thousands of classes (some machine-generated), and up to 15 levels of inheritance. Deciphering method calls in such a complex system was often a monumental task: multiple classes had to be consulted for even the most basic of operations. In fact, the logic of the system was so deeply wrapped that understanding a piece of code in some cases required days of wading through related files.

The most general rule of thumb of Python programming applies here, too: don't make things complicated unless they truly must be. Wrapping your code in multiple layers of classes to the point of incomprehensibility is always a bad idea. Abstraction is the basis of polymorphism and encapsulation, and it can be a very effective tool when used well. However, you'll simplify debugging and aid maintainability if you make your class interfaces intuitive, avoid making your code overly abstract, and keep your class hierarchies short and flat unless there is a good reason to do otherwise.

Chapter Summary

This chapter presented a handful of advanced class-related topics, including subclassing built-in types, pseudoprivate attributes, new-style classes, static methods, and function decorators. Most of these are optional extensions to the OOP model in Python, but they may become more useful as you start writing larger object-oriented programs.

This is the end of the class part of this book, so you'll find the usual lab exercises at the end of the chapter—be sure to work through them to get some practice coding real classes. In the next chapter, we'll begin our look at our last core language topic, exceptions. Exceptions are Python's mechanism for communicating errors and other conditions to your code. This is a relatively lightweight topic, but I've saved it for last because exceptions are supposed to be coded as classes today. Before we tackle that final subject, though, take a look at this chapter's quiz and the lab exercises.

Chapter Quiz

1. Name two ways to extend a built-in object type.
2. What are function decorators used for?
3. How do you code a new-style class?
4. How are new-style and classic classes different?
5. How are normal and static methods different?
6. How long should you wait before lobbing a "Holy Hand Grenade"?

Quiz Answers

1. You can embed a built-in object in a wrapper class, or subclass the built-in type directly. The latter of these tends to be simpler, as most original behavior is automatically inherited.

2. Function decorators are generally used to add to an existing function a layer of logic that is run each time the function is called. They can be used to log or count calls to a function, check its argument types, and so on. They are also used to "declare" static methods—simple functions in a class that are not passed an instance.

3. New-style classes are coded by inheriting from the object built-in class (or any other built-in type). In Python 3.0, this will likely not be required; all classes will be new-style classes by default.

4. New-style classes search the diamond pattern of multiple inheritance trees differently—they essentially search breadth-first (across), instead of depth-first (up). New-style classes also support a set of advanced extra tools, including properties and a _ _slots_ _ instance attributes list.

5. Normal (instance) methods receive a self argument (the implied instance), but static methods do not. Static methods are simple functions nested in a class object. To make a method static, it must be run through a special built-in function, or decorated with decorator syntax.

6. Three seconds. (Or, more accurately: "And the Lord spake, saying, 'First shalt thou take out the Holy Pin. Then, shalt thou count to three, no more, no less. Three shalt be the number thou shalt count, and the number of the counting shall be three. Four shalt thou not count, nor either count thou two, excepting that thou then proceed to three. Five is right out. Once the number three, being the third number, be reached, then lobbest thou thy Holy Hand Grenade of Antioch towards thy foe, who, being naughty in my sight, shall snuff it.'")*

---

* This quote is from *Monty Python and the Holy Grail*.

Part VI Exercises

These exercises ask you to write a few classes, and experiment with some existing code. Of course, the problem with existing code is that it must be existing. To work with the set class in exercise 5, either pull the class source code off the Internet (see the Preface), or type it up by hand (it's fairly brief). These programs are starting to get more sophisticated, so be sure to check the solutions at the end of the book for pointers. You'll find them in in Appendix B, in "Part VI, Classes and OOP."

1. *Inheritance.* Write a class called Adder that exports a method add(self, x, y) that prints a "Not Implemented" message. Then, define two subclasses of Adder that implement the add method:

   ListAdder
   > With an add method that returns the concatenation of its two list arguments.

   DictAdder
   > With an add method that returns a new dictionary containing the items in both its two dictionary arguments (any definition of addition will do).

   Experiment by making instances of all three of your classes interactively and calling their add methods.

   Now, extend your Adder superclass to save an object in the instance with a constructor (e.g., assign self.data a list or a dictionary), and overload the + operator with an __add__ method to automatically dispatch to your add methods (e.g., X + Y triggers X.add(X.data,Y)). Where is the best place to put the constructors and operator overloading methods (i.e., in which classes)? What sorts of objects can you add to your class instances?

   In practice, you might find it easier to code your add methods to accept just one real argument (e.g., add(self,y)), and add that one argument to the instance's current data (e.g., self.data + y). Does this make more sense than passing two arguments to add? Would you say this makes your classes more "object-oriented"?

2. *Operator overloading.* Write a class called Mylist that shadows ("wraps") a Python list: it should overload most list operators and operations, including +, indexing, iteration, slicing, and list methods such as append and sort. See the Python reference manual for a list of all possible methods to support. Also, provide a constructor for your class that takes an existing list (or a Mylist instance) and copies its components into an instance member. Experiment with your class interactively. Things to explore:

   a. Why is copying the initial value important here?

   b. Can you use an empty slice (e.g., start[:]) to copy the initial value if it's a Mylist instance?

---

c. Is there a general way to route list method calls to the wrapped list?

d. Can you add a `Mylist` and a regular list? How about a list and a `Mylist` instance?

e. What type of object should operations like + and slicing return? What about indexing operations?

f. If you are working with a more recent Python release (version 2.2 or later), you may implement this sort of wrapper class by embedding a real list in a standalone class, or by extending the built-in list type with a subclass. Which is easier, and why?

3. *Subclassing.* Make a subclass of `Mylist` from exercise 2 called `MylistSub`, which extends `Mylist` to print a message to `stdout` before each overloaded operation is called, and counts the number of calls. `MylistSub` should inherit basic method behavior from `Mylist`. Adding a sequence to a `MylistSub` should print a message, increment the counter for + calls, and perform the superclass' method. Also, introduce a new method that prints the operation counters to `stdout`, and experiment with your class interactively. Do your counters count calls per instance, or per class (for all instances of the class)? How would you program both of these? (Hint: it depends on which object the count members are assigned to: class members are shared by instances, but `self` members are per-instance data.)

4. *Metaclass methods.* Write a class called `Meta` with methods that intercept every attribute qualification (both fetches and assignments), and print messages listing their arguments to `stdout`. Create a `Meta` instance, and experiment with qualifying it interactively. What happens when you try to use the instance in expressions? Try adding, indexing, and slicing the instance of your class.

5. *Set objects.* Experiment with the set class described in "Extending Types by Embedding." Run commands to do the following sorts of operations:

a. Create two sets of integers, and compute their intersection and union by using & and | operator expressions.

b. Create a set from a string, and experiment with indexing your set. Which methods in the class are called?

c. Try iterating through the items in your string set using a `for` loop. Which methods run this time?

d. Try computing the intersection and union of your string set, and a simple Python string. Does it work?

e. Now, extend your set by subclassing to handle arbitrarily many operands using the `*args` argument form. (Hint: see the function versions of these algorithms in Chapter 16.) Compute intersections and unions of multiple operands with your set subclass. How can you intersect three or more sets, given that & has only two sides?

f. How would you go about emulating other list operations in the set class? (Hints: __add__ can catch concatenation, and __getattr__ can pass most list method calls off to the wrapped list.)

6. *Class tree links*. In "Namespaces: The Whole Story" in Chapter 24, and "Multiple Inheritance" in Chapter 25, I mentioned that classes have a __bases__ attribute that returns a tuple of their superclass objects (the ones in parentheses in the class header). Use __bases__ to extend the Lister mix-in class (see Chapter 25) so that it prints the names of the immediate superclasses of the instance's class. When you're done, the first line of the string representation should look like this (your address may vary):

```
<Instance of Sub(Super, Lister), address 7841200:
```

How would you go about listing inherited class attributes, too? (Hint: classes have a __dict__ attribute.) Try extending your Lister class to display all accessible superclasses and their attributes as well; for hints on climbing class trees, see Chapter 24's *classtree.py* example, and the footnote about using dir and getattr in Python 2.2 in the "Multiple Inheritance" section of Chapter 25.

7. *Composition*. Simulate a fast-food ordering scenario by defining four classes:

Lunch
: A container and controller class.

Customer
: The actor who buys food.

Employee
: The actor from whom a customer orders.

Food
: What the customer buys.

To get you started, here are the classes and methods you'll be defining:

```
class Lunch:
    def __init__(self)                          # Make/embed Customer and Employee
    def order(self, foodName)                   # Start a Customer order simulation
    def result(self)                            # Ask the Customer what kind of Food it has

class Customer:
    def __init__(self)                          # Initialize my food to None
    def placeOrder(self, foodName, employee)    # Place order with an Employee
    def printFood(self)                         # Print the name of my food

class Employee:
    def takeOrder(self, foodName)               # Return a Food, with requested name

class Food:
    def __init__(self, name)                    # Store food name
```

The order simulation works as follows:

a. The Lunch class' constructor should make and embed an instance of Customer and an instance of Employee, and should export a method called order. When called, this order method should ask the Customer to place an order by calling its placeOrder method. The Customer's placeOrder method should in turn ask the Employee object for a new Food object by calling Employee's takeOrder method.

b. Food objects should store a food name string (e.g., "burritos"), passed down from Lunch.order, to Customer.placeOrder, to Employee.takeOrder, and finally, to Food's constructor. The top-level Lunch class should also export a method called result, which asks the customer to print the name of the food it received from the Employee via the order (this can be used to test your simulation).

Note that Lunch needs to pass either the Employee or itself to the Customer to allow the Customer to call Employee methods.

Experiment with your classes interactively by importing the Lunch class, calling its order method to run an interaction, and then calling its result method to verify that the Customer got what he or she ordered. If you prefer, you can also simply code test cases as self-test code in the file where your classes are defined, using the module __name__ trick in Chapter 21. In this simulation, the Customer is the active agent; how would your classes change if Employee were the object that initiated customer/employee interaction instead?

8. *Zoo animal hierarchy.* Consider the class tree shown in Figure 26-1. Code a set of six class statements to model this taxonomy with Python inheritance. Then, add a speak method to each of your classes that prints a unique message, and a reply method in your top-level Animal superclass that simply calls self.speak to invoke the category-specific message printer in a subclass below (this will kick off an independent inheritance search from self). Finally, remove the speak method from your Hacker class so that it picks up the default above it. When you're finished, your classes should work this way:

```
% python
>>> from zoo import Cat, Hacker
>>> spot = Cat( )
>>> spot.reply( )                      # Animal.reply; calls Cat.speak
meow
>>> data = Hacker( )                    # Animal.reply; calls Primate.speak
>>> data.reply( )
Hello world!
```

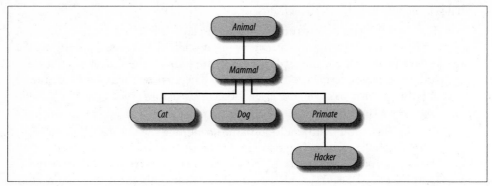

Figure 26-1. A zoo hierarchy composed of classes linked into a tree to be searched by attribute inheritance. Animal has a common "reply" method, but each class may have its own custom "speak" method called by "reply."

9. *The Dead Parrot Sketch.* Consider the object embedding structure captured in Figure 26-2. Code a set of Python classes to implement this structure with composition. Code your `Scene` object to define an `action` method, and embed instances of `Customer`, `Clerk`, and `Parrot` classes—all three of which should define a `line` method that prints a unique message. The embedded objects may inherit from a common superclass that defines `line` and simply provide message text, or define `line` themselves. In the end, your classes should operate like this:

```
% python
>>> import parrot
>>> parrot.Scene().action()          # Activate nested objects
customer: "that's one ex-bird!"
clerk: "no it isn't..."
parrot: None
```

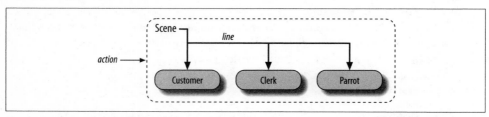

Figure 26-2. A scene composite with a controller class (Scene) that embeds and directs instances of three other classes (Customer, Clerk, Parrot). The embedded instance's classes may also participate in an inheritance hierarchy; composition and inheritance are often equally useful ways to structure classes for code reuse.

Why You Will Care: OOP by the Masters

When I teach Python classes, I invariably find that about halfway through the class, people who have used OOP in the past are following along intensely, while people who have not are beginning to glaze over (or nod off completely). The point behind the technology just isn't apparent.

In a book like this, I have the luxury of including material like the new Big Picture overview in Chapter 22—in fact, you should probably review that section if you're starting to feel like OOP is just some computer science mumbo-jumbo.

In real classes, however, to help get the newcomers on board (and keep them awake), I have been known to stop and ask the experts in the audience why they use OOP. The answers they've given might help shed some light on the purpose of OOP, if you are new to the subject.

Here, then, with only a few embellishments, are the most common reasons to use OOP, as cited by my students over the years:

Code reuse
> This one's easy (and is the main reason for using OOP). By supporting inheritance, classes allow you to program by customization, instead of starting each project from scratch.

Encapsulation
> Wrapping up implementation details behind object interfaces insulates users of a class from code changes.

Structure
> Classes provide new local scopes, which minimizes name clashes. They also provide a natural place to write and look for implementation code, and to manage object state.

Maintenance
> Classes naturally promote code factoring, which allows us to minimize redundancy. Thanks both to the structure and code reuse support of classes, usually only one copy of the code needs to be changed.

Consistency
> Classes and inheritance allow you to implement common interfaces, and hence, a common look and feel in your code; this eases debugging, comprehension, and maintenance.

Polymorphism
> This is more a property of OOP than a reason for using it, but by supporting code generality, polymorphism makes code more flexible and widely applicable, and hence, more reusable.

—continued—

Other

And, of course, the number one reason students gave for using OOP: it looks good on a résumé! (OK, I threw this one in as a joke, but it is important to be familiar with OOP if you plan to work in the software field today.)

Finally, keep in mind what I said at the beginning of Part VI: you won't fully appreciate OOP until you've used it for awhile. Pick a project, study larger examples, work through the exercises—do whatever it takes to get your feet wet with OO code; it's worth the effort.

Exceptions and Tools

## CHAPTER 27

Exception Basics

This last part of the book deals with *exceptions*, which are events that can modify the flow of control through a program. In Python, exceptions are triggered automatically on errors, and can be triggered and intercepted by your code. They are processed by four statements we'll study in this part, the first of which has two variations (listed separately here), and the last of which is an optional extension until Python 2.6:

try/except
 Catch and recover from exceptions raised by Python, or by you.

try/finally
 Perform cleanup actions, whether exceptions occur or not.

raise
 Trigger an exception manually in your code.

assert
 Conditionally trigger an exception in your code.

with/as
 Implement context managers in Python 2.6 and later (optional in 2.5).

This topic was saved for this last part of the book because you need to know about classes to code exceptions of your own. With a few exceptions (pun intended), though, you'll find that exception handling is simple in Python because it's integrated into the language itself as another high-level tool.

One procedural note up front: the exception story has changed in two major ways since this book was first written—the finally clause can now appear in the same try statement as except and else clauses, and user-defined exceptions should now be coded as class instances not strings. I will describe both the old and new ways of doing things in this edition, because you are still very likely to see the original techniques in code for some time to come. Along the way, I'll point out how things have evolved in this domain. I'll also document the new with statement, even though its official appearance is still one release in the future.

Why Use Exceptions?

In a nutshell, exceptions let us jump out of arbitrarily large chunks of a program. Consider the pizza-making robot we talked about earlier in the book. Suppose we took the idea seriously, and actually built such a machine. To make a pizza, our culinary automaton would need to execute a plan, which we would implement as a Python program: it would take an order, prepare the dough, add toppings, bake the pie, and so on.

Now, suppose that something goes very wrong during the "bake the pie" step. Perhaps the oven is broken, or perhaps our robot miscalculates its reach, and spontaneously bursts into flames. Clearly, we want to be able to jump to code that handles such states quickly. Also, as we have no hope of finishing the pizza task in such unusual cases, we might as well abandon the entire plan.

That's exactly what exceptions let you do: you can jump to an exception handler in a single step, abandoning all suspended function calls. An exception is a sort of structured "super-goto."* An exception handler (try statement) leaves a marker and executes some code. Somewhere further ahead in the program, an exception is raised that makes Python jump back to the marker immediately, abandoning any active functions that were called after the marker was left. Code in the exception handler can respond to the raised exception as appropriate (by calling the fire department, for instance). Moreover, because Python jumps to the handler statement immediately, there is usually no need to check status codes after every call to a function that could possibly fail.

Exception Roles

In Python programs, exceptions are typically used for a variety of purposes. Here are some of their most common roles:

Error handling

Python raises exceptions whenever it detects errors in programs at runtime. You can catch and respond to the errors in your code, or ignore the exceptions that are raised. If an error is ignored, Python's default exception-handling behavior kicks in—it stops the program, and prints an error message. If you don't want this default behavior, code a try statement to catch and recover from the exception—Python will jump to your try handler when the error is detected, and your program will resume execution after the try.

---

* If you've used C, you may be interested to know that Python exceptions are roughly similar to C's setjmp/ longjmp standard function pair: the try statement acts much like a setjmp, and raise works like a longjmp. But, in Python, exceptions are based on objects and are a standard part of the execution model.

Event notification

Exceptions can also be used to signal valid conditions without you having to pass result flags around a program or test them explicitly. For instance, a search routine might raise an exception on failure, rather than returning an integer result code (and hoping that the code will never be a valid result).

Special-case handling

Sometimes a condition may occur so rarely that it's hard to justify convoluting your code to handle it. You can often eliminate special-case code by handling unusual cases in exception handlers instead.

Termination actions

As you'll see, the try/finally statement allows you to guarantee that required closing-time operations will be performed, regardless of the presence or absence of exceptions in your programs.

Unusual control flows

And, finally, because exceptions are a sort of high-level "goto," you can use them as the basis for implementing exotic control flows. For instance, although backtracking is not part of the language itself, it can be implemented in Python with exceptions, and a bit of support logic to unwind assignments.*

We'll see such typical uses in action later in this part of the book. For now, let's get started with a look at Python's exception-processing tools.

Exception Handling: The Short Story

Compared to some other core language topics we've met in this book, exceptions are a fairly lightweight tool in Python. Because they are so simple, let's jump right into an initial example. Suppose we code the following function:

```
>>> def fetcher(obj, index):
...     return obj[index]
...
```

There's not much to this function—it simply indexes an object on a passed-in index. In normal operation, it returns the result of a legal index:

```
>>> x = 'spam'
>>> fetcher(x, 3)              # Like x[3]
'm'
```

---

* True backtracking is an advanced topic that is not part of the Python language (even with the addition of generator functions in 2.2), so I won't say more about it here. Roughly, backtracking undoes all computations before it jumps; Python exceptions do not (i.e., variables assigned between the time a try statement is entered, and the time an exception is raised, are not reset to their prior values). See a book on artificial intelligence, or the Prolog or Icon programming languages if you're curious.

However, if we ask this function to index off the end of the string, an exception will be triggered when the function tries to run obj[index]. Python detects out-of-bounds indexing for sequences, and reports it by *raising* (triggering) the built-in IndexError exception:

```
>>> fetcher(x, 4)
Traceback (most recent call last):
  File "<stdin>", line 1, in ?
  File "<stdin>", line 2, in fetcher
IndexError: string index out of range
```

Because our code does not explicitly catch this exception, it filters back up to the top level of the program, and invokes the *default exception handler*—which simply prints the standard error message. By this point in the book, you've probably seen your share of standard error messages. They include the exception that was raised, along with a *stack trace*—a list of the lines and functions active when the exception occurred. When coding interactively, the file is just "stdin" (standard input stream) or "pyshell" (in IDLE), so the file line numbers are not very meaningful here.

In a more realistic program launched outside the interactive prompt, the default handler at the top also *terminates* the program immediately. That course of action makes sense for simple scripts; errors often should be fatal, and the best you can do when they occur is inspect the standard error message. Sometimes, this isn't what you want, though. Server programs, for instance, typically need to remain active even after internal errors. If you don't want the default exception behavior, wrap the call in a try statement to catch exceptions yourself:

```
>>> try:
...       fetcher(x, 4)
... except IndexError:
...       print 'got exception'
...
got exception
>>>
```

Now, Python jumps to your *handler* (the block under the except clause that names the exception raised) automatically when an exception is triggered while the try block is running. When working interactively like this, after the except clause runs, we wind up back at the Python prompt. In a more realistic program, try statements not only catch exceptions, but also *recover* from them:

```
>>> def catcher():
...       try:
...           fetcher(x, 4)
...       except IndexError:
...           print 'got exception'
...       print 'continuing'
...
>>> catcher()
got exception
continuing
>>>
```

This time, after the exception is caught and handled, the program resumes execution after the entire try statement that caught it—which is why we get the "continuing" message here. We don't see the standard error message, and the program continues on its way normally.

Exceptions can be raised by Python or by your program, and can be caught or not. To trigger an exception manually, simply run a `raise` statement (or an `assert`, which is a conditional `raise`). User-defined exceptions are caught the same way as built-ins:

```
>>> bad = 'bad'
>>> try:
...     raise bad
... except bad:
...     print 'got bad'
...
got bad
```

If they're not caught, user-defined exceptions are propagated up to the top-level default exception handler, and terminate the program with a standard error message. In this case, the standard message includes the text of the string used to identify the exception:

```
>>> raise bad
Traceback (most recent call last):
  File "<pyshell#18>", line 1, in ?
    raise bad
bad
```

In other cases, the error message may include text provided by classes used to identify exceptions. As we'll see in the next chapter, user-defined exceptions may be defined with strings or classes, but class-based exceptions allow scripts to build exception categories, inherit behavior, and have attached state information. Class-based exceptions are preferred over strings today, and will be required as of Python 3.0:

```
>>> class Bad(Exception): pass
...
>>> def doomed(): raise Bad()
...
>>> try:
...     doomed()
... except Bad:
...     print 'got Bad'
...
got Bad
>>>
```

Finally, try statements can include `finally` blocks. The `try/finally` combination specifies termination actions that always execute "on the way out," regardless of whether an exception occurs in the try block:

```
>>> try:
...     fetcher(x, 3)
... finally:
```

```
...        print 'after fetch'
...
'm'
after fetch
```

Here, if the try block finishes without an exception, the finally block will run, and the program will resume after the entire try. In this case, this statement seems a bit silly—we might as well have simply typed the print right after a call to the function, and skipped the try altogether:

```
fetcher(x, 3)
print 'after fetch'
```

There is a problem with coding this way, though: if the function call raises an exception, the print will never be reached. The try/finally combination avoids this pitfall—when an exception does occur in a try block, finally blocks are executed while the program is being unwound:

```
>>> def after():
...        try:
...                fetcher(x, 4)
...        finally:
...                print 'after fetch'
...        print 'after try?'
...
>>> after()
after fetch
Traceback (most recent call last):
  File "<stdin>", line 1, in ?
  File "<stdin>", line 3, in after
  File "<stdin>", line 2, in fetcher
IndexError: string index out of range
```

Here, we don't get the "after try?" message because control does not resume after the try/finally block when an exception occurs. Instead, Python jumps back to run the finally action, but then propagates the exception up to a prior handler (in this case, to the default handler at the top). If we change the call inside this function so as not to trigger an exception, the finally code still runs, but the program continues after the try:

```
>>> def after():
...        try:
...                fetcher(x, 3)
...        finally:
...                print 'after fetch'
...        print 'after try?'
...
>>> after()
after fetch
after try?
>>>
```

In practice, try/except combinations are useful for catching and recovering from exceptions, and try/finally combinations come in handy to guarantee that termination actions will fire regardless of any exceptions that may occur in the try block's code. For instance, you might use try/except to catch errors raised by code that you import from a third-party library, and try/finally to ensure that calls to close files or terminate server connections are always run. We'll see some such practical examples later in this part of the book.

Although they serve conceptually distinct purposes, as of Python 2.5, we can now mix except and finally clauses in the same try statement—the finally is run on the way out regardless of whether an exception was raised, and regardless of whether the exception was caught by an except clause.

That is the majority of the exception story; exceptions really are a simple tool. In the rest of this part, we'll fill in some of the details about the statements involved, examine the other sorts of clauses that can appear under a try, and discuss string- and class-based exception objects.

Python exceptions are a high-level control flow device. They may be raised by Python, or by your own programs; in both cases, they may be ignored (to trigger the default error message), or caught by try statements (to be processed by your code). The try statement comes in two logical formats that, as of Python 2.5, can be combined—one that handles exceptions, and one that executes finalization code whether exceptions occur or not. Python's raise and assert statements trigger exceptions on demand. With that overview in mind, let's take a deeper look at these statements' general forms.

The try/except/else Statement

In the following discussion, I'll first present try/except/else and try/finally as separate statements because they serve distinct roles and cannot be combined in versions of Python prior to 2.5. As you've seen, in Python 2.5 except and finally can be mixed in a single try statement; I'll explain the implications of this change after we've explored the two original forms in isolation.

try is a compound statement; its most complete form is sketched below. It starts with a try header line, followed by a block of (usually) indented statements, then one or more except clauses that identify exceptions to be caught, and an optional else clause at the end. The words try, except, and else are associated by indenting them to the same level (i.e., lining them up vertically). For reference, here's the general format:

```
try:
    <statements>        # Run this action first
except <name1>:
    <statements>        # Run if name1 is raised during try block
```

```
except <name2>, <data>:
    <statements>          # Run if name2 is raised, and get extra data
except (name3, name4):
    <statements>          # Run if any of these exceptions occur
except:
    <statements>          # Run for all (other) exceptions raised
else:
    <statements>          # Run if no exception was raised during try block
```

In this statement, the block under the try header represents the *main action* of the statement—the code you're trying to run. The except clauses define *handlers* for exceptions raised during the try block, and the else clause (if coded) provides a handler to be run if *no* exceptions occur. The <data> entry here has to do with a feature of raise statements, which we will discuss later in this chapter.

Here's how try statements work. When a try statement is started, Python marks the current program context so it can return to it if an exception occurs. The statements nested under the try header are run first. What happens next depends on whether exceptions are raised while the try block's statements are running:

- If an exception *does* occur while the try block's statements are running, Python jumps back to the try, and runs the statements under the first except clause that matches the raised exception. Control resumes below the entire try statement after the except block runs (unless the except block raises another exception).

- If an exception happens in the try block, and *no* except clause matches, the exception is propagated up to a try that was entered earlier in the program, or to the top level of the process (which makes Python kill the program and print a default error message).

- If no exception occurs while the statements under the try header run, Python runs the statements under the else line (if present), and control then resumes below the entire try statement.

In other words, except clauses catch any exceptions that happen while the try block is running, and the else clause runs only if no exceptions happen while the try block runs.

except clauses are *focused* exception handlers—they catch exceptions that occur only within the statements in the associated try block. However, as the try block's statements can call functions coded elsewhere in a program, the source of an exception may be outside the try statement itself. I'll have more to say about this when we explore try nesting in Chapter 29.

try Statement Clauses

When you write try statements, a variety of clauses can appear after the try statement block. Table 27-1 summarizes all the possible forms—you must use at least one. We've already met some of these: as you know, except clauses catch exceptions, finally clauses run on the way out, and else clauses run if no exceptions are encountered. Syntactically, there may be any number of except clauses, but there should be only one else. Through Python 2.4, the finally clause must appear alone (without else or except); it's really a different statement. As of Python 2.5, however, a finally can appear in the same statement as except and else.

Table 27-1. try statement clause forms

Clause form	Interpretation
except:	Catch all (other) exception types.
except name:	Catch a specific exception only.
except name, value:	Catch the listed exception and its extra data (or instance).
except (name1, name2):	Catch any of the listed exceptions.
except (name1, name2), value:	Catch any of the listed exceptions, and get its extra data.
else:	Run if no exceptions are raised.
finally:	Always perform this block.

We'll explore the entries with the extra value part when we meet the raise statement. The first and fourth entries in Table 27-1 are new here:

- except clauses that list no exception name (except:) catch *all* exceptions not previously listed in the try statement.
- except clauses that list a set of exceptions in parentheses (except (e1, e2, e3):) catch *any* of the listed exceptions.

Because Python looks for a match within a given try by inspecting except clauses from top to bottom, the parenthesized version is like listing each exception in its own except clause, but the statement body needs to be coded only once. Here's an example of multiple except clauses at work, which demonstrates just how specific your handlers can be:

```
try:
    action( )
except NameError:
    ...
except IndexError:
    ...
except KeyError:
    ...
except (AttributeError, TypeError, SyntaxError):
    ...
else:
    ...
```

In this example, if an exception is raised while the call to the action function is running, Python returns to the try, and searches for the first except that names the exception raised. It inspects except clauses from top to bottom and left to right, and runs the statements under the first one that matches. If none match, the exception is propagated past this try. Note that the else runs only when *no* exception occurs in action—it does not run when an exception without a matching except is raised.

If you really want a general "catch-all" clause, an empty except does the trick:

```
try:
    action()
except NameError:
    ...                         # Handle NameError
except IndexError:
    ...                         # Handle IndexError
except:
    ...                         # Handle all other exceptions
else:
    ...                         # Handle the no-exception case
```

The empty except clause is a sort of wildcard feature—because it catches everything, it allows your handlers to be as general or specific as you like. In some scenarios, this form may be more convenient than listing all possible exceptions in a try. For example, the following catches everything without listing anything:

```
try:
    action()
except:
    ...                     # Catch all possible exceptions
```

Empty excepts also raise some design issues, though. Although convenient, they may catch unexpected system exceptions unrelated to your code, and may inadvertently intercept exceptions meant for another handler. For example, even system exit calls in Python trigger exceptions, and you usually want these to pass. We'll revisit this as a gotcha at the end of this part of the book. For now, I'll just say: use with care.

 In Python 3.0, the third row of Table 27-1 is scheduled to change: except name, value: will instead be coded as except name as value:. This change is being made to remove syntax confusion when a tuple of alternative exceptions is coded—the fourth row in Table 27-1 will no longer require enclosing parentheses in 3.0. This change will also modify the scoping rules: with the new as syntax, the value variable at the end of the except block will be deleted.

Also in 3.0, the raise statement form raise E, V will need to be coded as raise E(V) to explicitly generate a class instance to be raised. The prior form had been retained just for backward compatibility with string exceptions in Python 2.x. (See later in this chapter for more on raise, and the next chapter for a discussion of class-based exceptions.)

Although you can't use the as form of except in Python 2.x to future-proof your code, the "2to3" conversion tool to be shipped with 3.0 will automate the except and raise translations for existing 2.x code.

The try/else Clause

At first glance, the purpose of the else clause is not always obvious to Python newcomers. Without it, though, there is no way to tell (without setting and checking Boolean flags) whether the flow of control has proceeded past a try statement because no exception was raised, or because an exception occurred and was handled:

```
try:
    ...run code...
except IndexError:
    ...handle exception...
# Did we get here because the try failed or not?
```

Much like the way else clauses in loops make the exit cause more apparent, the else clause provides syntax in a try that makes what has happened obvious and unambiguous:

```
try:
    ...run code...
except IndexError:
    ...handle exception...
else:
    ...no exception occurred...
```

You can *almost* emulate an else clause by moving its code into the try block:

```
try:
    ...run code...
    ...no exception occurred...
except IndexError:
    ...handle exception...
```

This can lead to incorrect exception classifications, though. If the "no exception occurred" action triggers an IndexError, it will register as a failure of the try block, and hence erroneously trigger the exception handler below the try (subtle, but true!). By using an explicit else clause instead, you make the logic more obvious, and guarantee that except handlers will run only for real failures in the code you're wrapping in a try, not for failures in the else case's action.

Example: Default Behavior

Because the control flow through a program is easier to capture in Python than in English, let's run some examples that further illustrate exception basics. I've mentioned that exceptions not caught by try statements percolate up to the top level of the Python process, and run Python's default exception-handling logic (i.e., Python terminates the running program, and prints a standard error message). Let's look at an example. Running the following module, *bad.py*, generates a divide-by-zero exception:

```
def gobad(x, y):
    return x / y
```

```
def gosouth(x):
    print gobad(x, 0)

gosouth(1)
```

Because the program ignores the exception it triggers, Python kills the program, and prints a message:[*]

```
% python bad.py
Traceback (most recent call last):
  File "bad.py", line 7, in <module>
    gosouth(1)
  File "bad.py", line 5, in gosouth
    print gobad(x, 0)
  File "bad.py", line 2, in gobad
    return x / y
ZeroDivisionError: integer division or modulo by zero
```

The message consists of a stack trace and the name of (and any extra data about) the exception that was raised. The stack trace lists all lines active when the exception occurred, from oldest to newest. Note that because we're not working at the interactive prompt, in this case, the file and line number information is useful. For example, here we can see that the bad divide happens at the last entry in the trace—line 2 of the file *bad.py*, a return statement.

Because Python detects and reports all errors at runtime by raising exceptions, exceptions are intimately bound up with the ideas of error handling and debugging in general. If you've worked through this book's examples, you've undoubtedly seen an exception or two along the way—even typos usually generate a SyntaxError or other exception when a file is imported or executed (that's when the compiler is run). By default, you get a useful error display like the one above, which helps you track down the problem.

Often, this standard error message is all you need to resolve problems in your code. For more heavy-duty debugging jobs, you can catch exceptions with try statements, or use debugging tools I'll introduce in Chapter 29, such as the pdb standard library module.

Example: Catching Built-in Exceptions

Python's default exception handling is often exactly what you want—especially for code in a top-level script file, an error generally should terminate your program immediately. For many programs, there is no need to be more specific about errors in your code.

---

[*] The text of error messages and stack traces tends to vary slightly over time. Don't be alarmed if your error messages don't exactly match mine. When I ran this example in Python 2.5's IDLE, for instance, its error message text showed the full directory paths in filenames.

Sometimes, though, you'll want to catch errors and recover from them instead. If you don't want your program terminated when Python raises an exception, simply catch it by wrapping the program logic in a try. This is an important capability for programs such as network servers, which must keep running persistently. For example, the following code catches and recovers from the TypeError Python raises immediately when you try to concatenate a list and a string (the + operator wants the same sequence type on both sides):

```
def kaboom(x, y):
    print x + y                # Trigger TypeError

try:
    kaboom([0,1,2], "spam")
except TypeError:              # Catch and recover here
    print 'Hello world!'
print 'resuming here'          # Continue here if exception or not
```

When the exception occurs in the function kaboom, control jumps to the try statement's except clause, which prints a message. Since an exception is "dead" after it's been caught like this, the program continues executing below the try, rather than being terminated by Python. In effect, the code processes and clears the error.

Notice that once you've caught an error, control resumes at the place where you caught it (i.e., after the try); there is no direct way to go back to the place where the exception occurred (here, in the function kaboom). In a sense, this makes exceptions more like simple jumps than function calls—there is no way to return to the code that triggered the error.

The try/finally Statement

The other flavor of the try statement is a specialization that has to do with finalization actions. If a finally clause is included in a try, Python will always run its block of statements "on the way out" of the try statement, whether an exception occurred while the try block was running or not. Its general form is:

```
try:
    <statements>               # Run this action first
finally:
    <statements>               # Always run this code on the way out
```

With this variant, Python begins by running the statement block associated with the try header line. What happens next depends on whether an exception occurs during the try block:

- If no exception occurs while the try block is running, Python jumps back to run the finally block, and then continues execution past the entire try statement.

- If an exception *does* occur during the try block's run, Python still comes back and runs the finally block, but then propagates the exception up to a higher try or the top-level default handler; the program does not resume execution below the try statement. That is, the finally block is run even if an exception is raised, but unlike an except, the finally does not terminate the exception—it continues being raised after the finally block runs.

The try/finally form is useful when you want to be completely sure that an action will happen after some code runs, regardless of the exception behavior of the program. In practice, it allows you to specify cleanup actions that always must occur, such as file closes, and server disconnections.

Note that the finally clause cannot be used in the same try statement as except and else in Python 2.4 and earlier, so the try/finally is best thought of as a distinct statement form if you are using an older release. In Python 2.5, however, finally can appear in the same statement as except and else, so today, there is really a single try statement with many optional clauses (more about this shortly). Whichever version you use, though, the finally clause still serves the same purpose—to specify "cleanup" actions that must always be run, regardless of any exceptions.

 As we'll see later in this chapter, in Python 2.6, the with statement and its context managers provide an object-based way to do similar work for exit actions; however, this statement also supports entry actions.

Example: Coding Termination Actions with try/finally

We saw some simple try/finally examples earlier. Here's a more realistic example that illustrates a typical role for this statement:

```
class MyError(Exception): pass

def stuff(file):
    raise MyError()

file = open('data', 'w')        # Open an output file
try:
    stuff(file)                 # Raises exception
finally:
    file.close()                # Always close file to flush output buffers
...                             # Continue here only if no exception
```

In this code, we've wrapped a call to a file-processing function in a try with a finally clause to make sure that the file is always closed, and thus finalized, whether the function triggers an exception or not. This way, later code can be sure that the file's output buffer's content has been flush from memory to disk. A similar code structure can guarantee that server connections are closed, and so on.

This particular example's function isn't all that useful (it just raises an exception), but wrapping calls in try/finally statements is a good way to ensure that your closing-time (i.e., termination) activities always run. Again, Python always runs the code in your finally blocks, regardless of whether an exception happens in the try block.*

When the function here raises its exception, the control flow jumps back, and runs the finally block to close the file. The exception is then propagated on to either another try or the default top-level handler, which prints the standard error message and shuts down the program; the statement after this try is never reached. If the function here did *not* raise an exception, the program would still execute the finally block to close your file, but it would then continue below the entire try statement.

Also, notice that the user-defined exception here is again defined with a class—as we'll see in the next chapter, exceptions today should all be class instances.

Unified try/except/finally

In all versions of Python prior to Release 2.5 (for its first 15 years of life, more or less), the try statement came in two flavors, and was really two separate statements—we could either use a finally to ensure that cleanup code was always run, or write except blocks to catch and recover from specific exceptions and optionally specify an else clause to be run if no exceptions occurred.

That is, the finally clause could not be mixed with except and else. This was partly because of implementation issues, and partly because the meaning of mixing the two seemed obscure—catching and recovering from exceptions, seemed a disjoint concept from performing cleanup actions.

In Python 2.5, though (the version of Python used in this edition of this book), the two statements have merged. Today, we can mix finally, except, and else clauses in the same statement. That is, we can now write a statement of this form:

```
try:
    main-action
except Exception1:
    handler1
except Exception2:
    handler2
...
else:
    else-block
finally:
    finally-block
```

---

* Unless Python crashes completely, of course. It does a good job of avoiding this, though, by checking all possible errors as a program runs. When a program does crash hard, it is often due to a bug in linked-in C extension code, outside of Python's scope.

The code in this statement's *main-action* block is executed first, as usual. If that code raises an exception, all the except blocks are tested, one after another, looking for a match to the exception raised. If the exception raised is Exception1, the *handler1* block is executed; if it's Exception2, *handler2* is run, and so on. If no exception is raised, the *else-block* is executed.

No matter what's happened previously, the *finally-block* is executed once the main action block is complete, and any raised exceptions have been handled. In fact, the code in the *finally-block* will be run even if there is an error in an exception handler, or the *else-block* and a new exception is raised.

As always, the finally clause does not end the exception—if an exception is active when the *finally-block* is executed, it continues to be propagated after the *finally-block* runs, and control jumps somewhere else in the program (to another try, or to the default top-level handler). If no exception is active when the finally is run, control resumes after the entire try statement.

The net effect is that the finally is always run, regardless of whether:

- An exception occurred in the main action and was handled.
- An exception occurred in main action and was not handled.
- No exceptions occurred in the main action.
- A new exception was triggered in one of the handlers.

Again, the finally serves to specify cleanup actions that must always occur on the way out of the try, regardless of what exceptions have been raised or handled.

Combining finally and except by Nesting

Prior to Python 2.5, it is actually possible to combine finally and except clauses in a try by syntactically nesting a try/except in the try block of a try/finally statement (we'll explore this technique more fully in Chapter 29). In fact, the following has the same effect as the new merged form shown in the previous section:

```
try:
    try:
        main-action
    except Exception1:
        handler1
    except Exception2:
        handler2
    ...
    else:
        no-error
finally:
    clean-up
```

Again, the finally block is always run on the way out, regardless of what happened in the main action, and regardless of any exception handlers run in the nested try (trace through the four cases listed previously to see how this works the same). However, this equivalent is more obscure, and requires more code than the new merged form. Mixing finally into the same statement is easier to write and read, and so is the preferred technique today.

Unified try Example

Here's a demonstration of the merged try statement form at work. The following codes four common scenarios, with print statements that describe the meaning of each:

```
print '-' * 30, '\nEXCEPTION RAISED AND CAUGHT'
try:
    x = 'spam'[99]
except IndexError:
    print 'except run'
finally:
    print 'finally run'
print 'after run'

print '-' * 30, '\nNO EXCEPTION RAISED'
try:
    x = 'spam'[3]
except IndexError:
    print 'except run'
finally:
    print 'finally run'
print 'after run'

print '-' * 30, '\nNO EXCEPTION RAISED, ELSE RUN'
try:
    x = 'spam'[3]
except IndexError:
    print 'except run'
else:
    print 'else run'
finally:
    print 'finally run'
print 'after run'

print '-' * 30, '\nEXCEPTION RAISED BUT NOT CAUGHT'
try:
    x = 1 / 0
except IndexError:
    print 'except run'
finally:
    print 'finally run'
print 'after run'
```

When this code is run, the following output is produced. Trace through the code to see how exception handling produces each of the test's outputs here:

```
-------------------------------
EXCEPTION RAISED AND CAUGHT
except run
finally run
after run
-------------------------------
NO EXCEPTION RAISED
finally run
after run
-------------------------------
NO EXCEPTION RAISED, ELSE RUN
else run
finally run
after run
-------------------------------
EXCEPTION RAISED BUT NOT CAUGHT
finally run

Traceback (most recent call last):
  File "C:/Python25/mergedexc.py", line 32, in <module>
    x = 1 / 0
ZeroDivisionError: integer division or modulo by zero
```

This example uses built-in operations in the main action to trigger exceptions or not, and relies on the fact that Python always checks for errors as our code is running. The next section shows how to raise exceptions manually instead.

The raise Statement

To trigger exceptions explicitly, you can code `raise` statements. Their general form is simple—a `raise` statement consists of the word `raise`, optionally followed by the name of the exception to be raised, and an optional extra data item to pass with the exception:

```
raise <name>              # Manually trigger an exception
raise <name>, <data>      # Pass extra data to catcher too
raise                     # Re-raise the most recent exception
```

The second form allows you to pass an extra data item along with the exception to provide details for the handler. In the `raise` statement, the data is listed after the exception name; back in the try statement, the data is obtained by including a variable to receive it. For instance, if the try includes an except `name`, X: statement, the variable X will be assigned the extra data item listed in the `raise`. The third `raise` form simply reraises the current exception; it's handy if you want to propagate an exception you've caught to another handler.

So, what's an exception name? It might be the name of a built-in exception from the built-in scope (e.g., IndexError), or the name of an arbitrary string object you've assigned in your program. It can also reference a user-defined class, or class instance—a possibility that further generalizes raise statement formats. I'll postpone the details of this generalization until after we've had a chance to study class exceptions in the next chapter.

Regardless of how you name exceptions, they are always identified by normal objects, and at most one is active at any given time. Once caught by an except clause anywhere in the program, an exception dies (i.e., won't propagate to another try), unless it's reraised by another raise statement or error.

Example: Raising and Catching User-Defined Exceptions

Python programs can trigger built-in and user-defined exceptions using the raise statement. User-defined exceptions should be class instance objects today, like the one that calling MyBad creates in the following code:

```
class MyBad: pass

def stuff():
    raise MyBad()              # Trigger exception manually

try:
    stuff()                    # Raises exception
except MyBad:
    print 'got it'             # Handle exception here
...                            # Resume execution here
```

This time the raise occurs inside a function, but this makes no real difference—control jumps back to the except block immediately. Notice that user-defined exceptions are caught with try statements, just like built-in exceptions.

Example: Passing Extra Data with raise

As stated earlier, a raise statement can pass an extra data item along with the exception for use in a handler. In general, the extra data allows you to send context information about the exception to a handler. If you're writing a data file parser, for example, you might raise a syntax error exception on errors and also pass along an object that gives line and file information to the handler (we'll meet such an example in Chapter 28).

This is useful because when an exception is raised, it may cross arbitrary file boundaries—the raise statement that triggers an exception, and the try statement that catches it may be in completely different files. It is not generally feasible to store extra details in global variables because the try statement might not know which file the globals reside in. Passing extra data along with the exception itself enables the try statement to access it more reliably. Strictly speaking, every exception has this extra data: as with function return values, it defaults to the special None object if nothing is passed explicitly. The following code, *raisedata.py*, illustrates this concept at work with simple string-based exceptions:

```
myException = 'Error'                     # String object

def raiser1():
    raise myException, "hello"            # Raise, pass data

def raiser2():
    raise myException                     # Raise, None implied

def tryer(func):
    try:
        func()
    except myException, extraInfo:        # Run func; catch exception + data
        print 'got this:', extraInfo

% python
>>> from raisedata import *
>>> tryer(raiser1)                        # Explicitly passed extra data
got this: hello
>>> tryer(raiser2)                        # Extra data is None by default
got this: None
```

Here, the tryer function always requests the extra data object; it comes back as an explicit string from raiser1, but defaults to None in raiser2's raise statement.

In the next chapter, we'll see that the same hook can also be used to access instances raised in conjunction with class-based exceptions—the variable in the except is then assigned to the raised instance, which gives access to attached state information, as well as callable class methods.

Example: Propagating Exceptions with raise

A raise statement that does not include an exception name or extra data value simply reraises the current exception. This form is typically used if you need to catch and handle an exception, but don't want the exception to die in your code:

```
>>> try:
...     raise IndexError, 'spam'
... except IndexError:
...     print 'propagating'
...     raise
...
propagating
Traceback (most recent call last):
  File "<stdin>", line 2, in ?
IndexError: spam
```

Running a raise this way reraises the exception, and propagates it to a higher handler, or the default handler at the top, which stops the program with a standard error message.

The assert Statement

As a somewhat special case, Python includes the assert statement. It is mostly syntactic shorthand for a common raise usage pattern, and can be thought of as a *conditional* raise statement. A statement of the form:

```
assert <test>, <data>          # The <data> part is optional
```

works like the following code:

```
if __debug__:
    if not <test>:
        raise AssertionError, <data>
```

In other words, if the test evaluates to false, Python raises an exception: the data item (if it's provided) as the exception's extra data. Like all exceptions, the AssertionError exception raised will kill your program if it's not caught with a try.

As an added feature, assert statements may be removed from a compiled program's byte code if the -O Python command-line flag is used, thereby optimizing the program. AssertionError is a built-in exception, and the __debug__ flag is a built-in name that is automatically set to 1 (true) unless the -O flag is used.

Example: Trapping Constraints (but Not Errors)

Assertions are typically used to verify program conditions during development. When displayed, their error message text automatically includes source code line information, and the value listed in the assert statement. Consider the file *asserter.py*:

```
def f(x):
    assert x < 0, 'x must be negative'
    return x ** 2

% python
>>> import asserter
>>> asserter.f(1)
Traceback (most recent call last):
  File "<stdin>", line 1, in ?
  File "asserter.py", line 2, in f
    assert x < 0, 'x must be negative'
AssertionError: x must be negative
```

It's important to keep in mind that assert is mostly intended for trapping user-defined constraints, not for catching genuine programming errors. Because Python traps programming errors itself, there is usually no need to code `asserts` to catch things like out-of-bounds indexes, type mismatches, and zero divides:

```
def reciprocal(x):
    assert x != 0          # A useless assert!
    return 1 / x           # Python checks for zero automatically
```

Such asserts are generally superfluous—because Python raises exceptions on errors automatically, you might as well let it do the job for you.* For another example of common assert usage, see the abstract superclass example in Chapter 24; there, we used assert to make calls to undefined methods fail with a message.

with/as Context Managers

Python 2.6 (still in the future as this edition is being written) will introduce a new exception-related statement—the `with`, and its optional `as` clause. This statement is designed to work with context-manager objects, which support a new method-based protocol.

In short, the `with/as` statement is designed to be an alternative to a common `try/finally` usage idiom; like that statement, it is intended for specifying termination-time or "cleanup" activities that must run regardless of whether an exception occurs in a processing step. Unlike `try/finally`, though, the `with` statement supports a richer object-based protocol for specifying both entry and exit actions around a block of code.

Python enhances some built-in tools with context managers, such as files that automatically close themselves, and thread locks that automatically lock and unlock, but programmers can code context managers of their own with classes, too.

Basic Usage

This feature will not become an official part of Python until version 2.6. In Python 2.5, it is not yet available by default; it must be enabled with the special future import statement form we met in the modules part of this book (because of the two new reserved words `with` and `as`, this feature is being introduced gradually, as usual):

```
from __future__ import with_statement
```

When you run this import statement in 2.5, you enable the new `with` statement, and its two reserved words. The basic format of the `with` statement looks like this:

```
with expression [as variable]:
    with-block
```

---

* In most cases, at least. As suggested in Part IV, if a function has to perform long-running or unrecoverable actions before it reaches the place where an exception will be triggered, you still might want to test for errors. Even in this case, though, be careful not to make your tests overly specific or restrictive, or you will limit your code's utility.

The *expression* here is assumed to return an object that supports the context management protocol (more on this protocol in a moment). This object may also return a value that will be assigned to the name *variable* if the optional as clause is present.

Note that the *variable* is not assigned the result of the *expression*; the result of the *expression* is the object that supports the context protocol, and the *variable* may be assigned something else. The object returned by the *expression* may then run startup code before the *with-block* is started, as well as termination code after the block is done, whether the block raised an exception or not.

Some built-in Python objects have been augmented to support the context management protocol, and so can be used with the with statement. For example, file objects have a context manager that automatically closes the file after the with block, regardless of whether an exception is raised:

```
with open(r'C:\python\scripts') as myfile:
    for line in myfile:
        print line
        line = line.replace('spam', 'SPAM')
        ...more code here...
```

Here, the call to open returns a simple file object that is assigned to the name myfile. We can use myfile with the usual file tools—in this case, the file iterator reads line by line in the for loop.

However, this object also supports the context management protocol used by the with statement. After this with statement has run, the context management machinery guarantees that the file object referenced by myfile is automatically closed, even if the for loop raised an exception while processing the file.

We won't cover Python's multithreading modules in this book (for more on that topic, see follow-up application-level texts such as *Programming Python*), but the lock and condition variable synchronization tools they define also support the with statement by supporting the context management protocol:

```
lock = threading.Lock( )
with lock:
    # critical section of code
    ...access shared resources...
```

Here, the context management machinery guarantees that the lock is automatically acquired before the block is executed and released once the block is complete.

The decimal module (see Chapter 5 for more on decimals) also uses context managers to simplify saving and restoring the current decimal context, which specifies the precision and rounding characteristics for calculations.

The Context Management Protocol

The interface expected of objects used in with statements is somewhat complex, and many programmers only need to know how to use existing context managers. For tool builders who might want to write new ones, though, let's take a quick look at what is involved. Here's how the with statement actually works:

1. The expression is evaluated, and results in an object known as a *context manager*, which must have __enter__ and __exit__ methods.

2. The context manager's __enter__ method is called. The value it returns is assigned to a variable if the as clause is present, or simply discarded otherwise.

3. The code in the nested with block is executed.

4. If the with block raises an exception, the __exit__(*type*, *value*, *traceback*) method is called with the exception details. Note that these are the same values returned by sys.exc_info, described in Python manuals and later in this part of the book. If this method returns a false value, the exception is reraised; otherwise, the exception is terminated. The exception should normally be reraised so that it is propagated outside the with statement.

5. If the with block does not raise an exception, the __exit__ method is still called, but its *type*, *value*, and *traceback* arguments are all passed in as None.

Let's look at a quick demo of the protocol in action. The following defines a context manager object that traces the entry and exit of the with block in any with statement it is used for:

```
from __future__ import with_statement        # Required in Python 2.5

class TraceBlock:
    def message(self, arg):
        print 'running', arg
    def __enter__(self):
        print 'starting with block'
        return self
    def __exit__(self, exc_type, exc_value, exc_tb):
        if exc_type is None:
            print 'exited normally\n'
        else:
            print 'raise an exception!', exc_type
            return False  # propagate

with TraceBlock() as action:
    action.message('test 1')
    print 'reached'

with TraceBlock() as action:
    action.message('test 2')
    raise TypeError
    print 'not reached'
```

Why You Will Care: Error Checks

One way to see how exceptions are useful is to compare coding styles in Python and languages without exceptions. For instance, if you want to write robust programs in the C language, you generally have to test return values or status codes after every operation that could possibly go astray, and propagate the results of the tests as your programs run:

```
doStuff()
{                                    # C program
    if (doFirstThing() == ERROR)     # Detect errors everywhere
        return ERROR;                # even if not handled here
    if (doNextThing() == ERROR)
        return ERROR;
    ...
    return doLastThing();
}

main()
{
    if (doStuff() == ERROR)
        badEnding();
    else
        goodEnding();
}
```

In fact, realistic C programs often have as much code devoted to error detection as to doing actual work. But in Python, you don't have to be so methodical and neurotic. You can instead wrap arbitrarily vast pieces of a program in exception handlers, and simply write the parts that do the actual work, assuming all is well:

```
def doStuff():          # Python code
    doFirstThing()      # We don't care about exceptions here,
    doNextThing()       # so we don't need to detect them
    ...
    doLastThing()

if __name__ == '__main__':
    try:
        doStuff()       # This is where we care about results,
    except:             # so it's the only place we must check
        badEnding()
    else:
        goodEnding()
```

Because control jumps immediately to a handler when an exception occurs, there's no need to instrument all your code to guard for errors. Moreover, because Python detects errors automatically, your code usually doesn't need to check for errors in the first place. The upshot is that exceptions let you largely ignore the unusual cases and avoid error-checking code.

Notice that this class' __exit__ method returns False to propagate the exception; deleting the return statement there would have the same effect, as the default None return value of functions is False by definition. Also, notice how the __enter__ method returns self as the object to assign to the as variable; in other use cases, this might return a completely different object instead.

When run, the context manager traces the entry and exit of the with statement block with its __enter__ and __exit__ methods:

```
% python withas.py
starting with block
running test 1
reached
exited normally

starting with block
running test 2
raise an exception! <type 'exceptions.TypeError'>

Traceback (most recent call last):
  File "C:/Python25/withas.py", line 22, in <module>
    raise TypeError
TypeError
```

Context managers are somewhat advanced devices that are not yet officially part of Python, so we'll skip additional details here (see Python's standard manuals for the full story—for example, a new contextlib standard module provides additional tools for coding context managers). For simpler purposes, the try/finally statement provides sufficient support for termination-time activities.

Chapter Summary

In this chapter, we began our look at exception processing by exploring the statements related to exceptions in Python: try to catch them, raise to trigger them, assert to raise them conditionally, and with to wrap code blocks in context managers that specify entry and exit actions.

So far, exceptions probably seem like a fairly lightweight tool, and in fact, they are; the only substantially complex thing about them is how they are identified. The next chapter continues our exploration by describing how to implement exception objects of your own; as you'll see, classes allow you to code more useful exceptions than simple strings today. Before we move ahead, though, work though the following short quiz on the basics covered here.

Chapter Quiz

1. What is the try statement for?
2. What are the two common variations of the try statement?
3. What is the raise statement for?
4. What is the assert statement designed to do, and what other statement is it like?
5. What is the with/as statement designed to do, and what other statement is it like?

Quiz Answers

1. The try statement catches and recovers from exceptions—it specifies a block of code to run, and one or more handlers for exceptions that may be raised during the block's execution.

2. The two common variations on the try statement are try/except/else (for catching exceptions), and try/finally (for specifying cleanup actions that must occur whether an exception is raised or not). In Python 2.4, these are separate statements that can be combined by syntactic nesting; in 2.5 and later, except and finally blocks may be mixed in the same statement, so the two statement forms are merged. In the merged form, the finally is still run on the way out of the try, regardless of what exceptions may have been raised or handled.

3. The raise statement raises (triggers) an exception. Python raises built-in exceptions on errors internally, but your scripts can trigger built-in or user-defined exceptions with raise, too.

4. The assert statement raises an AssertionError exception if a condition is false. It works like a conditional raise statement wrapped up in an if statement.

5. The with/as statement is designed to automate startup and termination activities that must occur around a block of code. It is roughly like a try/finally statement in that its exit actions run whether an exception occurred or not, but it allows a richer object-based protocol for specifying entry *and* exit actions.

CHAPTER 28

Exception Objects

So far, I've been deliberately vague about what an exception actually *is*. Python generalizes the notion of exceptions—as mentioned in the prior chapter, they may be identified by string objects or class instance objects; class instance objects are preferred today, and will be required soon. Both approaches have merits, but classes tend to provide a better solution when it comes to maintaining exception hierarchies.

In short, class-based exceptions allow us to build exceptions that are organized into categories, have attached state information, and support inheritance. In more detail, compared to the older string exception model, class exceptions:

- Better support future changes by providing categories—adding new exceptions in the future won't generally require changes in try statements.

- Provide a natural place for us to store context information for use in the try handler—they may have both attached state information and callable methods, accessible through instances.

- Allow exceptions to participate in inheritance hierarchies to obtain common behavior—inherited display methods, for example, can provide a common look and feel for error messages.

Because of these differences, class-based exceptions support program evolution and larger systems better than string-based exceptions. String exceptions may seem easier to use at first glance, when programs are small, but they can become more difficult when programs grow large. In fact, all built-in exceptions are identified by classes, and are organized into an inheritance tree, for the reasons just listed. You can do the same with user-defined exceptions.

In the interest of backward compatibility, I'll present both string and class-based exceptions here. Both currently work, but string exceptions generate deprecation warnings in the current release of Python (2.5), and will no longer be supported at all in Python 3.0. We'll cover them here because they are likely to appear in existing code you encounter, but new exceptions you define should be coded as classes today, partly because classes are better, but also because you probably won't want to change your exception code when Python 3.0 is rolled out.

String-Based Exceptions

In all the examples we've seen up to this point, user-defined exceptions have been coded as strings. This is the simpler way to code an exception. For example:

```
>>> myexc = "My exception string"
>>> try:
...     raise myexc
... except myexc:
...     print 'caught'
...
caught
```

Any string value can be used to identify an exception. Technically, the exception is identified by the string *object*, not the string *value*—you must use the same variable (i.e., reference) to raise and catch the exception (I'll expand on this idea in a gotcha at the conclusion of Part VII). Here, the exception name, myexc, is just a normal variable—it can be imported from a module, and so on. The text of the string is almost irrelevant, except that it is printed as the exception message:

```
>>> raise myexc
Traceback (most recent call last):
  File "<stdin>", line 1, in ?
My exception string
```

 If your string exceptions may print like this, you'll want to use more meaningful text than most of the examples shown in this book.

String Exceptions Are Right Out!

As mentioned earlier, string-based exceptions still work, but they generate warnings as of Python 2.5, and are scheduled to go away completely in Python 3.0, if not earlier. In fact, here is the real output of the preceding code when run in IDLE under Python 2.5:

```
>>> myexc = 'My exception string'
>>> try:
        raise myexc
    except myexc:
        print 'caught'

Warning (from warnings module):
  File "__main__", line 2
DeprecationWarning: raising a string exception is deprecated
caught
```

You can disable such warnings, but they are generated to let you know that string exceptions will become errors in the future, and thus will be completely disallowed. This book's coverage of string exceptions is retained just to help you understand code written in the past; today, all built-in exceptions are class instances, and all user-defined exceptions you create should be class-based as well. The next section explains why.

Class-Based Exceptions

Strings are a simple way to define exceptions. As described earlier, however, classes have some added advantages that merit a quick look. Most prominently, they allow you to identify exception *categories* that are more flexible to use and maintain than simple strings. Moreover, classes naturally allow for attached exception details and support inheritance. Because they are the better approach, they will soon be the required approach.

Coding details aside, the chief difference between string and class exceptions has to do with the way that exceptions raised are matched against except clauses in try statements:

- String exceptions are matched by simple *object identity*: the raised exception is matched to except clauses by Python's is test (not ==).
- Class exceptions are matched by *superclass relationships*: the raised exception matches an except clause if that except clause names the exception's class or any superclass of it.

That is, when a try statement's except clause lists a superclass, it catches instances of that superclass, as well as instances of all its subclasses lower in the class tree. The net effect is that class exceptions support the construction of exception hierarchies: superclasses become category names, and subclasses become specific kinds of exceptions within a category. By naming a general exception superclass, an except clause can catch an entire category of exceptions—any more specific subclass will match.

In addition to this category idea, class-based exceptions better support exception *state information* (attached to instances), and allow exceptions to participate in *inheritance hierarchies* (to obtain common behaviors). They offer a more powerful alternative to string-based exceptions for a small amount of additional code.

Class Exception Example

Let's look at an example to see how class exceptions work in code. In the following file, *classexc.py*, we define a superclass called General and two subclasses called Specific1 and Specific2. This example illustrates the notion of exception categories—General is a category name, and its two subclasses are specific types of exceptions within the category. Handlers that catch General will also catch any subclasses of it, including Specific1 and Specific2:

```
class General:          pass
class Specific1(General): pass
class Specific2(General): pass

def raiser0():
    X = General()           # Raise superclass instance
    raise X
```

```
def raiser1():
    X = Specific1()        # Raise subclass instance
    raise X

def raiser2():
    X = Specific2()        # Raise different subclass instance
    raise X

for func in (raiser0, raiser1, raiser2):
    try:
        func()
    except General:        # Match General or any subclass of it
        import sys
        print 'caught:', sys.exc_info()[0]

C:\python> python classexc.py
caught: __main__.General
caught: __main__.Specific1
caught: __main__.Specific2
```

We'll revisit the sys.exc_info call used here in the next chapter—it's how we can grab hold of the most recently raised exception in a generic fashion. Briefly, for class-based exceptions, the first item in its result is the class of the exception raised, and the second is the actual instance raised. Apart from this method, there is no other way to determine exactly what happened in an empty except clause like this one that catches everything.

Notice that we call classes to make *instances* in the raise statements here; as we'll see when we formalize raise statement forms later in this section, an instance is always present when raising a class-based exception. This code also includes functions that raise instances of all three of our classes as exceptions, as well as a top-level try that calls the functions, and catches General exceptions (the same try also catches the two specific exceptions, because they are subclasses of General).

One more note: the current Python documentation states that it is preferred (though not required) that user-defined exception classes inherit from the built-in exception named Exception. To do this, we would rewrite the first line of our *classexc.py* file as follows:

```
class General(Exception): pass
class Specific1(General): pass
class Specific2(General): pass
```

Although this isn't required, and standalone exception classes work fine today, preferred things have a way of becoming requirements in Python over time. If you want to future-proof your code, inherit from Exception in your root superclass, as shown here. Doing so also provides your class with some useful interfaces and tools for free, by inheritance—for example, the Exception class comes with __init__ constructor logic, which automatically attaches constructor arguments to class instances.

Why Class Exceptions?

Because there are only three possible exceptions in the prior section's example, it doesn't really do justice to the utility of class exceptions. In fact, we could achieve the same effects by coding a list of string exception names in parentheses within the except clause. The file *stringexc.py* shows how:

```
General   = 'general'
Specific1 = 'specific1'
Specific2 = 'specific2'

def raiser0( ): raise General
def raiser1( ): raise Specific1
def raiser2( ): raise Specific2

for func in (raiser0, raiser1, raiser2):
    try:
        func( )
    except (General, Specific1, Specific2):      # Catch any of these
        import sys
        print 'caught:', sys.exc_info( )[0]
```

```
C:\python> python stringexc.py
caught: general
caught: specific1
caught: specific2
```

For large or high exception hierarchies, however, it may be easier to catch categories using classes than to list every member of a category in a single except clause. Moreover, you can extend exception hierarchies by adding new subclasses without breaking existing code.

Suppose you code a numeric programming library in Python, to be used by a large number of people. While you are writing your library, you identify two things that can go wrong with numbers in your code—division by zero, and numeric overflow. You document these as the two exceptions that your library may raise, and define them as simple strings in your code:

```
# mathlib.py

divzero = 'Division by zero error in library'
oflow   = 'Numeric overflow error in library'
...
def func( ):
    ...
    raise divzero
```

Now, when people use your library, they will typically wrap calls to your functions or classes in try statements that catch your two exceptions (if they do not catch your exceptions, exceptions from the library kill their code):

```
# client.py

import mathlib
...
try:
    mathlib.func(...)
except (mathlib.divzero, mathlib.oflow):
    ...report and recover...
```

This works fine, and lots of people start using your library. Six months down the road, though, you revise it. Along the way, you identify a new thing that can go wrong—underflow—and add that as a new string exception:

```
# mathlib.py

divzero = 'Division by zero error in library'
oflow   = 'Numeric overflow error in library'
uflow   = 'Numeric underflow error in library'
```

Unfortunately, when you rerelease your code, you create a maintenance problem for your users. If they've listed your exceptions explicitly, they now have to go back and change every place they call your library to include the newly added exception name:

```
# client.py

try:
    mathlib.func(...)
except (mathlib.divzero, mathlib.oflow, mathlib.uflow):
    ...report and recover...
```

This may not be the end of the world. If your library is used only in-house, you can make the changes yourself. You might also ship a Python script that tries to fix such code automatically (it would probably be only a few dozen lines, and it would guess right at least some of the time). If many people have to change their code each time you alter your exception set, though, this is not exactly the most polite of upgrade policies.

Your users might try to avoid this pitfall by coding empty except clauses to catch all possible exceptions:

```
# client.py

try:
    mathlib.func(...)
except:                          # Catch everything here
    ...report and recover...
```

But this workaround might catch more than they bargained for—even things like variable name typos, memory errors, and system exits trigger exceptions, and you want such things to pass, not be caught and erroneously classified as library errors. As a rule of thumb, it's usually better to be specific than general in exception handlers (an idea we'll revisit in the gotchas section in the next chapter).[*]

So what to do, then? Class exceptions fix this dilemma completely. Rather than defining your library's exceptions as a simple set of strings, arrange them into a class tree with a common superclass to encompass the entire category:

```
# mathlib.py

class NumErr(Exception): pass
class Divzero(NumErr): pass
class Oflow(NumErr): pass
...
def func():
    ...
    raise DivZero()
```

This way, users of your library simply need to list the common superclass (i.e., category) to catch all of your library's exceptions, both now and in the future:

```
# client.py

import mathlib
...
try:
    mathlib.func(...)
except mathlib.NumErr:
    ...report and recover...
```

When you go back and hack your code again, new exceptions are added as new subclasses of the common superclass:

```
# mathlib.py

...
class Uflow(NumErr): pass
```

The end result is that user code that catches your library's exceptions will keep working, *unchanged*. In fact, you are free to add, delete, and change exceptions arbitrarily in the future—as long as clients name the superclass, they are insulated from changes in your exceptions set. In other words, class exceptions provide a better answer to

---

[*] As a clever student of mine suggested, the library module could also provide a tuple object that contains all the exceptions the library can possibly raise—the client could then import the tuple and name it in an except clause to catch all the library's exceptions (recall that a tuple in an except means catch *any* of its exceptions). When a new exception is added later, the library can just expand the exported tuple. This works, but you'd still need to keep the tuple up-to-date with raised exceptions inside the library module. Also, class-based exceptions offer more benefits than just categories—they also support attached state information, method calls, and inheritance, which simple string exceptions do not.

maintenance issues than strings do. Moreover, class-based exceptions can support state retention and inheritance in ways that strings cannot—concepts we'll explore by example later in this chapter.

Built-in Exception Classes

I didn't really pull the prior section's examples out of thin air. Although user-defined exceptions may be identified by string or class objects, all built-in exceptions that Python itself may raise are predefined class objects instead of strings. Moreover, they are organized into a shallow hierarchy with general superclass categories and specific subclass types, much like the exceptions class tree we developed earlier.

All the familiar exceptions you've seen (e.g., SyntaxError) are really just predefined classes, available both as built-in names (in the module __builtin__), and as attributes of the standard library module exceptions. In addition, Python organizes the built-in exceptions into a hierarchy, to support a variety of catching modes. For example:

Exception
> The top-level root superclass of exceptions.

StandardError
> The superclass of all built-in error exceptions.

ArithmeticError
> The superclass of all numeric errors.

OverflowError
> A subclass that identifies a specific numeric error.

And so on—you can read further about this structure in either the Python library manual, or the help text of the exceptions module (see Chapters 4 and 14 for help on help):

```
>>> import exceptions
>>> help(exceptions)
...lots of text omitted...
```

The built-in class tree allows you to choose how specific or general your handlers will be. For example, the built-in exception ArithmeticError is a superclass for more specific exceptions such as OverflowError and ZeroDivisionError. By listing ArithmeticError in a try, you will catch any kind of numeric error raised; by listing just OverflowError, you will intercept just that specific type of error, and no others.

Similarly, because StandardError is the superclass of all built-in error exceptions, you can generally use it to select between built-in errors and user-defined exceptions in a try:

```
try:
    action()
```

```
except StandardError:
    ...handle Python errors...
except:
    ...handle user exceptions...
else:
    ...handle no-exception case...
```

You can also almost simulate an empty except clause (that catches everything) by catching the root class Exception. This doesn't quite work, however, because it won't catch string exceptions, and standalone user-defined exceptions are not currently required to be subclasses of the Exception root class.

Whether or not you will use categories in the built-in class tree, it serves as a good example; by using similar techniques for class exceptions in your own code, you can provide exception sets that are flexible and easily modified.

Other than in the respects that we have covered here, built-in exceptions are largely indistinguishable from the original string-based model. In fact, you normally don't need to care that they are classes unless you assume built-in exceptions are strings and try to concatenate without converting (e.g., KeyError + "spam" fails, but str(KeyError) + "spam" works).

Specifying Exception Text

When we met string-based exceptions at the start of this chapter, we saw that the text of the string shows up in the standard error message when the exception is not caught (i.e., when it's propagated up to the top-level default exception handler). But what does this message contain for an uncaught class exception? By default, you get the class' name, and a not very pretty display of the instance object that was raised:

```
>>> class MyBad: pass
>>> raise MyBad()

Traceback (most recent call last):
  File "<pyshell#13>", line 1, in <module>
    raise MyBad()
MyBad: <__main__.MyBad instance at 0x00BB5468>
```

To improve this display, define either the __repr__ or __str__ string-representation overloading method in your class to return the string you want to display for your exception if it reaches the default handler:

```
>>> class MyBad:
...     def __repr__(self):
...         return "Sorry--my mistake!"
...
>>> raise MyBad()

Traceback (most recent call last):
  File "<pyshell#28>", line 1, in <module>
    raise MyBad()
MyBad: Sorry--my mistake!
```

As we learned earlier, the __repr__ operator overloading method used here is called for printing and for string conversion requests made to your class' instances; __str__ defines the user-friendly display preferred by print statements. (See "Operator Overloading" in Chapter 24 for more on display-string methods.)

Note that if we inherit from built-in exception classes, as recommended earlier, the error test is modified slightly—constructor arguments are automatically saved and displayed in the message:

```
>>> class MyBad(Exception): pass
>>> raise MyBad( )

Traceback (most recent call last):
  File "<pyshell#18>", line 1, in <module>
    raise MyBad( )
MyBad

>>> class MyBad(Exception): pass
>>> raise MyBad('the', 'bright', 'side', 'of', 'life')

Traceback (most recent call last):
  File "<pyshell#22>", line 1, in <module>
    raise MyBad('the', 'bright', 'side', 'of', 'life')
MyBad: ('the', 'bright', 'side', 'of', 'life')
```

If your end users might see exception error messages, you will probably want to define your own custom display format methods with operator overloading, as shown here. Being able to automatically attach state information to instances like this, though, is a generally useful feature, as the next section explores.

Sending Extra Data and Behavior in Instances

Besides supporting flexible hierarchies, class exceptions also provide storage for extra state information as instance attributes. When a class-based exception is raised, Python automatically passes the class instance object along with the exception as the extra data item. As for string exceptions, you can access the raised instance by listing an extra variable back in the try statement. This provides a natural hook for supplying data and behavior to the handler.

Example: Extra data with classes and strings

Let's explore the notion of passing extra data with an example, and compare the string- and class-based approaches along the way. A program that parses data files might signal a formatting error by raising an exception instance that is filled out with extra details about the error:

```
>>> class FormatError:
...     def __init__(self, line, file):
...         self.line = line
...         self.file = file
...
```

```
>>> def parser():
...     # when error found
...     raise FormatError(42, file='spam.txt')
...
>>> try:
...     parser()
... except FormatError, X:
...     print 'Error at', X.file, X.line
...
Error at spam.txt 42
```

In the except clause here, the variable X is assigned a reference to the instance that was generated when the exception was raised.[*] In practice, though, this isn't noticeably more convenient than passing compound objects (e.g., tuples, lists, or dictionaries) as extra data with string exceptions, and may not by itself be a compelling enough reason to warrant class-based exceptions. Here's the string-based equivalent:

```
>>> formatError = 'formatError'

>>> def parser():
...     # when error found
...     raise formatError, {'line':42, 'file':'spam.txt'}
...
>>> try:
...     parser()
... except formatError, X:
...     print 'Error at', X['file'], X['line']
...
Error at spam.txt 42
```

This time, the variable X in the except clause is assigned the dictionary of extra details listed in the raise statement. The net effect is similar, but we don't have to code a class along the way. The class approach might be more convenient, however, if the exception should also have behavior. The exception class can also define *methods* to be called in the handler:

```
class FormatError:
    def __init__(self, line, file):
        self.line = line
        self.file = file
    def logerror(self):
        log = open('formaterror.txt', 'a')
        print >> log, 'Error at', self.file, self.line

def parser():
    raise FormatError(40, 'spam.txt')
```

---

[*] As we'll see in the next chapter, the raised instance object is also available generically as the second item in the result tuple of the sys.exc_info call—a tool that returns information about the most recently raised exception. This interface must be used if you do not list an exception name in an except clause, but still need access to the exception that occurred, or to any of its attached state information or methods.

```
try:
    parser( )
except FormatError, exc:
    exc.logerror( )
```

In such a class, methods (like `logerror`) may also be inherited from superclasses, and instance attributes (like `line` and `file`) provide a place to save state information that provides extra context for use in later method calls. We can mimic much of this effect by passing simple functions in the string-based approach, but the complexity of the code is substantially increased:

```
formatError = "formatError"

def logerror(line, file):
    log = open('formaterror.txt', 'a')
    print >> log, 'Error at', file, line

def parser( ):
    raise formatError, (41, 'spam.txt', logerror)

try:
    parser( )
except formatError, data:
    data[2](data[0], data[1])          # Or simply: logerror()
```

Naturally, such functions would not participate in inheritance like class methods do, and would not be able to retain state in instance attributes (`lambda`s and global variables are usually the best we can do for stateful functions). We could, of course, pass a class instance in the extra data of the string-based exception to achieve the same effect, but if we went this far to mimic class-based exceptions, we might as well adopt them—we'd be coding a class anyhow.

As mentioned previously, class exceptions will be required in a future version of Python. But, even if that were not the case, there are good reasons to use them today. In general, string-based exceptions are simpler tools for simpler tasks. Class-based exceptions, however, are useful for defining categories, and they are preferable for advanced applications that can benefit from state retention and attribute inheritance. Not every application requires the power of OOP, but the extra utility of class exceptions will become more apparent as your systems evolve and expand.

General raise Statement Forms

With the addition of class-based exceptions, the `raise` statement can take the following five forms. The first two raise string exceptions, the next two raise class exceptions, and the last reraises the current exception (useful if you need to propagate an arbitrary exception):

```
raise string              # Matches except with same string object
raise string, data        # Passes optional extra data (default=None)
```

```
raise instance            # Same as: raise instance.__class__, instance
raise class, instance     # Matches except with this class or its superclass

raise                     # Reraises the current exception
```

The third of these is the most commonly used form today. For class-based exceptions, Python always requires an instance of the class. Raising an instance really raises the instance's class; the instance is passed along with the class as the extra data item (as we've seen, it's a good place to store information for the handler). For backward compatibility with Python versions in which built-in exceptions were strings, you can also use these forms of the raise statement:

```
raise class               # Same as: raise class()
raise class, arg          # Same as: raise class(arg)
raise class, (arg, arg, ...)   # Same as: raise class(arg, arg, ...)
```

These are all the same as saying raise class(arg...), and therefore the same as the raise instance form above. Specifically, if you list a class instead of an instance, and the extra data item is not an instance of the class listed, Python automatically calls the class with the extra data items as constructor arguments to create and raise an instance for you.

For example, you can raise an instance of the built-in KeyError exception by saying simply raise KeyError, even though KeyError is now a class; Python calls KeyError to make an instance along the way. In fact, you can raise a KeyError, and any other class-based exception, in a variety of ways:

```
raise KeyError( )               # Normal form: raise an instance
raise KeyError, KeyError( )      # Class, instance: use instance
raise KeyError                   # Class: an instance will be generated
raise KeyError, "bad spam"       # Class, arg: an instance will be generated
```

For all of these raise forms, a try statement of the form:

```
try:
    ...
except KeyError, X:
    ...
```

assigns X to the KeyError instance object raised.

If that sounds confusing, just remember that exceptions may be identified by string or class instance objects. For strings, you may pass extra data with the exception or not. For classes, if there is no instance object in the raise statement, Python makes an instance for you.

In Python 2.5, you can almost ignore the string forms of raise altogether because string-based exceptions generate warnings, and will be disallowed in a future release. But alas, backward compatibility still counts in books that teach a programming language being used by more than one million people today!

Chapter Summary

In this chapter, we tackled coding user-defined exceptions. As we learned, exceptions may be implemented as string objects or class instance objects; however, class instances are preferred today, and will be required in a future version of Python. Class exceptions are preferable because they support the concept of exception hierarchies (and are thus better for maintenance), allow data and behavior to be attached to exceptions as instance attributes and methods, and allow exceptions to inherit data and behavior from superclasses.

We saw that in a try statement, catching a superclass catches that class, as well as all subclasses below it in the class tree—superclasses become exception category names, and subclasses become more specific exception types within those categories. We also saw that the raise statement has been generalized to support a variety of formats, though most programs today simply generate and raise class instances.

Although we explored both string and class-based alternatives in this chapter, exception objects are easier to remember if you limit your scope to the class-based model Python encourages today—code each exception as a class, and inherit from Exception at the top of your exception trees, and you can forget the older string-based alternative.

The next chapter wraps up this part of the book and the book at large by exploring some common use cases for exceptions, and surveying commonly used tools for Python programmers. Before we get there, though, here's this chapter's quiz.

Chapter Quiz

1. How are raised string-based exceptions matched to handlers?
2. How are raised class-based exceptions matched to handlers?
3. How can you attach context information to class-based exceptions, and use it in handlers?
4. How can you specify the error message text in class-based exceptions?
5. Why should you not use string-based exceptions anymore today?

Quiz Answers

1. String-based exceptions match by object identity (technically, via the is expression), not by object value (the == expression). Hence, naming the same string value might not work; you need to name the same object reference (usually a variable). Short strings are cached and reused in Python, so naming the same value might work occasionally, but you can't rely on this (more on this in a "gotcha" at the end of the next chapter).

2. Class-based exceptions match by superclass relationships: naming a superclass in an exception handler will catch instances of that class, as well as instances of any of its subclasses lower in the class tree. Because of this, you can think of superclasses as general exception categories, and subclasses as more specific exception types within those categories.

3. You attach context information to class-based exceptions by filling out instance attributes in the instance object raised, often in class constructor methods. In exception handlers, you list a variable to be assigned to the raised instance, then go through this name to access attached state information, and call any inherited class methods.

4. The error message text in class-based exceptions can be specified with the __repr__ or __str__ operator overloading methods. If you inherit from the built-in Exception class, anything you pass to the class constructor is displayed automatically.

5. Because Guido said so—they are scheduled to go away in a future Python release. Really, there are good reasons for this: string-based exceptions do not support categories, state information, or behavior inheritance in the way class-based exceptions do. In practice, this makes string-based exceptions easier to use at first, when programs are small, but more complex to use as programs grow larger.

Designing with Exceptions

This chapter rounds out this part of the book with a collection of exception design topics and common use case examples, followed by this part's gotchas and exercises. Because this chapter also closes out the book at large, it includes a brief overview of development tools as well to help you as you make the migration from Python beginner to Python application developer.

Nesting Exception Handlers

Our examples so far have used only a single try to catch exceptions, but what happens if one try is physically nested inside another? For that matter, what does it mean if a try calls a function that runs another try? Technically, try statements can *nest* in terms of syntax and the runtime control flow through your code.

Both of these cases can be understood if you realize that Python *stacks* try statements at runtime. When an exception is raised, Python returns to the most recently entered try statement with a matching except clause. Because each try statement leaves a marker, Python can jump back to earlier trys by inspecting the stacked markers. This nesting of active handlers is what we mean when we talk about propagating exceptions up to "higher" handlers—such handlers are simply try statements entered earlier in the program's execution flow.

Figure 29-1 illustrates what occurs when try/except statements nest at runtime. The amount of code that goes into a try block can be substantial (e.g., it can contain function calls), and it often invokes other code that may be watching for the same exceptions. When an exception is eventually raised, Python jumps back to the most recently entered try statement that names that exception, runs that statement's except clause, and then resumes after that try.

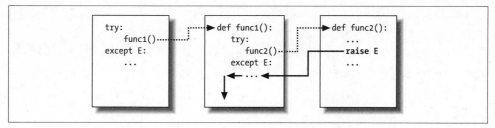

Figure 29-1. Nested try/except statements: when an exception is raised (by you or by Python), control jumps back to the most recently entered try statement with a matching except clause, and the program resumes after that try statement. Except clauses intercept and stop the exception— they are where you process and recover from exceptions.

Once the exception is caught, its life is over—control does not jump back to *all* matching trys that name the exception; only the first one is given the opportunity to handle it. In Figure 29-1, for instance, the `raise` statement in the function func2 sends control back to the handler in func1, and then the program continues within func1.

By contrast, when try/finally statements are nested, each `finally` block is run in turn when an exception occurs—Python continues propagating the exception up to other trys, and eventually perhaps to the top-level default handler (the standard error message printer). As Figure 29-2 illustrates, the `finally` clauses do not kill the exception—they just specify code to be run on the way out of each `try` during the exception propagation process. If there are many try/finally clauses active when an exception occurs, they will *all* be run, unless a try/except catches the exception somewhere along the way.

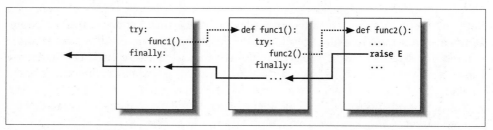

Figure 29-2. Nested try/finally statements: when an exception is raised here, control returns to the most recently entered try to run its finally statement, but then the exception keeps propagating to all finallys in all active try statements, and eventually reaches the default top-level handler, where an error message is printed. Finally clauses intercept (but do not stop) an exception—they are for actions to be performed "on the way out."

In other words, where the program goes when an exception is raised depends entirely upon *where it has been*—it's a function of the runtime flow of control through the script, not just its syntax. The propagation of an exception essentially proceeds backward through time to try statements entered but not yet exited. This propagation stops as soon as control is unwound to a matching except clause, but not as it passes through finally clauses on the way.

Example: Control-Flow Nesting

Let's turn to an example to make this nesting concept more concrete. The following module file, *nestexc.py*, defines two functions. action2 is coded to trigger an exception (you can't add numbers and sequences), and action1 wraps a call to action2 in a try handler, to catch the exception:

```
def action2():
    print 1 + [   ]                   # Generate TypeError

def action1():
    try:
        action2()
    except TypeError:                 # Most recent matching try
        print 'inner try'

try:
    action1()
except TypeError:                     # Here, only if action1 re-raises
    print 'outer try'
```

```
% python nestexc.py
inner try
```

Notice, though, that the top-level module code at the bottom of the file wraps a call to action1 in a try handler, too. When action2 triggers the TypeError exception, there will be two active try statements—the one in action1, and the one at the top level of the module file. Python picks and runs just the most recent try with a matching except, which in this case is the try inside action1.

As I've mentioned, the place where an exception winds up jumping to depends on the control flow through the program at runtime. Because of this, to know where you will go, you need to know where you've been. In this case, where exceptions are handled is more a function of control flow than of statement syntax. However, we can also nest exception handlers syntactically—an equivalent case we'll look at next.

Example: Syntactic Nesting

As I mentioned when we looked at the new unified try/except/finally statement in Chapter 27, it is possible to nest try statements syntactically by their position in your source code:

```
try:
    try:
        action2()
    except TypeError:                 # Most recent matching try
        print 'inner try'
except TypeError:                     # Here, only if nested handler re-raises
    print 'outer try'
```

Really, this code just sets up the same handler-nesting structure as (and behaves identically to) the prior example. In fact, syntactic nesting works just like the cases sketched in Figures 29-1 and 29-2; the only difference is that the nested handlers are physically embedded in a try block, not coded in functions called elsewhere. For example, nested `finally` handlers all fire on an exception, whether they are nested syntactically, or by means of the runtime flow through physically separated parts of your code:

```
>>> try:
...     try:
...         raise IndexError
...     finally:
...         print 'spam'
... finally:
...     print 'SPAM'
...
spam
SPAM
Traceback (most recent call last):
  File "<stdin>", line 3, in ?
IndexError
```

See Figure 29-2 for a graphic illustration of this code's operation; the effect is the same, but the function logic has been inlined as nested statements here. For a more useful example of syntactic nesting at work, consider the following file, *except-finally.py*:

```
def raise1():  raise IndexError
def noraise():  return
def raise2():  raise SyntaxError

for func in (raise1, noraise, raise2):
    print '\n', func
    try:
        try:
            func()
        except IndexError:
            print 'caught IndexError'
    finally:
        print 'finally run'
```

This code catches an exception if one is raised, and performs a `finally` termination-time action regardless of whether an exception occurred. This may take a few moments to digest, but the effect is much like combining an except and a finally clause in a single try statement today (recall that such combinations were syntactically illegal until Python 2.5):

```
% python except-finally.py

<function raise1 at 0x00BA2770>
caught IndexError
finally run
```

```
<function noraise at 0x00BB47F0>
finally run

<function raise2 at 0x00BB4830>
finally run

Traceback (most recent call last):
  File "C:/Python25/except-finally.py", line 9, in <module>
    func()
  File "C:/Python25/except-finally.py", line 3, in raise2
    def raise2():  raise SyntaxError
SyntaxError: None
```

As we saw in Chapter 27, as of Python 2.5, except and finally clauses can be mixed in the same try statement. This makes some of the syntactic nesting described in this section unnecessary, though it still works, may appear in code written prior to Python 2.5, and can be used as a technique for implementing alternative exception-handling behaviors.

Exception Idioms

We've seen the mechanics behind exceptions. Now, let's take a look at some of the other ways they are typically used.

Exceptions Aren't Always Errors

In Python, all errors are exceptions, but not all exceptions are errors. For instance, we saw in Chapter 9 that file object read methods return an empty string at the end of a file. In contrast, the built-in raw_input function (which we first met in Chapter 3, and deployed in an interactive loop in Chapter 10) reads a line of text from the standard input stream, sys.stdin, at each call, and raises the built-in EOFError at end-of-file. Unlike file methods, this function does not return an empty string—an empty string from raw_input means an empty line. Despite its name, the EOFError exception is just a signal in this context, not an error. Because of this behavior, unless end-of-file should terminate a script, raw_input often appears wrapped in a try handler and nested in a loop, as in the following code:

```
while 1:
    try:
        line = raw_input()        # Read line from stdin
    except EOFError:
        break                     # Exit loop at end-of-file
    else:
        ...process next line here...
```

Other built-in exceptions are similarly signals, not errors. Python also has a set of built-in exceptions that represent *warnings* rather than errors. Some of these are used to signal use of deprecated (phased out) language features. See the standard library manual's description of built-in exceptions, and the warnings module for more on warnings.

Functions Signal Conditions with raise

User-defined exceptions can also signal nonerror conditions. For instance, a search routine can be coded to raise an exception when a match is found, instead of returning a status flag for the caller to interpret. In the following, the try/except/else exception handler does the work of an if/else return-value tester:

```python
class Found(Exception): pass

def searcher():
    if ...success...:
        raise Found()
    else:
        return

try:
    searcher()
except Found:                    # Exception if item was found
    ...success...
else:                            # else returned: not found
    ...failure...
```

More generally, such a coding structure may also be useful for any function that cannot return a sentinel value to designate success or failure. For instance, if all objects are potentially valid return values, it's impossible for any return value to signal unusual conditions. Exceptions provide a way to signal results without a return value:

```python
class Failure(Exception): pass

def searcher():
    if ...success...:
        return ...founditem...
    else:
        raise Failure()

try:
    item = searcher()
except Failure:
    ...report...
else:
    ...use item here...
```

Because Python is dynamically typed and polymorphic to the core, exceptions, rather than sentinel return values, are the generally preferred way to signal such conditions.

Debugging with Outer try Statements

You can also make use of exception handlers to replace Python's default top-level exception-handling behavior. By wrapping an entire program (or a call to it) in an outer try in your top-level code, you can catch any exception that may occur while your program runs, thereby subverting the default program termination.

In the following, the empty except clause catches any uncaught exception raised while the program runs. To get hold of the actual exception that occurred, fetch the `sys.exc_info` function call result from the built-in sys module; it returns a tuple, whose first two items automatically contain the current exception's name, and its associated extra data (if any). For class-based exceptions, these two items are the exception class and the raised instance of the class, respectively (more on `sys.exc_info` in a moment):

```
try:
    ...run program...
except:                         # All uncaught exceptions come here
    import sys
    print 'uncaught!', sys.exc_info()[0], sys.exc_info()[1]
```

This structure is commonly used during development, to keep programs active even after errors occur—it allows you to run additional tests without having to restart. It's also used when testing other program code, as described in the next section.

Running In-Process Tests

You might combine some of the coding patterns we've just looked at in a test-driver application, which tests other code within the same process:

```
import sys
log = open('testlog', 'a')
from testapi import moreTests, runNextTest, testName

def testdriver():
    while moreTests():
        try:
            runNextTest()
        except:
            print >> log, 'FAILED', testName(), sys.exc_info()[:2]
        else:
            print >> log, 'PASSED', testName()

testdriver()
```

The `testdriver` function here cycles through a series of test calls (the module `testapi` is left abstract in this example). Because an uncaught exception in a test case would normally kill this test driver, you need to wrap test case calls in a `try` if you want to continue the testing process after a test fails. As usual, the empty `except` catches any uncaught exception generated by a test case, and it uses `sys.exc_info` to log the exception to a file. The `else` clause is run when no exception occurs—the test success case.

Such boilerplate code is typical of systems that test functions, modules, and classes by running them in the same process as the test driver. In practice, however, testing can be much more sophisticated than this. For instance, to test external programs, you could instead check status codes or outputs generated by program-launching tools such as `os.system` and `os.popen`, covered in the standard library manual (such tools do not generally raise exceptions for errors in the external programs—in fact, the test cases may run in parallel with the test driver).

At the end of this chapter, we'll also meet some more complete testing frameworks provided by Python, such as Doctest and PyUnit, which provide tools for comparing expected outputs with actual results.

More on sys.exc_info

The sys.exc_info result used in the last two sections is the preferred way to gain access to the most recently raised exception generically. If no exception is being handled, it returns a tuple containing three None values; otherwise, the values returned are (*type, value, traceback*), where:

- *type* is the exception type of the exception being handled (a class object for class-based exceptions).

- *value* is the exception parameter (its associated value or the second argument to raise, which is always a class instance if the exception type is a class object).

- *traceback* is a traceback object that represents the call stack at the point where the exception originally occurred (see the standard traceback module's documentation for tools that may be used in conjunction with this object to generate error messages manually).

The older tools sys.exc_type and sys.exc_value still work to fetch the most recent exception type and value, but they can manage only a single, global exception for the entire process. The preferred sys.exc_info instead keeps track of each thread's exception information, and so is thread-specific. Of course, this distinction matters only when using multiple threads in Python programs (a subject beyond this book's scope). See the Python library manual or follow-up texts for more details.

Exception Design Tips

By and large, exceptions are easy to use in Python. The real art behind them is in deciding how specific or general your except clauses should be, and how much code to wrap up in try statements. Let's address the second of these concerns first.

What Should Be Wrapped

In principle, you could wrap every statement in your script in its own try, but that would just be silly (the try statements would then need to be wrapped in try statements!). This is really a design issue that goes beyond the language itself, and becomes more apparent with use. But here are a few rules of thumb:

- Operations that commonly fail should generally be wrapped in try statements. For example, operations that interface with system state (file opens, socket calls, and the like) are prime candidates for trys.

- However, there are exceptions to the prior rule—in a simple script, you may *want* failures of such operations to kill your program instead of being caught and ignored. This is especially true if the failure is a showstopper. Failures in Python result in useful error messages (not hard crashes), and this is often the best outcome you could hope for.

- You should implement termination actions in try/finally statements to guarantee their execution. This statement form allows you to run code whether exceptions occur or not.

- It is sometimes more convenient to wrap the call to a large function in a single try statement, rather than littering the function itself with many try statements. That way, all exceptions in the function percolate up to the try around the call, and you reduce the amount of code within the function.

The types of programs you write will probably influence the amount of exception handling you code as well. Servers, for instance, must generally keep running persistently, and so will likely require try statements to catch and recover from exceptions. In-process testing programs of the kind we saw in this chapter will probably handle exceptions as well. Simpler one-shot scripts, though, will often ignore exception handling completely because failure at any step requires script shutdown.

Catching Too Much: Avoid Empty excepts

On to the issue of handler generality. Python lets you pick and choose which exceptions to catch, but you sometimes have to be careful to not be too inclusive. For example, you've seen that an empty except clause catches *every* exception that might be raised while the code in the try block runs.

That's easy to code, and sometimes desirable, but you may also wind up intercepting an error that's expected by a try handler higher up in the exception nesting structure. For example, an exception handler such as the following catches and stops every exception that reaches it, regardless of whether another handler is waiting for it:

```
def func():
    try:
        ...            # IndexError is raised in here
    except:
        ...            # But everything comes here and dies!

try:
    func()
except IndexError:     # Exception should be processed here
    ...
```

Perhaps worse, such code might also catch unrelated system exceptions. Even things like memory errors, genuine programming mistakes, iteration stops, and system exits raise exceptions in Python. Such exceptions should not usually be intercepted.

For example, scripts normally exit when control falls off the end of the top-level file. However, Python also provides a built-in `sys.exit(statuscode)` call to allow early terminations. This actually works by raising a built-in `SystemExit` exception to end the program, so that `try/finally` handlers run on the way out, and special types of programs can intercept the event.[*] Because of this, a try with an empty except might unknowingly prevent a crucial exit, as in the following file (*exiter.py*):

```
import sys

def bye():
    sys.exit(40)                 # Crucial error: abort now!

try:
    bye()
except:
    print 'got it'               # Oops—we ignored the exit
print 'continuing...'
```

```
% python exiter.py
got it
continuing...
```

You simply might not expect all the kinds of exceptions that could occur during an operation.

Probably worst of all, an empty except will also catch genuine programming errors, which should be allowed to pass most of the time. In fact, empty except clauses can effectively turn off Python's error-reporting machinery, making it difficult to notice mistakes in your code. Consider this code, for example:

```
mydictionary = {...}
...
try:
    x = myditctionary['spam']    # Oops: misspelled
except:
    x = None                     # Assume we got KeyError
...continue here with x...
```

The coder here assumes that the only sort of error that can happen when indexing a dictionary is a missing key error. But because the name `myditctionary` is misspelled (it should say `mydictionary`), Python raises a `NameError` instead for the undefined name reference, which the handler will silently catch and ignore. The event handler will incorrectly fill in a default for the dictionary access, masking the program error. If this happens in code that is far removed from the place where the fetched values are used, it might make for a very interesting debugging task!

---

[*] A related call, `os._exit`, also ends a program, but via an immediate termination—it skips cleanup actions, and cannot be intercepted with try/except or try/finally blocks. It is usually only used in spawned child processes, a topic beyond this book's scope. See the library manual or follow-up texts for details.

As a rule of thumb, be as specific in your handlers as you can be—empty except clauses are handy, but potentially error-prone. In the last example, for instance, you would be better off saying except KeyError: to make your intentions explicit and avoid intercepting unrelated events. In simpler scripts, the potential for problems might not be significant enough to outweigh the convenience of a catchall, but in general, general handlers are generally trouble.

Catching Too Little: Use Class-Based Categories

On the other hand, neither should handlers be too specific. When you list specific exceptions in a try, you catch only what you actually list. This isn't necessarily a bad thing, but if a system evolves to raise other exceptions in the future, you may need to go back and add them to exception lists elsewhere in your code.

For instance, the following handler is written to treat myerror1 and myerror2 as normal cases, and treat everything else as an error. If a myerror3 is added in the future, it is processed as an error, unless you update the exception list:

```
try:
    ...
except (myerror1, myerror2):      # Breaks if I add a myerror3
    ...                           # Nonerrors
else:
    ...                           # Assumed to be an error
```

Luckily, careful use of the class-based exceptions we discussed in Chapter 28 can make this trap go away completely. As we saw, if you catch a general superclass, you can add and raise more specific subclasses in the future without having to extend except clause lists manually—the superclass becomes an extendible exceptions category:

```
try:
    ...
except SuccessCategoryName:       # OK if I add a myerror3 subclass
    ...                           # Nonerrors
else:
    ...                           # Assumed to be an error
```

Whether you use class-based exception category hierarchies, a little design goes a long way. The moral of the story is to be careful to not be too general or too specific in exception handlers, and to pick the granularity of your try statement wrappings wisely. Especially in larger systems, exception policies should be a part of the overall design.

Exception Gotchas

There isn't much to trip over with exceptions, but here are two general usage pointers (one of which summarizes concepts we've already met).

String Exceptions Match by Identity, Not by Value

Now that exceptions are supposed to be identified with classes instead of strings, this gotcha is something of a legacy issue; however, as you're likely to encounter string-based exceptions in existing code, it's worth knowing about. When an exception is raised (by you or by Python itself), Python searches for the most recently entered try statement with a matching except clause—i.e., an except clause that names the same string object (for string-based exceptions), or the same class or a superclass of it (for class-based exceptions). For string exceptions, it's important to be aware that matching is performed by identity, not equality.

For instance, suppose we define two string objects we want to raise as exceptions:

```
>>> ex1 = 'The Spanish Inquisition'
>>> ex2 = 'The Spanish Inquisition'

>>> ex1 == ex2, ex1 is ex2
(True, False)
```

Applying the == test returns True because they have equal values, but is returns False because they are two distinct string objects in memory (assuming they are long enough to defeat the internal caching mechanism for Python strings, described in Chapter 6). Thus, an except clause that names the same string object will always match:

```
>>> try:
...     raise ex1
... except ex1:
...     print 'got it'
...
got it
```

but one that lists an equal-value but not identical object will fail:

```
>>> try:
...     raise ex1
... except ex2:
...     print 'Got it'
...
Traceback (most recent call last):
  File "<pyshell#43>", line 2, in <module>
    raise ex1
The Spanish Inquisition
```

Here, the exception isn't caught because there is no match on object identity, so Python climbs to the top level of the process, and prints a stack trace and the exception's text automatically. As I've hinted, however, some different string objects that happen to have the same values will in fact match because Python caches and reuses small strings (as described in Chapter 6):

```
>>> try:
...     raise 'spam'
... except 'spam':
```

```
...        print 'got it'
...
got it
```

This works because the two strings are mapped to the same object by caching. In contrast, the strings in the following example are long enough to be outside the cache's scope:

```
>>> try:
...        raise 'spam' * 8
... except 'spam' * 8:
...        print 'got it'
...
Traceback (most recent call last):
  File "<pyshell#58>", line 2, in <module>
    raise 'spam' * 8
spamspamspamspamspamspamspamspam
```

If this seems obscure, all you need to remember is this: for strings, be sure to use the same object in the raise and the try, not the same value.

For class exceptions (the preferred technique today), the overall behavior is similar, but Python generalizes the notion of exception matching to include superclass relationships, so this gotcha doesn't apply—yet another reason to use class-based exceptions today!

Catching the Wrong Thing

Perhaps the most common gotchas related to exceptions involve the design guidelines discussed in the prior section. Remember, try to avoid empty except clauses (or you may catch things like system exits) and overly specific except clauses (use superclass categories instead to avoid maintenance issues in the future as new exceptions are added).

Core Language Summary

Congratulations! This concludes your look at the core Python programming language. If you've gotten this far, you may consider yourself an Official Python Programmer (and should feel free to add Python to your résumé the next time you dig it out). You've already seen just about everything there is to see in the language itself, and all in much more depth than many practicing Python programmers initially do. You've studied built-in types, statements, and exceptions, as well as tools used to build up larger program units (functions, modules, and classes); you've even explored important design issues, OOP, program architecture, and more.

The Python Toolset

From this point forward, your future Python career will largely consist of becoming proficient with the *toolset* available for application-level Python programming. You'll find this to be an ongoing task. The standard library, for example, contains hundreds of modules, and the public domain offers still more tools. It's possible to spend a decade or more seeking proficiency with all these tools, especially as new ones are constantly appearing (trust me on this!).

Speaking generally, Python provides a hierarchy of toolsets:

Built-ins
> Built-in types like strings, lists, and dictionaries make it easy to write simple programs fast.

Python extensions
> For more demanding tasks, you can extend Python by writing your own functions, modules, and classes.

Compiled extensions
> Although we didn't cover this topic in this book, Python can also be extended with modules written in an external language like C or C++.

Because Python layers its toolsets, you can decide how deeply your programs need to delve into this hierarchy for any given task—you can use built-ins for simple scripts, add Python-coded extensions for larger systems, and code compiled extensions for advanced work. We've covered the first two of these categories in this book, and that's plenty to get you started doing substantial programming in Python.

Table 29-1 summarizes some of the sources of built-in or existing functionality available to Python programmers, and some topics you'll probably be busy exploring for the remainder of your Python career. Up until now, most of our examples have been very small and self-contained. They were written that way on purpose, to help you master the basics. But now that you know all about the core language, it's time to start learning how to use Python's built-in interfaces to do real work. You'll find that with a simple language like Python, common tasks are often much easier than you might expect.

Table 29-1. Python's toolbox categories

Category	Examples
Object types	Lists, dictionaries, files, strings
Functions	`len`, `range`, `apply`, `open`
Exceptions	`IndexError`, `KeyError`
Modules	`os`, `Tkinter`, `pickle`, `re`
Attributes	`__dict__`, `__name__`, `__class__`
Peripheral tools	NumPy, SWIG, Jython, IronPython, etc.

Development Tools for Larger Projects

Once you've mastered the basics, you'll find your Python programs becoming substantially larger than the examples you've experimented with so far. For developing larger systems, a set of development tools is available in Python and the public domain. You've seen some of these in action, and I've mentioned a few others. To help you on your way, here is a summary of some of the most commonly used tools in this domain:

PyDoc and docstrings

> PyDoc's help function and HTML interfaces were introduced in Chapter 14. PyDoc provides a documentation system for your modules and objects, and integrates with Python's docstrings feature. It is a standard part of the Python system—see the library manual for more details. Be sure to also refer back to the documentation source hints listed in Chapter 4 for information on other Python information resources.

PyChecker

> Because Python is such a dynamic language, some programming errors are not reported until your program runs (e.g., syntax errors are caught when a file is run or imported). This isn't a big drawback—as with most languages, it just means that you have to test your Python code before shipping it. Furthermore, Python's dynamic nature, automatic error messages, and exception model make it easier and quicker to find and fix errors in Python than it is in some other languages (unlike C, for example, Python does not crash on errors).

> The PyChecker system provides support for catching a large set of common errors ahead of time, before your script runs. It serves similar roles to the "lint" program in C development. Some Python groups run their code through PyChecker prior to testing or delivery, to catch any lurking potential problems. In fact, the Python standard library is regularly run through PyChecker before release. PyChecker is a third-party open source package; you can find it at either *http://www.python.org*, or the Vaults of Parnassus web site.

PyUnit (a.k.a. unittest)

> In Part V, we saw how to add self-test code to a Python file by using the `__name__ =='__main__'` trick at the bottom of the file. For more advanced testing purposes, Python comes with two testing support tools. The first, PyUnit (called unittest in the library manual), provides an object-oriented class framework for specifying and customizing test cases and expected results. It mimics the JUnit framework for Java. This is a sophisticated class-based system; see the Python library manual for details.

Doctest

The doctest standard library module provides a second and simpler approach to regression testing. It is based upon Python's docstrings feature. Roughly, to use doctest, you cut and paste a log of an interactive testing session into the docstrings of your source files. Doctest then extracts your docstrings, parses out test cases and results, and reruns the tests to verify the expected results. Doctest's operation can be tailored in a variety of ways; see the library manual for more details.

IDEs

We discussed IDEs for Python in Chapter 3. IDEs such as IDLE provide a graphical environment for editing, running, debugging, and browsing your Python programs. Some advanced IDEs, such as Eclipse and Komodo, support additional development tasks, including source control integration, interactive GUI builders, project files, and more. See Chapter 3, the text editors page at *http://www.python.org*, and the Vaults of Parnassus web site for more on available IDEs and GUI builders for Python.

Profilers

Because Python is so high-level and dynamic, intuitions about performance gleaned from experience with other languages usually don't apply to Python code. To truly isolate performance bottlenecks in your code, you need to add timing logic with clock tools in the `time` or `timeit` modules, or run your code under the `profile` module. We saw an example of the time modules at work when comparing iteration tools' speed in Chapter 17.

`profile` is a standard library module that implements a source code profiler for Python; it runs a string of code you provide (e.g., a script file import, or a call to a function), and then, by default, prints a report to the standard output stream that gives performance statistics—number of calls to each function, time spent in each function, and more. The `profile` module can be customized in various ways; for example, it can save run statistics to a file to be analyzed later with the `pstats` module.

Debuggers

The Python standard library also includes a command-line source code debugger module called `pdb`. This module works much like a command-line C language debugger (e.g., *dbx*, *gdb*): you import the module, start running code by calling a `pdb` function (e.g., `pdb.run("main( )")`), and then type debugging commands from an interactive prompt. `pdb` also includes a useful postmortem analysis call, `pdb.pm`, which starts the debugger after an exception has been encountered. Because IDEs such as IDLE include point-and-click debugging interfaces, pdb is relatively infrequently used today; see Chapter 3 for tips on using IDLE's debugging GUI interfaces.*

Shipping options

In Chapter 2, we introduced common tools for packaging Python programs. py2exe, PyInstaller, and freeze can package byte code and the Python Virtual Machine into "frozen binary" standalone executables, which don't require that Python be installed on the target machine and fully hide your system's code. In addition, we learned in Chapter 2 and Part V that Python programs may be shipped in their source (*.py*) or byte code (*.pyc*) forms, and import hooks support special packaging techniques, such as automatic extraction of *.zip* files and byte code encryption. We also briefly met the standard library's distutils modules, which provide packaging options for Python modules and packages, and C-coded extensions; see the Python manuals for more details. The emerging Python "eggs" packaging system provides another alternative that also accounts for dependencies; search the Web for more details.

Optimization options

For optimizing your programs, the Psyco system described in Chapter 2 provides a just-in-time compiler for translating Python byte code to binary machine code, and Shedskin offers a Python-to-C++ translater. You may also occasionally see *.pyo* optimized byte code files, generated and run with the -0 Python command-line flag (discussed in Chapter 18); because this provides a very modest performance boost, however, it is not commonly used. As a last resort, you can also move parts of your program to a compiled language such as C to boost performance; see the book *Programming Python* and the Python standard manuals for more on C extensions. In general, Python's speed also improves over time, so be sure to upgrade to the most recent release when possible (version 2.3 was clocked at 15–20 percent faster than 2.2, for example).

Other hints for larger projects

Finally, we've also met a variety of language features in this text that tend to become more useful once you start coding larger projects. Among these are: module packages (Chapter 20); class-based exceptions (Chapter 28); class pseudoprivate attributes (Chapter 25); documentation strings (Chapter 14); module path configuration files (Chapter 18); hiding names from from * with __all__ lists and _X-style names (Chapter 21); adding self-test code with the __name__ =='__main__' trick (Chapter 21); using common design rules for functions and modules (Chapters 16, 17, and 21); and so on.

---

* To be honest, IDLE's debugger is not used very often, either. Most practicing Python programmers end up debugging their code by inserting strategic print statements and running it. Because turnaround from change to execution is so quick in Python, adding prints is usually faster than either typing pdb debugger commands, or starting a GUI debugging session. Another valid debugging technique is to do nothing at all— because Python prints useful error messages instead of crashing on program errors, you usually get enough information to analyze and repair errors.

To learn about other large-scale Python development tools available in the public domain, be sure to also browse the pages at the Vaults of Parnassus web site.

Chapter Summary

This chapter wrapped up the exceptions part of the book (and the book as a whole) with a look at common exception use cases, and a brief summary of commonly used development tools. As this is the end of the book, you get a break on the chapter quiz—just one question this time. As always, be sure to work through this part's closing exercises to cement what you've learned in the past few chapters. The appendixes that follow give installation hints and the answers to the end-of-part exercises.

For pointers on where to turn after this book, see the list of recommended follow-up texts in the Preface. You've now reached the point where Python starts to become truly fun, but this is also where this book's story ends. You now have a good grounding to tackle some of the other books and resources that are available to help you do real applications-level work, like building GUIs, web sites, database interfaces, and more. Good luck with your journey—and of course, "Always look on the bright side of Life!"

Chapter Quiz

1. (This question is a repeat from your first quiz in Chapter 1—see, I told you this would be easy :-)). Why did spam appear in so many examples in this book?

Quiz Answers

1. Because Python is named after the British comedy group Monty Python (based on surveys I've conducted in classes, this is a much-too-well-kept secret in the Python world!). The spam reference comes from a Monty Python skit, where a couple who are trying to order food in a cafeteria keep getting drowned out by a chorus of Vikings singing a song about spam. And if I could insert an audio clip of that song here as the theme song for this book's closing credits, I would....

Part VII Exercises

As we've reached the end of this part of the book, it's time for a few exception exercises to give you a chance to practice the basics. Exceptions really are simple tools; if you get these, you've got them mastered.

See "Part VII, Exceptions and Tools" in Appendix B for the solutions.

1. try/except. Write a function called oops that explicitly raises an IndexError exception when called. Then, write another function that calls oops inside a try/except statement to catch the error. What happens if you change oops to raise a KeyError instead of an IndexError? Where do the names KeyError and IndexError come from? (Hint: recall that all unqualified names come from one of four scopes, by the LEGB rule.)

2. *Exception objects and lists.* Change the oops function you just wrote to raise an exception you define yourself, called MyError, and pass an extra data item along with the exception. You may identify your exception with a string or a class. Then, extend the try statement in the catcher function to catch this exception, and its data in addition to IndexError, and print the extra data item. Finally, if you used a string for your exception, go back and change it to a class instance; what now comes back as the extra data to the handler?

3. *Error handling.* Write a function called safe(func, *args) that runs any function using apply (or the newer *name call syntax), catches any exception raised while the function runs, and prints the exception using the exc_type and exc_value attributes in the sys module (or the newer sys.exc_info call result). Then, use your safe function to run your oops function from exercise 1 or 2. Put safe in a module file called *tools.py*, and pass it the oops function interactively. What sort of error messages do you get? Finally, expand safe to also print a Python stack trace when an error occurs by calling the built-in print_exc function in the standard traceback module (see the Python library reference manual for details).

4. *Self-study examples.* At the end of Appendix B, I've included a handful of example scripts developed as group exercises in live Python classes for you to study and run on your own in conjunction with Python's standard manual set. These are not described, and they use tools in the Python standard library that you'll have to look up. But, for many readers, it helps to see how the concepts we've discussed in this book come together in real programs. If these whet your appetite for more, you can find a wealth of larger and more realistic application-level Python program examples in follow-up books like *Programming Python*, and on the Web in your favorite browser.

## PART VIII

Appendixes

Installation and Configuration

This appendix provides additional installation and configuration details as a resource for people new to such topics.

Installing the Python Interpreter

Because you need the Python interpreter to run Python scripts, the first step in using Python is usually installing Python. Unless one is already available on your machine, you'll need to fetch, install, and possibly configure a recent version of Python on your computer. You'll only need to do this once per machine, and, if you will be running a frozen binary (described in Chapter 2), you may not need to do it at all.

Is Python Already Present?

Before you do anything else, check whether you already have a recent Python on your machine. If you are working on Linux, Mac OS X, and some Unix systems, Python is probably already installed on your computer. Type **python** at a shell prompt (sometimes called a terminal window), and see what happens. Alternatively, try searching for "python" in the usual places—*/usr/bin*, */usr/local/bin*, etc.

On Windows, check whether there is a Python entry in the Start button's All Programs menu (at the bottom left of the screen). If you find a Python, make sure it's version 2.5 or later; although any recent Python will do for most of this text, you'll need at least version 2.5 to run some of the examples in this edition.

Where to Fetch Python

If there is no Python to be found, you will need to install one yourself. The good news is that Python is an open source system that is freely available on the Web, and very easy to install on most platforms.

You can always fetch the latest and greatest standard Python release from *http://www.python.org*, Python's official web site; look for the Downloads link on that page, and choose a release for the platform on which you will be working. You'll find prebuilt Python executables (unpack and run), self-installer files for Windows (click the file's icon to install), RPMs for Linux (unpack with *rpm*), the full source code distribution (compile on your machine to generate an interpreter), and more. You can find links to offsite web pages where versions for some platforms, such as PalmOS, Nokia cell phones, and Windows Mobile, are maintained either at Python.org itself, or via a Google web search.

You can also find Python on CD-ROMs supplied with Linux distributions, included with some products and computer systems, and enclosed with some other Python books. These tend to lag behind the current release somewhat, but usually not seriously so.

In addition, a company called ActiveState distributes Python as part of its *ActivePython* package. This package combines standard CPython with extensions for Windows development, an IDE called PythonWin (described in Chapter 3), and other commonly used extensions. See ActiveState's web site for more details on the ActivePython package.

Finally, if you are interested in alternative Python implementations, run a web search to check out Jython (the Python port to the Java environment) and IronPython (Python for the C#/.NET world), both of which are described in Chapter 2. Installation of these systems is beyond the scope of this book.

Installation Steps

Once you've downloaded Python, you need to install it. Installation steps are very platform-specific, but here are a few pointers for major Python platforms:

Windows

On Windows, Python comes as a self-installer MSI program file—simply double-click on its file icon, and answer Yes or Next at every prompt to perform a default install. The default install includes Python's documentation set and support for Tkinter GUIs, shelve databases, and the IDLE development GUI. Python 2.5 is normally installed in the directory *C:\Python25*, though this can be changed at install time.

For convenience, after the install, Python shows up in the Start button's All Programs menu. Python's menu there has five entries that give quick access to common tasks: starting the IDLE user interface, reading module documentation, starting an interactive session, reading Python's standard manuals in a web browser, and uninstalling. Most of these actions involve concepts explored in detail elsewhere in this text.

When installed on Windows, Python also automatically registers itself to be the program that opens Python files when their icons are clicked (a program launch technique described in Chapter 3). It is also possible to build Python from its source code on Windows, but this is not commonly done.

One note for Windows Vista users: security features of the current version of Vista change some of the rules for using MSI installer files. See the sidebar "The Python 2.5 MSI Installer on Windows Vista" in this appendix for assistance if the current Python installer does not work, or does not place Python in the correct place on your machine.

Linux

On Linux, Python is available as one or more RPM files, which you unpack in the usual way (consult the RPM manpage for details). Depending on which RPMs you download, there may be one for Python itself, and another that adds support for Tkinter GUIs and the IDLE environment. Because Linux is a Unix-like system, the next paragraph applies as well.

Unix

On Unix systems, Python is usually compiled from its full C source code distribution. This usually only requires unpacking the file, and running simple config and make commands; Python configures its own build procedure automatically, according to the system on which it is being compiled. However, be sure to see the package's *README* file for more details on this process. Because Python is open source, its source code may be used and distributed free of charge.

On other platforms, these details can differ widely; installing the "Pippy" port of Python for PalmOS, for example, requires a hotsync operation with your PDA, and Python for the Sharp Zaurus Linux-based PDA comes as one or more *.ipk* files, which you simply run to install. Because additional install procedures for both executable and source forms are well documented, though, we'll skip further details here.

Configuring Python

After you've installed Python, you may want to configure some system settings that impact the way Python runs your code. (If you are just getting started with the language, you can probably skip this section completely; there is usually no need to make any system settings for basic programs.)

Generally speaking, parts of the Python interpreter's behavior can be configured with environment variable settings and command-line options. In this section, we'll take a brief look at Python environment variables. Python command-line options, which are listed when you launch a Python program from a system prompt, are used more rarely, and have very specialized roles; see other documentation sources for details.

The Python 2.5 MSI Installer on Windows Vista

As I write this in mid-2007, the Python self-installer for Windows is a *.msi* installation file. This format works fine on Windows XP (simply double-click on the file, and it runs), but it can have issues on the current version of Windows Vista. In particular, running the MSI installer by clicking on it caused Python to be installed at the root of the *C:* drive on my machine, instead of in the correct *C:\Python25* directory. Python still works in the root directory, but this is not the correct place to install it.

This is a Vista security-related issue; in short, MSI files are not true executables, so they do not correctly inherit administrator permissions, even if run by the administrator user. Instead, MSI files are run via the Widows Registry—their filenames are associated with the MSI installer program.

To install Python 2.5.1 on my Vista-based OQO handheld, I had to use a command-line approach to force the required administrator permissions. Here's the workaround: go to your Start button, select the All Programs entry, choose Accessories, right-click on the Command Prompt entry there, choose "Run as administrator," and select Continue in the access control dialog. Now, within the Command Prompt window, issue a cd command to change to the directory where your Python MSI installer file resides (e.g., `cd C:\user\downloads`), and then run the MSI installer manually by typing a command line of the form `msiexec /i python-2.5.1.msi`. Finally, follow the usual GUI interactions to complete the install.

Naturally, this behavior may change over time. This procedure may not be required in future versions of Vista, and additional workarounds may be possible (such as disabling Vista security, if you dare). It's also possible that the Python self-installer may eventually be provided in a different format that fixes this problem in the future—as a true executable, for instance. Be sure to try your installer by simply clicking its icon before attempting any workarounds to see if it works properly.

Python Environment Variables

Environment variables—known to some as shell variables, or DOS variables—live outside Python, and thus can be used to customize the interpreter's behavior each time it is run on a given computer. Python recognizes a handful of environment variable settings, but only a few are used often enough to warrant explanation here. Table A-1 summarizes the main Python-related environment variable settings.

Table A-1. Important environment variables

Variable	Role
PATH (or path)	System shell search path (for finding "python")
PYTHONPATH	Python module search path (for imports)
PYTHONSTARTUP	Path to Python interactive startup file
TCL_LIBRARY, TK_LIBRARY	GUI extension variables (Tkinter)

These variables are straightforward to use, but here are a few pointers:

- The PATH setting lists a set of directories that the operating system searches for executable programs. It should normally include the directory where your Python interpreter lives (the *python* program on Unix, or the *python.exe* file on Windows).

  You don't need to set this variable at all if you are willing to work in the directory where Python resides, or type the full path to Python in command lines. On Windows, for instance, the PATH is irrelevant if you run a **cd** C:\Python25 before running any code (to change to the directory where Python lives), or always type **C:\Python25\python** instead of just **python** (giving a full path). Also, note that PATH settings are mostly for launching programs from command lines; they are usually irrelevant when launching via icon clicks and IDEs.

- The PYTHONPATH setting serves a role similar to PATH: the Python interpreter consults the PYTHONPATH variable to locate module files when you import them in a program. (For more on the module search path, refer to Chapter 18.) If used, this variable is set to a platform-dependent list of directory names, separated by colons on Unix, and semicolons on Windows. This list normally includes just your own source code directories.

  You don't need to set this variable unless you will be performing cross-directory imports—because Python always searches the home directory of the program's top-level file automatically, this setting is required only if a module needs to import another module that lives in a different directory. As mentioned in Chapter 18, *.pth* files are a recent alternative to PYTHONPATH.

- If PYTHONSTARTUP is set to the pathname of a file of Python code, Python executes the file's code automatically whenever you start the interactive interpreter, as though you had typed it at the interactive command line. This is a rarely used but handy way to make sure you always load certain utilities when working interactively; it saves an import.

- If you wish to use the Tkinter GUI toolkit, you might have to set the two GUI variables in Table A-1 to the names of the source library directories of the Tcl and Tk systems (much like PYTHONPATH). However, these settings are not required on Windows systems (where Tkinter support is installed alongside Python), and are usually not required elsewhere if Tcl and Tk reside in standard directories.

Note that because these environment settings (as well as *.pth* files) are external to Python itself, when you set them is usually irrelevant. They may be set before or after Python is installed, as long as they are set the way you require before Python is actually *run*.

> ### Getting Tkinter (and IDLE) GUI Support on Linux
>
> The IDLE interface described in Chapter 2 is a Python Tkinter GUI program. Tkinter is a GUI toolkit, and it's a complete, standard component of Python on Windows and some other platforms. On some Linux systems, though, the underlying GUI library may not be a standard installed component. To add GUI support to your Python on Linux if needed, try running a command line of the form **yum tkinter** to automatically install Tkinter's underlying libraries. This should work on Linux distributions (and some other systems) on which the *yum* installation program is available.

How to Set Configuration Options

The way to set Python-related environment variables, and what to set them to, depends on the type of computer you're working on. And again, remember that you won't necessarily have to set these at all right away; especially if you're working in IDLE (described in Chapter 3), configuration is not required up front.

But suppose, for illustration, that you have generally useful module files in directories called *utilities* and *package1* somewhere on your machine, and you want to be able to import these modules from files located in other directories. That is, to load a file called *spam.py* from the *utilities* directory, you want to be able to say:

```
import spam
```

from another file located anywhere on your computer. To make this work, you'll have to configure your module search path one way or another to include the directory containing *spam.py*. Here are a few tips on this process.

Unix/Linux shell variables

On Unix systems, the way to set environment variables depends on the shell you use. Under the *csh* shell, you might add a line like the following in your *.cshrc* or *.login* file to set the Python module search path:

```
setenv PYTHONPATH /usr/home/pycode/utilities:/usr/lib/pycode/package1
```

This tells Python to look for imported modules in two user-defined directories. But, if you're using the *ksh* shell, the setting might instead appear in your *.kshrc* file, and look like this:

```
export PYTHONPATH="/usr/home/pycode/utilities:/usr/lib/pycode/package1"
```

Other shells may use different (but analogous) syntax.

DOS variables (Windows)

If you are using MS-DOS, or some older flavors of Windows, you may need to add an environment variable configuration command to your *C:\autoexec.bat* file, and reboot your machine for the changes to take effect. The configuration command on such machines has a syntax unique to DOS:

```
set PYTHONPATH=c:\pycode\utilities;d:\pycode\package1
```

You can type such a command in a DOS console window, too, but the setting will then be active only for that one console window. Changing your *.bat* file makes the change permanent and global to all programs.

Other Windows options

On more recent versions of Windows, you may instead set PYTHONPATH and other variables via the system environment variable GUI without having to edit files or reboot. On XP, select the Control Panel, choose the System icon, pick the Advanced tab, and click the Environment Variables button to edit or add new variables (PYTHONPATH is usually a user variable). You do not need to reboot your machine, but be sure to restart Python if it's open so that it picks up your changes (it configures its path at startup time only).

If you are an experienced Windows user, you may also be able to configure the module search path by using the Windows Registry Editor. Go to Start → Run… and type **regedit**. Assuming the typical registry tool is on your machine, you can then navigate to Python's entries and make your changes. This is a delicate and error-prone procedure, though, so unless you're familiar with the Registry, I suggest using other options.

Path files

Finally, if you choose to extend the module search path with a *.pth* file instead of the PYTHONPATH variable, you might instead code a text file that looks like the following on Windows (file *C:\Python25\mypath.pth*):

```
c:\pycode\utilities
d:\pycode\package1
```

Its contents will differ per platform, and its container directory may differ per both platform and Python release. Python locates this file automatically when it starts up.

Directory names in path files may be absolute, or relative to the directory containing the path file; multiple *.pth* files can be used (all their directories are added), and *.pth* files may appear in various automatically checked directories that are platform- and version-specific. For example, Release 2.5 typically looks for path files in *C:\Python25* and *C:\Python25\Lib\site-packages* on Windows, and in */usr/local/lib/python2.5/site-packages,* and */usr/local/lib/site-python* on Unix and Linux.

Because these settings are often optional, and because this isn't a book on operating system shells, I'll defer to other sources for more details. Consult your system shell's manpages or other documentation for more information, and if you have trouble figuring out what your settings should be, ask your system administrator or another local expert for help.

Solutions to End-of-Part Exercises

Part I, Getting Started

See "Part I Exercises" in Chapter 3 for the exercises.

1. *Interaction.* Assuming Python s configured properly, the interaction should look something like the following (you can run this any way you like (in IDLE, from a shell prompt, and so on):

```
% python
...copyright information lines...
>>> "Hello World!"
'Hello World!'
>>>                           # Use Ctrl-D or Ctrl-Z to exit, or close window
```

2. *Programs.* Your code (i.e., module) file *module1.py* and the operating system shell interactions should look like this:

```
print 'Hello module world!'
```

```
% python module1.py
Hello module world!
```

Again, feel free to run this other ways—by clicking the file's icon, by using IDLE's Run → Run Module menu option, and so on.

3. *Modules.* The following interaction listing illustrates running a module file by importing it:

```
% python
>>> import module1
Hello module world!
>>>
```

Remember that you will need to reload the module to run it again without stopping and restarting the interpreter. The question about moving the file to a different directory and importing it again is a trick question: if Python generates a *module1.pyc* file in the original directory, it uses that when you import the module, even if the source code (*.py*) file has been moved to a directory not in

Python's search path. The *.pyc* file is written automatically if Python has access to the source file's directory, and contains the compiled byte code version of a module. See Part V for more on modules.

4. *Scripts*. Assuming your platform supports the #! trick, your solution will look like the following (although your #! line may need to list another path on your machine):

```
#!/usr/local/bin/python          (or #!/usr/bin/env python)
print 'Hello module world!'

% chmod +x module1.py

% module1.py
Hello module world!
```

5. *Errors*. The interaction below demonstrates the sorts of error messages you'll get when you complete this exercise. Really, you're triggering Python exceptions; the default exception-handling behavior terminates the running Python program, and prints an error message and stack trace on the screen. The stack trace shows where you were in a program when the exception occurred. In Part VII, you will learn that you can catch exceptions using try statements and process them arbitrarily; you'll also see that Python includes a full-blown source code debugger for special error-detection requirements. For now, notice that Python gives meaningful messages when programming errors occur (instead of crashing silently):

```
% python
>>> 1 / 0
Traceback (innermost last):
  File "<stdin>", line 1, in ?
ZeroDivisionError: integer division or modulo
>>>
>>> x
Traceback (innermost last):
  File "<stdin>", line 1, in ?
NameError: x
```

6. *Breaks*. When you type this code:

```
L = [1, 2]
L.append(L)
```

you create a cyclic data structure in Python. In Python releases before 1.5.1, the Python printer wasn't smart enough to detect cycles in objects, and it would print an unending stream of [1, 2, [1, 2, [1, 2, [1, 2, and so on, until you hit the break-key combination on your machine (which, technically, raises a keyboard-interrupt exception that prints a default message). Beginning with Python 1.5.1, the printer is clever enough to detect cycles and prints [[...]] instead.

The reason for the cycle is subtle and requires information you will glean in Part II. But in short, assignments in Python always generate references to objects (which you can think of as implicitly followed pointers). When you run the first assignment above, the name L becomes a named reference to a two-item list object. Python lists are really arrays of object references with an append method that changes the array in-place by tacking on another object reference. Here, the append call adds a reference to the front of L at the end of L, which leads to the cycle illustrated in Figure B-1. In some programs that traverse arbitrary objects, you might have to detect such cycles yourself by keeping track of where you've been to avoid looping.

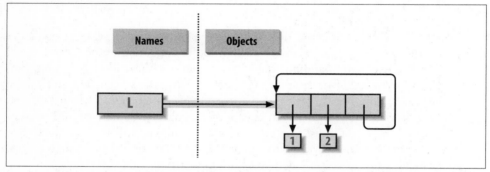

Figure B-1. A cyclic object, created by appending a list to itself. By default, Python appends a reference to the original list, not a copy of the list.

Believe it or not, cyclic data structures can sometimes be useful (but not when printed!).

Part II, Types and Operations

See "Part II Exercises" in Chapter 9 for the exercises.

1. *The basics.* Here are the sorts of results you should get, along with a few comments about their meaning. Note that ; is used in a few of these to squeeze more than one statement onto a single line; the ; is a statement separator:

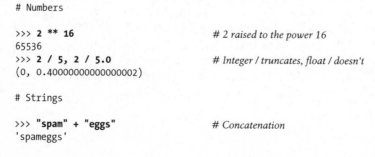

```
# Numbers

>>> 2 ** 16                           # 2 raised to the power 16
65536
>>> 2 / 5, 2 / 5.0                    # Integer / truncates, float / doesn't
(0, 0.40000000000000002)

# Strings

>>> "spam" + "eggs"                   # Concatenation
'spameggs'
```

```
>>> S = "ham"
>>> "eggs " + S
'eggs ham'
>>> S * 5                                   # Repetition
'hamhamhamhamham'
>>> S[:0]                                   # An empty slice at the front -- [0:0]
''
>>> "green %s and %s" % ("eggs", S)         # Formatting
'green eggs and ham'

# Tuples

>>> ('x',)[0]                               # Indexing a single-item tuple
'x'
>>> ('x', 'y')[1]                           # Indexing a 2-item tuple
'y'

# Lists

>>> L = [1,2,3] + [4,5,6]                   # List operations
>>> L, L[:], L[:0], L[-2], L[-2:]
([1, 2, 3, 4, 5, 6], [1, 2, 3, 4, 5, 6], [], 5, [5, 6])
>>> ([1,2,3]+[4,5,6])[2:4]
[3, 4]
>>> [L[2], L[3]]                            # Fetch from offsets; store in a list
[3, 4]
>>> L.reverse(); L                          # Method: reverse list in-place
[6, 5, 4, 3, 2, 1]
>>> L.sort(); L                             # Method: sort list in-place
[1, 2, 3, 4, 5, 6]
>>> L.index(4)                              # Method: offset of first 4 (search)
3

# Dictionaries

>>> {'a':1, 'b':2}['b']                     # Index a dictionary by key
2
>>> D = {'x':1, 'y':2, 'z':3}
>>> D['w'] = 0                              # Create a new entry
>>> D['x'] + D['w']
1
>>> D[(1,2,3)] = 4                          # A tuple used as a key (immutable)
>>> D
{'w': 0, 'z': 3, 'y': 2, (1, 2, 3): 4, 'x': 1}
>>> D.keys(), D.values(), D.has_key((1,2,3))    # Methods
(['w', 'z', 'y', (1, 2, 3), 'x'], [0, 3, 2, 4, 1], 1)

# Empties

>>> [[]], ["",[],(),{},None]                # Lots of nothings: empty objects
([[]], ['', [], (), {}, None])
```

2. *Indexing and slicing.* Indexing out of bounds (e.g., L[4]) raises an error; Python always checks to make sure that all offsets are within the bounds of a sequence.

On the other hand, slicing out of bounds (e.g., L[-1000:100]) works because Python scales out-of-bounds slices so that they always fit (the limits are set to zero and the sequence length, if required).

Extracting a sequence in reverse—with the lower bound greater than the higher bound (e.g., L[3:1])—doesn't really work. You get back an empty slice ([ ]) because Python scales the slice limits to make sure that the lower bound is always less than or equal to the upper bound (e.g., L[3:1] is scaled to L[3:3], the empty insertion point at offset 3). Python slices are always extracted from left to right, even if you use negative indexes (they are first converted to positive indexes by adding the sequence length). Note that Python 2.3's three-limit slices modify this behavior somewhat: L[3:1:-1] does extract from right to left:

```
>>> L = [1, 2, 3, 4]
>>> L[4]
Traceback (innermost last):
  File "<stdin>", line 1, in ?
IndexError: list index out of range
>>> L[-1000:100]
[1, 2, 3, 4]
>>> L[3:1]
[]
>>> L
[1, 2, 3, 4]
>>> L[3:1] = ['?']
>>> L
[1, 2, 3, '?', 4]
```

3. *Indexing, slicing, and* del. Your interaction with the interpreter should look something like the following code. Note that assigning an empty list to an offset stores an empty list object there, but assigning an empty list to a slice deletes the slice. Slice assignment expects another sequence, or you'll get a type error; it inserts items *inside* the sequence assigned, not the sequence itself:

```
>>> L = [1,2,3,4]
>>> L[2] = []
>>> L
[1, 2, [], 4]
>>> L[2:3] = []
>>> L
[1, 2, 4]
>>> del L[0]
>>> L
[2, 4]
>>> del L[1:]
>>> L
[2]
>>> L[1:2] = 1
Traceback (innermost last):
  File "<stdin>", line 1, in ?
TypeError: illegal argument type for built-in operation
```

4. *Tuple assignment.* The values of X and Y are swapped. When tuples appear on the left and right of an assignment symbol (=), Python assigns objects on the right to targets on the left according to their positions. This is probably easiest to understand by noting that the targets on the left aren't a real tuple, even though they look like one; they are simply a set of independent assignment targets. The items on the right are a tuple, which gets unpacked during the assignment (the tuple provides the temporary assignment needed to achieve the swap effect):

```
>>> X = 'spam'
>>> Y = 'eggs'
>>> X, Y = Y, X
>>> X
'eggs'
>>> Y
'spam'
```

5. *Dictionary keys.* Any immutable object can be used as a dictionary key—including integers, tuples, strings, and so on. This really is a dictionary, even though some of its keys look like integer offsets. Mixed-type keys work fine, too:

```
>>> D = {}
>>> D[1] = 'a'
>>> D[2] = 'b'
>>> D[(1, 2, 3)] = 'c'
>>> D
{1: 'a', 2: 'b', (1, 2, 3): 'c'}
```

6. *Dictionary indexing.* Indexing a nonexistent key (D['d']) raises an error; assigning to a nonexistent key (D['d']='spam') creates a new dictionary entry. On the other hand, out-of-bounds indexing for lists raises an error too, but so do out-of-bounds assignments. Variable names work like dictionary keys; they must have already been assigned when referenced, but are created when first assigned. In fact, variable names can be processed as dictionary keys if you wish (they're made visible in module namespace or stack-frame dictionaries):

```
>>> D = {'a':1, 'b':2, 'c':3}
>>> D['a']
1
>>> D['d']
Traceback (innermost last):
  File "<stdin>", line 1, in ?
KeyError: d
>>> D['d'] = 4
>>> D
{'b': 2, 'd': 4, 'a': 1, 'c': 3}
>>>
>>> L = [0, 1]
>>> L[2]
Traceback (innermost last):
  File "<stdin>", line 1, in ?
IndexError: list index out of range
>>> L[2] = 3
Traceback (innermost last):
  File "<stdin>", line 1, in ?
IndexError: list assignment index out of range
```

7. *Generic operations*. Question answers:

- The + operator doesn't work on different/mixed types (e.g., string + list, list + tuple).

- + doesn't work for dictionaries, as they aren't sequences.

- The append method works only for lists, not strings, and keys works only on dictionaries. append assumes its target is mutable, since it's an in-place extension; strings are immutable.

- Slicing and concatenation always return a new object of the same type as the objects processed.

```
>>> "x" + 1
Traceback (innermost last):
  File "<stdin>", line 1, in ?
TypeError: illegal argument type for built-in operation
>>>
>>> {} + {}
Traceback (innermost last):
  File "<stdin>", line 1, in ?
TypeError: bad operand type(s) for +
>>>
>>> [].append(9)
>>> "".append('s')
Traceback (innermost last):
  File "<stdin>", line 1, in ?
AttributeError: attribute-less object
>>>
>>> {}.keys()
[]
>>> [].keys()
Traceback (innermost last):
  File "<stdin>", line 1, in ?
AttributeError: keys
>>>
>>> [][:]
[]
>>> ""[:]
''
```

8. *String indexing*. Because strings are collections of one-character strings, every time you index a string, you get back a string that can be indexed again. S[0][0][0][0][0] just keeps indexing the first character over and over. This generally doesn't work for lists (lists can hold arbitrary objects) unless the list contains strings:

```
>>> S = "spam"
>>> S[0][0][0][0][0]
's'
>>> L = ['s', 'p']
>>> L[0][0][0]
's'
```

9. *Immutable types.* Either of the following solutions works. Index assignment doesn't, because strings are immutable:

```
>>> S = "spam"
>>> S = S[0] + 'l' + S[2:]
>>> S
'slam'
>>> S = S[0] + 'l' + S[2] + S[3]
>>> S
'slam'
```

10. *Nesting.* Here is a sample:

```
>>> me = {'name':('mark', 'e', 'lutz'), 'age':'?', 'job':'engineer'}
>>> me['job']
'engineer'
>>> me['name'][2]
'lutz'
```

11. *Files.* Here's one way to create and read back a text file in Python (ls is a Unix command; use dir on Windows):

```
# File: maker.py
file = open('myfile.txt', 'w')
file.write('Hello file world!\n')     # Or: open().write()
file.close()                          # close not always needed


# File: reader.py
file = open('myfile.txt')             # 'r' is default open mode
print file.read()                     # Or print open().read()


% python maker.py
% python reader.py
Hello file world!

% ls -l myfile.txt
-rwxrwxrwa   1 0        0           19 Apr 13 16:33 myfile.txt
```

12. *The dir function revisited.* The following is what you get for lists; dictionaries do the same, with different method names. Note that the dir result expanded in Python 2.2—you'll see a large set of additional underscore names that implement expression operators and support the subclassing in Part VI. The __methods__ attribute disappeared in 2.2 as well because it wasn't consistently implemented—use dir to fetch attribute lists today instead:

```
>>> [].__methods__
['append', 'count', 'index', 'insert', 'remove', 'reverse', 'sort',...]
>>> dir([])
['append', 'count', 'index', 'insert', 'remove', 'reverse', 'sort',...]
```

Part III, Statements and Syntax

See "Part III Exercises" in Chapter 14 for the exercises.

1. *Coding basic loops.* As you work through this exercise, you'll wind up with code that looks like the following:

```
>>> S = 'spam'
>>> for c in S:
...     print ord(c)
...
115
112
97
109

>>> x = 0
>>> for c in S: x += ord(c)              # Or: x = x + ord(c)
...
>>> x
433

>>> x = []
>>> for c in S: x.append(ord(c))
...
>>> x
[115, 112, 97, 109]

>>> map(ord, S)
[115, 112, 97, 109]
```

2. *Backslash characters.* The example prints the bell character (\a) 50 times; assuming your machine can handle it, and when it's run outside of IDLE, you may get a series of beeps (or one long tone, if your machine is fast enough). Hey—I warned you.

3. *Sorting dictionaries.* Here's one way to work through this exercise (see Chapter 8 if this doesn't make sense). Remember, you really do have to split up the keys and sort calls like this because sort returns None. In Python 2.2 and later, you can iterate through dictionary keys directly without calling keys (e.g., for key in D:), but the keys list will not be sorted like it is by this code. In more recent Pythons, you can achieve the same effect with the sorted built-in, too:

```
>>> D = {'a':1, 'b':2, 'c':3, 'd':4, 'e':5, 'f':6, 'g':7}
>>> D
{'f': 6, 'c': 3, 'a': 1, 'g': 7, 'e': 5, 'd': 4, 'b': 2}
>>>
>>> keys = D.keys()
>>> keys.sort()
>>> for key in keys:
...     print key, '=>', D[key]
...
```

```
a => 1
b => 2
c => 3
d => 4
e => 5
f => 6
g => 7

>>> for key in sorted(D):              # In more recent Pythons
...     print key, '=>', D[key]
```

4. *Program logic alternatives.* Here's some sample code for the solutions. Your results may vary a bit; this exercise is mostly designed to get you playing with code alternatives, so anything reasonable gets full credit:

```
L = [1, 2, 4, 8, 16, 32, 64]
X = 5

i = 0
while i < len(L):
    if 2 ** X == L[i]:
        print 'at index', i
        break
    i = i+1
else:
    print X, 'not found'


L = [1, 2, 4, 8, 16, 32, 64]
X = 5

for p in L:
    if (2 ** X) == p:
        print (2 ** X), 'was found at', L.index(p)
        break
else:
    print X, 'not found'


L = [1, 2, 4, 8, 16, 32, 64]
X = 5

if (2 ** X) in L:
    print (2 ** X), 'was found at', L.index(2 ** X)
else:
    print X, 'not found'


X = 5
L = []
for i in range(7): L.append(2 ** i)
print L
```

```
    if (2 ** X) in L:
        print (2 ** X), 'was found at', L.index(2 ** X)
    else:
        print X, 'not found'


    X = 5
    L = map(lambda x: 2**x, range(7))
    print L

    if (2 ** X) in L:
        print (2 ** X), 'was found at', L.index(2 ** X)
    else:
        print X, 'not found'
```

Part IV, Functions

See "Part IV Exercises" in Chapter 17 for the exercises.

1. *The basics*. There's not much to this one, but notice that using print (and hence your function) is technically a *polymorphic* operation, which does the right thing for each type of object:

```
% python
>>> def func(x): print x
...
>>> func("spam")
spam
>>> func(42)
42
>>> func([1, 2, 3])
[1, 2, 3]
>>> func({'food': 'spam'})
{'food': 'spam'}
```

2. *Arguments*. Here's a sample solution. Remember that you have to use print to see results in the test calls because a file isn't the same as code typed interactively; Python doesn't normally echo the results of expression statements in files:

```
def adder(x, y):
    return x + y

print adder(2, 3)
print adder('spam', 'eggs')
print adder(['a', 'b'], ['c', 'd'])

% python mod.py
5
spameggs
['a', 'b', 'c', 'd']
```

3. *varargs*. Two alternative adder functions are shown in the following file, *adders.py*. The hard part here is figuring out how to initialize an accumulator to an empty value of whatever type is passed in. The first solution uses manual type testing to look for an integer, and an empty slice of the first argument (assumed to be a sequence) if the argument is determined not to be an integer. The second solution uses the first argument to initialize and scan items 2 and beyond, much like one of the min function variants shown in Chapter 16.

The second solution is better. Both of these assume all arguments are of the same type, and neither works on dictionaries (as we saw in Part II, + doesn't work on mixed types or dictionaries). You could add a type test and special code to allow dictionaries, too, but that's extra credit:

```
def adder1(*args):
    print 'adder1',
    if type(args[0]) == type(0):        # Integer?
        sum = 0                         # Init to zero
    else:                               # else sequence:
        sum = args[0][:0]               # Use empty slice of arg1
    for arg in args:
        sum = sum + arg
    return sum


def adder2(*args):
    print 'adder2',
    sum = args[0]                       # Init to arg1
    for next in args[1:]:
        sum += next                     # Add items 2..N
    return sum


for func in (adder1, adder2):
    print func(2, 3, 4)
    print func('spam', 'eggs', 'toast')
    print func(['a', 'b'], ['c', 'd'], ['e', 'f'])
```

```
% python adders.py
adder1 9
adder1 spameggstoast
adder1 ['a', 'b', 'c', 'd', 'e', 'f']
adder2 9
adder2 spameggstoast
adder2 ['a', 'b', 'c', 'd', 'e', 'f']
```

4. *Keywords*. Here is my solution to the first part of this exercise (file *mod.py*). To iterate over keyword arguments, use the **args form in the function header, and use a loop (e.g., for x in args.keys(): use args[x]), or use args.values() to make this the same as summing *args positionals:

```
def adder(good=1, bad=2, ugly=3):
    return good + bad + ugly
```

```
print adder( )
print adder(5)
print adder(5, 6)
print adder(5, 6, 7)
print adder(ugly=7, good=6, bad=5)

% python mod.py
6
10
14
18
18
```

5. (and 6.) Here are my solutions to exercises 5 and 6 (file *dicts.py*). These are just coding exercises, though, because Python 1.5 added the dictionary methods D.copy( ) and D1.update(D2) to handle things like copying and adding (merging) dictionaries. (See Python's library manual or O'Reilly's *Python Pocket Reference* for more details.) X[:] doesn't work for dictionaries, as they're not sequences (see Chapter 8 for details). Also, remember that if you assign (e = d) rather than copying, you generate a reference to a *shared* dictionary object; changing d changes e, too:

```
def copyDict(old):
    new = {}
    for key in old.keys( ):
        new[key] = old[key]
    return new

def addDict(d1, d2):
    new = {}
    for key in d1.keys( ):
        new[key] = d1[key]
    for key in d2.keys( ):
        new[key] = d2[key]
    return new

% python
>>> from dicts import *
>>> d = {1: 1, 2: 2}
>>> e = copyDict(d)
>>> d[2] = '?'
>>> d
{1: 1, 2: '?'}
>>> e
{1: 1, 2: 2}

>>> x = {1: 1}
>>> y = {2: 2}
>>> z = addDict(x, y)
>>> z
{1: 1, 2: 2}
```

7. *More argument-matching examples.* Here is the sort of interaction you should get, along with comments that explain the matching that goes on:

```
def f1(a, b): print a, b              # Normal args

def f2(a, *b): print a, b             # Positional varargs

def f3(a, **b): print a, b            # Keyword varargs

def f4(a, *b, **c): print a, b, c     # Mixed modes

def f5(a, b=2, c=3): print a, b, c    # Defaults

def f6(a, b=2, *c): print a, b, c     # Defaults and positional varargs


% python
>>> f1(1, 2)                          # Matched by position (order matters)
1 2
>>> f1(b=2, a=1)                       # Matched by name (order doesn't matter)
1 2

>>> f2(1, 2, 3)                        # Extra positionals collected in a tuple
1 (2, 3)

>>> f3(1, x=2, y=3)                    # Extra keywords collected in a dictionary
1 {'x': 2, 'y': 3}

>>> f4(1, 2, 3, x=2, y=3)              # Extra of both kinds
1 (2, 3) {'x': 2, 'y': 3}

>>> f5(1)                              # Both defaults kick in
1 2 3
>>> f5(1, 4)                           # Only one default used
1 4 3

>>> f6(1)                              # One argument: matches "a"
1 2 ()
>>> f6(1, 3, 4)                        # Extra positional collected
1 3 (4,)
```

8. *Primes revisited.* Below is the primes example, wrapped up in a function and a module (file *primes.py*), so it can be run multiple times. I added an if test to trap negatives, 0, and 1. I also changed / to // to make this solution immune to the Python 3.0 / true division changes we studied in Chapter 5, and to enable it to support floating-point numbers. The // operator works in the current and future division schemes, but the future / operator fails (uncomment the from statement, and change // to / to see the differences in 2.2 and 3.0):

```
#from __future__ import division

def prime(y):
    if y <= 1:                                        # For some y > 1
```

```
            print y, 'not prime'
        else:
            x = y // 2                              # Future / fails
            while x > 1:
                if y % x == 0:                       # No remainder?
                    print y, 'has factor', x
                    break                            # Skip else
                x -= 1
            else:
                print y, 'is prime'

prime(13); prime(13.0)
prime(15); prime(15.0)
prime(3);  prime(2)
prime(1);  prime(-3)
```

Here is the module in action; the `//` operator allows it to works for floating-point numbers too, even though it perhaps should not.

```
% python primes.py
13 is prime
13.0 is prime
15 has factor 5
15.0 has factor 5.0
3 is prime
2 is prime
1 not prime
-3 not prime
```

This function still isn't very reusable, yet—it could return values, instead of printing—but it's enough to run experiments. It's also not a strict mathematical prime (floating-points work), and is still inefficient. Improvements are left as exercises for more mathematically minded readers. Hint: a `for` loop over `range(y, 1, -1)` may be a bit quicker than the `while` (in fact, it's roughly twice as fast in 2.2), but the algorithm is the real bottleneck here. To time alternatives, use the built-in `time` module and coding patterns like those used in this general function-call timer (see the library manual for details):

```
def timer(reps, func, *args):
    import time
    start = time.clock()
    for i in xrange(reps):
        apply(func, args)
    return time.clock() - start
```

9. *List comprehensions*. Here is the sort of code you should write; I may have a preference, but I'm not telling:

```
>>> values = [2, 4, 9, 16, 25]
>>> import math

>>> res = []
>>> for x in values: res.append(math.sqrt(x))
...
```

```
>>> res
[1.4142135623730951, 2.0, 3.0, 4.0, 5.0]

>>> map(math.sqrt, values)
[1.4142135623730951, 2.0, 3.0, 4.0, 5.0]

>>> [math.sqrt(x) for x in values]
[1.4142135623730951, 2.0, 3.0, 4.0, 5.0]
```

Part V, Modules

See "Part V Exercises" in Chapter 21 for the exercises.

1. *Import basics*. This one is simpler than you may think. When you're done, your file (*mymod.py*) and interaction should look similar to the following; remember that Python can read a whole file into a list of line strings, and the len built-in returns the length of strings and lists.

```
def countLines(name):
    file = open(name)
    return len(file.readlines())

def countChars(name):
    return len(open(name).read())

def test(name):                                    # Or pass file object
    return countLines(name), countChars(name)      # Or return a dictionary
```

```
% python
>>> import mymod
>>> mymod.test('mymod.py')
(10, 291)
```

Note that these functions load the entire file in memory all at once, and so won't work for pathologically large files too big for your machine's memory. To be more robust, you could read line by line with iterators instead and count as you go:

```
def countLines(name):
    tot = 0
    for line in open(name): tot += 1
    return tot

def countChars(name):
    tot = 0
    for line in open(name): tot += len(line)
    return tot
```

On Unix, you can verify your output with a wc command; on Windows, right-click on your file to view its properties. But note that your script may report fewer characters than Windows does—for portability, Python converts Windows \r\n line-end markers to \n, thereby dropping one byte (character) per line. To match byte counts with Windows exactly, you have to open in binary mode ('rb'), or add the number of bytes corresponding to the number of lines.

Incidentally, to do the "ambitious" part of this exercise (passing in a file object, so you only open the file once), you'll probably need to use the seek method of the built-in file object. We didn't cover it in the text, but it works just like C's fseek call (and calls it behind the scenes): seek resets the current position in the file to a passed-in offset. After a seek, future input/output operations are relative to the new position. To rewind to the start of a file without closing and reopening it, call file.seek(0); the file read methods all pick up at the current position in the file, so you need to rewind to reread. Here's what this tweak would look like:

```
def countLines(file):
    file.seek(0)                                # Rewind to start of file
    return len(file.readlines())

def countChars(file):
    file.seek(0)                                # Ditto (rewind if needed)
    return len(file.read())

def test(name):
    file = open(name)                           # Pass file object
    return countLines(file), countChars(file)   # Open file only once

>>> import mymod2
>>> mymod2.test("mymod2.py")
(11, 392)
```

2. from/from *. Here's the from * part; replace * with countChars to do the rest:

```
% python
>>> from mymod import *
>>> countChars("mymod.py")
291
```

3. __main__. If you code it properly, it works in either mode (program run or module import):

```
def countLines(name):
    file = open(name)
    return len(file.readlines())

def countChars(name):
    return len(open(name).read())

def test(name):                                 # Or pass file object
    return countLines(name), countChars(name)   # Or return a dictionary

if __name__ == '__main__':
    print test('mymod.py')

% python mymod.py
(13, 346)
```

4. *Nested imports.* Here is my solution (file *myclient.py*):

```
from mymod import countLines, countChars
print countLines('mymod.py'), countChars('mymod.py')
```

```
% python myclient.py
13 346
```

As for the rest of this one, mymod's functions are accessible (that is, importable) from the top level of myclient, since from simply assigns to names in the importer (it works almost as though mymod's defs appeared in myclient). For example, another file can say this:

```
import myclient
myclient.countLines(...)

from myclient import countChars
countChars(...)
```

If myclient used import instead of from, you'd need to use a path to get to the functions in mymod through myclient:

```
import myclient
myclient.mymod.countLines(...)

from myclient import mymod
mymod.countChars(...)
```

In general, you can define *collector* modules that import all the names from other modules so they're available in a single convenience module. Using the following code, you wind up with three different copies of the name somename (mod1.somename, collector.somename, and __main__.somename); all three share the same integer object initially, and only the name somename exists at the interactive prompt as is:

```
# File: mod1.py
somename = 42
```

```
# File: collector.py
from mod1 import *          # Collect lots of names here
from mod2 import *          # from assigns to my names
from mod3 import *
```

```
>>> from collector import somename
```

5. *Package imports.* For this, I put the *mymod.py* solution file listed for exercise 3 into a directory package. The following is what I did to set up the directory and its required _ _*init*_ _.py file in a Windows console interface; you'll need to interpolate for other platforms (e.g., use mv and vi instead of move and edit). This works in any directory (I just happened to run my commands in Python's install directory), and you can do some of this from a file explorer GUI, too.

When I was done, I had a *mypkg* subdirectory that contained the files _ _*init*_ _.py and *mymod.py*. You need an _ _*init*_ _.py in the *mypkg* directory, but not in its parent; *mypkg* is located in the home directory component of the module search path. Notice how a print statement coded in the directory's initialization file fires only the first time it is imported, not the second:

```
C:\python25> mkdir mypkg
C:\Python25> move mymod.py mypkg\mymod.py
C:\Python25> edit mypkg\__init__.py
...coded a print statement...
```

```
C:\Python25> python
>>> import mypkg.mymod
initializing mypkg
>>> mypkg.mymod.countLines('mypkg\mymod.py')
13
>>> from mypkg.mymod import countChars
>>> countChars('mypkg\mymod.py')
346
```

6. *Reloads.* This exercise just asks you to experiment with changing the *changer.py* example in the book, so there's nothing to show here.

7. *Circular imports.* The short story is that importing recur2 first works because the recursive import then happens at the import in recur1, not at a from in recur2.

The long story goes like this: importing recur2 first works because the recursive import from recur1 to recur2 fetches recur2 as a whole, instead of getting specific names. recur2 is incomplete when imported from recur1, but because it uses import instead of from, you're safe: Python finds and returns the already created recur2 module object, and continues to run the rest of recur1 without a glitch. When the recur2 import resumes, the second from finds the name Y in recur1 (it's been run completely), so no error is reported. Running a file as a script is not the same as importing it as a module; these cases are the same as running the first import or from in the script interactively. For instance, running recur1 as a script is the same as importing recur2 interactively, as recur2 is the first module imported in recur1.

Part VI, Classes and OOP

See "Part VI Exercises" in Chapter 26 for the exercises.

1. *Inheritance.* Here's the solution code for this exercise (file *adder.py*), along with some interactive tests. The __add__ overload has to appear only once, in the superclass, as it invokes type-specific add methods in subclasses:

```
class Adder:
    def add(self, x, y):
        print 'not implemented!'
    def __init__(self, start=[]):
        self.data = start
    def __add__(self, other):                  # Or in subclasses?
        return self.add(self.data, other)      # Or return type?

class ListAdder(Adder):
    def add(self, x, y):
        return x + y

class DictAdder(Adder):
    def add(self, x, y):
        new = {}
        for k in x.keys(): new[k] = x[k]
        for k in y.keys(): new[k] = y[k]
        return new
```

```
% python
>>> from adder import *
>>> x = Adder()
>>> x.add(1, 2)
not implemented!
>>> x = ListAdder()
>>> x.add([1], [2])
[1, 2]
>>> x = DictAdder()
>>> x.add({1:1}, {2:2})
{1: 1, 2: 2}

>>> x = Adder([1])
>>> x + [2]
not implemented!
>>>
>>> x = ListAdder([1])
>>> x + [2]
[1, 2]
>>> [2] + x
Traceback (innermost last):
  File "<stdin>", line 1, in ?
TypeError: __add__ nor __radd__ defined for these operands
```

Notice in the last test that you get an error for expressions where a class instance appears on the right of a +; if you want to fix this, use __radd__ methods, as described in "Operator Overloading" in Chapter 24.

If you are saving a value in the instance anyhow, you might as well rewrite the add method to take just one argument, in the spirit of other examples in Part VI:

```
class Adder:
    def __init__(self, start=[]):
        self.data = start
    def __add__(self, other):          # Pass a single argument
        return self.add(other)         # The left side is in self
    def add(self, y):
        print 'not implemented!'


class ListAdder(Adder):
    def add(self, y):
        return self.data + y


class DictAdder(Adder):
    def add(self, y):
        pass                           # Change me to use self.data instead of x


x = ListAdder([1, 2 ,3])
y = x + [4, 5, 6]
print y                                # Prints [1, 2, 3, 4, 5, 6]
```

Because values are attached to objects rather than passed around, this version is arguably more object-oriented. And, once you've gotten to this point, you'll probably find that you can get rid of add altogether, and simply define type-specific __add__ methods in the two subclasses.

2. *Operator overloading.* The solution code (file *mylist.py*) uses a few operator overloading methods that the text didn't say much about, but they should be straightforward to understand. Copying the initial value in the constructor is important because it may be mutable; you don't want to change or have a reference to an object that's possibly shared somewhere outside the class. The __getattr__ method routes calls to the wrapped list. For hints on an easier way to code this in Python 2.2 and later, see "Extending Types by Subclassing" in Chapter 26:

```
class MyList:
    def __init__(self, start):
        #self.wrapped = start[:]      # Copy start: no side effects
        self.wrapped = []             # Make sure it's a list here
        for x in start: self.wrapped.append(x)
    def __add__(self, other):
        return MyList(self.wrapped + other)
    def __mul__(self, time):
        return MyList(self.wrapped * time)
    def __getitem__(self, offset):
        return self.wrapped[offset]
    def __len__(self):
        return len(self.wrapped)
    def __getslice__(self, low, high):
        return MyList(self.wrapped[low:high])
    def append(self, node):
        self.wrapped.append(node)
    def __getattr__(self, name):      # Other members: sort/reverse/etc
        return getattr(self.wrapped, name)
    def __repr__(self):
        return repr(self.wrapped)

if __name__ == '__main__':
    x = MyList('spam')
    print x
    print x[2]
    print x[1:]
    print x + ['eggs']
    print x * 3
    x.append('a')
    x.sort()
    for c in x: print c,
```

```
% python mylist.py
['s', 'p', 'a', 'm']
a
['p', 'a', 'm']
['s', 'p', 'a', 'm', 'eggs']
['s', 'p', 'a', 'm', 's', 'p', 'a', 'm', 's', 'p', 'a', 'm']
a a m p s
```

Note that it's important to copy the start value by appending instead of slicing here because otherwise the result may not be a true list, and so will not respond to expected list methods, such as append (e.g., slicing a string returns another string, not a list). You would be able to copy a MyList start value by slicing because its class overloads the slicing operation, and provides the expected list interface; however, you need to avoid slice-based copying for objects such as strings. Also, note that sets are a built-in type in Python today, so this is largely just a coding exercise (see Chapter 5 for more on sets).

3. *Subclassing.* My solution (*mysub.py*) appears below. Your solution should be similar:

```
from mylist import MyList

class MyListSub(MyList):
    calls = 0                                        # Shared by instances

    def __init__(self, start):
        self.adds = 0                                # Varies in each instance
        MyList.__init__(self, start)

    def __add__(self, other):
        MyListSub.calls = MyListSub.calls + 1        # Class-wide counter
        self.adds = self.adds + 1                    # Per-instance counts
        return MyList.__add__(self, other)

    def stats(self):
        return self.calls, self.adds                 # All adds, my adds

if __name__ == '__main__':
    x = MyListSub('spam')
    y = MyListSub('foo')
    print x[2]
    print x[1:]
    print x + ['eggs']
    print x + ['toast']
    print y + ['bar']
    print x.stats()
```

```
% python mysub.py
a
['p', 'a', 'm']
['s', 'p', 'a', 'm', 'eggs']
['s', 'p', 'a', 'm', 'toast']
['f', 'o', 'o', 'bar']
(3, 2)
```

4. *Metaclass methods.* I worked through this exercise as follows. Notice that operators try to fetch attributes through __getattr__, too; you need to return a value to make them work:

```
>>> class Meta:
...     def __getattr__(self, name):
...         print 'get', name
```

```
...      def __setattr__(self, name, value):
...          print 'set', name, value
...
>>> x = Meta()
>>> x.append
get append
>>> x.spam = "pork"
set spam pork
>>>
>>> x + 2
get __coerce__
Traceback (innermost last):
  File "<stdin>", line 1, in ?
TypeError: call of non-function
>>>
>>> x[1]
get __getitem__
Traceback (innermost last):
  File "<stdin>", line 1, in ?
TypeError: call of non-function

>>> x[1:5]
get __len__
Traceback (innermost last):
  File "<stdin>", line 1, in ?
TypeError: call of non-function
```

5. *Set objects*. Here's the sort of interaction you should get. Comments explain which methods are called.

```
% python
>>> from setwrapper import Set
>>> x = Set([1, 2, 3, 4])            # Runs __init__
>>> y = Set([3, 4, 5])

>>> x & y                            # __and__, intersect, then __repr__
Set:[3, 4]
>>> x | y                            # __or__, union, then __repr__
Set:[1, 2, 3, 4, 5]

>>> z = Set("hello")                 # __init__ removes duplicates
>>> z[0], z[-1]                      # __getitem__
('h', 'o')

>>> for c in z: print c,             # __getitem__
...
h e l o
>>> len(z), z                        # __len__, __repr__
(4, Set:['h', 'e', 'l', 'o'])

>>> z & "mello", z | "mello"
(Set:['e', 'l', 'o'], Set:['h', 'e', 'l', 'o', 'm'])
```

My solution to the multiple-operand extension subclass looks like the class below (file *multiset.py*). It only needs to replace two methods in the original set. The class' documentation string explains how it works:

```
from setwrapper import Set

class MultiSet(Set):
    """
    inherits all Set names, but extends intersect
    and union to support multiple operands; note
    that "self" is still the first argument (stored
    in the *args argument now); also note that the
    inherited & and | operators call the new methods
    here with 2 arguments, but processing more than
    2 requires a method call, not an expression:
    """

    def intersect(self, *others):
        res = []
        for x in self:                      # Scan first sequence
            for other in others:            # For all other args
                if x not in other: break    # Item in each one?
            else:                           # No: break out of loop
                res.append(x)               # Yes: add item to end
        return Set(res)

    def union(*args):                       # Self is args[0]
        res = []
        for seq in args:                    # For all args
            for x in seq:                   # For all nodes
                if not x in res:
                    res.append(x)           # Add new items to result
        return Set(res)
```

Your interaction with the extension will look something like the following. Note that you can intersect by using & or calling intersect, but you must call intersect for three or more operands; & is a binary (two-sided) operator. Also, note that we could have called MultiSet simply Set to make this change more transparent if we used setwrapper.Set to refer to the original within multiset:

```
>>> from multiset import *
>>> x = MultiSet([1,2,3,4])
>>> y = MultiSet([3,4,5])
>>> z = MultiSet([0,1,2])

>>> x & y, x | y                           # Two operands
(Set:[3, 4], Set:[1, 2, 3, 4, 5])

>>> x.intersect(y, z)                      # Three operands
Set:[]
>>> x.union(y, z)
Set:[1, 2, 3, 4, 5, 0]
```

```
>>> x.intersect([1,2,3], [2,3,4], [1,2,3])        # Four operands
Set:[2, 3]
>>> x.union(range(10))                            # NonmultiSets work, too
Set:[1, 2, 3, 4, 0, 5, 6, 7, 8, 9]
```

6. *Class tree links.* Here is the way I changed the Lister class, and a rerun of the test to show its format. To display inherited class attributes, too, you'd need to do something like what the attrnames method currently does, but recursively, at each class reached by climbing __bases__ links. Because dir includes inherited attributes in Python 2.2, you might also simply loop through its result: say for x in dir(self) and use getattr(self,x). This won't directly help, though, if you wish to represent the class tree's structure in your display (as in the *classtree.py* example in Chapter 24):

```
class Lister:
    def __repr__(self):
        return ("<Instance of %s(%s), address %s:\n%s>" %
                            (self.__class__.__name__,     # My class's name
                             self.supers(),               # My class's supers
                             id(self),                    # My address
                             self.attrnames()) )          # name=value list
    def attrnames(self):
        ...unchanged...
    def supers(self):
        result = ""
        first = 1
        for super in self.__class__.__bases__:            # One level up from class
            if not first:
                result = result + ", "
            first = 0
            result = result + super.__name__              # name, not repr(super)
        return result

C:\python\examples> python testmixin.py
<Instance of Sub(Super, Lister), address 7841200:
    name data3=42
    name data2=eggs
    name data1=spam
>
```

7. *Composition.* My solution is below (file *lunch.py*), with comments from the description mixed in with the code. This is one case where it's probably easier to express a problem in Python than it is in English:

```
class Lunch:
    def __init__(self):                        # Make/embed Customer and Employee
        self.cust = Customer()
        self.empl = Employee()
    def order(self, foodName):                 # Start a Customer order simulation
        self.cust.placeOrder(foodName, self.empl)
    def result(self):                          # Ask the Customer about its Food
        self.cust.printFood()
```

```
class Customer:
    def __init__(self):                              # Initialize my food to None
        self.food = None
    def placeOrder(self, foodName, employee):        # Place order with Employee
        self.food = employee.takeOrder(foodName)
    def printFood(self):                             # Print the name of my food
        print self.food.name

class Employee:
    def takeOrder(self, foodName):                   # Return a Food, with requested name
        return Food(foodName)

class Food:
    def __init__(self, name):                        # Store food name
        self.name = name

if __name__ == '__main__':
    x = Lunch()                                      # Self-test code
    x.order('burritos')                              # If run, not imported
    x.result()
    x.order('pizza')
    x.result()
```

```
% python lunch.py
burritos
pizza
```

8. *Zoo animal hierarchy*. Here is the way I coded the taxonomy on Python (file *zoo.py*); it's artificial, but the general coding pattern applies to many real structures, from GUIs to employee databases. Notice that the self.speak reference in Animal triggers an independent inheritance search, which finds speak in a subclass. Test this interactively per the exercise description. Try extending this hierarchy with new classes, and making instances of various classes in the tree:

```
class Animal:
    def reply(self):   self.speak()          # Back to subclass
    def speak(self):   print 'spam'          # Custom message

class Mammal(Animal):
    def speak(self):   print 'huh?'

class Cat(Mammal):
    def speak(self):   print 'meow'

class Dog(Mammal):
    def speak(self):   print 'bark'

class Primate(Mammal):
    def speak(self):   print 'Hello world!'

class Hacker(Primate): pass                  # Inherit from Primate
```

9. *The Dead Parrot Sketch*. Here's how I implemented this one (file *parrot.py*). Notice how the line method in the Actor superclass works: by accessing self attributes twice, it sends Python back to the instance twice, and hence invokes *two* inheritance searches—self.name and self.says() find information in the specific subclasses:

```
class Actor:
    def line(self): print self.name + ':', repr(self.says())

class Customer(Actor):
    name = 'customer'
    def says(self): return "that's one ex-bird!"

class Clerk(Actor):
    name = 'clerk'
    def says(self): return "no it isn't..."

class Parrot(Actor):
    name = 'parrot'
    def says(self): return None

class Scene:
    def __init__(self):
        self.clerk    = Clerk()        # Embed some instances
        self.customer = Customer()     # Scene is a composite
        self.subject  = Parrot()

    def action(self):
        self.customer.line()           # Delegate to embedded
        self.clerk.line()
        self.subject.line()
```

Part VII, Exceptions and Tools

See "Part VII Exercises" in Chapter 29 for the exercises.

1. try/except. My version of the oops function (file *oops.py*) follows. As for the noncoding questions, changing oops to raise a KeyError instead of an IndexError means that the try handler won't catch the exception (it "percolates" to the top level, and triggers Python's default error message). The names KeyError and IndexError come from the outermost built-in names scope. Import __builtin__, and pass it as an argument to the dir function to see for yourself:

```
def oops():
    raise IndexError

def doomed():
    try:
        oops()
    except IndexError:
        print 'caught an index error!'
    else:
        print 'no error caught...'
```

```
    if __name__ == '__main__': doomed( )
```

```
% python oops.py
caught an index error!
```

2. *Exception objects and lists.* Here's the way I extended this module for an exception of my own (here a string, at first):

```
MyError = 'hello'

def oops( ):
    raise MyError, 'world'

def doomed( ):
    try:
        oops( )
    except IndexError:
        print 'caught an index error!'
    except MyError, data:
        print 'caught error:', MyError, data
    else:
        print 'no error caught...'

if __name__ == '__main__':
    doomed( )
```

```
% python oops.py
caught error: hello world
```

To identify the exception with a class, I just changed the first part of the file to this, and saved it as *oop_oops.py*:

```
class MyError: pass

def oops( ):
    raise MyError( )
```

```
...rest unchanged...
```

Like all class exceptions, the instance comes back as the extra data; the error message now shows both the class and its instance (<...>).

```
% python oop_oops.py
caught error: __main__.MyError <__main__.MyError instance at 0x00867550>
```

Remember, to make this look nicer, you can define a __repr__ or __str__ method in your class to return a custom print string. See Chapter 24 for details.

3. *Error handling.* Here's one way to solve this one (file *safe2.py*). I did my tests in a file, rather than interactively, but the results are about the same.

```
import sys, traceback

def safe(entry, *args):
    try:
        apply(entry, args)                  # Catch everything else
    except:
        traceback.print_exc( )
        print 'Got', sys.exc_type, sys.exc_value
```

```
import oops
safe(oops.oops)

% python safe2.py
Traceback (innermost last):
  File "safe2.py", line 5, in safe
    apply(entry, args)                          # Catch everything else
  File "oops.py", line 4, in oops
    raise MyError, 'world'
hello: world
Got hello world
```

Today, I would probably code this as follows, using the newer *args call syntax and exc_info:

```
def safe(entry, *args):
    try:
        entry(*args)                            # Catch everything else
    except:
        traceback.print_exc( )
        print 'Got', sys.exc_info( )[0], sys.exc_info( )[1]
```

4. Here are a few examples for you to study as time allows; for more, see follow-up books and the Web:

```
# Find the largest file in a single directory

    dirname = r'C:\Python25\Lib'
    import os, glob

    allsizes = []
    allpy = glob.glob(os.path.join(dirname, '*.py'))
    for filename in allpy:
        filesize = os.path.getsize(filename)
        allsizes.append((filesize, filename))

    allsizes.sort( )
    print allsizes[:2]
    print allsizes[-2:]
```

```
# Find the largest file in an entire directory tree

    import sys
    if sys.platform[:3] == 'win':
        dirname = r'C:\Python25\Lib'
    else:
        dirname = '/usr/lib/python'
    import os, glob

    allsizes = []
    for (thisDir, subsHere, filesHere) in os.walk(dirname):
        for filename in filesHere:
            if filename.endswith('.py'):
                fullname = os.path.join(thisDir, filename)
                fullsize = os.path.getsize(fullname)
                allsizes.append((fullsize, fullname))
```

```
    allsizes.sort( )
    print allsizes[:2]
    print allsizes[-2:]
```

Find the largest Python source file on the module import search path

```
    import sys, os, pprint
    visited  = {}
    allsizes = []
    for srcdir in sys.path:
        for (thisDir, subsHere, filesHere) in os.walk(srcdir):
            thisDir = os.path.normpath(thisDir)
            if thisDir.upper( ) in visited:
                continue
            else:
                visited[thisDir.upper( )] = True
            for filename in filesHere:
                if filename.endswith('.py'):
                    pypath  = os.path.join(thisDir, filename)
                    try:
                        pysize = os.path.getsize(pypath)
                    except:
                        print 'skipping', pypath
                    allsizes.append((pysize, pypath))

    allsizes.sort( )
    pprint.pprint(allsizes[:3])
    pprint.pprint(allsizes[-3:])
```

Sum columns in a text file separated by commas

```
    filename = 'data.txt'
    sums = {}

    for line in open(filename):
        cols = line.split(',')
        nums = [int(col) for col in cols]
        for (ix, num) in enumerate(nums):
            sums[ix] = sums.get(ix, 0) + num

    for key in sorted(sums):
        print key, '=', sums[key]
```

Similar to prior, but using lists instead of dictionaries for sums

```
    import sys
    filename = sys.argv[1]
    numcols  = int(sys.argv[2])
    totals   = [0] * numcols
```

```
    for line in open(filename):
        cols = line.split(',')
        nums = [int(x) for x in cols]
        totals = [(x + y) for (x, y) in zip(totals, nums)]

    print totals
```

Test for regressions in the output of a set of scripts

```
    import os
    testscripts = [dict(script='test1.py', args=''),
                   dict(script='test2.py', args='spam')]

    for testcase in testscripts:
        commandline = '%(script)s %(args)s' % testcase
        output = os.popen(commandline).read()
        result = testcase['script'] + '.result'
        if not os.path.exists(result):
            open(result, 'w').write(output)
            print 'Created:', result
        else:
            priorresult = open(result).read()
            if output != priorresult:
                print 'FAILED:', testcase['script']
                print output
            else:
                print 'Passed:', testcase['script']
```

Build a GUI with Tkinter with buttons that change color and grow

```
    from Tkinter import *
    import random
    fontsize = 25
    colors = ['red', 'green', 'blue', 'yellow', 'orange', 'white', 'cyan', 'purple']

    def reply(text):
        print text
        popup = Toplevel()
        color = random.choice(colors)
        Label(popup, text='Popup', bg='black', fg=color).pack()
        L.config(fg=color)

    def timer():
        L.config(fg=random.choice(colors))
        win.after(250, timer)

    def grow():
        global fontsize
        fontsize += 5
        L.config(font=('arial', fontsize, 'italic'))
        win.after(100, grow)
```

```
win = Tk()
L = Label(win, text='Spam',
            font=('arial', fontsize, 'italic'), fg='yellow', bg='navy',
            relief=RAISED)
L.pack(side=TOP, expand=YES, fill=BOTH)
Button(win, text='press', command=(lambda: reply('red'))).pack(side=BOTTOM,
        fill=X)
Button(win, text='timer', command=timer).pack(side=BOTTOM, fill=X)
Button(win, text='grow' , command=grow).pack(side=BOTTOM, fill=X)
win.mainloop()
```

➡️ ```
Similar to prior, but use classes so each window has own state information

from Tkinter import *
import random

class MyGui:
    """
    A GUI with buttons that change color and make the label grow
    """
    colors = ['blue', 'green', 'orange', 'red', 'brown', 'yellow']

    def __init__(self, parent, title='popup'):
        parent.title(title)
        self.growing = False
        self.fontsize = 10
        self.lab = Label(parent, text='Gui1', fg='white', bg='navy')
        self.lab.pack(expand=YES, fill=BOTH)
        Button(parent, text='Spam', command=self.reply).pack(side=LEFT)
        Button(parent, text='Grow', command=self.grow).pack(side=LEFT)
        Button(parent, text='Stop', command=self.stop).pack(side=LEFT)

    def reply(self):
        "change the button's color at random on Spam presses"
        self.fontsize += 5
        color = random.choice(self.colors)
        self.lab.config(bg=color,
                font=('courier', self.fontsize, 'bold italic'))

    def grow(self):
        "start making the label grow on Grow presses"
        self.growing = True
        self.grower()

    def grower(self):
        if self.growing:
            self.fontsize += 5
            self.lab.config(font=('courier', self.fontsize, 'bold'))
            self.lab.after(500, self.grower)

    def stop(self):
        "stop the button growing on Stop presses"
        self.growing = False
```
```

```
class MySubGui(MyGui):
    colors = ['black', 'purple']        # Customize to change color choices

MyGui(Tk(), 'main')
MyGui(Toplevel())
MySubGui(Toplevel())
mainloop()
```

```
# Email inbox scanning and maintenance utility

    """
    scan pop email box, fetching just headers, allowing
    deletions without downloading the complete message
    """

    import poplib, getpass, sys

    mailserver = 'your pop email server name here'            # pop.rmi.net
    mailuser   = 'your pop email user name here'              # brian
    mailpasswd = getpass.getpass('Password for %s?' % mailserver)

    print 'Connecting...'
    server = poplib.POP3(mailserver)
    server.user(mailuser)
    server.pass_(mailpasswd)

    try:
        print server.getwelcome()
        msgCount, mboxSize = server.stat()
        print 'There are', msgCount, 'mail messages, size ', mboxSize
        msginfo = server.list()
        print msginfo
        for i in range(msgCount):
            msgnum  = i+1
            msgsize = msginfo[1][i].split()[1]
            resp, hdrlines, octets = server.top(msgnum, 0)       # Get hdrs only
            print '-'*80
            print '[%d: octets=%d, size=%s]' % (msgnum, octets, msgsize)
            for line in hdrlines: print line

            if raw_input('Print?') in ['y', 'Y']:
                for line in server.retr(msgnum)[1]: print line      # Get whole msg
            if raw_input('Delete?') in ['y', 'Y']:
                print 'deleting'
                server.dele(msgnum)                                 # Delete on srvr
            else:
                print 'skipping'
    finally:
        server.quit()                                # Make sure we unlock mbox
    raw_input('Bye.')                                # Keep window up on windows
```

CGI server-side script to interact with a web browser

```python
#!/usr/bin/python
import cgi
form = cgi.FieldStorage()                              # Parse form data
print "Content-type: text/html\n"                      # hdr plus blank line
print "<HTML>"
print "<title>Reply Page</title>"                      # html reply page
print "<BODY>"
if not form.has_key('user'):
    print "<h1>Who are you?</h1>"
else:
    print "<h1>Hello <i>%s</i>!</h1>" % cgi.escape(form['user'].value)
print "</BODY></HTML>"
```

Database script to populate and query a MySql database

```python
from MySQLdb import Connect
conn = Connect(host='localhost', user='root', passwd='darling')
curs = conn.cursor()
try:
    curs.execute('drop database testpeopledb')
except:
    pass                                               # Did not exist

curs.execute('create database testpeopledb')
curs.execute('use testpeopledb')
curs.execute('create table people (name char(30), job char(10), pay int(4))')

curs.execute('insert people values (%s, %s, %s)', ('Bob', 'dev', 50000))
curs.execute('insert people values (%s, %s, %s)', ('Sue', 'dev', 60000))
curs.execute('insert people values (%s, %s, %s)', ('Ann', 'mgr', 40000))

curs.execute('select * from people')
for row in curs.fetchall():
    print row

curs.execute('select * from people where name = %s', ('Bob',))
print curs.description
colnames = [desc[0] for desc in curs.description]
while True:
    print '-' * 30
    row = curs.fetchone()
    if not row: break
    for (name, value) in zip(colnames, row):
        print '%s => %s' % (name, value)

conn.commit()                                          # Save inserted records
```

```
# Database script to populate a shelve with Python objects

rec1 = {'name': {'first': 'Bob', 'last': 'Smith'},
        'job':  ['dev', 'mgr'],
        'age':  40.5}

rec2 = {'name': {'first': 'Sue', 'last': 'Jones'},
        'job':  ['mgr'],
        'age':  35.0}

import shelve
db = shelve.open('dbfile')
db['bob'] = rec1
db['sue'] = rec2
db.close()
```

```
# Database script to print and update shelve created in prior script

import shelve
db = shelve.open('dbfile')
for key in db:
    print key, '=>', db[key]

bob = db['bob']
bob['age'] += 1
db['bob'] = bob
db.close()
```

Index

We'd like to hear your suggestions for improving our indexes. Send email to *index@oreilly.com*.

classes *(continued)*
    objects (see objects)
    persistence, 527
    pseudoprivate attributes, 543–545
        why use, 544
    user-defined (see user-defined classes)
    versus modules, 537
    why use, 452–453
        composition, 452
        customization via inheritance, 453
        inheritance, 452
        multiple instances, 452
        operator overloading, 453
classtree function, 511
closure, 321
__cmp__ method, 492
code
    common coding gotchas, 291–292
    compiling, 25
    documenting (see documenting code)
    nested, 214
    reuse, 386, 459–462
    strings, 143
coding basics, 465–480
    calling objects, 466
    classes intercepting Python
        operators, 472–476
      example, 474–475
    inheritance (see inheritance)
    multiple instance objects, 465–469
        concrete items, 466
        default behavior, 466
        example, 467–469
        inheritance, 466
        self, 466
    operator overloading, 475
    simple Python class, 476–478
cohesion, 369
COM support on MS Windows, 11
command-line arguments, 137
comments, 38, 99, 239
comparisons, 186–189
    languages, 18
    operators, 96
compiled extensions, 630
compiling
    byte code, 25
    extensions, 7
    Psyco just-in-time compiler, 29
    Shedskin, 29
complex numbers, 95, 104

components
    integration, 4, 10
    merging, 31
composition, 452, 523–527
    example, 524–527
compound statements, 37, 236–247
compound types, 371
concatenation, 71, 123
    strings, 132
concept hierarchy, 201
configuration (see installation and
        configuration)
constraints, trapping, 595
context management, 596–600
    protocol, 598–600
contextlib standard module, 600
continue statement, 202, 250, 251
control flows, unusual, 577
control language, 6
conversion, strings, 97
copies versus references, 184–186
coupling, 369
CPython, 28
cross-file changes, minimizing, 318
cross-file name changes, 402
csh shell, 644
current working directory, 392
customization via inheritance, 453
cyclic data structures, 193

D

Dabo, 10
data attributes, 482
data structures, 66
database programming, 11
databases, 11
__debug__ flag, 595
debugger (IDLE), 54
debuggers, 632
decimal numbers, 87
decimal object, 107
declaration statements
    missing, 112–116
def statements, 202, 301, 302–304, 483
    return, yield, 299
    versus lambda, 345
default argument values, 323
default exception handler, 578
defaults, 373
__del__ method, 492, 505
del statement, 203

F

inheritance *(continued)*
>example, 547
>explicit conflict resolution, 547
>each object.attribute reference invokes
>>new, independent search, 469
>example, 470–471
>extension coding pattern, 489
>hierarchy, 451
>instances inherit attributes from all
>>accessible classes, 469
>logic changes are made by subclassing,
>>not by changing superclasses, 469
>modeling real-world
>>relationships, 521–523
>mulitple, 560–561
>multiple, 529–531
>redefining inherited names, 488
>specializing inherited methods, 488
>superclasses listed in parentheses in class
>>header, 469
>tree-searching model, 488
_ _init_ _ constructor logic, 605
_ _init_ _ method, 458, 475, 492
_ _init_ _.py files, 416
input prompt, 35
installation and configuration, 23, 639–645
>checking to see if Python is already
>>installed, 639
>configuring Python, 641–645
>>DOS variables, 644
>>environment variable settings, 642
>>path files, 645
>>setting options, 644
>>shell variables, 644
>>Windows options, 645
>installation steps, 640
>installing Python interpreter, 639–641
>where to fetch Python, 639
instance methods, 555
instances, 454, 455
>_ _class_ _ attribute, 509
>attributes, 487
>emulating privacy, 499–500
>multiple, 452
>sending extra data and behavior
>>in, 611–613
int function, 105, 136, 212
integers, 94
>literals, 94
>log, 103
>numeric precision and long integers, 94

integrated development environment (see
>IDEs)
integration
>components, 10
>with C, 15
interactive coding, 34–37
>testing code, 36
interactive loops, 210–214
>doing math on user inputs, 211
>nested code, 214
>simple, 210
>testing inputs, 212
interactive prompt
>compound statements, 37
>indentation, 37
>prompt changes, 37
>testing code at, 36
>using, 37
interactive testing, 441
intercepting instance-indexing
>operations, 493
interfaces, programming, 9
internationalization, 130
Internet scripting, 10
Internet, utility modules, 10
interpreter, 22–24
>conventions, 227
intersect function, 307
introspection, 435
IronPython, 11, 29
is not operator, 96
is operator, 96
"is-a" links, 522
_ _lt_ _ method, 492
iter function, 262, 362
_ _iter_ _ method, 493–498
iterations
>alternatives, 366–369
>>timing, 366
>overloading, 493
>protocol, 83, 261
>strings, 133
iterators, 360–366
>built-in types and, 364
>generator expressions, 365
>user-defined, 494–498
>>multiple iterators on one object, 496

J

join method, 146, 264
just-in-time (JIT) compiler, 30
Jython, 10, 28

V

van Rossum, Guido, 18, 546
varargs, 331
variable name rules, 225
variable names, 313
variables, 114
    basic expressions and, 99–100
    creating, 113
    types, 113
    usage, 113
Vaults of Parnassus, 12, 31, 634
Vista, Python 2.5 MSI Installer, 642

W

warnings, 621
web site resources, xxxviii
while loops, 248–250
    emulating C, 255
    examples, 249
    general format, 249
while/else statement, 202
whitespace, 241
wide character strings, 130
win32all Windows extensions package, 423
win32com, 31
WingIDE, 55
with/as, 203, 575, 596–600
    context management protocol, 598–600
wrapping, 624
wxPython, 10, 31

X

XML (Extensible Markup Language), 10, 15
xml library package, 12
xmlrpclib module, 12

Y

yield statement, 202

Z

zip function, 265, 268
    dictionary construction, 270
Zope, 10

About the Author

Mark Lutz is the world leader in Python training, the author of Python's earliest and best-selling texts, and a pioneering figure in the Python community.

Mark is the author of the O'Reilly books *Programming Python* and *Python Pocket Reference*, both currently in third editions. He has been using and promoting Python since 1992, started writing Python books in 1995, began teaching Python classes in 1997, and has instructed more than 200 Python training sessions as of mid-2007.

In addition, he holds B.S. and M.S. degrees in computer science from the University of Wisconsin, and during the last 25 years has worked on compilers, programming tools, scripting applications, and assorted client/server systems.

Whenever Mark gets a break from spreading the Python word, he leads an ordinary life in Colorado. Mark can be reached by email at *lutz@rmi.net*, or on the Web at *http://www.rmi.net/~lutz* and *http://home.earthlink.net/~python-training*.

Colophon

The animal on the cover of *Learning Python*, Third Edition, is a wood rat (*Neotoma Muridae*). The wood rat lives in a wide range of conditions (mostly rocky, scrub, and desert areas) over much of North and Central America, generally at some distance from humans. They are good climbers, nesting in trees or bushes up to six meters off the ground; some species burrow underground or in rock crevices or inhabit other species' abandoned holes.

These grayish-beige, medium-size rodents are the original pack rats: they carry anything and everything into their homes, whether or not it's needed, and are especially attracted to shiny objects such as tin cans, glass, and silverware.

The cover image is a 19th-century engraving from *Cuvier's Animals*. The cover font is Adobe ITC Garamond. The text font is Linotype Birka; the heading font is Adobe Myriad Condensed; and the code font is LucasFont's TheSans Mono Condensed.

Related Titles from O'Reilly

Scripting Languages

Essential PHP Security

Exploring Expect

Jython Essentials

Learning Python, *2nd Edition*

Learning PHP and MySQL

Learning Ruby

Learning PHP 5

PHP Cookbook, *2nd Edition*

PHP Hacks

PHP in a Nutshell

PHP Pocket Reference, *2nd Edition*

PHPUnit Pocket Guide

Programming PHP, *2nd Edition*

Programming Python, *3rd Edition*

Python & XML

Python Cookbook, *2nd Edition*

Python in a Nutshell, *2nd Edition*

Python Pocket Reference, *3rd Edition*

Python Standard Library

Ruby in a Nutshell

Ruby on Rails: Up and Running

Upgrading to PHP 5

Web Database Applications with PHP and MySQL, *2nd Edition*

DATE DUE

OCT 29 2009			
	NOV 24 2009	FEB 07 2014	
DEC 22 2009			
	AUG 05 2010	JAN 03 2011	
AUG 05 2010			
		AUG 05 2011	
MAR 12 2010	SEP 1 2011		
SEP 22 2010	NOV 01 2011		
		DEC 01 2011	
OCT 28 2010	FEB 02 2012		